WATERWAY GUIDE

Volume 44, No. 4

Publisher's Note .... page 9	Weather Information 118
Editor's Log 11	Radiobeacons 121
Keep the Eagle *Flying,* By Walter Cronkite 12	Public Coast Marine Operators 122
How to Use WATERWAY GUIDE 16	Distances 123
The Great Lakes and Connecting Waterways 19	Mail Drops 128
The Hudson River .... page 23	Useful Publications 129
The Champlain Waterways 43	Customs 130
The Erie Canal 54	Metrics 131
Lake Ontario 69	Corps of Engineers 132
St. Lawrence Seaway 86	Distress, Urgency, Safety 133
Trent-Severn Waterway 99	Restaurants 134
Mariner's Handbook .... page 113	Lake Erie .... page 139
Rules of the Road 114	Detroit River, Lake St. Clair, St. Clair River 163
Bridge and Lock Manners 115	Lake Huron 177
Coast Guard 116	Lake Michigan/Eastern Shore 191
Coast Guard — Canadian 117	Lake Michigan/Western Shore 205

GREAT LAKES EDITION

3

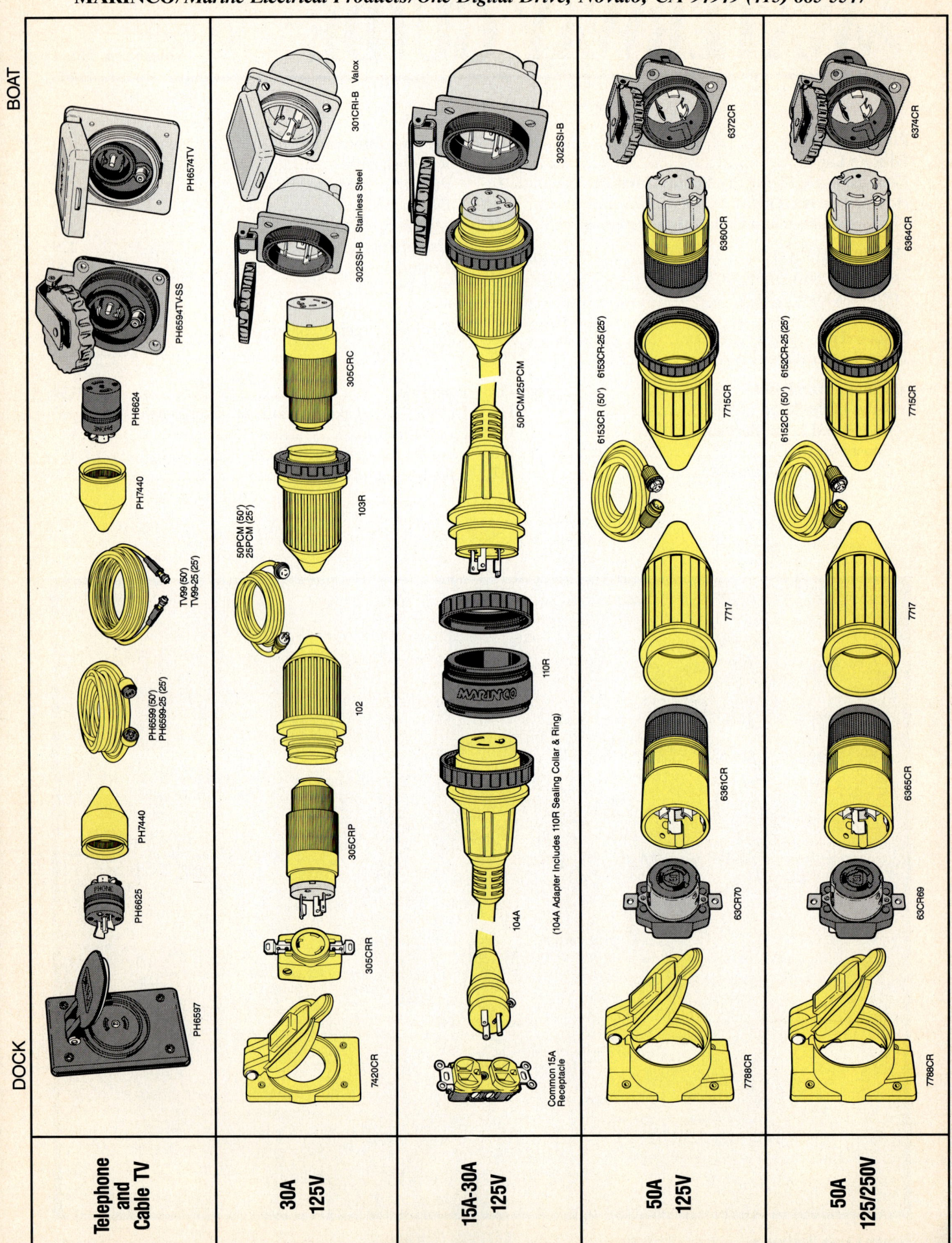

Of all Navigators Only Northstar is Rated Best 12 Years in a Row*

No matter what type of boat you own there's a Northstar for you. Center Console, Sport Fisher, Sail or Ocean crossing Yacht. **Industry Standard 800 & 800X**. The two Northstars that all other Loran Navigators are compared to. World renowned for performance and ease of use. The 800 is powerful and economical. And when the going gets wet, the 800X has a completely waterproof control head. The Northstar 800 Series is rated the best value in Loran Navigation.

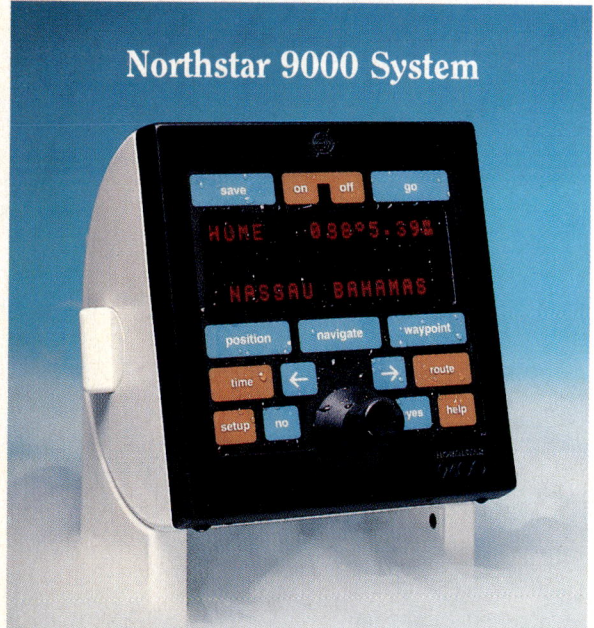

SYSTEM 9000 The complete Navigating system for the 90's. It manages your navigation information...from waypoints, routes & course to tides and avoidance areas. It's a high performance navigation system. Loran, GPS or both. Versatile and dynamic, System 9000 will support and run a virtually unlimited number of electronic navigation devices. Moving Map Displays. Track Plotters. On Screen Charting. Auto Pilots. Radar and more.

Northstar Navigators have set the standard for two decades. Today's Northstars are leading the way to the 21st Century. In the World of Navigation you have the best of choices, and they're all called Northstar.

Northstar IS Navigation

* N.M.E.A. LORAN AWARD "Best in Performance & Reliability"

For a hands-on demonstration call the toll FREE number for your local Northstar Dealer

Northstar Consumer Information
For complete information on DMEC products by mail, call anytime toll free 1-800-325-DMEC and give our operator your name and address. In Massachusetts, or for technical help, call (508) 897-6600.

DIGITAL MARINE ELECTRONICS CORPORATION
30 Sudbury Rd., Acton, MA 01720 (508) 897-6600
Fax: (508) 897-7241

All Northstars are covered by a 3 YEAR limited warranty, (parts & labor, FOB Acton, MA), the best in the industry.

GREAT LAKES EDITION

SWITLIK
— A Family Tradition of Excellence

Since 1920 and for three generations, The Switlik Family has designed and manufactured Safety and Survival Equipment. The advanced design of our Marine Life Rafts helped build our Tradition of Excellence.

LIFE RAFTS
.... Crafted With Pride In The U.S.A.

RESCUE PLATFORM™

The Rescue Platform is an affordable way to provide emergency flotation for up to 10 adults. It's compact fiberglass container or soft valise allow it to be carried aboard even the smallest vessel. American Power Boat Association (APBA) approved.

- Capacity: 10 persons
- Buoyancy: 130 lbs./person
- Floor Area: 3.75 sq. ft./person
- Container Size: 24" × 13" × 10"

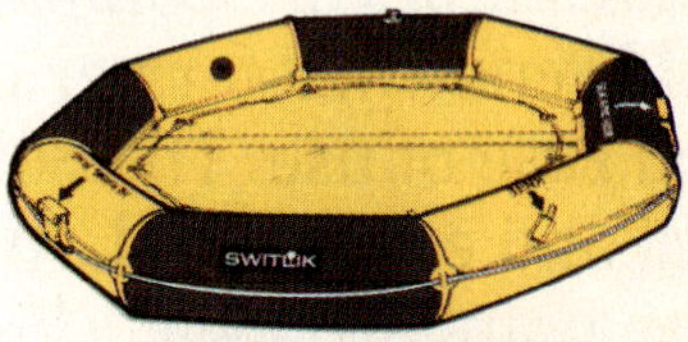

COASTAL LIFE RAFTS

The advanced design of our Coastal Life Raft makes it the only single tube raft which meets the Offshore Racing Council's (ORC) requirements. This design features a furlable canopy, a "sailaway" configuration, and the largest occupant area of any raft in this class.

- Capacity: 4 & 6 persons
- Buoyancy: 240 lbs./person
- Floor area: 4.0 sq. ft./person
- Container Size: 31" × 21" × 10"

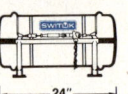

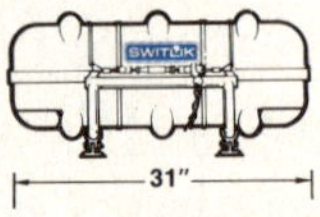

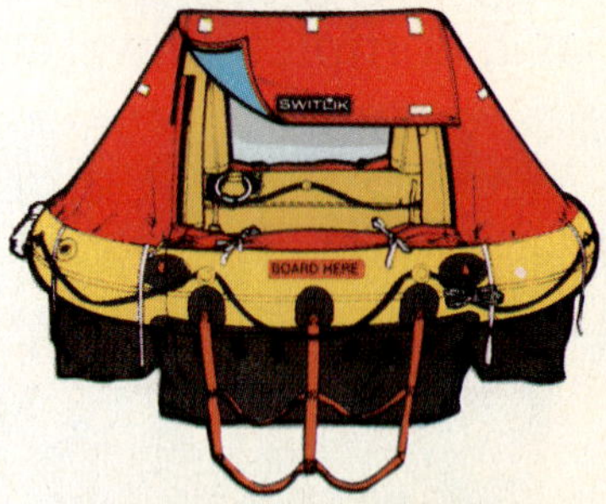

SEARCH & RESCUE LIFE RAFTS

The Search & Rescue Life Raft configuration was designed for and is used extensively aboard U. S. Coast Guard vessels and aircraft. It's furlable canopy allows easy boarding from higher freeboard vessels. The Toroidal Stability Device (TSD) and extended range survival kit are standard.

- Capacity: 6 & 8 persons
- Buoyancy: 250 lbs./person
- Floor Area: 3.6 sq. ft./person
- Container Size: 36.5" × 23.5" × 13.5" (6 person)

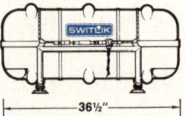

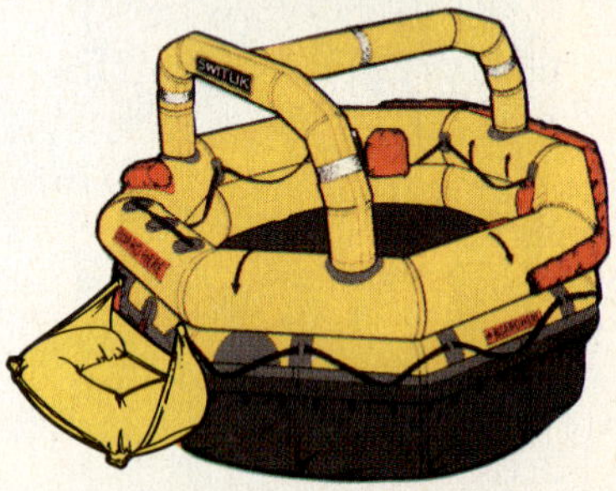

U.S.C.G. APPROVED LIFE RAFTS

There is no better life raft available than one approved by the United States Coast Guard for use aboard inspected vessels. Ours are now available for private vessels and feature the Coast Guard approved Toroidal Stability Device. (4, 6, 8, & 10 person capacities)

- Capacity: 4, 6, 8, 10, 15, 20, & 25 persons
- Buoyancy: 217 lbs./person
- Floor Area: 4.0 sq. ft./person
- Container Size: 36.5" × 23.5" × 17" (6 person)

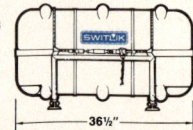

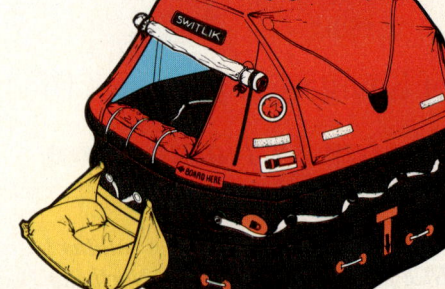

Ask Your Dealer For Further Information

SWITLIK PARACHUTE CO., INC. Established 1920
P.O. Box 1328   1325 East State Street   Trenton, N.J. 08607   (609)587-3300   Telex: 843 421: SPECO

WATERWAY GUIDE

Founded in 1947 — **From the publishers of Boating Industry Magazine**

Publisher	Charles Jones
Editorial Consultant	Walter J. Cronkite, Jr.
Editorial Director	Arthur E. Sweum
Editor	Judith Powers
Associate Editor	Leslie Jackson
Assistant Editor	Kim Jones
Production Director	Marty Greene
Production Manager	Suzette Leithauser
Art Director	Paula Tappen
Manager of Copy Sales	Etta Davis
Advertising Director	Kenneth R. Steele
Regional Representatives (Great Lakes Edition)	
Hudson River and the Erie Canal	Kim Mann
Lake Michigan	Wallace Wheatley
Lake Erie and Lake Huron	David G. Brown

WATERWAY GUIDE (ISBN Number: 0-915962-56-X) is published annually in four regional editions—Southern, Mid-Atlantic, Northern and Great Lakes—by Communication Channels, Inc. Copyright © 1991 by Waterway Guide, Inc. All rights reserved. Reproduction in whole or part without written permission from the publisher is prohibited. The title WATERWAY GUIDE is a registered trademark. Library of Congress Catalog Number: 54-3653.

Direct all mail concerning advertisements to: Ken Steele, Advertising Director, WATERWAY GUIDE, 19 Arrow Road, Hilton Head Island, South Carolina 29928; or call 1-803-686-5825.

Direct mail for the editors to: Editorial Office, WATERWAY GUIDE, 6255 Barfield Rd., Atlanta, GA. 30328. Price per copy is $27.95. When ordering by mail or telephone, add $3.00 for shipping and handling charges. Direct all orders to: Book Department, WATERWAY GUIDE, 6255 Barfield Rd., Atlanta, GA 30328; or call 1-800-233-3359, or 1-404-256-9800.

We believe the information contained herein to be reliable, and every effort has been made to insure accuracy. However, the publisher assumes no liability for omissions or changes. Charts are not intended for use in navigation. To insure your safety, all navigational information contained herein should be read in conjunction with current National Ocean Service Charts. Recent *Notices to Mariners* issued by the U.S. Coast Guard should also be consulted.

WATERWAY GUIDE, INC.
is published by
Communication Channels, Inc.

President	Jerrold France
Executive Vice President	Lawrence Moores

Cover: Chicago's Skyline from Lake Michigan

Photograph by Carol Singer

WATERWAY GUIDE

The **WATERWAY GUIDE** contains data on marinas, bridge clearances and schedules, anchorages and uncharted hazards. Also included, are sights to see, tide and distance tables, mail drops and the handy Mariner's Handbook. The series is published in four editions:

1 1991 Northern Edition: The C & D Canal and Delaware Bay, the New Jersey shore, New York Harbor, Long Island Sound, Narragansett and Buzzards Bay, and the coasts of Massachusetts and Maine to the Canadian border. $27.95

2 1991 Mid-Atlantic Edition: The major rivers of the Eastern and Western Shores, the Chesapeake Bay from the C & D Canal to Norfolk, plus the Intracoastal Waterway through Virginia, the Carolinas, and Georgia. $27.95

3 1991 Southern Edition: Begins at the Georgia/Florida line, covers all of Florida, the Gulf of Mexico, the Bahamas and the Keys, and the Okeechobee and Tenn-Tom Waterways. $27.95

1991 Great Lakes Edition: Lakes Michigan, Huron, Erie and Ontario and their connecting waterways, plus the upper Hudson River. $27.95

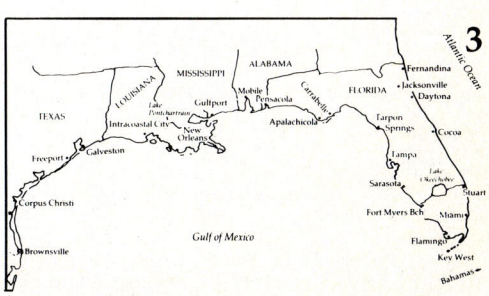

Send your check and order along with your name and street address to:

WATERWAY GUIDE
6255 Barfield Road
Atlanta, GA 30328

$3.00 shipping per book for each order

1-800-233-3359

GREAT LAKES EDITION

We'll protect your anything that

Your boat is prey to any number of hazards. And that's even before you put it in the water.

But Allstate will protect your boat with the same comprehensive service we do your home and car.

In addition to covering your boat, its motor, trailer and equipment, you can get liability coverage and medical expense protection for you, your passengers and water-skiers.

boat from almost comes up.

And you'll be pleased to know that our agent can even arrange boat financing.

So call or see an Allstate agent soon. And keep your pleasure boat just that.

Allstate®
BOATOWNERS INSURANCE

Subject to policy terms and limitations. Available in most states.
Boat financing provided by Sears Consumer Financial Corporation.
© 1989 Allstate Insurance Company, Northbrook, Illinois

PRESERVATION
PLAN ON IT

LYNDHURST, TARRYTOWN, NY. A NATIONAL TRUST PROPERTY.

Planning on restoring a house, saving a landmark, reviving your neighborhood?

No matter what your plans, gain a wealth of experience and help preserve our historic and architectural heritage. Join the National Trust for Historic Preservation and support preservation efforts in your community.

Make preservation a blueprint for the future.

Write:

**National Trust for Historic Preservation
Department PA
1785 Massachusetts Ave., N.W.
Washington, D.C. 20036**

Publisher's Note

I was born on the shores of Lake Michigan and have been in the pleasure boating business for more than 40 years. Though not our largest annual edition of WATERWAY GUIDE, the Great Lakes book is near to my heart as are all things marine.

Today there are more pleasure boats plying the nation's waterways than ever before. The Great Lakes, as well as the Intracoastal Waterway, are good examples of this phenomenon. We can look forward to even more activity on the water in the years ahead. Boating is a growing sport!

If you haven't yet acquainted yourself with the WATERWAY GUIDE Cruising Club, now is the time to do so. Elsewhere in this issue you will find a message from contributor and Club Commodore, Walter Cronkite, inviting you to become a member. In the spirit of WATERWAY GUIDE, we are committed to making it the finest cruising club afloat.

The current boating season could well be a harbinger for the industry. Boats offer an attractive alternative to vacation homes. Currently, all interest on loans for boats that have sleeping accommodations, a galley, and a head qualify for the second home mortgage deduction (as long as the amount of the loan does not exceed $1 million when combined with the mortgage on the primary home). In addition, some tax experts advise that interest payments for "dockominium" units also may be deductible if included in a boat's overall financing package.

Even though such deductions are coming under increasing scrutiny by Congress, large-scale public opposition makes it unlikely that lawmakers will repeal the mortgage deduction altogether.

Boats appealing to the second home shopper are tailored to a life of comfort on the water. Equipped with such amenities as air-conditioning, microwaves, VCRs, and freezers with automatic ice makers, these vessels afford owners the advantages of a home with the mobility that only a boat can offer.

Will the vacation home boom turn out to be a bust? The consensus says no. And it seems unlikely when you consider that the 55-plus age group currently holds 75 percent of the nation's wealth and will represent one-third of the population by 2010.

Boating is a never-ending adventure. Continue to enjoy it to the fullest, especially on the Great Lakes.

—Charles Jones

★ **CAPTAIN TO CAPTAIN** ★

FLY YOUR BRIGHTLY COLORED SAFE BOATERS I.D. FLAG AND CAST YOUR VOTE FOR SAFETY

- The only visual, uniform standard of recognition of who is who on the seas.
- When you see the flag, you know what to expect. If you don't see it, BEWARE.
- Available with proof of a boating course or a captain's license.
- Licensed captains and boating instructors qualify for a three star flag.
- A boating course certificate qualifies you for one star flag.
- CERTIFICATE OF OWNERSHIP AND TWO CAR DECALS WITH EVERY FLAG.
- NEXT DAY SHIPPING • MONEY-BACK GUARANTEE

Mail a photocopy of your documentation now, along with a check for $19.50 + $3.50 shipping and handling. N.J. residents add 6% sales tax.

Send to: **SAFE CAPTAINS USA P.O. BOX 157 MILLTOWN, N.J. 08850-0157**
- For free literature call 1-800-477-0157 9-5 M-F

SAFE CAPTAINS USA IS A NON PROFIT ORGANIZATION

Slip Into Delegal Creek Marina.

Delegal Creek Marina is located on the southern tip of Skidaway Island, about 15 miles south of Savannah. With its floating dock system, our new marina has 40- and 50-foot slips available for permanent as well as transient docking. We offer a full-range of services, professional security, and a fully-stocked Yacht Chandlery. Less than a mile off the I.C.W. and less than 5 miles from the Atlantic, our marina gives you easy access to great inshore and offshore fishing, plus all of the gold of Georgia's coastal islands without the crowds.

Call us today at 912/598-0023 for rates and additional information.

GREAT LAKES EDITION

"Quest" traveling through the Panama Canal.

DESTINATION Los Angeles

HIGH SPEED LONG RANGE RAISED BRIDGE COCKPIT MOTORYACHT
LOA - 103'
BEAM - 22'
DRAFT - 4'
ENGINES - (2) MTU 12V 396 TB 93 (1930 BHP) each
DRIVES - (2) KAMEWA #63 WATER JETS
TOP SPEED - 34 KNOTS

P.O. BOX 805, DANIA FL 33004
(305) 920-0622 FAX: (305) 920-6553
CONTACT: KIT DENISON

Editor's Log

As winter gives way to the promise of spring, Great Lakes mariners stir anew and start dreaming of summer cruising. Where will it be this season? Mackinac Island? Put-In-Bay? Lake Champlain?

Wherever your compass heading takes you, it's a certainty that some planning will be involved. In fact, the myriad of options offered for cruising in this region have prompted us to offer a new feature for readers: the Triangle Loop Cruise. You will note that we've devoted the second chapter of this edition to a Loop Cruise that runs from Troy to Oswego to Sorel, and back to Troy.

This first Loop Cruise will give readers a taste of what will come in subsequent editions. Other Loop Cruises on the agenda are: Albany to Toronto to Montreal and back; Syracuse to Detroit through Georgian Bay and back; and eventually, the "ultimate loop" that takes the cruising mariner from New York across and through the Great Lakes, down the Midwest's rivers into the Tenn-Tom, and finally out into Mobile Bay and the Gulf of Mexico. In this way, we'll tie all four editions of the GUIDE together in a set of books that connects each region's waters and gives mariners a complete four-volume guide to cruising all the important waters of the eastern half of the United States.

It's exciting to be able to offer Great Lakes cruisers something new and useful; something that you've asked for and wanted. Putting cruising information in this format should be especially valuable to those who have limited time available and want a definite itinerary. Motorists have planned their trips in this way for decades with the help of AAA, and now mariners can step aboard their boats with a preplanned route just as they pile into their cars for highway journeys.

Providing updates and changes for this edition are several correspondents who are more than familiar with the beauty and challenge of Great Lakes cruising. Stark and Joann Ferriss, who have made many trips north from their home port of Stuart, Florida, are in large part responsible for the inclusion of the Loop Cruise. Their first-hand experience and numerous discussions with like-minded mariners give them a unique perspective on the needs of readers who cruise this area. David Brown, from his vantage point in Port Clinton, Ohio, provides us with coverage of Lake Erie and the Detroit River. David is also a contributor to *Lakeland Boating Magazine* and *Soundings*. And, last but not least, a long-term GUIDE correspondent, Captain Donald Launer, collected notes from his delivery log for updates on the Hudson River and the Erie and Oswego canals.

Readers will see other changes with this edition, along with the new Triangle Loop Cruise. After polling Great Lakes mariners about previous editions, we determined that the chapters on Lake Superior and Georgian Bay should be eliminated. The area is simply too vast, and the audience too small to justify inclusion of these chapters. But we trust that our new features will more than compensate for those deletions.

Here's hoping that these changes will give you new ideas and choices when it comes to planning your cruises. Let us know what you think and what we might provide in future editions to make your time on the water even more enjoyable. Have an exciting and safe cruising season.

Judith Powers

Sailboats must step or unstep their masts at the juncture of the New York State Canal System.

Walter Cronkite

Keep the Eagle Flying

Walter Cronkite, here on his ketch, Wyntje, *supports the Coast Guard's tall ship training program.*

The U.S. Coast Guard Barkentine *Eagle* is sailing almost in the Land of the Midnight Sun—60 degrees north. It is June 20, 1989. Tomorrow will be the longest day of the year, before the sun starts its annual return trip south.

The *Eagle* is on a course of 070 degrees heading northeast from the Baltic Sea into the Gulf of Finland. She is carrying full canvas in the 12-knot breeze. Her courses, topsails, gallants, and royals are billowing under their yardarms; her jibs and staysails are drawing well; and her spanker is helping to relieve her natural weather helm for the two cadets stationed at her huge wheel.

It is just after 1:00 a.m., and the sky is still bright in the west. The clouds are tinted golden, as if the sun had just gone down. In fact, it hasn't gone down very far—barely ducking under the earth's horizon at this far north latitude, then speeding around to the other side of the Arctic for a moment or two before it reemerges for another long day.

A full moon has just risen, but its luminescence is embarrassed by the glow to the east. So bright is the sky that the moon's reflection is but a pale cousin of that which cuts a romantic path across more southern waters.

That reflection, however, is enough to backlight the silhouette of another great sailing vessel some six miles to starboard on a reciprocal course.

The *Eagle*'s captain, David Wood, hails her by radio.

"I am *Mir*," the other vessel answers.

Mir, one of the newest of the world's small fleet of Class A (the largest) sail training ships, is cruising near the Latvian coast.

Her captain, in a friendly chat in impeccable English, reveals to Captain Wood that she is two days out of Leningrad and sailing to London for a tall ship rendezvous to celebrate London's 400th anniversary before proceeding to Hamburg to help that German city commemorate a similar event.

"Will I see you there?" *Mir*'s captain asks.

"I'm afraid not," demurs Captain Wood. "We are going to Leningrad and then back to Denmark to join in a local celebration of the American Revolution, and then on to Rouen, France, for the celebration of Bastille Day—the bicentenary of their revolution. Will you be in Rouen?"

"Negative. One of our other Soviet ships will be there, I think."

Captain Wood's words, whether intended as such or not, are a subtle reminder to the Soviet captain that two of the other great nations of the world also were forged out of revolution. In turn, the *Mir* skipper's words are a

---

Editor's note: Walter Cronkite sailed aboard the Eagle *as a guest during part of its summer voyaging and was able to observe her majesty first-hand.*

The Eagle, the U.S. Coast Guard's tall sail training ship, is an important part of training Coast Guard cadets.

reminder that the Soviet Union has four tall sail training ships; more than any other nation. Because of this, the Russians can spread their goodwill visits to more ports and national celebrations than can the United States, with its single Class A square rigger, the *Eagle*.

U.S. warships seldom call at Soviet ports, and the *Eagle*'s ceremonial visit to Leningrad is the first such visit of an American government vessel there since 1975.

Because it is an unarmed sail training ship, the *Eagle* is ideally suited for this mission that represents the improving relationship between the United States and Gorbachev's Soviet Union. And in more subtle terms, the visit speaks of hope for the survival and burgeoning of that relationship.

Few means of promoting friendship between nations are as effective, and certainly none as picturesque, as the ceremonial visit of a tall ship. The romance of the sea is not restricted to those of us who love boats and boating. Wherever tall ships go, thousands of men, women, and children are drawn to these vessels, where they either stand in awe at dockside or go aboard and tour the vessel. With faces aloft, they squint against a bright sky to focus on the peak of the topmast and to marvel at the cadets who nimbly scurry up the ratlines where they hang like circus acrobats on the footropes and crawl out to the farthest reaches of the yardarms.

The more imaginative gawkers, especially the sailors in the crowd who have experienced rough weather at sea, can picture the crew's young men and women fighting storm-flogged sails from their swaying perches as the gale-driven rain lashes their faces.

The tall ships carry an important part of a civilization's history, and to no people is this more important than to Americans. Most of our ancestors came to these shores by boat; and some of them, not so many generations ago. Our commerce has always been dependent on ships and the men who sail them. In the early days, our major cities and the colonies were linked primarily by sailing ships, while river boatmen played a major role in pushing our frontiers westward.

The *Eagle*, along with some smaller sailing ships owned by private organizations, carries the burden of that heritage. Beyond that important chore, which alone would justify her existence, the *Eagle* is a practical part of the training of the cadets at The Coast Guard Academy in New London, Connecticut. They all serve aboard her at various times during their education to gain unparalleled experience in ship handling. To travel aboard the *Eagle* is to affirm the claim by the Academy that there is no seamanship training comparable to that which can be obtained aboard her.

Raw third-classmen, in their second year at the Academy, come aboard the *Eagle* for the first time as innocents in a strange environment. Confusion, and perhaps fear, is written on their faces as they confront not only the ever-present unknowns of the sea, but also the prospect of that first long climb aloft.

By the second or third day out, these young crewmen are turning out smartly to their assigned posts with each call to duty and are scrambling nimbly up the ratlines or throwing their strong backs into hauling sheets and halyards. Their confidence seems to build almost hour by hour as they stand watch with instructors, regular officers, and upperclassmen.

The mariner who has the opportunity to observe these young sailors in this unique training exercise goes forth on his own boat with a renewed confidence in the capabilities of the Coast Guard.

The fraternity of pleasure boaters should be prepared to help in the not-too-distant future when the fate of our country's tall ship training program may be at stake. Perhaps it's too early to become alarmed, but it is not too early to become concerned about losing our only square rigger.

The problem is that *Eagle* is beginning to show her age. She was built almost 60 years ago, which is a very long time in the life of a sailing ship. In a few years, she must be replaced. And in these days of tight federal budgets, one can safely bet that the Coast Guard request for millions of dollars to build a sailing ship is going to encounter some rough weather in Washington.

We boaters can help gird for this legislative battle, or perhaps even forestall it, if we take an active interest in promoting the continuation of the Coast Guard sail training program and the construction of a new square rigger on which to conduct it.

There are various ways we can express our interest. There is, of course, the Coast Guard Auxiliary for those with the time and inclination to lend a helpful hand. There is the Coast Guard Foundation that aids Coast Guard families—and the greater its membership rolls, the more impressive the public support of the service. Another means of expression are letters we can write to our legislators.

To foster not only the United States' but also the entire international training ship program (other nations also have budgetary problems that threaten their square riggers), we could urge local waterfront communities to

MARINE PLATING

SPECIALISTS IN MARINE CHROME PLATING SINCE 1955

Inquiries Invited • We Ship Anywhere

GULF PLATING INC.

TELEPHONE: 305/467-9751

518 S.W. FIRST AVENUE
FORT LAUDERDALE, FLA. 33301

RARITAN...Engineering Products and

Winning Customer Confidence

**Sanitation Systems • Converters
Rudder Indicators • Icemakers
Installation Aids • Water Heaters
Air Horns • Pumps**

RARITAN Engineering Company, Inc.

3101 S.W. Second Ave.
Ft. Lauderdale, FL 33315
Telephone: 305-525-0378
FAX: 305-764-4370

530 Orange St.
Millville, NJ 08332
Telephone: 609-825-4900
FAX: 609-825-4409

invite the *Eagle* or other tall ships to visit.

A properly promoted tall ship visit can be a major regional event, drawing thousands of visitors to a town's harbor, boosting both the local economy and civic spirit. Sometimes these visits also inspire waterfront development.

Contact Operation Sail, the volunteers who helped stage the great sailing ship parades in New York, Boston, Baltimore, and elsewhere in 1976 and 1986, for information about inviting these international good-will ambassadors to your port. OpSail is at 207 Front Street, New York, NY 10038.

Presumably we mariners are a bit more cognizant than our landlubber friends of the romance of the sea. Certainly it is in our self-interest to preserve our superbly trained Coast Guard.

If we don't take a lively interest in the sail training program and the *Eagle*, then who in the world will?

—Walter Cronkite

Help on the Water

When you need help on the water, you want it fast. Depending on the severity of the problem, the Coast Guard offers the following guidelines.

For distress (grave or imminent danger threatening you or your boat), contact the Coast Guard on Channel 16 or use signal flares.

For nondistress, however, different rules apply. For this aid, the Coast Guard will coordinate efforts to help by contacting a marina or commercial firm to assist you. If this is unsuccessful, a Marine Assistance Request Broadcast (MARB) will be made in your behalf. This announces that you need help, advises of your location, and invites others to come to your aid.

If a commercial firm offers to lend assistance, the Coast Guard will turn the incident over to them. You must pay for this assistance, however. And if you agree to commercial aid, then refuse when it arrives at the scene, you may still be obligated to pay a fee.

A fellow mariner or public agency may also offer to help, but be aware that they may not have the proper equipment or skills to provide safe and effective help.

If you require a tow, the Coast Guard or Coast Guard Auxiliary normally will tow you to the nearest place for repairs.

It is wise to consider the following before accepting any assistance:

★ Towing can cause damage and personal injury.

★ Does the provider have proper equipment?

★ Does the provider have proper insurance?

★ Is there adequate crew to handle the situation?

★ If there is a fee involved, does the commercial firm have a Coast Guard license? (All firms must be licensed if they charge for towing.)

The Fresh Connection™
Desalinization Unequaled

Join our impressive list of satisfied customers, yacht and ship builders...don't settle for an "imitation" when you can have the original **Watermaker**.

QUALITY
Watermakers, Inc. was established in 1984, with developing technology since 1961. We take pride in our product, personalized service and overall integrity. Only the finest materials are incorporated into our products.

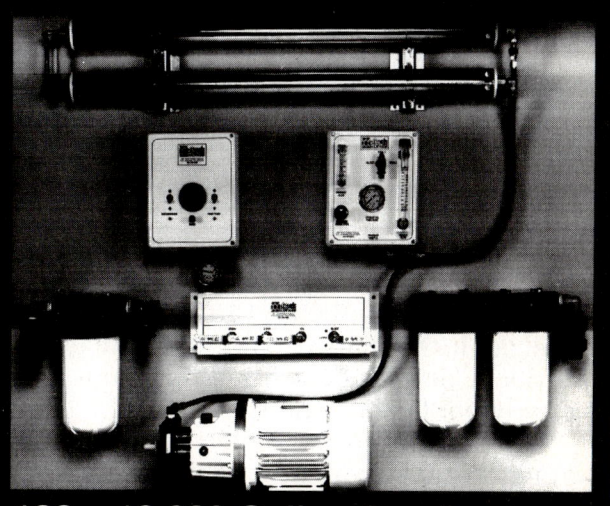

100 – 10,000 Gallon/Day Systems

Great Water Doesn't Just Happen...We Make It!
WORLD LEADER IN TECHNOLOGY

- The FIRST to introduce low-maintenance machines with no v-belts or accumulators.
- The ONLY manufacturer to feature a titanium pump on some of its machines.
- The FIRST to introduce stainless steel pressure vessels for sea water.
- The FIRST to create a component system that allows flexible, easy installation.
- The FIRST cleaning and testing lab in South Florida for all types of membranes. Our cleaning kits are the finest available today.

2233 S. Andrews Ave.
Fort Lauderdale, FL 33316

305-467-8920 • FAX: 305-522-3248

GREAT LAKES EDITION

Slip into the Good Life at The Jockey Club

Rent a transient slip at the internationally famous Jockey Club Marina and get more than a prestigious place to dock. More than free 24-hour security, cable TV and water.

Rent a slip at The Jockey Club and you're entitled to all the amenities of this world-famous private club. Like tennis courts. Swimming pools. Restaurants. Entertainment. And hotel suites.

We've got 60 transient slips ranging in size from 40' to 200'. So, after you've sailed the high seas, slip into the good life. At The Jockey Club. LIMITED NUMBER OF SLIPS ALSO AVAILABLE FOR OWNERSHIP.

- Free water and cable TV
- Telephone hook-up
- Electricity
- 24-hour Security
- Dockmaster
- Marked entry Channel
- Gas diesel fuels
- Showers/laundromat

The Jockey Club
Look for Red Marker #16, South of Broad Causeway

FAX 305-891-8129
11111 Biscayne Blvd., Miami, FL 33161
(305) 893-3344

How To Use WATERWAY GUIDE

Your cruise will be much safer and much more pleasurable if you have WATERWAY GUIDE as your constant companion—but not as a substitute for navigational charts. It isn't intended to be used alone but to be read in conjunction with the latest NOS chart or WATERWAY GUIDE ChartBook. THE GUIDE gives mile-by-mile navigational advice, pointing out hazards and handicaps, points of interest, and where to tie up overnight.

Contents

The main body of the book is divided into geographical sections, and each section is broken down into shorter chapters. Each of the major sections begins with a full-page chart of the area covered, an assessment of that area's characteristics, and vital statistics (bridges, distances) needed for safe and easy passages.

The chapters cover the actual route, described mile by mile, with signficant harbors, ports, anchorages, hazards, and points of interest along the way. Facilities listings and chartlets at the end of each section describe the marine facilities in each area. Note that the chartlets are intended for orientation only and should never be used for navigation.

To Get from Here to There

To locate a particular place or body of water, check the Index in the back of the book. If you are planning a cruise and want to find suitable harbors in which to lay over, consult the chart and mileage table at the beginning of each section. Then read our text and study the chart; plot your course; decide where you want to spend the night by consulting the appropriate facility listings and chartlets for services and dockage. The listings give marine facilities by area, with a chartlet identifying number and a description of available services.

The listing gives marine facilities by area, with an identifying number and a description of available services. To find a marina that interests you, look up its number on the chartlet. Each chartlet carries a north arrow so you can relate it to the NOS chart.

Reading the Facility Listings

The facilities listings provide skippers with information about services available at each facility. WATERWAY

JOIN THE WATERWAY GUIDE CRUISING CLUB

Become a charter member of the newest club for boating enthusiasts!

Send today to receive complete details on Club benefits, which include a newsletter, special discounts, a certificate signed by Commodore Walter Cronkite, and a Cruising Club burgee. Send in this postcard with your name and interests.

JOIN US TODAY !

Name _____

Address _____ City _____

State _____ Zip _____ Phone (_____) _____

Type of Boat _____ Size _____ Cruising Area _____

Areas of Special Interest (check all that apply)
- ❏ Cruising news
- ❏ Navigational bulletins
- ❏ The Chesapeake Bay
- ❏ Florida
- ❏ Long Island Sound
- ❏ Gulf Coast
- ❏ The ICW
- ❏ New England Waters
- ❏ Discounts on WWG products

Other _____

JOIN THE WATERWAY GUIDE CRUISING CLUB

Become a charter member of the newest club for boating enthusiasts!

Send today to receive complete details on Club benefits, which include a newsletter, special discounts, a certificate signed by Commodore Walter Cronkite, and a Cruising Club burgee. Send in this postcard with your name and interests.

JOIN US TODAY !

Name _____

Address _____ City _____

State _____ Zip _____ Phone (_____) _____

Type of Boat _____ Size _____ Cruising Area _____

Areas of Special Interest (check all that apply)
- ❏ Cruising news
- ❏ Navigational bulletins
- ❏ The Chesapeake Bay
- ❏ Florida
- ❏ Long Island Sound
- ❏ Gulf Coast
- ❏ The ICW
- ❏ New England Waters
- ❏ Discounts on WWG products

Other _____

```
|||| 
```

NO POSTAGE
NECESSARY
IF MAILED
IN THE
UNITED STATES

BUSINESS REPLY MAIL
FIRST CLASS   PERMIT 11077   ATLANTA, GA

POSTAGE WILL BE PAID FOR BY ADDRESSEE:

✴ **WATERWAY GUIDE**

6255 Barfield Road
Atlanta, GA 30328

```
|..||.|..|.|.|..|.|.|.|..||.|...||....||.|||..|
```

```
||||
```

NO POSTAGE
NECESSARY
IF MAILED
IN THE
UNITED STATES

BUSINESS REPLY MAIL
FIRST CLASS   PERMIT 11077   ATLANTA, GA

POSTAGE WILL BE PAID FOR BY ADDRESSEE:

✴ **WATERWAY GUIDE**

6255 Barfield Road
Atlanta, GA 30328

```
|..||.|..||.|.|.||.|.|.|..|.|.|..|..|||
```

GUIDE tries to list all marinas, yacht clubs, restaurants, and repair shops that have their own docks.

Not all facilities are listed—some are too small for cruising boats, some are committed exclusively to local business.

No. of transient berths indicates the number of slips reserved for transient use, but doesn't insure a slip will be available. Call ahead to reserve a slip.

Approach depth is the depth from the main channel to the dock (sometimes the approach *is* the main channel).

Dockside depth is given at low water, but is sometimes optimistically reported. Call ahead to check all depths if they appear marginal.

Railway/Lift capacity is intended to help mariners who need emergency hauling on their voyage. A bent prop, a hard grounding, or just a need for a fresh coat of antifouling paint may call for a quick haul-out. This category lists either the type of haul-out rig (**Rail** or **Lift**) or lift capacity in tons to help you locate a suitable facility.

Marine supplies/Groceries/Ice indicates whether these important commodities are available on premises or within walking distance.

LPG and CNG stands for liquid propane gas and compressed natural gas—widely used stove fuels.

Voltage and Amperage tells skippers whether their electrical system is compatible with the shore installation or whether it requires an adapter.

Showers/Laundromat indicates that these important facilities are available on premises or within walking distance.

Pump-out Station indicates the availability of equipment to empty your holding tanks.

Restaurant/Snack bar informs the mariner that one or both of these facilities can be found on premises or within walking distance.

Although facilities that advertise in WATERWAY GUIDE are noted as such in the listings, we list all the marinas we can, whether or not they advertise. The listings are not paid for and are published purely as a service to the readers.

GRAND BANKS®

The Grand Banks 42 Classic. . . a natural for coastal and inland cruising. Diesel power delivers speeds up to 18 knots. Two staterooms and two heads provide comfortable accomodations with plenty of storage. For information on Grand Banks sales and service, your contacts are:

Eldean Boat Sales
Macatawa, Michigan
616-335-5843

Inland Yacht
Pittsburgh, Pennsylvania
412-279-7090

Northshore Marine, Inc.
Port Credit, Ontario
416-891-0666

GREAT LAKES EDITION

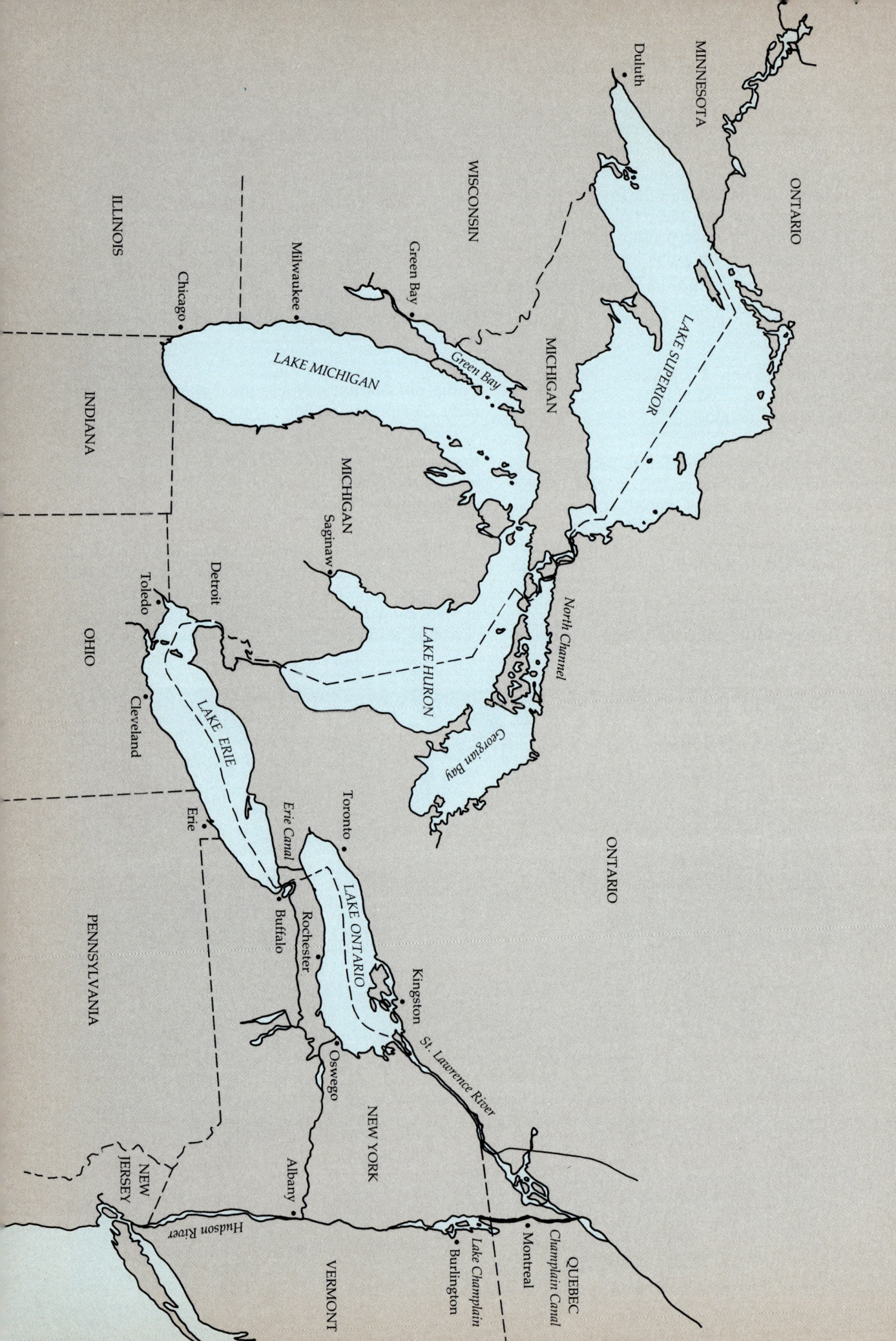

The Great Lakes and Connecting Waterways

Comprising one-fifth of the world's surface fresh water supply and encompassing 95,000 square miles, the prodigious Great Lakes are unique on the face of the earth. They are arranged like a flight of stairs, with Lake Superior standing at 602 feet above sea level, lakes Michigan and Huron at 581 feet, Erie at 572 feet, and Lake Ontario at 246 feet. Two of the rivers that connect them (St. Marys, between Lake Superior and Lake Huron; and the Niagara, between Lake Erie and Lake Ontario) require locks for navigation of their rapids and waterfalls. The enormous volume of water from all the lakes discharges from Lake Ontario into the St. Lawrence River, which carries it to the destination of all lakes and rivers, the open ocean. In the process, the St. Lawrence drops the remaining 246 feet to sea level through several series of swift rapids, which have been tamed for navigation by the St. Lawrence Seaway system of locks and canals.

While the St. Lawrence River and Seaway provide the only connection between the Great Lakes and the ocean for ships, three other waterways leading to the ocean are accessible to small craft. The New York State Canal, successor to the old Erie Canal, connects Lake Erie with the Hudson River, which flows into New York Bay. One branch of the canal discharges into Lake Ontario, while another leads to Lake Champlain, from which the Richelieu River and Chambly Canal carry small vessels into the St. Lawrence River. From Lake Michigan, the Chicago Sanitary and Ship Canal leads to the Illinois River, which flows into the Mississippi, discharging ultimately into the Gulf of Mexico. (WATERWAY GUIDE does not cover the Chicago-to-Mississippi route.) Canada's Rideau Waterway leads from Lake Ontario to the Ottawa River, which can then be navigated to the St. Lawrence. In addition, the Trent-Severn Waterway, an all-Canadian system of rivers, lakes, canals, and locks, connects Lake Ontario with Georgian Bay, Lake Huron's eastern arm.

Bordered by eight states—New York, Pennsylvania, Ohio, Michigan, Indiana, Illinois, Wisconsin, and Minnesota—and the province of Ontario, the Great Lakes offer a variety of scenic attractions and cruising conditions to suit every taste. Their natural settings range from cliffs and mountains to wide sand beaches and high dunes to dense forests and islands by the thousands. From the continent's largest cities to tiny rural villages, there is every sort of urban community. Industry, mining, farming, logging, and fishing can all be seen around the lake's shores, and on the open water are the mighty lake freighters and oceangoing vessels that tie it all together. Cruising conditions vary fron the vast oceanic expanse and big swells of Lake Superior to the chop of the small lakes, St. Clair and Erie, to the intricate island-studded channels of Georgian Bay, and the placid waters of the connecting canal systems.

International Cruising

The international boundary between the United States and Canada runs through the middle of the Great Lakes and their connecting waterways, including the St. Lawrence River to the latitude of St. Regis, New York. Lake Michigan, however, lies entirely within U.S. territory. A great deal of pleasure boat traffic moves both ways across the border every summer. There are only minor differences in cruising conditions.

Customs. Both countries require that visitors from

The Illinois Waterway Chicago to the Gulf

Not many mariners realize that there is another waterway leading to and from the Great Lakes, and that you can reach the Gulf Coast from Lake Michigan by boat. The Illinois Waterway connects the Chicago River with the Illinois River and links with the great Mississippi River. Large yachts can make the passage from Chicago south to St. Louis, Kansas City, Tulsa, Baton Rouge, or New Orleans. Skippers can also link up with the Tennessee River and the Tennessee-Tombigbee Waterway for an alternative route to the Gulf.

The Illinois Waterway was created by reversing the flow of the Chicago River through a series of locks so that it would flow, not into Lake Michigan, but into the Illinois River, 54 miles west of Chicago. From Chicago Harbor or Calumet Harbor on Lake Michigan, vessels proceed southwest through several major locks and dams, including the big Thomas J. O'Brien Lock and Dam, completed in 1960. Lockport, 36 miles from Lake Michigan, is where the waterway begins its descent to the Illinois River and on to the Mississippi.

WATERWAY GUIDE does not cover the Illinois River, nor the Mississippi River, although the 700 miles of the Tennessee-Tombigbee Waterway are covered in our Southern edition. These inland rivers are covered by an excellent publication entitled:

Quimby's Boating Guide
Waterways Journal, Inc.
319 N. Fourth Street
St. Louis, MO 63102

across the border report to Customs immediately upon arrival at the first port of call. Both agencies provide reporting service by telephone. See the "Customs" section in the Mariner's Handbook for specific procedures and regulations.

Charts and sailing directions. American and Canadian charts and publications differ little in style of presentation, with one major exception. Canada is entirely metric, so all measurements in the newer charts, signs, and publications are given in metric terms. The U.S. mariner must be prepared to convert. This is especially important with speed limits, where the zones are now marked in *kilometers/hour* rather than *mph*, and when buying fuel in liters. See the " Metrics" section in the Mariners' Handbook for a table of equivalents.

In the United States, conversely, the Canadian mariner will want to use the table of equivalents to translate kilometers and liters into miles per hour and gallons.

There are still a few old-style Canadian charts in use, which show depths in fathoms to an obsolete chart datum. The corrections that must be applied are noted on these charts.

For explanations of how to order charts, Coast Pilots, and Sailing Directions, see the "Government Publications" section in the Mariner's Handbook.

All Canadian charts reprinted in WATERWAY GUIDE are done so with the permission of the Canadian Hydrographic Service.

Note that overhead power transmission and telecommunication cables other than those charted on Canadian Hydrographic Service Charts exist on the waterways of Canada. Mariners should exercise caution and look aloft when navigating Canadian waters.

Weather. The U.S. Coast Guard broadcasts a weather report at intervals on Channel 22 and the Canadian Coast Guard maintains a continuous weather broadcast on Channel 21. Information is also available by MAFOR (MArine FORecast) coded reports and LAWEB (LAkes WEather Broadcast) plain language synopses. Commercial radio stations regularly broadcast MAFOR and LAWEB reports for big ships, and many pleasure mariners rely heavily on them. See the Mariner's Handbook for more information, lists of weather stations, and explanations of MAFOR and LAWEB.

Water levels. Although the Great Lakes are tideless, lake levels fluctuate from year to year and on an irregular cycle over several years. With droughts, lake levels have reached record lows, but then make their way back up. Mariners should be informed about current levels, which are reported on weather broadcasts. Mariners should be especially cautious in entering harbors with marginal depths.

Coast Guard. The Ninth District Headquarters is at Cleveland; Search and Rescue Stations, with telephone

---

Where to go, How to get there, What to do.

WATERWAY GUIDE

Details of Harbors, Anchorages, Weather, Marinas and their services, Events and Attractions on shore. Four regional editions, Southern, Mid-Atlantic, Northern and Great Lakes. Chart-books, too.

In Georgia call   404-256-9800
Elsewhere call toll-free   1-800-233-3359

6255 Barfield Road, Atlanta, GA 30328

numbers, are listed in the Mariner's Handbook. All group offices monitor Channel 16.

The Canadian Coast Guard operates seven main coast radio stations which handle all radio traffic: distress, commercial, ship-to-shore (as Public Coast Operators do in the United States), weather, and other marine safety information.

All Canadian Coast Guard stations monitor Channel 16. If you are in trouble, call the Coast Guard on Channel 16; your call will be relayed to the Rescue Coordination Centre at Trenton. The Centre coordinates all Canadian search-and-rescue operations and also works closely with the U.S. Coast Guard headquarters in Cleveland.

MSDs. You must have a Coast Guard approved MSD—Type I, II, or III. To cruise in various waters covered by this edition of WATERWAY GUIDE, you must have a Type III (holding tank) MSD. These waters are: Lake Champlain; the Thousand Islands area; the Michigan waters of Lake Erie; Lake St. Clair; Lake Huron; Lake Michigan (except Illinois and Indiana waters); Lake Superior waters belonging to Michigan (including Isle Royale) but not Minnesota and Wisconsin waters.

The Province of Ontario (the Canadian side of lakes Ontario, Erie, Huron, and Superior) also requires a Type III (holding tank) MSD, or a secured flow-through system retro-fitted with a holding tank. Portables are prohibited. The Ontario government enforces the rule very strictly, so be sure you're in compliance.

Buoyage. Canada and the United States follow the same principles of buoyage with respect to shape and color, but use a different mix of navigational aids. Canada places many more **spar buoys** (painted red and green, numbered odd and even) than it does nuns and cans, and occasionally uses a boat-shaped buoy that is not found in United States waters. Moreover, Canadian buoyage is usually of smaller size than its American counterpart.

Canada makes far more extensive use of **beacons** and **ranges**. Daybeacons are of two types: Steel triangles, painted red and white, or squares, painted green and black, are set on posts in the water or on land. These are most commonly found in narrow channels. Rectangular or square daybeacons may be fastened to the post of a relatively small lighted aid placed on shore, a sort of combination of a lighthouse and a buoy. These are usually red and white, but may have green on them if it's necessary to indicate that they should be left to port.

Ranges are of two kinds: lighted and unlighted. **Range lights** are usually fixed red, green, or white, and these structures are fitted with triangular white daybeacons, banded in red, for easy daytime identification. **Unlighted ranges** usually have the same kind of daybeacons, although there's a wider variety of style among these, especially on the upper lakes. White-painted triangles are common on the smaller ranges. Virtually every Canadian port is equipped with an **entrance range**, mostly lighted, but unlighted in a few remote places. Many passages are also marked exclusively by ranges rather than buoys. Beacons and ranges have two important advantages over buoys: They are highly visible, and they are not as subject to shifting and displacement as buoys are.

Pets. If you have a pet aboard, both the United States and Canada require certification that it has been vaccinated for rabies.

Holidays. Public, legal holidays in the **United States** are as follows: New Year's Day, Martin Luther King's Birthday (third Monday in January), President's Day (second Monday in February), Memorial Day (the last Monday in May), Independence Day (July 4), Labor Day (first Monday in September), Columbus Day (second Monday in October), Veterans Day (November 11), Thanksgiving Day (fourth Thursday in November), Christmas Day (December 25).

Canadian holidays are as follows: New Year's Day, Victoria Day (third Monday in May), St. John the Baptist Day (in Quebec, June 24), Dominion Day (July 1), Civic Holiday (in Ontario, August 3), Canadian Thanksgiving (second Monday in October), Remembrance Day (November 11), Christmas Day (December 25).

Liquor

In Canada, liquor, wine and beer are available in government liquor stores; wine and beer are available at retail stores in most of the larger cities. Most hotels and restaurants are licensed to serve alcohol.

In the United States, different states have different regulations concerning the sale of alcohol: Illinois and Indiana, liquor and beer in commercial liquor stores; Michigan, liquor and beer in state liquor stores; Minnesota, liquor and beer in commercial liquor stores; Ohio, liquor in state stores and beer in commercial liquor stores; New York, beer and wine in supermarkets, liquor in commercial liquor stores; Pennsylvania, beer carried-out from bars in small quantities, bought at commercial distributors in case lots; liquor in state liquor stores; Vermont, beer and wine in grocery and drug stores, liquor in state liquor stores; Wisconsin, beer and wine in liquor stores, grocery stores, drug stores, and convenience stores, liquor in commercial liquor stores.

Warning. The marine police and Coast Guard services in the United States and Canada are cracking down on intoxicated mariners. Many agencies now carry breathalyzers and have greater authority to arrest those suspected of impared operation of a boat. If convicted of this offense in Ontario, a mariner's boating privileges can be suspended for up to three months. A good rule of thumb, which is applied by many agencies, is to avoid operating a vessel if you have consumed more than 12 ounces of beer, six ounces of wine, or one ounce of 80 proof or stronger liquor within the past hour.

GREAT LAKES EDITION

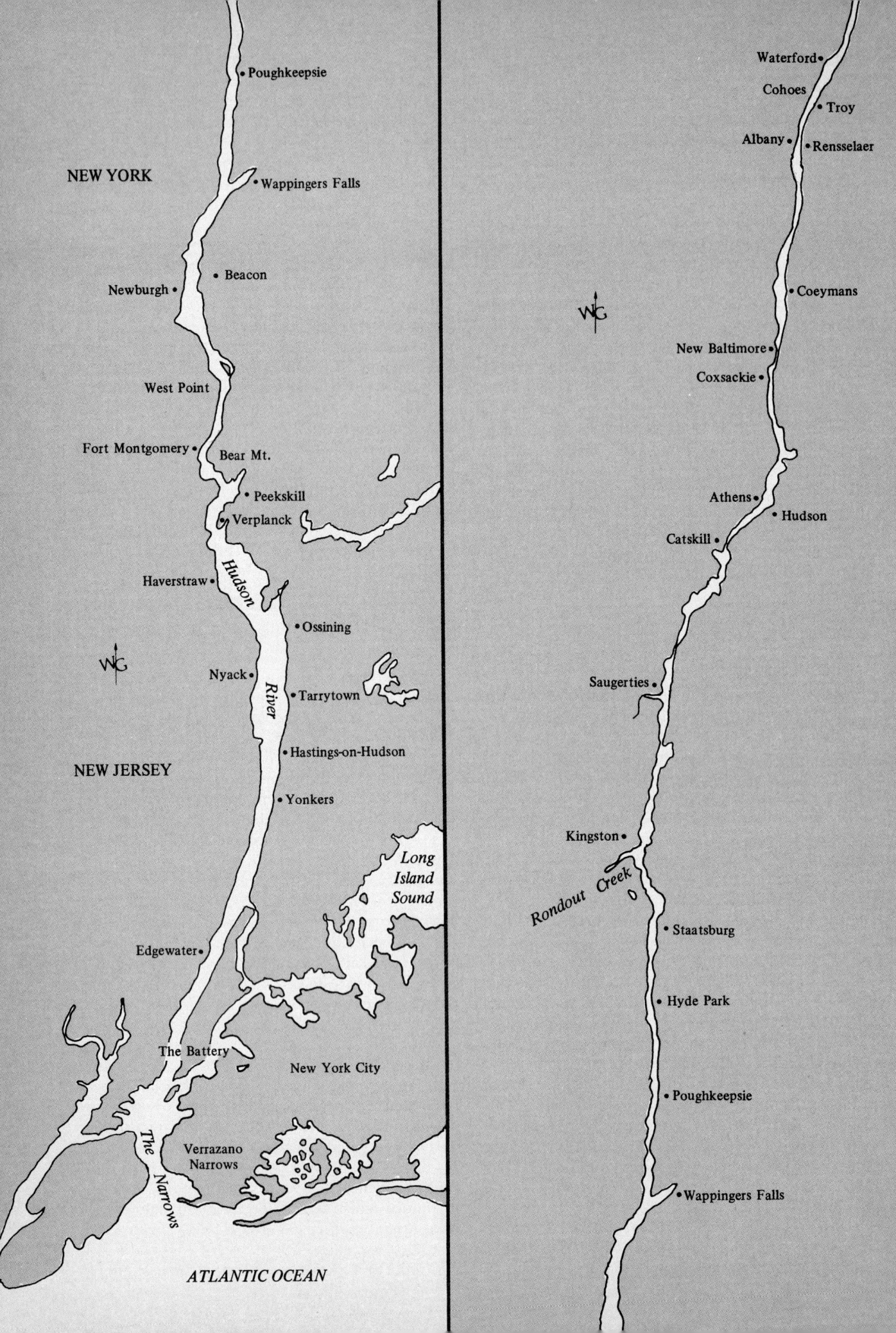

The Hudson River

New York Bay to Waterford

CHARTS: 12326, 12328-SC, 12333, 12334, 12336, 12335, 12339, 12341, 12342, 12343, 12345, 12346, 12347, 12348, 12351-SC, 12363, 12364; or Waterway Guide Chartbook.

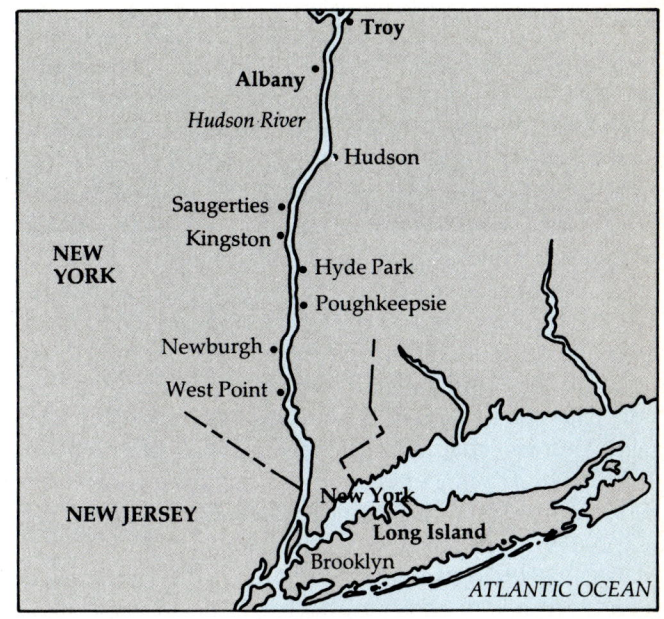

Named for Englishman Henry Hudson, who thought it might be the "Northwest Passage," the Hudson served many years as a highway for settlers, trade, and war. When New York was New Amsterdam, the banks of the Hudson were settled and farmed by the Dutch (You'll pass many of their original estates). Later, during the Revolution, the Hudson and Lake Champlain were the route for military expeditions to and from Canada.

Now as before, the river is a shipping route, and you'll encounter ships and barges carrying petroleum products, sugar and syrup, and building materials.

From Manhattan's skyscrapers to Albany, past spectacular mountain scenery including the Palisades, High Tor, Dunderberg, Storm King, Bear Mountain, and the "Kaatskills," the wide Hudson heads directly north for 155 miles.

Cruising Characteristics

Cruising the lower Hudson River is generally straightforward. Buoyage is plentiful, midchannel depths range from 15 to 175 feet and, north of Manhattan, marinas and hospitable yacht clubs are numerous. Almost every town has some accommodation for cruising mariners, but overnight berths should be selected for maximum protection from the river's natural chop and the wake from passing traffic. Most facilities have breakwaters or barrier bulkheads. Charts may or may not be accurate in showing some privately maintained markers. Some have been discontinued and some may not have been replaced after winter ice. It should also be noted that many commercial marinas and facilities list or advertise themselves as "yacht clubs." While many offer adequate services and are perfectly acceptable stopovers, they are not limited to yacht club members, nor do they observe reciprocity privileges.

On the upper river, creeks (both natural and dredged) make protected layovers. There are, however, a few conditions which must be kept in mind:

Tidal currents. Tidewater extends to Troy; the mean tidal range varies from three to five feet, and currents can be strong (two knots at The Battery, with an average of one and a half knots as far north as Albany). When you're northbound you are going away from the tidal current change and will hold a fair current longer than when southbound. Skippers should have a copy of the latest tidal current tables aboard.

Weather. The wind usually blows up or down the river, but near shore it tends to sweep towards the banks. Watch for summer squalls with sudden west winds up to 30 knots. Your only warning may be black clouds along the high west bank bluffs. Get to the weather side of the river whenever you see indications of rough conditions ahead.

Hazards. Navigation is straightforward for the 91 miles to Kingston, but thereafter extensive middle grounds and steep-to shoals must be given a wide berth. Be very cautious outside the lighted, buoyed channel. In the lower river, Haverstraw to Kingston, rocky shoals are common off the channel and departure from the marked route must be taken with caution and local knowledge. Above Kingston there are few rocks, but the mud and sand off-channel can be quite shoal, and grounding is a real danger.

Hazards are few, consisting mainly of debris, both floating and submerged, and in spring, fishtraps. The latter, flagged and lighted and set out for the shad run, are concentrated in the 25 to 30 statute miles below **Stony Point.** In the New York City and Albany-Troy

HUDSON RIVER

areas, drifting debris calls for an endless watch, particularly at tide change and in the spring.

Commercial traffic should be given full right-of-way, especially in poor visibility. Communicate, if you need to, on Channel 13.

The Battery to the George Washington Bridge.

One of the most thrilling passages for East Coast cruisers is the transit of New York Harbor and the entry into the mighty Hudson River. Called the Rhine of America, the Hudson is actually a fjord, or drowned river.

You will cruise through one of the world's busiest ports, passing within a few hundred feet of the Statue of Liberty; Ellis Island's spectacular Moorish architecture, gleaming from its recent restoration; and the renowned **Battery**, its name derived from a battery of 92 guns placed there by the British in 1693 to ward off attacks by the French. The renovated 1884 Fireboat Station adjacent to Battery Park displays a clock, built by Seth Thomas, that sounds the time with ship's bells. The World Trade Center and the dazzling residential condominiums are in dramatic contrast to historic old Manhattan.

Because the commercial traffic along the river causes a constant heavy chop, anchoring is not feasible until you are north of the George Washington Bridge. Most of the shore is lined with commercial wharves where no docking is permitted.

For those who wish to explore downtown **Manhattan**, a welcome new marina is on the New Jersey shore just north of the old Colgate Palmolive plant. Complete with floating docks, all amenities, and a nearby shopping mall, the marina provides safe and easy access to 33rd Street in Manhattan via the subway.

Heading up the river, you'll pass on the east side the old commercial and cruise ship wharves which are slowly being demolished and rebuilt. Here are world-famous yachts, such as the late Malcolm Forbes's *Highlander II*, moored at a mega-yacht marina. Next comes the Intrepid Museum at Pier 86, where the aircraft carrier *Intrepid* houses the museum. Between 59th Street and 72nd Street is the site of Donald Trump's mammoth planned Television City project.

George Washington Bridge to Tappen Zee Bridge. The **George Washington Bridge** was opened in 1931, during the Depression. It was not until 30 years later that the lower, second deck was added. **Spuyten Duyvil** (pronounced "spite-en die-vil") is the northern part of the **Harlem River**, the route followed by the famous Circle Line cruise boats during their scenic circumnavigation of the island of Manhattan.

The aura of the New York metropolis quickly dissipates beyond the George Washington Bridge, although the tall buildings of the city's northern reaches continue to form a backdrop that contrasts sharply with the 300- to 500-foot **Palisades**. Composed of columnar basalt, this striking series of cliffs is named for its visual similarity to old wooden barrier fortifications. If the wind is right, you can find a number of suitable anchorages close to shore at the base of the cliffs. Be prepared, however, to be rolled by the occasional wakes of the huge tugs as they scurry up and down the river.

Although **Yonkers** may appear on the chart to be a potential stopover, the marinas available here are, for the most part, small and private. Look for the restored Ambrose Light Ship docked north of the city.

Opposite **Hastings-on-the-Hudson** is the New Jersey-New York border. From this point to its headwaters in the Adirondack Mountains, the Hudson flows entirely within New York State.

Piermont Pier, the prominent mile-long point just north of the state border, was in 1850 the terminus of the Erie Railroad tracks. During that era, this spot was a major rail and ship cargo transfer point. A large NOAA research vessel is frequently berthed at the end of the pier. Although anchorage for protection from south winds can be found on the north side of the point, you should use caution in your approach—the shoaling is abrupt.

Tappan Zee Bridge to Bear Mountain Bridge. The Tappan Zee Bridge was completed just 35 years ago and carries across the river the New York State Thruway, an important interstate highway linking New York City to Albany and Buffalo. Just north of the bridge is **Tarrytown**. According to 19th-century author Washington Irving, the name derives from Dutch farm wives' complaining references to their husbands' tarrying too long at the village tavern there. The Tarrytown Marina and the Washington Irving Boat Club are the first full-service marinas north of New York City and provide ready access via frequent commuter trains to the heart of the Big Apple. Across the river at **Upper Nyack** is the Julius Peterson Boatyard, with a large marine railway, a marine store, and a broad range of repairs available. Immediately to the north is a large mooring and anchoring area suitable for south to north winds.

Ossining, on the eastern shore, was originally named Sing Sing, the same as the famous, sprawling,

---

TARRYTOWN MARINA
Just North of the Tappan Zee Bridge
"A TEXACO STARPORT"

- Diesel Fuel & Gas
- Transient Slips Available to 70'
- Dockside Water and Electricity
- Showers, Restrooms, Laundromat
- Restaurant, Ice, Beer, and Soda

Short walk to Village Center, convenient to Taxis, Trains to N.Y.C., and Transportation to Local Airports—Kennedy and LaGuardia.

We Accept MC, VISA, Amex & Texaco Credit Cards
P.O. BOX 404, TARRYTOWN, NY 10591   914-631-1300

hillside prison located here. At the turn of the century, a boycott of prison-made goods led the town to change its name to Ossining, allowing buyers to distinguish goods made at the prison from goods made in the town outside the prison.

Croton Point juts out into the river just north of Ossining, and except in west to north winds, it is one of the best anchorages on the river—certainly the best since leaving New York City. Don't short-cut the point when going in, because this shoal really does exist. The Croton Point Park invites a dinghy trip ashore. On the river's west side, to the north of Croton Point, is the large Haverstraw Marina complex. Be aware that a large commercial-ship loading dock just to the north makes the marina entrance a bit confusing. During a 1989 marina renovation, the marine store was eliminated. However, a wide selection of marine items can be found at the Willow Cove Marina, located about a mile farther north. Depths and docking here are limited and may require anchoring out and dinghying in.

This whole area was once the site of scores of brick factories. The north side of **Stony Point** is often used by cruising boats as an overnight anchorage in south to west winds.

Around the bend of the river on the east side is the **Indian Point Nuclear Power Plant**. Of course, no docking is allowed here. A mile beyond is the city of **Peekskill**, named for Jan Peek, a Dutch trader who settled here in 1665. The channel is shallow and the cruising amenities limited.

Across the river is densely forested **Dunderberg Mountain**, the 1,000-foot-high legendary dwelling of the Dutch goblin responsible for summer storms. The mountain marks the southern limit of the Highland section of the river. For the next ten miles, the river cuts through the Appalachian mountain chain, and may well be the most beautiful stretch of river scenery in the United States.

A couple of miles north of Dunderberg Mountain, and 46 miles from the Battery, is **Bear Mountain**, 1,300 feet high. You'll find a state park, a scenic drive to the mountain top, and recreational facilities. For those planning to visit the park, limited anchoring room is in the bight between **Iona Island** and the excursion boat dock at the foot of this spectacular mountain. A floating dinghy dock is behind the tour boat dock.

It is here that you and your crew may first encounter the white swans that paddle leisurely around the river's coves as far north as Catskill. Keeping a count of the number you've spotted can be a challenging pastime, particularly for the younger members of the crew. During a 1989 passage, one observer reported sighting 56.

The narrow section of the river between Iona Island and the eastern shore is known as **The Race**. The swiftest current on the Hudson River runs here. The island was the site of a Navy arsenal from 1900 until after World War II, and some fences and buildings still remain.

Bear Mountain Bridge to Newburgh/Beacon Bridge. The **Bear Mountain Bridge**, when completed in 1924, was the world's largest suspension bridge. In addition to carrying highway traffic, it also serves as the Hudson River crossing of the famous Maine-to-Georgia Appalachian Mountain hiking trail.

During the Revolutionary War, the Americans stretched a huge chain across the river just north of the bridge site to prevent British warships from passing. Unfortunately, the British seized the chain (sending it to Gibraltar to protect their own harbor), then sailed up the river and burned the town of Kingston.

Because much of the local traffic passes on the wrong side of Marker "25", anchoring there is not recommended.

Opened in 1802, **West Point**, the United States Military Academy, is well worth the effort to visit from the water. Dockage availability varies from limited to nonexistent. Check with the dockmaster's office. Limited dockage and anchorage are usually available at the yacht club across the river. There is also a marina on the west bank south of West Point, which might be more convenient.

The narrow section of the river just north of the Academy, designated as **World's End**, is the deepest section of the entire river. During the Revolutionary War, the Americans stretched another chain across the river at this point, but not in time to prevent the British from their attack on Kingston.

Foundry Cove is too shallow for most boats to use as an anchorage. The foundries here cast cannon and shot during the Civil War. Here, too, the first American iron warship—a revenue cutter—was built in the 1850s.

Just beyond is the village of **Cold Spring**, with a riverfront green, a marina with a swimming pool and a restaurant, and during the summer, village-sponsored water fiestas.

At the northern end of the river's Highland Section, spectacular **Storm King Mountain**'s 1,355-foot peak rises above the western shore. The scenic highway that girds it was completed in 1940.

Four miles north on the eastern shore is **Pollepel Island**, widely known as **Bannerman's Island**. Between 1900 and 1918, Bannerman, a munitions dealer, built a replica of a medieval castle here as a summer resort and

Hudson River

storehouse. In 1967, the state obtained the property, and tours were conducted until the castle burned in 1969. Today, because of the deteriorating condition of the building, landing on the island is no longer permitted. Note, however, that you can find an interesting anchorage behind the island by heading close into shore at **Breakneck Point** and then carefully following the seven- to ten-foot channel northward toward the island.

In this vicinity, the Catskill Aqueduct, a tunnel measuring 17.5 feet by 17 feet, was completed in 1919. Passing hundreds of feet beneath the river, the aqueduct provides 500 million gallons of water each day for metropolitan New York City.

Four miles north are the twin cities of **Newburgh** and **Beacon**. Newburgh, in spite of being situated more than 60 miles inland, was a 19th-century seaport and the home of whaling ships. George Washington's 1782-1783 headquarters, the Hasbrough House, still stands here and is open to the public.

Substantial waterfront development has sprung up in **Newburgh** during the last several years, mostly to accommodate local small craft. The Yacht Club, with its popular restaurant, continues to be a good stop for transient vessels.

Newburgh/Beacon Bridge to Kingston/Rhinecliff Bridge. The first span of the Newburgh/Beacon Bridge opened only 27 years ago, replacing not only the last remaining ferry service across the Hudson but also the oldest ferry in the United States. Two miles to the north and extending far out into the river from the east shore is a great array of moored sailboats belonging to the Chelsea Yacht Club.

The marina and the yacht club at **New Hamburg** are both convenient to grocery stores and other provisioners. You'll also find some marinas across the river at **Marlboro**. There are no cruising amenities or protected anchorages between Marlboro and Poughkeepsie. Just south of Poughkeepsie is a wall on the river's east side adjacent to a park and a ball field. It's relatively isolated, and mooring here requires heavy fendering to protect you from the large river wakes.

Opened in 1930, the **Mid-Hudson Suspension Bridge** is one of the oldest bridges spanning the Hudson. The temporary capital of New York State in 1777, **Poughkeepsie** is the home of Vassar College, which is now coed. Although it was once an active river port, the east bank has no marinas. On the west bank is Mariners Harbor, a waterfront restaurant that sells both diesel and gas and may provide overnight dockage. The massive Conrail railroad bridge has been in place for more than 100 years and once made Poughkeepsie an important railroad center.

Skippers, beware—the Poughkeepsie Yacht Club is not located at Poughkeepsie, but rather seven miles north of the city where the east shore "special anchor-

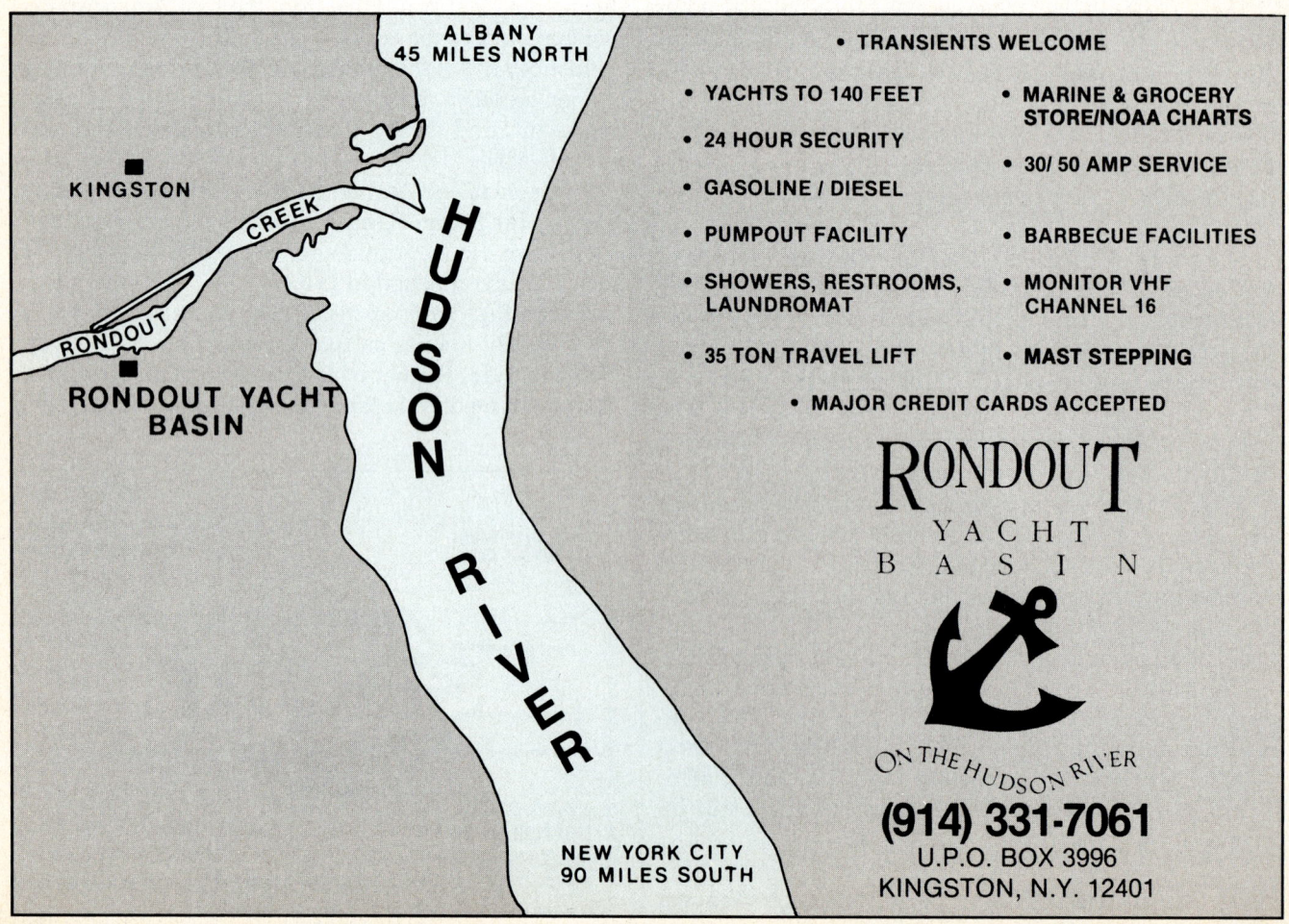

age" appears on the chart, just south of **Esopus Island**. You won't find any transient marinas or protected anchorages along this seven-mile stretch. Although fuel is not available here, the friendly Poughkeepsie Yacht Club welcomes all transient vessels. The handsome club houses a lounge and a laundry, and floating dock space and mooring buoys are both available. A mile farther north on the same side of the river is the Norrie Yacht Basin, a popular Hudson River marina on the grounds of Norrie State Park. Consider calling ahead for reservations if you plan to spend the night here. Both the PYC and the Norrie Yacht Basin are a short drive from historic **Hyde Park**, the former home of Franklin D. Roosevelt. The house is open for tours.

The shoals of **Esopus Meadows** are marked by the Esopus Lighthouse, the southernmost of several old lighthouses built along the river. This one, knocked askew by winter ice, was built in 1872.

For those ready to stop for the night before exploring Kingston's Rondout Creek, an anchorage is located a quarter mile south of **Port Ewen** on the river's west side. It offers seven-foot depths and good protection in south to northwest winds.

In 1777, **Kingston**, then the capital of New York State, was burned to the ground by the British, whose ships had managed to slip up the river. **Rondout Creek**, with another of the Hudson's lighthouses at the entrance, serves as the city's harbor. More amenities are located here than in any harbor beyond New York City. Rondout Marina provides a courtesy car for transients, and the Hideaway Marina has a fully stocked marine store. The town dock at Kingston, next to the Maritime Museum, charges one dollar per hour for tie-up, but overnight stays are not allowed. Stores and reaturants are convenient, and the indoor/outdoor Hudson River Maritime Museum at waterside is worth a visit. This dock is also an easy dink trip from one of the Roundout Creek marinas.

An interesting anchorage is located three miles up the creek in seven-foot depths just before the bridge at New Salem. Just before the first bridge (56 foot clearance) is the Hudson River Maritime Center Museum. Nowhere on the Hudson River can travelers learn more about the historic Hudson. It's open daily from May through October, except Tuesday, and it's a highly recommended stop. For a small fee, the museum provides docking for dinghies at a floating town dock located in the historic area on the north side of Rondout Creek.

Upon leaving Kingston, boats can pass to either side of the extensive five-mile stretch of mid-river shoals.

Kingston/Rhinebeck Bridge to Albany. This bridge, three miles north of Kingston, was completed in 1957. The river to the north is interrupted by well-marked shoals that require large ships to cross and recross the river. The small islands are all too shallow to provide anchorage.

Marking the entrance to **Esopus Creek**, the harbor for **Saugerties**, is another of the river's lighthouses, built in 1869. The name "Saugerties" is derived from the Dutch word for "sawmills." Although smaller than either Kingston to the south or Catskill to the north, this harbor is the home of several marinas providing transient space. In addition, just past the last marina to the west is a very cozy and attractive deepwater anchorage.

Upon heading north from Saugerties, you can see a lovely old estate at the top of a hillside lawn on the east bank opposite Marker "43". This is Clermont, oldest of the Hudson River estates and home of seven generations of Livingstons, including Chancellor Robert Livingston, negotiator of the Louisiana Purchase and co-inventor with Fulton of the first practical steamboat. The original building, like the city of Kingston, was burned by the British in 1777. It's now a state historic site, open from May to October.

At **North Germantown Reach**, halfway between Saugerties and Catskill, a large cement-loading jetty juts out into the river. By cautiously following the chart (and the depthsounder), you'll find an anchorage with seven- to nine-foot depths and protected from north winds.

Catskill is a popular harbor during the summer season. Consider making reservations on the weekend. Transient boats occasionally anchor on the south side of the entrance channel in the vicinity of Marker "3". Two anchors, to hold the boat out of the channel and off the shoal, are frequently used. Remember the four-foot tide.

At the creek's entrance is a sign for the local Hop-O-Nose Marina. Named for an Indian fur trader, Hop's

Riverview
Marine Services Inc.
103 Main St., Catskill, N.Y.
(518) 943-5311   VHF Ch. 16

- TRANSIENT DOCKAGE
- COMPLETE REPAIRS
- TOWING SERVICE
- MAST STEPPING
- 20 TON LIFT
- SUPPLIES
- PUMPOUT
- SHOWERS
- ICE

- DIESEL FUEL
- GASOLINE
- PROPANE NEARBY
- CONVENIENT TO SHOPPING & RESTAURANTS
- LAUNDRY

LOCATED ON THE CATSKILL CREEK & HUDSON RIVER

Hudson River

CATSKILL MARINA
Foot of Greene Street • Catskill, N.Y. 12414

On picturesque Catskill Creek catering to transients

★ Shaded park-like setting
★ Pleasant 2 block walk to center of town
★ Gasoline and diesel; 110/220 v. electricity
★ Vessels to 100+ feet; 10 foot dockside depth
★ Heated pool
★ Sundries shop — nautical charts
★ Laundromat
★ Spotless showers and dressing rooms
★ Cable TV
★ Nearby historic sites and 19th century neighborhoods
★ Restaurant and cocktail lounge

DOCKMASTER & RESERVATIONS 518-943-4170

"A Pleasant Place to Visit."

Shady Harbor Marina
Home of the friendly people

SALES & SERVICE
• Mainship • Bayliner • Silverton

COMPLETE SERVICE MARINA
20 ton lift   Engine &
Woodwork   hull repairs
Painting   Generator service
                          Out-drive

SHIP'S STORE
NOAA charts   Swimming pool
Showers   Picnic

"Everything for the Yachtsman"

Rt. 144, New Baltimore, NY 12124
18 miles south of Albany on the Hudson River

(518) 756-8001

---

nose is the rock promontory just east of the marina. Two marinas here offer mast stepping and unstepping services for sailboats heading north past Albany. The only other crane for this purpose located north of this point is at Castleton-on-Hudson. That one, however, is a do-it-yourself operation.

Immediately north of Catskill is the imaginatively named **Rip Van Winkle Bridge**, opened in 1935. While still south of the bridge, cast your gaze toward the top of **Church Hill** (marked on the chart), and you'll see the outline of Olana. This spectacular 19th-century building was the home of Frederic Church, one of the foremost Hudson River School artists.

The main ship channel passes east of **Middle Ground Flats**, but pleasure craft frequently use the shorter route to the west. This route also has less current. The lighthouse at the junction of these two routes is built on a shoal that in 1845 was the scene of a fiery wreck which killed 50 of 300 passengers of the steamboat *Swallow*. The northwest side of Middle Ground Flats can be used as an anchorage, but take special care to stay well out of the way of passing vessels.

You'll find a better anchorage, although with a more difficult approach, behind **Stockport Middle Ground** above Marker "6". The entrance is narrower than it appears on the chart, and the sides shoal abruptly. A depthsounder is essential here.

Just north of the town of **Coxsackie** (pronounced "Cook-sacky") is another protected anchorage, located between Coxsackie Island and the west bank of the river.

Although the anchorage marked by white buoys just north of Marker "28" is for big ship use, pleasure craft can find many attractive spots on the east side of **Houghtaling Island**. At **New Baltimore** is Shady Harbor Marina, the first full-service marina since Catskill.

At this writing, availability of transient facilities at **Coeymans** (pronounced "Kwee-mans") is doubtful.

Just north of the highway and railroad bridges is **Castleton-on-Hudson**. The Castleton Boat Club offers a large crane for do-it-yourself mast stepping. **Note:** A $25 fee and the signing of an insurance release form allows the sailboat skipper to use the crane at Castleton to unstep or step his mast before or after the Troy Lock. The

---

QUALITY DIESEL FUEL

Big, Big, Big Discounts!!

TRUCK DELIVERY • ALBANY
TROY • WATERFORD • CRESENT

518-272-4432

JOHN RAY & SONS
2900 6TH AVE., TROY, NY
— Since 1904 —

crane is manually operated on a do-it-yourself basis. A minimum of two people is necessary, one at the crane and one to guide the mast on deck. The dock is wide open to the river wakes, which sometimes requires that your mast-stepping crew be nimble. There are no other mast stepping facilities on the river north of the club and the crane operates on a first-come-first-served basis. During the height of the season, waiting your turn is to be expected.

Fourteen miles to the north, you'll emerge from the serenity of the upper Hudson into the sometimes-hectic activity of seagoing ships unloading their cargoes of imported automobiles, bananas, fuel, and molasses at the **Port of Albany**. In 1851, 15,000 Erie canal boats and 500 sailing ships cleared this port. **Albany**, capital of New York, has a four- to five-foot tide, even though it's 144 miles from the ocean.

On the east bank, just before the 60-foot fixed bridge, is the Albany Yacht Club, which offers a warm welcome to all mariners. It's a fine base from which to visit the impressive Nelson A. Rockefeller Empire State Plaza, more often referred to as the South Mall. Built in the 1960s, this complex is a magnificent showplace of modern granite architecture. In addition to the state government office buildings, the complex is home to one of the country's great modern museums and an acoustically superb auditorium. Affectionately called "The Egg," this bowl-shaped structure can be seen amidst the ten other buildings of the mall from the river. A tour of this complex will be a highlight of your Hudson river cruise.

Just north of the bridge is a huge, recently restored 19th-century building, once the headquarters of the Delaware and Hudson railroad, and now the headquarters of the mammoth New York State University system.

Albany to Waterford

North of Albany, past the Interstate 90 and Menands bridges, is the Watervliet Arsenal on the west shore. Arms for the U.S. Military have been manufactured here for more than 175 years, since the arsenal's establishment in 1813.

In 1609, a longboat from Henry Hudson's ship the *Half Moon*, explored as far north as the present city of **Troy**, found the head of navigation, and determined that, indeed, this was not the way to the Orient.

Troy is the home of Renasselaer Polytechnic Institute, an outstanding science and engineerring college, and Emma Willard School, the first women's college in the United States. Both are visible from the river. In 1825, a Troy woman invented the detachable collar, making the city a famed collar- and shirt-manufacturing center. The Cluett-Peabody plant on River Street produced Arrow shirts. "Uncle Sam" Wilson, a local meat packer during the War of 1812, stamped beef for the army with his initials: "U.S. Beef." Later, a caricature of Sam Wilson came to personify the United States. His grave is in Troy's Oakwood Cemetery.

Nautical Terms

Roach. The curve made in the side or bottom of a sail. This curve is an essential aerodynamic feature of the design of the sail and is very carefully computed by the sailmaker.

© The Overlook Press. Reprinted by permission.

The proposed Troy Municipal Docks were nowhere in evidence in the summer of 1989. Although a cruise boat and an occasional tugboat tie up to the wall, the 4½-foot tide, the lack of either cleat or bollards, and the height of the wall make docking virtually impossible at this time.

All lift bridges between Albany and the Troy Lock still open on demand during the day. Troy Lock, 153 miles from the Battery, is the first lock in a long series that carries you to Buffalo via the Erie Canal or to Lake Champlain and beyond via the Champlain Canal. Officially, the lock opens on the hour for pleasure craft.

Leaving Troy Lock, you next enter the quiet, non-tidal waters of the lower Champlain Canal. Anchoring room is on the western shore between Green Island and Van Schaick (pronounced "skoik") Island. A full-service marina is located on the west shore just south of bridge C-1.

Albany Yacht Club

Below Dunn Memorial Bridge
Across Hudson River from
New York State Capitol
P.O. BOX 293   RENSSELAER, NY 12144

**DOCKAGE • 220/110 ELECTRICITY •
SHOWERS • MOBIL GAS & DIESEL •
HAY BAGS • ICE • CHARTS •
RESTAURANTS, GROCERIES,
AND LAUNDROMAT
IN WALKING DISTANCE
RESERVATIONS RECOMMENDED
MAJOR CREDIT CARDS ACCEPTED**

Dock House: 518-445-9587
Club House: 518-465-9228

ALL BOATERS WELCOME

WE MONITOR CHANNEL 16

Locking Techniques

The following guidelines will be helpful in your transit of the locks.

Unlike most other canal systems, New York lock tenders **do not** furnish locking lines. This circumstance poses no problem to the downbound vessel. One simply loops a stern line and a bow line around convenient bollards at the top of the lock. From the deck of the vessel, pay out the free end of each line as the vessel descends.

Smaller vessels frequently use a single line looped around a single midship bollard.

Upbound travel, however, is another matter. The problem is that the bollards so easy to use in the downbound passage are now 20 to 40 feet above your reach. Most often it is impossible, or at least, very impractical, to put a crew member ashore who can climb to the top of the lock and drop the lines to you.

These locks were built to accommodate large vessels, tugs, and barges that tie to mooring posts recessed into the lock walls. These posts, however, are too high and too far apart to be reached from the deck of the average pleasure craft. In most locks, the only remaining places to loop lines around are the four iron ladders—two on each wall of the lock. A few of the newer locks have additional vertical pipes or cables.

A second problem encountered in upbound lock travel is the swirling current created when the lock is being filled. (Virtually no current is in a lock when it is being emptied.) Sailboat keels are particularly affected by these currents.

Following is a sketch of the most popular locking line configuration used by small- to medium-sized upbound vessels. It can also be used when locking down.

1. Attach the ends of a single line to both a bow and stern cleat, leading it outside all railings, shrouds, etc.

2. Leave eight to ten feet of slack in the line, using the slack to form a four- to five-foot bight amidships.

3. The bight, when looped around a ladder rung, can be pulled tight, to act as both a breast line and forward and stern spring line.

4. As the vessel is raised, the line handler transfers the loop to successively higher ladder rungs.

5. Note the position of the two fenders. It is important that they be approximately equidistant from the ladder.

The water that enters the lock is directed by the lock valves toward the sides of the lock, pressing the vessel against the wall. In the case of a deep-draft sailboat, this pressure can be sufficient to jam or damage a fender. It's therefore a good idea to have any extra crew members stationed with boathooks at bow and stern to push the boat away from the wall in order to relieve pressure on a stuck fender.

To allow fenders to slide more easily up the wall, some skippers rig a vertical two-by-four or two-by-six board outside of horizontally hung fenders. Another good idea when approaching the ladder is to have a boathook ready amidships to grab the ladder in case the linehandler can't quite reach far enough to get his line around the ladder. Even the folks with twin-screw vessels occasionally miss the ladder.

/ # HUDSON RIVER

New York to Waterford

		SEASONAL / YEAR-ROUND	SAIL / POWER / BOTH	LARGEST VESSEL ACCOMMODATED	NO. OF TRANSIENT BERTHS	MARKED ENTRY CHANNEL	APPROACH DEPTH (Reported)	DOCKSIDE DEPTH (Reported)	RAILWAY / LIFT CAPACITY (in tons)	GAS ★ DIESEL ● BOTH ▲ FUEL BRAND	ENGINE REPAIRS: Gas ★ Diesel ● Both ▲	PROPELLER / HULL REPAIRS	MARINE SUPPLIES / GROCERIES / BOTH	LPG ★ CNG ● BOTH ▲	110V ★ 220V ● BOTH ▲ / ICE	SHOWERS / LAUNDROMAT / MAX AMPS	RESTAURANT / SNACK BAR	PUMP-OUT STATION	RADIO WATCH—VHF (CB)
1.	Staten Island Boat Sales	984-7676	Y	P	58		●	20	10	IND	▲			▲	PH	M	★50		R	68
2.	Mansion Marina	984-6611	Y	P	55	5		12	7	TEX	▲	15		▲	PH	MGI	★30	S	R	
3.	Nichols Great Kills Park Marina	351-8476	Y	▲	30	10	●	12	12	TEX	▲	20				I	▲30	S		
GERRITSEN INLET AND JAMAICA BAY
4.	Paradise Yacht Club	646-9629			45			35			YACHT CLUB				▲		S	R		
5.	Sheepshead Bay Yacht Club	891-0991	S	▲	100			45	15			R				I	▲30	S	RS	(19)
6.	Bob's Landing	738-9149	Y	P	32		●	30	25			7		★	P	M	★		RS	
7.	MZ Marine	738-9149	Y	P	32		●	30	25			7		★	P	M	★	S	RS	16
8.	Argo Boat MFG Company, Inc.	527-9870	Y	P	28		●	4	4				R	★	PH	M	★			
9.	Kings Plaza Marina	253-5434		▲	45			40	20					★		MG	★		R	
10.	Viking Marina	444-3506	Y	▲	65	4	●	20	20	TEX	★	30	R	▲	PH	MI	★20	S	S	
GRAVESEND BAY
11.	Oceanview Marina	266-6000	Y	▲	32	1		10	6	IND	★	L	R	▲	H	MI	★20			
12.	Marine Basin Marina	372-5700	Y	▲	70	10		15	15	TEX	▲	30		▲	PH	MGI	▲50		R	
THE NARROWS TO TARRYTOWN
13.	Newport Yacht Club & Marina	(201) 626-5550	Y	▲	200	70	●	10	10					▲	PH	I	▲100	SL	● RS	16
14.	Lincoln Harbor Yacht Club	319-5100	Y	▲	200		●	40	6	TEX	▲			▲	PH	MI	▲	SL	● RS	16
15.	Port Imperial Marina	902-8787	S	▲	150			12	12	MOB	▲	35			PH	MI	▲200	S	● RS	16
16.	79th Street Boat Basin	(212) 362-0909	Y	▲	140	6		20	3	DINGHY DOCK AVAILABLE							★30	S	S	16
17.	Ferry Binghamton Restaurant	(201) 941-2300	Y		25	4				RESTAURANT DOCK									R	
18.	Grand Cove Marina & Yacht Club	944-BOAT	Y	▲	60		●	13	7	TEX	▲			▲	PH	MGI	▲	SL	RS	
19.	Von Dohln Marina	943-3424	Y	▲	30			5	4			5		★	P		★20			
20.	Englewood Boat Basin	894-9510	S	▲	50	1	●	6	5		▲						★30	S	S	
21.	Alpine Boat Basin	(201) 768-9798	S	▲	45	1		4	4	GUL	★						★50	S	S	
22.	Tower Ridge Yacht Club	(914) 478-9729	S	▲	35			40	2	MOB	★			YACHT CLUB		I	★			(13)
23.	**Tarrytown Marina (p. 24)**	**631-1300**	Y	▲	80	12	●	15	12	TEX	▲	7			P	MI	▲100	SL	R	16
24.	Washington Irving Boat Club	332-0517	Y	▲	35	5		5	4	CIT	★	15	R	★	P	I	★30	S	RS	16
NYACK
25.	Julius Petersen Inc. ✓	358-2100	Y	▲	100	6		8	8			60		▲	P	MI	▲		RS	
TAPPAN ZEE TO PEEKSKILL
26.	Westerly Marina, Inc. ✓	941-2203	Y	▲	40	7	●	6	6		★			▲	PH	MI	▲		R	68
27.	Sellazzo's Marine Restaurant	941-9539						6	6					RESTAURANT DOCK					R	
28.	Shattemuc Yacht Club	941-8777	S	▲							★			YACHT CLUB				S		
29.	Haverstraw Marina	429-2001	Y	▲	150	40	●	20	20	TEX	▲	30	R	▲	PH	MI	▲50	SL	● R	16
30.	Boatland On The Hudson	786-2600	S	P	40		●	5	40			35		★	P	MI	★		RS	16
31.	Minisceongo Yacht Club	786-8767	S	▲	50	10		5	10			35				MI	★	S	S	16
32.	Willow Cove Marina	786-5270	S	▲	60	12		4	5			35	R	▲	P	MI	★50	S	● RS	12/16
33.	Seaweed Yacht Club	786-8731	Y	▲	40	10		8	8			30	R	YACHT CLUB		I	★	S		16
34.	Kenway Marina	786-2787	S	▲	50		●	4	5			50	R			M	▲50	S		
35.	Cortlandt Yacht Club	737-9442	S	▲	45	5		4	5			20				I	▲	S	S	16
36.	Salty Dog Marina	737-3904	Y	▲	100	5		5	5					▲	H	★ MGI	▲30	S	RS	
37.	Viking Boatyard	739-5090	Y	▲	40	2		5	4			60		▲	PH	MI	★30	S	R	16
38.	Hudson River Boat Sales	737-7676	S	P	50			13	13		★	25		▲	P	M		S	R	16
39.	Peekskill Yacht Club	737-9515	S				●				★					GI	★	SL	R	16/68
40.	Charles Point Marina	736-7370	Y	P	50	6	●	4	4			25		▲	PH	MI	▲50	S	●	16
41.	Garrison Yacht Club	424-3440	S	▲	200		●	15	15	CIT	★			YACHT CLUB		GI	★			16
42.	Cornwall Yacht Club	534-8835	S	▲	42	6		6	6	IND	★					I	★30	S	RS	16
43.	Newburgh Yacht Club	565-3920	S	▲	60			8	5	GUL	▲		T			MI	★		R	
44.	White's Marina	297-8520						20	4	IND	★	15	R		PH	MI	★30			
45.	New Hamburg Yacht Club	297-9874	S	▲	42	20		12	6	TEX				▲	PH	MGI	★20			
46.	**West Shore Marine (p. 25)**	**236-4486**	S	▲	60	10		20	12		▲	25	R	▲	P	MI	★30		RS	16
47.	Marlboro Yacht Club	236-7070	S	▲	40	4		25	25	IND	★		R			I	▲50		RS	
POUGHKEEPSIE TO STAATSBURG
48.	Mariner's Harbor	691-6011								RESTAURANT										
49.	Hyde Park Marina	485-8211	S	▲	40			3	3		▲	20	R	★	P	MI	★	S	RS	
50.	Poughkeepsie Yacht Club	889-4745	S	▲				10	10			25				I	★30	SL	S	16

To provide the most complete and accurate information, **all facilities have been contacted within the past year.** If an asterisk (*) appears, it indicates a facility which did not respond to our requests for information (these listings may not reflect current conditions). Although facility operators supplied this data, we cannot guarantee accuracy or assume responsibility for errors. Entrance and dockside soundings tend to fluctuate. Always approach marinas carefully. Reference numbers on spotting charts indicate marina locations. ✓ Member American Boat Builders & Repairers Association.

GREAT LAKES EDITION 31

HUDSON RIVER

New York to Waterford

		SEASONAL / YEAR-ROUND	SAIL / POWER / BOTH▲	LARGEST VESSEL ACCOMMODATED	NO. OF TRANSIENT BERTHS	MARKED ENTRY CHANNEL	APPROACH DEPTH (Reported)	DOCKSIDE DEPTH (Reported)	GAS ★ DIESEL ● BOTH ● FUEL BRAND	RAILWAY / LIFT CAPACITY (in tons)	ENGINE REPAIRS: Gas ★ Diesel ● Both▲	LAUNCHING RAMP	PROPELLER / HULL REPAIRS	MARINE SUPPLIES / CNG ● BOTH ●	LPG ★ GROCERIES / ICE	110V ● 220V ● BOTH ● MAX AMPS	SHOWERS / LAUNDROMAT	RESTAURANT / SNACK BAR	PUMP-OUT STATION	RADIO WATCH—VHF (CB)
51. Norrie Point Yacht Basin	339-3060	S	▲	60	5	●	7	6	MOB		▲		R		MI	▲50	S	●		16
KINGSTON																				
52. Hidden Harbor Yacht Club	338-0923						4	4			★		YACHT CLUB			★				
53. Hideaway Marina, Inc.	331-4565	Y	▲	55	3	●	6	5		35	R	▲	PH		MGI	★60	SL		S	16
54. Kingston Power Boat Association	338-3946	S	▲	40				10							GI	★	S		RS	16
55. Rondout Yacht Basin (p. 26)	**331-7061**	S	▲	140	10	●	15	15		35	R	▲	P		MGI	▲50	SL	●	RS	16
56. Lou's Boat Basin	331-4670	S	▲				8	8	IND		▲		R	★	M	REPAIR FACILITY				
57. Ulster Marine	339-3943	S	P	35	2	●	20	12			R	★	P		M	★			S	
58. Certified Marine Service	339-3060	Y	▲	85		●	18	12	MOB	▲	30	R	▲	PH	▲	MI	▲50		S	16
SAUGERTIES																				
59. Saugerties Marine	246-7533	Y	▲	60	5	●	10	10	MOB	▲	5	R	▲	P	★	MI	★30		S	16
60. Lynch's Marina	246-8290	S	▲	65	2		12	12	CHE	▲		R					★30	S		
CATSKILL CREEK TO COEYMANS																				
61. Riverview Marine Services (p. 27)	**(518) 943-5311**	Y	▲	80	12		10	8	AGW	▲	20	R	▲	PH	★	MI	★	SL	●	R	16
62. Catskill Marina (p. 28)	**943-4170**	S	▲	100	15		10	10	MOB	▲						MGI	▲50	SL		R	
63. Hop-O-Nose Marine	943-4640	S	▲	115	50	●	10	15	MOB	▲	15		★	P	★	MGI	▲50	SL		RS	16
64. Catskill Yacht Club	943-9711	S	▲	40	5	●	24	8	MOB	★		YACHT CLUB			I	★30	S		R	
65. Hudson Power Boat Association	828-9023	S	▲	55	5		32	20	AMO	★		R			I	★30	S	●	R	16
66. Hagar's Harbor	945-1858	Y	▲	100		●	18	18		★		R			I	▲50			R	16
67. Coxsackie Yacht Club	731-9819	S	▲	40	4		14	14	IND	★		R	YACHT CLUB		I	★20	S		S	16
68. Shady Harbor Marina (p. 28)	**756-8001**	Y	▲	50	15		10	12	ATL	▲	20		▲	H		MI	★30	S			16
69. Finke's Marine	756-6111	S	▲	100	30	●	14	7			25	R	▲	PH		MGI	★100	SL		RS	
70. Ravena-Coeymans Yacht Club	756-9932	S	▲	44	2	●	4	4				R			★	I	★30	S			
CASTLETON / ALBANY / TROY																				
71. Castleton Boat Club	732-7077	S	▲	100			32	9	CIT	▲		R			★	GI	★20	S		RS	16
72. Hudson Marine Sales	732-2889	S	P	40						L		★	PH		MGI					
73. Albany Yacht Club (p. 29)	**445-9587**	S	▲	125	6		15	15	MOB	▲					GI	★15	S			16
74. Van Schaick Island Marina	237-2681	S	▲	100	20	●	20	10	GUL	▲	30		▲	PH		M	▲50	S			16
75. Arrowhead Marina & RV Park*	382-8966	S	▲	35	5		15	5	CIT	★		R				MGI	★30	SL	●		

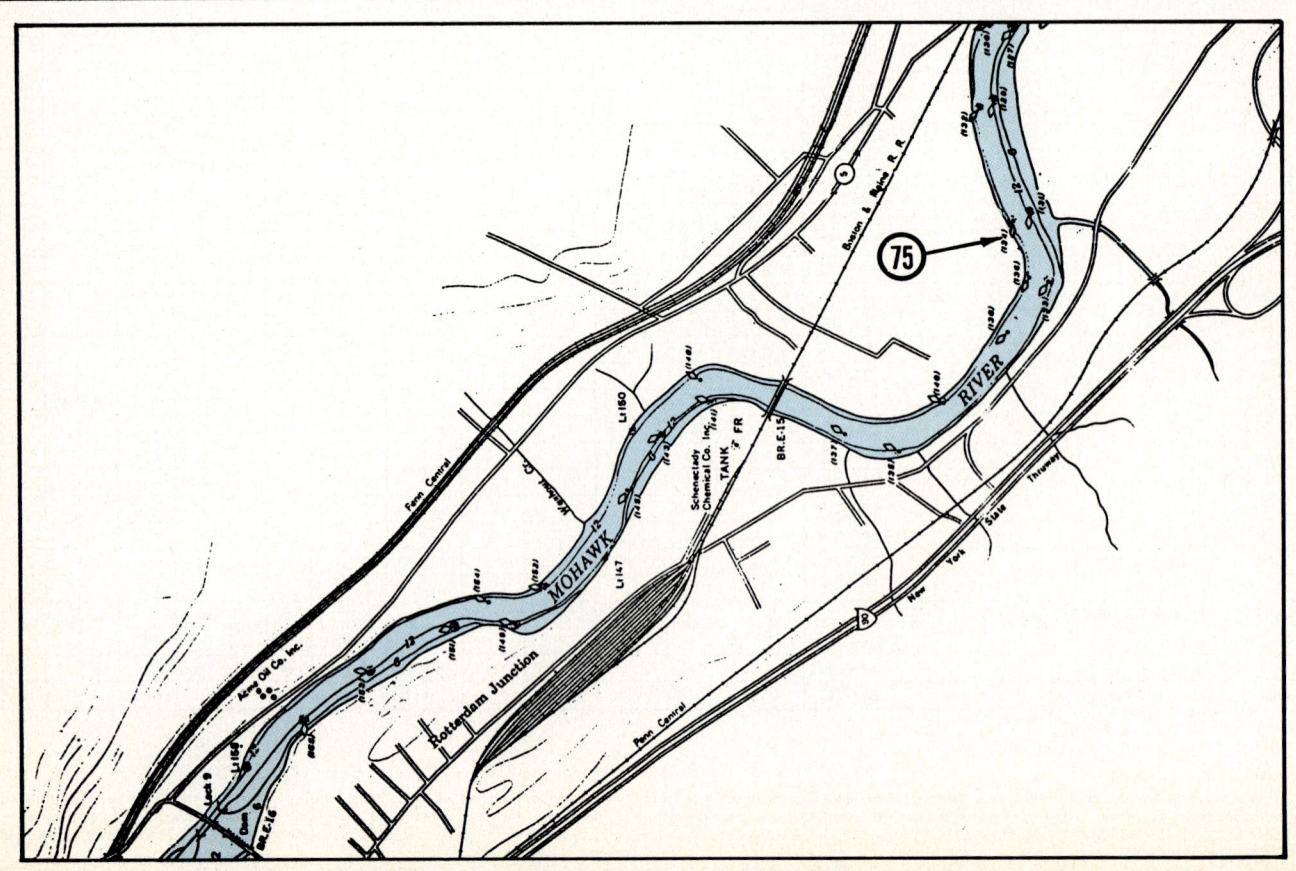

Under no circumstances are these charts to be used for navigation.

HUDSON RIVER

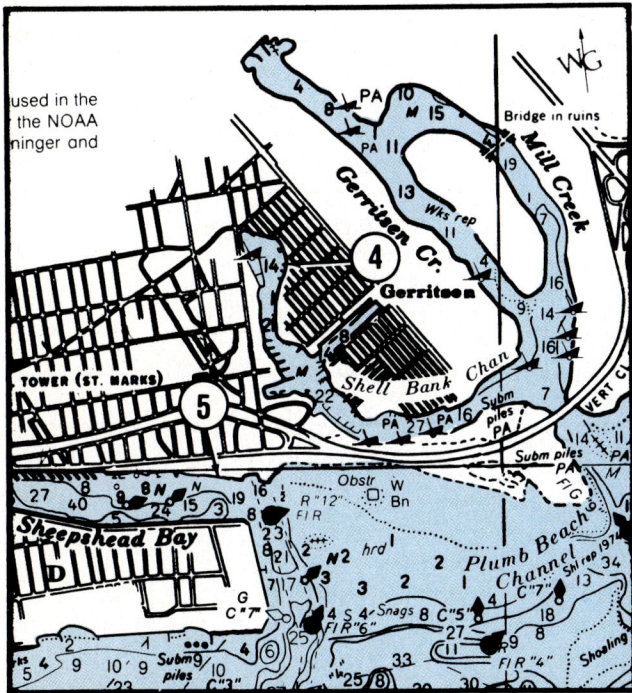

Chart 12327, edition 79

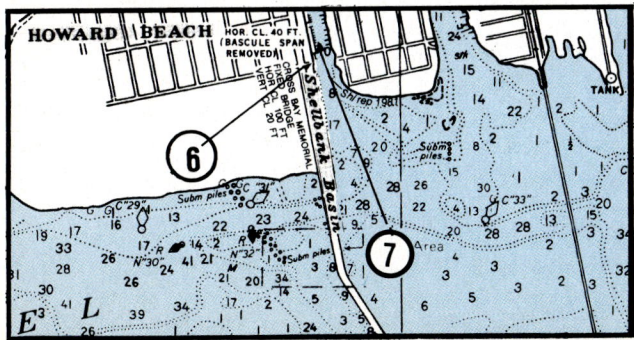

Chart 12327, edition 79

Chart 12350, edition 49
Under no circumstances are these charts to be used for navigation.
GREAT LAKES EDITION

Aids to Navigation

Unlighted buoy (C. can, N. nun, S. spar, Bell, Gong, Whistle)
Danger or junction buoy
Mooring buoy
Light (On fixed structure)
Fish trap buoy
Daybeacon (Bn)
R. Bn. radiobeacon
Mid-channel buoy
Lighted buoy

Lights (Lights are white unless otherwise indicated)
F. fixed	OBSC. obscured
Fl. flashing	WHIS. whistle
Qk. quick	DIA. diaphone
Gp. group	M. nautical miles
E. Int. equal interval	Rot. rotating
Mo.(A) morse code	SEC. sector
Occ. occulting	m. minutes
Alt. alternating	sec. seconds
I. Qk. interrupted quick	

Buoys:
T.B. temporary buoy	Or. orange
C. can	R. red
N. nun	G. green
S. spar	W. white
B. black	Y. yellow

Bottom characteristics:
Cl. clay	Sh. shells	bu. blue
Co. coral	hrd. hard	gn. green
G. gravel	rky. rocky	gy. gray
Grs. grass	sft. soft	rd. red
M. mud	stk. sticky	wh. white
Rk. rock	bk. black	yl. yellow
S. sand	br. brown	

Dangers:
Sunken wreck
Visible wreck
Rocks
Wreck, rock, obstruction, or shoal swept clear to the depth indicated
Rocks that cover and uncover, with heights in feet above datum of soundings

AERO. aeronautical	D.F.S. distance finding station
Bn. daybeacon	
R. Bn. radiobeacon	AUTH. authorized
R. TR. radio tower	Obstr. obstruction
C.G. Coast Guard Station	P.A. position approximate
	E.D. existence doubtful

Caution:
Mariners are warned to stay clear of the protective riprap surrounding navigational light structures shown thus.
Restricted Areas
Fish Trap Areas

33

Hudson River

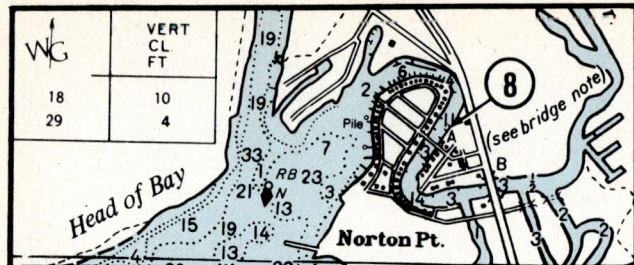
Chart 12350, edition 49

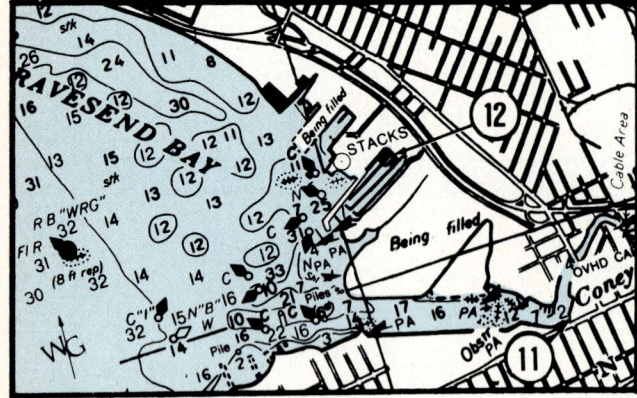
Chart 12327, edition 79

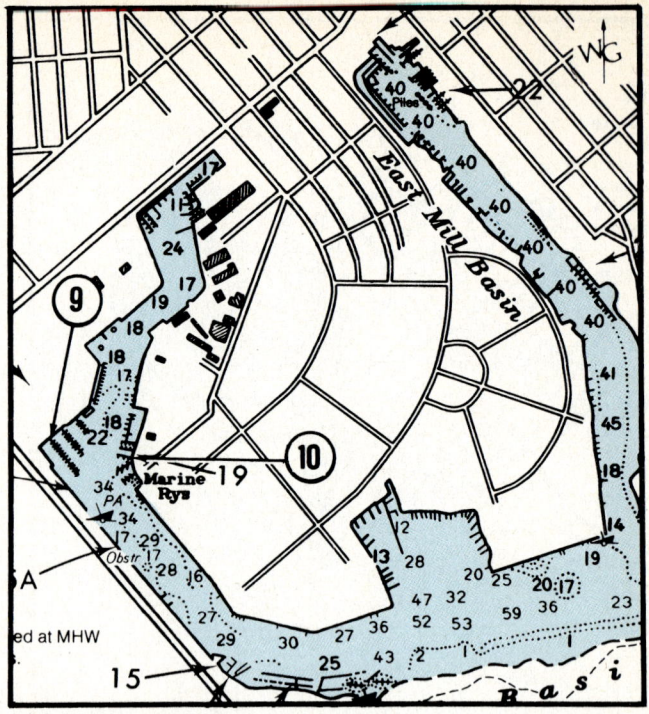
Chart 12350, edition 49

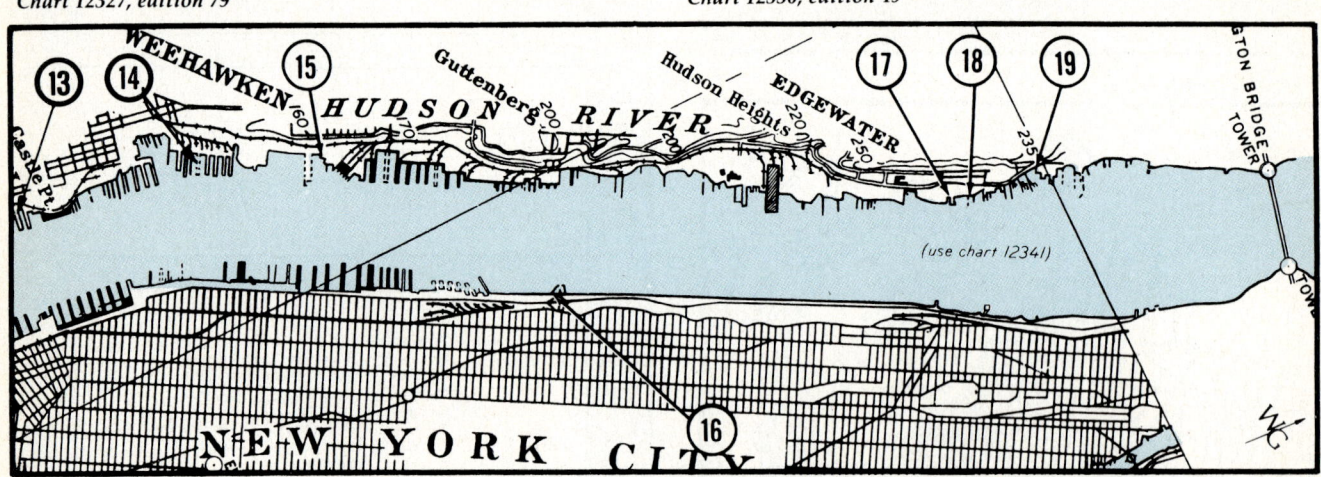
Chart 12343, edition 14

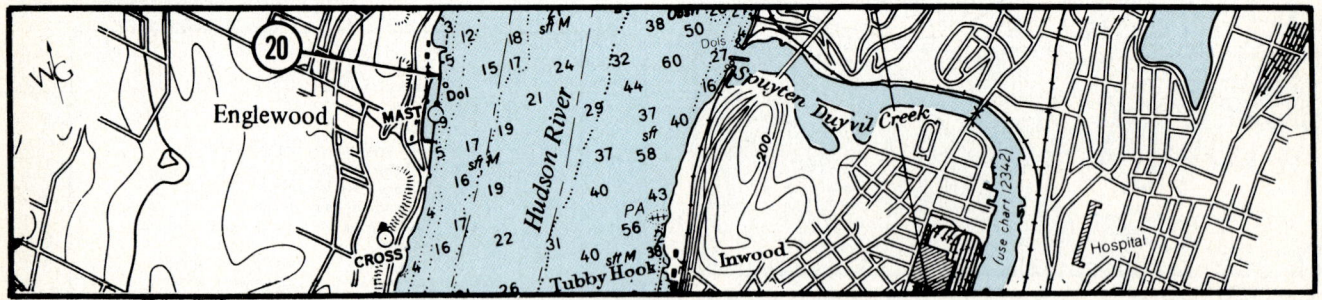
Chart 12343, edition 14

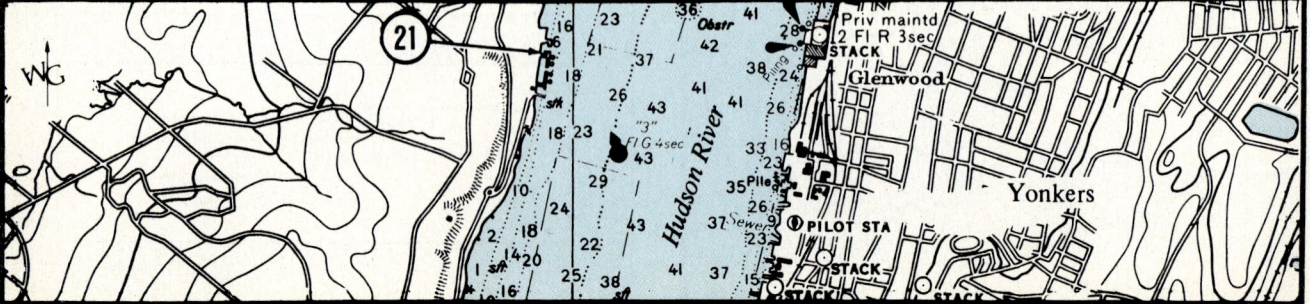
Chart 12343, edition 14

Under no circumstances are these charts to be used for navigation.

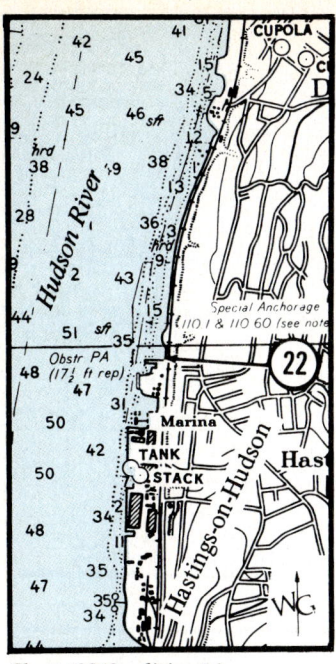

HUDSON RIVER

Chart 12343, edition 14

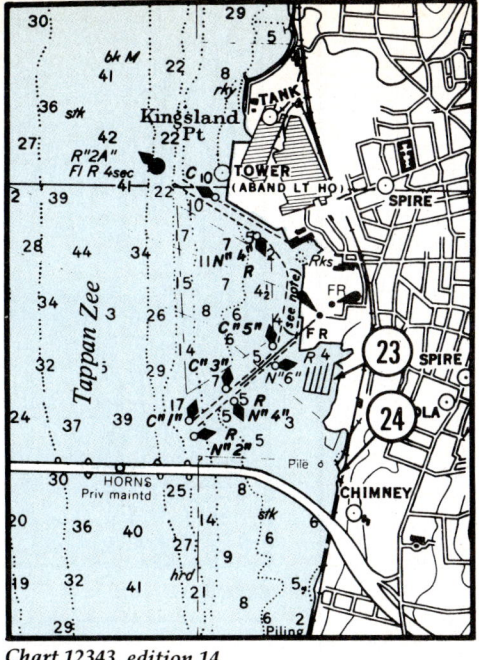

Chart 12343, edition 14

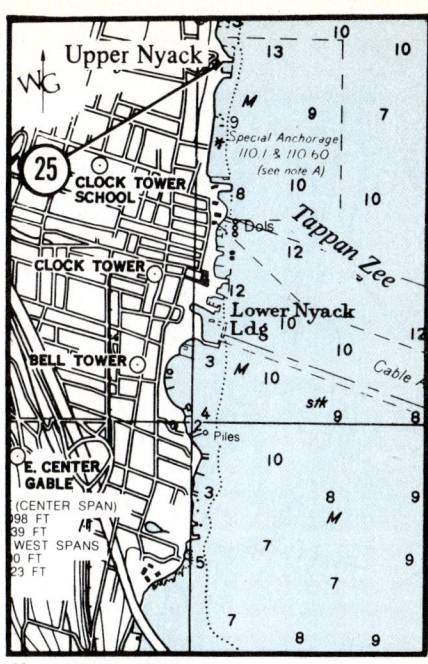

Chart 12343, edition 14

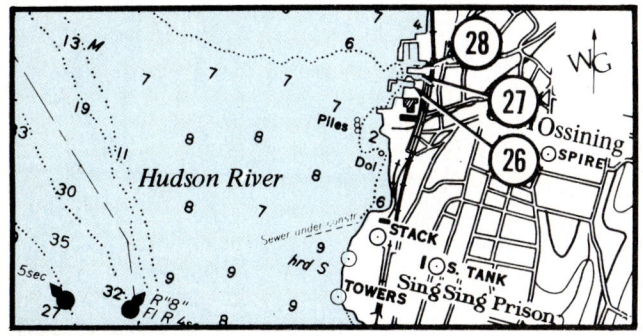

Chart 12343, edition 14

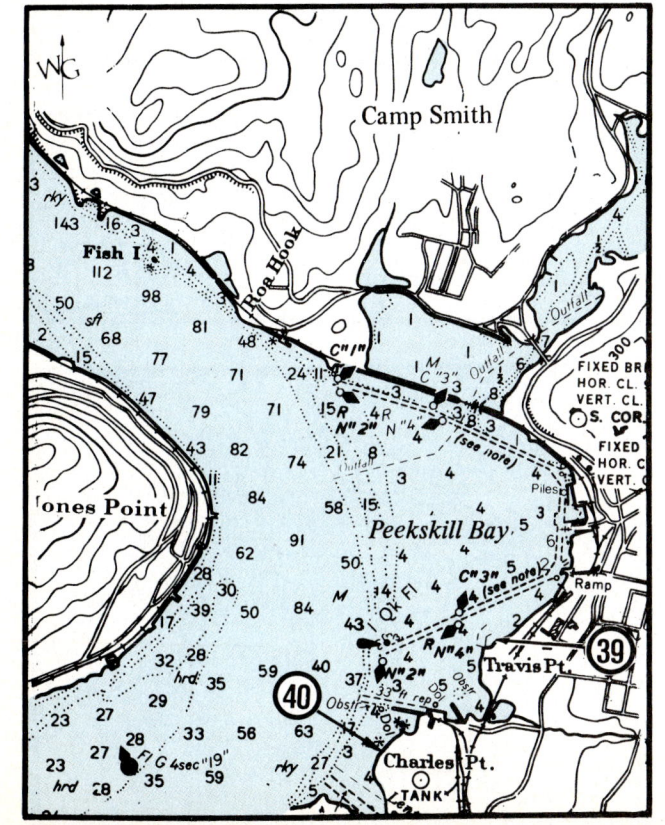

Chart 12343, edition 14

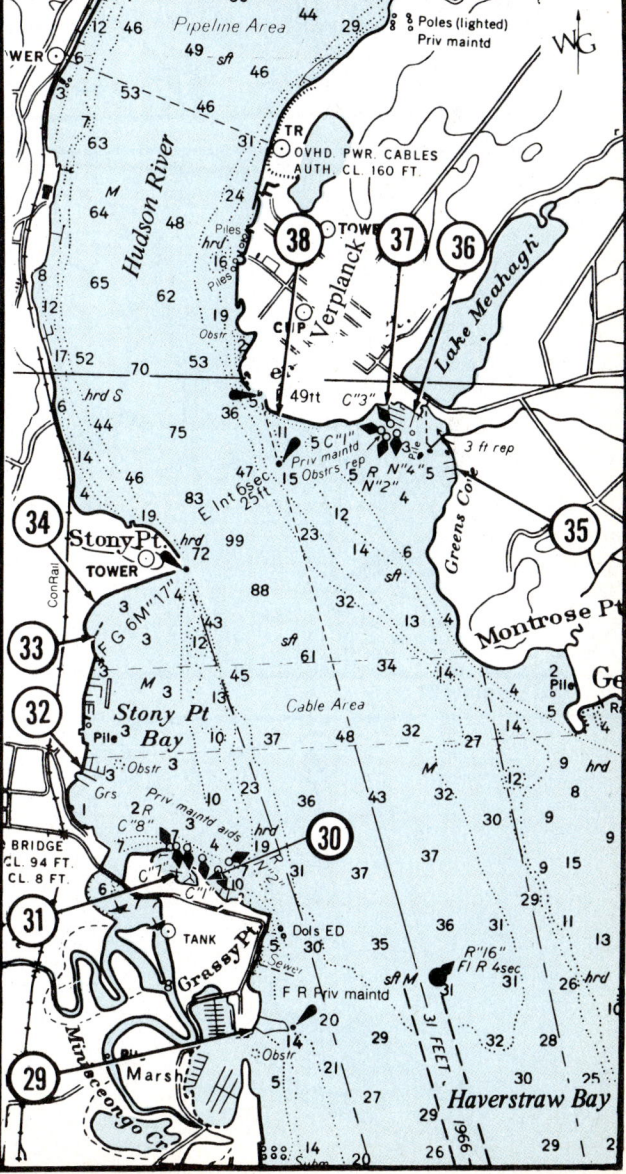

GREAT LAKES EDITION — *Under no circumstances are these charts to be used for navigation.*

HUDSON RIVER

Chart 12343, edition 14

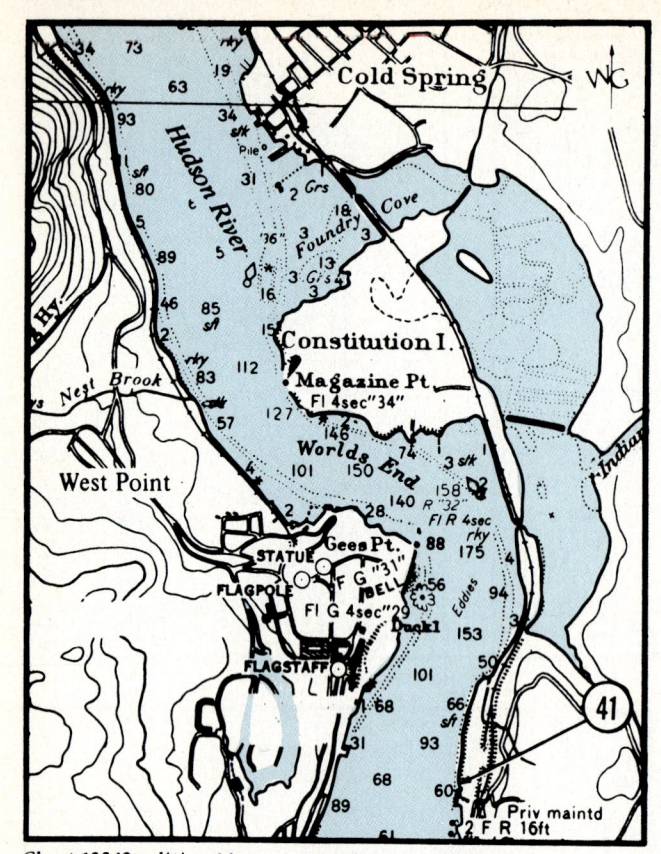

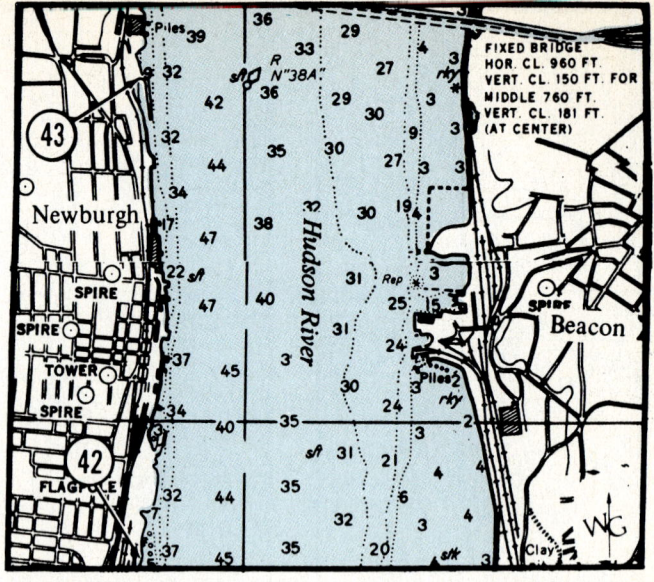

Chart 12343, edition 14

Chart 12347, edition 24

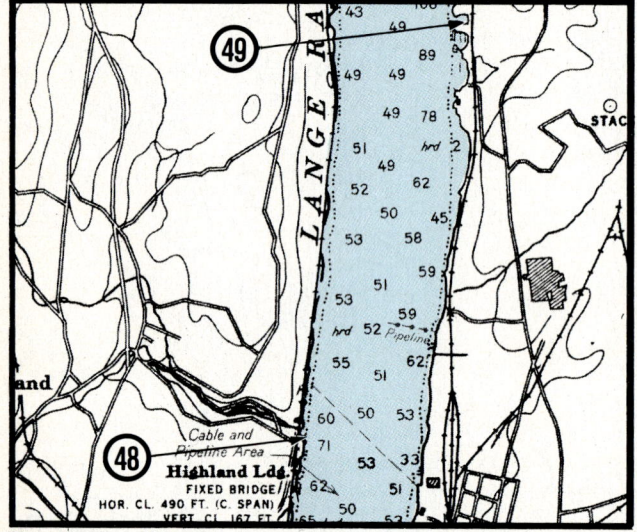

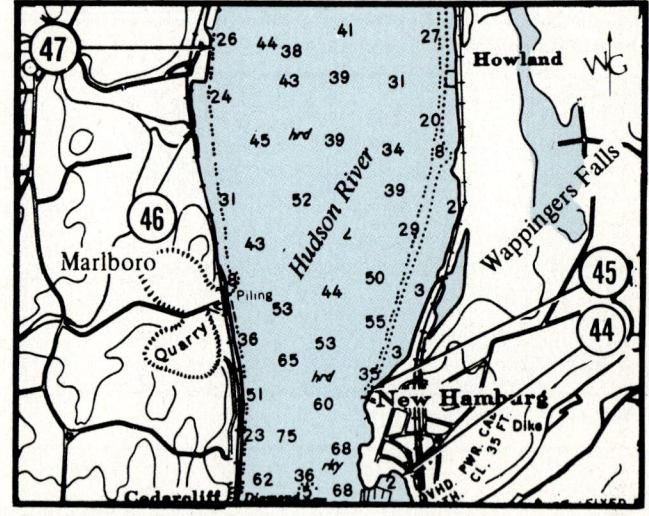

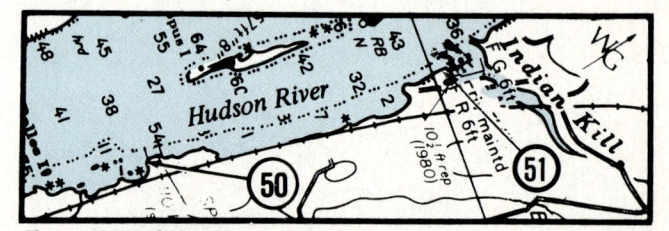

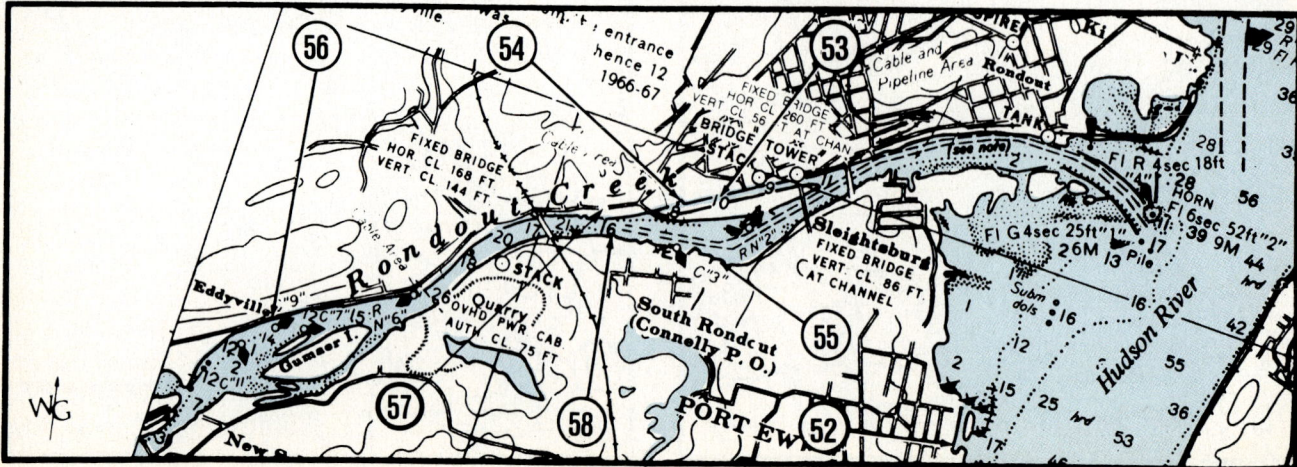

Chart 12347, edition 24

Chart 12347, edition 24

Chart 12347, edition 24

36 — *Under no circumstances are these charts to be used for navigation.*

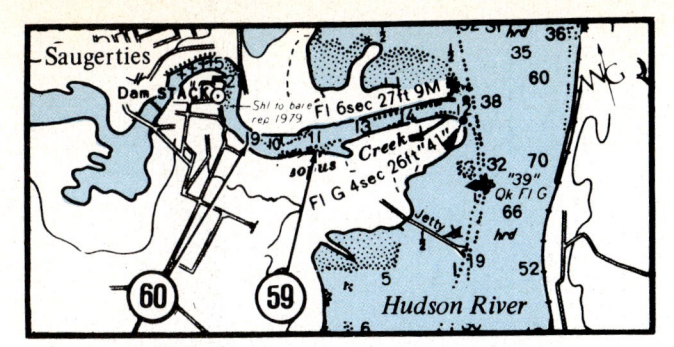

HUDSON RIVER

Chart 12347, edition 24

Chart 12348, edition 28

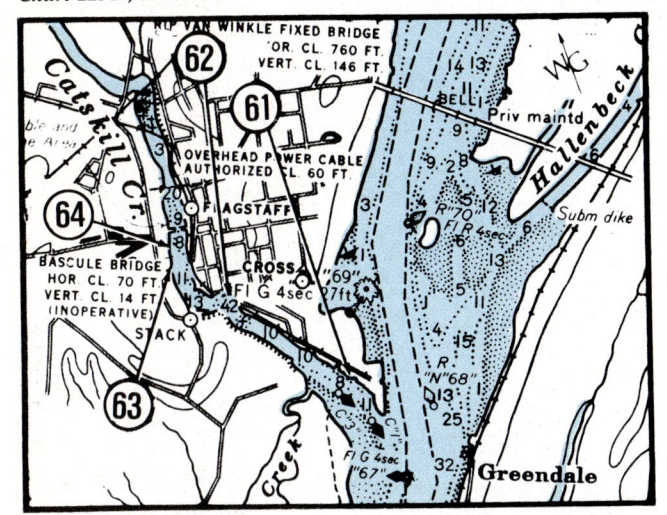

Chart 12347, edition 24

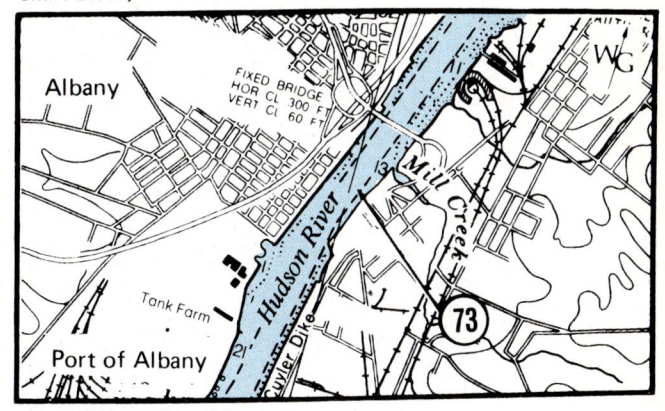

Chart 12348, edition 28

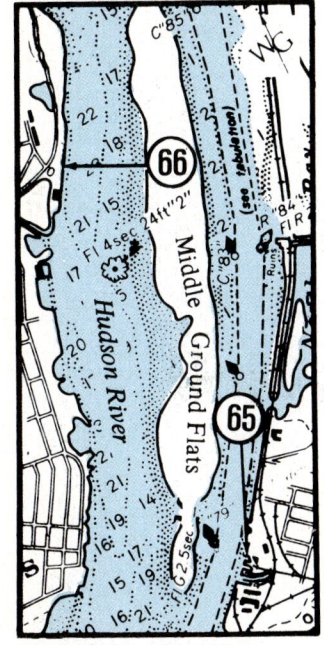

Chart 12347, edition 24

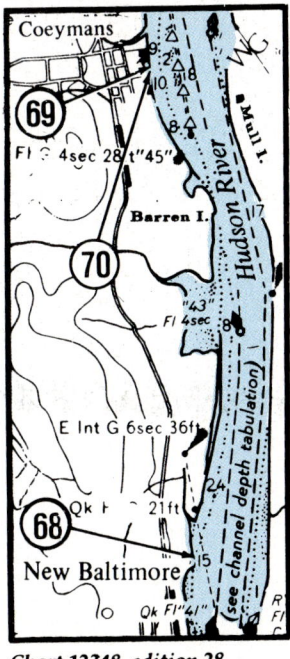

Chart 12348, edition 28

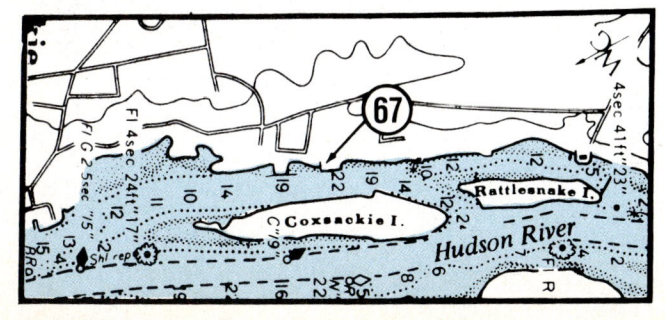

Chart 12348, edition 28

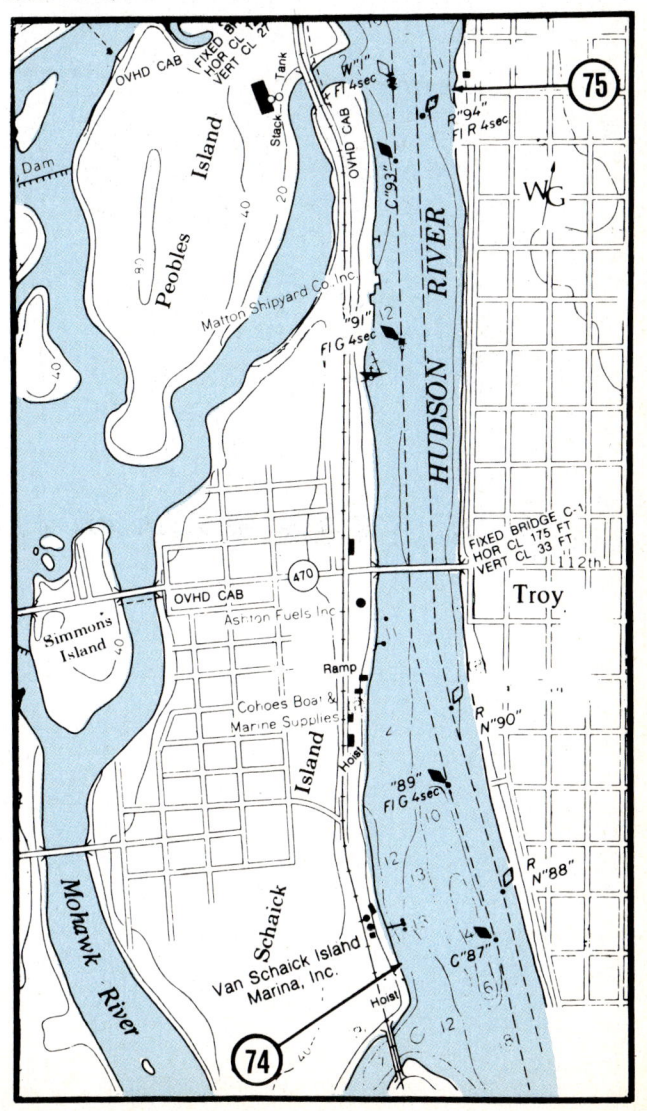

Chart 14786, edition 9

GREAT LAKES EDITION *Under no circumstances are these charts to be used for navigation.* 37

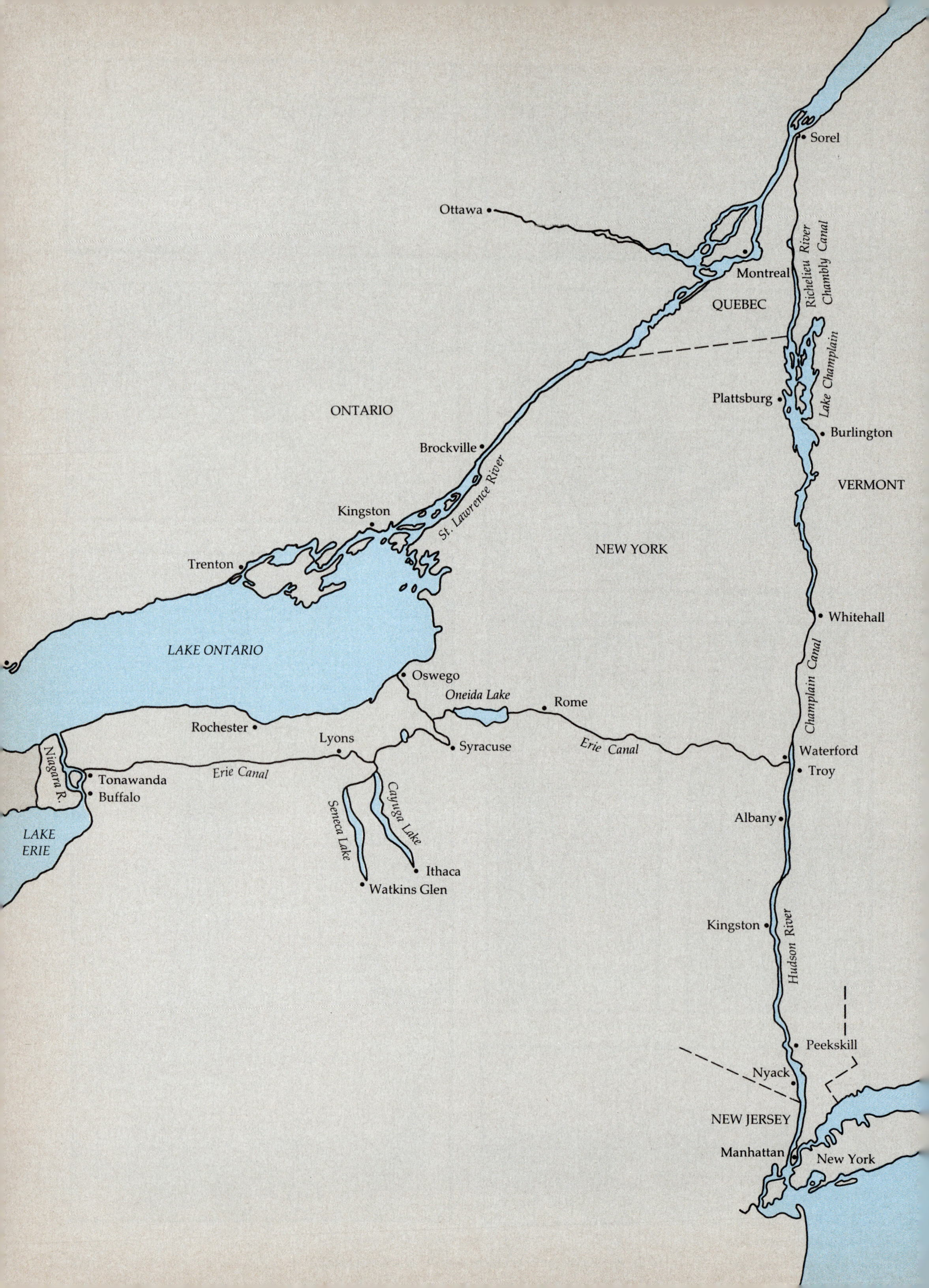
Sorel
Ottawa
Montreal
Richelieu River
Chambly Canal
QUEBEC
Lake Champlain
Plattsburg
Burlington
ONTARIO
Brockville
St. Lawrence River
VERMONT
Kingston
NEW YORK
Trenton
Whitehall
LAKE ONTARIO
Champlain Canal
Oswego
Oneida Lake
Rome
Rochester
Lyons
Syracuse
Erie Canal
Waterford
Troy
Niagara R.
Tonawanda
Buffalo
Erie Canal
Cayuga Lake
Seneca Lake
LAKE ERIE
Albany
Ithaca
Watkins Glen
Kingston
Hudson River
Peekskill
Nyack
NEW JERSEY
Manhattan
New York

Triangle Loop Cruise

Troy to Oswego to Sorel to Troy

Editor's Note: In order to make the Great Lakes edition more valuable to readers, a new feature—the Triangle Loop Cruise—is offered here for the first time. It is not intended to replace coverage of these areas, but to supplement existing material and offer alternative routes. Input from experienced Great Lakes mariners indicates that a definite itinerary or "trip plan" provides a more prudent and pleasurable cruise.

This first Triangle Loop Cruise takes the reader from Troy to Oswego via the Erie Canal, then across Lake Ontario to Ogdensburg, then up the St. Lawrence to Montreal and Sorel, and finally a turn back to the south in the direction of Rouses Point and Port Henry on Lake Champlain, and into the Champlain Canal for the return journey to Troy.

In subsequent editions, the GUIDE will offer additional Loop Cruises for the Great Lakes mariner.

With the possible exception of ensuring that your boat is generally seaworthy and mechanically sound, perhaps no concern is more important to the overall success and enjoyment of any loop cruise than the matter of planning the "Time to Leave" schedule of the voyage. In the case of a Triangle Loop Cruise, this schedule includes not only the decision of when to leave and when to return to Albany, but, of far more importance, the time to leave any location along the way.

How long you stay to enjoy a newly discovered harbor, explore a favorite city, linger to sail the waters of a Great Lake, or explore an inviting group of islands, can be quickly and automatically determined by your own "Time to Leave" (TTL) plan. An added bonus of the TTL plan is that it eliminates the gnawing fear that your pace is either too rapid or too slow; a fear that you'll be back in Troy before the summer is half over, or so late that you'll be caught in the first snowstorm of the season.

This Triangle Loop Cruise covers a distance of approximately 720 miles. In order to create your own TTL plan, the journey can be considered to consist of the following six distinct and separate legs:

One Troy to Oswego (Erie Canal) *180 miles*

Two Oswego to Ogdensburg (Lake Ontario/Thousand Islands) *130 miles*

Three Ogdensburg to Montreal (St. Lawrence Seaway) *120 miles*

Four Montreal to Rouses Point (Canadian waters) *120 miles*

Five Rouses Point to Port Henry (Lake Champlain) *70 miles*

Six Port Henry to Troy (Champlain Canal) *100 miles*

Note that the legs are arranged for a cruise progressing in a clockwise direction. Faster powerboats can travel in either direction, but slower powerboats and sailboats almost always prefer the clockwise direction. The prevailing southwest winds of the summer months are a definite inducement to select the clockwise route.

You will not travel the six legs at a uniform pace unless you plan to make a quick one- or two-week trip. Section Two (Lake Ontario and the Thousand Islands) and Section Five (Lake Champlain) will probably each take more time to cruise than the cumulative total of sections One, Three, Four, and Six.

But if you have never been there before, you may wonder how to gauge the amount of time you can allow yourself to tarry in those two beautiful cruising areas. Your TTL plan is the tool that will give you the answer.

Time to Leave (TTL) Plan

First: Decide when you will leave Troy to head north, and when it is that you want to be back in Troy, ready to head south down the Hudson River. (The water temperature of the Great Lakes is of paramount importance in determining these answers.) If you and your crew

TRIANGLE LOOP CRUISE

want to swim occasionally in Lake Ontario and to splash around among the Thousand Island anchorages, then don't plan to leave Troy on the clockwise route until after the middle of June. If warm water and fair summer weather is high on your "must have" list when you explore the shores of Lake Champlain, then your return to Troy should be before September sets in. In other words, for warm-natured travelers, the cruising season in this Triangle is limited to about two and a half months.

Second: If your cruise will be two, four, or six weeks, you can easily establish your TTL dates directly from the adjacent TTL map.

Third: If your trip is not a multiple of those on the map, divide 720 miles by the duration of your particular cruise and make your own TTL plan.

Fourth: Finally, write your actual TTL dates in the TTL circles and post the chart where the skipper and crew can refer readily to it at any time during the cruise.

Unless you have engine trouble or decide to visit the Finger Lakes on your way, you'll be far ahead of the schedule when you arrive at Oswego to begin Section Two. Beckoning Lake Ontario and the beauty of the Thousand Islands will surely demand that you now spend all of those days saved while transiting the Erie Canal. At the appropriate time, however, the TTL calendar will quietly serve to remind all that it is time to press on northward through the St. Lawrence Seaway toward Montreal.

Again, unless you are unexpectedly delayed—caught by heavy Seaway traffic, fallen victim to the fascinations of Montreal, or having chosen to lay over at Sorel or St. Jean to brush up on your French, you will complete sections Three and Four well ahead of schedule. The days you now have in the bank can be spent to the fullest in exploring the New York and Vermont shores of spectacular and historic Lake Champlain. Soon, however, without any new calculation on your part, your TTL calendar will automatically provide you with a nudge to cast off and head back to Troy. You should arrive not only long past the first of July, but also long before the first snowfall.

Triangle Loop Cruise
Section 1: Troy to Oswego

Approximately 180 miles

This first segment of your cruise covers the 180 miles from Troy Lock west to Oswego, on the southeastern shore of Lake Ontario. Along the way, your cruise will utilize the Erie Canal as it parallels the Mohawk River, runs into Oneida Lake and across it, and emerges alongside the Oswego River. Along the way, a series of locks will lift you to the point of 420 feet above sea level at Rome, N.Y., before you drop back down to 363 feet in preparation to enter the Oswego Canal on your way into Lake Ontario.

Overnight stopping places are many and well-spaced, but possible choices would be at Amsterdam, Fultonville, or Canajoharie for the first night; Utica, Rome, or Sylvan Beach for the second night enroute; and then Brewerton, Phoenix, or Fulton should you want to stop before you actually reach Oswego. If you choose to travel relatively equal distances each day, then possible stops could be in Amsterdam (35 miles from Troy), Utica (55 miles farther), and Syracuse (63 miles).

Section 2: Oswego to Ogdensburg

Approximately 130 miles

Oswego, an historic city that was the first New York settlement on Lake Ontario, is the gateway to Lake Ontario via the Oswego Canal with its eight locks. Once you enter the lake, it's a straightforward run to Henderson Bay and Sackets Harbor. If the weather acts up enroute, a harbor of refuge can be found near the halfway point at North Pond. It can be shallow in places, so enter carefully, watching for the red and black buoys that mark the channel. Anchor south of the harbor entrance in one of the coves.

The village of Chaumont, on Chaumont Bay, offers both marine facilities and an anchorage. Though much of the bay is exposed, anchorage can be found adjacent to the state park in a cove on Point Peninsula.

The southeast entrance to the St. Lawrence River lies 20 miles beyond here, at Tibbets Point.

Section 3: Ogdensburg to Montreal

Approximately 120 miles

Once in the St. Lawrence River, the cruising mariner will encounter swift currents, but fortunately when going north, it's "going with the flow" as the waters head "down" toward sea level in Montreal. Along the way, attractive stops such as Cape Vincent, Clayton, Wellesley Island, and Alexandria Bay provide opportunities for sight-seeing and provisioning. Ogdensburg has a municipal marina and is a good place to lay over and plan the next day's journey.

At Iroquois, the first in a series of locks appears that continue to bring you closer to sea level. Between Cornwall and the St. Regis Islands, the seaway becomes Canadian, and accordingly requires the use of Canadian charts. Montreal is a city of vast cultural opportunities and not-to-be-missed sights. Specifics on what to see and do in this French metropolis are covered in the GUIDE'S St. Lawrence chapter.

Mariners traveling to Sorel, 50 miles beyond Montreal, won't be disappointed. An important industrial city, Sorel offers ample marine facilities and is the entrance to the Richelieu River. One of Sorel's bridges reportedly is slow to open, so you'll probably want to unstep your mast in Montreal. Following the river south will lead the mariner into the 7.7-mile-long Chambly Canal with its nine locks and onto Lake Champlain. It costs $15 per day to use the locks, and sailboats will take longer than one day to transit the canal.

Section 4: Montreal to Rouses Point

Approximately 120 miles
French villages and fertile farmland drift past as you travel the 46 miles south from Sorel into the Chambly Basin. The Chambly Canal, with its nine locks, begins here. The last lock, at St. Jean, puts you 85 feet above sea level. From St. Jean, it's 23 miles to the Richelieu River and Rouses Point, where you cross back into the United States and must clear customs. Customs offices are located at Gaines Marina and Lighthouse Point Marina. Restep your mast and get ready for sailing the lake. Unstepping will be required again, however, when you enter the Champlain Canal.

Section 5: Rouses Point to Port Henry

Approximately 70 miles
Now in Lake Champlain, the southbound mariner will encounter anchorages in Treadwell Bay, Deep Bay, and Short Point Cove. The state park marina at Kingsland Bay is particularly pleasant. Then it's on to Cumberland Head and Plattsburgh, largest city on the New York side of the lake. The lake's Vermont side now begins to come into view, and with it, Malletts Bay—a popular spot along Champlain's eastern shore, some nine miles northeast of Burlington. Once inside the bay's narrow entry, you'll find anchorages and marinas offering a wide range of services.

Continuing on a southerly heading, the mariner will find a variety of attractive choices for overnight stops. Among them are Burlington Bay, Shelburne, and lovely Converse Bay. After cruising past a few other safe harbors to the south, you will finally enter New York waters. The tiny village of Essex makes for a pleasant overnight stop, or you may choose instead to venture farther and enjoy the seclusion of Partridge Harbor. Westport is but two miles south of here, and it's a favorite destination because of its ample facilities. At the midsection of the lake, Port Henry is a good place to get your mast stepped and offers transient dockage as well.

St. Lawrence Seaway: Vital Statistics

The official name is the St. Lawrence Seaway. It ranks with the Panama and Suez canals among the world's biggest.

In Seaway locks, pleasure craft must be at least 20 feet long and weigh at least one ton.

Speed limit in canal sections is six mph in Canadian waters, nine in American areas.

The Seaway has seven locks: five Canadian; two, Eisenhower and Snell, belonging to the United States.

The line-handling charge per lock is $7.00 (a total of $49.00).

Clearances are for big, big ships: 117-foot overhead and 26-foot draft.

Seaway charts may be ordered from the Hydrographic Chart Distribution Office, Dept. of Fisheries and Oceans, Box 8080, Ottawa, Ontario, Canada K1G 3H6. You should also have aboard a copy of the U.S. Light List, the appropriate "Sailing Directions" (see the Useful Publications section in the Mariner's Handbook for ordering information), the Seaway Handbook (only if your boat is more than 65 feet long) and the Pleasure Craft Guide (both are available from the St. Lawrence Development Corp., P.O. Box 520, Massena, New York, 13662).

When approaching a lock, tie up first to a special pleasure craft dock and report to the lockmaster on the telephone provided (even if all lights are green). Instructions on when and how to enter will come by loudhailer. Note: These docks are low, often wet and slippery, and inadequate for the size and numbers of boats using them. Fenders should be at water level when you approach all floating docks.

In the two American locks, Eisenhower and Snell, pleasure boats normally use floating bollards at the far end of the chamber. Again, instructions come by loudhailer. In the five Canadian locks, lines are dropped aboard and later retrieved by lockmen. You should have at least 50 feet ready. If you lock through with a freighter, you will go in first and exit first.

American pleasure craft should check in with Canadian Customs and Immigration at their first Canadian entry point. When leaving Canadian waters to head home, you must clear with U.S. Customs. Otherwise, you may shuttle back and forth across the border at will.

Vessels over 65 feet long must use and follow full Seaway VHF-FM procedure: Iroquois Lock: Channel 11; American locks: Channel 12; Montreal locks: Channel 14; lift bridges: Channel 14. Skippers of smaller craft should refrain from using Seaway frequencies except in emergencies but may talk to each other on channels 08 and 68.

Life preservers must be worn by all aboard before entering American locks, and during lockage.

TRIANGLE LOOP CRUISE

WATERWAY GUIDE

The **WATERWAY GUIDE** contains data on marinas, bridge clearances and schedules, anchorages and uncharted hazards. Also included, are sights to see, tide and distance tables, mail drops and the handy Mariner's Handbook. The series is published in four editions:

1 **1991 Northern Edition:** The C & D Canal and Delaware Bay, the New Jersey shore, New York Harbor, Long Island Sound, Narragansett and Buzzards Bay, and the coasts of Massachusetts and Maine to the Canadian border. $27.95

2 **1991 Mid-Atlantic Edition:** The major rivers of the Eastern and Western Shores, the Chesapeake Bay from the C & D Canal to Norfolk, plus the Intracoastal Waterway through Virginia, the Carolinas, and Georgia. $27.95

3 **1991 Southern Edition:** Begins at the Georgia/Florida line, covers all of Florida, the Gulf of Mexico, the Bahamas and the Keys, and the Okeechobee and Tenn-Tom Waterways. $27.95

1991 Great Lakes Edition: Lakes Michigan, Huron, Erie and Ontario and their connecting waterways, plus the upper Hudson River. $27.95

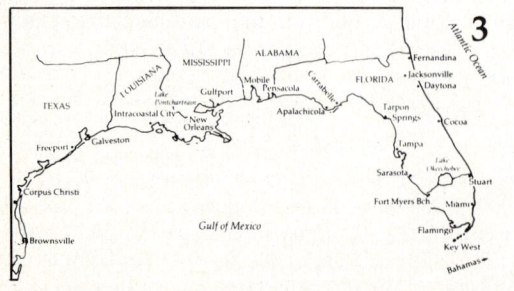

Send your check and order along with your name and street address to:

WATERWAY GUIDE
6255 Barfield Road
Atlanta, GA 30328

$3.00 shipping per book for each order

1-800-233-3359

Vital Statistics

Controlling overhead clearance on the Champlain Canal is 15½ feet. Have your mast stepped or unstepped south of Albany and in Whitehall, N.Y. (above the last fixed bridge at the north end of the canal).

Controlling depth is 12 feet.

At this writing no permit is required for pleasure craft using the canal and locks, but there has been some talk about establishing user fees in the future.

NOS chartbook 14786 covers the waters of the New York State Canal System including the Champlain Canal (see the "Useful Publications" section in the Mariner's Handbook for ordering information).

Locks 1 to 8 raise boats going north, locks 9 to 12 lower them. There is no lock 10.

In locks 1,3,6,7,9, and 11, the walls have recessed vertical pipes to which pleasure craft may secure their lines. As the water level rises or falls, lines slide freely up or down on the pipes and require no paying out or taking in.

Above Lock 2 you should be especially alert at high water stages. A strong side current can surge from the east across the approach wall.

Speed limit is 10 mph.

Lockmasters monitor VHF Channel 13 and openings should be requested in advance (see the "Locking Procedures" section in the Mariner's Handbook for tips on safe locking).

Section 6: Port Henry to Troy

Approximately 100 miles
Continuing south now, on your last leg, an area of historic forts comes into view. You'll pass two old forts at Crown Point before coming to the well known Fort Ticonderoga, built by the French in 1755. To visit the fort, anchor off its south side and take the dinghy in.

At Whitehall, you enter the Champlain Canal. Its 79-mile length consists of 11 locks and 26 bridges. Overhead clearance is 15.5 feet, and the controlling depth is 12 feet. There is no charge to transit the canal, which operates 24 hours a day. Navigation and locking are relatively simple, and the scenery improves as you begin to parallel the Hudson river on your way south. Mechanicville provides tie-up with power and water at no charge. Castleton-on-Hudson is a good place to restep the mast. Try the do-it-yourself setup at the Castleton Boat Club. The end of the canal brings you back to Troy, starting place for this Triangle Loop Cruise. For more detailed navigation information, see specific chapters of this edition that cover the areas transited during the Loop Cruise.

The Champlain Waterways

Waterford to Sorel

CHARTS: 14681, 14872, 14783, 14784, 14785; Canadian: 1325, 1326, 1338.

Few cruising grounds can match Lake Champlain and the canals and waterways leading to and from it for scenic and historic richness. From Waterford, New York, on the Hudson River, to Sorel, Quebec, on the St. Lawrence River, is about 270 miles—up the Champlain Canal, across the length of Lake Champlain, and along the Richelieu-Chambly Canal system to the St. Lawrence.

Samuel de Champlain was the first European to see Lake Champlain. In 1609 he traveled by canoe down the Richelieu River to the lake. The construction of the Champlain Canal connecting the Hudson with the lake was started in 1792 and the work was followed in 1833 by the construction of a canal joining the Richelieu to the Bassin de Chambly.

The route is clear, well-marked, and easy to follow through wilderness, lakes, mountains, French-Canadian farmland, and industrial cities.

Narrow, winding Champlain Canal is the first section of the Champlain waterway system. The canal widens into the open waters of Lake Champlain, which runs for 75 miles from Crown Point, New York, to the U.S./Canada border. The long lake separates New York and Vermont and features sandy beaches, rocky harbors, piney coves and islands, and ample facilities for transients. Reservations are recommended, especially during the last two weeks in July, the busiest time of the year.

Lake Champlain offers the cruising mariner hundreds of miles of splendid sailing, but the Coast Guard warns that strong winds blowing north and south can turn Lake Champlain into a sea of whitecaps. Pay attention to weather reports on WX-2 and stay put when these conditions arise.

Sailboat skippers should note that there are facilities for stepping and unstepping masts at Whitehall, Chipman Point, and Port Henry.

At the International Boundary, the lake gives way to the Canadian waters of the Richelieu River and Chambly Canal, leading north into the Province of Quebec to join the St. Lawrence River at Sorel.

CHAMPLAIN CANAL

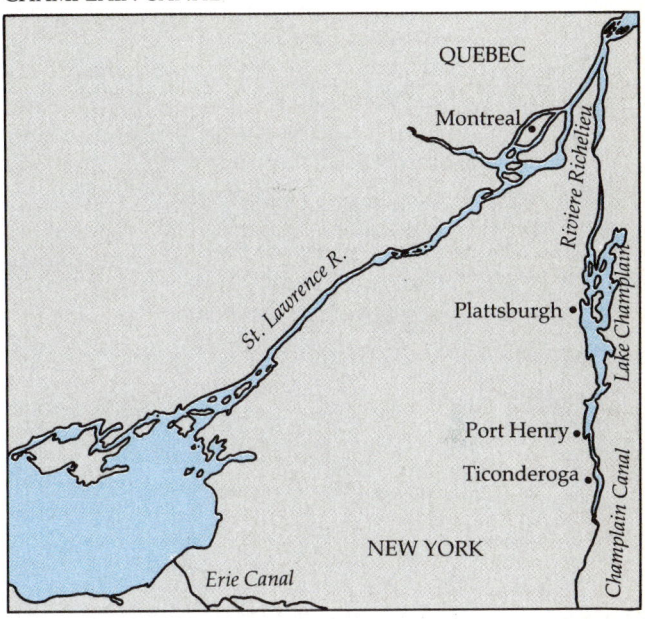

Champlain Canal.

The 60-mile-long Champlain Canal, part of the New York State Canal System, runs from Waterford to Whitehall, through 11 locks and under 26 bridges with a controlling depth of 12 feet and an overhead clearance of 15 and a half feet.

Locking and navigation are simple; buoyage runs the usual pattern to the canal end at Whitehall. The first 31 miles of the route follow the narrowing, scenic Hudson River while a man-made ditch forms the last 25 miles.

Facilities along the canal are generally improving and increasing in number. The tie-up spots of the past are becoming full-service marinas, and new facilities are opening.

Waterford to Whitehall

At Waterford, a signboard points west to the Erie Canal and north to the Champlain route. Lock tenders should be called on Channel 13 and advised that you are awaiting lockage. Their failure sometimes to acknowledge your call does not necessarily mean that they haven't heard you, but only that they are too busy at the time or

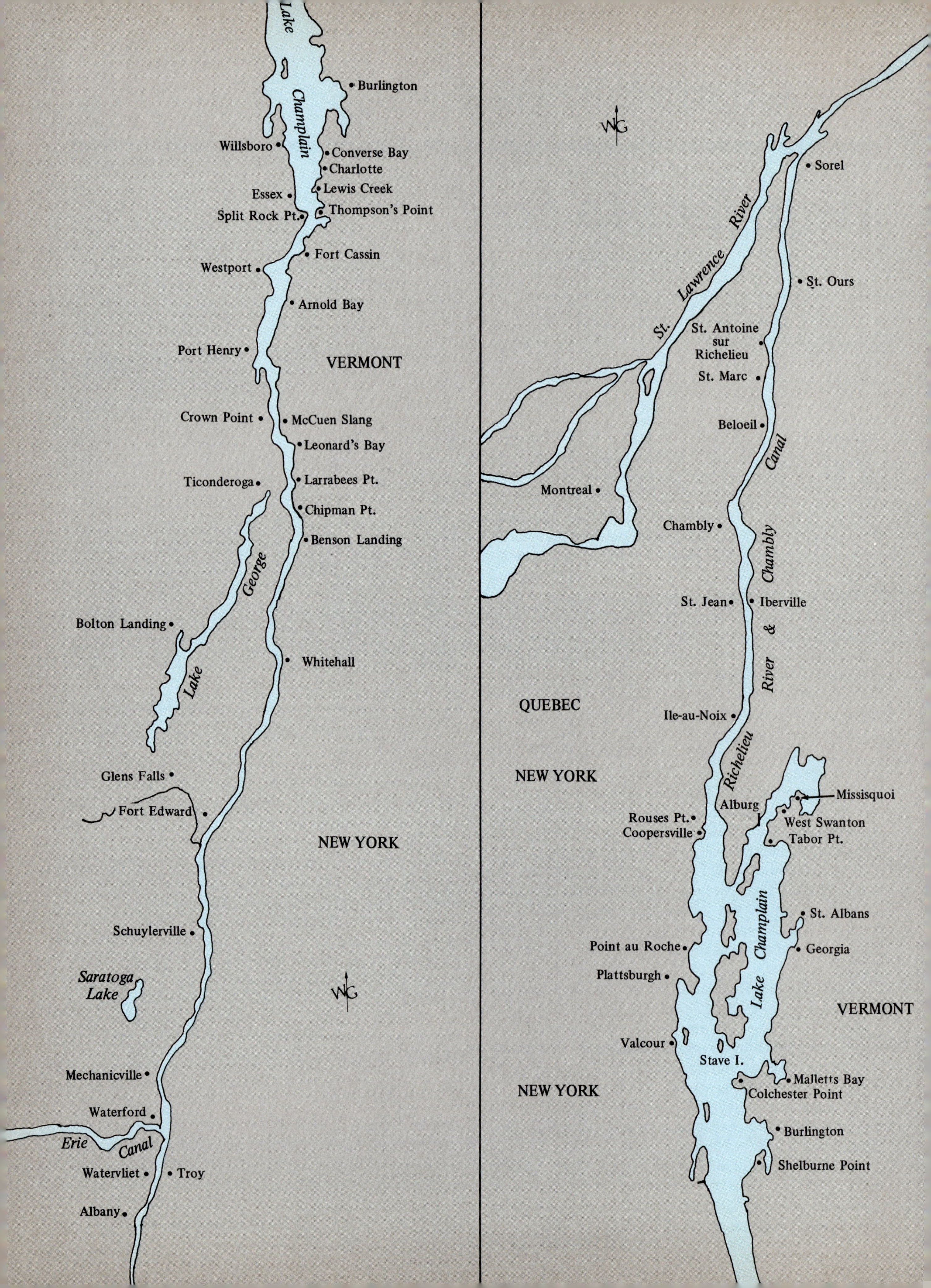
Lake Champlain
Burlington
Willsboro
Converse Bay
Charlotte
Essex
Lewis Creek
Split Rock Pt.
Thompson's Point
Fort Cassin
Westport
Arnold Bay
Port Henry
VERMONT
Crown Point
McCuen Slang
Leonard's Bay
Ticonderoga
Larrabees Pt.
Chipman Pt.
Benson Landing
Lake George
Bolton Landing
Whitehall
Glens Falls
Fort Edward
NEW YORK
Schuylerville
Saratoga Lake
Mechanicville
Waterford
Erie Canal
Watervliet
Troy
Albany
Sorel
St. Lawrence River
St. Ours
St. Antoine sur Richelieu
St. Marc
Beloeil
Montreal
Chambly
Richelieu River & Chambly Canal
St. Jean
Iberville
QUEBEC
Ile-au-Noix
NEW YORK
Missisquoi
Alburg
Rouses Pt.
West Swanton
Coopersville
Tabor Pt.
St. Albans
Point au Roche
Georgia
Plattsburgh
Lake Champlain
VERMONT
Valcour
Stave I.
Malletts Bay
NEW YORK
Colchester Point
Burlington
Shelburne Point

too far from the radio to respond. Some lock tenders use hand-held radios, but others do not.

Obey the speed limit. It is there to protect the fragile banks of the canal. Lock tenders record the time you leave a given lock and can easily determine that you are speeding if you arrive at the next lock before you should.

Mechanicville is a fine overnight stop. This friendly city provides a free town dock, including electricity. All services and stores are within a few blocks. Only Fort Edward and Whitehall on the canal are similarly convenient.

Just north of Mechanicville is Lock 3, the highest (19½ feet) in the Champlain system.

The Schuylerville Yacht Basin, with numerous transient slips, is located a mile south of Lock 5.

Beyond Lock 6, two miles of landcut bypass a long river curve. The canal rejoins the Hudson at Marker 190. Skippers heading south at this point should be alert, because the canal opening can be difficult to spot.

Just prior to Lock 7 is the marked side channel leading to Fort Edward. Up this channel and just past the railroad and highway bridges, the city has provided a long tie-up wall and a park with both free water and electricity. This is a favorite spot for those cruising the river. Restaurants, stores, and all services are immediately available.

A sign just as you enter Lock 7 reminds boaters that no overboard discharge of sewage is allowed. You can expect to be boarded and your holding tank inspected soon after you reach Lake Champlain. This sign allows little room for pleas of ignorance or other excuses.

At this point, the Hudson leaves the canal and heads westward toward Glens Falls and Hudson Falls cataracts.

Lock 8 is the last up lock. Between Lock 8 and Lock 9, the canal is frequently above the surrounding countryside, and provides some wonderful panoramic views.

At Lock 9 is a pleasant overnight tie-up spot on the southeast side of the lock near a small dam. After the strain of getting the boat safely through nine up locks since the tidal waters of Albany, your crew is bound to appreciate the ease of locking through this first of many down locks to come.

There is no Lock 10. It was laid out in the original survey but proved unnecessary. No one knows why the system wasn't renumbered.

A mile south of Lock 11, on the east shore, is Comstock Prison, known as Great Meadow Correctional Facility on the chart.

The southwest wall of Lock 11 is now occasionally used as an overnight tie-up. Now that noisy Route 22 has been shifted to the west, this spot is finally a comfortable stop.

Whitehall, at the northern end of the Champlain Canal is the midpoint between New York City and Montreal. The first U.S. Navy ships were built here from locally milled green lumber. The waterside Skenesborough Museum (Whitehall was known as Skenes-

DOCK IN HISTORIC SARATOGA COUNTY

Only few miles away from the beautiful victorian setting of Saratoga Springs. Enjoy the famous mineral water, the fastest horses in the world or the outstanding performing arts. And, of course, the incredible dining and nightlife is waiting for you.

Transient dockage up to 90 feet
Showers, rest rooms
Picnicking
Fuel & Lubricants
Ice-cubes & blocks
Dockside electricity & spring-fed water

Laundromat
8-10 ft. dock side depth
Marine boutique & supplies
Monitor ch 16
Marina open 24 hrs./day
Season coincide with canal schedule.

Calm, protected and wake free dockage

SCHUYLER YACHT BASIN
1 Ferry St., Schuylerville, NY 12871
(518) 695-3193

LOCK 12 MARINA
ON LAKE CHAMPLAIN

200 Feet North of Lock 12, Whitehall, N.Y.

Transient slips. (Reservations recommended July & August.)
New Swimming Pool
Texaco Gas & Diesel
Ships Store. (Close to many shops)
Mast Stepping Crane
Car Rentals. AMTRAK Train
Ramp. Boat Repairs.
Portage to Lake George. (Up to 30' boats)

Finch & Chubb RESTAURANT French Cuisine

LOCK 12 MARINA
Whitehall, N.Y. 12887
For Reservations call:
(518) 499 2049, VHF Channel 16

borough in Colonial days) exhibits relics and models of ships from the Revolutionary War and the War of 1812, as well as the work of local artists.

Over the past few years, the city of Whitehall has made great strides. The city has improved the lock, modernized the waterfront, and restored its downtown area. Boaters are welcome to tie up at the wall on the west side of the canal either north or south of the bridge. Across the canal is a fine alternate tie-up at the Liberty Marina. Although the variety of stores and services is more limited than in Fort Edward and Mechanicville, Whitehall is as pleasant a stop.

All vessels, whether they are heading north or south, must tie to the west wall of Lock 12.

On the lower side of the lock is the newly expanded Lock 12 Marina with a ship's store, a mast-stepping crane, and a fine restaurant.

Lake Champlain

Holding tanks required. Lake Champlain, an enclosed body of water, has more stringent sanitation regulations than federal law requires.

Note the 1989 Vermont Holding Tank Law: "Every marine toilet on board any vessel operated on the waters of the state shall also incorporate or be equipped with a holding tank. Any holding tank designed so as to provide for an optional means of discharge to the waters on which the vessel is operating shall have the discharge openings sealed shut and any discharge lines, pipes, or hoses shall be disconnected and stored while the vessel is in the waters of this state."

New York State has a similar law. Marine patrol vessels of both states routinely board and inspect vessels to insure compliance. In 1989, the Vermont fine for disobedience was $255.

For the next 15 miles the well-buoyed channel winds through a river-like stretch of marshes in the southern narrows of Lake Champlain. Follow the markers closely, take it slowly, and keep to mid-channel past **Maple Bend, Narrows of Dresden**, and **Pulpit Point.**

ANCHORAGE. Just south of **Benson Landing** you can drop the hook in six- to nine-foot depths northwest of markers "1" and "2" in grass.

Stony Point. Here the lake and the channel begin to broaden, the marshes end, buoyage thins out, and navigation becomes easier. But open water is still almost 17 miles away, and land points, projecting out from both shores, must be given a wide berth.

Four miles north of Stony Point you reach the facilities at **Chipman Point**, Vermont. Here you can get your mast stepped or unstepped, and taxi service to Fort Ticonderoga is available.

Fort Ticonderoga. On a broad spit of land about 23 miles above Whitehall stands Fort Ticonderoga. Situated high on a hill on the New York shore, the fort was built in 1755 by the French, captured in 1756 by the English, taken in 1775 by Ethan Allen and his Green Mountain Boys, and retaken in 1777 by the British.

If you want to visit the well-restored fort, anchor off and dinghy in to the beach on the south side of the fort; there's a hike up the hill. You can also dock at one of

Distances
Approximate Statute Miles
Distances in parentheses are off-channel

Location	Between Points	Cumulative
Waterford, NY	0	0
Champlain Canal		
Lock 1	3	3
Lock 2	4	7
Mechanicville, NY	2	9
Lock 3	1	10
Lock 4	1	11
Schuylerville, NY	13	24
Lock 5	1	25
Lock 6	4	29
Lock 7	7	36
Lock 8	2	38
Lock 9	6	44
Lock 11	9	53
Lock 12, Whitehall, NY	7	60
Lake Champlain		
Chipman Point, VT	19	79
Ticonderoga, NY	3	82
Crown Point, NY	15	97
Port Henry, NY	2	99

Location	Between Points	Cumulative
Lake Champlain		
Westport, NY	10	109
Split Rock Point, NY	7	116
Willsboro Point, NY	12	128
Burlington, VT	(7)	
Stave Island	10	138
Mallets Bay, VT	(5)	
Cumberland Head	7	145
Plattsburgh, NY	(3)	
Rouses Point, NY	21	166
Richelieu/Chambly System		
Ile-aux-Noix	11	177
St. Jean	12	189
Lock 9, Chambly Canal	1	190
Locks 8 to 4, Chambly Canal	9	199
Locks 3 to 1, Chambly Canal	2	201
St. Marc	15	216
St. Ours Lock	16	232
Sorel	15	247
Montréal	53	300

the nearby marinas and taxi over.

At Larrabees Point, Vermont, a cable ferry crosses to the road leading up to the fort. It operates continuously between sunrise and sunset; be sure to wait for the cables to sink before you pass by.

There are two other old forts at **Crown Point**, New York, about 14 miles to the north of Fort Ticonderoga (and here dockage is easy in five to seven foot depths). A 91-foot fixed bridge crosses from Crown Point to **Chimney Point**, Vermont.

Beyond the bridge at Crown Point, the lake widens to about two miles and continues to widen northward. In a hard north wind, lake crossing can be rough, but refuge can be found about a half mile northward on the Vermont side in **Hospital Creek**. The marina here has only four feet of water. If you don't draw more than that, you can anchor along the north shore of the creek in northerly weather. Most Lake Champlain anchorages are open to north or south winds.

The New York Shore. Port Henry, New York, two miles west of the Crown Point Bridge, offers facilities for transients, and you can get your mast stepped. The lake's midsection begins here and extends roughly 40 miles northward to Port Kent on the New York shore and Burlington and Malletts Bay on the Vermont side. Through most of Lake Champlain you can zigzag as you please, sampling an anchorage on one shore, and a marina on the other—or just enjoying the scenery.

Westport, the historic village about nine miles north of Port Henry, makes a pleasant stop. You'll find many fine examples of 19th- and early 20th-century architecture here, and at the hospitable marina you can pick up informative brochures and begin the highly acclaimed walking tour of the village. The marina has spring water from its own wells, making it a good place to take on drinking water. Groceries and other supplies are nearby. Deep, secluded **Partridge Harbor**, less than two miles to the north, offers good anchorage.

Next stop on the lake's New York shore is the hamlet of **Essex**, where period architecture remains relatively intact. There are shops, a Laundromat, and a ferry to **Charlotte**, Vermont.

Ten miles north of Essex, one of the largest expanses of open water on the lake begins near **Willsboro Bay**. Boat facilities welcoming transients are located in the southeast cove of Willsboro Bay.

The Vermont shore. Opposite Westport, New York, **Button Bay** marks the beginning of a stretch of interesting harbors, anchorages, and potential side trips along the Vermont shore. There is a state park here (the north shore is all beach), and the bay offers anchorage protected from every direction but southwest.

Just to the north of the bay are **Porter Bay**, where you can anchor snugly in all but northwest winds, and **Kingsland Bay**, with well-protected coves on its west and south shores.

Thompson's Point, across from Split Rock Point, is halfway between Whitehall, New York, and the Inter-

---

Welcome to the **WESTPORT MARINA**
Where Lake Champlain meets the Adirondack Mountains . . .we're *more* than a place to dock!

THE GALLEY
Light Meals, Breakfast
DOCKSIDE DINING

Friendly and fun
SATURDAY NIGHT BARBECUES

Complete & creative chandlery
MARINE SUPPLIES and GIFTS

Mountain Spring Water
25-TON LIFT   FULL SERVICE   GAS   DIESEL
Johnson Outboards, OMC, Volvo-Penta,
Onan, Marine Air
FACTORY-TRAINED SERVICE DEPARTMENT
Mast Stepping

Easy walk or free ride to markets, restaurants, overnight accommodations, summer theater, golf, tennis, craft shops, antiques, playground, laundromat, liquor store, pharmacy, AMTRAK train

WESTPORT MARINA, Westport, N.Y. 12993
For Reservations call (518) 962-4356, VHF Channel 16

POINT BAY MARINA

Southeast Side of Thompson's Point
Chart 14783 on Lake Champlain
Pump-out Station • Floating Docks
Power & Water • Showers
Lounge • Picnic Area • Ice • Grocery Service
Major Repairs • 24 Ton Open End Travelift
Mast Stepping • Hauling • Storage
Marine Supplies

OMC — MERCRUISER — VOLVO PENTA
Authorized Service-Parts

OMCobra   merCruiser   VOLVO PENTA

GAS   **Mobil**   DIESEL

Charlotte, Vt. 05445   802/425-2431

CHAMPLAIN WATERWAYS

national Boundary. Inside the point, in an almost landlocked cove, a full-service marina provides all repairs, supplies, and pump-out. Around the point to the north is beautiful **Converse Bay**, where protected anchorages can be found east and north of **Cedar** and **Garden** islands.

About 11 miles north, opposite New York's Willsboro Bay, is **Shelburne Point**, which you round to enter Vermont's **Shelburne Bay**. Inside, near the mouth, is a full-service marina and repair yard. About five miles north, just south of the village of **Shelburne**, is the Shelburne Museum.

North of Shelburne Point lies **Burlington Bay**. This section of Lake Champlain is more than ten miles of wide and open water from shore to shore. Farther north the lake is divided by islands, but here the expanse is almost unbroken.

Burlington, located on Burlington Bay, is Lake Champlain's largest city. Charts 14782 and 14783 show the approaches to this manufacturing and resort center. Groceries and a Laundromat are available within two blocks of the small local marina. Facilities are limited, but you can anchor in 20-25 feet behind the breakwater. Twenty moorings and a dinghy ramp have been placed by the city of Burlington.

Malletts Bay, Vermont, one of Champlain's most popular bodies of water, is about nine miles north and east of Burlington, along the lake's eastern shore. Nearly landlocked, this bay within a bay is more than five miles from the lake center, east of **Stave Island**. You'll find everything from elegant marinas to good repair operations and protected anchorages.

To reach Malletts Bay, pass north or south of Stave Island. Go through the narrow channel, and cut through the abandoned railroad dike, east of the island. Watch your depths in approaching the dike opening. There are some three-foot spots and the better water is found by approaching the trestle from the north and paralleling it to the passage through the dike. Once through, leave the can off **Allen Point** to port and travel the outer bay five miles east to the narrow entrance of Malletts Bay.

Plattsburgh Harbor Marina
formerly Dock and Coal Marina
NOT A NEW MARINA...
JUST A NEW NAME - FOR A GREAT OLD MARINA
WITH A BRIGHT NEW FUTURE!

- Dockage With Hook-Ups • VHF Ch. 16
- Ship's Store • Water/Ice • Phone
- Showers • Rest Room Facilities
- Repair Services • Travel Lift
- Gas • Diesel • Pumpout

SPACES CURRENTLY AVAILABLE

One Dock Street
Plattsburgh, N.Y. 12901
Phone: (518) 561-2800

Richelieu River/ Chambly Canal

Roughly a mile north of Rouses Point, you cross the International Boundary and enter Canada. The route to the St. Lawrence is part river and part canal, cutting through the green and tranquil countryside for about 70 miles, to Sorel, Quebec. The channel is, for the most part, narrow and easy to navigate. Cable ferries cross the route at frequent intervals, and the ten locks lift vessels a total of 85 feet. The trip has four distinct segments: **Richelieu River** to **St. Jean** (23 miles); **Chambly Canal**, with nine locks (ten miles); the **Richelieu** again, to St. Ours and the last of the locks (27 miles); and **St. Ours** to **Sorel** (11 miles).

Richelieu River to St. Jean. After crossing the International Boundary, hoist the Canadian ensign as a courtesy to your hosts. The ensign is flown at the starboard spreader or bow staff, according to the nature of your boat.

Just south of the border, however, take time to glance at Fort Montgomery, locally referred to as "Fort Blunder." It was built by the United States just prior to the War of 1812. After the war, it was discovered that the fort had been built above the 45th parallel—Canadian territory at that time.

ANCHORAGE. You'll find anchorage providing protection from east to south winds just north of the Rouses Point Bridge Causeway. Another anchorage with protection from southwest to north winds is just off the permanent moorings of the yacht club, just south of the Canadian customs dock.

Be sure to stop at the Canadian Customs dock a mile north of the border on the west side. Take the few steps necessary to clear for Canadian entry (for complete information see our Mariner's Handbook). Note that if you clear on Sunday or after hours, you must pay a fee.

Minimum channel depth on the **Richelieu River** is nine feet. The clear river is wide and slow, with summer cottages lining the banks. Behind the cottages lies flat farmland and well-to-do countryside where the language, both written and spoken, is French.

On summer weekends, the southern end of the Richelieu River can be unpleasantly crowded with power boats scurrying to and from the waters of Lake Champlain. Cruising vessels should consider traveling this stretch on weekdays, when it's less crowded.

About nine miles above the border you'll find a full-service marina offering repairs and a pump-out station. There is a hotel at **Ile-aux-Noix**. Ft. Lennox Public Park is here, and if the small dock is full, anchor just off the old channel in good holding.

Another 12 miles brings you to **St. Jean** on the west bank, or **Iberville** on the east. St. Jean gives you the full flavor of French Canada. The Chambly Canal, which bypasses the Richelieu's long chain of rapids, begins

CHAMPLAIN WATERWAYS

here. Note: The bascule bridge at St. Jean is closed Monday through Friday, 11:45 a.m.-1:15 p.m., so try to avoid lunchtime lockage.

The cranes for mast-stepping are no longer available at either end of the canal. It is suggested that you have the job done before you leave the States.

Chambly Canal

Canadian canals, including the Chambly Canal and the St. Ours Lock, are now subject to two types of user fees—a lock use fee and an overnight mooring fee, both subject to change.

The most recent fees were:
Lock fees (per day of lock use):
5.5 meters and less — $5.00
5.5 meters to 8 meters — $10
8 meters to 12 meters — $15
Over 12 meters — $20

Mooring fees (overnight fee to tie up to a lock wall):
5.5 meters and less — $5.00
5.5 meters to 8 meters — $8
8 meters to 12 meters — $11
Over 12 meters — $14

Lock tenders will provide you with the lock lines. Boats heading south (those being raised in the lock) may encounter a surprising amount of turbulence at the front of the locks. Because of this turbulence, the lock tender may offer you a third line. Take it and use it as a spring line to keep your bow from being sucked forward into the gate.

At the base of the Chambly rapids (in the Chambly

Champlain Waterway / Richelieu River / Chambly Canal		SEASONAL / YEAR-ROUND	SAIL / POWER / BOTH▲	LARGEST VESSEL ACCOMMODATED	NO. OF TRANSIENT BERTHS	MARKED ENTRY CHANNEL	APPROACH DEPTH (Reported)	DOCKSIDE DEPTH (Reported)	GAS ★ DIESEL ● BOTH▲	FUEL BRAND	RAILWAY / LIFT CAPACITY (in tons)	ENGINE REPAIRS: Gas ★ Diesel ● Both▲	LAUNCHING RAMP	PROPELLER / HULL REPAIRS	MARINE SUPPLIES	LPG ★ CNG ● BOTH▲ / GROCERIES / ICE	110V ★ 220V ● BOTH▲ MAX AMPS	SHOWERS / LAUNDROMAT	RESTAURANT / SNACK BAR	PUMP-OUT STATION	RADIO WATCH—VHF (CB)
CHAMPLAIN CANAL / WATERFORD TO WHITEHALL																					
1. Riverside Marina*		S	▲	40	10	●	12	5		IND	★			R			MGI	★20	S	S	16
2. Fisherman's Rest*			▲				12	6			★			R			I	▲30	S		
3. Schuyler Yacht Basin (p. 45)	(518) 695-3193	S	▲	90	40	●	12	10		MOB	▲						MGI	▲	SL		RS	16
4. Fort Edward Yacht Basin		S	▲	110		●		10			★			MUNICIPAL DOCK			MGI	★200	L		RS	
5. Liberty Marina	499-0301	S	▲	70	20	●	11	11					▲	P	▲		MGI	▲50	SL		RS	
6. Frere and Company	499-2100					MARINE SUPPLIES				COURTESY DOCK AT LIBERTY MARINA												
7. Lock 12 Marina (p. 45)	499-2049	S	▲	100	50	●	20	18		TEX	▲			R	▲	P	MGI	▲50	SL	●	R	16
LAKE CHAMPLAIN / CHIPMAN PT. TO SHELBURNE PT., VT																						
8. Chipman Point Marina & Camp Grounds	(802) 948-2288	S	▲	65	7		12	7			▲	L		R			MI	★30	SL	●	R	16
9. Buoy 39 Marina, Inc.	948-2411	S	▲	36	6		6	5		TEX	▲	20		R	▲	P	MI	★30	SL	●		16
10. Champlain Bridge Marina	759-2049	Y	▲	35	4	●	4	5		GUL	★			R	★	PH	MI	★15	S	●		
11. Velez Marine Service	(518) 546-7588	S	▲	50			15	12		AME	▲			R	▲	PH	★	MGI	▲30	S	RS	16
12. Westport Marina, Inc. (p. 47)	962-4356	S	▲	100	40	●	15	5		CIT	▲	25		R	▲		★	MGI	▲30	SL	RS	16
13. Point Bay Marina (p. 47)	(802) 425-2431	Y	▲	80	4	●	10	10		MOB	▲	24		R	▲	P	MI	★20	S	●		16
14. Essex Shipyard	(518) 963-7700	Y	▲	100			12	12		TEX	RL			R	▲	PH	MGI	★30	S	●	R	16
15. Indian Bay Marina	963-7858	S	▲	45	5		8	8		CIT	★	20		R	▲	PH	MGI	▲30	SL	●	R	16
16. Willsboro Bay Marina, Inc.	963-4472	Y	▲	55	33		50	50		AGW	▲	25		R	▲		●	MGI	★30	S	RS	16
17. Shelburne Shipyard	(802) 985-3326	Y	▲	70	10		20	10			▲	50		▲	P	●	MI	★	S	●		
BURLINGTON BAY TO MALLETTS BAY, VT																						
18. Lake Champlain Transportation Co.	864-9804	Y	▲	100	6	●	7	10		MOB	★						I	★30	L		RS	16
19. Malletts Bay Marina	862-4072	S	▲	36	20		17	4		CIT	★	7		★	PH		MGI	★30	S	●	RS	
20. The Moorings, Inc.*	862-1407	S	▲	50	6		10	10				15			H		MGI		SL	●		
21. Champlain Club, Ltd.	658-4034	S	▲	65	10		30	6		MOB	★	25		R			MGI	▲30	S	●	RS	
22. Marble Island	864-4546	Y	▲	70	12		5	5									I	▲	S	●	R	
PLATTSBURGH, NY AREA																						
23. Valcour Lodge	(518) 561-9472	S	▲				10	6		RESTAURANT & HOTEL DOCK											·	
24. Plattsburgh Harbor Marina (p. 48)	561-2800	Y	▲	65	25	●	12	10		MOB	▲	20		▲	PH		MGI	▲30	S	●		16
25. Mooney Bay Marina	(518) 563-2960	S	▲	38	20		20	7		MOB	▲	20		▲	P	★	MGI	★30	SL	●	R	16

To provide the most complete and accurate information, **all facilities have been contacted within the past year.** If an asterisk (*) appears, it indicates a facility which did not respond to our requests for information (these listings may not reflect current conditions). Although facility operators supplied this data, we cannot guarantee accuracy or assume responsibility for errors. Entrance and dockside soundings tend to fluctuate. Always approach marinas carefully. Reference numbers on spotting charts indicate marina locations. ⌁ Member American Boat Builders & Repairers Association

GREAT LAKES EDITION

CHAMPLAIN WATERWAYS

Basin) is Fort Chambly, surrounded by a park. This fort, now beautifully restored, played a significant historical role for almost three centuries. Admission is free, and a visit is well worth your time.

Richelieu River to Sorel. For 46 miles north from Chambly Basin, the Richelieu River winds through fertile farmland and quiet, affluent French Canadian villages, each with towering church spires soaring above well-kept homes.

Just north of McMasterville is a Canadian National railroad bridge. The narrow approach and the swift current call for a good deal of caution.

A friendly yacht club and marina with a restaurant is the best tie-up in the Beloeil-St. Hilaire area.

At **St. Ours**, another lock (electrically operated) ends a quarter-mile-long canal cut. Pleasant dockage is available at the lock. Additional limited dockage can be found at the public wharf just south of the St. Ours cable ferry.

Sorel

The industrial city of Sorel is the fourth oldest (1642) in Canada. Boats new to the area should take time to sort out the channel buoys leading to the two marinas, particularly the channel to the westernmost marina. Sailors wishing to raise or lower their masts can find an excellent do-it-yourself lift at Beaudry Marine Services (the marina to the west).

ANCHORAGE. Two miles west of Sorel, you can find an anchorage behind Ile aux Foins.

Champlain Waterway / Richelieu River / Chambly Canal

	Phone	Seasonal/Year-Round	Sail/Power/Both	Largest Vessel Accommodated	No. of Transient Berths	Marked Entry Channel	Approach Depth	Dockside Depth	Gas/Diesel/Both	Fuel Brand	Railway	Lift Capacity	Launching Ramp	Engine Repairs	Propeller/Hull Repairs	LPG/CNG/Both	Marine Supplies/Groceries/Ice	110V/220V/Both	Showers/Max Amps	Pump-out/Laundromat	Restaurant/Snack Bar	Radio Watch VHF(CB)
NORTH HERO TO ST. ALBANS BAY, VT																					
26. Tudhope Marine	(802) 372-4161	S	▲	28	10	●	4	4	MOB	★		L	R	★			PH	MGI				16
27. North Hero House	372-8237	S		35		●	8	8				COUNTRY INN							★30		R	
28. Marina Internationale*	372-5953	S	▲	85	20	●	16	16				L		▲			H	MGI	★		●	
29. Anchor Island Marina	372-5131	Y	P	42	10		8	8	GET	▲		L	R	▲			PH	MI	★30		●	16
30. Tudhope Sailing Center	372-5320	S		40	10	●	12	7	MOB	▲		L	R	★				M	30		●	16
31. Burton Island State Park	524-6353	S	▲	60	70	●	8	6		★								I	▲30	S	●	
32. St. Albans Bay Dock							6	4				STATE DOCK						GI				
33. Snug Harbor Monty Bay Marine	(518) 846-7900	Y	▲	36	6		6	6		★		L		▲			PH	MGI	★30	S	●	16
ROUSES POINT, NY																						
34. Chazy Boat Basin	298-2010	S	▲	36	2	●	5	10		▲	7	R	▲				PH	MGI	★20	SL	●	16
35. Ken's Marine*	298-2797	S	▲	35	2	●	5	7	SHE	★								MGI	★20	S	●	
36. The Anchorage	297-4211	Y					HOTEL & RESTAURANT DOCK															
37. Gaines' Marina	297-7000	S	▲	80			12	10	TEX	▲	25		▲				P	MI	▲30	SL	●	
38. Lighthouse Point Marina	297-6392	S	▲	48	15	●	14	11	IND	▲	25	R	▲			PH	●	MGI	★30	SL	● R	68
RICHELIEU RIVER TO SOREL																						
39. Isle-Aux-Noix Wharf				50			12	5				DOCKAGE ONLY—GOVERNMENT PIER										
40. Gagnon Marina	(514) 291-3336	Y	▲	72	20	●	8	7	ESS	▲	50	R	▲			PH	★	MI	★30	SL	● RS	68
41. Marina Gosselin	291-3170	S	▲	65	20		20	6	IND	▲	35	R	▲			H		MGI	★30	SL	● S	68
42. Le Nautique St.-Jean	347-4888	S	▲	80	25	●	6	6	IND	▲	L	R	▲			PH		MI	★15	SL	● R	68
43. Chambly Marina*	658-7308	S	▲	80	30	●	7	8	SHE	★		R	★			P		GI	★	SL	● RS	68
44. Club Nautique Beloeil-St. Hilaire*				100			15	11	SHE	★	R	R	▲			PH		MI	▲50	S	R	
45. St. Marc—Auberge Handfield*				90			12	8	CME	★								I	▲30	SL	R	
46. Borchert Marine, Inc.	584-2017	S	▲	40			8	10	IND	▲		R	▲			P		M			● RS	16/68
47. St. Antoine Wharf				50			8	7				DOCKAGE ONLY—GOVERNMENT PIER										
48. St. Denis Wharf				50			8	7				DOCKAGE ONLY—GOVERNMENT PIER										
49. St. Ours Wharf				60			8	10				DOCKAGE ONLY—GOVERNMENT PIER										
50. Beaudry Marine Services*			▲	40			6	6	TEX	▲		R	▲					MGI	★15	S	● R	
51. Parc Nautique de Sorel*	742-0413	S	▲	65	20	●	25	10	TEX	▲		R	▲			PH		MI	▲50	SL	● S	68

To provide the most complete and accurate information, **all facilities have been contacted within the past year.** If an asterisk (*) appears, it indicates a facility which did not respond to our requests for information (these listings may not reflect current conditions). Although facility operators supplied this data, we cannot guarantee accuracy or assume responsibility for errors. Entrance and dockside soundings tend to fluctuate. Always approach marinas carefully. Reference numbers on spotting charts indicate marina locations. ⚓ Member American Boat Builders & Repairers Association.

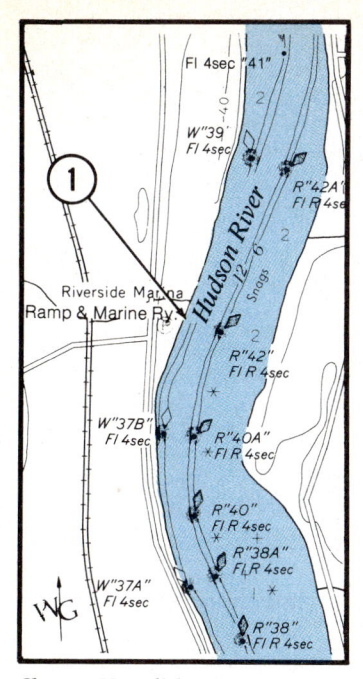

CHAMPLAIN WATERWAYS

Chart 14786, edition 9 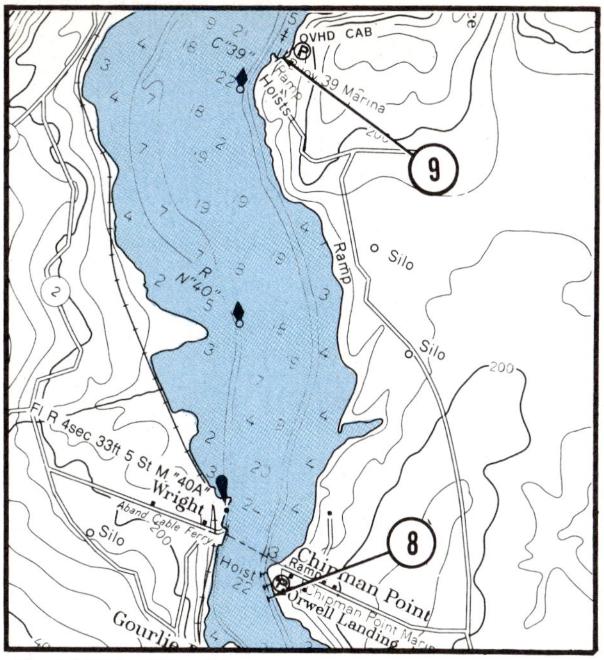   *Chart 14784, edition 17* 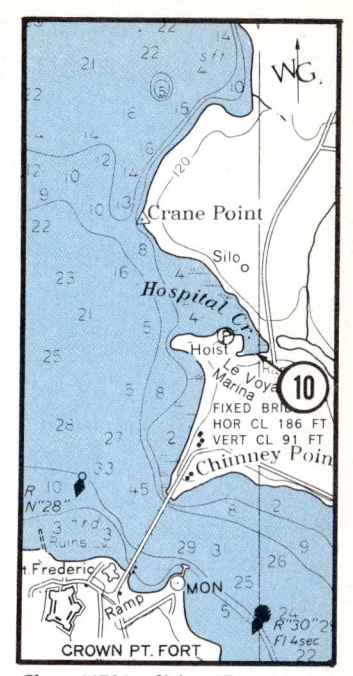   *Chart 14784, edition 17*

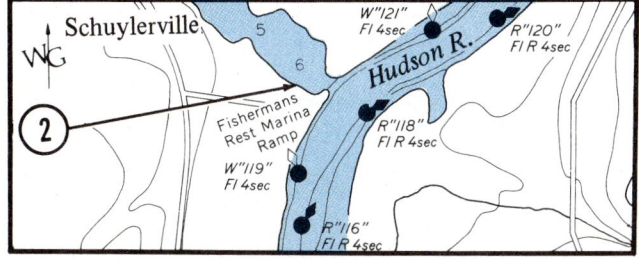

Chart 14786, edition 9

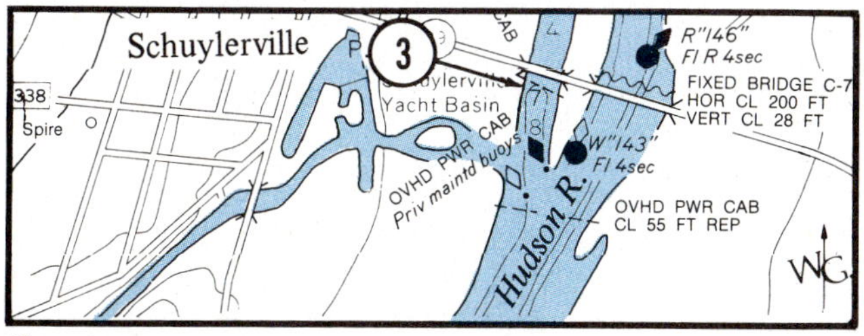

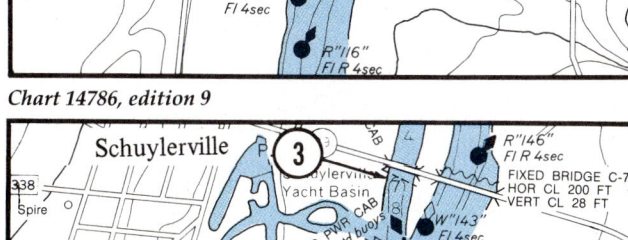

Chart 14786, edition 9 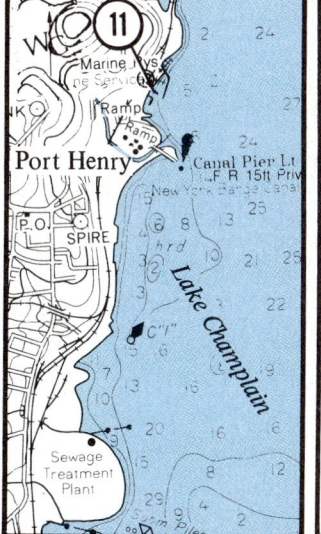   *Chart 14784, edition 17*   *Chart 14783, edition 16*

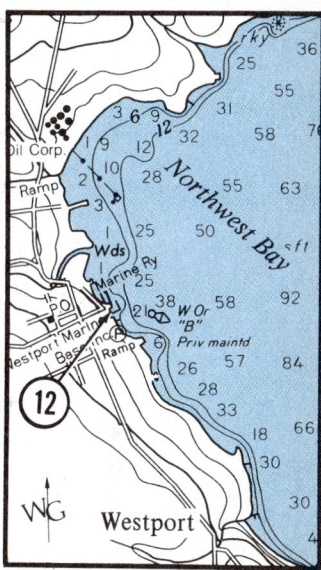

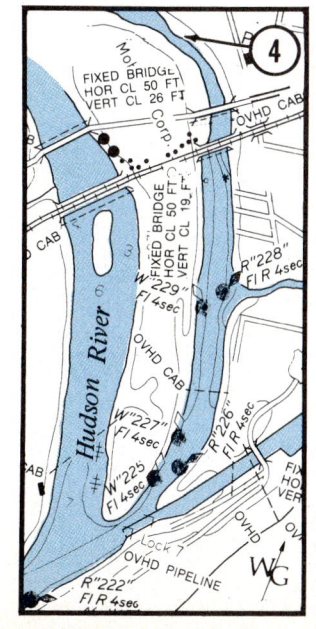

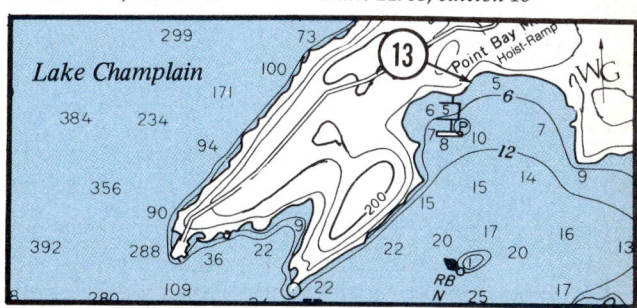

Chart 14783, edition 16

Chart 14786, edition 9 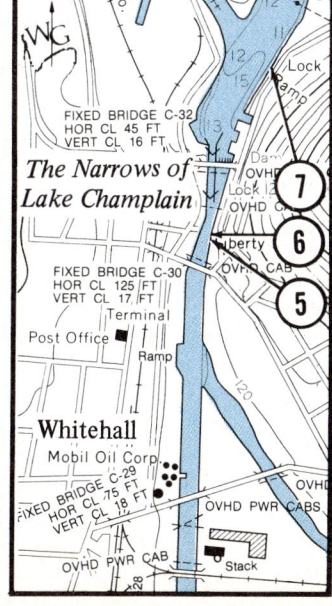   *Chart 14786, edition 9*   *Chart 14783, edition 16*

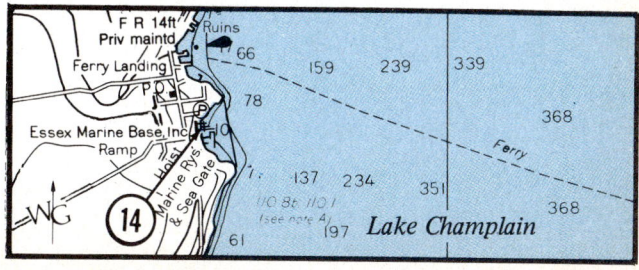

Great Lakes Edition   *Under no circumstances are these charts to be used for navigation.*   51

CHAMPLAIN WATERWAYS

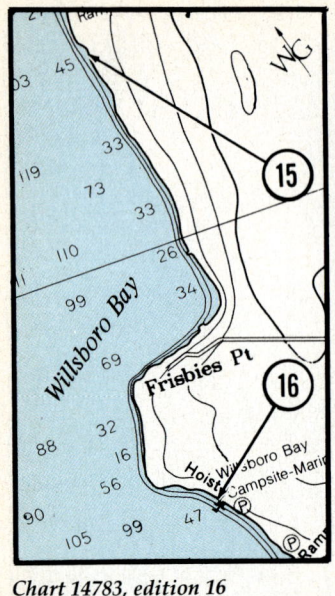

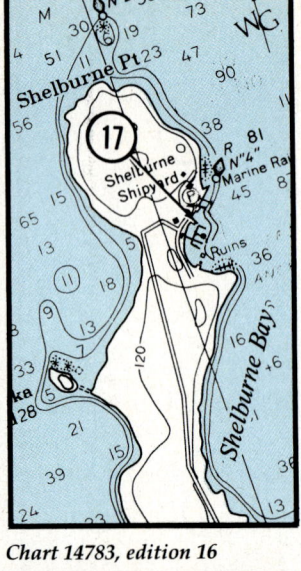

Chart 14783, edition 16

Chart 14783, edition 16

Chart 14782, edition 21

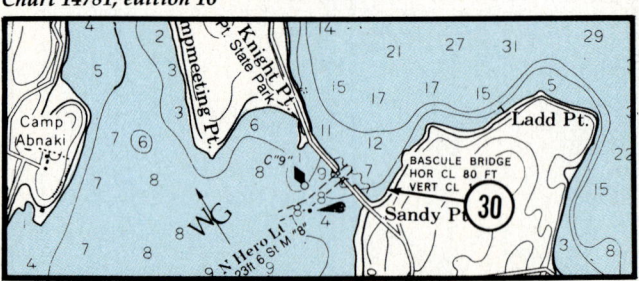

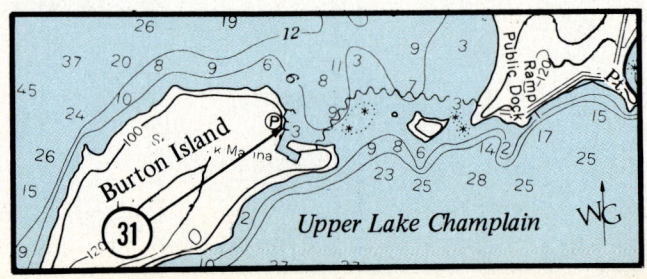

Chart 14782, edition 21

Chart 14782, edition 21

Chart 14782, edition 21

Chart 14781, edition 16

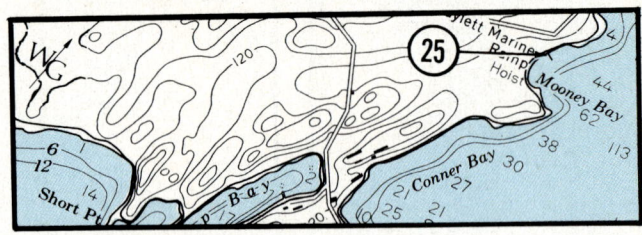

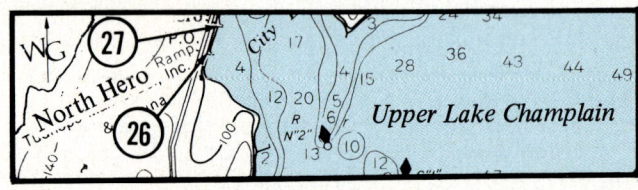

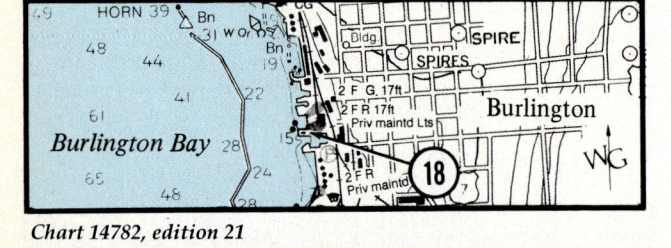

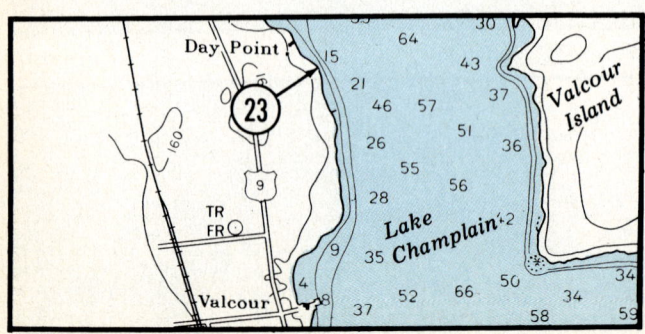

Chart 14781, edition 16

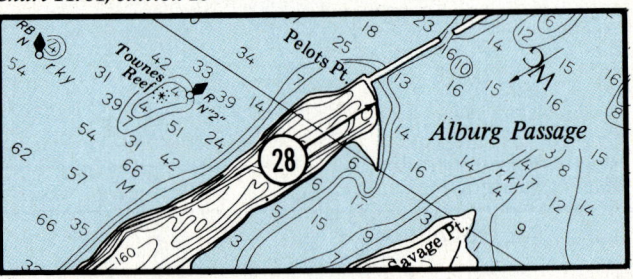

Chart 14781, edition 16

Chart 14781, edition 16

Chart 14781, edition 16

Chart 14781, edition 16

Under no circumstances are these charts to be used for navigation.

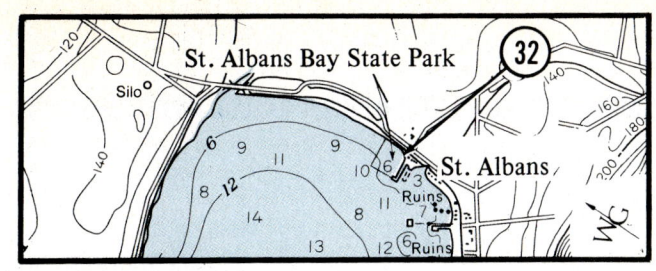

Champlain Waterways

Chart 14781, edition 16

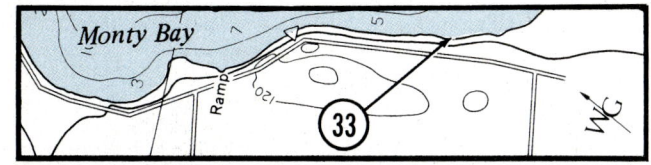

Chart 14781, edition 16

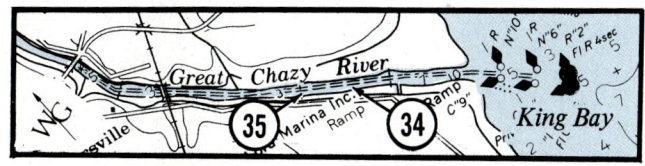

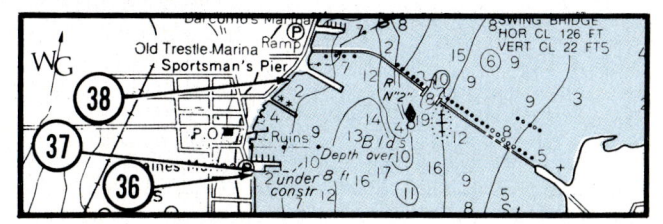

Chart 14781, edition 16

Canadian Chart 1326

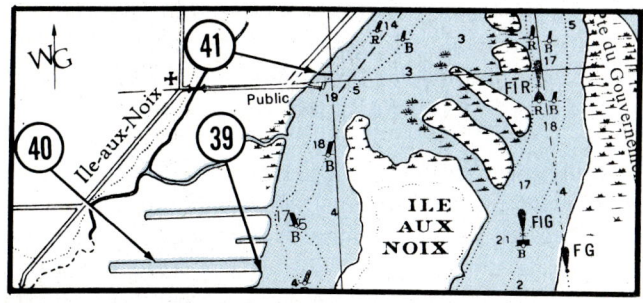

Canadian Chart 1326

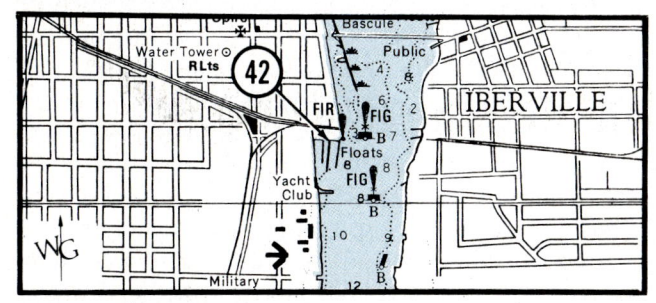

Canadian Chart 1326

Canadian Chart 1326

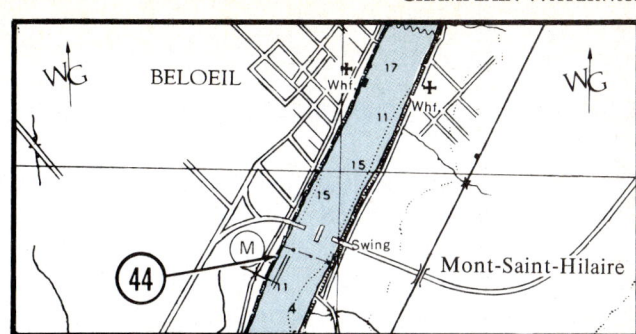

Canadian Chart 1325

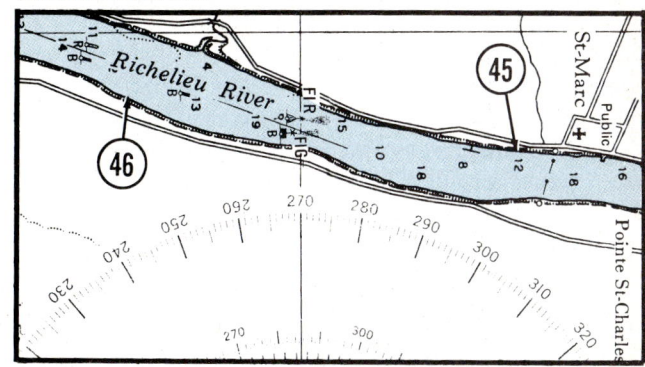

Canadian Chart 1325

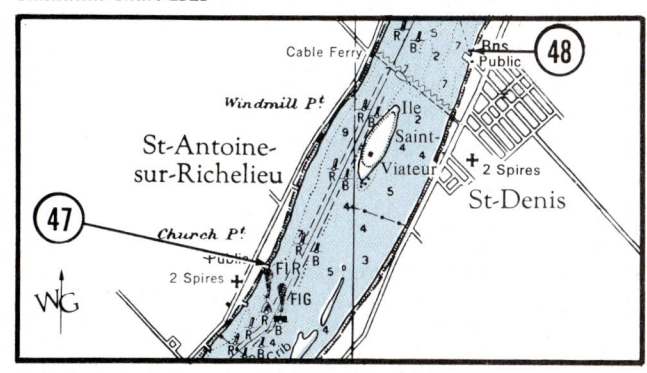

Canadian Chart 1325

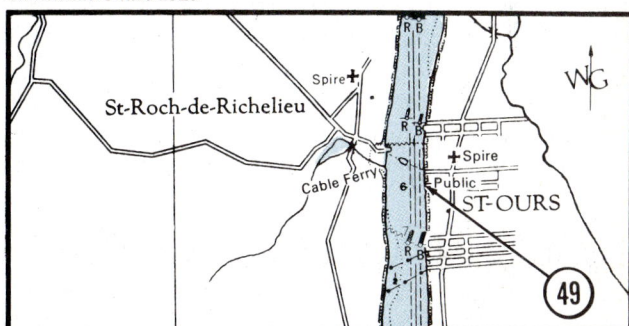

Canadian Chart 1325

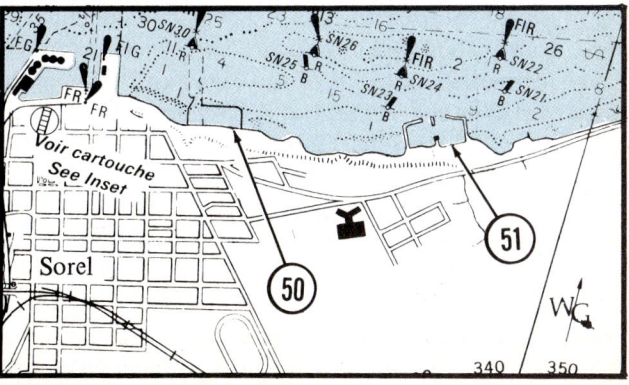

Canadian Chart 1338

Great Lakes Edition — *Under no circumstances are these charts to be used for navigation.*

The Erie Canal

Waterford to Buffalo

CHARTS: 14786, 14788, 14832, 14833.

Erie Canal

Opened in 1825, the Erie Canal linked the Great Lakes with the Atlantic Seaboard by connecting natural rivers and lakes with man-made cuts. The canal shortened travel time from Buffalo to New York City by one third, slashed shipping costs, and quickly became an important trade route, heavily traveled by all types of vessels.

Incredibly, 83 locks and 18 aquaducts were constructed to lift the canal 676 feet over the 363-mile distance to Lake Erie. It was an engineering masterpiece that quickly made New York Harbor the greatest port in America, and it opened the west to the rest of the world. Every child learns of the importance of the Erie Canal in school, but few people realize that it still operates for commercial and pleasure boats as it has for more than 150 years.

Today the Erie Canal, major component of the New York State Canal System, stretches from Waterford on the Hudson west to Tonawanda on the Niagara River, and has offshoot canals running north to Oswego on Lake Ontario and south to New York's wine region, the Finger Lakes. It is the only major canal system not supported by federal funds and is run on a shoestring budget by the State of New York. Little commercial traffic now travels the canal system but a fifty-million-dollar, five-year "Rebuilding New York Initiative" is underway. New and improved parks, marinas, restaurants, and shopping areas are being developed throughout the system.

The westward trip on the Erie system begins at Lock 2. The Federal Lock at Troy is the system's first lock. It is operated by the U.S. Corps of Engineers. The Erie Canal follows the **Mohawk River** almost 90 miles to **Frankfort**, past rolling farmland, busy cities, and prosperous rural communities. It becomes landcut through pasture and woodland to **Sylvan Beach**, crosses **Oneida Lake**'s almost 21 miles of open water, and follows the canalized **Oneida, Seneca** and **Clyde** rivers through marshes full of wildlife. From **Lyons** on, it is an artificial channel and, in the **Rochester-Lockport** segment, the canal is 60 feet higher than the surrounding orchard countryside. Beyond Lockport, it's mainly rock cut to Tonawanda.

Branching off from mainstream Erie at **Three Rivers Point**, New York, 162 statute miles from Waterford, the 23-mile-long **Oswego Canal** (20-foot vertical clearance) leads to Lake Ontario.

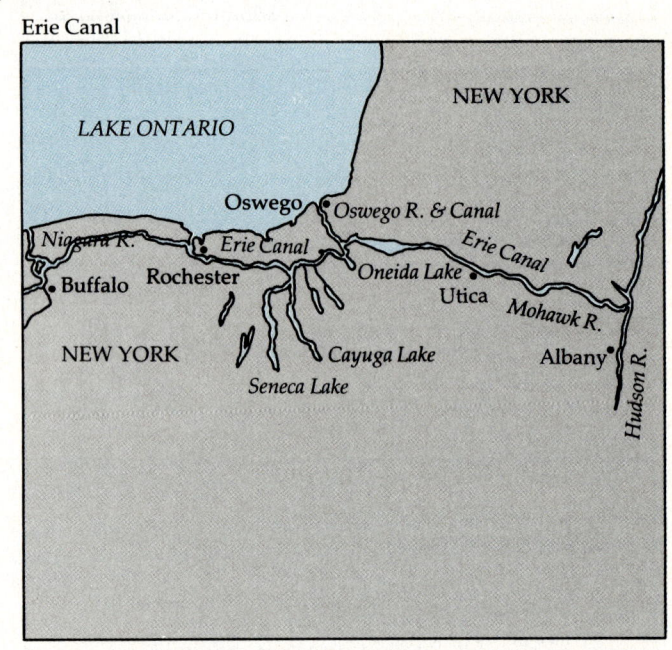

The **Cayuga-Seneca Canal** leaves the Erie Canal near Montezuma, New York, 202 miles west of Waterford, for the wine-and-waterfall country of the two largest Finger Lakes. The scenery here differs from the main channel and makes each lake an interesting sidetrip.

Navigation. Cruising the Erie Canal is easy, because of its excellent buoyage system, but occasionally buoys are unnumbered. Often a number will be seen painted on a flat rock or tree onshore. The only hazard along the route, unless weather and fog are unusually bad, is debris. Watch for obstructions at the lower end of the Erie, particularly around Schenectady, and at the western end of the canal, from Lockport to Tonawanda. During flood stages on the Erie and especially on the Mohawk River, upstream travel requires extra care because of strong currents and debris. Currents below some of the lock entrances can be strong, and at high-water stages, particularly in the spring, strong side currents can be expected from locks 8 to 18. At times, guard gates have to be closed in some sections until the water level drops; inquire as you go. Many lock walls are rough concrete, so don't stint on fenders. Your lines may also become frayed because of the rough walls. Be prepared and plan ahead since many locks on the canal have restrictive passage hours for pleasure boats.

Boat speed is regulated to six mph in landcuts and ten mph in river sections. Boat facilities are ample, protected anchorages frequent, and in many places you can tie up alongside the canal and walk to nearby towns. The State of New York has done a great deal to improve the appearance and efficiency of the locks in the past few years. A volunteer group called the "Green Thumbs" has helped spruce up the entire system, and many of the locks serve as recreation sites for mariners and nearby communities. In areas where marinas are sparse, you can frequently find dockage, generally with water, at a canal terminal. Ask the lockmaster to see the powerhouse or the lock operations, and you will usually be given a great show. There is a dearth of diesel fuel on the canal; diesel-powered boats should top off when it is available. Monitor Channel 13 to stay in touch with barges and bridges throughout the system.

Waterford to Three Rivers Point

A large sign at Waterford alerts you to the junction of the Champlain and Erie canals. Going west or north from Waterford, red markers are to starboard and white to port. The lock tenders on both systems are courteous, helpful, and generally quick to respond on VHF Channel 13.

At Waterford, you can tie up to the wall using the blue-and-yellow painted bollards, either to wait for the lock or for an overnight stay. Heavy fendering is advisable because of strong turbulence created by the emptying of Erie Lock 2 into the narrow channel. If you have to wait for down-locking boats or commercial traffic, a stroll through downtown Waterford will recall scenes of a 19th-century industrial river town. A few basic supplies are avilable in town.

The lockmaster at Erie 2 has several publications that will enhance your trip. These include maps, historical information, and an up-to-date newsletter, listing events along the canal. Ask for these materials if the lockmaster should forget to offer them.

Lock 2 is the first of five locks, collectively the **Waterford Flight**, which raises boats 165 feet in less than two miles. Locking time — about two hours — cannot be rushed; the locks are on a synchronized schedule. These five locks have the roughest walls. Before entering the lock, mariners can fuel up and take on supplies at the full service marina in Cohoes.

Beyond Lock 6 the canal enters the **Mohawk River** and sweeps in a two-mile curve along the river's north bank past the village of **Crescent**, which has several facilities. About two and a half miles beyond Crescent, along a section called the Snake Trail, the Mohawk route runs almost parallel to the old canal, now abandoned but filled with water, as far as **Vischer Ferry**. A mile farther at Lock 7, you'll be raised 27 feet in about 20 minutes for the approach to **Schenectady**. Less than four miles away is a hospitable yacht club on the north bank. The club is the only layover spot you'll find if you want to visit the city. Dockage is limited here, so be sure to call ahead. The **Schenectady Museum and Planetarium** offers a history and science collection, changing art exhibits, and a children's section as well as planetarium shows.

Distances
Statute miles (approximate)

Location	Between Points	Cumulative
Lock 2, Waterford	0.0	0.0
Lock 3	0.5	0.5
Lock 4	0.5	1.0
Locks 5 and 6	0.3	1.3
Lock 7	10.8	12.4
Schenectady Y. C. Bridge E 8	4.1	16.5
Lock 8	6.7	23.2
Lock 9	4.9	28.1
Lock 10	6.2	34.3
Lock 11, Amsterdam	4.3	38.6
Lock 12	4.4	43.0
Fonda Terminal	5.2	48.2
Lock 13	4.7	52.9
Lock 14, Canajoharie Term.	8.0	60.9
Lock 15, Fort Plain	3.4	64.3
St. Johnsville Terminal	5.4	69.7
Lock 16, Little Falls	7.9	77.6
Little Falls Terminal	1.1	78.7
Lock 18	3.2	81.9
Ilion Terminal & Marina	6.0	87.9
Lock 19	6.0	93.9
Utica Harbor Lock	6.7	100.6
Lock 20, Utica	3.6	104.2
Rome Terminal	10.0	114.2
Lock 21	8.6	122.8
Lock 22	1.4	124.2
Sylvan Beach, Fl R "106"	5.2	129.4
Brewerton, Fl R "136"	19.6	149.0
Lock 23	3.1	153.1
Three Rivers Point, Bridge 70	6.8	159.9
Klein Island mid-point	7.2	167.1
Lock 24, Baldwinsville	5.0	172.1
Cayuga-Seneca Canal junc.	29.4	201.5
Lock 25	1.6	203.1
Lock 26	5.8	208.1
Lock 27, Lyons	9.4	220.0
Lock 28A	1.4	221.4
Lock 28B, Newark	4.2	225.6
Lock 29, Palmyra	9.9	235.5
Lock 30, Macedon	3.1	238.6
Fairport, Bridge E 128	7.6	246.2
Lock 32	8.2	254.4
Lock 33	1.3	255.7
Rochester, Genesee R. junc.	3.8	259.5
Spencerport, Bridge E 174	10.9	270.4
Albion, Bridge E 200	21.9	292.3
Gasport, Bridge E 222	21.1	313.4
Lock 34 and 35, Lockport	6.7	320.1
Tonawanda, Main St. Bridge	21.3	341.4
Buffalo, Erie Basin Entrance	12.4	353.8

ERIE CANAL

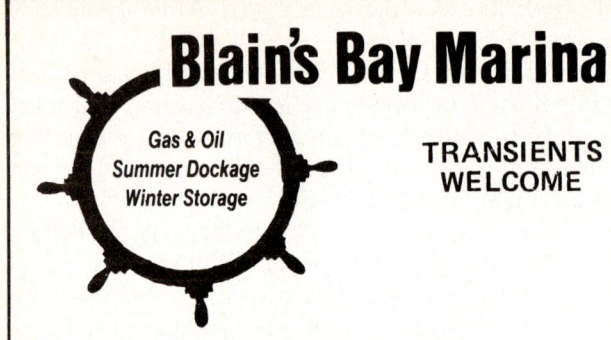

Blain's Bay Marina

Gas & Oil
Summer Dockage
Winter Storage

TRANSIENTS WELCOME

Celebrity Sales & Service
Close to Capital districts finest restaurants and ALBANY AIRPORT.

Authorized Service For:
MERCRUISER — OMC
VOLVO PENTA

Located between Locks 6 & 7 on the Erie Canal

We Monitor Channel 16 • Agent for NOAA Charts

RD1, Cohoes, NY 12047 (518) 785-6785
"On the Mohawk"

Across from the western outskirts of Schenectady, on the north shore, is **Scotia**. Protected anchorage can be found behind **Daley Island**, and just beyond is Lock 8 (lift 14 feet) where there may be minor turbulence. This moveable dam, with its bridge-like steel superstructure, is one of a series of locks whose floodgates are raised during the winter months to allow free passage of ice.

The Mohawk River swings northward, then west, past Locks 9 (lift 15 feet), 10 (lift 15 feet), and 11 (lift 12 feet), to **Amsterdam**, where a house built in 1773 is located on the lock grounds. Most anchorages in this immediate area are close to the main channel, but are disturbed by wakes of passing boats. Reportedly, the terminal is in a rough neighborhood and tying up here is not a good idea.

For the next 62 miles, to **Utica**, the canal follows the Mohawk Valley, an important route since Indian days. This beautiful stretch is set against the backdrop of the Adirondacks to the north. There is a shortage of marine facilities; however, sometimes you can tie up overnight at a lock wall or temporarily near a bridge fender.

Five miles past Lock 12 is **Fonda Terminal**, which has no electricity; the outlets have been locked up because of vandalism. You can shop either at Fonda or across the river at **Fultonville**, where Philbrook's Grocery on Main Street will pick you up and return you to your boat.

East of the Fultonville/Fonda Bridge on the south side of the waterway is a marina/motel complex in Ful-

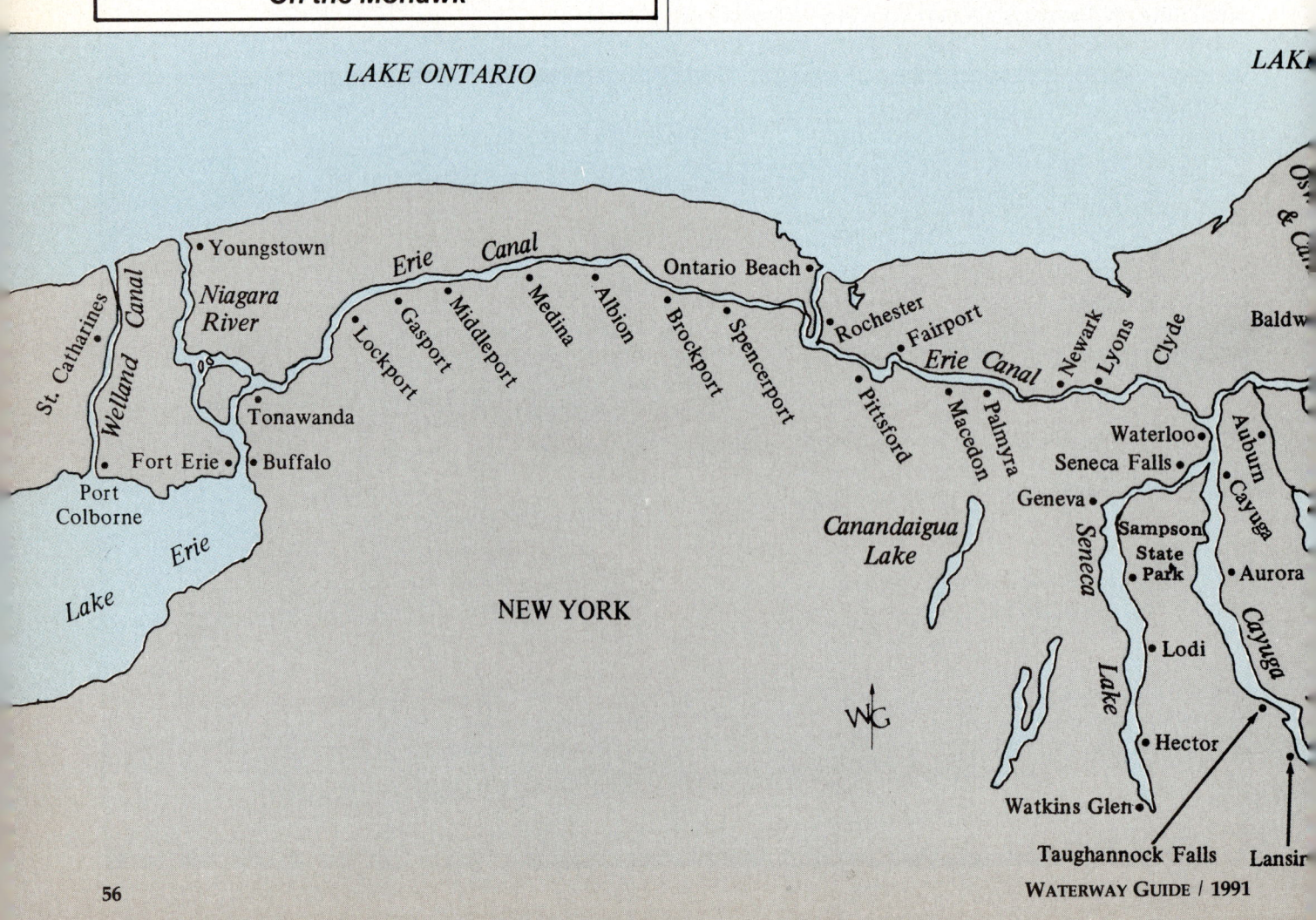

WATERWAY GUIDE / 1991

tonville. On the north side of the waterway, west of the bridge, is a long concrete bulkhead with bollards at the Fonda Terminal. There are no facilities here, but tie up is free, and it's a short walk to stores. Check at the office to find out what time the gates are locked if you plan to walk to town.

Lock 13 (lift eight feet) is a good place to fill your water tanks. Past "The Noses," 600-foot rocks towering beside the river, is Canajoharie Terminal with dock space but no marine services. Lock 14 (lift eight feet) follows. Canajoharie, an Indian word for "pot that washes itself," is named for a gorge south of the village where the water seethes continuously. About a mile up the creek a waterfall drops 45 feet.

At **Fort Plain**, three miles beyond Canajoharie, you'll find the destroyed remains of a Revolutionary War fort and Lock 15 (lift eight feet), last of the locks with a moveable dam and overhead structure. Beyond the lock, protected anchorage can be found behind **Abeel Island** in eight to ten feet of water. At **St. Johnsville**, three miles beyond the island, you'll find Lock 16 (lift 20.5 feet) and a friendly marina offering most services. The town, with groceries and a hardware store, is a five minute walk. The marina can become crowded on summer weekends. Check ahead or go in early. About six miles down the canal, Lock 17 (lift 40.5 feet) at **Little Falls** provides the largest single lift in the system. Going west you tie up against the south wall. The lower gate lifts vertically to open; your boat will get wet passing under it. There are stores near the Little Falls Terminal and a restaurant is within walking distance.

At Lock 18 (lift 20 feet) the canal leaves the winding Mohawk River to follow a three-mile straight land cut past **Herkimer** and **Mohawk**.

Two miles beyond the lock lies **Ilion**, with fuel, tie-ups and an arms museum. The next town along the canal is **Frankfort**, where you'll find tenuous anchorage off the main channel in the Mohawk River Outlet. Though tow traffic is now infrequent, keep a sharp lookout should a large vessel crowd the channel around this bend. Beyond Lock 19 (lift 21 feet), a five-mile

---

The Poplars Inn
Riverfront Dining & Motel
Boat Tours
at Thruway Exit 28
Riverside Drive
Fultonville, New York
12072
Phone 518-853-4511

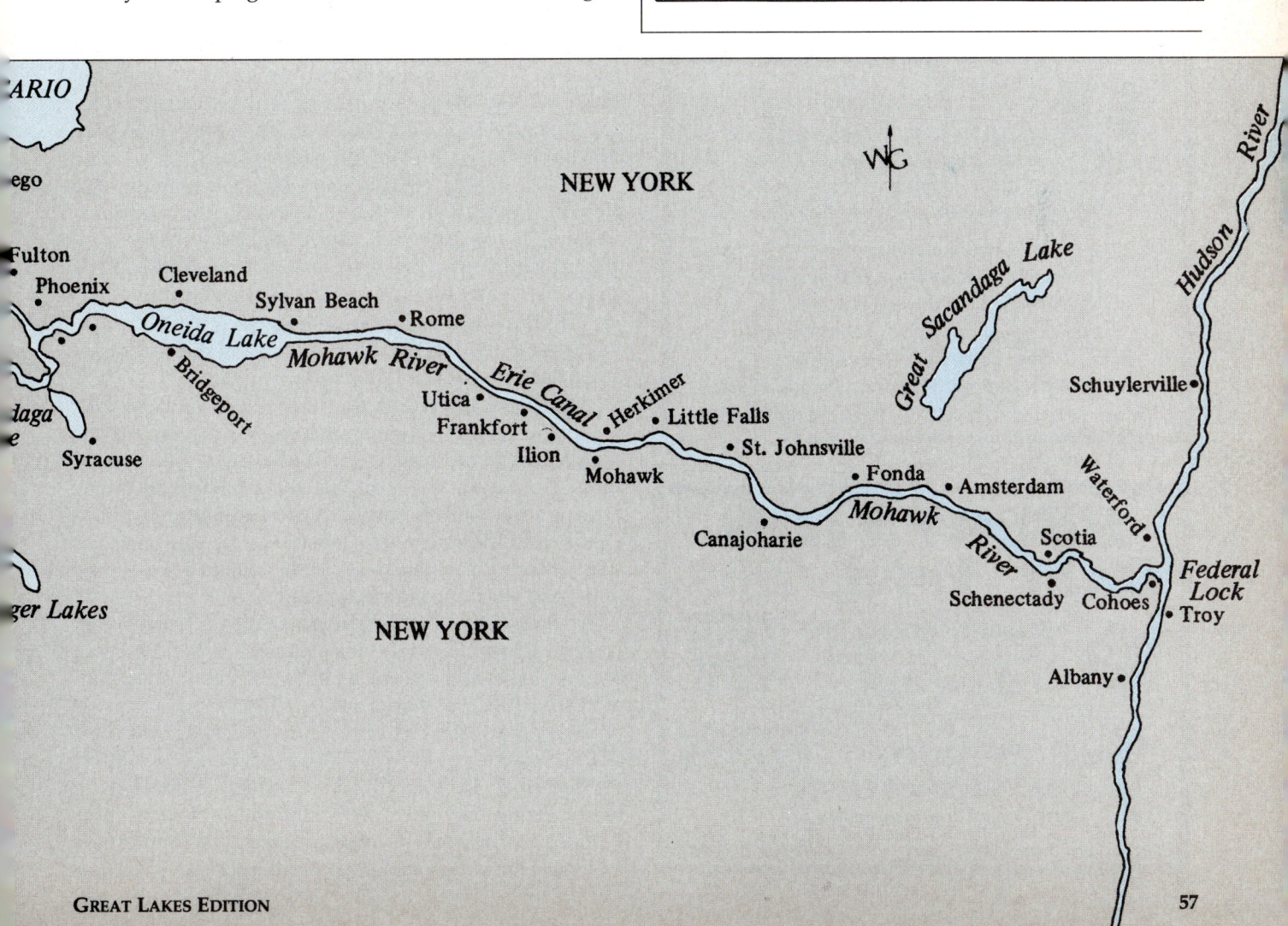

ERIE CANAL

Vital Statistics

Overhead clearances are 20 feet from Waterford to Three Rivers Point and in the Oswego Canal; 15 and a half feet between Three Rivers Point and Tonawanda.

Controlling depths are 13 feet from Waterford to Three Rivers Point and in the Oswego Canal; 12 feet elsewhere.

There is no Lock 31.

NOS chartbook 14786 covers the Erie Canal as far west as Lyons, and the Oswego and Cayuga-Seneca Canals (see the "Useful Publications" section of the Mariner's Handbook for ordering information). The Erie Canal from Lyons west to Tonawanda is covered by the "Grand Canal Chart Kit" available from the Office of Parks and Recreation, Empire State Plaza, Albany NY.

245 bridges cross the canal.

Stay clear of the "open" dams with no overhead structures located in the Mohawk River section of the canal to maintain water levels.

New York State Canal System locks monitor VHF Channel 13 and lock openings should be requested in advance (operators will not always acknowledge a request). Many lock operators are now mobile and operate several locks in a given area. While an advance request for opening will usually avoid a hangup, delays are sometimes inevitable. (See the "Locking Procedures" box in the Mariner's Handbook.)

---

skinner's harbour
TRANSIENTS WELCOMED
500 FT. SERVICE DOCK
NO YACHT TOO LARGE

Restaurant on Premises
Protected Dockage • Gas & Diesel Fuel
15 Ton Lift • Pump-Out Service
Marine Supplies • Minor Repair Service
Clean Showers & Rest Rooms
Half Mile to Shopping (Transportation Available)
Sylvan Beach, N.Y. 13157   Phone: 315/762-9986

BREWERTON Boat Yard, Inc.

South Side of Oneida River
Just West of RR Bridge
MARINE RAILWAY
ENGINE, HULL & MACHINERY REPAIR
ONAN MARINE SALES & SERVICE VOLVO PENTA
US MARINE POWER

TRANSIENTS WELCOME
Close to Restaurants and Shopping
Brewerton, New York 13029   315/676-3762

---

stretch of canal soon leads to busy **Utica**. The Utica Harbor spur, which was formerly used by commercial fuel barges, has been closed. To visit the city of Utica, tie up at the dock immediately west of the Genesee Street Bridge.

At Lock 20 (lift 16 feet) the canal, now man-made cut, reaches a plateau. Up to this point, boats have been raised at each lock. From here the next three locks will lower them. Lock 20 has a canal park on its west side with floating docks and ample water. This is a particularly well-maintained area with several grill-equipped fireplaces, picnic tables, heads, and good drinking water. A large restaurant is just across the road. From here, the route continues for ten miles past **Oriskany Battlefield**, south of the canal, to **Rome**.

In the Rome area, about a half mile west of Bridge E-50, you'll encounter a twin-span bridge (vertical clearance 35 feet). Dockage is available just east of the bridge, and it is an ideal spot to layover and visit the Rome area. A restaurant in town offers free pickup service. Telephones are available at the dockage site, and the restaurant can be reached at (315) 339-3166. Taxis can bring you into town for groceries, ice, and supplies, or to visit the "Erie Canal Village," a recreation of a 19th-century canal town. About eight miles beyond Rome and two miles past **New London**, you reach Lock 21, then in another mile Lock 22, each dropping you 25 feet to the level of **Oneida Lake**.

The open water of the 21-mile-long, five-mile-wide lake is a welcome sight after so many miles of confined cruising. Be warned that easterly or westerly winds can kick up heavy wave action. Check the weather before crossing the lake. Dockage can be found in **Sylvan Beach** if you wish to wait out bad weather.

Sylvan Beach, on the shore of Lake Oneida, is a pleasant resort town, with plenty of entertainment, restaurants, stores, and full-service boat facilities welcoming cruising boats. The town has natural sand beaches with clean water for swimming and good fishing.

A well-marked route runs the length of the lake, with a 278-degree course for the longest leg of the 14 miles to a red flasher south of **Constantia**.

Before leaving the main mid-lake channel to visit shoreside facilities, study the chart for a safe route around mid-lake and inshore shallows and danger spots. The largest town on the lake is **Cleveland** on the north shore, with a harbor protected against all but winds from the southeast. **Constantia**, farther west, has a fish hatchery which raises trout, walleye, bass, and salmon to stock the state's waters.

At **Brewerton**, the canal leaves Oneida Lake to join **Oneida River**. Services are available at boatyards in Brewerton, and the town's shops are about a quarter-mile from the waterfront. This is a good layover spot with several marinas and nearby restaurants with pickup services.

Steel-lined Lock 23 (drop seven feet) is about three miles beyond Brewerton on a cutoff of the Oneida River. It opens on the hour for boats headed west, and on the half hour for boats headed east. About seven miles farther along the canal, past mile-long **Big Bend Cut**, is **Three Rivers Point**, junction of the **Oneida**, **Oswego**, and **Seneca** rivers.

Here you may choose: The **Oswego Canal**, takes you north to **Oswego** and **Lake Ontario**, and offers an open water run to the **Welland Canal** and Lake Erie or a lake crossing to the canals of Canada and the St. Lawrence Seaway; the Erie Canal takes you south toward **Onondaga Lake** and **Syracuse**, and west to Buffalo.

Oswego Canal

Mariners heading for Lake Ontario, the Thousand Islands, Georgian Bay, or other U.S. and Canadian ports to the north, east, and west turn northward off the Erie Canal at Three Rivers Point, New York. Here, 162 statute miles from the Erie's origin at Waterford, **Oswego Canal**, the shortest all-water passage between New York and the Great Lakes, leads to Lake Ontario, about 24 miles away. The canal, with seven locks and 14 bridges, follows the dredged **Oswego River**, which formerly plunged 150 feet over cataracts.

The first town on the canal is **Phoenix**. Here you first go through a highway bridge opening only on the half hour, then enter Lock 1. Proceed carefully until you are in the lock, which drops the water level ten feet over the **Rifts**, falls that once supplied power for industry here. Less than three miles farther, you can anchor behind **Walter Island** if you can clear four-foot depths inside the island's southeastern approach. Just beyond is **Himmansville** on the canal.

Fulton to Minetto. Six miles beyond Himmansville is **Fulton**, with locks 2 and 3 (combined drop 45 feet). Between the locks you'll find a good tie-up with free electricity and water at the municipal boat basin. Stores and restaurants are found at a revitalized waterfront area nearby. The route hugs the eastern shore, staying well clear of shoals and snags on the river's western side. At high water, a strong side current in the spillway on the west side below Lock 3 can be a hazard. At **Minetto**, four miles from Oswego, you descend through Lock 5 (drop 18 feet). A Lock 4 was found to be unnecessary.

Oswego. The canal route cuts through the city, and the locks here are synchronized. In strong winds off the lake, eddies can be tricky, even in locks with closed gates. Beyond Lock 6 (drop 20 feet) the channel narrows and favors the eastern shore through Locks 7 (drop 14.5 feet) and 8 (last lock, drop 11.1 feet). Beyond Lock 8 the canal ends, and the route broadens into Oswego's deep harbor (Chart 14813).

A full-service marina with repairs, on-site restaurant, and nearby provisioning is conveniently situated if you must wait for favorable crossing conditions on

---

Heading NORTH Via
NEW YORKS' PICTURESQUE ERIE BARGE CANAL ?
CENTRAL NY AREA

Be On Lookout For

ess kay yards, inc.
MARK OF DEPENDABILITY

IN-House PROP & SHAFT Shop

Knowledgeable Staff, incl.
        Underwater Repair Service
14 Ton Lift
        Regular & Diesel Fuel
Extensive Chart Inventory (US & CAN)
        Monitor VHF Channel 16
Dockage Up to 110 Feet
        110/220 Electric Service
15 Mins to SYRACUSE Int'l Airport
⚓ Oneida River – East of LOCK 23 – Marker 150 ⚓

The One-Stop Yard – (315) 676-2711
Operated for Boatmen by Boatmen

Perhaps You've Heard Of Us

ERIE CANAL

OSWEGO MARINA
Oswego, New York 13126
Full Marina Facilities

Phone: 315-342-0436

Diesel Fuel - Gulf - Reg. Gas

LOCATION: On port side when entering Oswego Harbor from Lake Ontario and passing channel entrance into Oswego Canal. When entering Harbor from Canal, marina is located about 200 yards north of Lock 8. Gas dock 150 feet long, with water 21 feet deep alongside.

FACILITIES: Marine hoist of 12-ton capacity can provide haulouts for craft up to 40 feet in length. All types of repair work available at this marina, including electrical and machine shop work, hull, ship's carpentry and engine repairs. Mast work and sailboat rigging a specialty. Moorage docks have water 10 to 15 feet deep. Electricity and fresh water at docks. Diesel fuel obtainable from pumps at gas dock. Showers, washers, dryers, and restrooms for visitors. Grocery and meat stores about two blocks distant. Marine supply store on premises. Immigration services are available for craft coming from Canada. Charts and ice available at store.

AMUSEMENT: Restaurant and cocktail lounge on premises. Theatres and general shopping district of downtown Oswego about five blocks away. Next to Ft. Ontario.

MasterCard   VISA

Lake Ontario, or if you'd simply like a convenient layover point from which to visit the city. Free dockage is available at the east wall between Lock 8 and the marina—but a tie-up is all there is; you'll find no electricity or other amenities.

At Oswego you have reached Lake Ontario. The lake is a major crossroads, with waterways leading in all directions. To the north, across Lake Ontario, are the **Rideau Waterway** to Ottawa and the entrance to the **St. Lawrence Seaway**, which leads through the Thousand Islands to Montreal. To the west are **Niagara River** and commercial **Welland Canal**, the gateway to Lake Erie. To the northwest is the **Trent-Severn Waterway** to Georgian Bay and Lake Huron.

Syracuse to Lyons

On the Erie Canal, it's about six miles from Three River Point to **Onondaga Outlet**, a pleasant sidetrip which leads to **Onondaga Lake** and the port of **Syracuse**. To visit the state's fourth largest city, lay over at the marina at **Liverpool**, on the lake's eastern shore. Syracuse was founded in 1797 on a salt spring reservation, and for almost a century salt mining was the town's main industry. A number of museums and historic sites, particularly the Art Museum and the Erie Canal Museum on an old section of canal, are of interest.

The canal itself follows the Seneca River past **Klein Island**, which is surrounded by two branches of the Onondaga Outlet. Five miles on, at **Baldwinsville**, an old canal town which the Indians called "Stones in the Water," you reach steel-lined Lock 24 (lift 11 feet).

The route loops its way to four-mile-long **Cross Lake**. The canal passage cuts across the mile-wide lake's southern end, but there are good depths to the northwest. A glance at the chart will reveal good anchorages here and in the lake's western bay.

The Erie leaves Cross Lake and follows Seneca River 18 miles to its next major crossroads—the junction with the **Cayuga-Seneca Canal**, scenic waterway to the **Finger Lakes** near **Montezuma**. (For our continuing coverage of the Canal System westward, see the section entitled "Montezuma to North Tonawanda" at the end of this chapter.)

Finger Lakes Cayuga/Seneca

One of the loveliest sidetrips in the northeastern U.S.—to Cayuga and Seneca, largest of the famous Finger Lakes—can be reached by turning south from the Erie Canal at **Montezuma Marsh**, about 203 miles west of Waterford and the Hudson River.

The route to the lakes runs south from the Montezuma National Wildlife Refuge in the Seneca River section of the Erie Canal via the **Cayuga-Seneca Canal**. This is a double-pronged waterway: The east fork leads to Ithaca at the southern tip of Cayuga Lake, and the

ERIE CANAL

western branch continues to Montour Falls at the south end of Seneca Lake—a total cruising distance of about 80 miles, with four locks and 16 bridges. The lakes are the wellspring for much of the Erie Canal; water flowing out of the lakes floods Montezuma Marsh and creates the Seneca River and ultimately the Oswego.

Leaving the Erie Canal and entering the Cayuga-Seneca Waterway, you pass beneath the New York State Thruway, and in about four miles arrive at Lock 1, to be lifted seven and a half feet to the level of Cayuga Lake. Here the routes to the two lakes separate. Straight ahead is Cayuga Lake, and on the west is the Seneca Canal leading to **Seneca Lake**, 12 miles away. Be sure to check buoyage carefully.

Cayuga Lake. This is the longest of the Finger Lakes (40 miles), with an average width of two miles and a maximum depth of 435 feet. Around its shores are four state parks, ample facilities for mariners, and unlimited recreational opportunities—picnicking, swimming, fishing, and nature-trail hiking. The cruising is safe and interesting, taking you through beautiful countryside. Enter Cayuga Lake via a narrow, well-marked channel leading through a side shoal.

Shoals end about six miles from the lake's northern tip, near **Canoga** on the western shore and **Union Springs** on the east. Here the channel widens, the waters deepen, buoyage thins out, and facilities become

HIBISCUS HARBOR

Two Miles 142° South-Southeast of Buoys 50 & 51 on Cayuga Lake

TRANSIENTS WELCOME

- BERTHS FOR 200 CRUISERS
- COMPLETE MARINE SUPPLIES
- BOAT SALES & SERVICE
- LARGEST MARINE TRAVELIFT ON THE FINGER LAKES
- SWIMMING POOL
- RESTAURANT & BAR
- DAY OR SEASON RATES
- WE MONITOR VHF CH. 16
- FUEL
- YACHT TRANSPORT ALL TYPES/ON AIR TRAILERS

HIBISCUS HARBOR

UNION SPRINGS, NY 13160   *"THE FINGER LAKES FINEST"*

TROJAN YACHT

FAX (315) 889-7759
(315) 889-5086 / 5008

GREAT LAKES EDITION

plentiful. At Union Springs, dockage and repairs are available within walking distance of the center of town.

From here south, the lake is deep to the shores, but there are few towns. On the west shore, about 23 miles to the south, **Taughannock Falls**, the highest falls east of the Rockies, drops 215 feet—50 feet more than Niagara—over a craggy precipice. Dockage is available at **Allen H. Treman State Marine Park** on the south end of Cayuga Lake.

Ithaca, located on Cayuga's southern tip, is a lively boat-minded community, well-supplied with marine facilities. Known as the site of Cornell University and birthplace of the ice cream sundae, Ithaca was also the world's pre-Hollywood silent movie capital.

Cruising boats are welcome here; most facilities are situated on or near the entrance of the short canal leading south from the lake. The Cornell University boathouse and a Coast Guard Auxiliary base are also located on the canal.

Seneca Canal. Just below Lock 1, where the routes to the two lakes branch off, the **Seneca Canal** leads west through three locks to Seneca Lake, 63 feet higher than Cayuga. The route starts through **Seneca Falls**, where locks 2 (lift 26 feet) and 3 (lift 23 feet) are in flight. They open on the hour from 7:00 a.m. to 10:00 p.m. Seneca Falls is the home of the **National Women's Hall of Fame**, a museum dedicated to the history of the women's movement in the United States. The museum is located near the waterfront. You can tie up between bridges S7 and S8, within walking distance of shopping.

Lock 4 (lift 14.5 feet), the last on Seneca Canal, is located at **Waterloo**, where Memorial Day was first observed. The holiday is commemorated in a museum housed in an 1840 mansion.

Seneca Lake. A narrow channel through shallow water leads from the canal to Seneca Lake. The lake is 35 miles long and more than two miles across at its widest point. With depths to 635 feet, Seneca Lake is one of the world's deepest. Fed by big springs, and surrounded by high hills, its shores are covered with vineyards, orchards, woods, and open fields. At the northern tip of the lake is **Geneva**, home of Hobart and William Smith College. At the southern end of Seneca Lake is **Watkins Glen**, known for auto racing, its rock gorge with stone walks, stairs, and bridges past and over cataracts and grottos.

Beyond Watkins Glen, a three-mile cut, once part of the canal system, leads south to **Montour Falls**. Here **Chequaga Falls** drop 156 feet. At night the falls are spectacularly illuminated.

Montezuma to North Tonawanda

A mile past the Cayuga-Seneca entrance, the Erie Canal continues through Lock 25 (lift six feet), before turning northwest through **Montezuma Marsh**. Beyond Lock 26 (lift six feet), the canal winds westward for about 11 miles to **Lyons**. Here, within a mile of each other are two locks—27 (lift 12.5 feet) and 28A (lift 19.6 feet).

From Lyons west to Tonawanda the route is canalized and simple to follow; there are no navigational charts, and the speed limit is six mph. In many places the canal is elevated, and boats cruise high above the countryside below.

The route broadens briefly in **The Wide Waters**, just past **Newark**. Favor the north shore here. Camp sites and small boat docks line the south bank. **Palmyra** is next, with Lock 29 (lift 16 feet) and protected anchorage in the abandoned Erie cut just to the south. (Mormon Joseph Smith had his first revelations at Palmyra, and a week-long pageant is held each August to commemorate his discovery of the golden plates of the sacred Book of Mormon.)

Caution: Wide waters near Wayneport are poorly marked, with boats occasionally running aground on the channel's south side.

Fairport, about six miles beyond Palmyra, offers a yacht club and, in the center of town, a full-service marina and easy provisioning. Stopping here or at **Pittsford**, 11 miles farther on, gives you easy access to nearby **Rochester**. The **Genesee River** leading to the city crosses the canal about three miles beyond Lock 33 (25.1 feet). Beyond Rochester, the Genesee flows into Lake Ontario, but a dam prevents navigation, and there is no access from the canal to the lake at this point.

For almost 70 miles west of Rochester, the Erie runs through **Spencerport, Brockport, Holley, Albion,** Med-

Waterford to Buffalo

		SEASONAL / YEAR-ROUND	SAIL / POWER / BOTH▲	LARGEST VESSEL ACCOMMODATED	NO. OF TRANSIENT BERTHS	MARKED ENTRY CHANNEL	APPROACH DEPTH (Reported)	DOCKSIDE DEPTH (Reported)	FUEL BRAND	GAS ★ / DIESEL ● / BOTH▲	RAILWAY / LIFT CAPACITY (in tons)	ENGINE REPAIRS: Gas ★ / Diesel ● / Both▲	PROPELLER / HULL REPAIRS	LAUNCHING RAMP	MARINE SUPPLIES / GROCERIES / ICE	LPG ★ / CNG ● / BOTH▲	110V ★ / 220V ● / BOTH▲	SHOWERS / LAUNDROMAT	PUMP-OUT STATION	RESTAURANT / SNACK BAR	RADIO WATCH—VHF (CB)
WATERFORD TO UTICA																					
1. Albany Marine Service	(518)783-5333	Y	▲	65	2			5			★	25	R	★	PH		M	★30	S		
2. Crescent Boat Club*	371-9864	S	▲	96	6		10	6	CIB				R				I				
3. Blain's Bay Marina (p. 56)	785-6785	S	▲	80	6		10	10			★	10	R	▲	PH		MI	★30	S	●	16
4. Schenectady Yacht Club	384-9971	S	▲	75	6		12	12	IND	▲		15					GI	★	S	●	16
5. Poplars Resort & Marina (p. 57)	853-4511	S	▲	100	20		12	10	MOB	▲			R	▲	P		MGI	▲40	SL	R	
6. Canajoharie Terminal				100			10	10				CANAL TERMINAL						▲50			
7. St. Johnsville Marina	568-7406	S	▲	165	7		10	11	EXX	▲			R	▲		★	I	▲60	S	RS	13
8. Little Falls Terminal				100			10	10				CANAL TERMINAL									
9. Ilion Marina*	(315)894-9758	S	▲	125	20	●	9	10	CHE	▲			R	▲			MGI	▲	SL	●	RS
10. Frankfort Terminal				100			10	10				CANAL TERMINAL									
11. Marcy Marina*			S	▲	50	10		10	5	AGW	★		L	R		P		MG	★30			
ONEIDA LAKE																					
12. Skinner's Harbour (p. 58)*	762-9986	Y	▲	100	20	●	20	10	SUN	▲		15	R	★	PH		MI	▲50	S	●	R
13. Johnnie's Pier 31	697-7007	S	▲	38	2	●	4	4					R	▲			I	★	S		R
14. Fisher Bay Marina	633-9657	Y	▲	50	10	●	8	5	AGW	★		25	R	▲	PH		MI	▲	S	●	RS	16
15. Anchorage Marina	699-2978	Y	▲	45	12	●	5	20	EXX	★		L		▲	PH		MI	★30	S	●	RS
16. Aero Marina	699-7736	Y	▲	55	10	●	5	4	SUN	▲		L	R	▲	PH		MI	▲50	S	●	
17. Trade-A-Yacht Marina	676-3531	Y	▲	50	3	●	5	6	IND	★		L		▲	PH		MI	★30	SL	●	S	16
18. Brewerton Boat Yard, Inc. (p. 58)	676-3762	Y	▲	85	5		10	10			★	30	R	▲	PH		M	★20		●	
19. Ess-Kay Yards, Inc. (p. 59)	676-2711	Y	▲	120	10		12	10	AGW	▲		12		▲	P		MI	▲50		R	16
THREE RIVER POINT AREA																					
20. Pirates Cove Marina & Restaurant	695-3901	S	P	50	6	●	12	8	AGW	★		25	R	★			MI	★30		R	16
OSWEGO CANAL																					
21. Oswego Marina (p. 60)	342-0436	S	▲	180	25	●	15	15	GUL	▲		20		▲	P		MGI	▲50	SL	●	RS	16
22. Oswego Nautical	342-1222	Y					MARINE DEALER							▲	PH		MI			R	
ERIE CANAL TO BALDWINSVILLE																					
23. Onondaga Yacht Club*	457-9786											YACHT CLUB									
24. Onondaga Lake Marina	457-4422	S	▲	50	2	●	18	8					R				I	★30		●	16
25. Cold Springs Harbour	622-2211	S	P	38	3	●	8	4	TEN	★		12	R	★	PH		MI	★30	S	●	
26. J&S Marine	622-1095		▲	50			15	10	EXX	★		R	R	★	H		MI	★30	S	●	
27. Riverview Marina	622-2161	S	▲	50			8	8	SUN	★		RL	R	★	PH		MI	★30		●	
28. Cooper's Marina	635-7371	Y	▲	65	10	●	10	10	CHE	▲		9	R	▲	P	★	MGI	★30	SL	●	R	16
CAYUGA / SENECA CANAL																					
29. Lockview Marina*	253-8065											UNDER RECONSTRUCTION-CALL AHEAD									

To provide the most complete and accurate information, **all facilities have been contacted within the past year.** If an asterisk (*) appears, it indicates a facility which did not respond to our requests for information (these listings may not reflect current conditions). Although facility operators supplied this data, we cannot guarantee accuracy or assume responsibility for errors. Entrance and dockside soundings tend to fluctuate. Always approach marinas carefully. Reference numbers on spotting charts indicate marina locations. ⚓ Member American Boat Builders & Repairers Association.

ERIE CANAL

ina, **Middleport, Gasport** and as far as Lockport—without a lock. There are 77 bridges along the route.

Facilities for transients are scattered along this stretch, and most towns offer some sort of dockage at canal terminals. For supplies, you can usually tie up temporarily near one of the bridges and walk to the nearest store. At **Lockport**, locks 34 and 35 (combined lift 49.1 feet) are the last in the Canal System.

About 12 and a half miles beyond the last locks, the canal joins **Tonawanda Creek**, skirting the town of **North Tonawanda** to the **Niagara River** where the Erie Canal reaches its western end about 345 miles from its start at Waterford. At North Tonawanda, with the last of the 15-foot clearance bridges behind you, you can have your mast raised. Both North Tonawanda and Buffalo have full-service marina facilities, and either town makes a good layover point from which to explore the surrounding area.

Buffalo. South of the canal terminus, Buffalo is a railroad hub and industrial center as well as New York's second largest city. A channel on the east end of the Niagara River, now a Federal waterway, leads from the canal about eight miles south to **Black Rock Lock** at **Squaw Island**, where boats are raised about five feet to the level of **Lake Erie**. From the lock it's about four miles to the terminal at **Erie Basin** in Buffalo Harbor and to big Lake Erie itself, gateway to the U.S. interior. (Our coverage of Buffalo proper and Lake Erie begins in the section entitled "Lake Erie".)

Waterford to Buffalo	Phone	Seasonal/Year-round	Sail/Power/Both	Largest Vessel	No. of Transient Berths	Marked Entry Channel	Approach Depth	Dockside Depth	Railway/Lift Capacity	Gas/Diesel/Both	Fuel Brand	Engine Repairs	Launching Ramp	Propeller/Hull Repairs	Marine Supplies/Groceries/Ice	LPG/CNG/Both	110V/220V/Both	Showers/Max Amps	Restaurant/Snack Bar	Pump-out Station	Radio Watch VHF(CB)
30. Troy's Marina*	(315) 889-5560	S	P	60	6	●	7	7	TEX	★		L			MI		★30	S	●		(13)
31. Hibiscus Harbor (p. 61)	889-5086	Y	▲	55	8	●	5	10		▲	35	R	▲	P	MI		★30	S	●	R	16
32. Castelli's Marina	889-5532	Y	▲	44	2	●	6	4	CHE	▲	25		▲	H	MGI		★30	S	●	R	16
33. Finger Lakes Marine Service, Inc.	(607) 533-4422	Y	▲	45	2	●	6	6	CIB	★	20	R	★	PH	MI		★30	SL			
34. Allan H. Treman State Park Marina	272-1460	S	▲	51	11	●	12	9				R					★50	S	●		
35. Johnson Boat Yard & Marina (p. 62)	272-5191	Y	▲	45	3	●	12	6	GUL	▲	20		▲	P	MI		★50	S	●	R	16
36. Ithaca Boating Center, Inc.	272-1581	Y	▲	65	2	●	9	8	GUL	★	20		▲	P	MGI		★30	SL		RS	16
37. Kelly's Dockside Cafe	273-9642	Y																		R	
38. Inland Harbor	(315) 789-7255	Y	▲	60	10		9	4	IND	▲	15		▲	PH	MGI		★30	S	●		16
SENECA LAKE																					
39. Barrett Marine	789-6605	Y	P	52	2	●	4	4	AGW	★	20	R	▲	H	MI		▲30	S		R	
40. Seneca Marina Mart*	789-5520	Y	▲	40	4	●	7	6	EXX	★	26		▲	PH	MGI		▲30	S		RS	(13)
41. Seneca Lake State Park	789-2331	Y	▲	55	20	●	20	6				R	STATE MARINA				▲30	S	●	RS	
42. Seneca Yacht Club*	789-4564	S	▲	40			12	5					YACHT CLUB				▲30				
43. Glen Harbor Marina	(607) 535-2751	Y	P	45				6	TEX	★	6	R	★	P	MI		★20				
44. Lembeck's Marina	535-2503	S	▲	48	5	●	15	5									▲50	S			
45. Ervay's, Inc.	535-2671	Y	P	50	5	●	11	5	IND	★	11	R	★	P	MI		★30	S	●	RS	
ERIE CANAL - LYONS TO BUFFALO																					
46. Miller's Marina	(315) 946-9363	S	▲	72	5	●	12	12		▲	14	R	★	P	MI		▲50		●	RS	
47. Fairport Village Landing Marina*	(716) 223-8011	S	▲	100	3		10	10	SUN	▲											
48. Packett's Landing Canal Park			▲	100			20	15		48 HRS MAX STAY						G	★20				
49. Captain Jeff's Marina	426-5400	Y	▲	70	15	●	8	8	TEX	▲	L	R	▲	PH	MGI		★20	SL	●		
50. Midshipman's Marina*				50			8	8	EXX	▲	L	R	★	PH	MI		▲30				
51. Nelson C. Goehle Municipal Marina*	433-9795	S		50	4		5	5	MOB	▲		R					▲30	SL	●	RS	
52. Hi-Skipper Marine	694-4311	Y	P	47		●	17	5			20			PH	M			S			
53. Wardell Boat Yard	692-9428	Y	-	60	3		8	8	IND	▲	20			PH	MGI		▲30			S	
54. Smith Boys, Inc. (p. 62)	695-3472	Y	▲	65	20	●	16	16		▲	50		★	PH	MI		★30	S	●	R	
55. Marina Bay Club	875-1777		▲	50			8	4			L		★	PH	MI		★20			R	
56. Anchor Marine	773-7063	Y	P	40			12	6		★			▲		MI		★30	S		RS	
57. Beaver Island State Park	773-3271	S	P	40	80		6	6									★20		●	S	
58. Placid Harbor Marina	693-6226		▲	50		●	16	6	ASH	★	L	R	▲	PH	MI		▲50		●	R	
59. Harbor Place	876-5944	Y	▲	60	4		20	10		▲	60	R	▲	PH	MI		▲50	S	●	RS	
60. Rich Marine Sales	873-4060	Y	▲	45	6	●	25	10		▲	25	R	★	P	MI		★20			RS	
61. Erie Basin Marina*	842-4141	S	▲	300	11	●	29	21	NOC	▲		R	▲	PH	MGI		▲50	S	●	RS	

To provide the most complete and accurate information, all facilities have been contacted within the past year. If an asterisk (*) appears, it indicates a facility which did not respond to our requests for information (these listings may not reflect current conditions). Although facility operators supplied this data, we cannot guarantee accuracy or assume responsibility for errors. Entrance and dockside soundings tend to fluctuate. Always approach marinas carefully. Reference numbers on spotting charts indicate marina locations. ⚓ Member American Boat Builders & Repairers Association.

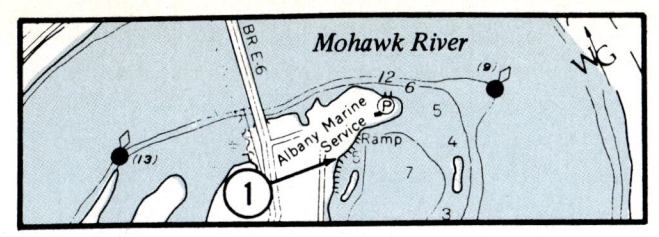

ERIE CANAL

Chart 14786, edition 9

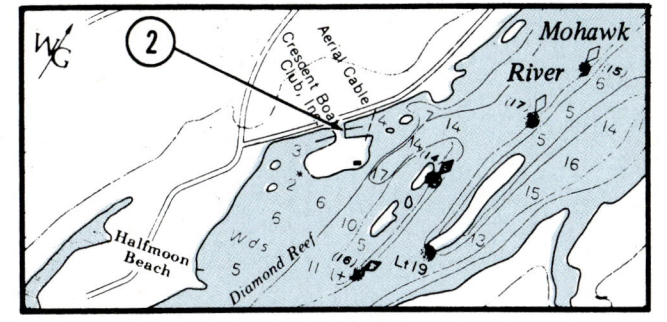

Chart 14786, edition 9

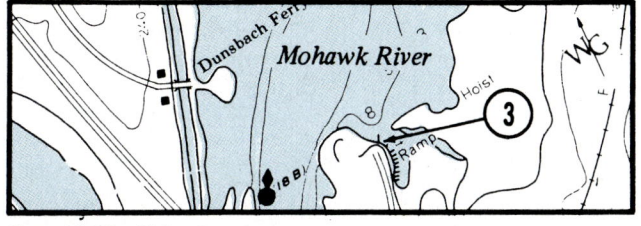

Chart 14786, edition 9

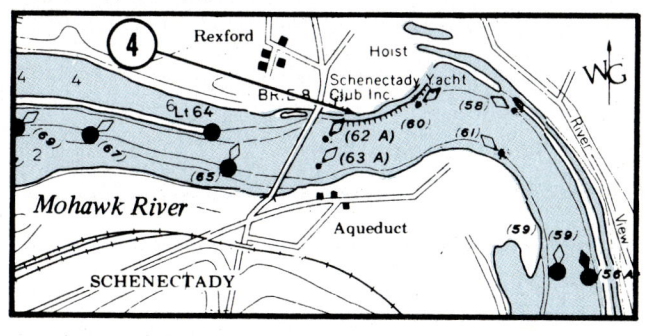

Chart 14786, edition 9

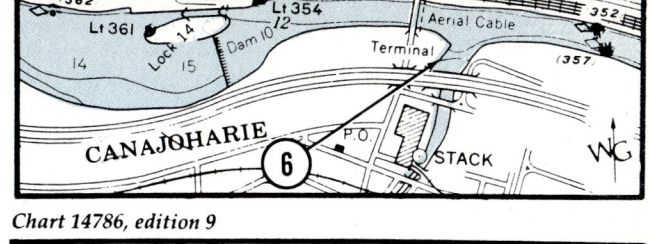

Chart 14786, edition 9

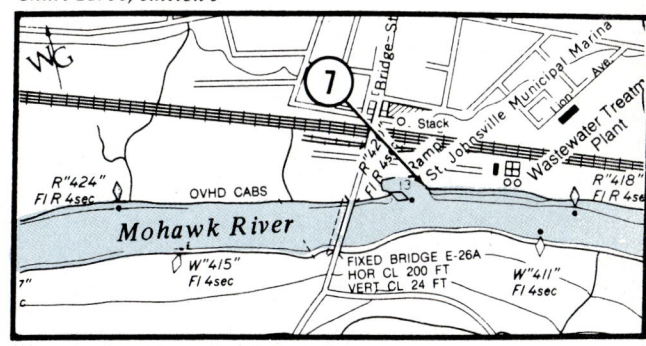

Chart 14786, edition 9

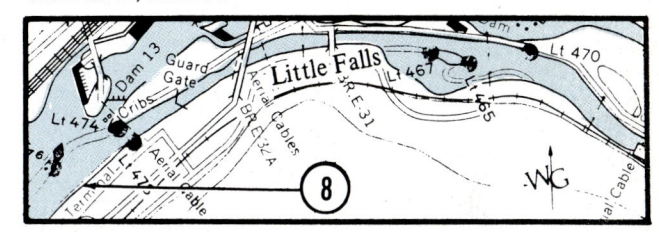

Chart 14786, edition 9

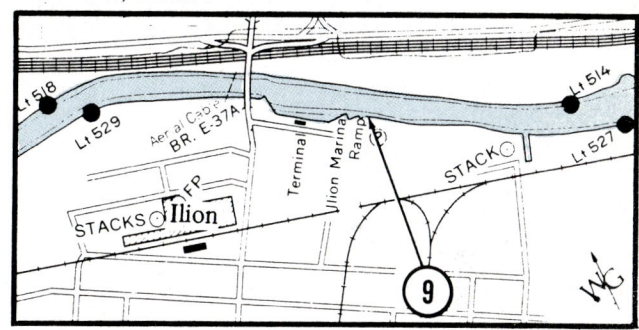

Chart 14786, edition 9

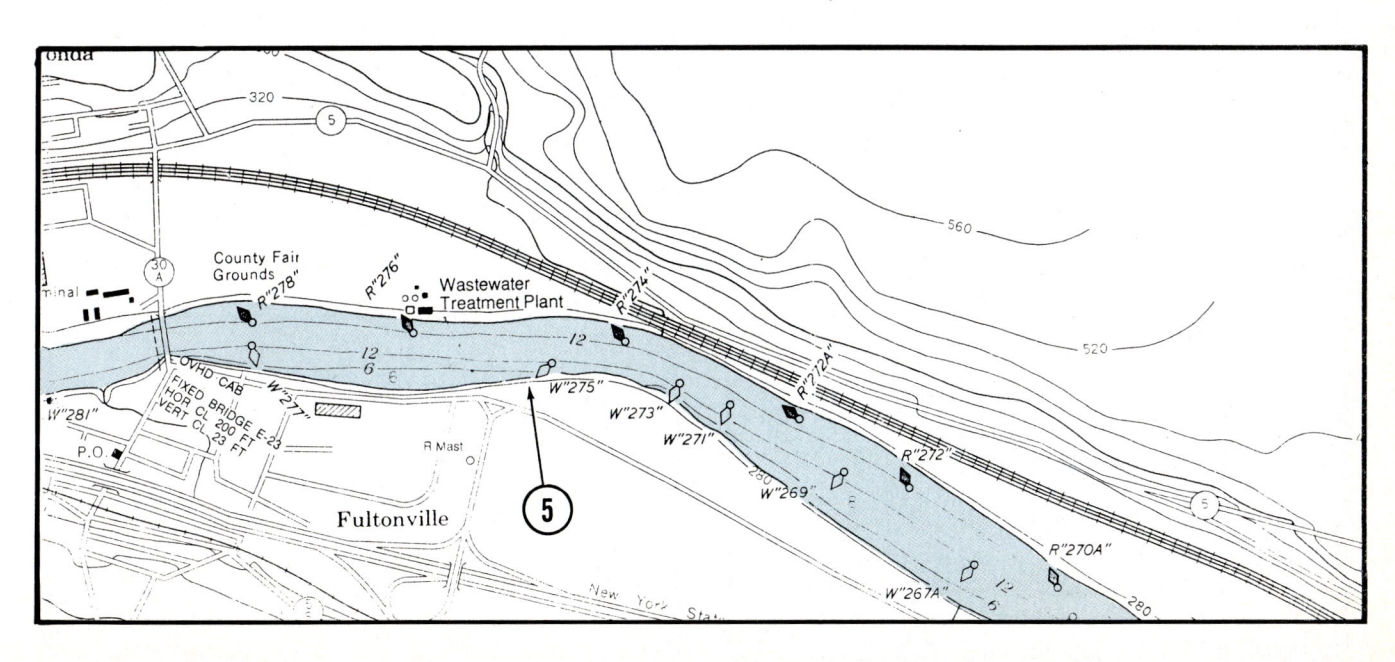

Chart 14786, edition 9

GREAT LAKES EDITION *Under no circumstances are these charts to be used for navigation.* 65

Erie Canal

Chart 14786, edition 9 (10)

Chart 14786, edition 9 (11)

Chart 14786, edition 9 (12)

Chart 14786, edition 9 (13)

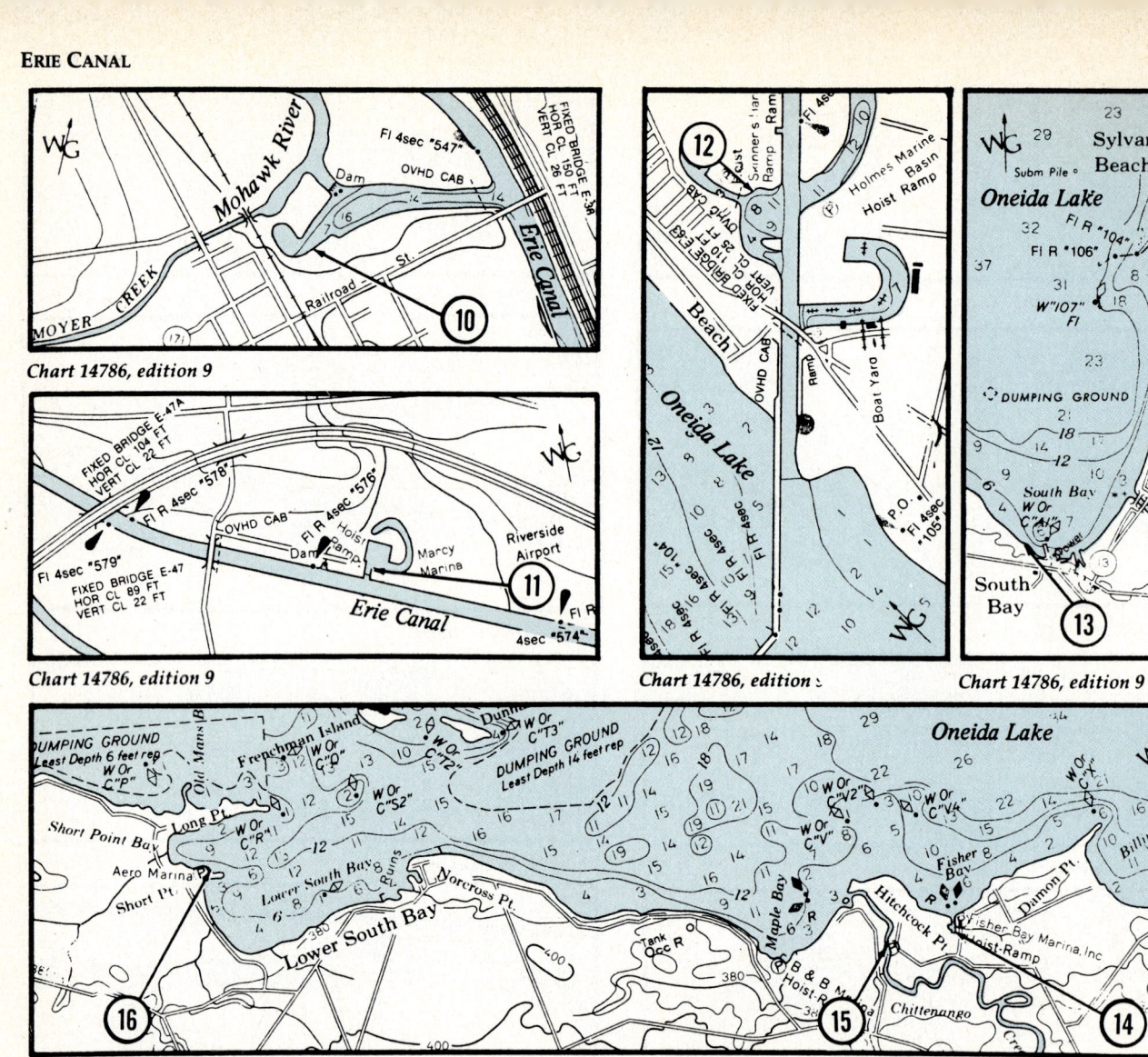

Chart 14786, edition 9 (14, 15, 16)

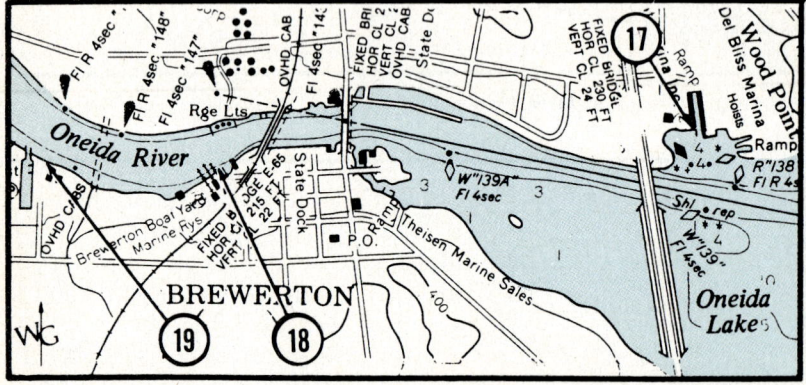

Chart 14786, edition 9 (17, 18, 19)

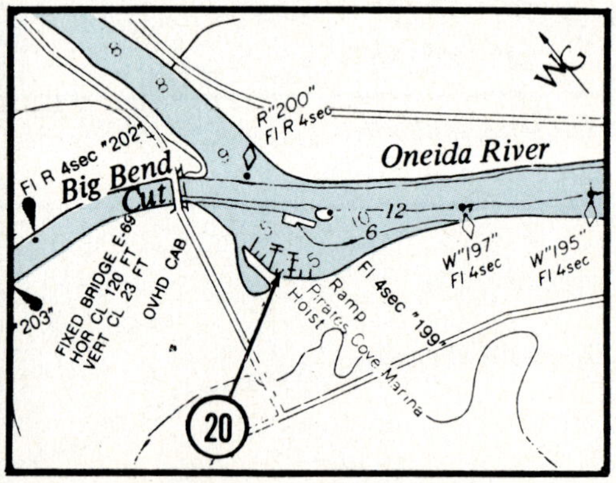

Chart 14786, edition 9 (20)

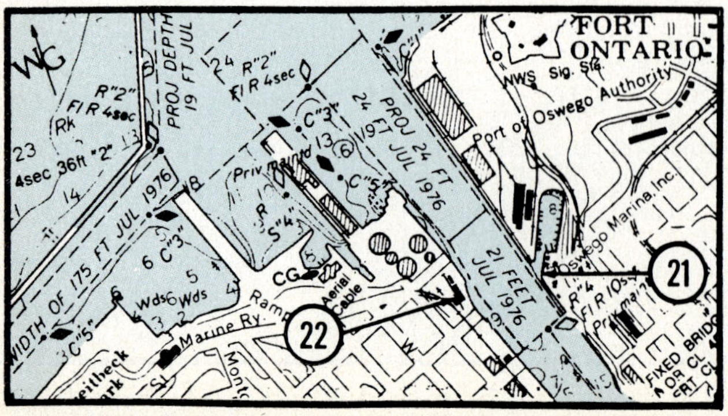

Chart 14786, edition 9 (21, 22)

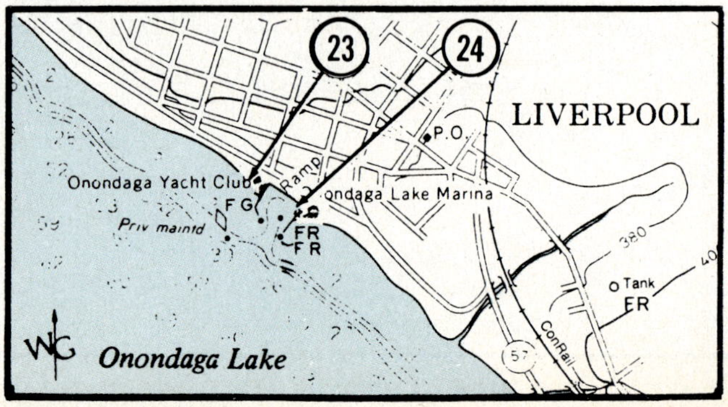

Chart 14786, edition 9 (23, 24)

Under no circumstances are these charts to be used for navigation.

ERIE CANAL

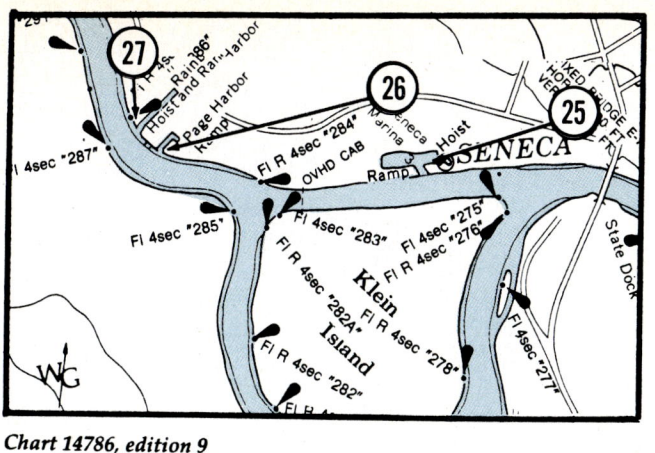

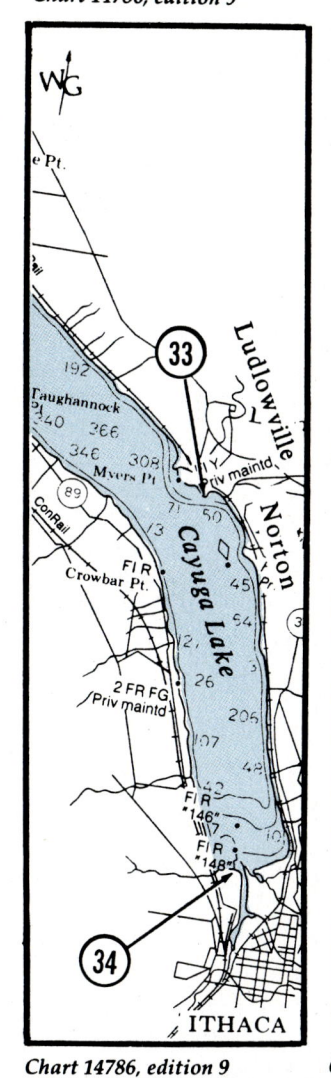

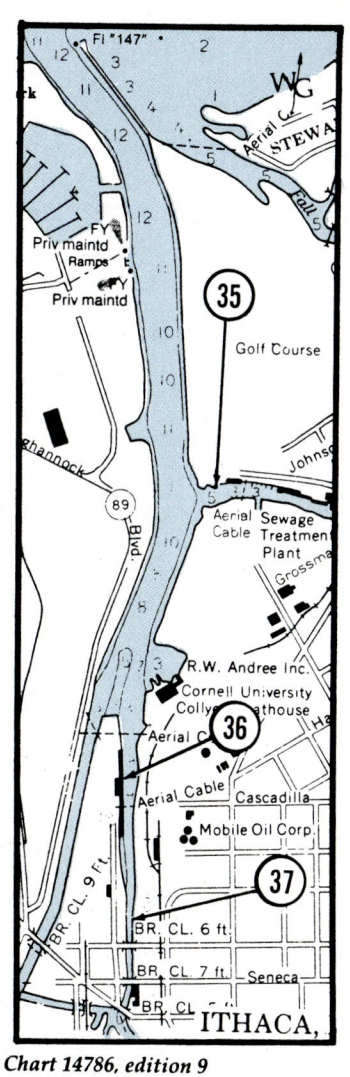

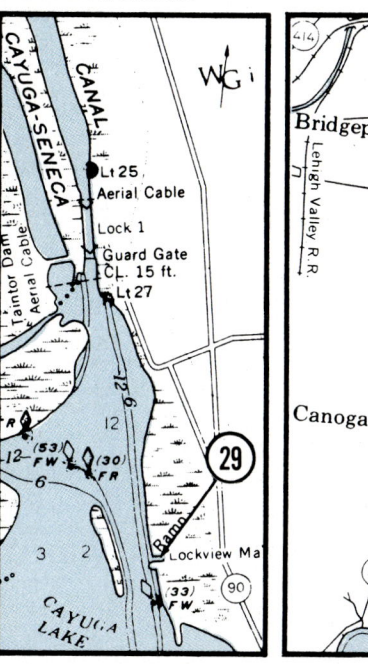

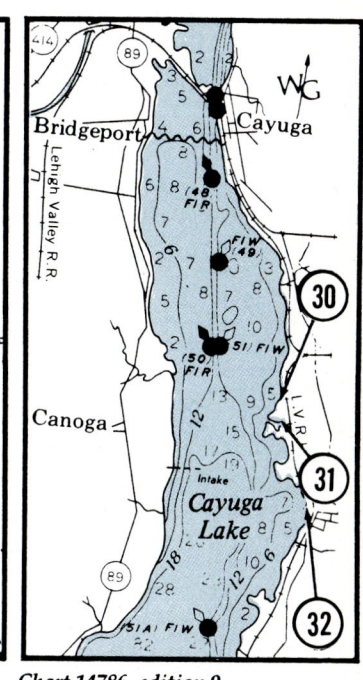

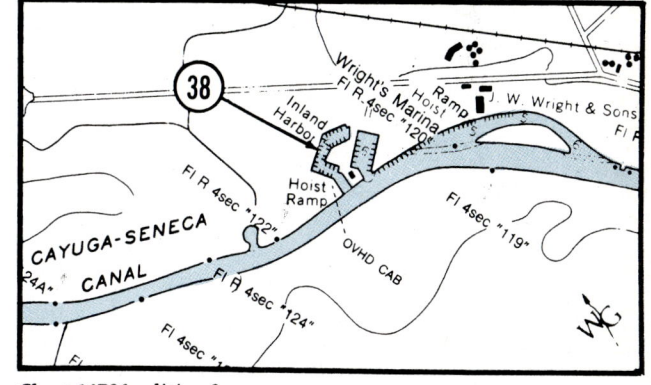

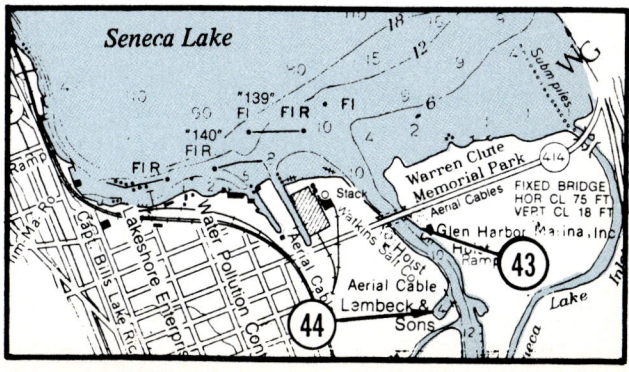

Chart 14786, edition 9 (multiple panels)

GREAT LAKES EDITION — *Under no circumstances are these charts to be used for navigation.* — 67

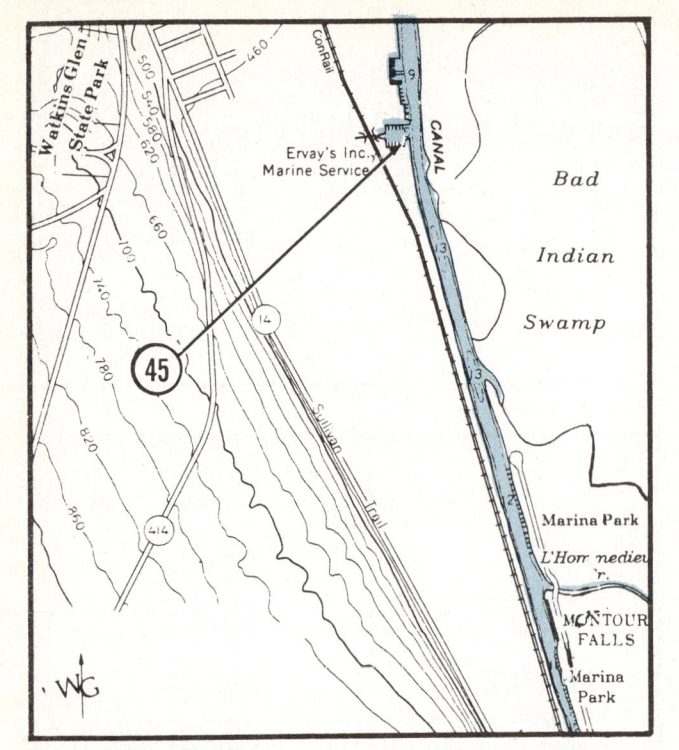

Erie Canal

Chart 14786, edition 9

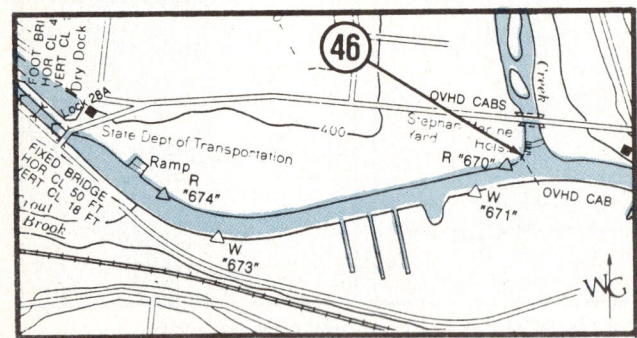

Chart 14786, edition 9

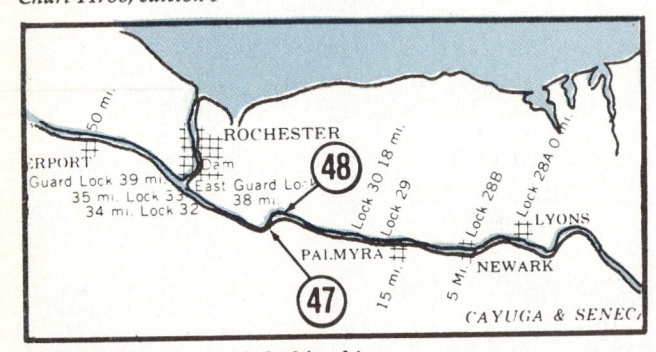

No NOS charts are published for this area.

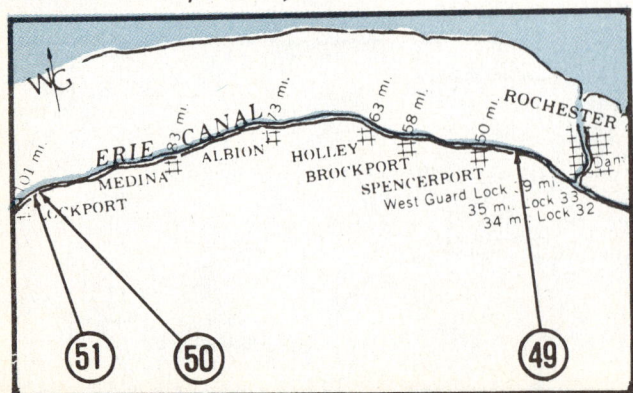

No NOS charts are published for this area.

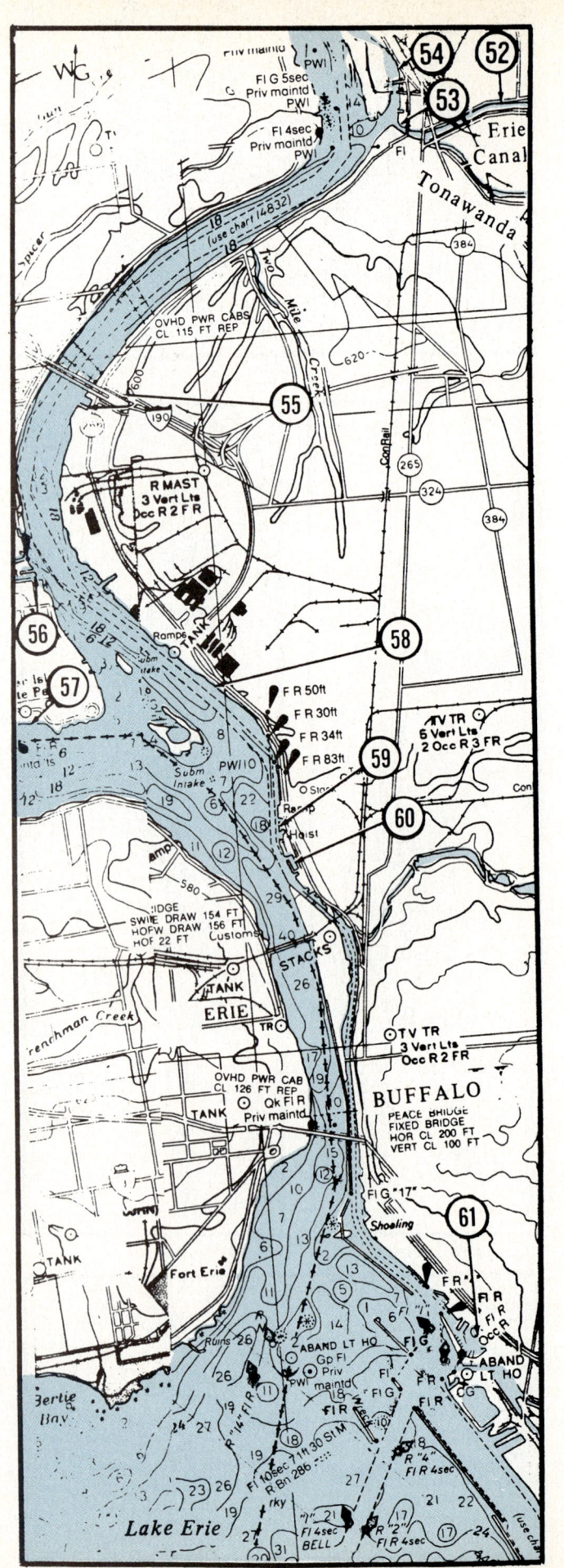

Chart 14822, edition 25

Lake Ontario

CHARTS: U.S. 14800, 14805, 14814, 14802, 14806, 14815, 14803, 14811, 14816, 14804, 14813, 14822; Canadian: 2042, 2062, 2058, 2063, 2060, 2064, 2061, 2069.

Lake Ontario

Smallest of the Great Lakes, **Lake Ontario** is nevertheless almost 200 miles long by about 55 miles across at its widest. Its orientation on an east-west axis makes for good cross-lake sailing, although west-bound sailors can have a tough beat. Strong westerly winds can also pile up the water at the eastern end into steep seas. As on any large body of water, weather forecasts must be carefully monitored before setting forth on the lake. Summer storms come up suddenly.

Boating on the lake starts as early as late April and extends into October, but June, July, and August are the prime cruising months. Temperatures average in the 70s and 80s during summer days, cooling to the 60s at night. By midsummer, the water has warmed to a comfortable 70 degrees for swimming.

Ontario is unique among the lakes in that four canals radiate from its shores: the Oswego and the Welland on the south, the Rideau and Trent-Severn on the north side. (The Oswego was described in the previous section, and the others are covered later on.) The Ontario also receives the discharge from all the other lakes via the Niagara River and passes it to the St. Lawrence River for ultimate flow to the sea.

The shoreline of Lake Ontario is remarkably smooth, so that most of the harbors are manmade. At the eastern end lie a few natural bays and the prized sheltered cruising ground of the **Bay of Quinte** (pronounced *Kwin-tey*). Except for the cities of Oswego and Rochester, the New York side of the lake is mostly rural, with rolling fields and orchards reaching back from the lakeshore between small villages. The Ontario side, by contrast, is the site of Canada's most heavily urbanized corridor, although between the cities are stretches of placid farmland. Boating is extremely popular on both sides of the lake, and, especially on the Ontario side, transient dockage is sometimes hard to find. It's a good idea to make reservations in advance. Our coverage of Lake Ontario begins at Oswego and circles counterclockwise.

Oswego is the site of the first settlement on the American side of Lake Ontario and has always been an important port. Its harbor at the mouth of the Oswego River is protected by a set of breakwaters that can be confusing. The piers extending into the lake are not parallel, but converge at their outer ends, and a detached breakwater angles across them. All are marked by lighted aids. You can enter from either end of the detached breakwater, but a strong current can run easterly. A strong river current runs into the harbor entrance when the river is in flood. Tie-up without services is available along the east wall of the harbor, with a full-service marina in the basin behind it. This is where sailboats transiting the Oswego Canal have their masts stepped and unstepped.

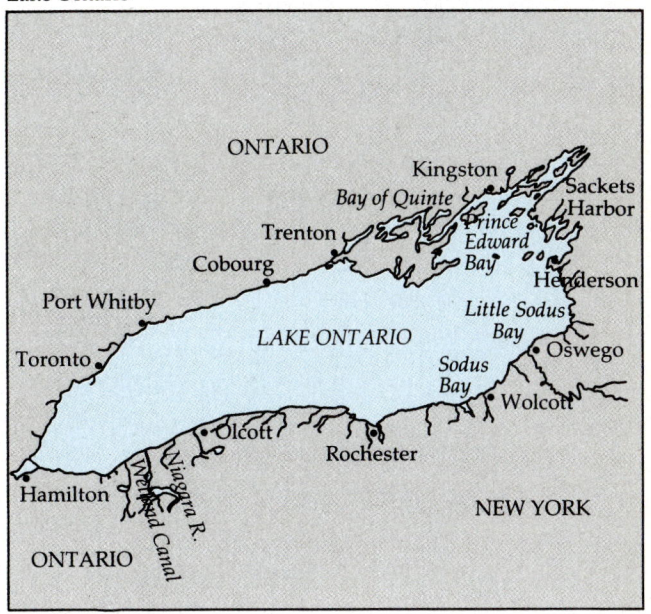

In addition to a historical museum and a marine museum in town, **Fort Ontario**, open to the public, is a few blocks from the marina. It is the successor to earlier forts that were raised on this site beginning in 1727. Shopping, restaurants, and movies are all a convenient walking distance over the bridge from the marina.

Oswego to Kingston

Crossing the eastern end of the lake from Oswego to one of the bays in the northeast corner or proceeding directly to **Kingston** can be rough and potentially dangerous in high winds. It's 40 miles northeasterly to sheltered **Henderson Bay** across notorious **Mexico Bay**, and 55 almost due north to Kingston via Galloo Island.

Port Ontario/North Pond. A new harbor of refuge for small boats has been constructed at the south end of Mexico Bay. Enter from the east end of the breakwater, and then turn south to get in. No commercial facilities are available.

About halfway between Oswego and Henderson Bay in Mexico Bay, **North Pond** offers another refuge. It is quite shallow, about 12 feet at its deepest, and the entrance channel is comprised of shifting sand that shoals to three feet in low-water years. Locally placed buoys mark the channel, but they are small and difficult to see

GREAT LAKES EDITION

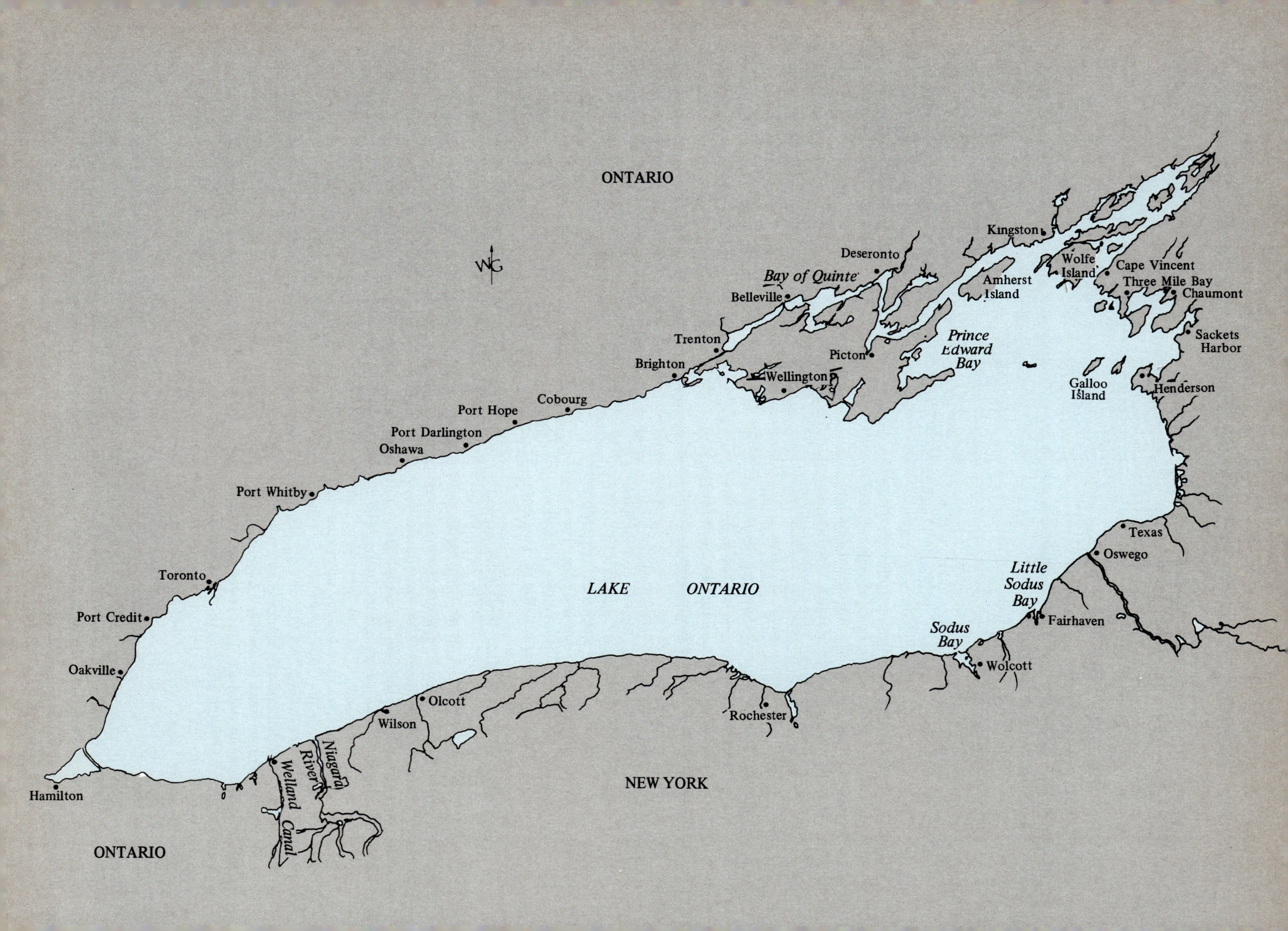
ONTARIO
Kingston
Deseronto
Bay of Quinte
Belleville
Wolfe Island
Cape Vincent
Three Mile Bay
Chaumont
Amherst Island
Trenton
Prince Edward Bay
Sackets Harbor
Picton
Brighton
Wellington
Galloo Island
Henderson
Port Hope
Cobourg
Port Darlington
Oshawa
Port Whitby
Texas
Oswego
Toronto
Little Sodus Bay
LAKE ONTARIO
Port Credit
Fairhaven
Sodus Bay
Wolcott
Oakville
Olcott
Rochester
Wilson
Niagara River
Welland Canal
Hamilton
NEW YORK
ONTARIO

from offshore. The small-boat marinas in the bay do not cater to transient boats, except for selling gasoline, but anchorage can be found in one of the coves south of the harbor entrance.

Henderson Bay. Seven miles long and two miles wide, this harbor is deep inside, but has a tricky entrance marked by a buoy at **Lime Barrel Shoal**. Study the chart carefully for the unmarked shoals off **Six Town Point** and **Gull Island**. Henderson Bay has no real village, but the area offers a number of marinas. The yacht club in the southeast corner welcomes transients, and you'll find a pleasant anchorage with good holding in **Whites Bay** on the west shore.

Sackets Harbor. A quaint village, Sackets Harbor lies at the mouth of **Black River Bay** behind sheltering **Navy Point**. Lighted aids guide you in from the lake, but Navy Point shoals out as far as 200 feet and should be given a wide berth. On the south side of the peninsula is a full-service marina, and across the small harbor, the town provides tie-up with some services. During the War of 1812, Sackets Harbor was the major American naval base on the Great Lakes and an important shipbuilding center. **Battlefield Park** is posted with signs telling the story of the engagements that took place during that war, and an annual reenactment is held in July. A historical museum and a number of well-preserved or restored old buildings can be found in the village.

Chaumont Bay. Protected from the lake by **Point Peninsula**, this harbor is easily entered and leads to **Sawmill Bay** east of **Independence Point**, where service establishments welcome transients. Groceries are available about half a mile from the waterfront at the village of **Chaumont**, named for a 19th-century French nobleman and local landowner.

Twenty miles past Point Peninsula and **Grenadier Island**, **Tibbetts Point** marks the southeast entrance to the St. Lawrence River, covered in the next chapter.

Kingston

Strategically located at the confluence of Lake Ontario, the St. Lawrence River, and the Rideau Waterway (described in later sections), **Kingston** has always been an important place. The first European settlement on the Great Lakes, **Fort Frontenac**, was erected in 1673. The history of Kingston as a city began when United Empire Loyalists from New York crossed the lake to settle in 1784. It soon became a major naval base. Later the Royal Military College, other military installations, and a distinguished university were established here. All of these institutions make Kingston one of the most interesting cities on the Great Lakes, architecturally and culturally.

It is also an enthusiastic boating center, with two excellent marinas and a yacht club. Portsmouth Olympic Harbour, built in 1976 for the Olympic Games, is about 2½ miles from downtown, but the municipal **Confederation Basin** is in the heart of the city under the imposing domed city hall. Unfortunately, both harbors tend to have a bad surge in a heavy southwest blow.

The lakefront off Kingston has many shoals, but the channels are well marked, and the main channel leading from the southwest has a lighted range to guide you in. Note that the approach is buoyed as if coming from the sea on the St. Lawrence River, so that red is left to port when coming from south or west until you actually enter the harbor at Carruthers Shoal when they shift to starboard. Furthermore, some magnetic anomalies in the area make it advisable to rely on the buoyage rather than on your compass.

Kingston is well worth a visit of several days. At least 13 museums, many art galleries, live theater, and a collection of excellent restaurants are located here. Information on all of this is available at the Chamber of Commerce in the old railroad station at Confederation Basin. Simply walking the streets of this well-preserved historic city is a pleasure, but a train tour offers an alternative. Behind city hall, the farmers' market convenes on Tuesday, Thursday, and Saturday, and the flea market on Sunday is another lively event.

Bay of Quinte

The 60-mile-long, Z-shaped **Bay of Quinte** provides some of Lake Ontario's finest cruising in scenic, shel-

---

LAKE ONTARIO MARINERS MARINA

The advantages of Lake Ontario Mariners Marina!

+ Newly renovated with open and covered slips.
+ Nestles in protected waters and ideal for sport fishing.
+ Fish cleaning stations.
+ Beautiful grounds with park and picnic areas.
+ Deck, modern bath facilities and all conveniences.
+ Ship's store and trained repairmen for servicing boats.
+ Protected harbor offers fishing & boating when the Lake is rough.

For more information on seasonal/annual dockage/storage packages.

Call 315/938-5222

Military Road - off Rte. 3   Henderson, NY 13650

Collins Bay Marina

Seasonal and Overnight Docking
Reservations by phone or VHF ch. 68

• gas • ice • pumpout • washrooms • showers •
• park, playground and hiking trails •

Come and be our guests!

1089 BATH RD., KINGSTON, ONT. K7M 4Y2   (613) 389-4455

Lake Ontario

tered waters. From Kingston, the approach is guarded by **Amherst Island**. Pass north of the island's northernmost shoals, the **Brother Islands**. Extra caution is needed; rocks are awash north of the lights, and Amherst Bar extends all the way from the easternmost Brother Island to Amherst Island. Although clearly charted, it is the site of many groundings every year. Be sure to stay in the channel. It's a 20-mile run along this North Channel to **Upper Gap**, the eastern entrance to the Bay of Quinte. Note that the North Channel and all of the Bay of Quinte is buoyed from east to west, with red on the starboard side for a westbound vessel.

Adolphus Reach to Picton. From Upper Gap, **Adolphus Reach** extends southwesterly for 14 miles between Prince Edward County, known as **Quinte's Isle**, and the mainland. A popular and well-sheltered anchorage at **Prinyer's Cove** is located on the island side. The only hazard along the reach is the ferry at **Glenora**. **Picton** is a charming village at the foot of **Picton Bay**, the county town of rural Quinte's Isle. You'll find two choices for overnight dockage, attractive streets to explore, and good shopping.

Picton to Belleville. Northward from Picton Bay, **Hayward Long Reach** extends for about ten miles before the Bay of Quinte turns westward again. Part of the way up on the starboard side, **Hay Bay** indents the rural mainland with several popular anchorages. Just beyond the end of the reach, the quiet village of **Deseronto** on **Mohawk Bay** has a marina.

The route swings west for three miles to well-buoyed **Telegraph Narrows**, and five miles beyond opens into **Big Bay**. Anchorage can be found in an indentation of **Big Island**, and there is also a marina in a man-made harbor.

From here, the channel continues west to Belleville, the largest town on the bay. The harbor is fronted with shoals, but the channel is well marked. You can choose from several accommodations, and this is where sailboats transiting the Trent-Severn Waterway have their masts stepped and unstepped. Downtown Belleville is attractive, with several restaurants and a farmers' market open on Tuesday, Thursday, and Saturday. No grocery shopping is convenient to the waterfront.

Belleville to Brighton. Beyond Belleville, the bay is somewhat less scenic along the 11-mile run to Trenton. The waters outside Trenton are the shallowest in the bay, so it's important to follow the buoyage carefully. In addition to the Canadian Forces Base Yacht Club behind Baker Island, the city has two municipal marinas. The one located in Fraser Park, a short way up the Trent River, is convenient to shopping and restaurants. Here is where the **Trent-Severn Waterway** begins. It is described in a later chapter.

A few miles past Trenton, the five-mile **Murray Canal** connects the Bay of Quinte with Lake Ontario via shallow, but well-marked **Presqu'ile Bay**. Three bridges cross the canal; one usually stands open, the others respond quickly to oncoming boats. Strong currents sometimes flow past these bridges, and the water is generally deeper on the south side of the opening. You'll find tie-up at the west end of the canal. Presqu'ile Bay has a stubborn weed problem, so be sure to stay in the buoyed channel. The westbound red markers on the starboard side continue through this bay for about 4½ miles to the lighted Brighton range. Here, you can exit to Lake Ontario (with red still to starboard) or follow the channel to the Brighton Marina. It is several miles from the village, but transportation can be arranged for a trip to town or to **Presqu'ile Provincial Park** with its wide, sandy beaches, lush woods, and extraordinary bird life.

The North Shore East of Toronto

Around the north shore of Lake Ontario from Presqu'ile Bay to Toronto, the harbors are spaced relatively close together. They are all either man-made or dredged from river mouths, and all are entered past piers or jetties thrusting into the lake. Some of them are in rural areas and difficult to spot from offshore. Transient space is scarce in most of these harbors; it's wise to arrive early in the day or to make advance reservations.

Cobourg. Identified from offshore by its oil tanks west of the harbor entrance, Cobourg is one of the few places along the coast where shopping and restaurants are within easy reach of the marina. The town features interesting historic buildings and a walking-tour leaflet to guide you.

Port Hope. Although this city, too, is a treasury of 19th-century architecture, the waterfront is still commercial, and the railroad bridge crosses close to the marina and yacht club. The harbor can be restless and noisy in a south wind. Shopping is conveniently located.

Newcastle. The harbor, dredged from a creek mouth in a rural setting, consists of an expanding marina with surrounding condominiums under construction. Although Newcastle's harbor is situated a couple of miles from the inland village, the grounds feature tennis courts, a restaurant, and children's play equipment. The entrance channel is narrow, with a dogleg to port.

Port Darlington. Four miles west of Newcastle, Port Darlington is several miles from the nearest town, **Bowmanville**, but the marina here is part of a hotel that offers a dining room, bar, swimming pool, and volleyball court. The narrow entrance channel to the formerly commercial harbor is buoyed.

Oshawa. This substantial city's port is still in commercial use. A buoyed channel leads to the large marina in the northwest corner. The amenities are excellent, and include a small swimming pool and picnic area, but the harbor is three miles from downtown. Buses and taxis are available to see the sights, which include the Canadian Automotive Museum, tours of the General Motors plant, several historic house museums, and an art gallery.

Port Whitby. If you prefer to stop, Port Whitby is five miles west of Oshawa, with a tall chimney to help identify the harbor entrance. A buoyed channel leads to the marina.

Frenchman's Bay. Eighteen miles from Toronto, Frenchman's Bay is home to a complex of marinas and yacht clubs. The landmark for the approach is the nuclear power station located a half mile east of the entrance. A small shopping center with restaurants is a half mile from the harbor.

Toronto

Toronto is one of the most exciting cities on the Great Lakes, offering an abundance of things to see and do. More important to the mariner is that Toronto is a boating city that cherishes its 20 miles of waterfront and has done much to enhance it.

The 1,815-foot CN Tower, the world's tallest free-standing structure, dominates the skyline and serves as a landmark for boats far out on the lake.

The harbor attractions begin seven miles east of the main port in the first of Toronto's strand of waterfront parks. **Bluffers Bay**, at the foot of the Scarborough cliffs, was created by two encircling arms of landfill. High on the bluff, the dome of St. Augustine's Seminary identifies the harbor from offshore. A consortium of yacht clubs has developed the park's marine services, with occasional space for transients.

Proceeding west from Bluffers Bay, you pass a charming neighborhood known as **The Beaches**, with a boardwalk along the water and a pleasant beach for swimming. This is a good spot for day anchoring in calm weather. After you pass the prominent race track at **Woodbine Park**, proceed around the western point of the spit of land and enter artificial **Ashbridges Bay**. Here, you'll find anchoring room, a yacht club, swimming, and a park.

The next five miles of waterfront, ending as you reach the entrance to the Main Harbour Channel, is commercial. At the **Outer Harbour East Headland**, known locally as the **Leslie Street Spit**, **Aquatic Park** is being developed to combine natural amenities with marine services. Proceeding through the Main Harbour Channel with its big lighted range, **Eastern Gap** leads to the Inner Harbour. Here, the ships that serve the port move eastward into the ship channel to extensive berths. The rest of the harbor belongs to pleasure craft.

The Toronto Islands. Forming the natural outer boundary of the harbor, these islands have long been an important summer recreation area for Toronto residents, and around the turn of the century, hotels, an amusement park, churches, and hundreds of summer cottages dotted the islands. Now, houses remain only on the two easternmost islands, **Ward's** and **Algonquin**. About 350 people live here year-round. The rest of the area is parkland, with several yacht clubs and one full-service marina that leases space from the city.

Centre Island features several family attractions, including a turn-of-the-century theme park, a petting farm with pony rides, and a puppet theater. On westernmost **Toronto Island**, public dockage is available at **Hanlan Point** immediately south of the airport. It's first-come, first-served, with a two-day limit for your stay. This is a good base for exploring the city, because the ferry dock is close by. Hanlan Point is near **Western Gap**, the entrance to the Inner Harbor, where boat traffic is thick. Keep a careful watch and proceed slowly. Two restricted areas near the airport are marked by buoys.

South of Hanlan Point are **The Lagoons** with opportunities for anchoring. **Lighthouse Pond** is popular, as is the area behind **Forestry Island**. About the only place you can't explore with six-foot draft is between Algonquin and Snake islands, where a three-foot bar would prevent your passage.

The Toronto Mainland. Toronto ashore presents entertainment, museums, shops, architecture, theater,

---

East Shore Marina

Where you're always welcome...

Located on beautiful Frenchman's Bay in Pickering, East Shore Marina is Durham Region's largest and most progressive yacht facility

Full Marina Service Include:

- We Monitor VHF Ch. 68
- Space for 650 boats up to 30 tons
- Boat and engine repairs
- Docks with hydro, water, phone, cable T.V. and pump out services
- Snack bar
- Washrooms and showers
- Two yacht brokers on premises
- Winter bubbling to accommodate live aboards
- Picnic area and ample parking on 7 acre site
- Minutes from fine restaurants, shopping and GO transit
- Very competitive rates
- ALL docks color coded

EAST SHORE MARINA
1295 Wharf Street (Off Liverpool Rd S)

Pickering, Ontario L1W1A2
(416) 839-5036

HARBOURFRONT

Harbourfront is Toronto's fastest growing attraction and one of North America's leading waterfront developments. The 100 acre site is just minutes away from the core of one of Canada's most vibrant cities.

Harbourfront has 3 berthing areas, able to accommodate vessels of all sizes (up to 150 feet). Services include double 50 amp shorepower outlets, fresh water, dockmaster service, pumpout and a host of other amenities.

Located within walking distance are a variety of shops including marine supplies, books and clothing, charts and publications, pharmacy, photo shop, dry cleaning, five star hotel and a 24 hour food-mart. Within a short distance are beer and liquor outlets and access to the central business district.

While docked, enjoy all that Harbourfront has to offer - water's edge promenade, excellent dining in a variety of restaurants, fascinating shops, art galleries, film, theatre, music, dance and special events. There is something on board for all!

The best things in life are here!

For further information and rates
call (416) 973-4094
Fax (416) 973-4703
Dockmaster
(416) 973-4148

or write
Marine Department
Harbourfront Corporation
410 Queens Quay West
Suite 100
Toronto, Ontario
M5V 2Z3
Canada

restaurants, concerts, and a first-rate public transit system to take you to all of them. Some of the best attractions are right at the waterside in the Harbourfront development. Along the 2½-mile promenade is a kaleidoscope of marine services, art and craft galleries, restaurants, theaters, playgrounds, and special-event spaces, all woven into renovated old buildings and imaginative new ones. More than 3,500 events take place at Harbourfront every year. At York Quay Centre and Queen's Day Terminal, information centers are open every day to let you know what is going on.

West of Harbourfront, beyond Western Gap, **Ontario Place** raises its futuristic architecture and huge symbolic sphere on three man-made islands. This unusual multi-purpose cultural, educational, commercial, and entertainment complex defies easy definition. There are activities here to delight everyone. Enter the marina to starboard of a line of three old lake freighters sunk to serve as a breakwater. Reservations are a must for this popular place.

Across Lakeshore Boulevard from Ontario Place is the Canadian National Exhibition grounds, with several museums and special events taking place all summer, including Blue Jays baseball, and culminating in a giant fair from mid-August until Labor Day.

A breakwater runs along the shore all the way from Ontario Place to Palace Pier, a conspicuously tall condominium at the mouth of the **Humber River**. Several openings in the breakwater have moorings located inside, and the anchorage affords ten-foot depths. Two public swimming pools are located here, but it's a long walk to public transportation and shopping.

Humber Bay Park is the last of Toronto's suburban parks. A landfill has created a headland and a protected lagoon with two yacht clubs. Neighborhood shopping is available about a half mile away.

The West End

The 35 miles between Toronto and **Hamilton** is a densely populated urban area, but the string of close harbors and intermittent parks continue among the apartment towers and industrial enclaves. The fast, efficient metropolitan transit system also extends along the line between the two large cities.

Port Credit. Formerly commercial, Port Credit is an artificial harbor now devoted entirely to pleasure boating, with a large full-service marina and a yacht club. Shopping is conveniently located a few blocks away.

Oakville. Oakville is a city with two harbors and two identities. The older, elegant part of town surrounds **Oakville Creek**, which features a couple of yacht clubs. Atop the steep embankments of the creek is excellent shopping, a charming historic district, tennis courts, restaurants, summer theater, and an art gallery.

Bronte Harbour lies along **Bronte Creek**, a few miles away at the west end of town, where the houses are newer and less concentrated. The creek is subject to silting and a strong outflow, but a marina and yacht club are located here. A pleasant park is on the waterfront, and shopping is close by.

Hamilton. Steel capital of Canada, industrial Hamilton is located on 12-miles-square **Burlington Bay**. A natural sandbar almost closes off the bay from the lake. The high, arched bridge of the Burlington Skyway is visible from far out into the lake and helps to guide you to the Burlington Canal leading into the bay. Just before the canal is a lift bridge that opens every hour and half hour. To starboard at the bay end of the canal is the Canada Centre for Inland Waters, a research agency with short-term tie-up among the research vessels if you would like to visit.

Burlington Bay is considered one of the best areas for sailing on Lake Ontario, because it is generally much calmer than the open lake, and the waters are wide, clear, and deep. On the northwest Burlington shore is a marina in **LaSalle Park**.

The south end of **Hamilton Harbour**, the official name for Burlington Bay, is almost entirely commercial. But in the southwest corner, in a residential district, is a large, full-service marina and two yacht clubs. Bus service at the top of the bluff will take you to downtown Hamilton's shops, theaters, art gallery, and restaurants. Elaborate **Dundern Castle** is one of the city's most popular attractions. The exquisite **Royal Botannical Gardens**, reachable by taxi from the waterfront, has hiking trails and natural areas in addition to the formal displays.

Lake Ontario's South Shore

The south shore, both in Ontario and in New York, is mostly rural. Climatic conditions make this area ideal for growing fruit, and orchards and vineyards grow all along the coast.

Fifty Mile Point is a new artificial harbor about nine miles southeast of the Burlington Bay entrance. A marina in a large park offers picnic grounds, playground,

WE'RE "THE STORE" AND WE'RE SERIOUS ABOUT MARINE SUPPLIES

Call Coast to Coast Toll Free 1-800-263-1506
Fax us at (416) 278-5758, write or
Drop By and See For Your Self!!
IN THE PORT CREDIT MARINA. CALL (416) 278-7005
1 PORT STREET EAST, PORT CREDIT, ONTARIO L5G 4N1

LAKE ONTARIO

FAMILY TIES

A Marina flying this flag

ONTARIO MARINA OPERATORS ASSOCIATION

promises you
professional service.
Look for it!
The OMOA family looks
after your boating family.

For a free copy of our Marina Directory, with more than 400 Ontario Marina listings, fill out and mail this coupon today.

Please send the OMOA Marina Directory to:

Name _____

Address _____

_____

City _____

Ontario Marina Operators Association
4 Cataraqui Street, Suite 211
Kingston, Ontario, Canada   K7K 1Z7
Phone 613 547-6662   Fax 613 547-6813

---

bicycle track, and beach, but has no shopping nearby. A white light tower on the east breakwater is all that identifies the harbor from the lake. **Grimsby** is four miles farther on, with two marinas in the manmade harbor, identifiable from the lake by eight radio towers west of town.

Port Dalhousie is easy to spot from the lake with its two tall white lighthouses at either end of the eastern breakwater. The entrance to the original **Welland Canal**, the harbor was designed for big ships, but now is used almost exclusively by recreational boats. Current can run as high as three knots when Ontario Hydro opens the sluice gates at the southern end, and in a north wind, surge from the lake can be quite uncomfortable.

The Welland Canal

In order to circumvent Niagara Falls, ships seeking passage between Lake Ontario and Lake Erie must use the Welland Canal. Only relatively shallow-draft pleasure craft can transit the alternative route between these two lakes—the Erie Canal. This 30-mile waterway raises boats 326 feet from Lake Ontario "uphill" to Lake Erie in a series of eight locks. The trip can be arduous. Eddies and currents in the locks can make an upbound passage a test of physical endurance for the crew.

The minimum time for a passage through the Welland is eight hours, however, it's seldom accomplished in such a short time. Plan to spend 12 to 14 hours making the journey, and be prepared to man your boat continuously for that period of time.

Pleasure boats are required to notify canal officials and should use the special telephones provided at both **Port Weller** and **Port Colborne** to report to "Seaway Welland". Docks for pleasure craft are provided at these phones. The Port Weller dock is on the east side just upstream of the gate lifter berth; at Port Colborne, the phone is on the west side just south of the first set of vertical lift bridges. These phone docks are the only ones provided for yachts, and the use of any other Seaway docking facility is prohibited. You will be asked for a description of your boat, her name and the number of people aboard. The phone operator will probably tell you to go back to your boat and monitor VHF Channel 14 for further instructions. You may have to wait several hours, perhaps half a day, before being allowed to enter the canal.

The phone dock at Port Colbourne, conveniently located in the city's new Harborview Park and Marina, is a fine place to await your turn to enter the canal. Don't call the lock until you are ready to travel; your instruction to enter the canal may come on very short notice.

Requirements for passage. All pleasure boats transiting the Welland Canal must have a copy of the St. Lawrence Seaway **Pleasure Craft Guide** on board. This booklet covers the entire Seaway from Montreal to Lake Erie, in both French and English. Yachts over 65 feet long are subject to the rules and regulations contained in the **Seaway Handbook**. Requests for the **Seaway Handbook** should contain the overall length

A yacht club is on the east side of the harbor, and a city dock on the west. Port Dalhousie has made a tourist attraction of its historic buildings, restored to house boutiques and restaurants. **Lakeside Park** has a beach and antique carousel.

Port Weller. Situated at the northern entrance of the Welland Canal, Port Weller is served by the St. Catherines's Marina. This newly expanded and full-service marina is located on the east side of the east breakwater, about a mile from the city of St. Catherines. The city provides a wide variety of stores for provisioning. There are no facilities between the breakwaters, with the exception of a phone-in tie-up area, to be used only when you are ready to transit the canal.

Off **Four Mile Point**, between Port Weller and Niagara-on-the-Lake, numerous uncharted buoys mark the limits of a firing range. Stay clear.

The Niagara River. This river empties into Lake Ontario about nine miles east of Port Weller and forms part of the border between the United States and Canada. The river is navigable for about ten miles, but the only marine services are near the mouth. The strong river current, up to three knots, carries sand and silt that create shoals part of the way into the lake. These shoals are well marked by buoys. In addition, the current sets easterly beyond the river mouth, and strong north

---

of your boat. Copies of both publications can be obtained from the Information Officer, The St. Lawrence Seaway Authority, Tower A, Place de Ville, Ottawa, Ontario, Canada K1R 5A3. Free copies of the handbook are usually available at the Port Colbourne Harbor Marina and from the lock tenders at the first lock.

You must have a VHF-FM radiotelephone. Channel 14 is the Seaway working channel and it should be monitored at all times; you will receive instructions on entering locks via radio from Seaway Welland.

Other required equipment includes a **personal flotation device** (PFD) for every member of the crew who will be on deck. PFDs must be worn by linehandlers when going through the locks.

Seaway officials may stop a boat from using the canal if they feel it has an insufficient crew. Smaller yachts may go downbound with just two people aboard, but on upbound passages you must have at least three people aboard. Usually, finding an extra hand isn't difficult because pleasure craft are sent through in groups and other boats in the group may have some extra hands to share. The minimum size for pleasure craft is 20 feet or one ton, and sailing is not permitted.

A toll of $7.00 per lock is charged as a "line handling fee." The total cost for the eight locks of the Welland system is $48.00, payable in cash to the officer in charge of Lock 3.

Fenders. Welland Canal locks were designed for cargo ships, not yachts. The rough concrete walls chew up the sides of any boat that's not properly protected with fenders. Any type of fender is better than none, but the regular white vinyl fenders are not up to the job, and fender boards placed outside the round vinyl fenders have been known to snag on the lock walls. One of the best protection devices is a heavy canvas bag filled with straw, sold by marinas at either end of the canal. Vertical 4x4 inch timbers with the tops tapered like sled runners have also proved satisfactory if the side of the wood against the boat is covered with carpet. The use of old tires as fenders is prohibited by the canal officials.

Mooring lines, bow and stern, are supplied by the lockmasters. These are rough, oily, and otherwise nasty lengths of rope, so have a pair of sturdy work gloves for each member of the crew.

Upbound boats take in line as the water level in the lock rises; downbound boats let out line as the water drops. Do not cleat any lines; you must tend them at all times. Occasionally, a downbound boat will tie off a mooring line and then find itself hanging in mid-air as the water goes down.

Locking through. The locks and lift bridges on the Welland have visual traffic control systems to guide the approach of vessels, similar to traffic signals on the highway. (The system is clearly explained in the Pleasure Craft Guide.)

The control system for bridges is the simplest. A yellow light begins to flash when the bridge operator begins bridge operation. A red light flashes when the bridge starts to rise. You may not proceed past the Limit of Approach (L/A) sign when either the yellow or red lights are flashing. Once the bridge is fully raised, a green light will signal you to proceed. You are advised to stay near the edges of the channel when waiting for a bridge to operate; pleasure craft in the center of the channel may not be visible from the wheelhouse of large ships. If you can't see the wheelhouse, the captain can't see you.

The approach control system for locks is more complex. There can be up to three L/A signs. The first two carry just red lights. The one closest to the lock has both a red and green light. **Never pass a fixed or flashing red light**. Large panels containing multiple lights are mounted immediately adjacent to the locks. These panels have red, green, and amber lights. The red and green lights work in conjunction with the L/A sign lights. Each amber fixed light indicates two minutes until the lock will open. A flashing amber light indicates one minute. The amber lights go out in sequence, starting from the top of the panel, with the last one going out as the lock gates open.

Enter a lock only when the green lights come on. The side for mooring differs from lock to lock, except Locks 4, 5, and 6 which are port side to both ways.

Pleasure craft should stay ahead of large ships in the locks. This makes the most efficient use of the locks and prevents yachts from being caught in the prop wash of big ships. It also means that pleasure boats must be able to stay ahead of ships when going through the Welland. Most freighters steam at the six knot speed limit in the canal sections between locks, and sailboats may find they have to strain to stay ahead of a ship while the ship's captain advises them by radio to "Get a move on or get run over."

Lake Ontario

winds can create eddies and rips.

Niagara-on-the-Lake is a charming resort village on the Canadian side of the river, with many vintage buildings, fine restaurants, boutiques, a historic fort and museum. The outstanding attraction is the annual May-through-October Shaw Festival, during which the plays of George Bernard Shaw and other 20th-century playwrights are performed. Regrettably, transient dock space in the small, crowded harbor is hard to find. Slips can be reserved, but the fees are high.

Youngstown, on the east side of the Niagara River, is an excellent stopover. The Youngstown Yacht Club offers only moorings, but the club does accommodate visiting members of reciprocating clubs along their dock wall. Due to the popularity of the club, you'll often find extensive rafting at the wall, but the adage, "there's always room for one more," is certainly applicable here. The town, a short and steep walk away, and Yachting World, a most complete marine store, combine to make provisioning here both convenient and pleasant. RCR Yacht Service, adjacent to the yacht club, provides repairs and haulouts.

Wilson. About 12 miles east of the Niagara River, **Tuscarora Bay** is the harbor for the village of Wilson. Seen from the lake, the town lies west of three silos. Three yacht clubs and a marina are in the bay, and **Tuscarora State Park** has a few slips without services. You'll also find a good anchorage in the bay near the park. About a mile from the harbor is a small supermarket, and a restaurant is within walking distance.

The Tuscarora Yacht Club welcomes visitors from other clubs and provides a packet of information, including a map of the village and a list of the town's available services.

Olcott, only six miles east of Wilson, is on **Eighteen-mile Creek**, where the surge can be heavy in northwest-to-northeast winds. Two marinas and a town dock are here, and if you can get under the 52-foot fixed bridge up the creek, a pleasant anchorage lies beyond it. Favor the eastern shore as you move upstream to avoid shoals in the west side, and pass under the starboard arch of the bridge. On the lakefront is a park with beach and tennis courts.

Due to fish-stocking programs, the creek and surrounding waters abound with coho and chinook salmon. The result is wall-to-wall boats, with docking for transients at a premium.

Point Breeze/Oak Orchard. The double name refers to one place, the village of Point Breeze on Oak Orchard Creek, that can't make up its mind what to be called. A water treatment plant and four silos flanking the entrance identify the town as seen from the lake, and a detached breakwater lies across the ends of the two standard piers thrusting into the lake. You can enter from either side. Favor the east side of the creek as you move upstream in six-foot depths to one of the two

Distances
Approximate Statute Miles

Cross-lake (from Oswego)	
Oswego, west pierhead	0.0
Galloo Island, light abeam to the east	28.0
Main Duck Island, light abeam to the east	32.0
Stony Island	31.0
Tibbetts Point Light, abeam	44.0
Kingston, via Boat Channel	54.5
Upper Gap, Indian Point	49.0
Presquile Light	71.0
Toronto, Outer Harbor entrance	144.0
Welland Canal, entrance	139.0

Cross-lake Distances (point-to-point)	
Kingston to Rochester, entrance	98.0
Rochester, entrance to Presquile Light	53.0
Rochester, entrance to Toronto, entrance	97.0
Toronto, entrance to Welland Canal, ent.	27.2
Toronto, entrance to Niagara, entrance	30.1
Hamilton, entrance to Welland Canal, ent.	28.6

Location	Between Points	Cumulative
Coastwise (incl. Bay of Quinte)		
Oswego	0	0
Galloo Island	28	28
Sackets Harbor	20	48
Tibbetts Point	21	69

Location	Between Points	Cumulative
Kingston	20	89
Upper Gap	20	109
Picton	16	125
Deseronoto	13	138
Belleville	16	154
Trenton	10	164
Brighton	10	174
Presqu'ile Light	3	177
Cobourg	24	201
Port Hope	6	207
Oshawa	27	234
Port Whitby	6	240
Toronto	27	267
Port Credit	12	279
Oakville	9	288
Hamilton	12	300
Port Dalhousie	27	327
Welland Canal	4	331
Youngstown	14	345
Olcott	20	365
Rochester	60	425
Sodus Bay	31	456
Little Sodus Bay	14	470
Oswego	13	483

marinas or the yacht club beyond the 52-foot fixed bridge. You can also anchor upstream from the club.

The Oak Orchard Yacht Club, due to its popularity, now charges a nominal fee to reciprocal club members for the first night. A newly renovated dining room with excellent cuisine is open to members and their guests Thursday through Sunday for dinner, and on weekends for breakfast. The long Orleans County Marine Park dock is located on the east side of the creek. It has no cleats and appeared recently to be limited to fishermen's use. The small docks are rented by the season. Oak Orchard remains one of the prettiest, most active, and most secure harbors on the lake.

On the 35-mile stretch between Point Breeze and **Rochester** are two shoal draft harbors, **Brockport**, with a yacht club for sailboats under 30 feet, and **Braddock Bay**, where there are two marinas and a state park.

Rochester. The port of Rochester, largest city on the New York shore, is entered through the Lake Ontario mouth of the **Genessee River**, although the heart of the city lies several miles upstream beyond the falls and dam at the head of navigation. The entrance is readily identified, but strong northeast winds can send a bad surge into the harbor, making it hard to maneuver if the opposing river current is running hard. Several marinas and yacht clubs lie on both sides of the river. The railroad swing bridge remains open most of the time, but the Stutson Street Bascule Bridge farther along opens on the hour and half hour except at rush hours.

The Rochester Yacht Club welcomes members from reciprocating clubs and offers a dining room, a pool, and tennis courts. Several fine marinas and marine stores are located on the east side of the river. All have easy access to Stutson Street Plaza, where all amenities, including a movie theater, are available. City bus service is nearby.

A few miles east of Rochester, **Irondoquoit Bay** has

Lake Ontario

Lake Ontario	Phone	Seasonal/Year-round	Sail/Power/Both	Largest Vessel Accommodated	No. of Transient Berths	Marked Entry Channel	Approach Depth	Dockside Depth	Railway/Lift Capacity	Gas/Diesel/Both	Fuel Brand	Engine Repairs	Propeller/Hull Repairs	Launching Ramp	Marine Supplies/Groceries/Ice	LPG/CNG/Both	110V/220V/Both	Showers/Max Amps	Pump-Out Station	Restaurant/Snack Bar	Radio Watch-VHF (CB)
OSWEGO TO CAPE VINCENT																					
1. Oswego Marina	(315) 342-0436	Y	▲	160	16		25	20		CHE	▲	12		▲	PH	MGI	▲30	SL	●	R	
2. **Lake Ontario Mariners Marina (p. 71)**	938-5222	Y	P	36	2		5	5		AG	▲	12	R	▲		MI	▲30	S	●		16
3. Navy Point Marine	646-3364	Y	▲	75	20		12	12			▲	20		▲	P		★30	SL	●	RS	9
4. General Wolfe Marina	(613) 385-2611	S	▲	50			7	7		ESS	★		R	★		MGI	★30	S		R	
5. Portsmouth Olympic Harbour*	544-9842	S	▲	100	30	●	19	26		ESS	▲	2	R			MGI	▲	SL	●	RS	68
6. Kingston Yacht Club	548-3052	S	▲	45	2		15	10		ANG	▲	6				MI	★10	S	●	R	
7. Confederation Basin	No Listing		▲	100	125	●	14	14							MUNICIPAL DOCK	I	▲50	SL			
8. **Collins Bay Marina (p. 71)**	389-4455	S	▲	50	75		7	7			★	25	R			I	★30	S	●	RS	68
9. Loyalist Cove Yacht Club	352-3478	Y	▲	100	30		19	6			▲				H	MGI	★50	SL	●	RS	68
10. Waupoos Marina	476-2926	S	▲	70	20	●	12	7			▲		R	▲		MGI	★30	SL	●	S	68
BAY OF QUINTE																					
11. Quinte Marina	396-3707	Y	▲	100	20		18	10		ESS	▲	R	▲	PH		MGI	★30	L	●	R	
12. Baycrest Lodge, Marina & Restoration	476-5357	S	▲	45	9		5	5		IND	▲	20	R	▲	PH		MI	★20	SL		
13. Tip of the Bay Hotel	476-2156	S	▲	60	30	●	15	15			▲		R				▲30	SL		RS	
14. Prince Edward Cruising Club	(416) 922-5687	S	▲	100	10		12	7								GI	▲30	SL			
15. Prince Edward Yacht Club*	(613) 476-5585	S	▲	40	8		12	10								GI	★	S		R	68
16. Glenora Marina	476-2377	S	▲	50	6		25	9		ESS	★	7	R	★	P	MI	★			R	
17. Myers Pier Marina*	967-1906	S	▲	60	30		10	10			▲		R			MGI	▲30	SL	●	RS	68
18. Victoria Park Marina*	968-2121	S	▲	50	20		10	6					R			MGI	▲30	SL		RS	
19. Morch Marine	966-0208	S	▲	55	30	●	10	10		SHE	▲	25		▲	PH	★	MI	★15	SL	●	RS	68
20. Belleville Marine, Ltd.	967-0206	Y	▲	50			13	14		GUL	▲	L	R	▲	PH		MI	★30	S	●	R	
21. CFB Trenton Yacht Club	392-8995	S	▲	35	5	●	6	5								I	★30	S	●		(13)
TRENTON TO TORONTO / HAMILTON																					
22. Robert Patrick Marina	392-2841		▲	100			5	3								GI	★30				
23. Fraser Park Marina	392-2841	Y	▲	70	20	●	10	8			▲		R	▲	PH			★30	SL	●	RS	
24. Brighton Marina and Galley	475-3611	S	▲	60	23	●	6	6		TEX	▲	30	R	▲			★20	SL	●	RS	68
25. Town of Cobourg Marina	(416) 372-3231	S	▲	130	90	●	15	15		ESS	▲		R			MGI	★20	SL			
26. Port of Newcastle Marina	987-5251	Y	▲	50	20	●	9	8		ESS	▲	25					★30	S	●	S	68/16
27. Port Darlington Marina	623-3501	Y	▲	46	30	●	10	7		SHE	▲	L	R	▲	H	I	▲30	SL	●	R	(13)
28. Port Oshawa Marina	723-3112	Y	▲	100	10	●	16	9		PLU	▲	30	R	▲	PH	●	MGI	★60	SL	●	R	68
29. Port Pickering Marina	839-2123	Y	▲	60	10	●	14	10		PC	▲	40	R	▲	PH		MGI	★30	SL	●	RS	68
30. **East Shore Marina (p. 73)**	839-5036	Y	▲	50	50	●	6	8		PC	▲	35	R	▲	PH		MI	★30	S	●	RS	68
31. Neptune Marine Services	686-1465	Y	▲	50	6		9	5				L		▲	PH		MGI	★30			S	16

To provide the most complete and accurate information, **all facilities have been contacted within the past year.** If an asterisk (*) appears, it indicates a facility which did not respond to our requests for information (these listings may not reflect current conditions). Although facility operators supplied this data, we cannot guarantee accuracy or assume responsibility for errors. Entrance and dockside soundings tend to fluctuate. Always approach marinas carefully. Reference numbers on spotting charts indicate marina locations. ⚓ Member American Boat Builders & Repairers Association.

Lake Ontario

recently been opened to the lake. A good channel leads into the bay, but the marine services cater mostly to small speedboats, and in summer, the thrashing wakes caused by these craft make anchorage untenable.

Pultneyville, 25 miles east of Rochester, is a little tricky to get into and shouldn't be attempted in a northeast blow. Submerged piers are off the creek mouth, but the channel is well buoyed, and ranges will guide you in. The harbor can be hard to identify from offshore. The Pultneyville Yacht Club is hospitable, but the harbor is crowded, and draft is limited to five feet.

Sodus Bay, a few miles farther on, is the best natural harbor on the southern coast of the lake. Except for the shallows and ruins off **Sand Point** just inside the harbor (which must be skirted by a 45-degree turn to port upon entering), the ten-square-mile bay is clear and deep throughout. Several marinas and a yacht club cluster around the attractive resort village in the northwest corner, and another marina is on the east shore. In addition, a number of good anchorages are located throughout the pretty bay.

The Sodus Bay Yacht Club, an active and well-run club, is conveniently located near the village. The village is thriving with the onset of recreational salmon fishing, boasting one of the two McDonald's "McShacks" in the United States. The McShack offers the same McDonald's menu, but offers only an outside dining area and is open seasonally. The choice of many fine restaurants, sightseeing in a resort area, and a tour of the Lighthouse Museum all provide a good excuse for a day's layover.

Little Sodus Bay, 15 miles farther on, is only two miles long by less than half a mile wide, but it has a yacht club and several marinas, most of them in the southwest corner. You can also anchor in a number of sheltered coves around the bay. **Fairhaven Beach State**

Lake Ontario	Phone	Seasonal/Year-Round	Sail/Power/Both	Largest Vessel Accommodated	No. of Transient Berths	Marked Entry Channel	Approach Depth (Reported)	Dockside Depth (Reported)	Fuel Brand	Gas/Diesel/Both	Railway/Lift Capacity (in tons)	Engine Repairs: Gas/Diesel/Both	Propeller/Hull Repairs	Launching Ramp	Marine Supplies/Groceries/Ice	LPG/CNG/Both	110V/220V/Both Max Amps	Showers/Laundromat	Pump-out Station	Restaurant/Snack Bar	Radio Watch—VHF (CB)
32. Moore Haven Wharf, Inc.	(416) 839-3681	S	▲	60			6	6	PC	▲	30		★		PH	★	MGI	★15	S	●	R	
33. Toronto Island Marina	360-1430	S	▲	60			12	12	ESS	▲	15		▲		PH		MGI	★15	SL	●	RS	68
34. Harbourfront (p. 74)	**973-4148**	S	▲	150	10	●	27	21									MGI	▲50		●	RS	68
35. Marina 4*	368-2620	S	▲	50	10	●	17										MGI	★30	S		RS	
36. Marina Quay West	364-2885	S	▲	50	25	●	25	8			8			▲	H		MGI	★30	S		RS	
37. Alexandra Yacht Club	979-7551	S	▲	40			12	8			4	YACHT CLUB						★30	S	●		
38. Ontario Place Marina	965-7676	S	▲	80	50		25	15									I	★50	SL	●	RS	
39. Port Credit Harbour Marina	274-1595	Y	▲	100	20		22	22			L	R	▲		PH		MGI	★50	SL	●	RS	
40. Harbor Marine Services	278-8166	S	▲	96	20	●	20	14	Cip	▲	35	R	▲		PH	★	MGI	★150	SL	●	R	9
41. The Store (p. 75)	**278-7005**	S					CHANDLERY										MGI					
42. Oakville Harbour	845-6601	S	▲	40	8		9	6				R				★	MGI	★15	L	●	RS	
43. Bronte Harbour	845-6601	S	▲	50	4		9	6		▲		R	★		PH	★	MGI	★15			RS	
44. Metro Marine Ltd.	827-2401	Y	▲	70	12		9	6	PC	▲	15	R	▲		PH		MGI	▲30	SL	●	RS	
45. Hamilton Harbour Marine Dockyard	525-4330	Y	▲	60			35	25	GUL	▲		R	▲		PH		MGI	★15	S			16
TO WELLAND CANAL																						
46. Fifty Point Marina	643-2103	Y	▲	65	40	●	10	10	PC	▲	15	R					MGI	★30	SL	●	RS	98
47. Foran's Marine	945-5284	S	▲	36		●	6	6	PC	★	10	R	★				MI	★30	S	●	R	
48. Dalhousie Yacht Club	934-3531	Y	▲	65	12	●	12	6	CHA	▲		R					MI	★15	SL	●	R	68
49. St. Catherine's Marina	935-5522	Y	▲	48		●	10	7	ESS	▲	25	R	▲		PH		MI	★15	S	●	S	68
EAST TO ROCHESTER																						
50. Williams Marine Service	(716) 745-7000	Y	▲	40	5	●	50	12		▲		L		★	H	●	MI	★30		●		16
51. Wilson-Tuscarore State Park*	751-6308	S	▲	40	8	●	7	7				R						★20		●		
52. Hedley Boat Co., Inc.	778-7771	Y	▲	45	3	●	6	6		★	30		★		P	▲	MI	★20	S	●	S	16
53. Braddock Bay Marina	227-1579	Y	▲	36		●	3	5	SUN	★		R	▲		PH		MI	★	S	●	RS	16
ROCHESTER TO LITTLE SODUS BAY																						
54. Pelican Bay Marina	621-6040	S	P	34	9	●			GUL	★		L	R	★			MI	★110		●	R	16
55. Rochester Yacht Club*	266-9896	Y	▲	50	2		25	6	ATL	★		L		★	PH		MGI	★15				
56. Shumway Marine	342-3030	Y	▲	90	8	●	16	10	AGW	▲	40	R	▲			●	MI	▲15	S	●	RS	16/9
57. Voyager Boat Sales	342-5150	Y	▲	55	9		20	8			10	R	★		P		GI	▲	SL		R	
58. Riverview Yacht Basin	663-0088	Y	▲	70	5		27	12	SUN	▲	20	R	▲		PH		MGI	★15	SL	●	R	
59. Sodus Bay Marina	483-9376	Y	▲	30	6		8	8		▲		R	▲		H		MGI	★	SL	●	RS	16
60. Sills Marina	483-9102	Y	▲	60			14	14	MOB	▲		L	▲		PH		MGI	★	L		RS	
61. Anchor Marine Sales ✓	(315) 483-4052			50			6	6	TEX	▲		L	▲		H		MI	★		●		
62. Arney's Marina	483-9111	S	P	33	10		15	6	MOB	★										●		
63. Chinook Harbor Marina	947-5599	Y	▲		1	●	20	5	IND	★							I	★30	S		RS	13
64. Pleasant Beach Hotel	947-5592	S	▲	80	8		12	6				HOTEL DOCKS					MGI	★30	L		R	

To provide the most complete and accurate information, **all facilities have been contacted within the past year**. If an asterisk (*) appears, it indicates a facility which did not respond to our requests for information (these listings may not reflect current conditions). Although facility operators supplied this data, we cannot guarantee accuracy or assume responsibility for errors. Entrance and dockside soundings tend to fluctuate. Always approach marinas carefully. Reference numbers on spotting charts indicate marina locations. ✓ Member American Boat Builders & Repairers Association.

Lake Ontario

Park, to port near the entrance, offers some dockage, with easy access to the beach. A current sets easterly across the entrance to the bay in high west winds. Favor the east side of the channel as you move down into the bay. Thirteen miles beyond Little Sodus Bay, you will have come full circle to **Oswego**.

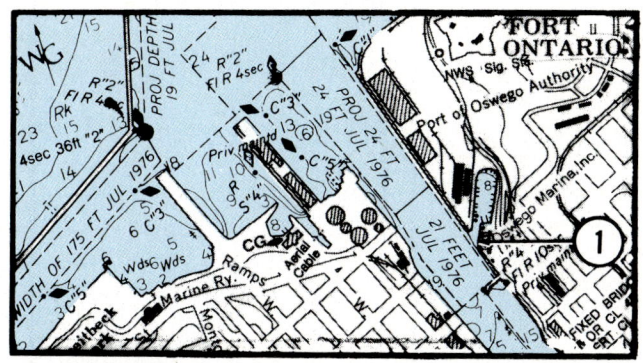

Chart 14786, edition 9

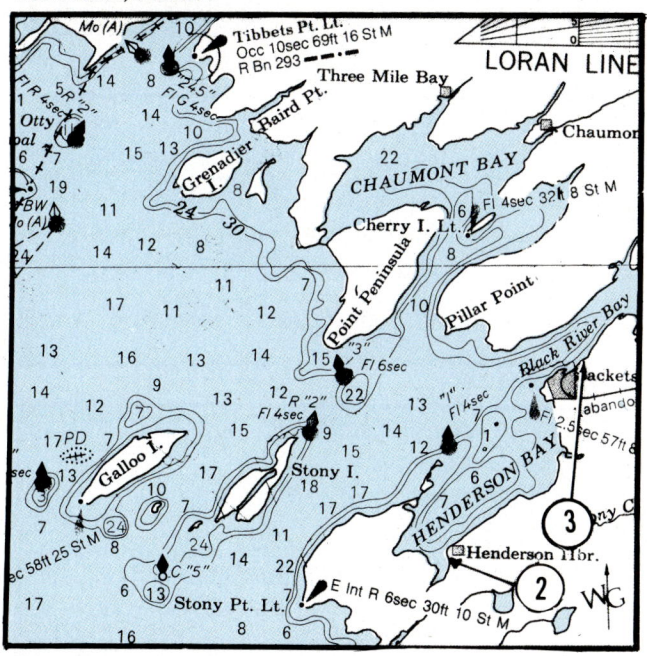

Chart 14800, edition 26

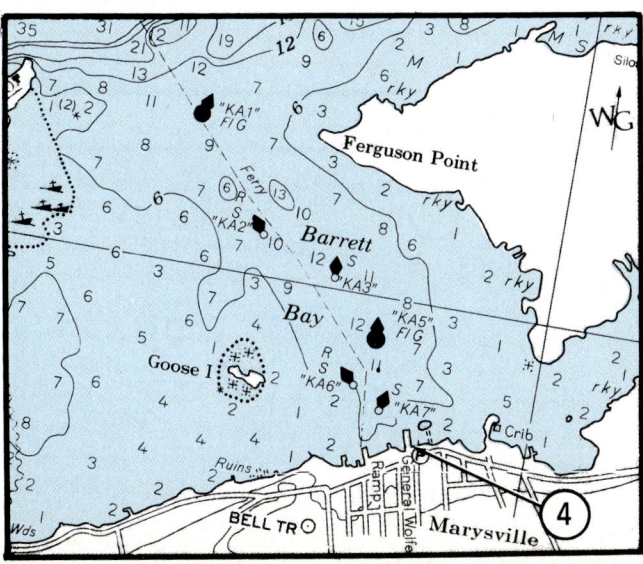

Under no circumstances are these charts to be used for navigation.

GREAT LAKES EDITION

Aids to Navigation

Unlighted buoy (C. can, N. nun, S. spar, Bell, Gong, Whistle)
Danger or junction buoy
Mooring buoy
Light (On fixed structure)
Fish trap buoy
Daybeacon (Bn)
R. Bn. radiobeacon
Mid-channel buoy
Lighted buoy

Lights (Lights are white unless otherwise indicated)
F. fixed — OBSC. obscured
Fl. flashing — WHIS. whistle
Qk. quick — DIA. diaphone
Gp. group — M. nautical miles
E. Int. equal interval — Rot. rotating
Mo.(A) morse code — SEC. sector
Occ. occulting — m. minutes
Alt. alternating — sec. seconds
I. Qk. interrupted quick

Buoys:
T.B. temporary buoy — Or. orange
C. can — R. red
N. nun — G. green
S. spar — W. white
B. black — Y. yellow

Bottom characteristics:
Cl. clay — Sh. shells — bu. blue
Co. coral — hrd. hard — gn. green
G. gravel — rky. rocky — gy. gray
Grs. grass — sft. soft — rd. red
M. mud — stk. sticky — wh. white
Rk. rock — bk. black — yl. yellow
S. sand — br. brown

Dangers:
Sunken wreck
Visible wreck
Rocks
Wreck, rock, obstruction, or shoal swept clear to the depth indicated
Rocks that cover and uncover, with heights in feet above datum of soundings
AERO. aeronautical — D.F.S. distance finding station
Bn. daybeacon
R. Bn. radiobeacon — AUTH. authorized
R. TR. radio tower — Obstr. obstruction
C.G. Coast Guard Station — P.A. position approximate
E.D. existence doubtful

Caution:
Mariners are warned to stay clear of the protective riprap surrounding navigational light structures shown thus.
Restricted Areas
Fish Trap Areas

Lake Ontario

Chart 14768, edition 16

Canadian Chart 2005

Canadian Chart 2006

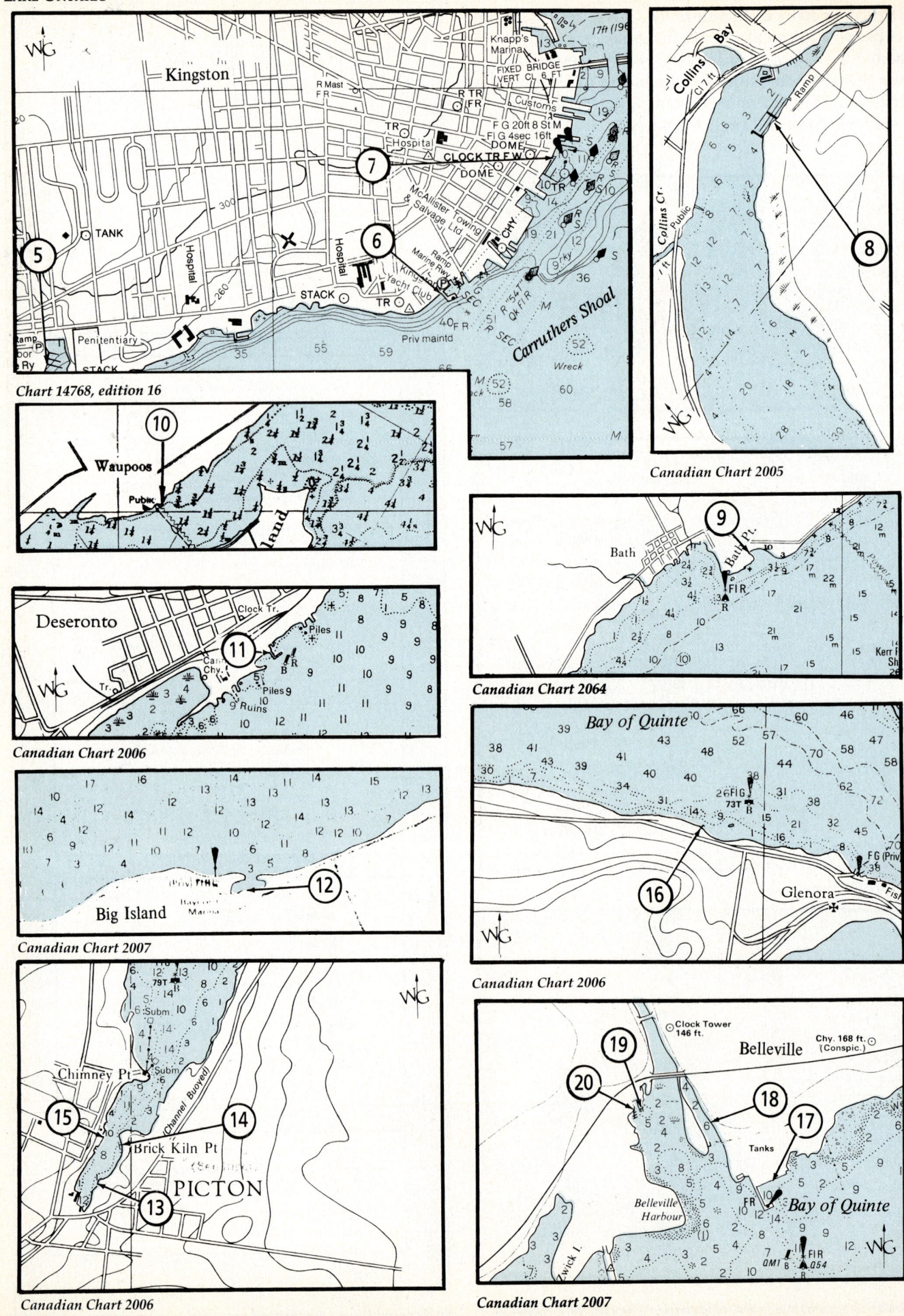

Canadian Chart 2064

Canadian Chart 2007

Canadian Chart 2006

Canadian Chart 2006

Canadian Chart 2007

82　　　*Under no circumstances are these charts to be used for navigation.*　　　WATERWAY GUIDE / 1991

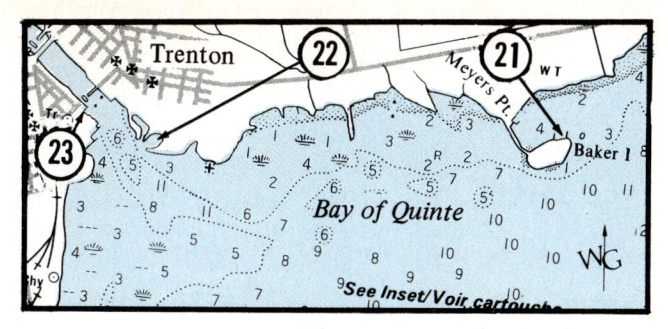

Lake Ontario

Canadian Chart 2069

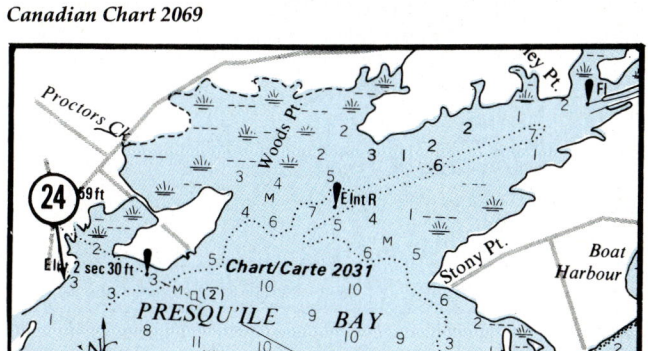

Canadian Chart 2069

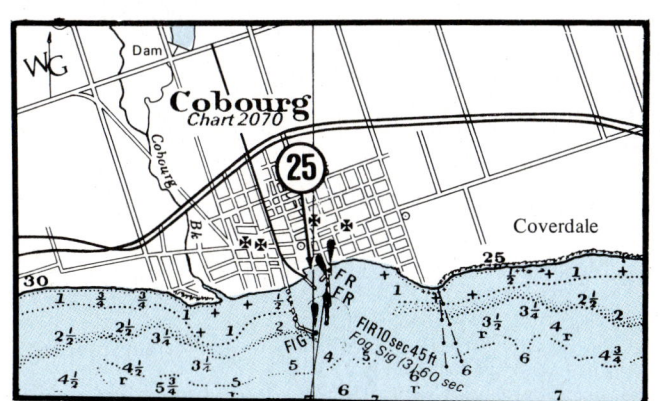

Canadian Chart 2058

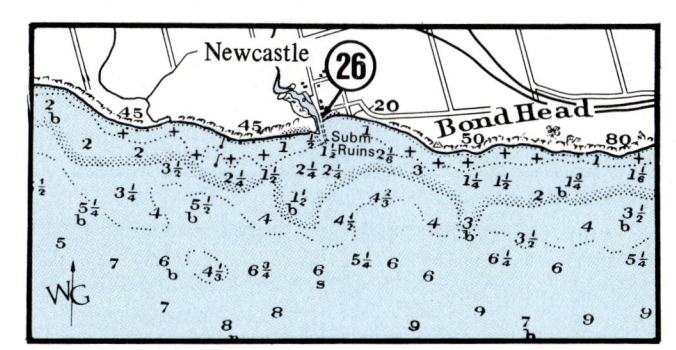

Canadian Chart 2058

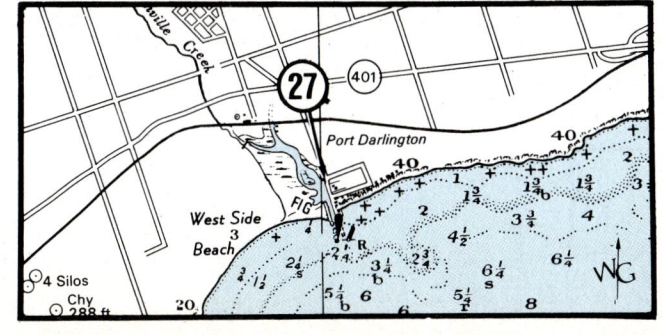

Canadian Chart 2058

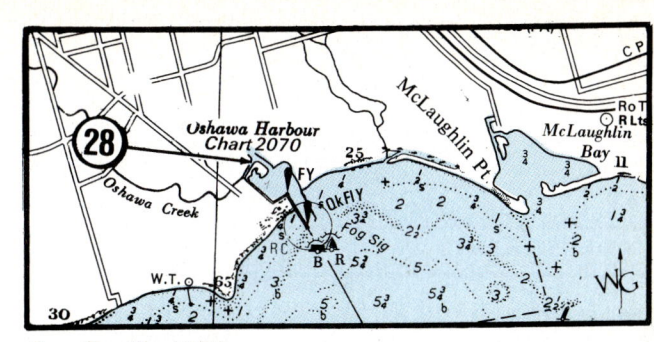

Canadian Chart 2058

Canadian Chart 2062

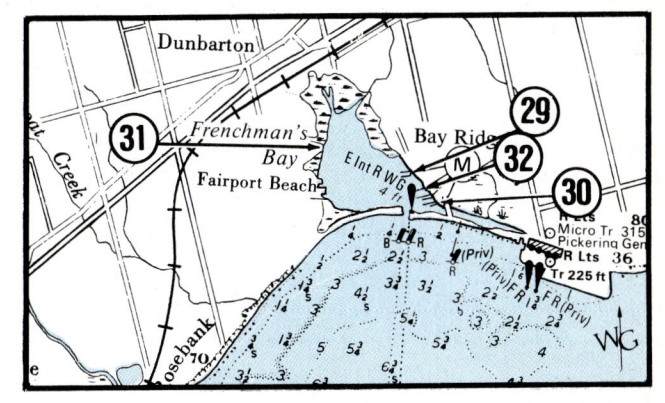

Canadian Chart 2062

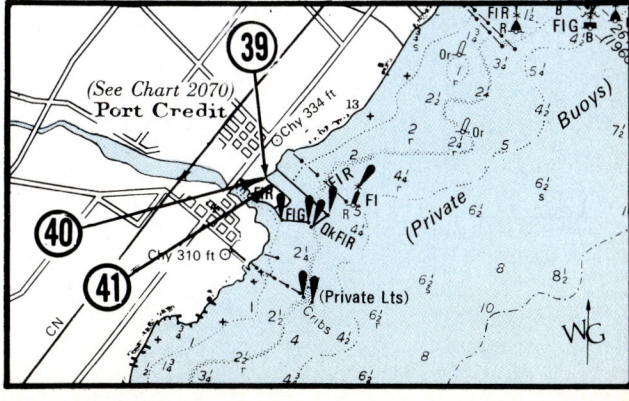

Canadian Chart 2063

GREAT LAKES EDITION — *Under no circumstances are these charts to be used for navigation.*

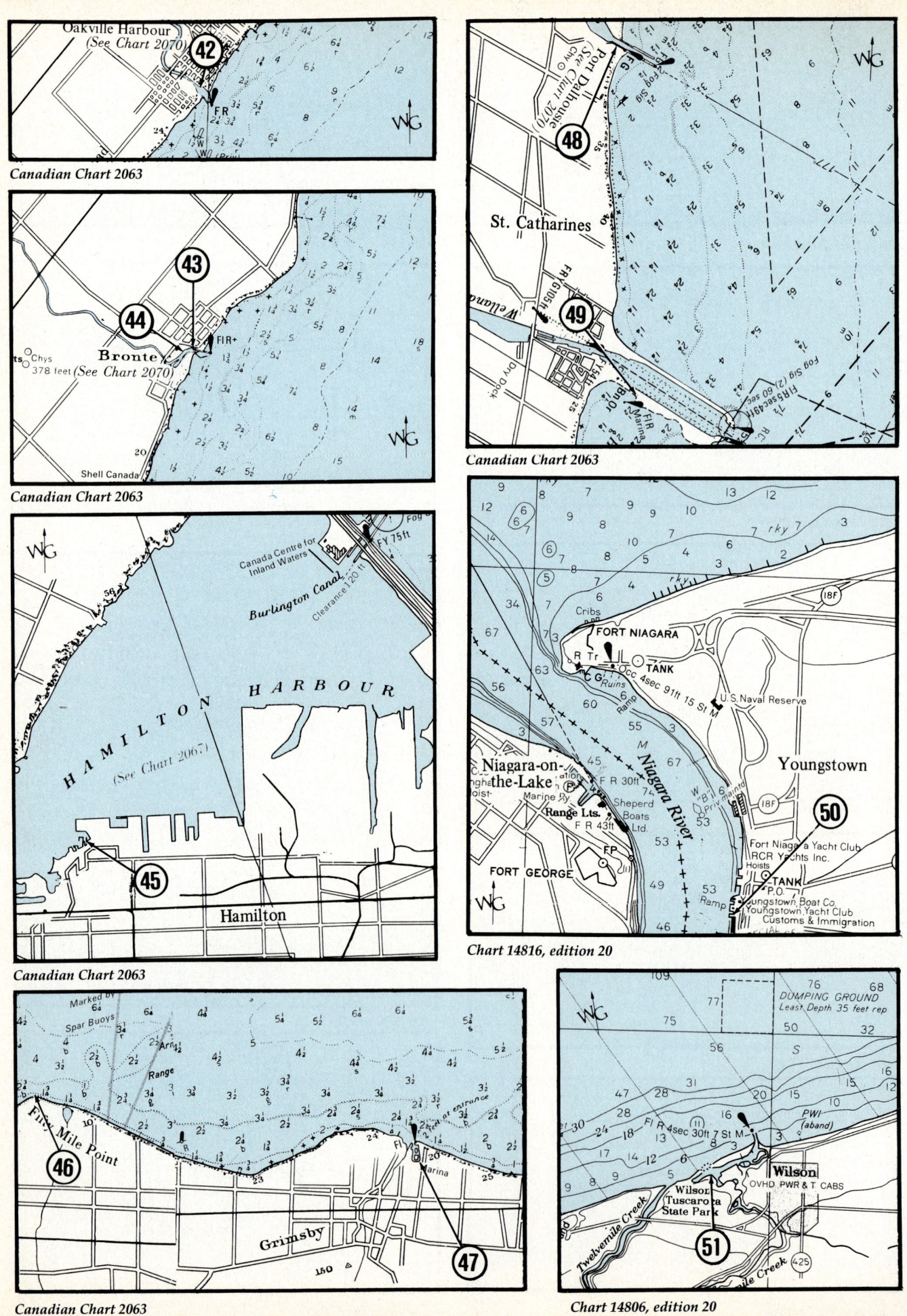

Lake Ontario

Canadian Chart 2063

Canadian Chart 2063

Canadian Chart 2063

Canadian Chart 2063

Canadian Chart 2063

Chart 14816, edition 20

Chart 14806, edition 20

84   *Under no circumstances are these charts to be used for navigation.*   Waterway Guide / 1991

LAKE ONTARIO

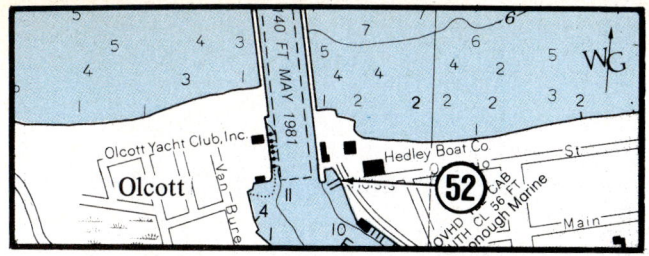

Chart 14806, edition 21

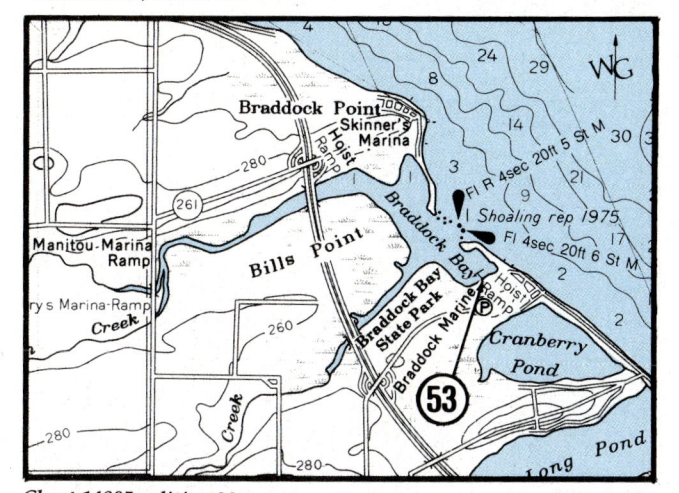

Chart 14805, edition 20

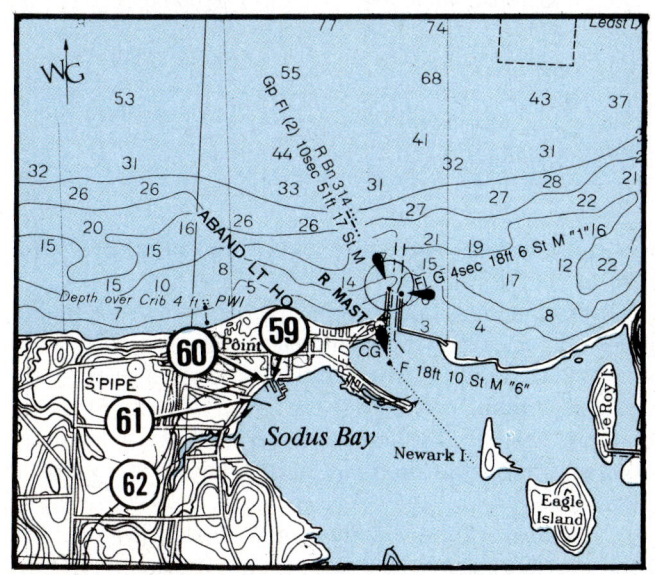

Chart 14804, edition 21

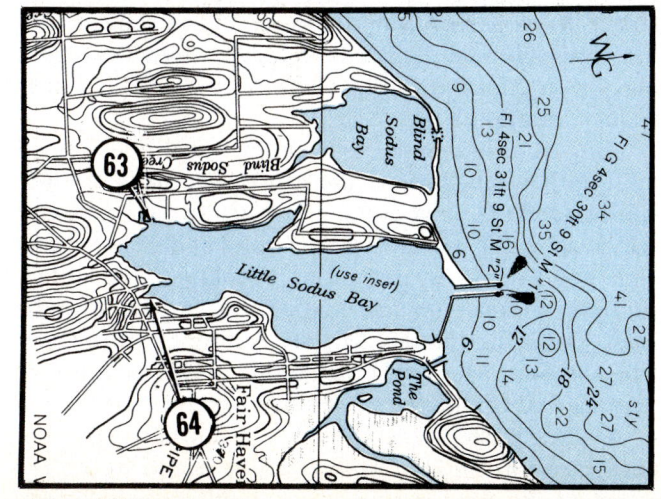

Chart 14803, edition 23

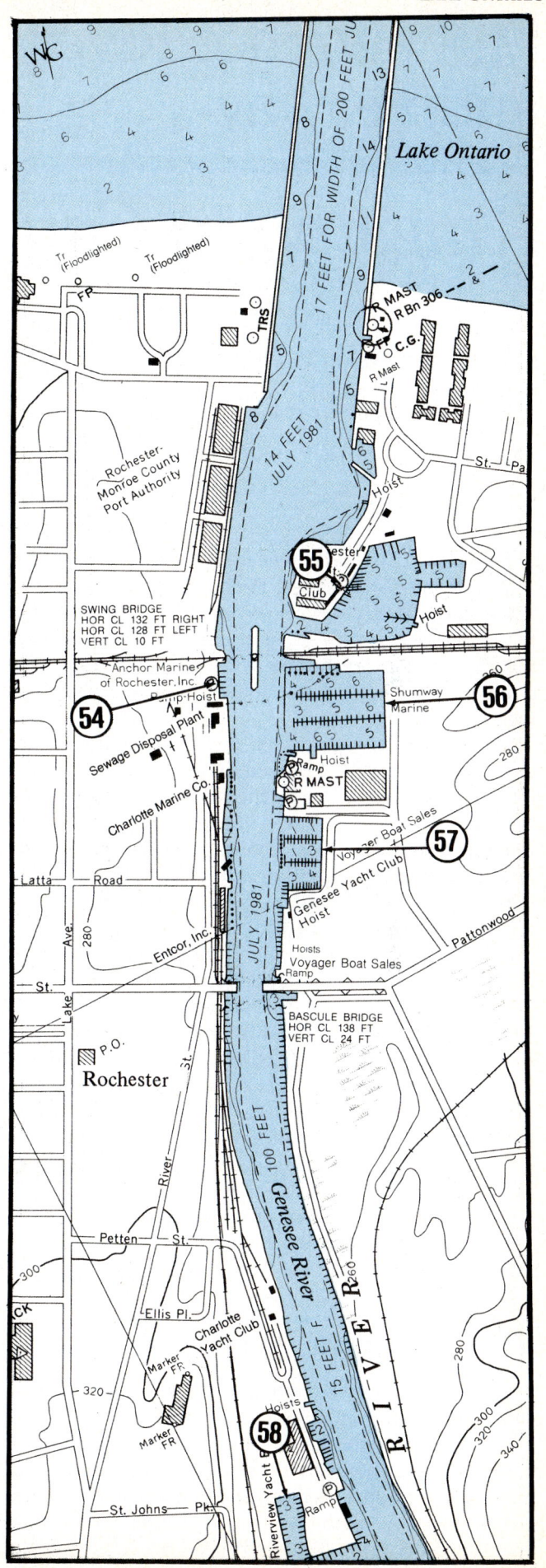

Chart 14815, edition 20

GREAT LAKES EDITION   *Under no circumstances are these charts to be used for navigation.*   85

St. Lawrence River and Seaway

Kingston to Cap Gaspé

CHARTS: 14802, 14761 through 14774; Canadian: 1338, 1339, 1340, 1352, 1400, 1409, 1410, 1411, 1412, 1413, 1414, 1415, 1416, 1417, 1418, 1419, 1420, 1421.

The St. Lawrence River is the only natural outlet for the Great Lakes. Discharging at the rate of 234,000 cubic feet per second, it is no wonder that the St. Lawrence runs in swift currents. Furthermore, the river must drop the lake waters 246 feet from Lake Ontario to sea level. Until tamed by canals, its rapids were legendary.

The first canals were built in the late 18th century and were gradually improved and expanded over the following 175 years. During the 1950s, the St. Lawrence Seaway, a massive engineering project shared by the United States and Canada, reduced the number of locks and canals to seven, created a large new lake, and opened the heart of the continent to ocean vessels. After it began operation in 1959, the smaller ports along the river lost most of their commerce, but the major lakeside cities of the interior became world ports.

For practical purposes, Montreal is considered sea level, although the river continues to drop a few feet thereafter, and that is where the Seaway officially begins. Between Montreal and Quebec, the river banks are alternately industrial and agricultural, while below Quebec they take on another quality. Most rivers are wild and rural in the upper reaches, becoming more urban and industrial the closer they get to the ocean. By contrast, the St. Lawrence's dramatic scenery begins at Quebec, and the closer it gets to the sea, the smaller the villages and the wilder the landscape.

The Thousand Islands

The St. Lawrence River begins at the **Thousand Islands**. Actually numbering 1,800, they fill an area 15 miles wide at the Lake Ontario end, tapering to five miles over a downstream distance of about 50 miles. Because these islands were once mountain peaks, water depths between them can change abruptly from more than 50 feet to zero. Deep-draft boats are limited in the passages and islands they can negotiate, but for shallow-draft vessels, the entire area is a gunkholer's paradise.

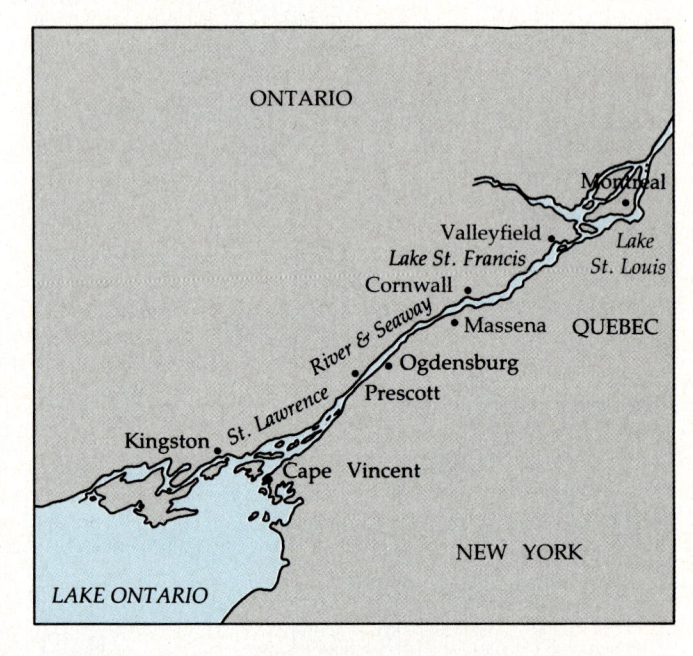

Full of secluded anchorages, passages through mazes of islands, and twisting channels — some too narrow for you to pass another boat — the area is nonetheless well-charted. Bass, pike, pickerel, perch, and muskie abound. The islands themselves range from tiny granite outcroppings to forested land large enough to support a village.

Two-thirds of the islands lie in Canadian waters. The best way to cruise is to crisscross the international border, visiting the most interesting sites on each side. A practical way for cruising mariners to see some of the less accessible islands is to take a sightseeing boat from Clayton or Alexandria Bay, New York, or from Gananoque, Ontario.

Long-term settlement as a summer resort has placed most of the islands in private hands, but many of them are included in one or another of the national, state, and provincial parks that border both sides of the river. Most have good docks, water, stone fireplaces, and in late summer, blueberries and raspberries to pick. **Beaurivage, Cedar, Endymion, Milton, Aubrey** (Burnt), **Camelot, Gordon, Mermaid, McDonald** and **Stovin** are so popular that finding space can be a real problem.

A cruise through the Thousand Islands begins either north or south of 16-mile-long Wolfe Island in the entrance to the St. Lawrence. The southern route starts from Cape Vincent, New York, on the main Seaway channel running between the U.S. mainland and Wolfe Island. The northern route from Kingston, Ontario, follows the Canadian Middle Channel, and is less busy but also less well marked. WATERWAY GUIDE coverage begins on the Canadian side.

Kingston/Canadian Shore

At Kingston, the route begins south of **Cedar Island**. (See the ''Lake Ontario'' chapter for the details on Kingston Harbor.) The red flashing light at the southwest end of Cedar Island starts you toward well-buoyed **Canadian Middle Channel**. Five miles ahead, **The Spectacles** are marked by another red flashing light, and Canadian Middle Channel goes off to starboard, south of **Howe Island**. The more popular, sheltered ten-mile **Bateau Channel** (to port) leads to the resort town of **Gananoque**. Caution should be observed near Grog Island Light—the channel is ill-defined.

Gananoque can also be reached from Canadian Middle Channel through the Admiralty Islands ten miles east of the Spectacles; or, if you turn sharply through Wolfe Island Cut at this point, you can pass into the main Seaway channel in U.S. waters.

Gananoque. Once an important mill town, **Gananoque** is the commercial and tourist center for the Canadian Thousand Islands. The town, with many historic buildings, offers good shopping and restaurants, as well as a recently-built municipal marina. The Thousand Islands Playhouse draws audiences all summer long. Located in the old Gananoque Canoe Club on the waterfront, the theater provides free overnight dockage for ticket holders.

Admiralty, Lake Fleet, and Navy Islands. Captain William Fitzwilliam Owen made the original marine survey here and named the **Navy Islands** for his buddies in the War of 1812, the **Lake Fleet** for their ships, and the **Admiralty** for the big brass. The Thousand Islands scenery really begins with the Admiralty Islands—granite outcrops with steep faces and woods in between. **Aubrey, Mermaid, Beaurivage**, and **McDonald** are all units of the park system and have docks. Designated anchorage is also available off Aubrey and Beaurivage. Another popular anchorage is off **Leek Island**'s south shore, with a sandy beach on its northeast side.

Next along Canadian Middle Channel, the Lake Fleet Islands, close to the international border, offer coves for anchorage, good fishing, and swimming. **Camelot** and **Endymion** are park islands with public docks and designated anchorages. Just east of Endymion is a New York State park at Canoe Point on **Grindstone Island**.

The Navy Islands present fewer anchoring possibilities than the others. **Mulcaster Island** is a good base here. Just across the channel and the border from them, New York's Wellesley Island State Park has marine facilities, pump-out service, and a picnic area and snack bar. Watterson Point State Park, farther east on Wellesley Island, has a long, well-protected public dock.

Ivy Lea to Mallorytown Landing. Within view of the **Thousand Islands Bridge**, a route leads to port into **Ivy Lea**, with marine facilities, fuel, and supplies. The steep river banks and the group of islands near Ivy Lea are spectacular, presenting interesting navigation through the narrow channels bordered by high granite and wooded hills. The main route continues east under the 120-foot Canadian span of the Thousand Islands Bridge to the resort of **Rockport**, which has full-service marinas and a park with barbecue grills and a panoramic view of the river.

Outside Rockport, Canadian Middle Channel continues eastward to **Ironsides Shoal**, where it joins the main Seaway channel. An alternate buoyed channel to port offers an interesting side trip to **Mallorytown Landing**. This route, between **Tar** and **Grenadier** islands, leads through shallows and reedy flats and offers great fishing in the summer season and duck hunting in the fall.

Mallorytown Landing, headquarters of the St. Lawrence Islands National Park and accessible only to shallow-draft boats, has campgrounds and a beach with lifeguards. The best swimming is after July 1, when the water has warmed up. From Mallorytown Landing, a buoyed channel past the islands and shoals joins the main Seaway channel near **Chippewa Bay**, on the U.S. side.

Cape Vincent/U.S. Shore

The southern U.S. channel around Wolfe Island begins at Tibbetts Point. This is the Seaway ship channel, where you must be on the lookout for freighters from the Great Lakes and all over the world. The village of **Cape Vincent**, located at the junction of the St. Lawrence River and Lake Ontario, is small but active. The convenience of a complete market, liquor store, and restaurants, plus the quaintness of the village, have made Cape Vincent a popular and crowded stopover for cruisers. The free town dock and the Department of Environmental Conservation dock can host as many as two dozen boats (rafting included) on a summer weekend. **Anchoring** behind the breakwater wall provides more solitude and offers good swimming. Anchor Marina is a full-service marina with space for transients, and Precision Marine specializes in engine and prop repairs.

A mile out of Cape Vincent harbor, the international border and the channel both swing northward of **Carelton Island** where you can see the ruins of Fort Haldimand. A Revolutionary War supply base for the British, the fort was captured by the Americans in the War of 1812. Nearby **Bayfield Island** and **Bayfield Bay** have good bass fishing.

On the south side of Carelton Island, a channel leads to Burnham Point State Park, **Millen Bay**, and Cedar

HUTCHINSON'S BOAT WORKS, INC.

Custom Alterations, Restoration & Repair

Brokerage • Covered Slips

Dry Land Marina • Storage
Travelift • Marine Railway
Machine Shop • Welding Shop
Upholstery Shop
Wood Working Shop
Wheel Reconditioning

DEALERS FOR

Sea Ray®

OMC
Mercruiser
Chrysler Marine Engines

MARINE STORE
Complete stock of boating supplies & equipment at Holland Street Boat Basin.

USED & BROKERAGE SALES
An Outstanding Selection
Write or Phone for Listings.

CUSTOMER SERVICES

Pump-Out Station
2200 feet of dock space for transient boats
Water and electricity at every dock
Showers and laundry facilities
Mail service and ice deliveries
Paved parking • Telephones on the docks
Four locations for gasoline and diesel service
Dock attendants on duty 16 hours per day 7 days a week

Phone 315-482-9931
HOLLAND STREET, ALEXANDRIA BAY, N.Y. 13607

Point State Park, which offers a refreshment stand and a pleasant beach.

Clayton. Between Wolfe and Grindstone islands, Wolfe Island Cut, the route from Gananoque and Canadian Middle Channel, makes into the main Seaway channel. From here, it's three straight miles to **Clayton**. In August, Clayton features an antique boat show that draws visitors from all over the country. Year-round, the Shipyard Museum exhibits ancient craft from Indian dugouts to St. Lawrence skiffs, and the Thousand Islands Museum displays the history of the area. Clayton has two village docks. One, on the river, provides free two-hour dockage. The other, in the bay west of town, offers overnight dockage for a nominal fee. All services are available in town.

Wellesley Island. The channel east from Clayton roughly parallels the U.S. mainland, goes north of **Round** and **Little Round** islands, and then threads through **Upper Narrows** (188 feet in spots) between **Wellesley Island** and the mainland.

The high-level Thousand Islands Bridge crosses from the U.S. mainland to Wellesley Island, Hill Island, and to the Canadian shore near Ivy Lea.

Alexandria Bay. Beyond the bridge are weedy **Swan Bay**, Keewaydin State Park, and the resort town of **Alexandria Bay**. When entering, watch the chart and buoyage. The ship channel is 150 feet deep, but channel areas are spotted with shoals and rocks.

Alexandria Bay, a summer community and famous boating port, has marine facilities, all services, repairs, restaurants, scenic beauty, and protected waters. The large and often crowded village dock provides free tie-up with a four-hour limit. You'll have ample opportunity in this time to tour the town and survey the opulence of the new Riveredge Resort and Hotel.

The summer homes, built in the early decades of the century, are palatial. The most famous one is the never-finished Boldt Castle, a turreted fortress on **Heart Island**. The chairman of the board of New York's Wal-

THE FOOD AND FUN SPOT
IN THE THOUSAND ISLANDS

Cavallario's
Seafood &
Steak House

AAA APPROVED
BOATERS'
HEADQUARTERS
IN
ALEXANDRIA BAY

OPEN 7 DAYS PER WEEK
April to October 31st
Lounge Noon -- 1:00 A.M.
Dining Room 4:30 -- 11:00 P.M.
Sunday Noon -- 10:00 P.M.

CALL 315/482-9867 FOR COURTESY CAR

Riveredge RESORT HOTEL

ALL NEW

A STAR HAS RISEN

WELCOME - COMPLETE TRANSIENT DOCKAGE FACILITIES

17 HOLLAND ST., ALEXANDRIA BAY, N.Y. 13607 (315) 482-9917

+ TURN AT CHANNEL MARKER 190 +
+ MONITORING CH 16 +
1-800-ENJOY US

- FULL ELECTRICITY
- COMPLETE SHOWER FACILITIES
- LAUNDRY
- CABLE T.V.
- PHONES
- WATER SUPPLY
- ICE
- LAUNCHING FACILITIES

- WINDOWS ON THE BAY MAIN DINING ROOM PANCAKE HOUSE
- STEAK & SEAFOOD
- JACQUES CARTIER FINE DINING
- OUTDOOR POOL & SPA
- SAUNA
- INDOOR POOL & SPA
- 122 LUXURIOUS ROOMS

DOCK AND SECURITY ATTENDANTS

ST. LAWRENCE SEAWAY

dorf-Astoria Hotel designed the castle for his wife, but lost heart for the project when she died midway through construction. Boat excursions run daily to the castle from Alexandria Bay and from Gananoque, and the house may be toured for a small fee; docking for private yachts is limited to short periods by permission only.

The Channels Join

Eastward of Alexandria Bay, the main Seaway channel runs along islands named Fairyland, Deer, Summerland, and Mary (a state park), and past **Goose Bay**, which is shallow but good for dinghy exploring.

East of Goose Bay, Canadian Middle Channel and the Seaway channel join and run together between **Grenadier Island** and its shallow, weedy, muskie-filled bays to port, and **Chippewa Bay**, also muskie territory, to starboard. Many islands dot both shores, but the channel is clearly identified with markers and flashing lights. Beyond Chippewa Bay, the river narrows, the channel zigzags across the international border, and the islands thin out. At Jacques Cartier State Park, which has a dock and refreshment stand but no fuel, the river is again briefly dotted with islands and shoals and warrants careful attention while navigating.

Brockville. At **Brockville** on the Ontario side, you see the last of the Thousand Islands granite-and-woods scenery. The historic old city, founded in 1784 by United Empire Loyalists, has an impressive courthouse square. Along with its boating services, Brockville boasts many cultural offerings ranging from historic architecture through international theater, open-air waterfront demonstrations and exhibits, restaurants and night spots, to a wide variety of sporting activities. Several good anchorages are located throughout the islands that make up the Brockville Narrows. Just east of the city, the Three Sisters Islands are sites of one of the largest ring gull colonies on the Great Lakes.

Brockville/Morristown to Montreal. This is the business stretch of the river. On both shores are historic industrial and commercial towns, and this is where the drastic Seaway alterations took place. All seven of the locks occur between Ogdensburg and Montreal.

Ogdensburg/Prescott to Red Mills. Ogdensburg, the oldest settlement in New York State and now a port of entry, was first settled by the French; taken by the British in 1760, it was ceded to the United States after the Revolution. Here you will find the **Remington Art Memorial**, with Frederick Remington paintings, bronzes, and sketches of the Old West. During the last week in July, Ogdensburg celebrates the Seaway Festival with eight days of parades, band competitions, boat races, and fireworks. A new municipal marina is located in the waterfront park.

Prescott, on the Canadian side, has a new first-class marina, offering all amenities. Near the bridge that links it to Ogdensburg, you see giant grain elevators, reminders of a time when Prescott and Ogdensburg were terminals of the old pre-Seaway canal system. Ships brought grain to these elevators for transfer to small "canallers" that carried their cargo to Montreal. The **Galop Canal**, below Prescott, carried canal boats around the St. Lawrence rapids, a 12-mile trip now eliminated by the single Seaway lock at Iroquois.

Five miles downstream from the bridge on the Canadian side is **Cardinal**, whose special aroma comes from a starch plant. One of the locks of the old Galop Canal is behind the town. On the south side of Galop Island, in a channel created by the Seaway flooding, is **Red Mills**, which offers dockage, groceries, and supplies.

Iroquois Lock. Five miles past Cardinal is the first Seaway lock at half-mile-long **Iroquois Dam**. The lock has a drop ranging from one to six feet.

Cruising boats lock through, awaiting clearance at the marked pleasure-boat dock. After the gates open, you may be waved through without having to tie up. A clipboard on the end of a pole will come down for your line-handling charge.

Beyond the lock the main route follows the international border in midstream to **Ogden Island**. Here the Seaway channel carries north of the island, while Little River leads south to **Waddington**, New York. **Waddington** provides a town dock that is only a few hundred feet from the center of town. Complete provisioning, banking, laundry, and restaurants make this upstate New York village a good layover spot.

Wiley-Dondero Canal. Ogden Island marks the beginning of another island-studded stretch of the river, leading to Lake St. Lawrence. At the entrance to the ten-mile-long Wiley-Dondero Canal, boats can pass into the lake alongside **Croil Island**.

On the Canadian shore, the typical old river town of **Long Sault** offers boat facilities. **Barnhart Island**, in U.S. territory, is mostly given over to Robert Moses State Park.

The Wiley-Dondero Canal, named for the congressmen who sponsored the Seaway Act, is entirely in U.S. territory, and includes the two American locks, Eisenhower and Snell. No stopping is permitted in the three-mile stretch of canal between them, and boats must keep the order of progression. Throughout the Seaway, of course, commercial vessels take precedence over pleasure craft.

At Marker 47, a sign directs pleasure craft to call Seaway Eisenhower. Directions may not require you to tie up at the pleasure craft docks. A similar sign at the Cornwall Bridge is two miles before the Snell Lock.

Cornwall, an industrial city on the Canadian shore, offers some boat facilities. It can be reached from the channel around either end of Cornwall Island.

Lake St. Francis. Where the Seaway channel passes between Cornwall and St. Regis Islands, the St. Lawrence River departs U.S. territory. (You may have noticed that U.S. weather broadcasts predict only as far as "St. Lawrence above St. Regis.")

Here you must switch to Canadian charts; 1413 is the first one. The lake is a 27-mile stretch of the St. Lawrence created by the two control dams that eliminated the **Soulange Rapids** and the old canal around them. Lake St. Francis offers services, mostly on the north shore at **Glen Walter** and **Summerstown**. **Lancaster** and **Blainsville** have fuel stations, as do **Pointe au Cedre** and **Pointe Anicet**. The Ontario-Quebec border passes through the eastern end of **Lake St. Francis**. From here until it reaches the Atlantic Ocean, the St. Lawrence River lies entirely within the Province of Quebec.

Past Blainsville, both shores are in Quebec. The Seaway route through the lake zigzags to maintain its 27-foot depths for big ships. The western end of the lake is very shallow outside the channel, but at the eastern end, pleasure craft can run a straighter track, avoiding the few shoals.

Salaberry-de-Valleyfield to Montreal. Salaberry-de-Valleyfield, at the east end of the lake, is a boating center and a good stopover, particularly when it's too late in the day to run farther. The Valleyfield Yacht Club no longer has berths for visitors and uses the adjacent marina for its guests. Recent summer rates were $1.00 per foot (Canadian) for overnight dockage. A good (though weedy) anchorage is behind Point aux Chats and the causeway on the west side of the harbor.

Beyond Salaberry-de-Valleyfield, the Seaway route enters the 15-mile **Beauharnois Canal** with no place to stop. Note that **Porte de Valleyfield**, just inside the canal entrance, does not allow small craft to tie up.

Montreal

Canada's second largest city, the second largest French-speaking city in the world and a major seaport, **Montreal** sits on a large island with an abrupt mountain in the middle that gives the city its name. Offering commercial, cultural, and entertainment amenities with an international flavor, Montreal is worth an extended visit. Be sure to visit Old Montreal, now restored and featuring an exciting night life. Ride a *caleche* to the top of Mount Royal for a fine view. In between are museums, galleries, historic monuments, theaters, sporting events, shops and restaurants.

At **Lac St. Louis** are located almost all of the city's yacht clubs and marinas. It is suburban, so you will have to find transportation downtown, either by bus, commuter train, or rental car. Lac St. Louis is shallow; follow the channels carefully as you make your way to the north shore facilities. North of **Ile Perrot**, the **Ottawa River**, which also offers marinas, flows into the lake. Boats transiting the Golden Triangle, via the **Rideau Canal** and the Ottawa River, enter this way.

South Shore Canal. The Seaway leaves the lake via

Pets On Board

Some dog breeds such as retrievers and spaniels take to boating readily. Poodles, beagles, and dachshunds seem to be natural sailors. In general, short-haired breeds seem to do better than those with long hair, and most puppies can usually acclimate themselves to the water. Old dogs who have a violent dislike of the water should not be forced to go along with you on a boat.

If your dog goes swimming in salt water, wash him off with fresh water at least once a day, dry him well, and keep him away from drafts. Salt water, if left on the dog, can cause skin problems.

Some pets will drink excessive amounts of salt water, causing them to become nauseated. Give your pet a small amount of Pepto-Bismol (check with your veterinarian) and don't feed him for a little while. Fresh water should be available to him at all times; renew it four or five times a day, if necessary, to make sure that it is fresh and pure. Avoid too much ice water, though, because it can lead to diarrhea.

Dogs need plenty of exercise ashore three or four times a day. Make sure you allow at least an hour each day for your pet's exercise. Dogs find it necessary to relieve themselves with regularity, and you should provide scheduled times for this purpose. Most of them prefer to have this opportunity after they have eaten, so a good walk following the evening meal is recommended.

Don't allow your pet on deck when coming in alongside a pier or another boat. Most dogs regard the boat as family property to be guarded and may try to bite anyone who reaches aboard to take a line or steps aboard for any reason. You may also trip easily over a dog or cat moving about on deck.

Don't go ashore at night and leave a noisy dog in the cabin, and don't allow your dog to run loose in a marina.

Cats make excellent cruising companions. They do not need trips ashore for exercise, and an on-board litter pan serves them very well. And although their dislike of water is well known, cats are able swimmers—you need not fear that your cat will sink like a rock should she fall overboard.

From *Boatman's Handbook* by Tom Bottomley.
Copyright © 1988. Reproduced by permission of Hearst Marine Books, an affiliate of William Morrow & Co., Inc., 105 Madison Ave., New York, NY 10016.

the **South Shore Canal**, paralleling the Lachine Rapids, about 11 miles from the entrance at Beauharnois. It's seven miles, past the Caughnawaga Indian Reserve community, to the first lock at **Cote St. Catherine** (drop 30 feet). Another ten miles of canal, busy with tankers and freighters, leads to the last lock, **St. Lambert**, which drops your boat 13 to 20 feet.

The Down River Suburbs. Beyond St. Lambert Lock, the **Montreal** skyline rises over the river from the north shore. A little farther on, the commercial wharves and grain elevators extend for several miles.

At **Longueuil**, on the east bank (the river flows almost due north at this point) are two marinas within a 15-minute walk of the superb Metro system that takes you into downtown Montreal. The St. Helens Marina

ST. LAWRENCE SEAWAY

(at Expo) is probably not open and is a long walk from the Metro station. Another marina and anchorage is located a few miles downstream at **Boucherville**.

At the north end of **Montreal Island** (although it is known to Montrealers as the East End), **Point-aux-Trembles** has a yacht club, and there is a full-service boat yard at **Repentigny**.

Montreal to Quebec City

The 150 miles between **Montreal** and **Quebec City** holds the heart of urban Quebec. Between the cities and towns are rural stretches, old-fashioned villages, and a lake rich with wildlife. From Sorel on, you must follow the ship channel, which has plenty of width for passing, as mud flats and sand bars encroach on the river from both banks.

Sorel. Below Montreal, the ship channel follows the east shore to Sorel, but you'll find an alternative small-craft channel on the west side of the islands. The channels join a few miles above Sorel, 50 miles from Montreal, where the river turns easterly again.

Although it is an industrial city, Sorel is important to yachtsmen. Entrance is made here to the **Richelieu River**, which leads via the **Chambly Canal** to **Lake Champlain**. The Richelieu offers marinas (see the Lake Champlain chapter for details), and beyond the mouth of the Richelieu on the St. Lawrence is a marina built by the province, with an inn and a restaurant next door. Shallow **Lac St. Pierre**, below Sorel, is good for bird-watching, but no anchorage suitable for strangers is available.

Trois Rivieres, about 35 miles from Sorel, is an industrial city on the north shore. A marina on **Ile St. Quentin** in the mouth of the **Maurice River** is far from the city, and a paper mill is nearby—but you don't have many alternatives when passage up and down the river must be timed with tidal flows.

Deschaillons is an alternative to Trois Rivieres if your boat can travel the 55 nautical miles from Sorel on one tide. A well-protected new marina has opened here. The narrow opening in the breakwater is on the downstream side. The current runs swiftly at this point, so if you pass it by, it will take you a while to struggle back upstream to the entrance. The south bank village is typical of Quebec.

Neuville, 50 miles below Trois Rivieres and 30 miles from Deschaillons, is another village on the north shore. Its manmade harbor is the next one downstream with a pleasure boat marina. Because it is only 18 miles from Quebec, you may wish to make the run all the way from either Trois Rivieres or Deschaillons.

Quebec City

Although the land begins to rise at Trois Rivieres, the real St. Lawrence scenery begins at Quebec. The river contracts to its narrowest (less than a mile across) under steep cliffs, where Samuel de Champlain established his "habitation" in 1608. The capital of New France for the next 150 years, Quebec City remains the capital of the Province of Quebec.

Two docking choices are available for visiting boats: the yacht club at suburban **Sillery** and the marina at **Bassin Louise** downtown in the Old City. Both offer full services, but the latter, with all the major points of interest within walking distance, is preferable for sight-

Distances
Approximate Statute Miles

Location	Between Points	Cumulative	Location	Between Points	Cumulative
From Kingston, Ont.			Lower Beauharnois Lock	1	168
Gananoque, Ont.	17	17	South Shore Canel Ent.	11	179
Ivy Lea, Ont.	9	26	Côte Ste. Catherine Lock	9	188
Rockport, Ont.	2	28	Côte St. Lambert Lock	9	197
Ironsides Island	4	32	Montréal, Ste. Hélène Is.	1	198
			Sorel, Richelieu River	41	239
From Cape Vincent, NY			Three Rivers, Qué.	30	269
Clayton, NY	15	15	Québec, Qué.	66	335
Alexandria Bay, NY	12	27	Ile aux Coudres	52	387
Ironsides Island	5	32			
			North Shore		
From Ironsides Island			Cap a L'Aigle	20	407
Brockville/Morristown	18	50	Tadoussac	41	448
Prescott, Ont.	9	59	Baie Comeau	100	548
Ogdensburg, NY	2	61	Sept Iles	100	648
Iroquois Lock, Ont.	13	74			
Morrisburg/Waddington	7	81			
Crysler Memorial Park	6	87	**South Shore**		
Eisenhower Lock, NY	17	104	Riviere du Loup	44	431
Snell Lock, NY	3	107	Rimouski	57	488
Cornwall, Ont.	4	111	Matane	43	531
Valleyfield, Qué.	41	152	Cape Gaspe	150	681
Upper Beauharnois Lock	15	167			

seeing. A vast man-made, formerly commercial harbor, Bassin Louise is entered through a lock that operates on the half-hour. There is a convenient floating dock for tie-up if it is necessary to wait.

The narrow lanes of Quebec's Old City are bordered by ancient stone houses and shops. A funicular carries you up the steep cliffside to another section of the Old City at the top, including the Chateau Frontenac and Dufferin Terrace. Beyond this well-preserved section is the newest part of modern Quebec. Shops, restaurants, art galleries, historical sites and museums, carriage sightseeing tours, summer events, and night life make Quebec a good place for an extended visit.

The Lower St. Lawrence

The last 350 miles of the St. Lawrence River is a continuous panorama of mountains, quaint villages and a few larger towns, farms along the riverbanks, and forests rising to steep heights. The river itself is studded with islands, midstream tidal flats, and shoaling shores for the first 200 miles below Quebec. Most of the town and village wharves visible along this route reportedly dry out at high tide as their access channels do, so they are not available to cruising boats. It's wise for strangers to keep to the ship channel in this stretch of the river. Thereafter, the river deepens, with few obstructions, as it continually widens to become the Gulf of St. Lawrence.

Ile d'Orleans. From Quebec City, the ship channel follows the south shore of pastoral Ile d'Orleans. At the eastern end of the island, it moves to the north shore. You might consider stopping at one of the marinas on Ile d'Orleans if you haven't time to reach **Ile aux Coudres**, 52 miles from Quebec, on one tide.

Ile aux Coudres has a good marina and is a popular stopover for boats passing both ways on the river. The village, with supplies available, is close by, up the hill.

From Ile aux Coudres, the river channels divide, one along each bank, with islands and mud flats in the middle. You'll find few safe places to cross over for the next 60 miles. Thereafter, you can move back and forth across the river, but the distances become greater as it widens.

The North Shore

A backdrop of mountains continues along the coast, with resort and fishing villages below them on the riverbank. Distances between harbors accessible at all tides become greater as you proceed downstream.

Cap a l'Aigle is only 20 miles from Ile aux Coudres, but it has a good marina and is a choice place to stop before the next 40-mile run. You'll pass the famous **Manoir Richelieu** at the other end of the bay from this resort area, and the village at the top of the hill has some excellent restaurants.

Navigation Below Sorel

The St. Lawrence River is tidal to Montreal, but the tidal range doesn't affect the passage of recreational craft until Sorel. A sailboat moving downstream from there against the incoming tide will not progress very well, despite the favorable river current. Conversely, attempts to sail or motor upstream without the boost of the incoming tide can, in some parts of the river, be utterly futile. Accordingly, recreational craft time a downstream passage from port to port to coincide with the ebb tide and time upstream passages with the flood. These conditions hold for the entire 200-mile distance between Sorel and Tadoussac at the mouth of the Saguenay River. Beyond the Saguenay, the effects of tide and current, while still present, are greatly reduced.

Tadoussac. At the mouth of the fabled **Saguenay River**, Tadoussac was the St. Lawrence River's first settlement, established in 1608. It is now a resort as well as a commercial and fishing town. The red roof of the Grand Hotel is a landmark from far upstream. The Saguenay current runs up to seven knots where it flows into the St. Lawrence, so you must time your arrival at Tadoussac with the turn of the flood current in order to get over the bar. If you have to wait, you can enjoy watching the white Beluga whales that congregate to feed near the mouth of the Saguenay. At Tadoussac, a broad sand beach lies behind the well-equipped marina. Here, too, you can visit the oldest church in Canada, and the village provides good shopping.

From Tadoussac, a side trip up the majestic Saguenay River is well worthwhile. The river is navigable for 60 miles to **Chicoutimi**, with several anchorages and a couple of small marinas on the way. One of the most beautiful stopovers is **Baie Éternité**, about halfway, where you'll find anchorage, a small dock in the provincial park, and moorings placed by the park service. The park features a nature center and hiking trails.

Baie Comeau. One hundred miles from Tadoussac, Baie Comeau is a young city, founded in 1937 to supply North America with newsprint. Several industries have sprung up there now, and a friendly yacht club is in the well-protected harbor. Shopping is a considerable distance from the marina, but taxis and rental cars are available.

Sept Isles. The river widens dramatically at **Pointe des Monts**. Sept Isles, 100 miles from Baie Comeau on the far north shore, is nevertheless the largest city below Quebec. It is an important mining, pulp, and paper port. The entrance through the islands is well lighted and buoyed. You'll find a substantial marina here and a museum to visit.

ST. LAWRENCE SEAWAY

The South Shore

The south shore is more agricultural along the 150 miles below Ile aux Coudres than the north shore. Then the forested **Chic-Choc Mountains** plunge steeply into the St. Lawrence during the last stretch of the river, with a string of fishing villages on the foreshore.

Riviere du Loup. This commercial town is 45 miles from Ile aux Coudres. You'll find a marina in the man-made harbor. If you prefer to anchor, the commercial port of **Gros Cacouna**, a few miles below Riviere du Loup, has room and good protection at the northern end of the basin.

Rimouski. Fifty-five miles from Riviere du Loup, Rimouski is the largest city on the south shore below Quebec. It's an industrial town with a big commercial harbor, and it's well-equipped marina is in its own basin to the east.

Matane. Forty-five miles farther on, Matane is a fishing and forest town, famous for the Matane River salmon. The marina here is located in the river mouth, east of the commercial harbor and close to downtown shopping and restaurants.

Matane to Cap Gaspé. Below Matane, a series of fishing villages of varying sizes provide harbors of varying quality. Some are merely wharves projecting into the river; others have protected breakwaters. **Sainte Anne des Monts**, **Marsoui**, **Mont Louis** (where anchorage is also available), **L'Anse a Valleau**, and **Rivière au Renard** are of the latter type. At Rivière au Renard, a marina is situated in a corner of the large, well-protected harbor.

From Rivière au Renard, it is about 20 miles to **Cap Gaspé**, with its towering bluffs and dramatic lighthouse looking out across the sea. The St. Lawrence River becomes a gulf here, part of the Atlantic Ocean.

St. Lawrence River	Phone	SEASONAL / YEAR-ROUND	SAIL / POWER / BOTH▲	LARGEST VESSEL ACCOMMODATED	NO. OF TRANSIENT BERTHS	MARKED ENTRY CHANNEL	APPROACH DEPTH (Reported)	DOCKSIDE DEPTH (Reported)	RAILWAY / LIFT CAPACITY (in tons)	GAS★ / DIESEL● / BOTH▲ FUEL BRAND	ENGINE REPAIRS: Gas★ / Diesel● / Both▲	PROPELLER / HULL REPAIRS	LAUNCHING RAMP	MARINE SUPPLIES	LPG★ / CNG● / BOTH▲	110V★ / 220V● / BOTH▲ / GROCERIES / ICE	SHOWERS / LAUNDROMAT MAX AMPS	PUMP-OUT STATION	RESTAURANT / SNACK BAR	RADIO WATCH—VHF (CB)
1. General Wolfe Marina	(613) 385-2611	S	▲	50			7	7	ESS	★		R	★			MGI	★30	S		R	
CAPE VINCENT																				
2. Cape Vincent Marina*	(315) 654-2151		▲	35			8	8	AME	★	L	R	★		PH	MI	★30		●	
3. Cape Vincent Village Dock				60			15	8												
4. Anchor Marina	654-2300		▲	100			15	12	TEX	▲	L		▲		PH	MI	▲30	S	●	16
CLAYTON, NY																				
5. French Creek Marina	686-3621	Y	▲	50	10		12	6				30	R	▲	P	MI	▲50	S	●	R	16
6. French Bay	686-5574	Y	▲	100	10	●	7	5	TEX	▲	L		▲		PH	MI	★30	S	●	
7. Remar Shipyard, Inc.	686-4170	S	▲	55	6		8	8		▲	11		★		P	MI	★30	SL	●	RS
8. Clayton Municipal Dock	No Listing		▲	100	15		7	8			MUNICIPAL DOCK						★30			
9. Village Shipyards	686-3218	S	▲	60	4		8	7	ESS	▲			▲		PH	MI	30		●	
10. Clayton Marina	686-3741	Y	P	32	5	●	5	6		★	4	R	★			MI	★15	S		R	16
11. Cantwell Pier 65	686-3992	S	P	35			10	10				R	★		PH		★	S		
GANANOQUE TO ROCKPORT, ONT.																				
12. Clark's Marina	(613) 382-5190	Y	▲	40	10		5	4	BP	★	L	R	★	★	I	★	S	●		
13. Gordon Marine, Ltd.	382-4315	Y	▲	60	25	●	15	15		▲	10		★	P	MI	★30	S	●	RS	
14. Gananoque Inn, Ltd.	382-2165	S	▲	55		●	6	6						★	MGI	▲30			RS	
15. Brennan Marine	382-3137	S	P	30		●	10	10	PC	★		R	★	P	MI	★30				
16. Peck's Marina	659-3185		P	40	8		7	5	TEX	★		R	★		I	★50			RS	
17. William's Marine Service	659-3163	Y	▲	75	4		8	5	ESS	★	L	R	▲	PH		★30		●		16
18. Hunt's Marina*	659-3262	S	▲	65		●	10	6	SUN	★					MGI	★		S		
19. Holidays Afloat Marina*	659-3207	S	▲	80	10	●	10	5	IND	★	R	R	★	PH	MGI	★30		●		
20. Andress Boat Works	659-3471	S	P	50	10		20	8	IND			R	★	PH	★	MI	★			R
21. Howard's Marine	659-3485	Y	P	60	10		25	10	ESS	★		R	★	P	MI	★30		●	RS	
22. Ed Huck Marine	659-3408	Y	▲	60	10		25	7	TEX	★	30	R	★	P	MI	★30	SL	●	RS	68
ALEXANDRIA BAY																				
23. Keewaydin State Park Marina*	(315) 482-3720	S	▲	40	24		18	5	ARC	★	L	R	★		PH	I	★30	S	●	(10)
24. The Thousand Islands Resort & Golf Club	482-2551	S	▲	80	10	●	9	4								GI	▲50	S		RS
25. Hutchinson's Boat Works, Bethune (p. 88)	482-9931	Y	▲	65	6		50	6	IND	▲	25		★	P	MI	★	S	●	RS	
26. Rogers Marine, Inc.	482-9461	Y	P	37	2	●	8	4	CIB	▲	20	R	▲	PH	MI	★20	S		S	16
27. Vans Motor Marine, Inc.	482-2271		▲	50			8	8	EXX	★	L	R	★		MI	★30		●		

To provide the most complete and accurate information, **all facilities have been contacted within the past year.** If an asterisk (*) appears, it indicates a facility which did not respond to our requests for information (these listings may not reflect current conditions). Although facility operators supplied this data, we cannot guarantee accuracy or assume responsibility for errors. Entrance and dockside soundings tend to fluctuate. Always approach marinas carefully. Reference numbers on spotting charts indicate marina locations. ✔ Member American Boat Builders & Repairers Association.

Aids to Navigation

Buoys:
- Unlighted buoy (C. can, N. nun, S. spar, Bell, Gong, Whistle)
- Danger or junction buoy
- Mooring buoy
- Light (On fixed structure)
- Fish trap buoy
- Daybeacon (Bn)
- R. Bn. radiobeacon
- Mid-channel buoy
- Lighted buoy

Buoys:
- T.B. temporary buoy
- C. can
- N. nun
- S. spar
- B. black
- Or. orange
- R. red
- G. green
- W. white
- Y. yellow

Lights (Lights are white unless otherwise indicated)
- F. fixed
- Fl. flashing
- Qk. quick
- Gp. group
- E. Int. equal interval
- Mo. (A) morse code
- Occ. occulting
- Alt. alternating
- I. Qk. interrupted quick
- OBSC. obscured
- WHIS. whistle
- DIA. diaphone
- M. nautical miles
- Rot. rotating
- SEC. sector
- m. minutes
- sec. seconds

Bottom characteristics
- Cl. clay
- Co. coral
- G. gravel
- Grs. grass
- M. mud
- Rk. rock
- S. sand
- Sh. shells
- hrd. hard
- rky. rocky
- sft. soft
- stk. sticky
- bk. black
- br. brown
- bu. blue
- gn. green
- gy. gray
- rd. red
- wh. white
- yl. yellow

Dangers:
- Sunken wreck
- Visible wreck
- Rocks
- Wreck, rock, obstruction, or shoal swept clear to the depth indicated
- Rocks that cover and uncover, with heights in feet above datum of soundings
- AERO. aeronautical
- Bn. daybeacon
- R. Bn. radiobeacon
- R. TR. radio tower
- C.G. Coast Guard Station
- D.F.S. distance finding station
- AUTH. authorized
- Obstr. obstruction
- P.A. position approximate
- E.D. existence doubtful

Caution: Mariners are warned to stay clear of the protective riprap surrounding navigational light structures shown thus.
- Restricted Areas
- Fish Trap Areas

St. Lawrence River

	SEASONAL / YEAR-ROUND	SAIL / POWER / BOTH▲	LARGEST VESSEL ACCOMMODATED	NO. OF TRANSIENT BERTHS	MARKED ENTRY CHANNEL	APPROACH DEPTH (Reported)	DOCKSIDE DEPTH (Reported)	RAILWAY / LIFT CAPACITY (in tons)	GAS ● DIESEL ● BOTH▲ FUEL BRAND	ENGINE REPAIRS: Gas ★ Diesel ● Both▲	LAUNCHING RAMP	PROPELLER / HULL REPAIRS	MARINE SUPPLIES / GROCERIES / BOTH▲ LPG ★ CNG ● BOTH▲ ICE	110V ● 220V ● BOTH▲ MAX AMPS	SHOWERS / LAUNDROMAT	RESTAURANT / SNACK BAR PUMP-OUT STATION	RADIO WATCH - VHF (CB)
ALEXANDRIA BAY																	
28. Horizon Marine Sales	482-9956	Y	P	50		6	6	ARC	★	25	R	★	P	MGI	★30	●	RS	16
29. O'Brien's Boats	482-9548	S	P	25					★			★	P	MI			R	
30. Riveredge Resort (p. 89)	482-9917	Y	▲	180	75	●	25	10				R		MGI	▲100	SL	RS	16
31. Hutchinson's Boat Works, Holland Street (p. 88)	482-9931	Y	▲	50	6		50	6	IND	★	25	R	★	P	MI	★	SL	●	RS
32. Bonnie Castle Yacht Basin	482-2526	Y	▲	100	30	●	10	10		▲	L	R	▲	PH	MI	▲100	SL	●	RS
GRENADIER IS. TO LAKE ST. LAWRENCE																	
33. Bill's Boat Livery	(613) 923-5377	S		50	10		10	7	ESS	★		R	★	H	MGI				
34. Gilbert Marine, Ltd.	342-3462	S	P	25	2		8	8	ESS	★		R	★	P	MGI	★15		●	RS
35. St. Lawrence Marina	549-7747	Y	▲	60			8	8	PC	▲	L		▲		MI	★15	S	●	
36. Wright's Sporting Goods	(315) 375-8841	Y		35			10	8	CIT	★	L	R	★	H	M	★30		●	(13)
37. Morristown Village Dock	375-8841	S	▲	50	5		10	8				R		★	MGI	★30			RS
38. Corkins "Sunrise" Marina*	393-5906	Y	▲	40	6	●	25	25	ATL	▲		R		PH	★	MGI	▲		RS
39. Ogdensburg Marina	393-1980	S	▲	40	20	●	25	12		▲		R			GI	▲	S	●	RS
40. Bridgeview Res. & Marina	(613) 925-2974	Y	▲	36	10	●	5	8	MAC	★	13	R	★	P	MI	▲30	S	●	RS
41. Coles Creek Marina*	388-5531	S	▲	45	2		10	8		★	10	R	▲	PH	MI	★30		●	S	16
42. Crysler Park Marina*	543-2254	S	▲	100	15		12	7	PC	▲	15	R	▲	PH	MI	▲		S	●	RS	68
43. Long Sault Marina	534-2540	S	P	50	10		10	7		▲	RL	R	★	PH	MI	★		S	●	S
CORNWALL TO MONTREAL																	
44. Lancaster Inn Marina	(613) 347-3767	S	P	48	10	●	12	5	MAC	★	10	R	★	H	★	MI	★15		●	RS	16
45. Mac's Marina	347-2788	Y	P	35	6		6	6		★		R	★	P	▲	MI	★			RS
46. Dan's Place	347-2098	Y	P	27	10	●	6	6	ESS	★	12	R	★	P		MI	★30		●	R
47. Club Nautique de Valleyfield	(514) 373-0304	S		100	22		14	18	SHE	▲	L	R	▲	PH	★	GI	▲50	SL	●	
48. Ste. Annes Marine Service, Ltd.	457-3456	Y	▲	50			10	10		★	L	R	▲	PH		MGI	★	L		R
49. Pointe-Claire Yacht Club	695-2441	S	▲	50	4		8	7	IND	★		R			MGI	★	SL	●	R
50. The Royal St. Lawrence Yacht Club	631-2720	Y	▲	60	5		7	8	BP	▲	25				I	★30		●	RS
51. Boulanger Yacht, Inc.	637-4408	S	▲	57	3		10	6			RL		▲	PH	MGI	★30		SL		RS
52. Lonqueuil Pleasurecraft Harbour	442-9575	S	▲	70	20	●	7	8	ULT	▲	RL	R	▲	PH	★	MGI	★50		●	RS	68

To provide the most complete and accurate information, **all facilities have been contacted within the past year.** If an asterisk (*) appears, it indicates a facility which did not respond to our requests for information (these listings may not reflect current conditions). Although facility operators supplied this data, we cannot guarantee accuracy or assume responsibility for errors. Entrance and dockside soundings tend to fluctuate. Always approach marinas carefully. Reference numbers on spotting charts indicate marina locations. ✓ Member American Boat Builders & Repairers Association.

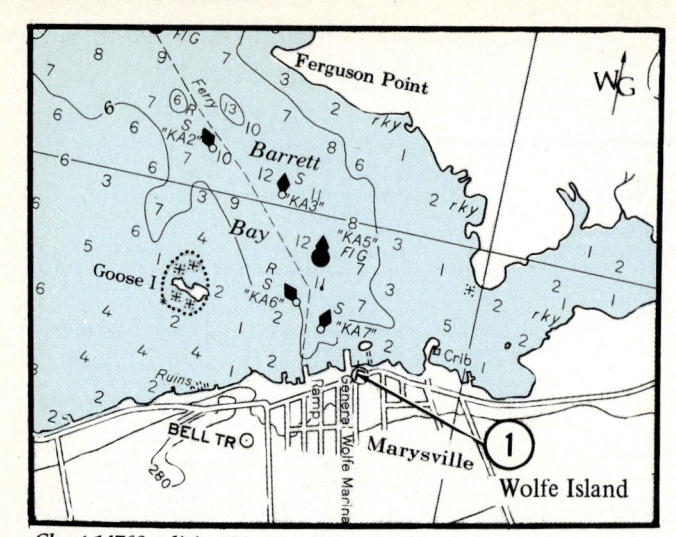

ST. LAWRENCE SEAWAY

Chart 14768, edition 16

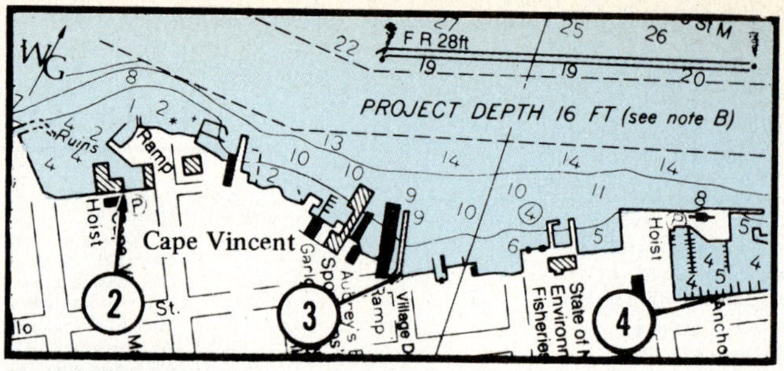

Chart 14767, edition 16

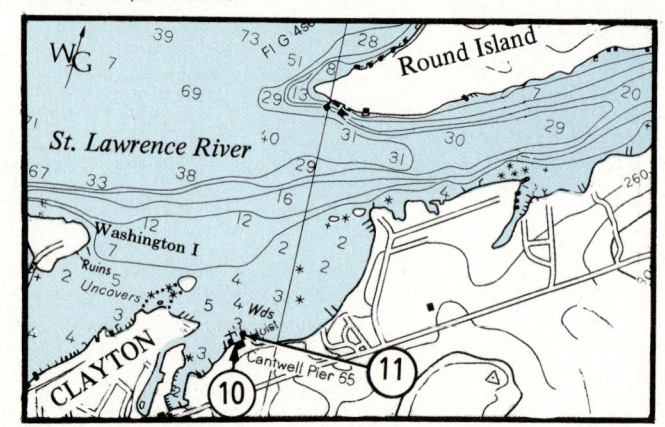

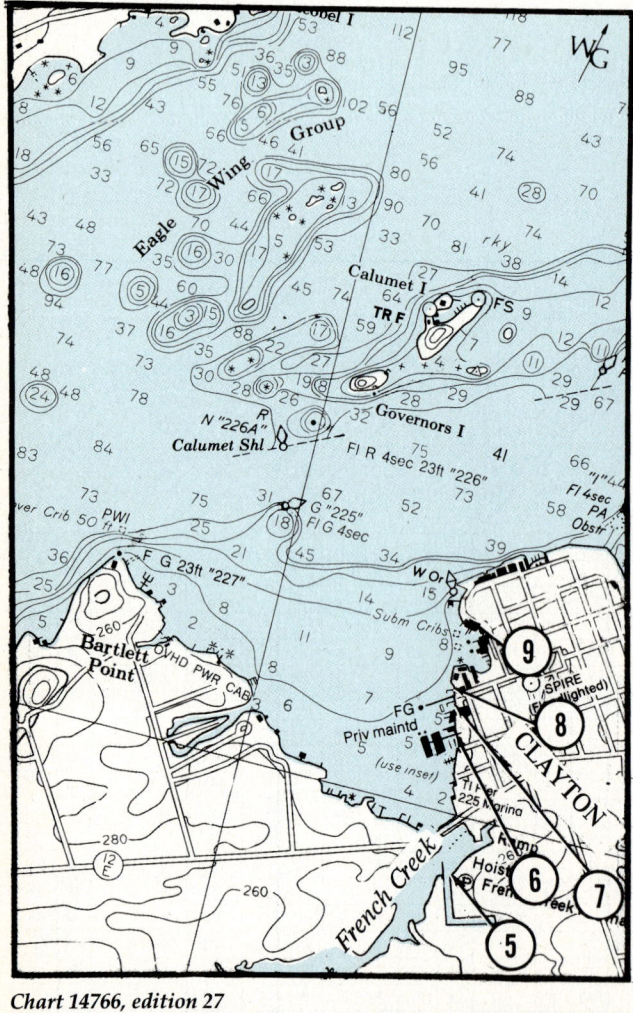

Chart 14766, edition 27

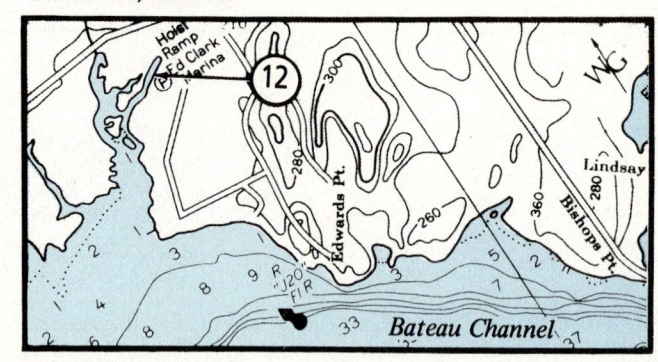

Chart 14767, edition 16

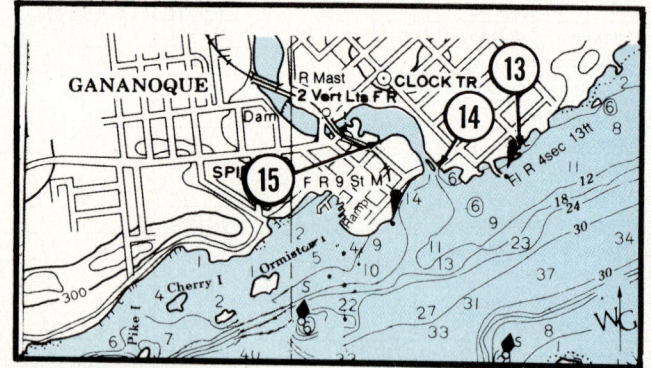

Chart 14767, edition 16

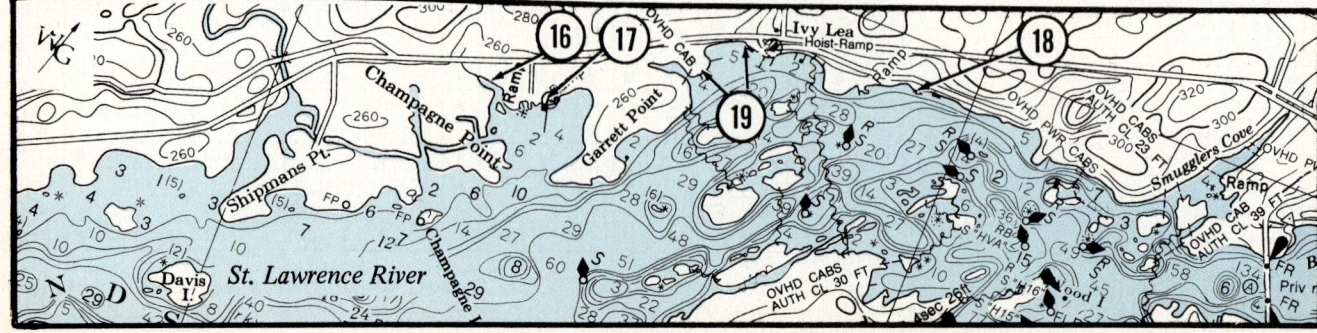

Chart 14766, edition 27

Under no circumstances are these charts to be used for navigation.

96   WATERWAY GUIDE / 1991

St. Lawrence Seaway

Chart 14766, edition 27

Chart 14764, edition 24

Chart 14766, edition 27

Chart 14765, edition 27

Chart 14764, edition 24

Chart 14764, edition 24

Chart 14764, edition 24

Chart 14763, edition 27

GREAT LAKES EDITION *Under no circumstances are these charts to be used for navigation.* 97

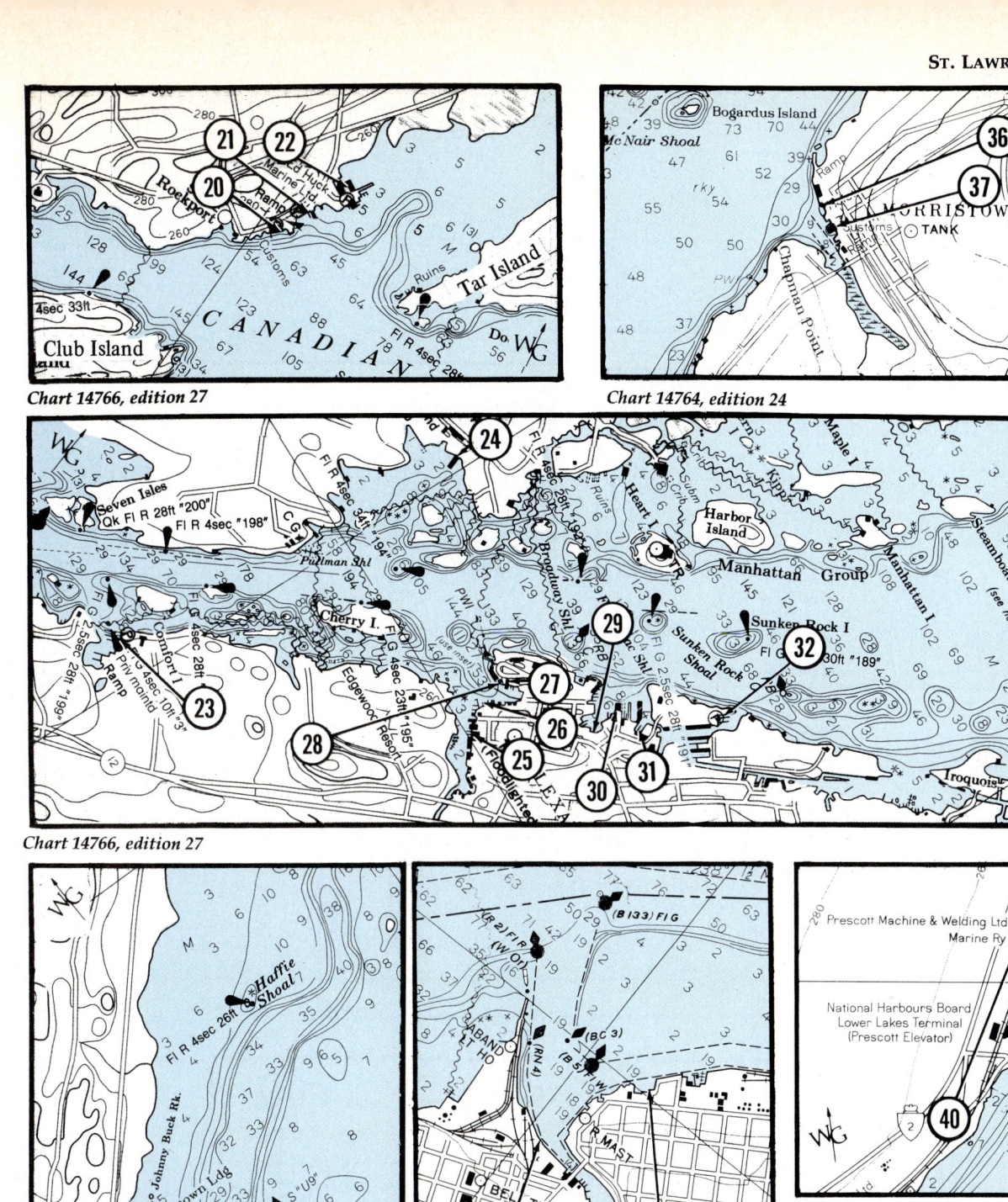

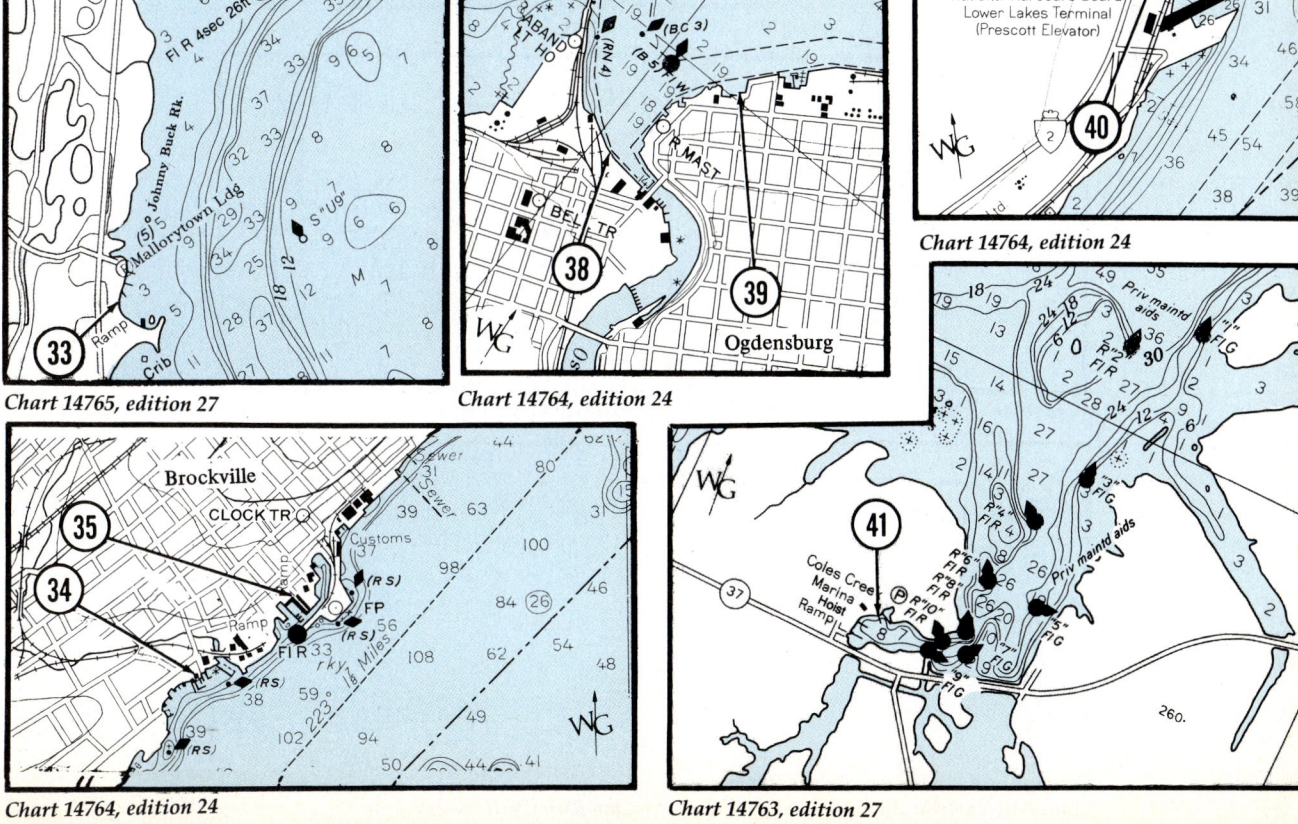

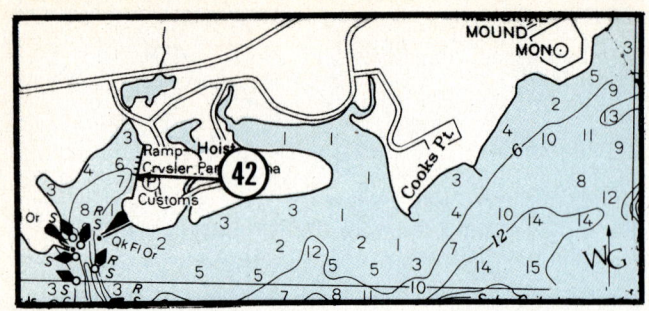

St. Lawrence Seaway

Chart 14762, edition 25

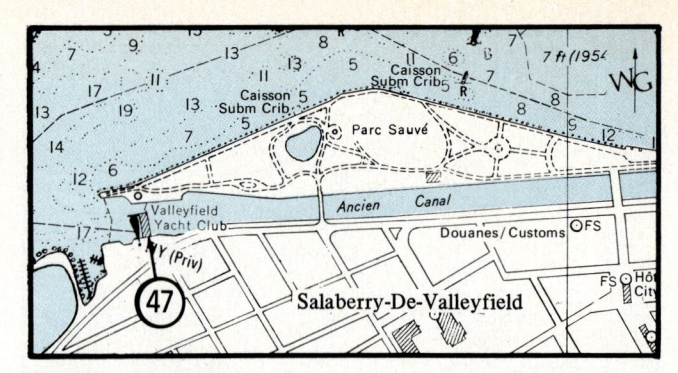

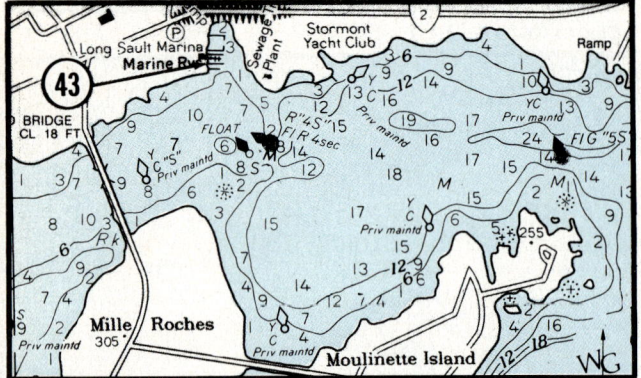

Chart 14761, edition 26

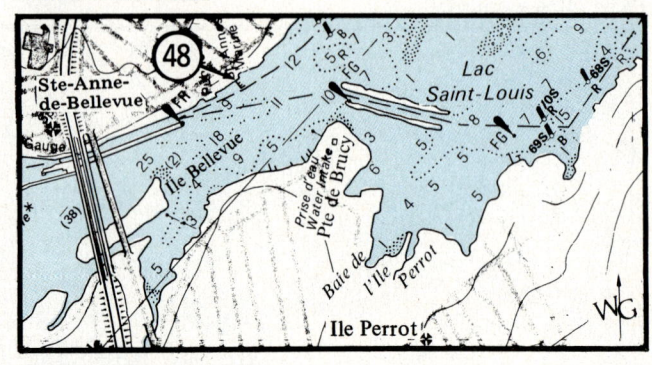

Canadian Chart 1411

Canadian Chart 1410

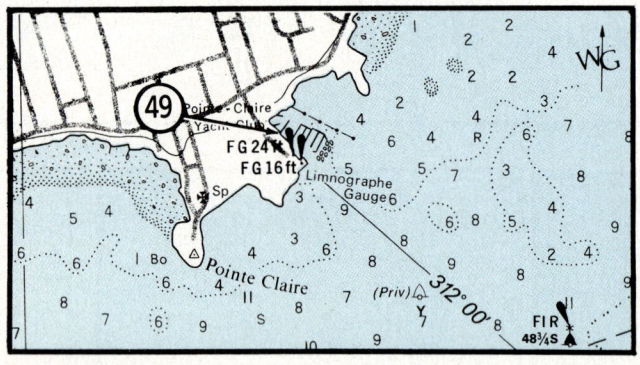

Canadian Chart 1410

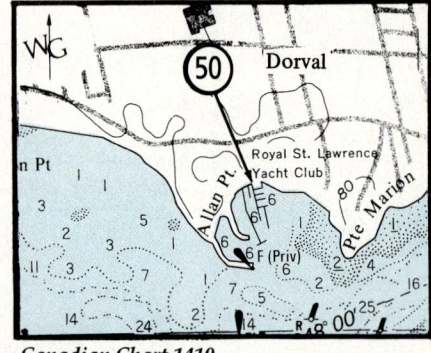

Canadian Chart 1410

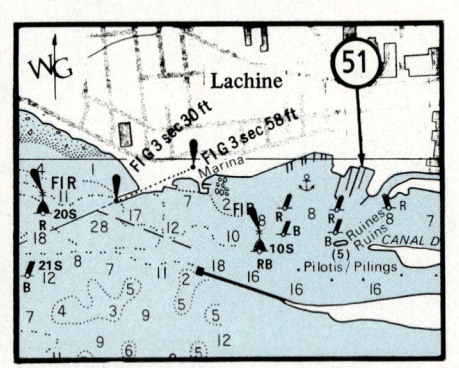

Canadian Chart 1410

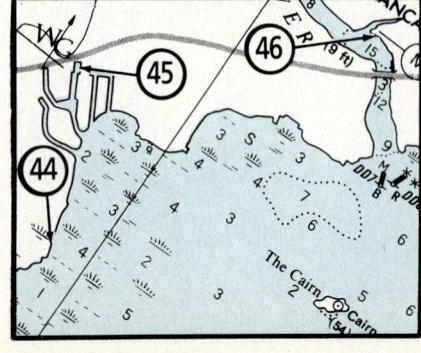

Canadian Chart 1413

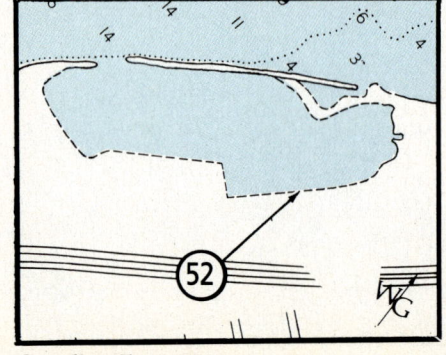

Canadian Chart 1340

98 *Under no circumstances are these charts to be used for navigation.* Waterway Guide / 1991

Trent-Severn Waterway

CHARTS: *Canadian: 2015, 2023, 2026, 2031, 2021, 2024, 2028, 2069, 2022, 2025, 2029.*

In 1827, canal fever was running high, and Canadian anxiety about conflict with the United States wasn't far behind. A proposal for an all-Canadian commercial water route connecting Lake Ontario with Georgian Bay through a chain of interior lakes and rivers found favor in legislative circles, and the Trent-Severn Waterway was begun. Construction was slow, however, and as a commercial link, the Waterway was obsolete long before its completion. Nevertheless, new locks and canals were built from time to time until the entire system limped to completion in 1920, with marine railways instead of locks at two places. One of those railways was replaced with a lock in 1964.

Although never important commercially, the Trent-Severn Waterway is an invaluable recreational resource. Winding among hills and farms, past quiet villages and a couple of energetic cities, through island-studded lakes and placid rivers, the scenic and sheltered waterway lures thousands of boats every summer.

The Waterway is operated by Parks Canada during daytime hours from mid-May to Canadian Thanksgiving in October. Controlling depth in the Waterway is six feet, and overhead clearance of fixed bridges is 22 feet. Sailboats can have their masts stepped and unstepped at Belleville or Trenton on Lake Ontario and at Midland or Penetanguishene on Georgian Bay.

Most towns and resort areas have commercial marinas, and all locks have tie-up walls for overnight dockage. Many of the locks also feature pleasant grounds and picnic areas, and almost all have restrooms. In high season, you may have to wait for lockage in some of the more congested boating areas, especially on weekends.

Trent River

The Waterway begins at **Trenton**, where the **Trent River** empties into the Bay of Quinte, a long arm of Lake Ontario. (See the "Lake Ontario" chapter for a description of the Bay of Quinte and Trenton.)

The Trent River has many bridges, dams, and in the first 50 miles, 18 locks with a total lift of 370 feet. Lockmasters and bridge tenders are helpful and very prompt, but at closing time, traffic stops. You can get a schedule of operating hours at the first lock.

Be sure to use the latest charts and follow the channel line. Canadian small-craft waters make use of spar buoys and shaped day beacons. In poor visibility, spar shapes may be hard to distinguish without a chart check. Most day beacons should be given more room than spars.

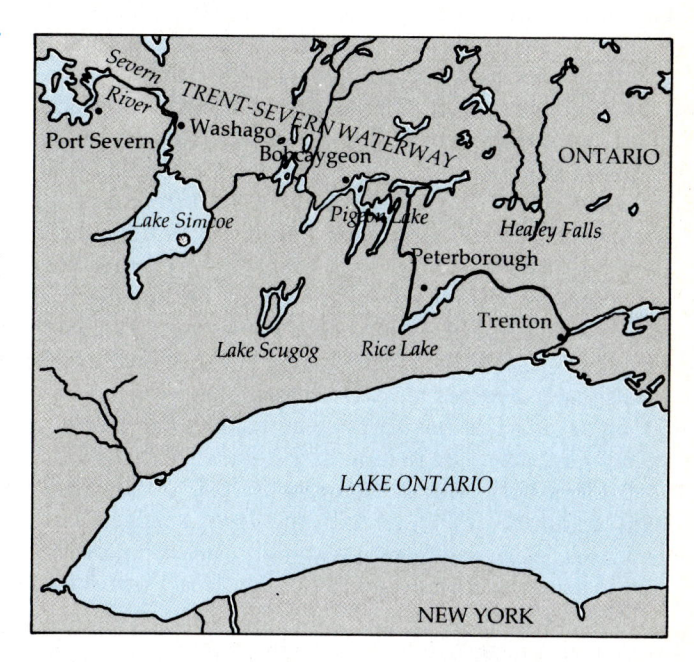

Trenton. A manufacturing town, Trenton has two marinas and a yacht club. In the river's first seven miles, boats climb 117 feet through six locks. Trenton has four bridges (least vertical clearance 22 feet). Trenton swing bridge openings are: 7:45, 9:00, 10:00, 10:45, 11:30, 13:50, 14:50, 15:50, 16:50, and 18:00 — all fairly prompt. The railroad bridge is normally open. The first lock (lift 17.5 feet) is less than two miles from the river mouth. Lock 2 (lift 20 feet) is 1,000 yards farther on; then come locks 3, 4, 5, and 6 (combined lift 79 feet), close together.

Frankford to Hastings. At the village of **Frankford**, which has fuel and groceries but little else, the river widens. The channel skirts islands and shoals, and for about four miles the scenic route heads north. After a sharp turn to port comes Lock 7 at **Glen Ross**, which lifts your boat ten feet.

For the next 60 miles the waters are alive with muskellunge. **Percy Reach**, a broad shallow stretch in the Waterway about 20 miles from Trenton, yields champion-sized muskies each year. Before early July, try fishing for pickerel in the fast water below power dams or spillways. Remember to get a fishing license first.

The well-buoyed route through Percy Reach ends at Lock 8 (lift 19.5 feet). A channel off to port runs west into picturesque **Meyersburg**, with limited supplies and a good tackle shop.

Above Percy Reach, the torrent that once tumbled 108 feet in about four miles is now contained by locks 9,

GREAT LAKES EDITION

TRENT-SEVERN WATERWAY

10, and 11/12 in flight, all closely spaced. The latter takes boats around the cataract and rocky gorge of **Ranney Falls**, to **Campbellford**.

Here the river cuts through town, where you can get supplies and limited repair service. The new municipal park and marina is a pleasant place to stop and is convenient to shopping. The town claims the distinction of having the world's biggest muskellunge hatchery.

Along this stretch, the river is clean and placid with good swimming and fishing. Past Lock 14 (25 foot lift) is **Crowe Bay**, actually a small lake, with a channel well-marked by spar buoys. About two miles up the bay the route veers sharply off to port, and you'll find good off-channel anchorage beyond the turn. Explore Crowe Bay by dinghy. Marshes full of waterfowl are on the east side; muskies six feet long and weighing 42 pounds have been caught here. The **Crowe River**, which drains a vast watershed to the north, enters Crowe Bay and the Trent, which has beautiful clear water except after a heavy rain. The bass fishing in this area is excellent.

It takes Lock 15 and Flight locks 16/17 (total rise 75 feet) to top **Healey Falls**, with the Trent's biggest dam and hydroelectric generating station. Site of an old Indian battleground, Healey Falls is pastoral, with heavily wooded stretches.

A well-marked, deep, protected waterway threads through islands and between shores lined with summer cottages to **Hastings**, 12 miles from Healey Falls. Here are Lock 18 (lift nine feet), limited marine facilities, and convenient shopping. The fast water below the dam is famous for pickerel. Six miles upriver delivers you to Rice Lake.

Rice Lake. Fifty-seven miles and 18 locks from Trenton, Rice Lake, 20 miles long and three miles wide, is the Trent system's second largest body of water. Dotted with islands, secluded coves, and resort towns, it offers good cruising and pleasant sailing. A giant granary in Indian times, the lake was named for the wild rice that grows around its shores and still attracts great flocks of southbound ducks and geese on their way to winter feeding grounds.

On windy days the lake kicks up quite a chop, and summer's short, sharp thunderstorms can make things uncomfortable. Keep an eye on the weather and an ear to the forecasts, usually given every hour after the news by local radio stations. The channel is well-marked, although some markers are a mile or more apart. Plotted courses are advisable in poor visibility.

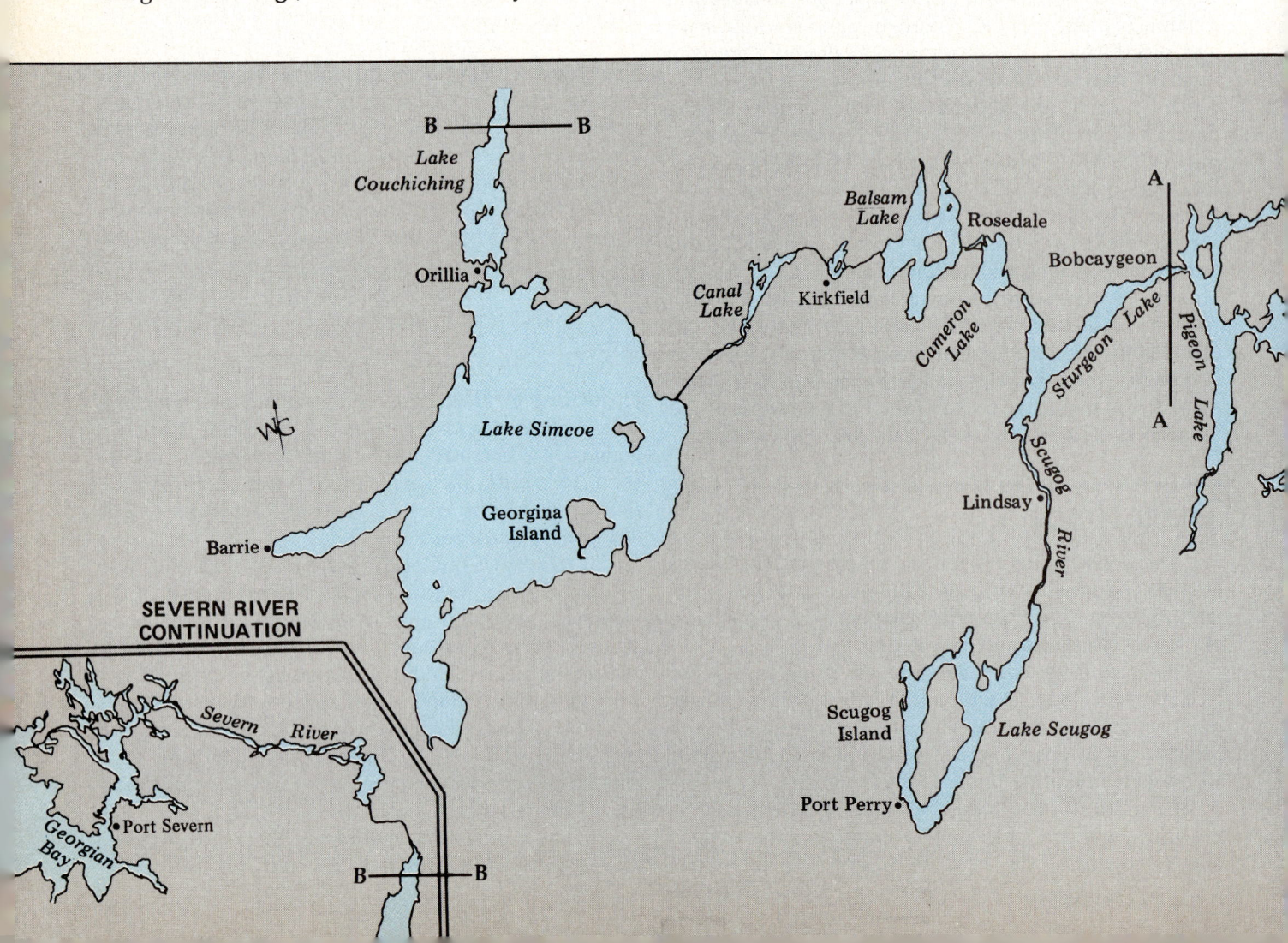

Just after you enter the lake, a government wharf to starboard offers tie-up (interesting muskie-raising ponds are nearby). For the next two miles, the narrow channel hugs the south shore, clear of northside shoals, leaving **Margaret Island** to starboard. About six and a half miles into the lake, just past **Rack Island**, is a government wharf at **Roach Point** on the northern shore. This Provincial Park, with camping and picnic grounds and good fishing at the mouth of **Indian River**, is a popular spot in season.

Leaving Serpent Mounds, follow closely along the channel. Pilings of the long-abandoned Cobourg-Chemung railway trestle string across the lake and channel markers are hard to find in poor visibility. You'll find **Harwood**—along with fuel, supplies and a clearly defined channel—at the south end of the trestle. Three miles farther west is **Gores Landing**, with a government wharf, tiny offshore islands, and a fine anchorage between Cow and Long islands. The eastern Waterway's best repair service for boats is located at Gores Landing on the south side of the lake. It has the only railway between Trenton and Lake Simcoe capable of handling boats up to 42 feet long with 14-foot beam. Right next door to the marina is an inn with the only restaurant with a liquor license on Rice Lake. Guests of the marina may use the amenities at the inn, including the swimming pool.

The main Trent Waterway channel heads out of Rice Lake straight north across the lake from Gores Landing up the Otonabee River.

Otonabee River

A quiet stream, winding for 20 miles through swampland and rolling hills, past cottages and farms, the **Otonabee River** between Rice Lake and Peterborough has three fixed bridges and three government wharves where you can tie up. The Hiawatha Indian Reserve is on its eastern shore. Gasoline is available at the town of **Bensford Bridge**, and you may find accommodations at **Wallace Point**.

Peterborough. Midway in the Otonabee run, Peterborough is one of the Waterway's two cities. Peterborough has two standard locks, Lock 19 (lift eight feet) and Lock 20 (lift 12 feet), and the world's highest lift lock, Lock 21 (lift 65 feet). The hydraulic lift lock works like a simple set of scales. A boat enters a huge tank shaped like a giant cake pan. Parallel to that chamber, but 65 feet up on a big piston, is another chamber, twin of the tank below. The higher water level in the upper tank forces the lower tank, boats and all, to rise on its piston while the upper tank sinks down.

The lock, opened in 1904, was an engineering wonder in its day. A local newspaper reporter wrote enthusiastically "there will be perpetual unrest in the public mind to see the wonderful...mechanism by which the law of equilibrium makes a passenger steamer mount...like a bird or a barge... drop as gently as a tuft of down...." Even 80 years later, it is still a remarkable operation to watch.

Between locks 19 and 20, the Otonabee widens

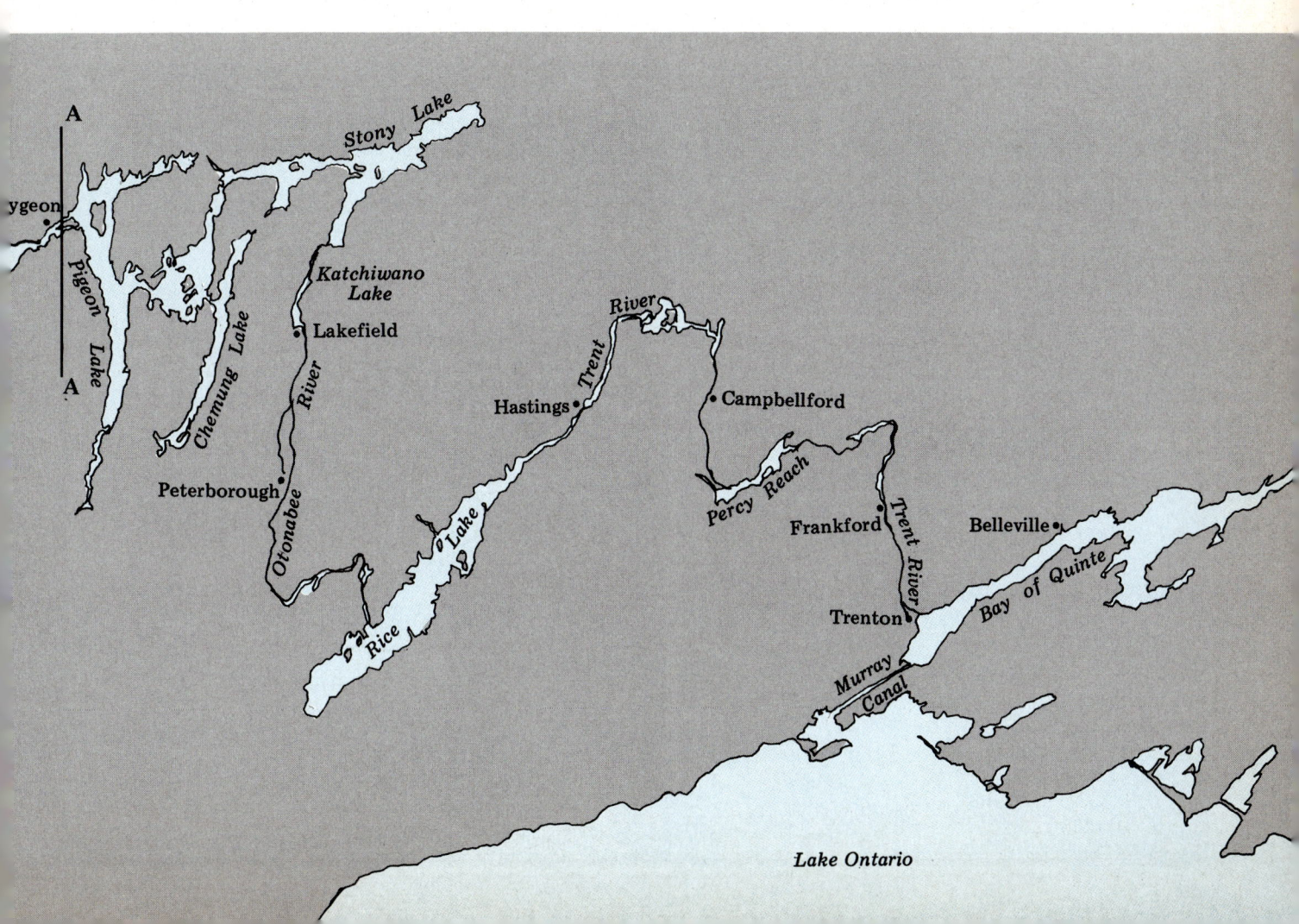

briefly into **Little Lake**. Here, in the heart of Peterborough, is an outstanding marina near the city's main street and a shopping center. A local art gallery, near the marina, frequently features native works of art.

Four miles past the lift lock and beyond the Trent University footbridge (clearance 22 feet) begins a very steep, short section with locks 22 through 25 (combined lift 54 feet). The hand-operated locks, which still use the old valves in the gates themselves, can be very frustrating on busy weekends. The old single barge tie-ups are too short and interlock communication is obsolete. The lock staffs try to accommodate through-boat traffic as much as possible in spite of endless rental boat problems. Lock 26 is located at **Lakefield,** a summer community with supplies.

Kawartha Lakes

The **Kawartha Lakes,** known to the Indians as "happy lands and bright waters," stretch across Ontario in a series of long loops. They offer unlimited cruising and sailing, both on and off the main Waterway route, almost 70 miles long. Mariners can enjoy a dozen or more lakes ranging from tiny **Lovesick** to 14-mile-long **Sturgeon Lake**. Overhead clearance is 22 feet.

The route begins past Lakefield at **Lake Katchewanooka** (also known as **Katchiwano**). A well-marked channel leads through the four-mile-long, half-mile-wide lake.

At **Youngs Point**, which has wharves, gas, groceries, a hotel, and a restaurant, is Lock 27 (lift seven and a half feet), and here the route swings out of Katchewanooka into **Clear Lake**. This lake has a buoyed channel. On its northwestern shore is **Kawartha Park**.

Well-named **Stony Lake** is large, island-filled, and full of reefs off the marked channel. Many regard Stony as queen of the Kawarthas. At its junction with Clear Lake, pine-crowned islands of red granite rise out of the blue water. The direct route cuts through only a small segment of the lake's southern reaches, but you can find fascinating cruising among the well-charted and marked waters of its islands and coves. At **Juniper Island**, **McCrackens Landing**, **Mount Julian**, and **Crowes Landing**, some docks welcome cruising boats. Exit from the lake is at **Burleigh Falls**. The falls are off to port as the route swings, also to port, for the approach to Lock 28 (lift 24 feet).

Lovesick Lake, named for an Indian boy spurned by a redheaded Irish girl, is a rocky-bottomed, island-studded beauty less than two miles long. The route threads due west past tiny islands to Lock 30 (lift three and a half feet), past **Deer Bay**, a fine anchorage, and into **Lower Buckhorn Lake**, about six miles long.

Halfway point on the Trent-Severn Waterway is Lock 31 (lift 11.5 feet) at **Buckhorn**. Now, for 15 miles to **Bobcaygeon** (Bob-kay-jun), there are no locks and only two

Distances
Statute miles (approximate)

Location	Between Points	Cumulative	Location	Between Points	Cumulative
Trenton, Ontario	0.0	0.0	Lock 24, Douro*	1.5	96.3
Lock 1, Trenton	1.8	1.8	Lock 25, Sawyer Creek*	1.0	97.3
Lock 2, Sydney	1.0	2.8	Lock 26, Lakefield	1.4	98.7
Lock 3, Glen Miller	1.0	3.8	Lock 27, Youngs Point	5.8	104.5
Lock 4, Batawa	1.4	5.2	Locks 28-29, Burleigh Falls	8.5	113.0
Lock 5, Trent	1.2	6.4	Lock 30, Lovesick	1.8	114.8
Lock 6, Frankford	0.9	7.3	Lock 31, Buckhorn	5.9	120.7
Lock 7, Glen Ross	6.5	13.8	Lock 32, Bobcaygeon	8.0	138.2
Lock 8, Percy Reach	11.4	25.2	Lock 34, Fenelon Falls	15.5	153.7
Lock 9, Meyers	1.2	26.4	Lock 35, Rosedale	3.5	157.2
Lock 10, Haigues Reach	1.6	28.0	Lock 36, Kirkfield	12.1	169.3
Locks 11-12, Ranney Falls	1.7	29.7	Lock 37, Bolsover*	7.7	177.0
Campbellford, fixed bridge	1.4	31.1	Lock 38, Talbot*	1.0	178.0
Lock 13, Crowe Bay	1.1	32.2	Lock 39, Portage*	1.6	179.6
Lock 14, Healey Falls	1.3	33.5	Lock 40, Thorah*	0.4	180.0
Lock 15, Healey Falls	2.6	36.1	Lock 41, Gamebridge*	0.8	180.8
Locks 16-17, Healey Falls	0.4	36.5	L. Simcoe Gamebridge	1.4	182.2
Lock 18, Hastings Swing Br.	7.6	51.1	Atherley Narrows	15.5	197.7
Otanabee River (ent.)	17.9	69.0	Orilla	2.3	200.0
Lock 19, Scott's Mills*	19.2	88.2	Lock 42, Couchiching	10.0	209.9
Lock 20, Ashburnham*	1.3	89.5	Lock 43, Swift Rapids	14.6	224.5
Lock 21, Peterborough	0.6	90.1	Lock 44, Big Chute	8.0	232.5
Lock 22, Nassau Mills*	4.2	94.3	Lock 45, Port Severn*	8.0	240.5
Lock 23, Otonabee*	0.5	94.8	*slow-operating valve gate lock		

fixed bridges. (From Buckhorn Lake you can make a number of side trips, one of which goes southward into **Chemung Lake**.)

A clear run northwest through **Gannon Narrows** and **Pigeon Lake** and a sharp turn to port through the narrow approach to **Bobcaygeon** (with facilities and supplies) brings you to Lock 32 (lift five and a half feet). Bobcaygeon is built on three islands, and Lock 32 passes right through the center of the village. At the busiest times, many boats spend the night tied up above and below the lock. Space is at a premium, but a marina below the lock can offer dockage at the end of the day on the long gas dock. Or if you can make the last lockage, the marina west of town may have space. Now the route leads into long, double-pronged **Sturgeon Lake**, which offers good sailing and many anchorages.

Side trip to Lake Scugog. From Sturgeon Lake, the 40-mile passage to Lake Scugog carries boats with less than four-foot draft and 10.6 foot overhead clearance. The side route runs southward through the lock (lift seven feet) at the town of **Lindsay** (Chart 2026).

Fenelon Falls to Lake Simcoe. Heading westward on the Waterway, exit from Sturgeon Lake is via Lock 34 (lift 23.5 feet) in the center of **Fenelon Falls**. Here you'll find facilities and supplies. Three miles across deep **Cameron Lake** you come to Lock 35 (lift four feet) and the resort of **Rosedale**, whose several relatively small marinas are convenient to groceries, hardware, and fishing tackle shops.

Lock 35, almost 160 miles from Trenton, is the last lift. **Balsam Lake**, high point of the system, is 598 feet above Trenton, and from here it's 260 feet down to Georgian Bay. This is the highest point in the world a boat can reach from the sea under its own power.

Balsam Lake. This lake is deep and large, but a careful look at the chart will reveal good anchorages. Boats with less than four-foot draft can visit **Coboconk**, a pleasant village at the lake's northern end. The main route cuts west across the lake, south of Grand Island, and goes around Long Point to a cut marked with a lighted beacon on the western shore. You can tie up on the breakwater at the entrance to the cut, but no services are available.

This two-and-a-half-mile link, which joins the Trent and Severn watersheds, makes the entire route possible. The channel goes through manmade **Mitchell Lake**. Dredging has improved depths in this stretch. Boats over 45 feet and four-foot draft should go slowly between miles 165 and 173 to avoid sucking water out from underneath their hulls. Twin-engine boats will be helped by shutting off one engine in canal sections.

Another artificial cut leads three miles to a guard gate, used to isolate the headwaters of the system, and the Waterway's second lift lock, similar to Peterborough's but smaller. This is Lock 36 (drop 49 feet) at **Kirkfield**. Note: Past the lock, channel markers reverse for the downstream run.

Vital Statistics

The Trent-Severn Waterway runs through three rivers, 20 lakes, 43 locks, and a marine railway. There are 33 canal miles with six mph speed limits, and 207 miles of rivers and lake. It empties into Georgian Bay at Port Severn. Write for complete information kits to: The Superintendent, Trent-Severn Waterway, Box 567, Peterborough, Ontario, Canada K9J 6Z6.

Highest point is Balsam Lake, 598 feet above Lake Ontario, 260 feet above Georgian Bay.

Buoys are all numbered. New charts show the numbers to aid your navigation. Markers reverse at Kirkfield lift lock.

Speed limits (six mph) are enforced on certain sections of the Waterway. They will be designated by signs placed either on a white buoy anchored on the edge of the channel or on posts along the shoreline.

The controlling overhead clearance is 22 feet; draft is six feet. The railway at Big Chute takes boats of 100 tons, 100-foot length, 24-foot beam, and six-foot draft.

All locks have plastic covered steel cables, fastened top and bottom, about 15 feet apart on both sides. Put lines around them; do not fasten to them.

Approach walls have blue lines painted on some sections to mark areas reserved for boats locking through.

The hand operated gates are usually not fully opened for smaller or single boats in good weather. If you need a wider opening, wait for the other gate. If you need a full opening, give four blasts on your horn.

Nearly all locks have clean restrooms with hot water but no showers. The lockmaster will leave a key with a boat staying overnight.

Charts show lock numbers only, but the locks themselves bear names (plus the numbers in some cases).

Overhead wire heights as shown on charts shouldn't be taken as completely accurate. Many are being replaced by submarine cables because of the increase in the number of sailboats on the Trent-Severn.

Weedy, shallow **Canal Lake** gives way after 13 miles to **Talbot River**, leading to **Lake Simcoe**.

Bolsover and **Talbot** have gas and supplies. There are five locks: 37 and 38, with a combined drop of 36 feet and, in a straight cut of the Talbot, 39, 40 and 41 with a total drop of 39 feet. The river and canal rejoin after Lock 41. The swing bridge operates on Trent hours. The canal opens into Lake Simcoe.

Lake Simcoe. This lake, 20 miles long and 16 wide, is the largest on the Trent-Severn Waterway. Its open water can create cruising hazards; thunderstorms sometimes bring eight-foot waves. The breakwater entrance can be sloppy in westerly winds. The breakwaters form an excellent harbor with minimum surge in the southwest corner.

The lake has several large islands, one of which, Georgina, is an Ojibway Nation Indian Reservation. Good cruising abounds in three major bays: **Kempenfelt Bay**, named for a British admiral, with a big boating

Trent-Severn Waterway

center at **Barrie**; **McPhee Bay** and **Cook Bay** with facilities on both sides. The sailing is superb, with fresh winds, gorgeous scenery, and numerous anchorages.

The Waterway route through Lake Simcoe is well-marked by lighted buoys as far as **The Narrows**, at the northern tip. Use caution in this short stretch. On weekends the boat traffic can be quite a sight, passing through in line, entering or leaving the marinas at Orillia. Often the current is strong and the hand-operated railway bridge creates some real bottlenecks. Northbound, stay south of the highway bridge until a clear passage through the span is available. Outside the marked channel is sufficient room to turn good-sized boats. Use your chart carefully. Heading south, tie up on the west-side docks.

Orillia. Just past the Narrows, a well-buoyed channel leads to the city of Orillia, which boasts good marine services with electricity, water, and heads. Showers cost extra, bring quarters for the slot. Shopping convenience here is hard to beat. You can dine in restored railway cars looking out over the lake and town docks.

Lake Couchiching. Beyond the railway bridge and The Narrows is Lake Couchiching (*Kooch-it-ching*, accent on the first syllable), about ten miles long, more shallow, but not as predictable as Simcoe. The lake is speckled with shoals, but the sailing is fine and ashore is an increasing number of resorts. Anchorages are attractive. **Washago**, a small town at the northern end of the lake with facilities and shore accommodations, is where the Waterway cuts northwest for its last 30-mile leg to Georgian Bay.

Severn River

A manmade two-mile canal with an enforced six-mph speed limit leads from Lake Couchiching to Lock 42 (drop 20.3 feet) and the **Severn River**. It goes under a very slowly swinging transcontinental main line railway bridge (closed clearance 14 feet), which is seldom left open on weekends. Be careful while waiting here; boat traffic is heavy and there is no place to tie up.

Delays are unavoidable at Lock 42, one of the busiest in the system. When you're unable to get into the small blue line area, be prepared for some current while the lock is filling.

For the six miles between Lake Couchiching and

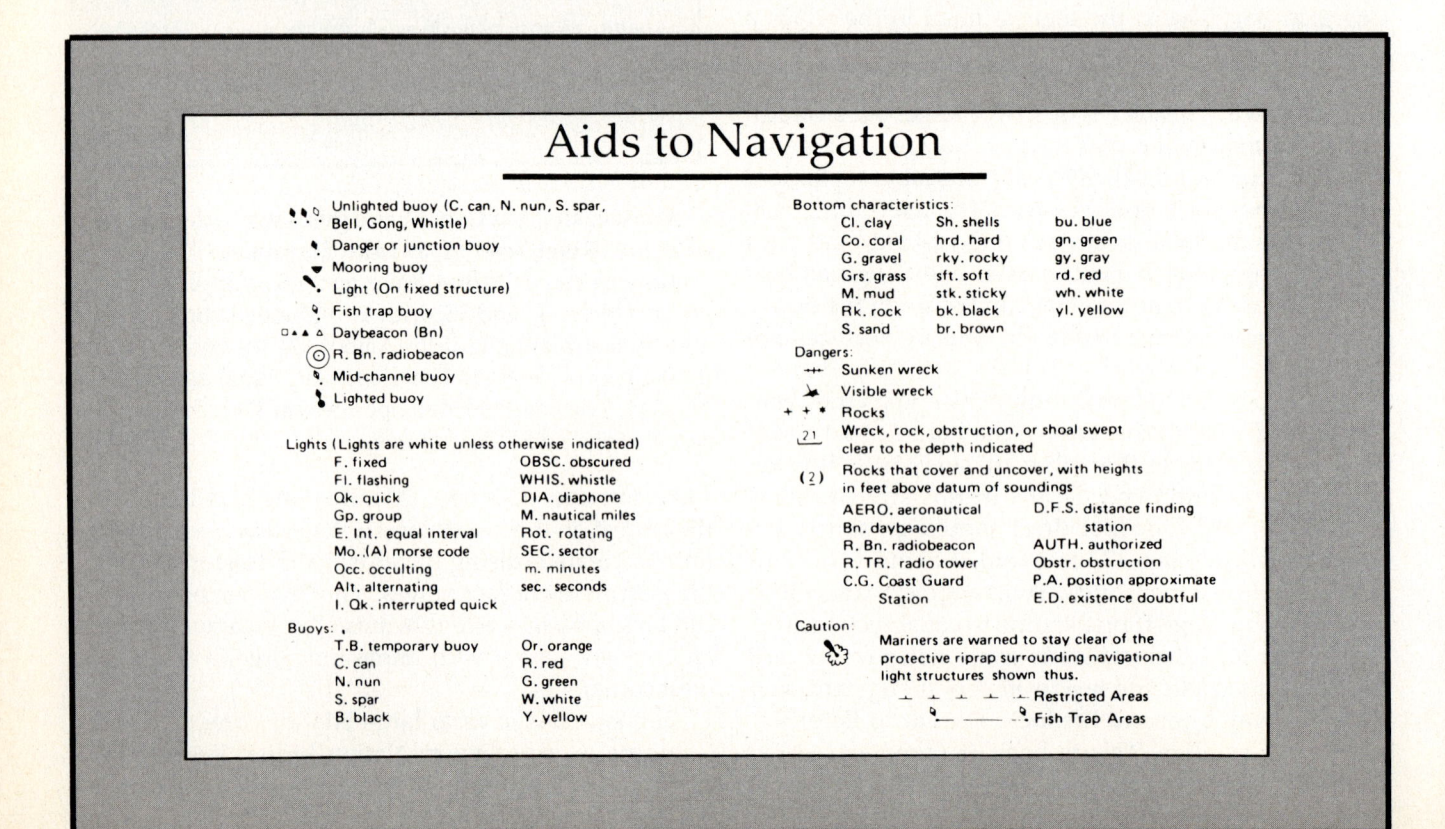

DAWSON'S
SINCE 1842
South End Lake Simcoe

1 hr. to Toronto International Airport

TROJAN • BLUEWATER • OCEAN • VIKING
MARINE TRADER • FOUR WINDS V.I.P. • DEFEAVER
UP TO 100 BROKERAGE BOATS ON DISPLAY IN
LARGE SALES HARBOUR - CRUISERS FROM 24'-66'
COMPLETE 300 SLIPS — FULL SERVICE MARINA
HAULOUT & REPAIRS UP TO 55' - PROPELLER & SHAFT
REPAIR - ELECTRONICS REPAIR & INSTALLATION
SHIP'S STORE - FUEL - TRANSIENT DOCKAGE
MONITOR VHF CH 68
TORONTO: (416) 887-5891 • KESWICK: (416) 476-4321
294 QUEENSWAY SOUTH, KESWICK, ONTARIO L4P 2B5

Aids to Navigation

Unlighted buoy (C. can, N. nun, S. spar, Bell, Gong, Whistle)
Danger or junction buoy
Mooring buoy
Light (On fixed structure)
Fish trap buoy
Daybeacon (Bn)
R. Bn. radiobeacon
Mid-channel buoy
Lighted buoy

Lights (Lights are white unless otherwise indicated)
F. fixed
Fl. flashing
Qk. quick
Gp. group
E. Int. equal interval
Mo. (A) morse code
Occ. occulting
Alt. alternating
I. Qk. interrupted quick

OBSC. obscured
WHIS. whistle
DIA. diaphone
M. nautical miles
Rot. rotating
SEC. sector
m. minutes
sec. seconds

Buoys:
T.B. temporary buoy
C. can
N. nun
S. spar
B. black
Or. orange
R. red
G. green
W. white
Y. yellow

Bottom characteristics:
Cl. clay
Co. coral
G. gravel
Grs. grass
M. mud
Rk. rock
S. sand
Sh. shells
hrd. hard
rky. rocky
sft. soft
stk. sticky
bk. black
br. brown
bu. blue
gn. green
gy. gray
rd. red
wh. white
yl. yellow

Dangers:
Sunken wreck
Visible wreck
Rocks
21 Wreck, rock, obstruction, or shoal swept clear to the depth indicated
(2) Rocks that cover and uncover, with heights in feet above datum of soundings

AERO. aeronautical
Bn. daybeacon
R. Bn. radiobeacon
R. TR. radio tower
C.G. Coast Guard Station
D.F.S. distance finding station
AUTH. authorized
Obstr. obstruction
P.A. position approximate
E.D. existence doubtful

Caution:
Mariners are warned to stay clear of the protective riprap surrounding navigational light structures shown thus.
Restricted Areas
Fish Trap Areas

TRENT-SEVERN WATERWAY

Sparrow Lake, the Severn, only 200 feet wide in some places, takes you past scores of summer cottages while outboards churn up the waters. Sparrow Lake's four-mile buoyed channel takes you through quieter waters.

The Severn runs west from Sparrow Lake through red and gray granite walls cut by glaciers that left gorges and cliffs, fjord-like coves, side channels, and fine anchorages. After six miles of this remote scenery the Waterway opens into the headwaters of **Swift Rapids** power dam, accessible only by boat or aircraft. Here a modern lock lowers boats 47 feet past the rapids.

Big Chute. The river continues westward for six scenic miles, and winds past the summer community of **Severn Falls** with its good marine facilities, restaurant overlooking the river, overnight accommodations, groceries, and supplies. Beyond Severn Falls, you'll find **Big Chute**, the unique marine railway. Extensive tie-up areas are available in front of and on both sides of the railway, and a fine marina stands nearby on the south shore. The newer of the two railways takes craft up to 90 metric tons, 100-foot length, 24-foot beam, and six-foot draft. The old system of handling boats under 20

Trent-Severn Waterway	Phone	SEASONAL/YEAR-ROUND	SAIL/POWER/BOTH	LARGEST VESSEL ACCOMMODATED	NO. OF TRANSIENT BERTHS	MARKED ENTRY CHANNEL	APPROACH DEPTH (Reported)	DOCKSIDE DEPTH (Reported)	RAILWAY/LIFT CAPACITY (in tons)	GAS★/DIESEL●/BOTH▲ FUEL BRAND	ENGINE REPAIRS: Gas★/Diesel●/Both▲	PROPELLER/HULL REPAIRS	LAUNCHING RAMP	MARINE SUPPLIES/GROCERIES/ICE	LPG★/CNG●/BOTH▲	110V★/220V●/BOTH▲ SHOWERS/LAUNDROMAT MAX AMPS	RESTAURANT/SNACK BAR PUMP-OUT STATION	RADIO WATCH—VHF (CB)
TRENT RIVER TO PETERBOROUGH																		
1. Government Wharf, Trenton*	(613) 394-2561	S	▲	100			10	7		SHE	▲		R		GI	★	S	● S
2. Island Park Marina, Stirling	395-2522	S	▲	35	3		15	8		ESS	★		R		MGI	★15	S	
3. Clarion Boat Co. Inc., Campbellford	(705) 653-3820	S	▲	50	6	●	6	5		ESS	★	REPAIR FACILITY			MI	▲		● RS
4. Jorgensen's Marina, Trent River*	778-3424	S		100	6		12	6		SHE	★		R	★	GI	★15	S	(10)
5. Hastings Marine, Ltd., Hastings	696-2366	Y	▲	50	10		6	6		SHE	★		R	★	MGI	★15	SL	● RS
6. Lang's Marina Resort, Roseneath	(416) 352-2308	S		60	10		8	6		ESS	★		R	★	GI	★30	S	● R
7. Sandercock's Camp Resort, Ltd., Roseneath	352-2469	S	P	17	5		7	7			★		R		GI	★20	S	S 4
8. Coxies Cove Marina, Gores Landing	342-2138	S	P	50	4		15	6		ESS	★	20		★ P	I	★	S	● RS (19)
9. Turtle Bay Marina*	(705) 748-2290	S	P	40	15		5	5		XL	★		R	▲ PH	★	MI	★15	S ●
10. Willow Bend Marina, Peterborough	743-4270	S	▲	100	10	●	6	6		ESS	▲	20	R	▲ PH		MI	★20	SL ● S 68
11. Peterborough Marina	745-8787	S	▲	100	95	●	8	6		ESS	▲		R		GI	▲	SL	● RS
KAWARTHA LAKES																		
12. Island View Park & Marina	652-8498	S	▲	70	8		5	5		SHE	★				GI	★30	SL	● R
13. Kawartha Park Marina, Stoney Lake	654-3549	S	▲	60	6	●	20	8		ESS	★	L	R	★ PH	★	MGI	★30	● S
14. Carveth's Marina, Ltd., Stoney Lake	652-6226	Y	P	26	4	●	8	4			★	8	R	★	★	MI	★15	
15. Bayview Marina, Stoney Lake	652-8174	Y	▲	48	5		22	8		TRB	★	35	R	▲ PH	★	M	★30	
16. Deer Bay Marina, Buckhorn Lake	654-3641	S	▲	24	8	●	25	5		ESS	★	2	R	▲ P	★	MGI	★15	SL ● S
17. Sunrise Resort, Buckhorn Lake	657-8713	S	▲	36	6		5	5		SHE	★		R			MGI	★	S
18. Buckhorn Yacht Harbour, Ltd.	657-8752	Y	P	100	6	●	10	8		PC	★	15	R	★ PH		MGI	▲30	S ●
19. Scotsman Point Resort, Buckhorn Lake	657-8630	S	▲	26			4	4		SHE	★		R			MGI	★30	SL S
20. Dutch Marine of Canada, Ltd., Chemong Lake	292-7111	Y	▲	45			17	6		BP	▲	L	R	▲ PH		MI	▲30	S ●
21. Chemong Yacht Haven, Chemong Lake	292-7251	Y	▲	28			6	3		DX	★	5	R	★ P		MI	★15	RS
22. Theona Park Marina, Buckhorn Lake	292-5282	S	P	26	10		7	5		TEX	★		R			MGI	★	SL S
23. Emerald Isle Marine, Buckhorn Lake	292-8452	S	P	40	2		8	5		SHE	★		R	★ P		MGI	★15	●
24. Midway Marina, Pigeon Lake*	No Listing	S	P	40	8		12	8		SHE	★	10	▲	▲ H		MGI	★20	S ●
25. Gordon Yacht Harbour, Pigeon Lake	738-2381	Y	P	45	10	●	21	10		IND	★		R	★ P		MI	▲30	S RS 16/68
26. The Buckeye, Bobcaygeon*	738-2481	S		48	8		4	4		ESS	★		R	★ P		MI	★	S
27. Centre Point Landing, Ltd., Bobcaygeon	738-3463	S	▲	58	10		7	5		IND	★	10	▲	▲ P		MGI	★15	SL ● R (19)
STURGEON LAKE TO BALSAM LAKE																		
28. Birch Point Marina, Bobcaygeon	738-2473	S	P	36	6	●	6	5		ESS	★		R	★ PH		MI	▲30	S ●
29. McLaren's Marina, Ltd., Sturgeon Lake	793-2282	S	P	28	4		10	8		TEX	★		R	★ PH		MGI	★20	S ● RS 16
30. Sturgeon Lake Marina, Sturgeon Lake*	793-2952	Y	P	38	5	●	5	5		SHE	★		R	★ PH		MGI	★30	S ● RS
31. Snug Harbor Marina, Sturgeon Lake*	No Listing	S	▲	40	5	●	6	5		PC	★		R	★ P	★	MGI	★15	SL ● S
32. Goresk Resort and Marina, Port Perry	(416) 985-3068	S	▲	35	50	●	6	5		BP	★	10	R	★ PH		MI	★20	S ● RS
33. West Shore Marine, Port Perry	985-2658	S	▲	40	20	●	6	5		PC	★	15	R	★ PH		MI	★15	S
34. Port Perry Marine	985-3236	Y	▲	30			6	5		SUP	★	L	R	PH		MGI	★30	L ● R
35. Port Perry Yacht Club	No Listing			33			5	5		ESS	★	RL	R		★	I	★50	SL
36. Kings Marina, Fenelon Falls	(705) 887-3321	Y	▲	40	5		6	5		ESS	★	L	R	★ PH	★	MI	★15	●
37. Skinner's Marine, Inc., Rosedale	887-6921	Y	▲	40		●	5	6		PC	▲	15	R	▲ PH		MI	★20	SL ●
38. Rosedale Flemings Marine, Balsam Lake*	887-6920	S	▲	50	4		6	5		PC	▲			P		MGI	▲30	SL ● RS
39. Thompson's Marina, Balsam Lake	454-3372	S	▲	35	20	●	7	5		SHE	★		R	★ PH		MGI	★20	

To provide the most complete and accurate information, **all facilities have been contacted within the past year.** If an asterisk (*) appears, it indicates a facility which did not respond to our requests for information (these listings may not reflect current conditions). Although facility operators supplied this data, we cannot guarantee accuracy or assume responsibility for errors. Entrance and dockside soundings tend to fluctuate. Always approach marinas carefully. Reference numbers on spotting charts indicate marina locations. ⌁ Member American Boat Builders & Repairers Association.

GREAT LAKES EDITION

TRENT-SEVERN WATERWAY

tons, 13-foot beam and four-foot draft remains in service for emergencies.

The railway operator is extremely competent and will give you instructions on his loudhailer. If it's windy he will center you on the car; make sure the hydraulically operated slings are holding you steady. Depending on your boat's size, you might be loaded aboard with four or five other boats. Be advised that the railway crew, if politely asked, will not only check your boat's bottom but will "bump" a damaged prop into reasonable shape during the short transit if you furnish the proper tools.

Below Big Chute, in short, narrow **Little Chute**, the current can reach five knots. Sound one long blast for the blind approach. Downstream traffic has the right of way and needs good power for control. Upbound boats should avoid meeting if possible; keep to the right if you do meet anyone coming the other way.

At this point, the Severn River widens into a large lake, **Gloucester Pool**, with coves, islets, and sheltered anchorages. Buoys lead to the lake's western end and the last lock on the waterway. The hand-operated, extremely busy and substandard lock is just beyond a swing bridge (16-foot clearance closed). The small resort town of **Port Severn** has good facilities, including an automatic pump-out.

Trent-Severn Waterway		SEASONAL/YEAR-ROUND	SAIL/POWER/BOTH▲	LARGEST VESSEL ACCOMMODATED	NO. OF TRANSIENT BERTHS	MARKED ENTRY CHANNEL	DOCKSIDE DEPTH (Reported)	APPROACH DEPTH (Reported)	RAILWAY/LIFT CAPACITY (in tons)	ENGINE REPAIRS: Gas★/Diesel●/Both▲	GAS★/DIESEL●/BOTH▲ FUEL BRAND	LAUNCHING RAMP	PROPELLER/HULL REPAIRS	MARINE SUPPLIES	LPG★/CNG●/BOTH▲	110V★/220V●/BOTH▲	GROCERIES/ICE	SHOWERS/MAX AMPS	RESTAURANT/SNACK BAR	PUMP-OUT STATION/LAUNDROMAT	RADIO WATCH—VHF (CB)
TALBOT RIVER AND LAKE SIMCOE																					
40. Sunset Cove, Bolsover	(705) 426-5221	S	▲	90	20	●	16	9	SHE	★	10	R	▲	PH		MGI	★30	SL		S	(13)
41. Port of Call Marina, Bolsover	426-7522	Y	P	40	6		6	9		★	4	R	★	P		MGI	★15	S		R	
42. Harbour Inn & Resort Club, Lake Simcoe	484-5365	S	▲	55	50	●	8	6	BP	★						GI	▲30	L	●	RS	
43. Beaverton Marina, Ltd., Lake Simcoe*	No Listing	S	▲	36	10	●	5	5	TEX	★	L	R	★	PH	★	MGI	★30	S	●		16
44. Sibbald Point Park, Lake Simcoe	(416) 722-3268	S	▲		20		4	3				R				GI	30			S	
45. Keswick Marina, Keswick	476-4343	Y	▲	42			10	7	PC	★	L	R	▲			MI	★	SL	●	RS	
46. Crate Marine Sales, Ltd., Keswick	476-4552	Y	P	60		●	5	5			35	R	▲			MGI	★30	SL	●	RS	
47. **Dawson's Marina, Ltd., Keswick** (p. 104)	**476-4321**	Y	P	65	25	●	8	8	SHE	▲	35	R	▲			MGI	▲50	SL	●	RS	68
48. Kon-Tiki, Gilford	(705) 456-2339	Y	▲	55	15		6	6	GUL	★			▲	H		MI	▲30	S	●	S	(13)
49. Lefroy Harbour Resorts, Inc., Lefroy	435-6074	Y	▲	60			6	6	PC	▲	25		▲	P		MI	▲	SL	●	R	
50. Monto Reno, Lefroy	456-2122	S	P	45			6	6	GUL	★	L	R	▲	PH		MGI	★30	S	●	RS	68
51. Big Bay Point Resorts	436-1176	Y	▲	60	25	●	6	6	CAN	▲	35	R	▲	P		MI	★15	SL	●	RS	
52. Harbor West, Barrie*	No Listing	Y	▲	32			5	5	BP	★	L	R	★	PH		I	★		●		(13)
53. City of Barrie Marina	726-4242	S	▲	40	10		11	6	TEX	★		R				GI	▲30	SL	●	S	
54. Marina del Rey, Orillia	325-3051	Y	▲	40	10		8	8		★	25		▲	P		M	★30	S	●	S	
55. Crate's Yacht Basin, Orillia	325-3775	Y	▲	50	25	●	6	7	SHE	▲	25	R	▲	PH		MI	★60	SL	●	S	16
56. Orchard Point, Orillia	326-9413	Y	P	50			8	6	TEX	★	L	R	★	PH		MGI	★30			R	
57. Blue Beacon Marina, Atherley	325-2526	S	▲	25			5	5	PC	★		R	★	P		MI	★		●	S	
LAKE COUCHICHING AND SEVERN RIVER																					
58. Inner Harbour, Orillia*	326-2588	Y		50	20	●	8	8	ESS	★		R	★	PH	★	GI	★30	SL	●		
59. Couchiching Marina, Orillia	326-7898	S	▲	40	10		5	5	SHE	★		R	★	PH		MGI	★30	S	●		
60. Crother's Twin Lakes Marina, Orillia	326-2511	Y	P	50			15	6	ESS	▲		R	▲			M	★	SL	●		
61. Hunter Boats, Orillia*	No Listing			60			15	8	GUL	★	R		★	PH		MI	★				
62. Port of Orillia Centennial Park Marina*	326-6314	S	▲	84	130	●	5	5				R				MGI	★30	SL	●	RS	68
63. Ojibway Bay Marina, Longford	326-5855	Y	P	30	67	●	8	5	UNI	★		R	★	H		GI	★15	S	●	RS	(13)
64. Skipper's Cove Marina, Longford*	No Listing	S	▲	25	3		8	8	PC	★		R	▲	P		MGI	★30			S	(13)
65. Pier Eleven Marina, Washago	689-2311	Y	▲	50	10		5	5	PC	▲	15	R	▲	P		MGI	★30	S	●	RS	68
66. Shamrock Marina, Severn Bridge*	No Listing	S	P	30	10		4	4	SHE	▲		R				GI	★30	SL		S	
67. Lauderdale Marina, Sparrow Lake	689-2601	S	▲	48	10		7	6	SHE	★		R	▲	PH		MGI	★15	S	●	S	(13)
68. Torpitt Lodge, Port Stanton	689-2633			50			10	7	TEX	★		R				GI		L		S	(1)
69. Waubic Inn, Coldwater*	No Listing	S	▲	50			15	10									★30			R	(13)
70. Tamarack Park Marina, Severn Falls	686-7935	S	P	50		●	25	15	SHE	★		R				GI				S	
71. Severn Cove Marina	686-7496	Y	P	40			20	10	PC	★		R	★			MGI				S	
72. Big Chute Marina, Severn	756-2641	Y	▲	60	6		20	10	SHE	★	5	R	★	P		MGI	★30		●	S	16
PORT SEVERN																					
73. Severn Lodge, Port Severn	756-2722	S	▲	60	10		12	12									★15	S		RS	
74. White's Falls Marina, Port Severn	756-2525	S	P	45			15	10	SUN	★		R	★	H	★	MGI					
75. Whitestone Lodge Marina, Port Severn*	756-8050	S		36		●	7	7		★		R				GI	★20			R	
76. Severn Boat Haven, Port Severn	538-2975	Y	▲	50	10	●	20	12	PC	▲	20		★	PH		MGI	★30	S	●	S	
77. Bush's Boat Livery, Port Severn	538-2378	S	P	40	10		12	12	GUL	★	12	R	★	PH		MGI	★			R	(13)
78. Severn Marina, Port Severn	538-2571	S	P	35	20	●	5	5	SHE	★	10	R	▲	P		MI	★50	S	●		(13)

To provide the most complete and accurate information, **all facilities have been contacted within the past year.** If an asterisk (*) appears, it indicates a facility which did not respond to our requests for information (these listings may not reflect current conditions). Although facility operators supplied this data, we cannot guarantee accuracy or assume responsibility for errors. Entrance and dockside soundings tend to fluctuate. Always approach marinas carefully. Reference numbers on spotting charts indicate marina locations. ✓ Member American Boat Builders & Repairers Association.

Aids to Navigation

Unlighted buoy (C. can, N. nun, S. spar, Bell, Gong, Whistle)
Danger or junction buoy
Mooring buoy
Light (On fixed structure)
Fish trap buoy
Daybeacon (Bn)
R. Bn. radiobeacon
Mid-channel buoy
Lighted buoy

Lights (Lights are white unless otherwise indicated)
F. fixed — OBSC. obscured
Fl. flashing — WHIS. whistle
Qk. quick — DIA. diaphone
Gp. group — M. nautical miles
E. Int. equal interval — Rot. rotating
Mo.(A) morse code — SEC. sector
Occ. occulting — m. minutes
Alt. alternating — sec. seconds
I. Qk. interrupted quick

Buoys:
T.B. temporary buoy — Or. orange
C. can — R. red
N. nun — G. green
S. spar — W. white
B. black — Y. yellow

Bottom characteristics:
Cl. clay — Sh. shells — bu. blue
Co. coral — hrd. hard — gn. green
G. gravel — rky. rocky — gy. gray
Grs. grass — sft. soft — rd. red
M. mud — stk. sticky — wh. white
Rk. rock — bk. black — yl. yellow
S. sand — br. brown

Dangers:
Sunken wreck
Visible wreck
Rocks
Wreck, rock, obstruction, or shoal swept clear to the depth indicated
Rocks that cover and uncover, with heights in feet above datum of soundings
AERO. aeronautical — D.F.S. distance finding station
Bn. daybeacon
R. Bn. radiobeacon — AUTH. authorized
R. TR. radio tower — Obstr. obstruction
C.G. Coast Guard Station — P.A. position approximate
E.D. existence doubtful

Caution: Mariners are warned to stay clear of the protective riprap surrounding navigational light structures shown thus.
Restricted Areas
Fish Trap Areas

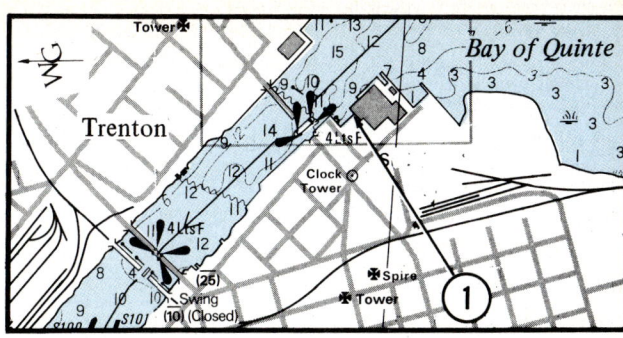

TRENT-SEVERN WATERWAY

① *Canadian chart 2021-SC*

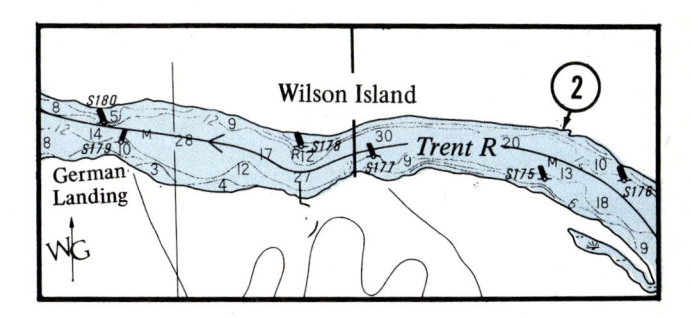

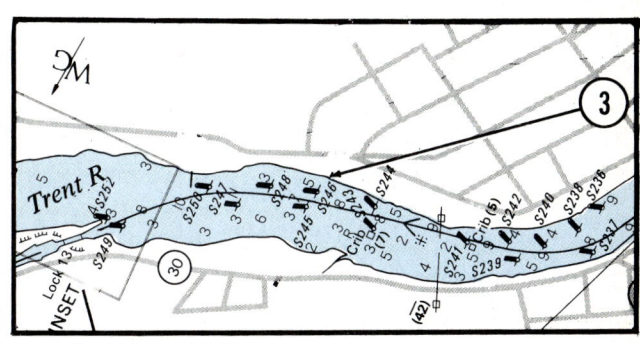

②

③ *Canadian chart 2021-SC*

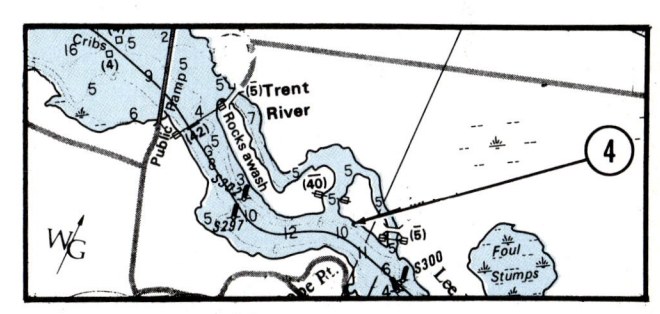

④ *Canadian chart 2022-SC*

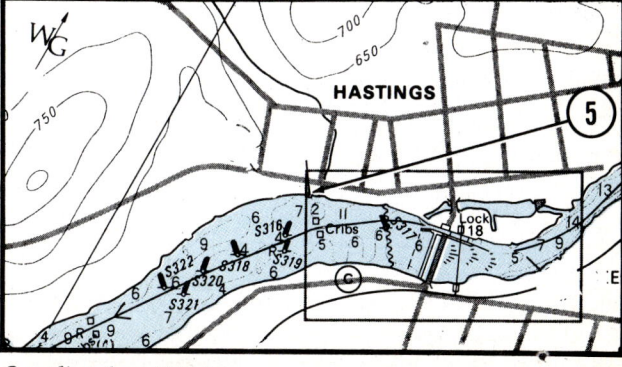

⑤ *Canadian chart 2022-SC*

GREAT LAKES EDITION — *Under no circumstances are these charts to be used for navigation.* — 107

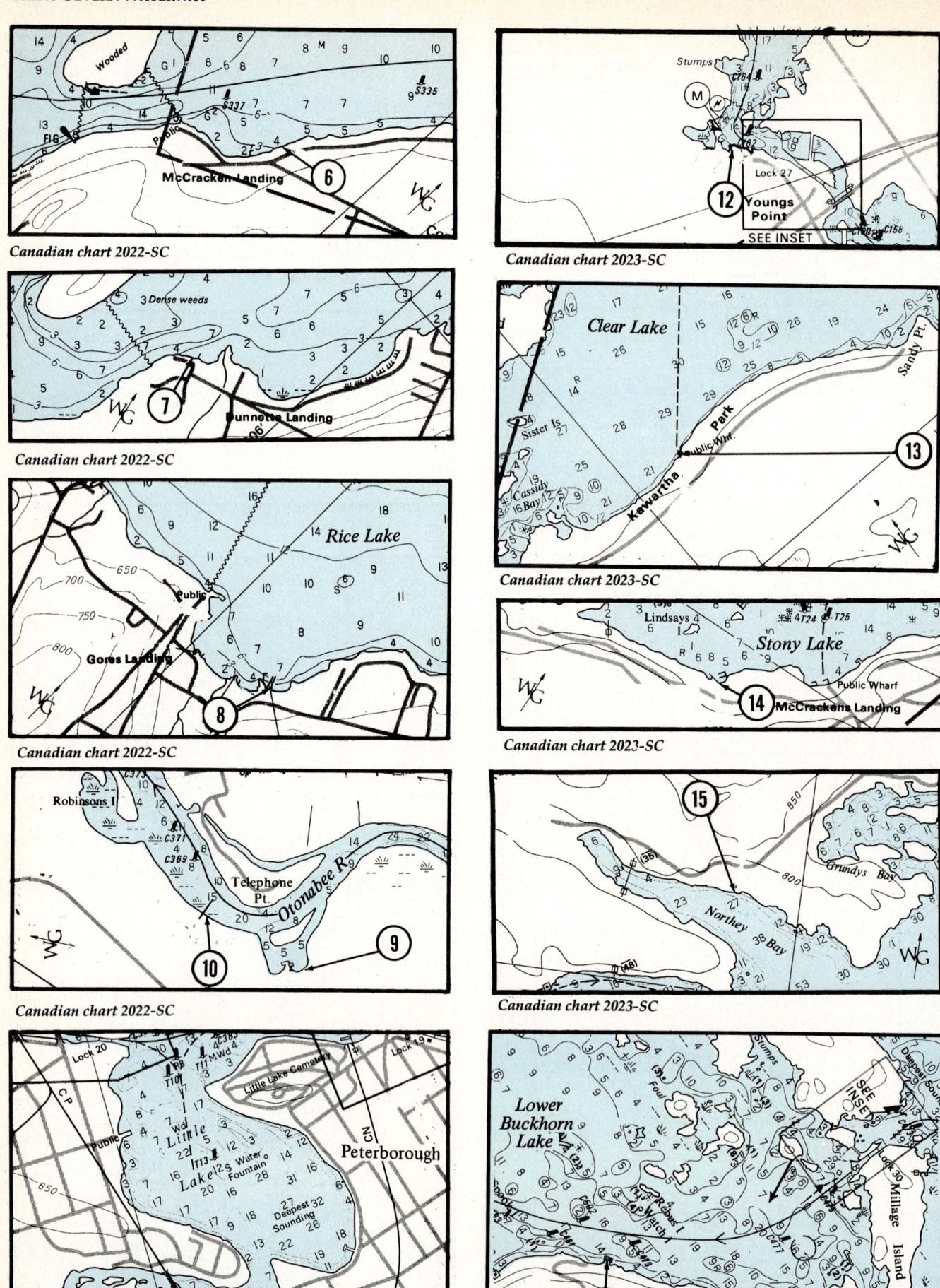

TRENT-SEVERN WATERWAY

Canadian chart 2022-SC

Canadian chart 2022-SC

Canadian chart 2022-SC

Canadian chart 2022-SC

Canadian chart 2022-SC

Canadian chart 2023-SC

Canadian chart 2023-SC

Canadian chart 2023-SC

Canadian chart 2023-SC

Canadian chart 2023-SC

108   Under no circumstances are these charts to be used for navigation.   WATERWAY GUIDE / 1991

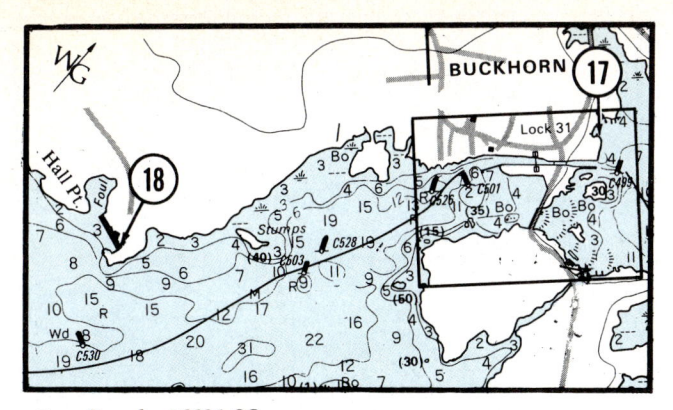

Trent-Severn Waterway

Canadian chart 2024-SC

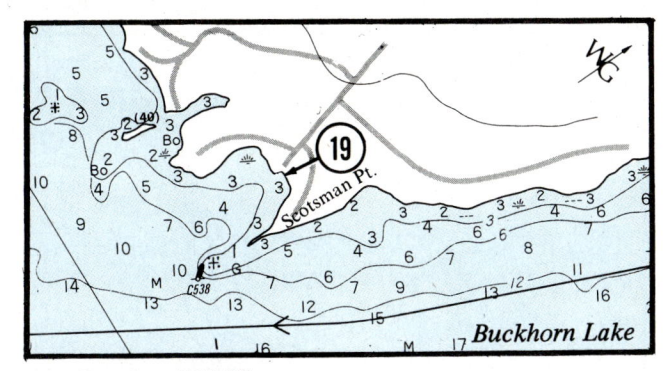

Canadian chart 2024-SC

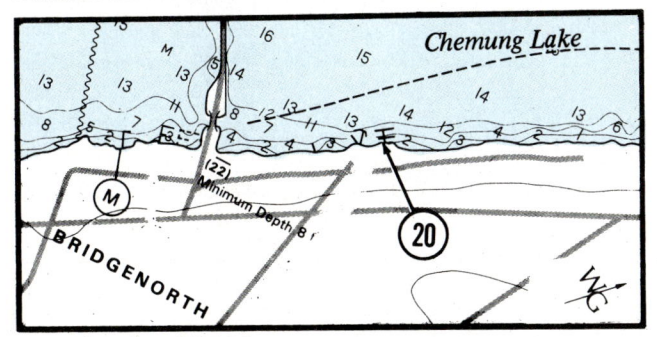

Canadian chart 2024-SC

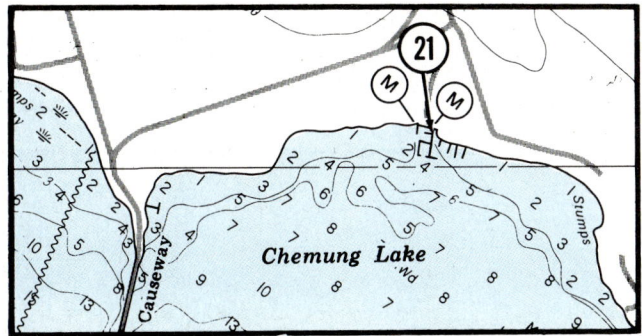

Canadian chart 2024-SC

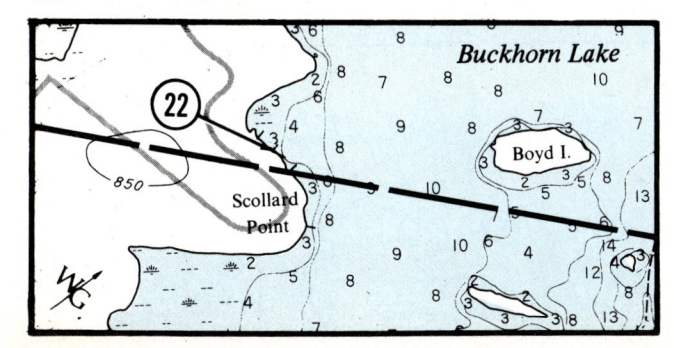

Canadian chart 2024-SC

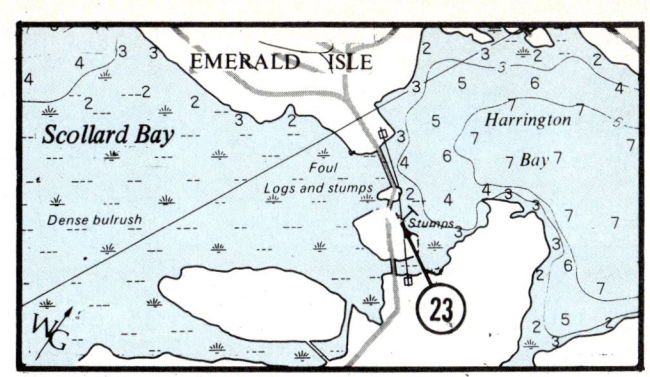

Canadian chart 2024-SC

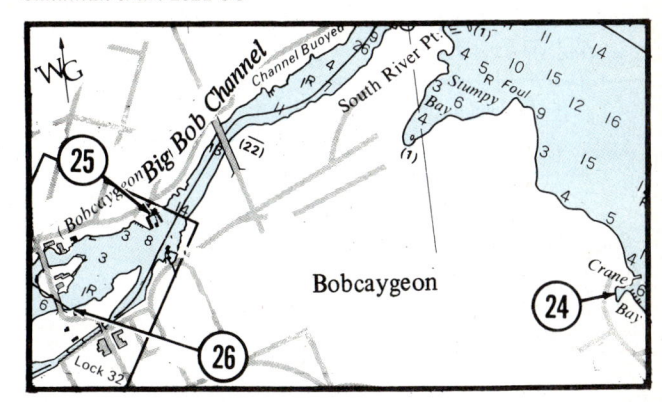

Canadian chart 2024-SC

Canadian chart 2025-SC

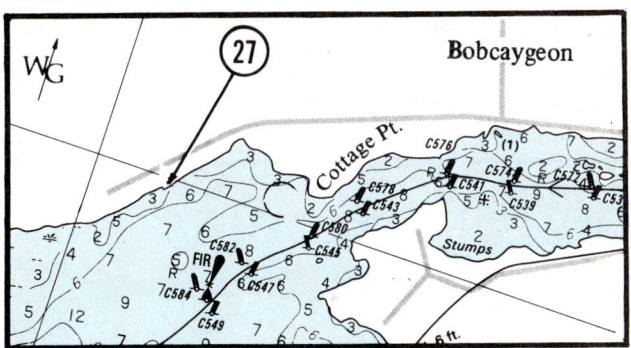

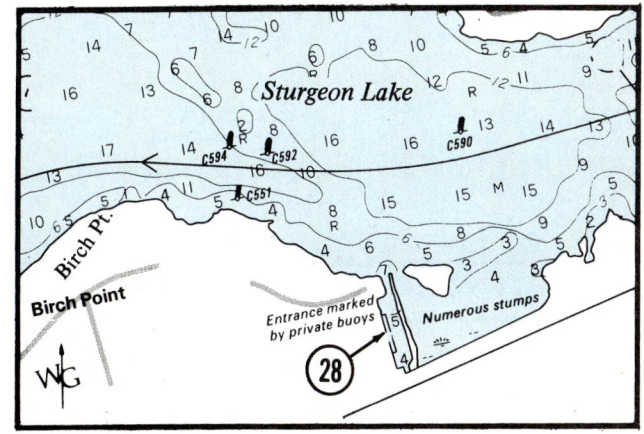

Canadian chart 2025-SC

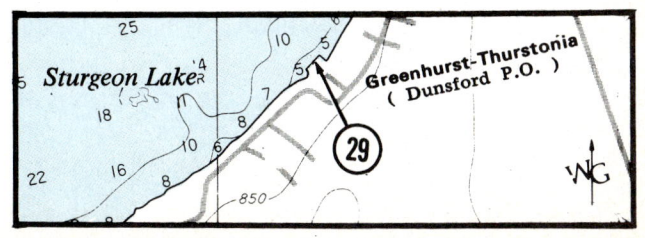

Canadian chart 2025-SC

Great Lakes Edition — *Under no circumstances are these charts to be used for navigation.*

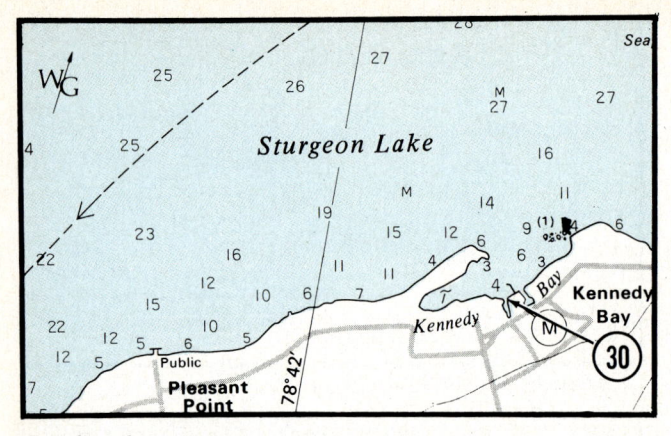

TRENT-SEVERN WATERWAY

Canadian chart 2025-SC

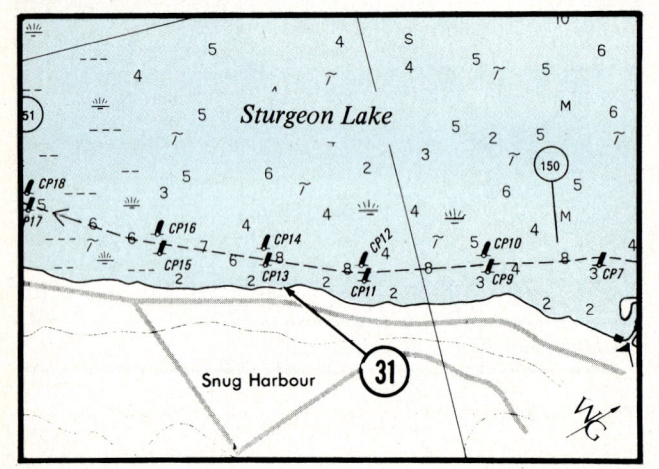

Canadian chart 2026-SC

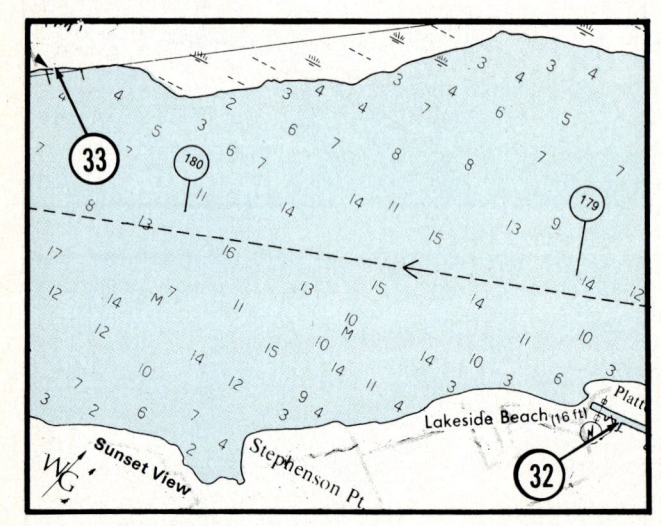

Canadian chart 2026-SC

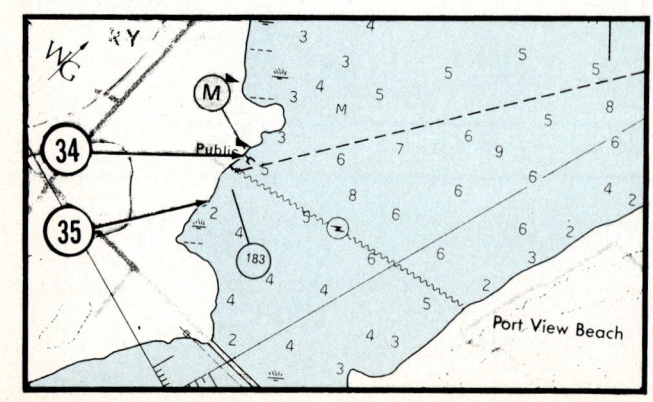

Canadian chart 2026-SC

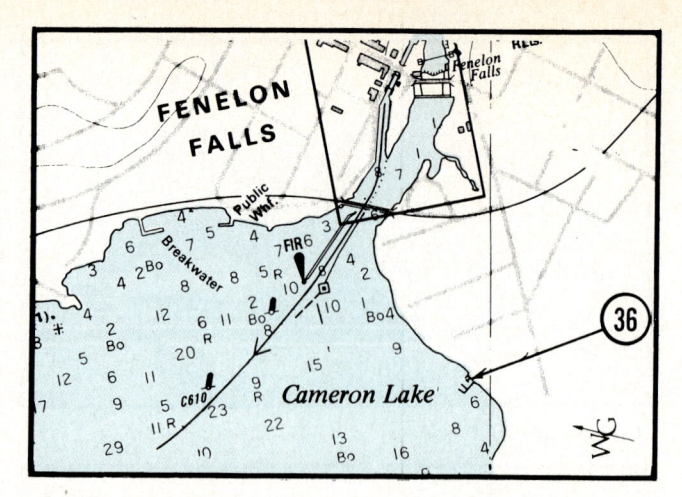

Canadian chart 2025-SC

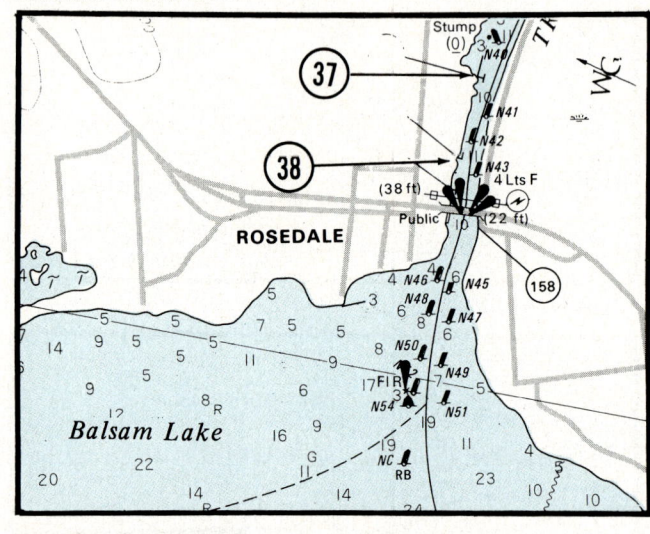

Canadian chart 2025-SC

Canadian chart 2025-SC

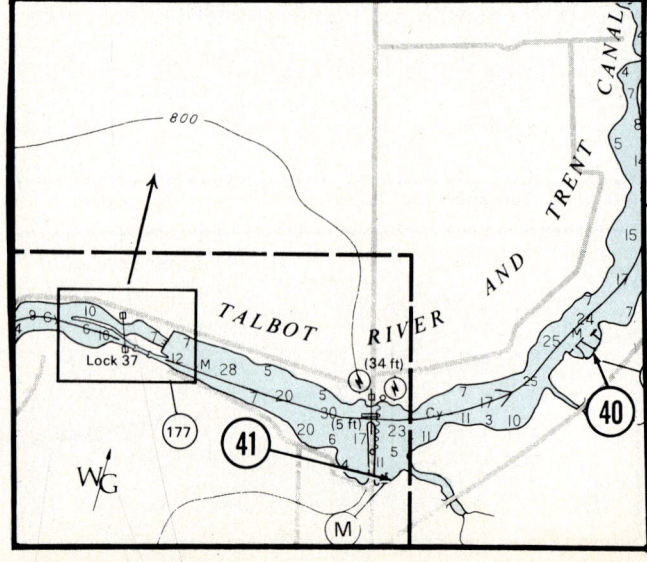

Canadian chart 2025-SC

Under no circumstances are these charts to be used for navigation.

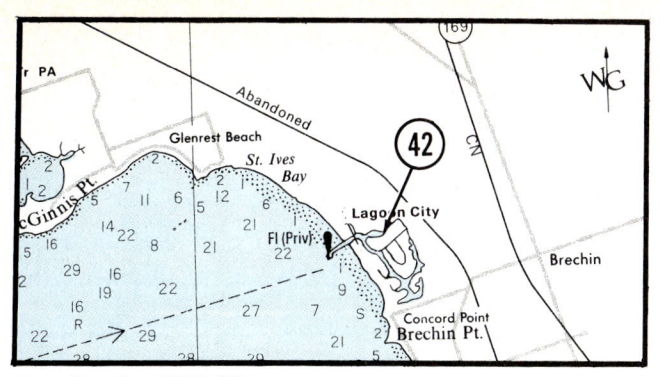

Trent-Severn Waterway

Canadian chart 2028-SC

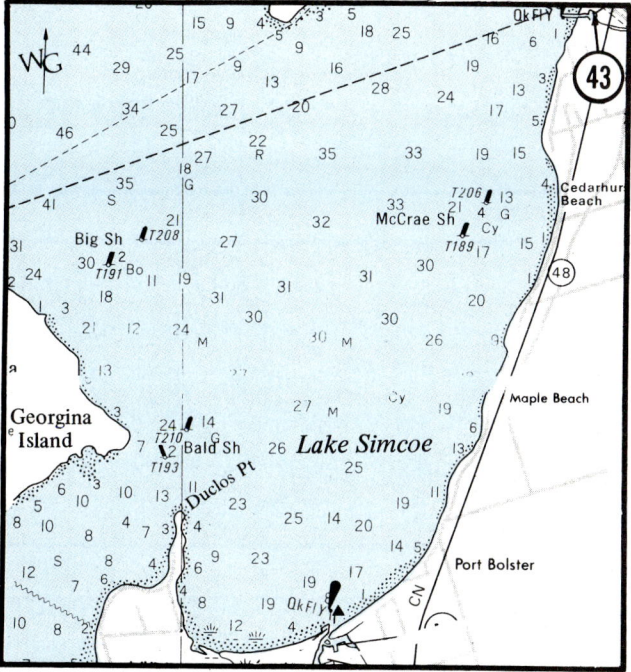

Canadian chart 2028-SC

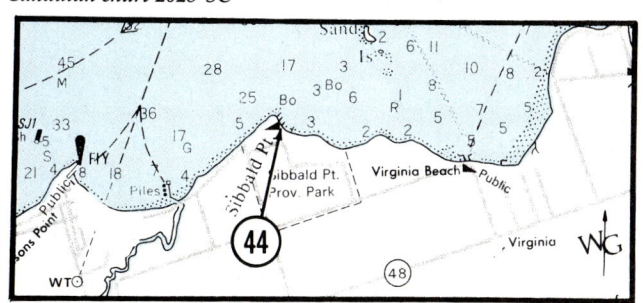

Canadian chart 2028-SC

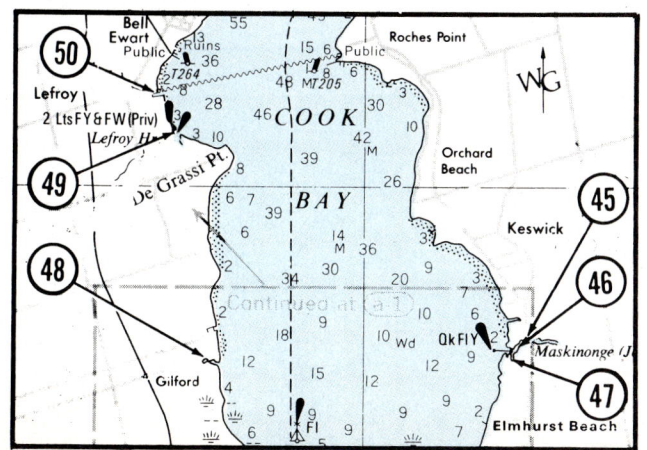

Canadian chart 2028-SC

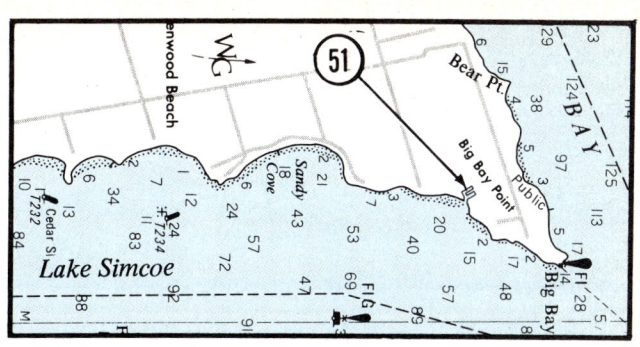

Canadian chart 2028-SC

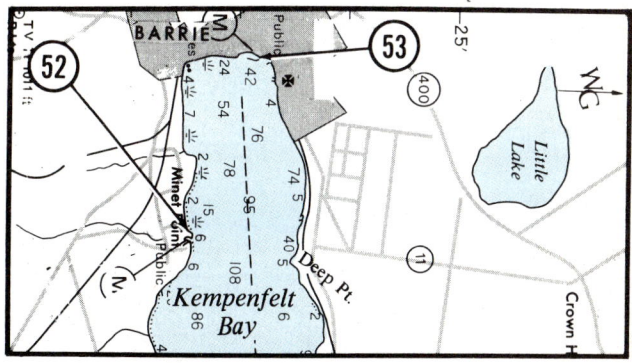

Canadian chart 2028-SC

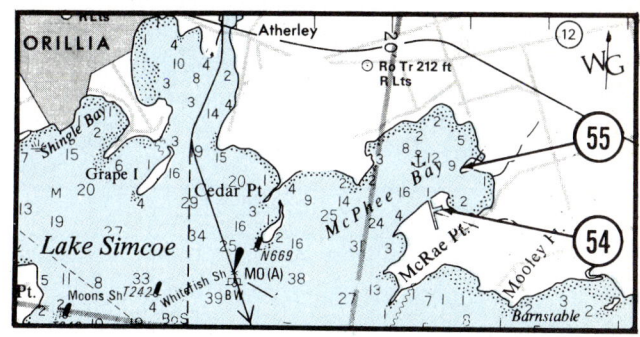

Canadian chart 2028-SC

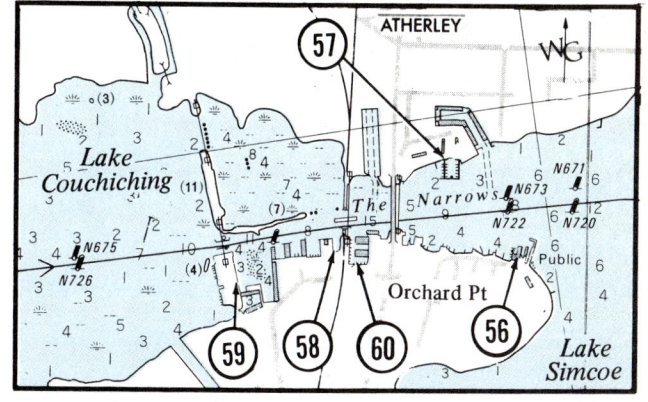

Canadian chart 2028-SC

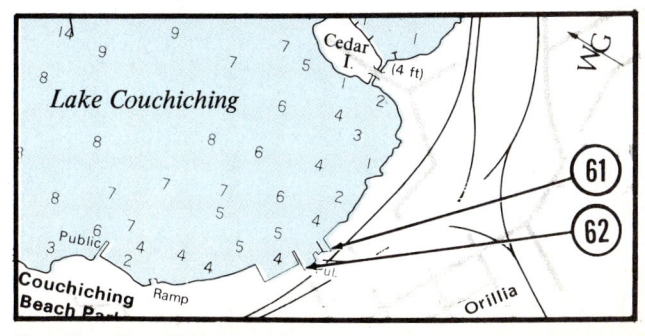

Canadian chart 2028-SC

Great Lakes Edition — *Under no circumstances are these charts to be used for navigation.*

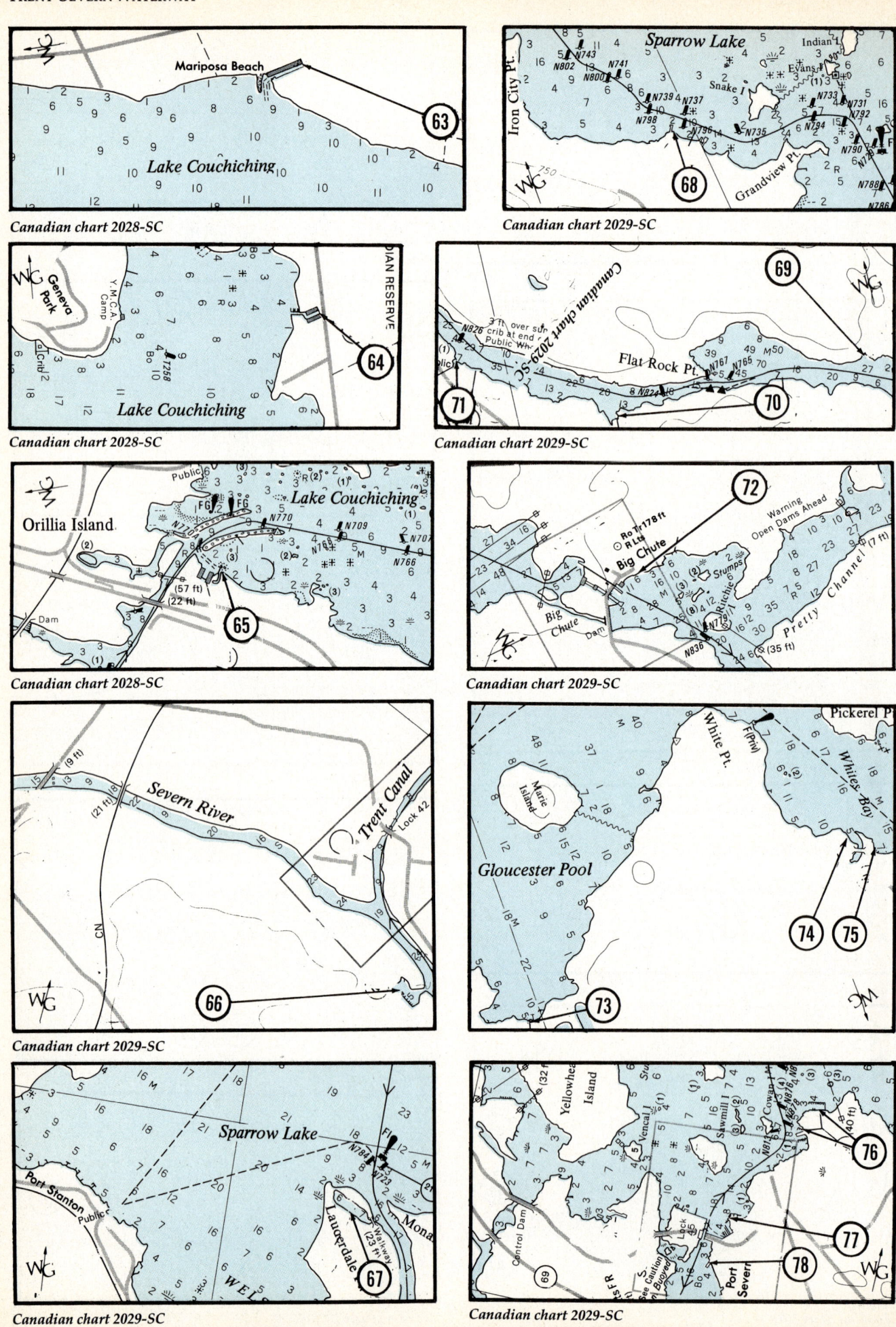

Trent-Severn Waterway

Canadian chart 2028-SC

Canadian chart 2028-SC

Canadian chart 2028-SC

Canadian chart 2029-SC

Canadian chart 2029-SC

Canadian chart 2029-SC

Canadian chart 2029-SC

Canadian chart 2029-SC

Canadian chart 2029-SC

Canadian chart 2029-SC

Mariner's Handbook

Eisenhower Lock; St. Lawrence Seaway. Courtesy NY State Dept. of Commerce.

GREAT LAKES EDITION
113

Rules of the Road

The wag who coined the phrase about a collision ruining your whole day understated the matter. A collision, which can ruin a great deal more than your day, is simply the result of neglect, and knowledgeable boat operators use every means available to obtain early warnings and take early action to avoid collision.

Mariners must maintain a watch above deck at all times, whether or not the vessel is on autopilot. When in doubt, take the conservative stance and assume that a risk of collision is present. Make decisions in plenty of time, alter course in ways that are readily apparent to the captain of the other vessel, reduce speed or reverse engines when necessary, and pass at a safe distance. Refer to charts often to guide you away from waters where you cannot maneuver safely, and when forced to operate in confined channels, do so with caution.

Perhaps most important, make yourself scrupulously aware of the Rules of the Road concerning privileged and burdened vessels, as prescribed under the International Rules ('72 COLREGS). Skippers on the Great Lakes, in the coastal waters of the Atlantic Ocean and the Gulf of Mexico, on the Intracoastal Waterway and the GIWW, and in all waters connected therewith that are navigable by seagoing vessels must use the same rules that apply to vessels on the high seas. WATERWAY GUIDE offers some basic guidelines to the Rules of the Road, with the caveat that every mariner should obtain a copy of the *Navigation Rules, International-Inland*, published by the U. S. Coast Guard, and perhaps the consolidated *Collision Regulations*, published by the Canadian Hydrographic Service.

Give-way and Stand-on vessels. When two vessels meet on the water, explicit rules govern which one has the right of way. The **give-way,** or burdened, vessel is responsible for altering course to avoid collision. The **stand-on,** or **privileged,** vessel must hold an intended course that will not confuse the other vessel.

Vessels under sail meeting one another. When two sailing vessels meet and a risk of collision exists, the give-way (burdened) vessel shall keep clear of the stand-on (privileged) vessel as follows:

- When each has the wind on a different side, the boat with the wind on the port side shall keep clear of the boat with the wind on the starboard.

- When both have the wind on the same side, the vessel to windward will keep clear of the leeward boat.

- A vessel with the wind on the port side that sees a vessel to windward but cannot determine whether the windward vessel has the wind to port or starboard will assume that the windward vessel is on starboard and keep clear.

Power vessels meeting one another or meeting vessels under sail.

- When two vessels under power— be they sailboats or powerboats—meet head on, neither is privileged. Both are obliged to alter course to starboard to avoid the risk of collision.

- When a vessel under power meets a vessel under sail, the sailing vessel is privileged and the vessel under power will alter course accordingly.

Vessels in a crossing situation

- When two vessels under power are crossing and a risk of collision exists, the vessel that has has the other on her starboard side is burdened and must keep clear and avoid crossing ahead of the other vessel.

- When a vessel under sail and a vessel under power are crossing, the boat under power is burdened and must keep clear.

- Any vessel crossing a river shall keep clear of a power-driven vessel ascending or descending the river.

Vessels in an overtaking situation.

- Any vessel overtaking any other vessel is burdened and shall keep out of the way of the vessel being overtaken.

- A vessel in doubt as to whether she is overtaking another shall assume that such is the case and act accordingly until finally past and clear.

Action required of give-way/stand-on vessels.

- Give-way vessels must take early and substantial action to keep clear.

- Stand-on vessels must keep their course and speed, unless they must maneuver to avoid a give-way vessel that is not keeping clear. In that case, they must take action to best avoid collision. When two boats under power are in this situation and the stand-on vessel has the unresponsive give-way vessel to port, the stand-on vessel must not alter course to port.

You may order a copy of the *International-Inland Rules* from the Superintendent of Documents, U.S. Government Printing Office, Washington, D.C. 20402, or call (202) 783-3238.

Bridge and Lock Manners

A casual observer may feel that the process of passing through a drawbridge is quite simple and always goes smoothly, but mariners and bridge tenders know differently. Opening a drawbridge can be painless, but it can also cause tempers to flare and lead to an exchange of words or even blows. In an effort to promote better understanding between mariners and bridge tenders, WATERWAY GUIDE offers some basic guidelines.

The first step to opening a drawbridge is to decide if you really need to have it opened. You should know your boat's exact height from the waterline to the top of the highest fixed structure.

Federal regulations require that you lower any gear, such as antennae, bimini tops, or fishing outriggers, if you can get under the bridge with them down. One of the most common complaints from bridge tenders is that mariners signal for opening when they could lower equipment easily and pass safely under the bridge. The tenders report such violations to the Coast Guard, who investigate and take the appropriate action.

The next step is to establish communication with the bridge tender, either by horn or by marine radio (Channels 13 and/or 16). Let the tender know you intend to pass through the bridge: he has no way of knowing if an approaching boat plans to go through, is heading for a nearby marina or side stream, or is going to turn around and go back.

The signal to request a bridge opening is one long blast on the horn, followed by one short blast. Three blasts on the horn is not correct anymore, it means "my engine is going astern" in the Rules of the Road. The bridge tender must reply with the same signal if he can open the bridge promptly. If he cannot, he must sound five short blasts.

Where bridges have restricted openings, the traditional five short blasts for emergency openings and for the passage of privileged vessels (tugs with tows and U.S. Government vessels) continues in effect.

Note that if two or more vessels approach the same bridge at nearly the same time, each one must signal and then be acknowledged independently. Many a bridge has closed prematurely—and disastrously—because the bridge tender didn't see a second boat right behind another, or one approaching from a different direction.

Once the bridge is open, keep in the channel and proceed at no-wake speed. Going through in company, keep a safe distance between you and other craft; currents and turbulence around bridge supports can be tricky. After you've passed through the bridge, maintain a no-wake speed until you're well clear and then you can resume normal speed.

Locking Through

Lock procedure varies with different canal systems and lock designs. The first rule of safe locking is to follow the lockmaster's instructions carefully. These may be given over VHF radio (channels to be used are given in each chapter as appropriate), by whistle signals, through red/green light indicators, or by voice communication. Most lockmasters are extremely courteous and knowledgeable, with long years of experience handling all sorts of vessels.

Dangers. The accidents in locking through usually take the following forms: loss of control or damage in lock turbulence, strong currents, and prop wash; getting "hung-up" on unattended dock lines as water level changes; inadequate fendering; excessive speed in the lock area; and falling overboard.

Some lock systems, such as the Welland Canal, require considerable advance planning and special equipment such as specified fenders or gloves. WATERWAY GUIDE gives these particulars and each lock system's "vital statistics" as needed in the chapter covering the canal system. These should be checked when planning passage through a lock system; such factors as special equipment, time constraints, boat length (and even boat weight on the Trent-Severn railway) may have to be considered.

Fenders. Most locks prohibit the use of old tires as fenders because they tear off, sink, and can foul the lock valves. Bags of hay can be used in some locks, but they are fragile, and can tear off and foul the water and the boat's propellers. The best fender arrangement consists of stout wooden boards (two-by-sixes) laid outside of oversize fenders. These fender boards may be laid horizontally, or even better in many locks, vertically, to slide along the lock's rough walls smoothly. The ends of the boards can be shaped (something like a ski tip) so they won't catch along the wall. Never use your foot or hands to fend off.

Lines. Dock lines can be lighter, and should be longer (twice the length of the lock's vertical drop) than the vessel's normal dock lines. Bow and stern lines are usually sufficient and may be looped over separate bollards or posts on the lock wall and adjusted from on deck. They must be attended at all times, and never cleated permanently. Many locks provide each boat with dock lines, which are handed over by the dockmaster, for bow and stern. WATERWAY GUIDE notes the locks that provide lines.

Coast Guard

The U.S. and Canadian coast guards stand watch at all times to aid mariners, either by helping them out of trouble or giving them information about cruising conditions. The stations listed below cover the areas in this edition of WATERWAY GUIDE. They have search and rescue capabilities and may provide lookout, communication and/or patrol functions to assist vessels in distress. If you have a question of a non-emergency nature and happen to be in port, the Coast Guard prefers you to telephone their offices for information.

To call the Coast Guard on VHF-FM, use Channel 16, guarded by all Group Commands. All Canadian search and rescue activities are coordinated through the Rescue Coordination Centre at Trenton, Ontario, which directs operations through Coast Guard cutter bases on the Great Lakes and seasonal mobile rescue units in areas of heavy pleasure boat activity. Canadian Coast Guard radio stations and Coast Guard vessels on the Great Lakes and connecting waters keep a continuous watch on Channel 16. Canadian Coast Guard radio stations also provide a continuous marine weather broadcast on Channel 21 or 83B.

U.S. Coast Guard vessels are identified by the wide diagonal red stripe on the bow; Canadian Coast Guard vessels are identified by the red hull with diagonal white stripes and white superstructure.

Coast Guard Centers:

First District (Boston) (617) 223-8515.
Ninth District (Cleveland) (216) 522-3984.
Canadian (Trenton) (613) 392-2811, ext. 3870/3875.

Search and Rescue Stations:

New York City/Hudson River
New York—On Governors Island. Phone: (212) 668-7936.
Port of Albany—(518) 472-6110.

Lake Champlain
Burlington—East of Burlington Harbor North Breakwater Light, on Battery Park. Phone: (802) 864-6791.

Thousand Islands
Alexandria Bay—On the southern shore of Wellesley Island, 1,100 yards southwest of Thousand Islands Country Club. Seasonal. Opens May 15. Phone: (315) 482-2574.

Lake Ontario
Oswego—On the south side of the basin about 0.7 mile southward of West Pierhead Light. Phone: (315) 343-1551; (800) 321-4400.
Rochester—East side of entrance to harbor. Phone: (716) 342-4140.
Sacketts Harbor—On the southern side of the harbor, about 800 feet south of Navy Point Light. Seasonal, May 1-Oct. 1. Phone: (315) 646-2290.
Sodus Bay—On west side of harbor entrance. Seasonal. Phone: (315) 483-9816.
Youngstown—East side of entrance to Niagara River. Phone: (716) 745-3327.

Lake Erie/Detroit River
Ashtabula—On east side of river, about 700 feet north of the highway bridge. Phone: (216) 964-9417.
Buffalo—On the south pier at the mouth of Buffalo River. Phone: (716) 846-4151.
Cleveland—Near the west end of airport on the south side of a small basin 1.1 miles east of East Breakwater Light. Phone: (216) 522-4412.
Detroit—At Belle Isle Light near the upper end of the island. Phone: (313) 331-3110.
Erie—On the north side of the entrance channel, near the Erie Harbor Inner Range Rear Light. Phone: (814) 838-2097.
Fairport—On the west side of the mouth of Grand River. Phone (216) 352-3111.
Lorain—East side of the mouth of Black River. Phone: (216) 288-1206.
Marblehead—On Point Marblehead, 1.1 (.8 nautical) miles north-northwest of Marblehead Light. Phone: (419) 798-4444.
Toledo—In Bay View Park, on northwestern side of Maumee River near its mouth. Phone: (419) 259-6448.

Lake St. Clair/St. Clair River
Port Huron—On west side of entrance to St. Clair River, near Fort Gratiot Light. Phone: (313) 984-2602.
St. Clair Shores—Near the end of Revere Avenue about 0.7 mile north of Miller Memorial Light. Phone: (313) 778-0590; (313) 748-9921.
Selfridge Air National Guard Base, Detroit Air Station—West of Anchor Bay, about 3.5 miles west-northwest of Clinton River entrance. Phone: (313) 466-4747.

Lake Huron
East Tawas—On Tawas Point, about 0.6 mile southeast of Tawas Light. Phone: (517) 362-4428.
Harbor Beach—At the outer end of causeway, about 0.7 mile west-northwest of Harbor Beach Light. Seasonal. Phone: (517) 479-3285.
Saginaw River—On northwestern side of entrance to Saginaw River. Phone: (517) 892-0555.
St. Ignace—Near State Highway dock on the east end of Graham Point. Phone: (906) 643-9192.

Lake Michigan

Calumet Harbor—Lake front in Calumet Park. About 1.1 miles south of Calumet River entrance. Phone: (312) 353-0278.

Charlevoix—North side of Pine River entrance to Lake Charlevoix. Phone: (616) 547-2541.

Chicago Air Station—About 7.5 miles west of Wilmette Harbor. Phone: (312) 657-2145.

Frankfort—North side of harbor entrance. Phone: (616) 352-4242.

Grand Haven—South side of the mouth of Grand River. Phone: (616) 846-3237.

Green Bay—On the east side of the mouth of the Fox River. Seasonal. Phone: (414) 435-7042.

Holland—North side of the harbor entrance. Phone: (616) 399-9330.

Kenosha—On east side of the inner basin. Phone: (414) 657-7651.

Ludington: North side of the harbor entrance. Phone: (616) 843-9088.

Manistee—North side of the harbor entrance. Phone: (616) 723-7412.

Michigan City—East side of the harbor entrance. Phone: (219) 879-8371.

Milwaukee—At south end of outer harbor, about 0.8 mile southwest of South Entrance Light. Phone: (414) 747-7100.

Muskegon—South side of entrance to harbor. Phone: (616) 759-8581.

Plum Island—On northern side of Plum Island. Seasonal. (414) 847-2638.

St. Joseph—North side of the river. Phone: (616) 983-6114.

Sheboygan—Near inner end of old north pier stub. Phone: (414) 452-5115.

Sturgeon Bay—At eastern entrance, north side. Phone: (414) 743-3366.

Traverse City—At southeastern limits of the city, adjacent to Cherry Capitol Airport. Phone: (616) 922-8226.

Two Rivers—Northeast side of entrance to harbor. Phone: (414) 793-1304.

Wilmette—North side of harbor entrance. Phone: (312) 251-0185.

Lake Superior/St. Marys River

Bayfield—On south side of city, about 1,000 feet southwest of South Breakwater Light. Phone: (715) 779-3950.

Duluth—On Minnesota Point, about 0.5 mile south of Duluth Ship Canal. Phone: (218) 720-5412.

Grand Marais—On west side of harbor entrance channel. Phone: (218) 720-5412.

Hancock, Station Portage—On east bank of upper canal about 0.8 mile southeast of breakwater entrance. (906) 482-1520.

Marquette—Near inner end of breakwater, about 1,000 feet southwest of Marquette Light. Phone: (906) 226-3312.

Munising—In the town of Munising at the Munising Range Front Light. Seasonal. Phone: (906) 387-2041.

Coast Guard — Canadian

St. Lawrence River
Prescott, mobile rescue
Rockport, mobile rescue

Lake Ontario
Kingston, cutter base
Coburg, cutter base
Port Weller, cutter base

Lake St. Clair/St. Clair River
Thames River, mobile rescue
Lambton, mobile rescue

Lake Erie/Detroit River
Port Dover, cutter base
Amherstburg, cutter base
Long Point, mobile rescue

Lake Huron/North Channel/Georgian Bay
Goderich, cutter base
Tobermory, cutter base
Meaford, cutter base
Bruce Mines, mobile rescue
Snug Harbour, mobile rescue
Gereaux Island, mobile rescue
Port Severn, mobile rescue

Lake Superior
Thunder Bay, cutter base

Weather Information

For mariners, few things are as important as the weather, and obtaining accurate weather data can mean the difference between a safe, pleasant cruise and a disaster. The U.S. National Weather Service and the Canadian Coast Guard provide mariners with continuous broadcasts of weather warnings, forecasts, and radar reports over VHF-FM radio. Canadian broadcasts are in English and in MAFOR code. Reception range is usually up to 40 miles from the antenna site, depending on the terrain and the type of receiver and antenna you're using.

National Weather Service Office telephone numbers which give forecasts—usually round-the-clock—are listed below. Also listed are the VHF-FM frequencies which broadcast weather information exclusively. If you have a crystal unit, be sure to have the appropriate crystals installed in your set.

Weather Radio on the Great Lakes. Two types of weather broadcasts are available on the regular VHF radiotelephone channels. MAFOR (MArine FORecast) broadcasts are predictions of the coming weather. These predictions are transmitted in a simple code. The LAWEB (LAkes WEather Broadcasts) reports are transmitted in plain English and contain reports of wind direction and speed, wave height, and visibility. Both types are transmitted by commercial radiotelephone operators primarily for use by commercial ships.

Both MAFOR and LAWEB broadcasts are made at specific times throughout the day. Additional weather broadcasts are made as needed. Storm and gale warnings are included in these broadcasts, but small craft warnings are not included.

MAFOR. The MAFOR code is a group of numbers. Each position within the group stands for a portion of the forecast. Each number carries a specific weather reference. MAFOR broadcasts start with the name of the lake in plain English. This is followed by the number "1" which is an identifying figure carrying no weather information. The next four digits tell how long the forecast is valid, the wind direction and speed, and the predicted weather conditions.

Several MAFOR code groupings may be broadcast for the same lake. This happens when weather conditions are changing rapidly. The identifying figure "1" helps separate the code groups. The first group is effective from the beginning of the forecast period. The second group takes effect at the end of the first period. This pattern continues for as many groups as needed to cover a full 24 hours.

The table shows the format for a typical MAFOR code grouping. The grouping shown in the illustration would sound like this on the radio: "MAFOR...Superior...One...Six...Eight...Three...Zero."The marine operator will repeat each code grouping at least twice. Decoding: "Superior" means Lake Superior; the "One" is the identifying figure indicating the beginning of the code group; the "Six" says this forecast is valid for 24 hours; the "Eight" indicates the winds will be from the north; the "Three" says the predicted wind speeds are 22 to 27 knots; the "Zero" says there will be good visibility, more than three nautical miles.

LAWEB. LAWEB broadcasts aren't forecasts; they are reports of actual conditions encountered on the lakes by commercial ships. Reports from selected land stations are also included. These reports are generally about 90 minutes old, so they closely reflect the actual conditions at the reporting location. LAWEB reports are transmitted in plain English, not code. Ship positions are given by a reference to the closest landmark. For instance, the marine operator may say, "Lake Erie two miles southeast of Point Pelee...east at three...fog."

Coast Guard. Additional sources of Great Lakes weather information are the U.S. and Canadian Coast Guard broadcasts, made in plain English. U.S. Coast Guard broadcasts are made at regular intervals; notice is given on Channel 16 and the actual broadcast on Channel 22.

Visual Signals. Visual small-craft advisories still exist in some places. When you see these displayed, you should tune your radio to the latest marine broadcast. The Weather Service encourages mariners to rely on their broadcasts rather than visual displays.

Small craft: Daytime, red pennant. Nighttime, red light over white. Winds up to 33 knots.

Gale: Daytime, two red pennants. Nighttime, white light over red. Winds 34 to 47 knots.

Storm: Daytime, square, red flag with black square centered. Nighttime, two red lights. Winds 48 to 63 knots.

Hurricane: Daytime, two red square flags with black squares centered. Nighttime, white light between two red lights. Winds over 64 knots; these signals are displayed only in connection with a hurricane.

Weather Information

Weather Offices

*Recording only

Weather Service Office	Telephone
Alpena	*(517)356-0942
Buffalo	(716)632-1319
Chicago	*(312)298-1413
Cleveland	*(216)931-1212
	(216)267-3900
Detroit	*(313)941-7192
Duluth	*(218)722-3588
Erie	*(814)453-2211
Flint	(313)234-3987
	*(313)234-4622
Grand Rapids	*(616)949-4253
Green Bay	(414)494-1482

Weather Service Office	Telephone
Marquette	*(906)475-5212
Milwaukee	*(414)744-8000
Muskegon	*(616)798-4070
New York	*(212)976-1212
Rochester	*(716)974-1212
	(716)328-7391
Sault Ste. Marie	(906)632-8921
Syracuse	*(315)455-6601
	*(315)457-9000
Toledo	*(419)936-1212
	*(419)865-3468

Stations in the Area Covered by This Edition

Note: WX-1 is 162.55 MHz
WX-2 is 162.40 MHz
WX-3 is 162.475 MHz

Location	Channel
Akron	WX-2
Alpena	WX-1
Buffalo	WX-1
Burlington	WX-2
Chicago	WX-1
Cleveland	WX-1
Detroit	WX-1
Duluth	WX-1
Erie	WX-2
Grand Rapids	WX-1
Green Bay	WX-1

Location	Channel
Houghton	WX-2
Kingston	WX-3
Marquette	WX-1
Menominee	WX-2
Milwaukee	WX-2
New York	WX-1
Rochester	WX-2
Sandusky	WX-2
Sault Ste. Marie	WX-1
South Bend	WX-2
Traverse City	WX-2

MAFOR Code

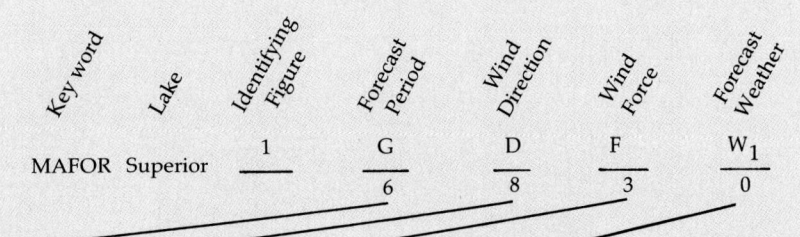

MAFOR Superior 1 / 6   G / 8   D / 3   F / W_1 / 0

(Key word / Lake / Identifying Figure / Forecast Period / Wind Direction / Wind Force / Forecast Weather)

G - Forecast Period
- 0- Beginning of period
- 1- Valid for 3 hours
- 2- Valid for 6 hours
- 3- Valid for 9 hours
- 4- Valid for 12 hours
- 5- Valid for 18 hours
- 6- Valid for 24 hours
- 7- Valid for 48 hours
- 8- Valid for 72 hours
- 9- Occasionally

D - Wind Direction
- 0- Calm
- 1- Northeast
- 2- East
- 3- Southeast
- 4- South
- 5- Southwest
- 6- West
- 7- Northwest
- 8- North
- 9- Variable

F - Wind Force
- 0- 0 to 10 knots
- 1- 11 to 16 knots
- 2- 17 to 21 knots
- 3- 22 to 27 knots
- 4- 28 to 33 knots
- 5- 34 to 40 knots
- 6- 41 to 47 knots
- 7- 48 to 55 knots
- 8- 56 to 63 knots
- 9- 64 knots and above

W - Forecast Weather
- 0- Moderate or good visibility, more than three nautical miles
- 1- Risk of accumulation of ice on superstructures (Temp 23 to 32 F)
- 2- Strong risk of accumulation of ice on superstructures (Temp below 23 F)
- 3- Mist (visibility 5/8 to 3 nautical miles)
- 4- Fog (visibility less than 5/8 nautical mile)
- 5- Drizzle
- 6- Rain
- 7- Snow or rain and snow
- 8- Squally weather with or without showers
- 9- Thunderstorms

GREAT LAKES EDITION

Weather Information

U.S. Coast Guard Broadcasts

Station	Frequency (MHz)	Warnings	Urgent/Safety Broadcasts
Marie	157.100-CH 22	Every 3 hours beginning at 12:05 a.m.	Upon receipt & next scheduled broadcast
Buffalo	"	Every 3 hours beginning at 2:55 a.m.	"
Detroit	"	Every 3 hours beginning at 1:35 a.m.	"
Alexandria Bay	"	Every 3 hours beginning at 2:35 a.m.	"
Duluth	"	Every 3 hours beginning at 1:35 a.m.	"
Milwaukee	"	Every 3 hours beginning at 2:55 a.m.	"
Muskegon	"	Every 3 hours beginning at 2:35 a.m.	"

Canadian Coast Guard Broadcasts

Station	Frequency	Continuous Broadcast Coverage Area
Cardinal	161.65-Ch 21	Lake Ontario and St. Lawrence River
Kingston	161.775-Ch 83B	"
Cornwall	161.65-Ch 21	"
Toronto	161.65-Ch 21	Lake Ontario
Cobourg	161.65-Ch 21	"
Font Hill	161.775-Ch 83B	"
Orillia	161.65-Ch 21	Trent Severn Waterway and Lake Simcoe
Port Burwell	161.65-Ch 21	Lake Erie
Sarnia	161.65-Ch 21	Lake Huron
Leamington	161.775-Ch 83B	Lake Erie
Kincardine	161.775-Ch 83B	Lake Huron
Sault Ste. Marie	161.775-Ch 83B	Lakes Huron and Superior
Bald Head	161.65-Ch 21	Lake Superior
Blind River	161.65-Ch 21	North Channel
Wiarton	161.65-Ch 21	Georgian Bay
Meaford	161.775-Ch 83B	"
Tobermory	161.65-Ch 21	Lake Huron and Georgian Bay
Killarney	161.775-Ch 83B	North Channel and Georgian Bay
Thunder Bay	161.65-Ch 21	Lake Superior
Horn	161.775-Ch 83B	"

MAFOR / LAWEB Broadcasts

Station	Frequency (MHz)	LAWEB	MAFOR	Warnings
Duluth	161.825-Ch 84	2:30 & 8:30 a.m. & p.m. EST	12:02 & 6:02 a.m. & p.m. EST	On receipt and every 30 mins for 2 hours
Copper Harbor	161.975-Ch 87	"	"	"
Grand Marais	161.825-Ch 84	"	"	"
Sturgeon Bay	161.975-Ch 87	"	"	"
Port Washington	161.875-Ch 85	"	"	"
Ontonagan	161.925-Ch 86	"	"	"
Pickford	161.925-Ch 86	"	"	"
Benton Harbor	161.925-Ch 86	"	"	"
Ripley	161.925-Ch 86	"	"	"
Cleveland	161.975-Ch 87	"	"	"
Lorain	161.900-Ch 26	"	"	"
Oregon	161.825-Ch 84	"	"	"
Algonac	161.925-Ch 86	"	"	"
Harbor Beach	161.975-Ch 87	"	"	"
Alpena	161.825-Ch 84	"	"	"
Rogers City	161.900-Ch 26	2:45 & 8:45 a.m. & p.m. EST	12:17 & 6:17 a.m. & p.m. EST	On receipt and 45 mins past even hours
Tawas City	161.900-Ch 26	"	"	"
Sault Ste. Marie	161.900-Ch 26	"	"	"
Charlevoix	161.900-Ch 26	"	"	"

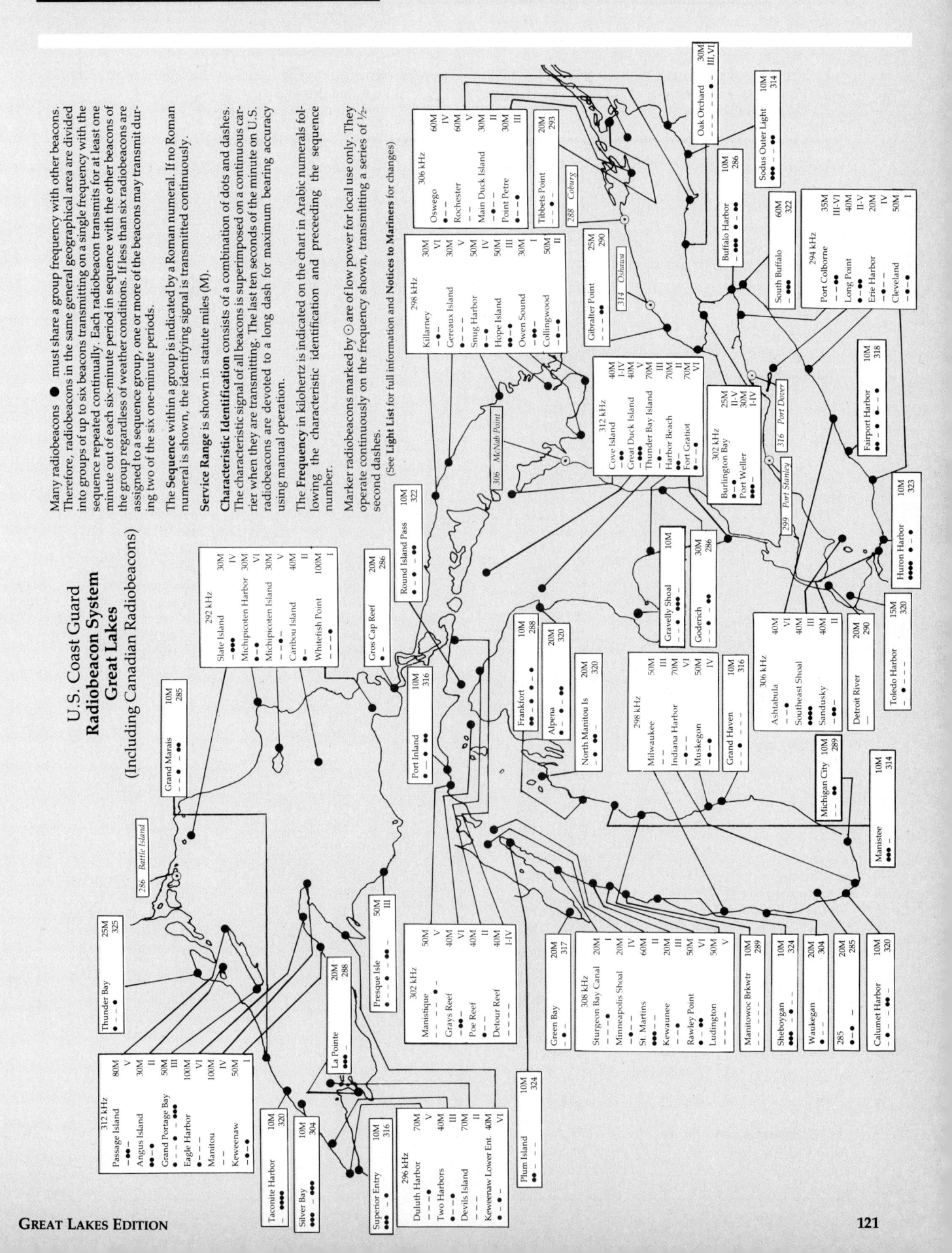

Radiobeacons

Many radiobeacons ● must share a group frequency with other beacons. Therefore, radiobeacons in the same general geographical area are divided into groups of up to six beacons transmitting on a single frequency with the sequence repeated continually. Each radiobeacon transmits for at least one minute out of each six-minute period in sequence with the other beacons of the group regardless of weather conditions. If less than six radiobeacons are assigned to a sequence group, one or more of the beacons may transmit during two of the six one-minute periods.

The **Sequence** within a group is indicated by a Roman numeral. If no Roman numeral is shown, the identifying signal is transmitted continuously.

Service Range is shown in statute miles (M).

Characteristic Identification consists of a combination of dots and dashes. The characteristic signal of all beacons is superimposed on a continuous carrier when they are transmitting. The last ten seconds of the minute on U.S. radiobeacons are devoted to a long dash for maximum bearing accuracy using manual operation.

The **Frequency** in kilohertz is indicated on the chart in Arabic numerals following the characteristic identification and preceeding the sequence number.

Marker radiobeacons marked by ⊙ are of low power for local use only. They operate continuously on the frequency shown, transmitting a series of ½-second dashes.

(See **Light List** for full information and **Notices to Mariners** for changes)

U.S. Coast Guard Radiobeacon System Great Lakes
(Including Canadian Radiobeacons)

GREAT LAKES EDITION   121

Public Coast Marine Operators

This list of Public Coast stations will help you determine the appropriate VHF channels to install aboard your boat, depending on the area in which you plan to cruise. (Dial "0" to call the marine operator.)

Location	Call Sign	Channel	Marine Operator
Illinois			
Chicago	WAY 200	26,27	(call sign only)
Waukegan	KTD 564	84	(call sign only)
Indiana			
Michigan City	KLU 757	25	(call sign only)
Portage	KQU 578	28	(call sign only)
Michigan			
Bay City	KUF 718	28	(call sign only)
Charlevoix	WLC	26	Charlevoix
Copper Harbor	KVY 602	86,87	Copper Harbor
Detroit	KQB 666	26,28	Detroit
Grand Marais	KVY 603	84,85,87	Grand Marais
Harbor Beach	KIL 926	86,87	(call sign only)
Hessel	KIL 923	84,86	(call sign only)
Ludington	KZT 262	25	(call sign only)
Marquette	KZN 587	28	(call sign only)
Marysville	KAD 836	25	Port Huron
Monroe	KAD 806	25	Toledo
Muskegon Height	KQU 546	26	(call sign only)
Ontonagon	KIL 922	84,86	(call sign only)
Ste. Clair	KIL 927	84,86	(call sign only)
St. Joseph	KSK 283	24	(call sign only)
Sault Ste. Marie	WLC	26	Soo
Spruce	KIL 925	84,87	(call sign only)
Stevensville	KIL 924	85,86	(call sign only)
Tawas City	WLC	26	Tawas City
Minnesota			
Duluth	KVY 601	84,87	Duluth
New York			
Buffalo	WBL	26,28	(call sign only)
Dryden	KMB 846	26	(call sign only)
Fishkill	KLG 325	27	(call sign only)
Newark	KGW 418	28	(call sign only)
New York City	KEA 693	25,26,84	New York
Ripley	KIL 929	84,86	(call sign only)
Rochester	KLU 788	25	Rochester channel 25
Schenectady	KFL 993	26	(call sign only)
Syracuse	KGW 416	25	(call sign only)
Utica	KGW 415	28	(call sign only)
West Beekmantown	KGW 417	28	Plattsburgh
Ohio			
Ashtabula	WXY 934	28	(call sign only)
Cleveland	KQU 440	86,87	(call sign only)
Oregon	KIL 928	84,86	(call sign only)
South Amherst	WMI	26	Lorain
Pennsylvania			
Erie	KLU 745	25	(call sign only)
Wisconsin			
Port Washington	KVY 605	85,87	Port Washington
Sturgeon Bay	KVY 604	86,87	(call sign only)

Distances

Table 1: New York (Hudson River) to Troy Lock, N.Y.

Figure at intersection of columns opposite ports in question is the mileage between the two. Distances are in nautical miles unless otherwise noted. Example (below): Poughkeepsie is 60 nautical miles from Albany.

NEW YORK (Battery) 40°42.0'N., 74°01.0'W.	Yonkers 40°56.1'N., 73°54.3'W.	Tarrytown 41°04.7'N., 73°52.2'W.	Nyack 41°05.4'N., 73°54.9'W.	Ossining 41°09.6'N., 73°52.3'W.	Haverstraw 41°11.8'N., 73°57.5'W.	Peekskill 41°17.3'N., 73°56.0'W.	West Point 41°23.1'N., 73°57.3'W.	Newburgh 41°30.1'N., 74°00.3'W.	Poughkeepsie 41°42.3'N., 73°56.5'W.	Hyde Park 41°47.3'N., 73°56.9'W.	Kingston 41°55.1'N., 73°59.0'W.	Saugerties 42°04.4'N., 73°52.1'W.	Catskill 42°13.0'N., 73°48.5'W.	Hudson 42°15.3'N., 73°47.6'W.	Athens 42°15.6'N., 73°47.4'W.	Coxsackie 42°21.0'N., 73°45.3'W.	Coeymans 42°28.5'N., 73°45.1'W.	Albany 42°37.9'N., 73°41.8'W.	Rensselaer 42°37.9'N., 73°41.9'W.	Troy 42°43.7'N., 73°41.1'W.	Watervliet 42°43.7'N.	Troy Lock 42°45.1'N., 73°41.1'W.
16																						
24	9																					
25	10	2																				
29	14	6	6																			
33	18	9	10	5																		
38	23	15	15	11	6																	
45	29	21	22	17	13	8																
53	37	29	29	25	21	15	8															
66	50	42	43	38	34	29	21	13														
71	55	47	48	43	39	34	26	18	5													
80	64	56	57	52	48	43	35	27	14	9												
89	74	66	66	62	58	52	45	37	24	19	12											
99	83	75	75	71	67	61	54	46	33	28	21	11										
102	86	78	78	74	70	64	57	49	36	31	24	14	5									
102	86	78	78	74	70	64	57	49	36	31	24	14	5	1								
108	93	85	85	80	76	71	63	55	42	37	30	21	11	7	6							
115	100	92	92	88	84	78	70	62	49	44	38	28	19	14	14	7						
126	110	102	102	98	94	88	81	73	60	55	48	38	29	24	24	18	10					
126	110	102	102	98	94	88	81	73	60	55	48	38	29	24	24	18	10	0				
132	116	108	108	104	100	94	87	79	66	61	54	44	35	30	30	24	16	6	6			
132	116	108	108	104	100	94	87	79	66	61	54	44	35	30	30	24	16	6	6	0		
134	118	110	110	106	102	96	89	81	68	63	56	46	37	32	32	26	18	8	8	2	2	

Table 2: New York Canals and Lake Champlain

Troy Lock	Waterford, junction canals	Schenectady, terminal	Amsterdam, terminal	Little Falls, lock	Utica, terminal	Rome, terminal	Syracuse, terminal	Newark, terminal	Rochester, terminal	Lockport, lower terminal	Tonawanda, terminal	BUFFALO, Erie Basin	Fulton, terminal	Oswego, lake terminal	Ithaca, terminal	Seneca Falls	Geneva	Watkins Glen	Mechanicville, terminal	Whitehall, terminal	Burlington, Vt., landing	Plattsburgh, landing	Rouses Point, terminal	Canadian line
3																								
19	17																							
35	32	16																						
70	68	51	36																					
90	87	70	55	19																				
102	99	83	67	31	12																			
153	150	134	118	83	63	51																		
198	196	181	163	128	109	96	56																	
226	224	209	192	156	137	125	84	29																
281	279	262	247	211	192	180	139	83	55															
297	295	278	262	227	208	196	155	99	70	16														
308	306	289	274	238	219	207	166	110	82	27	11													
152	149	133	117	82	63	50	22	67	96	150	166	177												
162	159	143	127	91	72	60	31	76	105	160	176	187	10											
213	210	194	178	143	123	111	70	56	85	140	156	167	82	91										
184	182	165	149	114	95	83	42	28	56	111	127	138	53	63	36									
194	191	175	159	123	104	92	51	37	66	120	136	148	63	72	45	10								
223	221	204	189	153	134	122	81	69	96	150	166	177	92	102	75	39	30							
10	8	26	40	76	95	107	159	204	232	287	303	314	158	167	219	190	199	229						
54	51	68	83	119	138	150	202	247	275	330	346	357	201	210	262	233	242	272	44					
116	113	130	145	181	200	212	264	309	337	392	408	419	263	272	324	295	304	334	106	63				
129	126	143	158	194	213	225	277	322	350	405	421	432	276	285	337	308	317	347	119	75	18			
146	143	160	175	211	230	242	294	339	367	422	438	449	293	302	354	325	334	364	136	92	35	23		
147	144	161	176	212	231	243	295	340	368	423	439	450	294	303	355	326	335	365	137	93	36	24	1	

GREAT LAKES EDITION

Distances

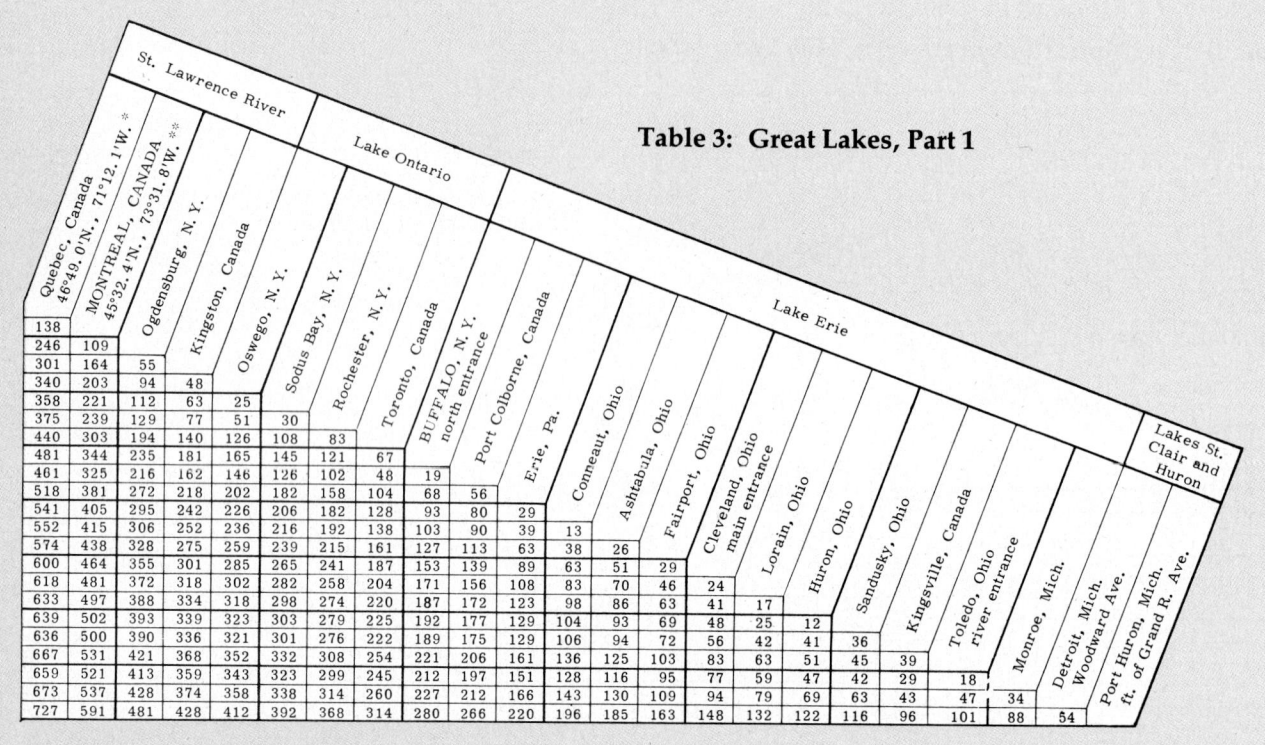

Table 3: Great Lakes, Part 1

Diagonal distance table with the following location headers (reading along the diagonal):
- St. Lawrence River: Quebec, Canada 46°49.0'N, 71°12.1'W *; Montreal, Canada 45°32.4'N, 73°31.8'W **; Ogdensburg, N.Y.
- Lake Ontario: Kingston, Canada; Oswego, N.Y.; Sodus Bay, N.Y.; Rochester, N.Y.; Toronto, Canada; Buffalo, N.Y. north entrance; Port Colborne, Canada
- Lake Erie: Erie, Pa.; Conneaut, Ohio; Ashtabula, Ohio; Fairport, Ohio; Cleveland, Ohio main entrance; Lorain, Ohio; Huron, Ohio; Sandusky, Ohio; Kingsville, Canada; Toledo, Ohio river entrance; Monroe, Mich.
- Lakes St. Clair and Huron: Detroit, Mich. Woodward Ave.; Port Huron, Mich. ft. of Grand R. Ave.

138																					
246	109																				
301	164	55																			
340	203	94	48																		
358	221	112	63	25																	
375	239	129	77	51	30																
440	303	194	140	126	108	83															
481	344	235	181	165	145	121	67														
461	325	216	162	146	126	102	48	19													
518	381	272	218	202	182	158	104	68	56												
541	405	295	242	226	206	182	128	93	80	29											
552	415	306	252	236	216	192	138	103	90	39	13										
574	438	328	275	259	239	215	161	127	113	63	38	26									
600	464	355	301	285	265	241	187	153	139	89	63	51	29								
618	481	372	318	302	282	258	204	171	156	108	83	70	46	24							
633	497	388	334	318	298	274	220	187	172	123	98	86	63	41	17						
639	502	393	339	323	303	279	225	192	177	129	104	93	69	48	25	12					
636	500	390	336	321	301	276	222	189	175	129	106	94	72	56	42	41	36				
667	531	421	368	352	332	308	254	221	206	161	136	125	103	83	63	51	45	39			
659	521	413	359	343	323	299	245	212	197	151	128	116	95	77	59	47	42	29	18		
673	537	428	374	358	338	314	260	227	212	166	143	130	109	94	79	69	63	43	47	34	
727	591	481	428	412	392	368	314	280	266	220	196	185	163	148	132	122	116	96	101	88	54

*Customs House (Signal Service Office)
**Intersection Seaway-Ship Channel, origin of Seaway mileage

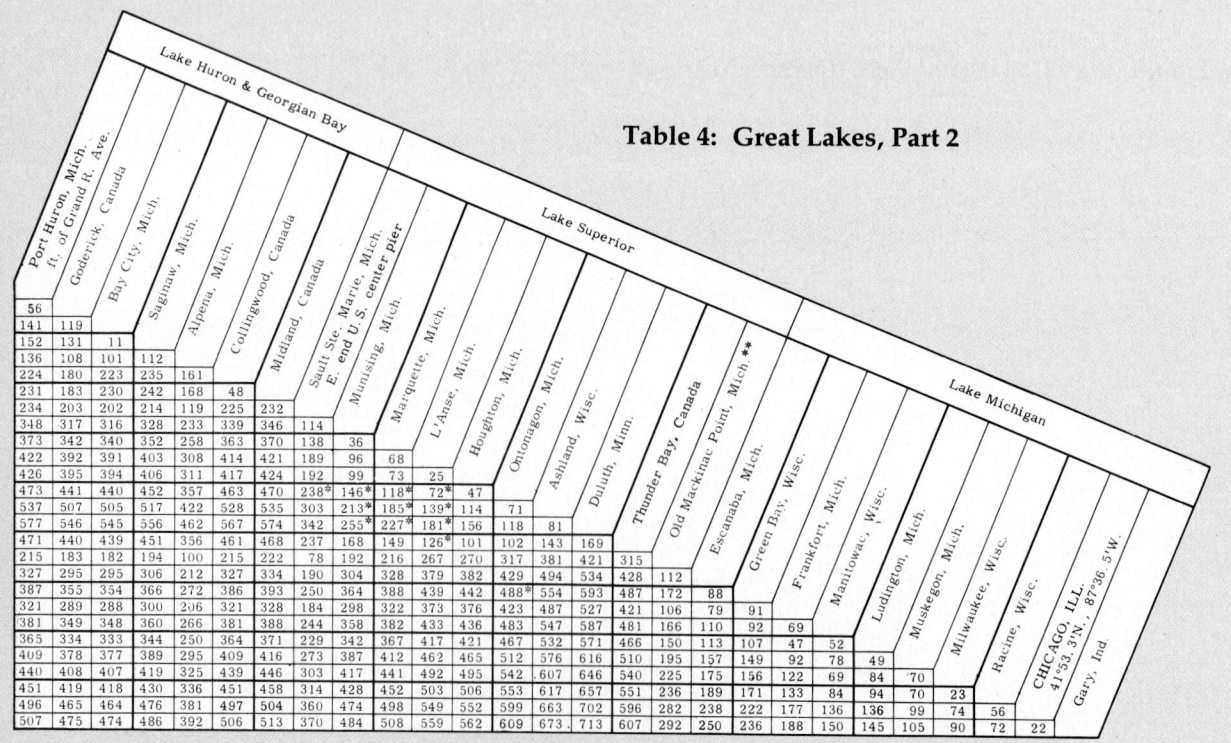

Each distance is by shortest marked or safe direct route starting, unless otherwise noted, from the main entrances between pierheads of breakwaters or piers, or from the principal landings of open roadsteads.

Table 4: Great Lakes, Part 2

Diagonal distance table with the following location headers:
- Port Huron, Mich. ft. of Grand R. Ave.; Goderich, Canada
- Lake Huron & Georgian Bay: Bay City, Mich.; Saginaw, Mich.; Alpena, Mich.; Collingwood, Canada; Midland, Canada; Sault Ste. Marie, Mich. E. end U.S. center pier
- Lake Superior: Munising, Mich.; Marquette, Mich.; L'Anse, Mich.; Houghton, Mich.; Ontonagon, Mich.; Ashland, Wisc.; Duluth, Minn.; Thunder Bay, Canada; Old Mackinac Point, Mich. **
- Lake Michigan: Escanaba, Mich.; Green Bay, Wisc.; Frankfort, Mich.; Manitowoc, Wisc.; Ludington, Mich.; Muskegon, Mich.; Milwaukee, Wisc.; Racine, Wisc.; Chicago, Ill. 41°53.3'N, 87°36.51'W; Gary, Ind.

56																						
141	119																					
152	131	11																				
136	108	101	112																			
224	180	223	235	161																		
231	183	230	242	168	48																	
234	203	202	214	119	225	232																
348	317	316	328	233	339	346	114															
373	342	340	352	258	363	370	138	36														
422	392	391	403	308	414	421	189	96	68													
426	395	394	406	311	417	424	192	99	73	25												
473	441	440	452	357	463	470	238*	146*	118*	72*	47											
537	507	505	517	422	528	535	303	213*	185*	139*	114	71										
577	546	545	556	462	567	574	342	255*	227*	181*	156	118	81									
471	440	439	451	356	461	468	237	168	149	126*	101	102	143	169								
215	183	182	194	100	215	222	78	192	216	267	270	317	381	421	315							
327	295	295	306	212	327	334	190	304	328	379	382	429	494	534	428	112						
387	355	354	366	272	386	393	250	364	388	439	442	488*	554	593	487	172	88					
321	289	288	300	206	321	328	184	298	322	373	376	423	487	527	421	106	79	91				
381	349	348	360	266	381	388	244	358	382	433	436	483	547	587	481	166	110	92	69			
365	334	333	344	250	364	371	229	342	367	417	421	467	532	571	466	150	113	107	47	52		
409	378	377	389	295	409	416	273	387	412	462	465	512	576	616	510	195	157	149	92	78	49	
440	408	407	419	325	439	446	303	417	441	492	495	542	607	646	540	225	175	156	122	69	84	70
451	419	418	430	336	451	458	314	428	452	503	506	553	617	657	551	236	189	171	133	84	94	70	23
496	465	464	476	381	497	504	360	474	498	549	552	599	663	702	596	282	222	177	136	136	99	74	56
507	475	474	486	392	506	513	370	484	508	559	562	609	673	713	607	292	250	236	188	150	145	105	90	72	22

* Via Keweenaw Waterway
**Sailing course point north of light

Each distances is by shortest marked or safe direct route starting, unless otherwise noted, from the main entrances between pierheads of breakwaters or piers, or from the principal landings of open roadsteads.

Distances

Table 5: Great Lakes, (Statute Miles)

	36 Montreal	35 Ogdensburg	34 Kingston	33 Toronto	32 Oswego	31 Rochester	30 Port Colborne	29 Buffalo	28 Erie	27 Conneaut	26 Ashtabula	25 Fairport	24 Cleveland	23 Lorain	22 Toledo	21 Detroit	20 Port Huron	19 Midland	18 Collingwood	17 Goderich	16 Bay City	15 Alpena	14 Ludington	13 Muskegon	12 Gary	11 Chicago	10 Milwaukee	9 Green Bay	8 Escanaba	7 Sault Ste. Marie	6 Marquette	5 Houghton	4 Ashland	3 Duluth	2 Two Harbors
1 Thunder Bay (Port Arthur), Canada	1222	1096	1034	903	1016	965	848	864	795	768	754	729	711	694	658	604	542	539	531	506	505	410	536	587	699	686	621	560	492	273	171	116	164	195	172
2 Two Harbors, Minn.	1320	1194	1132	1001	1114	1063	946	963	893	866	852	828	809	792	756	702	640	638	630	604	603	508	634	685	797	785	720	659	590	371	239	157	71	26	
3 Duluth, Minn.	1344	1218	1156	1025	1138	1087	970	986	917	890	876	851	833	816	781	726	664	661	653	628	627	532	657	709	820	808	743	682	614	394	261	179	93		
4 Ashland, Wis.	1298	1172	1110	979	1092	1041	924	941	871	844	830	806	788	771	734	680	618	616	608	583	581	486	612	663	775	763	698	637	568	349	213	131			
5 Houghton, Mich.	1170	1044	982	851	964	913	796	813	743	716	702	678	659	643	606	552	490	488	480	455	453	358	484	535	647	635	570	509	440	221	84				
6 Marquette, Mich.	1109	983	921	790	903	852	735	751	682	655	641	616	598	581	545	491	429	426	418	393	391	297	422	474	585	573	508	447	378	159					
7 Sault Ste. Marie, Mich. (a)	949	823	761	630	743	692	575	592	522	495	481	457	438	422	385	331	269	267	259	234	232	137	263	314	426	414	349	288	219						
8 Escanaba, Mich.	1056	930	868	737	850	799	682	699	629	602	588	564	545	528	492	438	376	384	376	340	339	244	130	181	288	274	201	101							
9 Green Bay, Wis.	1125	999	937	806	919	868	751	767	698	671	657	632	614	597	561	507	445	452	444	409	407	313	123	171	272	255	180								
10 Milwaukee, Wis.	1186	1060	998	867	980	929	812	828	759	732	718	693	675	658	622	568	506	513	505	470	468	374	97	80	103	85									
11 Chicago, Ill.	1251	1125	1063	932	1045	994	877	893	824	797	783	758	740	723	688	633	571	578	570	535	534	439	156	114	25										
12 Gary, Ind.	1263	1137	1075	944	1057	1006	889	905	836	809	795	770	752	735	699	645	583	590	582	547	546	451	167	121											
13 Muskegon, Mich.	1151	1025	963	832	945	894	777	794	724	697	683	659	640	623	587	533	471	479	471	435	434	339	56												
14 Ludington, Mich.	1100	974	912	781	894	843	726	742	673	646	632	607	589	572	536	482	420	427	419	384	383	288													
15 Alpena, Mich.	837	711	649	518	631	580	463	479	410	383	369	344	326	309	273	219	157	193	185	124	116														
16 Bay City, Mich.	842	716	654	523	636	585	468	484	415	388	374	349	331	314	278	224	162	265	257	137															
17 Goderich, Canada	745	619	557	426	539	488	371	387	318	291	277	252	234	217	181	127	65	211	207																
18 Collingwood, Canada	938	812	750	619	732	681	564	580	511	484	470	446	427	410	374	320	258	55																	
19 Midland, Canada	946	820	758	627	740	689	572	588	519	492	478	453	435	418	382	328	266																		
20 Port Huron, Mich. (b)	680	554	492	361	474	423	306	322	253	226	213	188	170	152	116	62																			
21 Detroit, Mich. (Woodward Ave.)	618	492	430	299	412	361	244	261	191	164	150	126	108	91	54																				
22 Toledo, Ohio (river mouth)	611	485	423	292	405	354	237	254	185	157	144	119	96	72																					
23 Lorain, Ohio	554	428	366	235	348	297	180	197	124	95	80	53	28																						
24 Cleveland, Ohio (main entrance)	534	408	346	215	328	277	160	176	102	73	59	33																							
25 Fairport, Ohio	504	378	316	185	298	247	130	146	73	44	30																								
26 Ashtabula, Ohio	478	352	290	159	272	221	104	119	45	15																									
27 Conneaut, Ohio	466	340	278	147	260	209	92	107	33																										
28 Erie, Pa.	439	313	251	120	233	182	65	78																											
29 Buffalo, N.Y. (north entrance)	396	270	208	77	190	139	22																												
30 Port Colborne, Canada	374	248	186	55	168	117																													
31 Rochester, N.Y.	275	149	89	95	59																														
32 Oswego, N.Y.	234	108	55	145																															
33 Toronto, Canada	349	223	161																																
34 Kingston, Canada	189	63																																	
35 Ogdensburg, N.Y.	126																																		
36 Montreal, Canada (c)	0																																		

(a) From abreast east end of U.S. center pier.
(b) From foot of Grand River Ave.
(c) From intersection Seaway-Ship Channel, Montreal Harbour.

EXPLANATION

Distances in these tables are expressed to the nearest even statute mile; fractions of 1/2 mile or more being taken as a full mile and those under the half dropped. The results are, therefore, at times inconsistent by 1 mile in their comparative differences. Thus, measured distances to two given points may differ uniformly by 0.8 mile; if the respective distances to the two points from a certain port measure 116.0 and 115.2, they appear in the table as 116 and 115, a difference of 1 mile; whereas from the next port listed, the distance to the same two points may measure 105.4 and 104.6, and both will appear in the table as 105.

Measurements are by the shortest marked or safe direct courses, starting (unless otherwise noted) from the main entrance between pierheads of breakwaters or piers, or from the principal landings of open roadsteads. Where landings are appreciably remote from protected entrances, the appropriate further distances, if desired, may be ascertained from the harbor descriptions or from charts.

Points in this table are arranged in the order of their location on the several lakes in the following sequence; Lake Ontario, Lake Erie, Lake Huron, Lake Michigan, and Lake Superior.

The distance between any two points appears in the line extending horizontally from the point first in order in the list and in the column headed by the other point.

Table 6: Lake Ontario and St. Lawrence River (Statute Miles)

Other tables to which initial points Nos. 1-3 are common:
35 - Lake Erie, St. Clair, Detroit, and Niagara Rivers.
36 - Lake Huron and St. Marys River.
37 - Lake Michigan.
38 - Lake Superior.

	36 Quebec	35 St. Lambert Lock	34 Cote Ste. Catherine Lock	33 Beauharnois Lock	32 Colquhoun Island	31 Snell Lock	30 Eisenhower Lock	29 Iroquois Lock	28 Ogdensburg	27 Brockville	26 Alexandria Bay	25 Thousand Island Park	24 Clayton	23 Gananoque	22 Kingston	21 Picton	20 Deseronto	19 Belleville	18 Trenton	17 Cobourg	16 Port Hope	15 Toronto	14 Hamilton	13 Port Weller	12 Lewiston	11 Niagara-on-the-Lake	10 Olcott	9 Rochester	8 Sodus Bay	7 Little Sodus Bay	6 Oswego	5 Sacketts Harbor	4 Cape Vincent	3 Port Colborne
1 OLD MACKINAC POINT (35, 36, 37, 38)(a)	1084	922	914	892	848	841	837	812	799	787	766	760	755	758	739	726	713	697	688	653	648	608	610	580	598	592	608	670	698	712	721	745	740	553
2 PORT HURON (35, 36, 38)(b)	837	675	667	645	601	594	590	565	552	540	519	513	508	511	492	479	466	450	441	406	401	361	363	333	351	345	361	423	451	465	474	498	493	306
3 PORT COLBORNE (35, 38)	531	369	361	339	295	288	284	259	246	234	213	207	202	205	186	173	160	144	135	100	95	55	57	27	45	39	55	117	145	159	168	192	187	
4 Cape Vincent, N.Y.	344	183	175	153	109	102	98	73	60	48	27	20	16	19	24	45	51	67	78	101	106	160	186	160	160	154	134	89	69	59	49	26		
5 Sacketts Harbor, N.Y.	370	209	201	179	135	128	124	99	86	74	53	46	42	45	36	56	61	78	88	106	112	165	191	165	164	158	138	88	64	52	41			
6 Oswego, N.Y.	391	232	224	202	158	151	147	122	108	97	76	69	65	68	55	66	71	88	82	91	96	145	166	141	139	133	113	59	29	15				
7 Little Sodus Bay, N.Y.	401	241	233	211	167	160	156	131	118	106	85	78	74	77	64	73	78	88	79	85	90	136	157	131	130	124	104	48	18					
8 Sodus Bay, N.Y.	411	251	243	221	177	170	166	141	128	116	95	88	84	87	72	80	86	83	74	77	81	124	145	118	118	112	92	35						
9 Rochester, N.Y. (Charlotte)	432	271	263	241	197	190	186	161	149	136	115	108	104	107	90	98	89	73	64	57	60	96	117	89	89	83	63							
10 Olcott, N.Y.	478	316	308	286	242	235	231	206	193	181	160	153	149	152	134	121	109	92	83	51	47	38	55	28	28	22								
11 Niagara-on-the Lake, Canada	500	336	328	306	262	255	251	226	213	201	180	173	169	172	154	141	128	111	102	66	63	30	39	11	6									
12 Lewiston, N.Y.	506	342	334	312	268	261	257	232	219	207	186	179	175	178	160	147	134	117	108	72	69	36	45	17										
13 Port Weller, N.Y.	504	342	334	312	268	261	257	232	219	207	186	179	175	178	159	146	133	117	107	72	68	28	30											
14 Hamilton, Canada	530	367	359	337	293	286	282	257	244	232	211	205	200	204	185	169	156	140	131	94	88	30												
15 Toronto, Canada (west entrance)	506	342	334	312	268	261	257	232	219	207	186	180	175	179	160	142	129	112	103	65	60													
16 Port Hope, Canada	449	289	281	259	215	208	204	179	166	154	132	126	121	125	106	85	72	56	47	7														
17 Coburg, Canada	444	283	275	253	209	202	198	173	160	148	127	120	116	120	101	79	67	50	41															
18 Trenton, Canada	417	255	247	225	181	174	170	145	132	120	101	94	90	89	71	40	28	11																
19 Belleville, Canada	406	244	236	214	170	163	159	134	121	109	90	84	80	78	60	29	17																	
20 Deseronto, Canada	390	228	220	198	154	147	143	118	105	93	74	68	63	62	44	13																		
21 Picton, Canada	383	222	214	192	148	141	137	112	99	87	68	62	57	56	37																			
22 Kingston, Canada	346	185	177	155	111	104	100	75	62	50	32	25	21	19																				
23 Gananoque, Canada	327	167	159	137	93	86	82	57	44	32	18	11	10																					
24 Clayton, N.Y.	327	167	159	137	93	86	82	57	44	32	11	4																						
25 Thousand Island Park, N.Y.	326	164	156	134	90	83	79	54	41	29	8																							
26 Alexandria Bay, N.Y.	317	156	148	127	83	76	72	46	33	22																								
27 Brockville, Canada	295	135	127	105	61	54	50	25	12																									
28 Ogdensburg, N.Y.	283	123	115	93	49	42	38	13																										
29 Iroquois Lock, Canada	270	110	102	80	36	29	25																											
30 Eisenhower Lock, N.Y.	245	85	77	55	11	4																												
31 Snell Lock, N.Y.	241	81	73	51	7																													
32 Colquhoun Island, Canada	233	74	66	44																														
33 Beauharnois Lock, Canada	190	30	22																															
34 Cote Ste. Catherine Lock, Canada	169	8																																
35 St. Lambert Lock, Canada	160																																	
36 Quebec, Canada	0																																	

(a) From sailing course point north of Old Mackinac Point.
(b) From foot of Grand River Ave. To Toronto west entrance.

EXPLANATION

Explanation generally applicable to all tables is published in Table 33.

Points in this table are arranged in geographical sequence proceeding westward along the south shore and returning eastward along the north shore of the lake and down St. Lawrence River.

For determining distances to points located in other lakes, distances from all places listed in this table are given to the initial points Nos. 1 to 3, which also appear in the other tables respectively indicated by numeral designation. The through distance from a given point in this table to a given point in any other table is the sum of the respective distances to each given point from the initial point which is common to the two tables. Thus, Port Colborne being the common point for determining distances from Lake Ontario and St. Lawrence River points to points in Lake Superior (Table 38), a through distance would be derived as follows:

Port Colborne to Colquhoun Island	295
Port Colborne to Thunder Bay (Ft. William)	847
Colquhoun Island to Thunder Bay (Ft. William)	1,142

Distances

Table 7: Lake Erie and St. Clair, Detroit, and Niagara Rivers (Statute Miles)

Other tables to which initial points Nos. 1-3 are common:
34 - Lake Ontario and St. Lawrence River.
36 - Lake Huron and St. Marys River.
37 - Lake Michigan.
38 - Lake Superior.

		37 Kingsville	36 Rondeau	35 Port Stanley	34 Port Burwell	33 Port Dover	32 Port Maitland	31 Niagara Falls	30 Tonawanda	29 Buffalo	28 Dunkirk	27 Erie	26 Conneaut	25 Ashtabula	24 Fairport	23 Cleveland	22 Lorain	21 Vermilion	20 Huron	19 Sandusky	18 Put-in-Bay	17 Port Clinton	16 Toledo	15 Monroe	14 Detroit River Light	13 Amherstburg	12 Trenton	11 Wyandotte	10 Detroit	9 Chatham	8 Mt. Clemens	7 St. Clair Flats	6 Algonac	5 Marine City	4 St. Clair	3 Port Huron	2 Port Colborne
1	OLD MACKINAC POINT (34, 36, 37, 38)[a]	358	414	459	475	527	538	588	580	569	539	500	473	460	435	417	399	391	387	380	363	369	363	348	334	326	324	320	309	322	296	286	274	266	259	247	553
2	PORT COLBORNE (34, 38)	201	146	109	89	52	18	41	33	22	25	65	92	104	130	160	180	190	198	204	204	213	237	227	219	227	229	234	244	292	278	267	281	287	294	306	
3	PORT HURON (34, 36, 38)[b]	111	167	212	228	280	291	341	333	322	292	253	226	213	188	170	152	144	140	133	116	122	116	101	87	79	77	73	62	75	49	39	27	19	12		
4	St. Clair, Mich.	99	155	200	216	268	279	330	322	311	281	241	214	201	176	158	141	133	129	122	105	111	105	89	75	67	65	61	50	63	37	27	15	7			
5	Marine City, Mich.	92	148	193	209	261	272	322	314	303	273	234	207	194	169	151	133	125	121	114	97	103	97	82	68	60	58	54	43	56	30	20	7				
6	Algonac, Mich.	86	143	188	203	255	267	317	309	298	268	228	201	188	163	145	128	120	116	109	92	98	92	76	62	55	53	48	37	49	22	14					
7	St. Clair Flats, Mich., Canada[c]	72	129	174	189	241	253	303	295	284	254	215	187	174	149	131	114	106	102	95	78	84	78	62	48	41	39	34	23	35	15						
8	Mt. Clemens, Mich.	83	140	185	200	252	264	314	306	295	265	226	199	185	161	142	125	117	113	106	89	95	89	73	59	53	50	45	35	49							
9	Chatham, Canada	97	154	199	214	265	278	328	320	309	279	239	212	198	174	156	139	130	127	120	102	108	102	87	73	66	63	59	48								
10	Detroit, Mich. (Woodward Ave.)	49	106	151	166	217	230	280	272	261	231	191	164	150	126	108	91	82	79	72	54	60	54	39	25	18	15	11									
11	Wyandotte, Mich.	39	96	141	156	208	220	270	262	251	221	182	154	141	116	98	81	73	69	62	45	51	45	29	15	8	5										
12	Trenton, Mich.	34	91	136	151	203	215	265	257	246	216	177	149	136	111	93	76	68	64	57	40	46	40	24	10	13											
13	Amherstburg, Canada	31	88	133	148	200	212	262	254	243	213	173	146	133	108	90	73	64	61	54	36	42	36	21	7												
14	Detroit River Light, Mich.	24	81	126	141	193	205	255	247	236	206	166	139	126	101	83	66	58	54	47	30	36	30	14													
15	Monroe, Mich. (piers)	33	89	134	149	200	213	263	255	244	214	174	147	133	109	89	68	60	54	48	30	35	21														
16	Toledo, Ohio (river mouth)	45	98	143	159	210	223	272	265	254	224	185	157	144	119	96	72	65	59	52	38	40															
17	Port Clinton, Ohio	37	75	120	136	187	199	249	241	230	200	160	131	118	92	67	43	36	29	22	12																
18	Put-in-Bay, Ohio	27	66	111	127	177	190	240	232	221	190	150	122	109	83	61	38	32	27	21																	
19	Sandusky, Ohio (wharves)	41	69	114	130	178	190	239	232	221	189	149	120	107	79	55	29	21	14																		
20	Huron, Ohio	47	68	111	124	172	184	233	226	215	183	142	113	99	72	47	20	11																			
21	Vermilion, Ohio	46	62	104	117	163	175	225	217	206	174	133	104	90	63	37	11																				
22	Lorain, Ohio	48	57	97	109	154	166	215	208	197	164	124	95	80	53	28																					
23	Cleveland, Ohio (main entrance)	65	53	85	93	134	146	194	187	176	143	102	73	59	33																						
24	Fairport, Ohio	83	48	62	66	104	116	165	157	146	114	73	44	30																							
25	Ashtabula, Ohio	108	63	56	47	79	90	138	130	119	86	45	15																								
26	Conneaut, Ohio	122	74	59	48	68	80	126	118	107	74	33																									
27	Erie, Pa.	149	98	70	53	47	54	98	89	78	45																										
28	Dunkirk, N.Y.	188	134	98	78	50	28	55	48	37																											
29	Buffalo, N.Y.	218	163	126	106	72	38	21	13																												
30	Tonawanda, N.Y.	230	174	137	117	83	49	8																													
31	Niagara Falls, N.Y.	237	182	145	125	90	57																														
32	Port Maitland, Canada	187	132	95	75	37																															
33	Port Dover, Canada	175	120	83	62																																
34	Port Burwell, Canada	123	65	23																																	
35	Port Stanley, Canada	108	49																																		
36	Rondeau, Canada	63																																			
37	Kingsville, Canada	0																																			

(a) From sailing course point north of Old Mackinac Point.
(b) From foot of Grand River Ave.
(c) From south end of canal dike.

EXPLANATION

Explanation generally applicable to all tables is published in Table 33.

Points in this table are arranged in geographical sequence proceeding southward in St. Clair River and Lake and Detroit River, eastward along the south shore of Lake Erie to Niagara River, and returning westward along the north lake shore.

For determining distances to points located in other lakes, distances from all places listed in this table are given to the initial points Nos. 1 to 3, which also appear in the other tables respectively indicated by numeral designation. The through distance from a given point in this table to a given point in any other table is the sum of the respective distances to each given point from the initial point which is common to the two tables. Thus, Old Mackinac Point being the common point for determining distances from Lake Erie to points in Lake Michigan (Table 37), a through distance would be derived as follows:

Old Mackinac Point to Tonawanda ---------- 580
Old Mackinac Point to Sheboygan ---------- 212

Tonawanda to Sheboygan ---------- 792

Table 8: Lake Huron, Georgian Bay and St. Marys River (Statute Miles)

Other tables to which initial points Nos. 1-3 are common:
34 - Lake Ontario and St. Lawrence River.
35 - Lake Erie, St. Clair, Detroit, and Niagara Rivers.
37 - Lake Michigan.
38 - Lake Superior.

		38 Thessalon	37 Algoma Mills	36 Gore Bay	35 Little Current	34 Killarney	33 French River	32 Key Harbor	31 Byng Inlet	30 Parry Sound	29 Depot Harbor	28 Victoria Harbor	27 Midland	26 Penetanguishene	25 Collingwood	24 Meaford	23 Owen Sound	22 Wiarton	21 Southampton	20 Kincardine	19 Goderich	18 Port Sanilac	17 Harbor Beach	16 Saginaw	15 Bay City	14 East Tawas	13 Au Sable	12 Alpena	11 Rockport	10 Stoneport	9 Rogers City	8 Cheboygan	7 Mackinac Island	6 St. Ignace	5 Port Dolomite	4 De Tour	3 Sault Ste. Marie	2 Old Mackinac Point
1	PORT HURON (34, 35, 38)[a]	*238	+238	+250	225	213	224	232	229	247	243	267	266	265	258	241	238	228	121	94	65	33	63	175	162	119	117	157	166	182	194	233	243	247	239	224	269	247
2	OLD MACKINAC POINT (34, 35, 37, 38)[b]	69	*101	*116	*143	*167	*196	*205	*211	235	231	256	255	254	247	230	227	217	189	192	211	215	186	223	210	163	142	115	83	78	54	18	7	6	27	45	90	
3	SAULT STE. MARIE (38)[c]	&48	&88	&106	&131	&155	&184	&193	&201	&242	+238	268	267	266	259	242	239	229	207	213	234	238	208	246	232	185	165	137	107	96	84	84	84	90	68	45		
4	DeTour, Mich.	%24	%58	%76	%101	%125	%154	%163	%171	201	198	224	222	221	214	197	194	185	162	168	189	193	164	201	187	140	120	92	61	51	40	39	39	44	23			
5	Port Dolomite, Mich.	+92	+90	+108	+135	189	197	199	198	218	215	243	241	238	233	220	219	207	176	183	203	218	190	219	206	163	143	113	76	70	47	31	26	28				
6	St. Ignace, Mich.	%68	*100	*115	*142	*166	*195	*204	*209	234	231	256	254	252	246	229	227	217	191	194	214	216	187	224	210	163	143	115	83	82	55	20	6					
7	Mackinac Island, Mich.	%63	*95	*110	*137	*161	*190	*199	*204	229	226	251	249	248	241	224	221	212	186	189	209	212	184	220	207	159	140	111	79	77	50	17						
8	Cheboygan, Mich.	%63	*92	*106	*133	*157	*186	*195	*197	221	217	242	241	240	233	216	213	204	175	178	198	202	173	210	196	149	129	101	69	66	40							
9	Rogers City, Mich.	*63	+74	+87	+114	+138	157	163	164	187	183	208	206	206	199	182	177	169	139	142	161	163	134	171	157	110	90	61	31	27								
10	Stoneport, Mich.	+75	+73	+92	+118	137	145	147	147	166	163	190	189	186	181	164	163	151	115	120	146	158	130	154	141	97	76	48	9									
11	Rockport, Mich.	*79	+79	+92	+119	123	136	143	143	166	162	187	186	185	178	161	158	148	112	113	132	134	106	142	129	82	62	31										
12	Alpena, Mich.	*107	+107	+120	+143	131	145	151	152	174	171	195	193	192	185	168	165	156	109	107	124	125	97	129	116	69	49											
13	Au Sable, Mich.	*135	+135	+148	158	146	160	163	166	183	180	204	202	201	189	177	174	165	98	85	93	86	58	83	69	21												
14	East Tawas, Mich.	*155	+155	+168	175	163	176	180	182	199	196	220	218	217	210	194	190	181	110	94	95	88	60	68	54													
15	Bay City, Mich.	*202	+202	+215	222	210	223	228	229	245	243	267	265	264	257	240	237	228	153	136	137	130	102	13														
16	Saginaw, Mich.	*216	+216	+228	235	223	237	242	242	258	256	280	278	278	271	254	250	241	167	149	151	144	115															
17	Harbor Beach, Mich.	*178	+178	+191	171	159	171	176	176	194	190	214	213	212	205	188	185	175	79	56	47	32																
18	Port Sanilac, Mich.	*207	+207	+219	197	185	196	201	201	219	215	239	238	237	230	213	210	200	97	70	47																	
19	Goderich, Canada	+198	+198	204	169	159	172	172	174	192	189	213	211	210	207	187	183	174	64	36																		
20	Kincardine, Canada	+173	+174	174	141	128	142	149	144	162	158	182	181	180	176	156	153	144	30																			
21	Southampton, Canada	+166	+166	155	122	110	123	130	125	143	140	163	162	161	157	137	134	125																				
22	Wiarton, Canada[d]	+188	158	142	110	94	88	79	81	74	71	76	74	73	53	36	29																					
23	Owen Sound, Canada[d]	+197	167	152	119	103	97	97	89	79	75	71	70	69	46	29																						
24	Meaford, Canada[d]	+200	169	153	121	105	96	96	86	71	68	55	53	52	24																							
25	Collingwood, Canada[d]	+217	186	171	138	120	108	107	97	80	76	57	55	54																								
26	Penetanguishene, Canada[d]	+224	187	172	139	120	106	104	94	72	69	12	10																									
27	Midland, Canada[d]	+225	188	173	140	121	107	105	95	73	70	7																										
28	Port McNicoll, Canada[d]	+227	190	174	142	122	108	106	97	75	71																											
29	Depot Harbor, Canada[d]	193	155	140	107	87	73	71	62	6																												
30	Parry Sound, Canada[d]	197	159	143	111	91	77	75	65																													
31	Byng Inlet, Canada[d]	155	118	102	70	50	31	27																														
32	Key Harbor, Canada[d]	148	110	94	62	42	22																															
33	French River, Canada[d]	139	101	86	53	33																																
34	Killarney, Canada[d]	110	72	56	24																																	
35	Little Current, Canada	86	48	33																																		
36	Gore Bay, Canada	61	27																																			
37	Algoma Mills, Canada	43																																				
38	Thessalon, Canada	0																																				

* Via False Detour and North Channels.
\+ Via Mississagi Strait and North Channel.
& Via Lake Nicolet, St. Joseph, and North Channels.
% Via Potagannissing Bay and North Channel.

(a) From foot of Grand River Ave.
(b) From sailing course point north of Old Mackinac Point.
(c) From abreast east end of U.S. center pier, and (except those marked &) via Middle Neebish and Detour; distances downbound through West Neebish are 1 mile less.
(d) Distances to Georgian Bay ports (except those marked *, +, &, %) are via the bay entrance from Lake Huron and St. Marys River points and via Little Current from North Channel points.

EXPLANATION

Explanation generally applicable to all tables is published in Table 33.

Points in this table are arranged in geographical sequence proceeding from St. Marys River southward along the west shore, and returning northward up the east shore, around Georgian Bay, and westward through North Channel.

For determining distances to points located in other lakes, distances from all places listed in this table are given to the initial points Nos. 1 to 3, which also appear in the other tables respectively indicated by numeral designation. The through distance from a given point in this table to a given point in any other table is the sum of the respective distances to each given point from the initial point which is common to the two tables.

Distances

Table 9: Lake Michigan (Statute Miles)

This table lists distances in statute miles between ports on Lake Michigan. Points are numbered 1–38 and arranged in geographical sequence proceeding southward along the west shore and returning northward along the east shore.

Other tables to which initial point No. 1 is common:
- 34 – Lake Ontario and St. Lawrence River.
- 35 – Lake Erie, St. Clair, Detroit, and Niagara Rivers.
- 36 – Lake Huron and St. Marys River.
- 38 – Lake Superior.

Column headings (points 38 → 2): Beaver Island Harbor, Petoskey, Charlevoix, Traverse City, Frankfort, Portage Lake, Manistee, Ludington, Pentwater, White Lake, Muskegon, Grand Haven, Holland, Saugatuck, South Haven, St. Joseph, Michigan City, Gary, Indiana Harbor, South Chicago, Chicago, Waukegan, Kenosha, Racine, Milwaukee, Port Washington, Sheboygan, Manitowoc, Two Rivers, Kewaunee, Algoma, Sturgeon Bay, Green Bay, Menominee, Escanaba, Manistique, Port Inland.

Row listing (point no., name):
1. OLD MACKINAC POINT (34, 35, 36, 38)(a)
2. Port Inland, Mich.
3. Manistique, Mich.
4. Escanaba, Mich.
5. Menominee, Mich. & Wis. (b)
6. Green Bay, Wis. (city)(b)
7. Sturgeon Bay, Wis. (town)
8. Algoma, Wis.
9. Kewaunee, Wis.
10. Two Rivers, Wis.
11. Manitowoc, Wis.
12. Sheboygan, Wis.
13. Port Washington, Wis.
14. Milwaukee, Wis.
15. Racine, Wis.
16. Kenosha, Wis.
17. Waukegan, Ill.
18. Chicago, Ill.
19. South Chicago, Ill.
20. Indiana Harbor, Ind.
21. Gary, Ind.
22. Michigan City, Ind.
23. St. Joseph, Mich.
24. South Haven, Mich.
25. Saugatuck, Mich.
26. Holland, Mich.
27. Grand Haven, Mich.
28. Muskegon, Mich.
29. White Lake, Mich.
30. Pentwater, Mich.
31. Ludington, Mich.
32. Manistee, Mich.
33. Portage Lake, Mich.
34. Frankfort, Mich.
35. Traverse City, Mich.
36. Charlevoix, Mich.
37. Petoskey, Mich.
38. Beaver Island Harbor, Mich.

Notes:
(a) From sailing course point north of Old Mackinac Point.
(b) Distances from Menominee and Green Bay to Lake Michigan points except those marked (*) are via Sturgeon Bay Canal.
* Via Rock Island Passage.

EXPLANATION

Explanation generally applicable to all tables is published in Table 33.

Points in this table are arranged in geographical sequence proceeding southward along the west shore and returning northward along the east shore.

For determining distances to points in other lakes, distances from all places listed in this table are given to Old Mackinac Point, and this initial point also appears in each of the other tables respectively indicated by numerical designation. The through distance from a given point in this table to a given point in any other table is the sum of the respective distances to each given point from Old Mackinac Point, common to the two tables. Thus, a through distance from a Lake Michigan point to a point in Lake Superior (Table 38) would be derived as follows:

Old Mackinac Point to Racine	272
Old Mackinac Point to Ashland	439
Racine to Ashland	711

Table 10: Lake Superior (Statute Miles)

This table lists distances in statute miles between ports on Lake Superior. Points are numbered 1–39.

Other tables to which initial points Nos. 1–4 are common:
- 34 – Lake Ontario and St. Lawrence River.
- 35 – Lake Erie, St. Clair, Detroit, and Niagara Rivers.
- 36 – Lake Huron and St. Marys River.
- 37 – Lake Michigan.

Column headings (points 39 → 4): Gargantua Harbor, Michipicoten Harbor, Quebec Harbor, Peninsula Harbor, Rossport, Thunder Bay (Pt. Arthur), Thunder Bay (Ft. William), Passage Island, Rock of Ages, Grand Marais Minn., Taconite, Silver Bay, Two Harbors, Duluth, Superior, Port Wing, Bayfield, Washburn, Ashland, Ontonagon, Keweenaw W. Upper Ent., Houghton, Dollar Bay, Lake Linden, Chassell, Portage Entry, Eagle Harbor, Copper Harbor, Mendota Canal, L'Anse, Huron Bay, Marquette, Munising, Grand Marais Mich., Whitefish Point, Sault Ste. Marie.

Row listing:
1. PORT COLBORNE (34, 35)
2. PORT HURON (34, 35, 36)(a)
3. OLD MACKINAC POINT (34, 35, 36, 37, 38)(b)
4. SAULT STE. MARIE (37)(c)
5. Whitefish Point, Mich.
6. Grand Marais, Mich.
7. Munising, Mich.
8. Marquette, Mich. (docks)
9. Huron Bay, Mich. (village)
10. L'Anse, Mich.
11. Mendota Canal, Mich.
12. Copper Harbor, Mich.
13. Eagle Harbor, Mich.
14. Portage Entry, Mich.
15. Chassell, Mich.
16. Lake Linden, Mich.
17. Dollar Bay, Mich.
18. Houghton, Mich.
19. Keweenaw Waterway, Upper Entry, Mich.
20. Ontonagon, Mich.
21. Ashland, Wis.
22. Washburn, Wis.
23. Bayfield, Wis.
24. Port Wing, Wis.
25. Superior, Wis.
26. Duluth, Minn.
27. Two Harbors, Minn.
28. Silver Bay, Minn.
29. Taconite, Minn.
30. Grand Marais, Minn.
31. Rock of Ages, Mich.
32. Passage Island, Mich.
33. Thunder Bay (Ft. William), Canada
34. Thunder Bay (Pt. Arthur), Canada
35. Rossport, Canada
36. Peninsula Harbor, Canada
37. Quebec Harbor, Canada
38. Michipicoten Harbor, Canada
39. Gargantua Harbor, Canada

Notes:
(a) From foot of Grand River Ave.
(b) From sailing course point north of Old Mackinac Point.
(c) From abreast east end of United States center pier.
* Via Keweenaw Waterway.

EXPLANATION

Explanation generally applicable to all tables is published in Table 33.

Points in this table are arranged in geographical sequence proceeding westward along the south shore and returning eastward along the north shore.

For determining distances to points located in other lakes, distances from all places listed in this table are given to the initial points Nos. 1 to 4, which also appear in the other tables respectively indicated by numerical designation. The through distance from a given point in this table to a given point in any other table is the sum of the respective distances to each given point from the initial point which is common to the two tables. Thus, Port Huron being the common point for determining distances from Lake Superior points to points in Lake Erie (Table 35), a through distance would be derived as follows:

Port Huron to Ontonagon	544
Port Huron to Dunkirk	292
Ontonagon to Dunkirk	836

GREAT LAKES EDITION — 127

Mail Drops

Skippers cruising in the Great Lakes region will be happy to learn that the post offices below are willing to handle transients' mail. Correspondents should address letters with your name, the name of your vessel, and the post office where you'll be picking up your mail. Direct mail to "General Delivery" and write "Hold for Arrival" in the lefthand corner of the envelope. The post office will generally hold such mail for 10 days. Leave a forwarding address with the postmaster. An asterisk signifies a post office not within walking distance of the waterfront.

Location	Street Address	Zip
Illinois		
Chicago (main office)	*433 W. Van Buren	60607
Waukegan	*326 N. Genesee St.	60085
Indiana		
Gary	*1499 M.L. King Dr.	46401
Michigan City	303 Washington St.	46360
Michigan		
Alpena	350 N. 2nd Ave.	49707
Bay City	1000 Washington	48707
Benton Harbor	525 Riverview Dr.	49022
Charlevoix	109 Mason St.	49720
Cheboygan	200 N. Main St.	49721
Escanaba	2515 1st Ave. N.	49829
Hancock	221 W. Quincy St.	49930
Houghton	701 Shelden Ave.	49931
Macatawa	2150 S. Shore Dr.	49434
Marquette	202 W. Washington St.	49855
Munising	220 Elm Ave.	49862
Ontonagon	207 Copper St.	49953
Port Huron	1300 Military St.	48060
Port Sanilac	34 N. Ridge St.	48469
Muskegon	800 1st St.	49440
Sault Ste. Marie	151 Ridge	49783
(Locks)	Locks 2-3	49783
Minnesota		
Duluth	*2800 W. Michigan	55806
Grand Portage		55605
New York		
Albany	Broadway	12207-9998
Alexandria Bay	15 Bethune St.	13607
Baldwinsville	26 E. Genesee St.	13027
Brewerton	9661 Main St.	13029
Buffalo (Niagara Sq.)	68 Court St.	14202
Cape Vincent	Broadway St.	13618
Coxsackie	27-39 Reed St.	12051
Gasport	4433 Main St.	14067
Ithaca	*213 North Tioga St.	14850
Lockport	1 East Ave.	14094
Medina	128 W. Center St.	14103
Middleport	42 Main St.	14105
Newburgh	217 Liberty St.	12550
Ogdensburg	420 Ford St.	13669
Oswego	391 W. First St.	13126
Rochester	*1335 Jefferson Rd.	14692
Tarrytown	50 N. Broadway	10591
Youngstown	135 Lockport St.	14174
Ohio		
Ashtabula	718 Lake Ave.	44004
Huron	378 Main St.	44839
Port Clinton	121 W. 2nd St.	43452
Toledo	*435 S. St. Clair St.	43601
Vermont		
Burlington	11 Elmwood Ave.	05401
Charlotte	*Ferry Road	05445
Grand Isle	*U.S. Route 2	05458
Vergennes	9 Green St.	05491
Wisconsin		
Green Bay	*300 Packerland Dr.	54303
Kenwanee	119 Ellis St.	54216
Manitowoc	1202 Franklin St.	54220
Racine	*603 Main St.	53401
Sheboygan	522 N. 9th St.	53081
Sturgeon Bay	359 Louisiana St.	54235
Superior	805 Belknap St.	54880
Two Rivers	1516 18th St.	54241
Ontario		
Brockville	34 Buell St.	K6V 4Y0
Cornwall	*45 Second St. E.	K6H 5R8
Gananoque	201 King St. E.	K7G 1G0
Goderich	35 East St.	N7A 1N0
Gore Bay		P0P 1H0

Hamilton	10 John St. S.	L8N 3T8	St Catharines (Station B)	32 Church St.	L2R 3B0
Kingston	120 Clarence St.	K7L 1X0		366 Scott St.	L2M 6P4
Leamington	*25 John St.	N8H 3V9	Sarnia	105 S. Christina St.	N7T 2M0
Little Current	14 Water St.	P0P 1K0	Thorold	18 Front St. N.	L2V 3Y6
Midland	525 Dominion Ave.	L4R 1P0	Thunder Bay (Station P)	33 S. Court St.	P7B 2W0
Orillia	25 Peter St. N.	L3V 4Y0			
Oshawa	*47 Simcoe St. S	L1H 4G0	Tobermory	Head St.	N0H 2R0
Owen Sound	General Delivery	N4K 5N9	Trenton	70 Front St.	K8V 4N0
Parry Sound (Sub P.O.)	74 James St.	P2A 2X1 P2A 2T0	Wiarton	543 Berford St.	N0H 2T0
Peterborough	191 Charlotte St.	K9J 2T0	**Québec**		
Port Colborne	184 Elm St.	L3K 5V6	Beloeil	595 Laurier Blvd.	J3G 2M0
Prescott	292 Centre St.	K0E 1T0	Sorel	*88 George St.	J3G 1C0

Useful Publications

In planning a cruise, skippers should consult the various government charts and publications that are available from U.S. and Canadian sources. The National Ocean Service (NOS) and the Canadian Hydrographic Service will send a free copy of their **chart catalog**, which diagrams the charts covering the Great Lakes.

Great Lakes charts come in four levels of scale: an entire lake at a scale of 1:400,000 to 1:600,000; segments of coastline at 1:80,000 to 1:120,000 U.S. and 1:40,000 to 1:100,000 Canadian; harbor or small area charts ranging from 1:5,000 to 1:30,000 U.S. and 1:6,000 to 1:18,000 Canadian; Canadian small-craft folio charts at 1:20,000 and American small craft charts spiral-bound into books at an assortment of scales. Many of the coastal charts have insets of harbors at larger scale.
NOS
Distribution Branch (N/CG33)
6501 Lafayette Avenue
Riverdale, Maryland 20737

U.S. Coast Pilot, Number 6 ($16.50) should be ordered from NOS.

Light List, Volume VII, furnishes complete information concerning aids to navigation—lights, fog signals, buoys, daybeacons, radiobeacons, racons, Loran-C stations—more than can be shown on the charts. It is available from:
Superintendent of Documents
Government Printing Office
Washington, D.C. 20402

Canadian Hydrographic Service
Chart Distribution Office
Department of Fisheries and Oceans
1675 Russell Road, P.O. Box 8080
Ottawa, Ontario, Canada K1G 3H6
  Sailing Directions, Great Lakes, Volumes I and II
  Georgian Bay, Small Craft Guide
  List of Lights, Buoys, and Fog Signals, Inland Waters
  Radio Aids to Marine Navigation, Atlantic and Great Lakes

Great Lakes Water Levels are available in three publications. One contains monthly and annual average levels, in tabular form, obtained from permanent water level gauges during the period 1860-1980. The other two publications contain daily and monthly average levels from permanent gauges for the years 1984-1985.

These publications are available from the National Ocean Service, N/OMA/21, Rockville, Maryland 20852. Price is $2.50 each, check payable to NOAA.

Hydrograph of Lake Levels. A hydrograph of monthly mean levels of the Great Lakes including Lake St. Clair, from 1900 to date, is available free of charge.

The Bulletin of Lake Levels is a monthly bulletin showing current levels of the Great Lakes and Lake St. Clair levels of the prior 12 to 23 months, along with probable levels for the next 6 months. It is available without charge from the Detroit District, U.S. Army Corps of Engineers, P.O. Box 1027, Detroit, Michigan 48231.

Customs

Foreign craft may enter Canada temporarily on condition that they are exported at the conclusion of the non-resident's visit or at the end of the boating season. If they remain in Canada beyond the expiration of the visit or season, they are subject to duty and taxes.

The Customs Act and regulations require that the owner/operator of each craft arriving from a foreign port or place report immediately on arrival in Canada to Canadian Customs. Only the owner/operator is permitted to go ashore to make the report; all passengers and goods must remain on board until Customs formalities have been completed.

At some Vessel Reporting Stations, Customs Inspectors are on duty during the boating season. They clear the vessel and issue a permit E99. At other stations a telephone reporting system is used. The owner/operator telephones the nearest Customs Office. After routine questioning the Inspector may issue a verbal clearnace, or if inspection or documentation is required, the Inspector will proceed to the location of the vessel. These reporting stations display a sign indicating the telephone numbers. Calls are recorded as proof of inward report to Customs.

The hours of service away from location to location as well as seasonally. If service is requested beyond the hours stipulated, there is a special service charge of $54.00 for the first two hours or any portion thereof, and $27.00 for each hour or portion thereof in excess of 2 hours. In addition to the special service charge, transportation charges may be assessed.

Should a resident wish to have legitimate repairs or maintenance work done on his/her boat by a bona fide marina or service depot during the off-season, he/she may be permitted to retain it in Canada. Under this procedure the owner is required to provide a copy of the work order, or a written statement from the individual or firm who will be effecting the repairs. Vessels retained in Canada in this manner shall be documented on form E99 endorsed "For Repair Only."

Additional information on Canadian Customs Regulations may be obtained from the nearest Customs Office (see below for list of Customs Offices and addresses), or from the Travelers Division, Connaught Building, MacKenzie Avenue, Ottawa, Ontario, Canada K1A 0L5.

Returning to the U.S. American boats returning from foreign ports must be cleared by three U.S. agencies: Customs, Dept. of Agriculture (for plant pests), and Immigration (for citizenship). As a convenience to mariners, one boarding inspector effects clearance for all three.

Returning boats should fly the yellow quarantine flag. As soon as the boat is securely berthed at a marina, the master may go ashore, but only to report the boat's arrival by telephone. (At most marinas the dockmaster will gladly make the call.) No one else is permitted to leave the boat and no articles should be taken ashore or visitors allowed on board before clearance is effected. All vessels arriving at any port in the United States must report their arrival. Failure to comply would subject the vessel's master to a $5,000 penalty.

Firearms. Canada has strict rules about any small arms aboard. Absolutely no handguns or pistols are permitted. Period. You must leave handguns in a U.S. port until your return to the United States or mail them through U.S. mail to another port of entry for pick-up there. Smuggling your handgun into Canada risks severe fines and confiscation.

Hunting rifles are permitted in hunting season only. While they do not require a permit, they *must be declared*. Contact the police at your port of entry for further small firearms information. All firearms taken outside the United States must be registered with the U.S. Customs Service in order to facilitate reentry.

Currency. If you're carrying more than $10,000 in U.S. currency, traveler's checks, or other instruments, you must report it to Customs; complete form 4790 at any Customs office. Note that this applies whether you're entering or leaving the U.S.

Note that the current exchange rate (as of this writing) between Canadian and U.S. currencies is .84 Canadian to every $1.00 U.S.. Canadian mariners entering the U.S. should be aware that some mariners have had difficulty getting American boatyards to accept Canadian checks. If the check is written for the exact amount of the bill, banks will discount the check. Canadian mariners should therefore be prepared to pay in U.S. dollars or to include the current rate of exchange when figuring the amount of a check to be based on Canadian funds.

Canadian Vessels. At the first U.S. port of arrival, the master must immediately report his arrival and make formal entry at the Customhouse within 48 hours. Here he may apply for a "cruising license" which will let him cruise U.S. waters without again making formal entry. However, it's important to note that regulations require the master to report his arrival to the nearest Customs office *at each subsequent port visited*, cruising license or no. Failure to report may incur a penalty of $1,000.

Boarding Hours. Clearance is handled without charge during regular boarding hours, which vary with the location and season. A service charge will be assessed **outside of normal working hours.** The vessel may be subject to an annual user fee of $25.00.

Customs

Contact the following offices for more information:

U.S. Customs District Offices:

Buffalo, NY 14202	111 W. Huron Street	(716) 846-4353
Chicago, IL 60607	610 S. Canal Street	(312) 353-6100
Cleveland, OH 44114	55 Erieview Plaza	(216) 522-4287
Detroit, MI 48226	477 Michigan Avenue	(313) 226-3177
Duluth, MN 55802	515 W. First Street	(218) 720-5201
Cudahy, WI 53110	6269 Ace Industrial Dr.	(414) 297-3932
New York, NY 10048	6 World Trade Center	(212) 466-5550
Ogdensburg, NY 13669	127 N. Water Street	(315) 393-0660
St. Albans, VT 05478	Main & Stebbins Sts. (Box 1490)	(802) 524-6527
Washington, DC 20229	1301 Constitution Avenue	(202) 298-1200

Canadian Regional Customs Offices:

Hamilton, Ont. L8N 3V8	10 John Street South	(416) 572-2812
London, Ont. N6A 4Y4	457 Richmond	(519) 679-5065
Ottawa, Ont. K1K 2C6	360 Coventry Rd.	(613) 993-0534
Toronto, Ont. M6W 1AS	55 Bloor Street W.	(416) 973-8022
Windsor, Ont. N8Y 4R8	185 Ovellette Ave.	(519) 973-8500

Metrics

The metric system of measurement may soon be the prevalent standard in the United States. In fact, NOAA Chart 14820, Lake Erie, is printed in meters and decimeters instead of fathoms and has a distance scale laid out in meters as well as in statute miles.

Although the nautical mile has been fixed by international agreement at 1,852 meters, the knot (velocity in nautical miles per hour) is a term used by all nations and doesn't require translation into metric terms.

To convert from Farenheit to Centigrade, use the equation:

$$C° = 5/9(F° - 32)$$

To convert from Centigrade to Farenheit:

$$F° = 9/5 \times C° + 32$$

Also note that:
1 litre = 2.113 pints or 0.264 U.S. gallons
1 U.S. gallon = 3.785 litres

CONVERSIONS

1 Foot = 0.305 meter   1 meter = 3.282 feet
1 yard = 0.914 meter   1 meter = 1.094 yards
1 fathom = 1.829 meters   1 meter = 0.547 fathom
1 fathom = 6 feet

1 statute mile = 1.609 kilometers   1 kilometer = 0.621 statute mile
1 nautical mile = 1.852 kilometers   1 kilometer = 0.540 nautical mile

Statute miles are used on fresh water and on inland waterways, including the ICW; nautical miles are used on salt water. To convert statute to nautical miles, multiply by 0.869; to convert nautical to statute, multiply by 1.151.

1 nautical mile = 1.151 statute miles
1 statute mile = 0.869 nautical miles

GREAT LAKES EDITION

Corps of Engineers

For information on conditions in U.S. navigable waters, contact the Corps of Engineers. Improvement, depths, maintenance, regulations, obstructions—if you have questions about the waters you plan to travel, the offices listed below will supply all the necessary data. You can write or phone the following district headquarters.

New York District Office: 26 Federal Plaza, New York, N.Y. 10278-0090. Phone: (212) 264-0100. Includes western Vermont, portions of western Massachusetts, eastern and southcentral New York (including Long Island), and northeastern New Jersey, embraced in the drainage basins tributary to Lake Champlain, Mohawk River, Hudson River, Passaic River, and Hackensack River, and to the Atlantic Ocean from the New York/Connecticut state line to, but not including, Manasquan Inlet, New Jersey. Also, anything pertaining to improvement of the Great Lakes-Hudson River Waterway, the tidal waters of New York Harbor, and the waters leading into that harbor.

Department of Transportation, Office of Public Affairs, Building 5, State Campus, Albany, N.Y. 12232. Phone: (518) 457-6400. In addition to the Corps of Engineers, the Dept. of Transportation provides information on New York State waterways including the Erie Canal, and the Champlain, Oswego, and Cayuga-Seneca canals.

Buffalo District Office—1776 Niagara St., Buffalo, N.Y. 14207. Phone: (716) 876-5454. Covers all New York State bordering Lake Ontario and the St. Lawrence River, including Finger Lakes, and all New York, Pennsylvania, and Ohio bordering Lake Erie.

Detroit District Office—Department of the Army Corps of Engineers, P.O. Box 1027, Detroit, MI 48231-1027. Phone: (313) 226-6413. Covers all Lakes Huron, Michigan, and Superior, and the western shore of Lake Erie from Toledo northward.

Special Notice: Lake Water Levels

The U.S. Army Corps of Engineers reports that water levels on the Great Lakes are four to ten inches lower than last year. Lake levels have been steadily declining in the past few years, and are three feet lower now than in 1986. The low levels are blamed on reduced precipitation — both rain and snow — throughout the Great Lakes in 1988 and 1989. Mariners are urged to use caution and consult their navigation charts prior to and when underway.

Distress, Urgency, Safety

> ### Fire Hazards
>
> Batteries and electrical connections are often overlooked as a potential fire hazard. If not properly ventilated, the hydrogen gas emitted by lead-acid batteries can be ignited by any spark. Batteries should be protected (from water and falling objects) but well-ventilated.
>
> Loose or corroded high voltage connections such as battery terminals and generator leads can get hot enough to start a fire. Keep connections clean and corrosion free (petroleum jelly liberally applied to terminals will prevent corrosion) and be alert for overheating and odors.

Distress Signals. Only in situations of grave and imminent danger are distress signals to be issued. Switch to Channel 16 and begin your message with the distress call: the word "Mayday" repeated three times, followed by vessel name and call sign. The distress message follows the distress call: "Mayday" spoken once, identification, position, the nature of the emergency, and the type of assistance desired. Be sure to include a description of your vessel and the number of people aboard. For example, "Mayday, Mayday, Mayday, this is *Zephyr*, Whiskey-Alpha 1234. Mayday, this is *Zephyr*. 160 degrees true, 12 miles from Key Largo. Taking on water fast. Estimate cannot stay afloat more than two hours. *Zephyr* is a 35-foot yawl, black hull, red trim. Two persons on board. This is *Zephyr*, over." Be sure to release the mike key and listen for a response.

Repeat the entire distress signal until it has been acknowledged. The Coast Guard or available rescue units will instruct you. If repeated distress calls are not acknowledged, switch to another channel and try again.

Receiving a Distress Signal. If you hear a Mayday call, use the following procedure: Monitor—do not transmit. Determine if your boat is in a position to render assistance. Monitor to see if another vessel is better equipped or located to handle the situation. If your vessel is best able to assist, acknowledge the call, e.g., "*Zephyr, Zephyr, Zephyr,* this is *Centurion, Centurion, Centurion,* Whiskey-Alpha 5678. Mayday received." Once contact is made, give your position and speed toward the scene.

Whether you are responding or not, enter all calls in your station log and continue to monitor the situation. If you are relaying a Mayday issued by another vessel, be sure to repeat the words "Mayday Relay" three times before your station identification.

Urgency Signal. Pan-Pan (pronounced "Pahn-Pahn"), repeated three times and followed by station ID and message, is used in important safety messages such as "man overboard." A Pan-Pan call has priority over all communications except distress signals.

Safety Signal. Security (pronounced "Say-curitay") is used for messages concerning safety of navigation and important meteorological warnings. If you hear an urgency or a security call—listen, do not transmit. Monitor the situation and respond appropriately.

Procedure words. Some words common to the radio world are often used in order to cut down the length of the transmission; like signal flags, each one expresses a whole thought. Be sure to use them accurately.

- Affirmative: You are correct.
- Break: I separate one message from the message following.
- Figures: Numbers follow (as in "vessel length is figures two two three feet").
- I spell: I shall spell the next word phonetically.
- Out: This is the end of my transmission; no answer is expected.
- Over: This is the end of my transmission and a response is necessary.
- Wait: I must pause a few seconds; stand by for further transmission.

The Phonetic Alphabet. For accuracy of transmission, sometimes you'll use the phonetic alphabet—especially when giving your call letters.

A-Alfa	J-Juliette	S-Sierra
B-Bravo	K-Kilo	T-Tango
C-Charlie	L-Lima	U-Uniform
D-Delta	M-Mike	V-Victor
E-Echo	N-November	W-Whiskey
F-Foxtrot	O-Oscar	X-Xray
G-Golf	P-Papa	Y-Yankee
H-Hotel	Q-Quebec	Z-Zulu
I-India	R-Romeo	

> ### Prop Wrap
>
> A line wrapped around your propeller can sometimes be unwound without a dive overboard or a haulout. If any of the line is within reach, have someone hold it while you go below and turn your propeller shaft with a vise-grip pliers, or turn by hand if you can get a grip on the shaft coupling. The shaft won't turn against the snarl. If it turns the other way, your helper may be able to pull the tangled line slowly and gently while you turn. Don't pull the line too hard. If the shaft won't turn either way, you'll have to go overboard or limp into port for help.

Restaurants 1991

This listing was compiled from information supplied by visitors' bureaus and chambers of commerce. These establishments are presented as a service to readers and should not be considered recommendations.

Illinois

Chicago:

Alfo's Ristorante
2512 S. Oakley Ave.
523-6994

Ambria
2300 N. Lincoln Park West
472-5959

Ann Sather's Restaurant
929 W. Belmont Ave.
348-2378

Annabelle's on Ontario
240 East Ontario
944-3170

Arnie's
1030 North State St.
266-4800

Avanzare
161 E. Huron
337-8056

Bacchanalia Ristorante
2413 S. Oakley Ave.
254-6555

Bacino's on Wacker
75 East Wacker Dr.
263-0070

The Bakery
2218 N. Lincoln Ave.
472-6942

Bencher's Fish House
233 S. Wacker Dr.
933-0096

Benkay
320 N. Dearborn
744-1900

Berghoff
17 West Adams
427-3170

Biggs
1150 N. Dearborn
787-0900

Bistro 110
110 E. Pearson St.
266-3110

Buckingham's
720 S. Michigan Ave.
922-4400

Butch McGuire's
20 W. Division St.
337-9080

The Butcher Shop
358 W. Ontario
440-4900

Cafe Ba-Ba-Reeba!
2024 N. Halsted St.
935-5000

Cafe Bernard
2100 N. Halsted St.
871-2100

Cafe Royal
1633 N. Halsted
266-3394

Cafe Spiaggia
980 N. Michigan Ave.
280-2764

Carlucci Restaurant
2215 N. Halsted
281-1220

Casanova's
2425 W. Lawrence
271-3661

Charlie Chiangs
158 E. Ontario
944-1917

Chestnut Street Grill
845 N. Michigan Ave.
280-2720

Chicago Chop House
60 W. Ontario St.
787-7100

Ciel Bleu Restaurant
181 East Lakeshore Dr.
951-2864

The City Tavern
33 W. Monroe
280-2740

Cricket's
100 East Chestnut St.
280-2100

The Dining Room
909 N. Michigan Ave.
943-7200

Ditka's/City Lights
223 W. Ontario St.
280-1790

Ghandi Indian Restaurant
2601 W. Devon
761-8714

Harry Caray's
33 West Kinzie
465-9269

L'Escargot on Michigan
701 N. Michigan Ave.
337-1717

La Salle
65 East Wacker
346-7100

Lawry's The Prime Rib
100 E. Ontario St.
787-5000

Martha's Vineyard
1160 North Dearborn
337-6617

Jim McMahon's
1970 N. Lincoln
751-1700

Nick's Fishmarket
1 First National Plaza
621-0200

P.J. Clarke's
1204 N. State St.
664-1650

The Palm
181 E. Lake Shore Dr.
944-0135

Pronto
200 E. Chestnut
664-6181

The Pump Room
1301 N. State Pkwy
266-0360

Scoozi
410 W. Huron
943-5900

Shaw's Crab House
21 E. Hubbard
527-2722

Spiaggia
980 N. Michigan Ave.
280-2750

Star of Chicago Ship
600 E. Grand/Navy Pier
644-5914

Su Casa
49 E. Ontario
943-4041

Tijuana Yacht Club
516 Clark
321-1160

Trader Vic's
17 E. Monroe
726-7500

Michigan

Bay City:

Brass Lantern
1019 N. Water Street
894-0772

Fireside Restaurant
802 N. Euclid
686-5170

Water Street Pub
916 N. Water St.
893-0344

White's Restaurant
305 N. Euclid
686-0700

Benton Harbor:

Beach Side Restaurant
6263 N M-63
849-1919

Berk's Place of Sister Lakes
67990 W M-152
944-5855

New Harbor Inn
655 Riverview Dr.
927-2421

Pietro's On The Lake
3640 N M-63
849-2155

Cheboygan:

Carnation Restaurant
423 N. Main
627-5324

The Loft
423 N. Main
627-7052

The Pines
5419 Long Lake Rd.
625-2121

Sunset Bluff
10905 Highbluff Dr.
625-9230

Walkway Cafe
330 N. Main
627-7518

Detroit:

Cadieux Cafe
4300 Cadieux
882-8560

Captains Restaurant
260 Schweizer Pl.
568-1862

Carl's Chop House
3020 Grand River
831-9749

The Caucus Club
150 W. Congress St.
965-4970

Checker Bar & Grill
134 Cadillac Square
961-9249

Dionysos Taverna
300 Renaissance Center
259-4715

Dunleavy's River Place
267 Jos. Campeau
259-0909

Elaine's
Two Washington Blvd.
965-0200

Jacoby's Since 1904
624 Brush St.
962-7067

London Chop House
155 W. Congress St.
962-0277

Mario's Restaurant
4222 Second Ave.
833-9425

Nemo's Bar & Grill
300 Renaissance Center
259-1525

1940 Chop House
1940 E. Jefferson Ave.
567-1940

Opus One
565 E. Larned
961-7766

Park Place Cafe
15402 Mack Ave.
881-0550

Rattlesnake Club
300 River Place
567-4400

Strohaus
2001 Rivard
568-5131

Sweet Water Tavern
400 E. Congress
962-2210

333 East
333 E. Jefferson Ave.
222-7404

Top of the Pontch
2 Washington Blvd.
965-0200

Woodbridge Tavern
289 St. Aubin
259-0578

Mackinaw City

The Admiral's Table
506 S. Huron
436-5687

Embers Restaurant
810 S. Huron
436-5773

Kenville's Cafe
112 S. Huron
436-7131

'Neath the Birches
Old U.S. 31
436-5401

Teysen's Cafeteria
416 Huron Ave.
436-7011

Three Coins Restaurant
815 S. Huron Ave.
436-5746

Muskegon:

Acorn Restaurant
431 E. Laketon Ave.
722-0100

Carmen's Cafe
315 W. Clay Ave.
726-6317

Cobwebs and Rafters
3006 Lakeshore Dr.
755-3985

Hearthstone
3350 Glade St.
733-1056

Mill Inn
2441 Lakeshore Dr.
755-7263

Morat's River Walk Cafe
Mears at the River
893-5163

Racquets
446 W. Western Ave.
726-2475

Ship's Rail
1936 Peck St.
722-6772

St. Joseph:

Inner Harbor
100 Main St.
983-7341

Mark III Restaurant
4179 M-139
429-2941

New Dock Side Inn
613 Pleasant St.
982-0313

The Oaks
3711 Niles Rd.
429-2531

Pier III
105 Main St.
983-2334

Sinbads West
4220 Lake Shore Dr.
429-3911

Traverse City:

Bean Pot
301 E. Front St.
946-1270

Bowers Harbor
13512 Peninsula Dr.
223-4222

Pointe of View
13641 W. Bay Shore Dr.
947-7079

Sail Inn
1104 Barlow St.
946-4195

Top of the Park
300 State Street
946-5000

Sweitzer's By The Bay
13890 W. Bay Shore Dr
947-0493

Windows Restaurant
7677 W. Bay Shore Dr.
941-0100

New York

Alexandria City:

Cavallario's Restaurant
26 Church
482-9867

Buffalo:

Atrium
120 Church St.
845-5100

Center City Cafe
28 High St.
882-3950

Colter Bay Grill
561 Delaware Ave.
882-1330

Garvey's
414 Pearl St.
856-3222

The Greenery
120 Church St.
845-5100

Hemingway's
492 Pearl St.
856-1937

Justine's
120 Church St.
845-5100

Park Lane at the Circle
Delaware Ave./Gates Cir.
883-3344

Shooters Waterfront Cafe
325 Fuhrmann Blvd.
854-0416

Valentine's
91 Niagara St.
56-8373

Dunkirk:

Fireside Manor Restaurant
Route 5
672-4449

Kettle & Keg Restaurant
243 Lake Shore Dr.
366-2056

Strychalski'a Restaurant
49 E. Doughty St.
366-2115

Oswego:

Oswego Marina Restaurant
Oswego Marina
342-0436

St. Johnsville:

Beardslee Manor
St. Johnsville Marina
568-7406

Union Springs:

Wheelhouse
Hibiscus Harbor Marina
889-5086

Westport:

The Galley
Westport Marina
962-4899

Ohio

Cleveland:

Cafe Sausalito
Galleria at Erieview
696-CAFE

Celery Stalk
1803 E. 12th St.
579-0880

Champion Of China
840 Huron Rd.
781-6646

D'Poo's on the River
1146 Old River Rd.
579-0828

French Connection
24 Public Square
696-5600

Haymarket
123 Prospect Ave. W.
241-4220

Jim's Steak House
1800 Scranton Rd.
241-6343

John Q's Public Bar & Grille
55 Public Square
861-0900

New York Spaghetti House
2173 E. Ninth St.
696-6624

Ninth Street Grill
Galleria at Erieview
579-9919

Pat Joyce's
602 St. Clair Ave.
771-6444

River's Edge
1198 Old River Rd.
696-DELI

Rockefellers
1111 Lakeside Ave.
241-5100

Roxy Bar & Grill
1900 E. Ninth St.
523-5580

Sammy's
1400 W. 10th St.
523-5560

Shooters on the Water
1148 Main Ave.
861-6900

Shorty's Delux Diner
1540 Columbus Rd.
621-5321

Stouffer Tower City Plaza
24 Public Square
696-5600

Sweetwater Cafe
1320 Huron Rd.
781-1150

Top of the Town
100 Erieview Plaza
771-1600

Watermark
1250 Old River Rd.
241-1600

Sandusky:

Bay Harbor Inn
Cedar Point Marina
627-2334

Bayview Bar & Grille
2001 Cleveland Rd.
627-2500

The Cold Creek Cafe
107 Main St.
684-7462

Damon's
Battery Park Marina
625-6142

Harbour Lights Restaurant
10 Harbour Pkwy.
625-5551

The Hickory
1649 Cleveland Rd.
625-3635

Home Village Chinese
1012 Cleveland Rd.
626-7000

Johnny Angel's
1935 Cleveland Rd.
626-6761

Log Cabin Inn
505 E. Bayview Dr.
684-7185

Marina Steak House
Cedar Point Marina
627-2334

Shooters On The Water
2003 Cleveland Rd.
626-5200

The Water's Edge
7724 Wahl Rd.
684-9361

Toledo:

Arlington Restaurant
901 Starr Ave.
691-2803

Athenian Cafe
Portside
255-5107

Captain Creole
Portside
241-8226

Chadwick Inn
301 River Rd.
893-2388

Checkerboard Grill
408 N. Summit St.
244-7573

City Club
415 N. Huron
248-9139

Craig's At Portside
Portside
242-8860

Cypher's Restaurant
5220 N. Summit St.
729-9121

Greenstreets
141 N. Summit St.
243-8860

Louie's Lightnin' Grill
Portside
242-8611

Northwood Inn
3025 N. Summit St.
729-3791

Old Roadhouse Inn
224 S. Erie
241-3045

Tony Packo's Cafe
1902 Front
691-6054

Real Seafood Company
Portside
241-1133

Ricardo's
1 Seagate
255-1116

River Cafe & Marina
6215 Edgewater Dr.
723-7405

Riverview Yacht Club
5981 Edgewater Dr.
726-2157

The Roaster
Portside
244-7147

Steak Escape
Portside
255-3155

Vie De France
Portside
242-2680

Webber's Restaurant
6339 Edgewater Dr.
723-7411

Pennsylvania

Erie:

The Dry Dock
3122 West Lake Rd.
833-6135

Farrell's Restaurant
1535 W. 26th St.
453-4911

The Hearth
2670 W. Eighth St.
838-2162

Henry's Restaurant
2212 W. Eighth St.
454-7141

Pufferbelly on French St.
414 French St.
454-1557

Smuggler's Wharf Inn
3 State St.
459-4273

Stonehouse Inn
4753 West Lake Rd.
838-9296

Wisconsin

Baileys Harbor:

Baileys Harbor Yacht Club
8115 Ridges Rd.
839-2336

Green Bay:

Baxter's Food & Spirits
240 N. Broadway
432-3344

Chili John's
519 S. Military Ave.
494-4624

Harbor Ridge Food & Spirits
2638 Bay Settlement Rd.
468-8860

Prime Quarter Steak House
2610 S. Oneida
498-8701

Viand's Restaurant
418 S. Military Ave.
497-9646

Kenosha:

Alex's Bar & Restaurant
2500 52nd
654-9981

Gazebo Restaurant
5722 Sixth Ave.
657-7072

Giovanni's on the Lake
3101 Eagle Rd.
878-4500

House of Gerhard
3927 75th St.
694-5212

Oage Thomsen's
2227 60th St.
657-9314

The Renaissance
2217 52nd St.
658-3177

The Ranch
7500 Sheridan Rd.
654-0288

Ray Radigan's
11712 Sheridan Rd.
694-0455

Windows on the Harbor
5125 Sixth Ave.
658-3281

Manitowoc:

The Breakwater
101 Maritime Dr.
682-7000

Lighthouse Inn
1515 Memorial Dr.
(800) 362-5575
Outside WI (800) 228-6416

Milwaukee:

Alioto's Restaurant
3041 N. Mayfair Rd.
476-6900

WATERWAY GUIDE

The **WATERWAY GUIDE** contains data on marinas, bridge clearances and schedules, anchorages and uncharted hazards. Also included, are sights to see, tide and distance tables, mail drops and the handy Mariner's Handbook. The series is published in four editions:

1 1991 Northern Edition: The C & D Canal and Delaware Bay, the New Jersey shore, New York Harbor, Long Island Sound, Narragansett and Buzzards Bay, and the coasts of Massachusetts and Maine to the Canadian border. $27.95

2 1991 Mid-Atlantic Edition: The major rivers of the Eastern and Western Shores, the Chesapeake Bay from the C & D Canal to Norfolk, plus the Intracoastal Waterway through Virginia, the Carolinas, and Georgia. $27.95

3 1991 Southern Edition: Begins at the Georgia/Florida line, covers all of Florida, the Gulf of Mexico, the Bahamas and the Keys, and the Okeechobee and Tenn-Tom Waterways. $27.95

1991 Great Lakes Edition: Lakes Michigan, Huron, Erie and Ontario and their connecting waterways, plus the upper Hudson River. $27.95

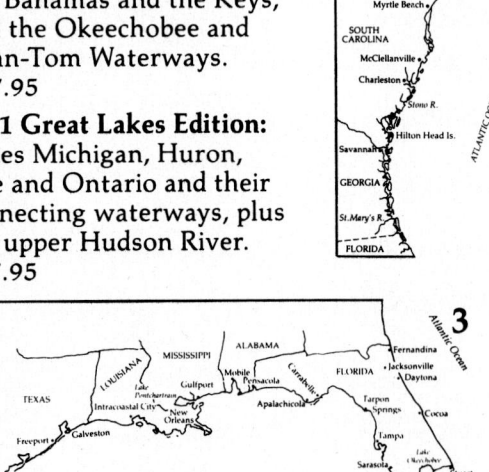

Send your check and order along with your name and street address to:

WATERWAY GUIDE
6255 Barfield Road
Atlanta, GA 30328

$3.00 shipping per book for each order

1-800-233-3359

Boulevard Inn
4300 W. Lloyd St.
445-4221

Boder's on the River
11919 N. River Road
242-0335

Dietze's Alpen Haus
800 W. Layton Ave.
744-1750

Fleur de Lis
925 E. Wells St.
278-8030

Highland House
12741 N. Port Washington
243-5844

John Hawks Pub
607 N. Broadway
272-3199

Nantucket Shores
924 E. Juneau
278-8660

Water Street Brewery
1101 N. Water St.
272-1195

Weissgerber's
1110 Old World Third St.
272-0330

Racine:

Castlewood Restaurant
2811 Wisconsin St.
886-9799

Channings
1346 Grand Ave.
633-9050

Corner House
1521 Washington Ave.
637-1295

The Docks Waterfront
Reefpoint Marina
631-5555

The Elmwood
2427 Lathrop Ave.
632-9639

Fish Joynt
1245 Douglas Ave.
634-8955

Golden Phoenix
3340 Douglas Ave.
639-4000

The Packing House
6825 Washington Ave.
886-9866

Rio Grande
1201 N. Wisconsin
637-7300

Sheboygan County:

Citystreets
607 Plaza 8
457-9050

Dockside Lounge & Deli
737 Riverside Dr.
458-7900

Jume's
504 N. Eighth St.
452-4914

Mark's Fine Foods
1910 Calumet Dr.
457-5181

Richard's
501 Monroe St.
467-6401

Riverdale Inn
5008 S. 12th St.
457-6655

Rupp's Lodge
925 N. Eighth St.
459-8155

The Villager
124 Pine St.
467-4011

Toronto:

Pier 4 Restaurant
Harbourfront Marina
973-4094

Prescott:

Bridgeview Restaurant
River Road East
925-2974

Lake Erie

CHARTS: 14820, 14822, 14823, 14824, 14825, 14826, 14830, 14832, 14833, 14835, 14836, 14837, 14839, 14841, 14842-SC, 14844, 14845, 14846-SC, 14847; Canadian: 2100, 2110, 2181, 2183.

Four-hundred years ago, the Iroquois Indians called Lake Erie the Lake of the Cat. Today, it's still a good idea to keep the analogy of a cat in mind as you cruise this southernmost of the Great Lakes. Like a cat, Erie can change almost instantly from quiet calm to stormy. And, just like a cat, it can quickly fall asleep again.

Native Americans used Erie both as a water highway and as a source of food. Fear of the fierce Iroquois kept French explorers well to the north of the lake until Joliet finally reached its shores in 1669. Thus, although now the most heavily populated of the lakes, Erie was the last of the Great Lakes to be discovered by European explorers.

In 1813 a major sea battle off West Sister Island in Erie's western end was instrumental in setting the international boundary between the United States and Canada. "We have met the enemy and he is ours," was Commodore Oliver H. Perry's message after capturing an entire British fleet. Three monuments and numerous historic sites commemorating Perry's victory dot the southern Erie shoreline.

Erie is heavily traveled by large commercial ships. Commercial shipping does not pose a great threat to cruising boats, though, since the freighters and ore carriers use well-defined shipping lanes, shown on Chart 14820. Of course, you must keep a sharp lookout when cruising near major ports such as Buffalo, Erie, Conneaut, Cleveland, Lorain, Toledo, or the mouth of the Detroit River.

Cruising Lake Erie

Four states share the southern shore of the lake: New York, Pennsylvania, Ohio, and Michigan. Much of the nation's heavy industry is concentrated along Lake Erie. Nevertheless, cruising skippers still find miles of unspoiled shoreline between the major urban centers.

Erie's northern shore is in the Canadian province of Ontario. The low-lying coastline contains no major cities. Small fishing villages and resort communities punctuate the rural countryside. Silos can be important local landmarks.

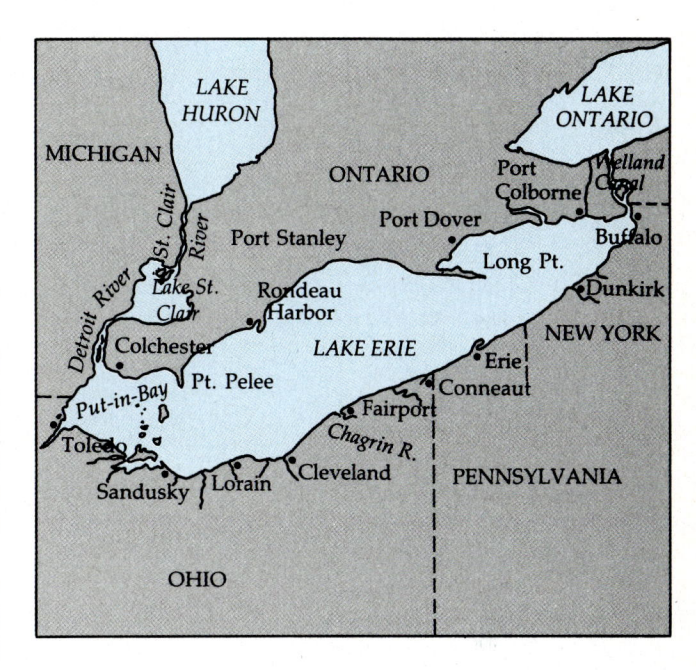

Lake Erie's islands are the main attraction for most cruising boats. Located in the western end of the lake, they are spread like stepping stones from the Ohio shore across to Canada. Some of the world's finest walleye fishing can be found on the reefs of this area. Each of the islands has a distinct personality, providing activities from anchoring off a sandy beach to enjoying a glass of wine in a local winery.

Cruising Conditions

Fourth largest of the Great Lakes (only Lake Ontario is smaller), Erie is 241 miles long and 56 miles across at its widest point. The deepest sounding is 210 feet, but the average depth is only 58 feet. This makes Erie the shallowest of the Great Lakes, and many of the prime cruising grounds around the islands are much shallower than average depth, often less than 20 feet. A complete set of up-to-date charts should be carried by anyone cruising this lake, particularly around the islands.

Because of the shallowness of Lake Erie, you should pay close attention to the current lake level. Daily reports of the lake level are included in NOAA Weather Radio broadcasts as well as in MAFOR reports.

The shallowness of Lake Erie accounts for its infamous, bone-jarring, choppy water. Short, confused seas build quickly with any significant increase in wind speed — a phenomenon especially noticeable in the areas around the islands. The size of a Lake Erie chop is less significant than its shape. High-speed travel in a powerboat is nearly impossible, and sailboats may find the wind knocked from their sails even though waves

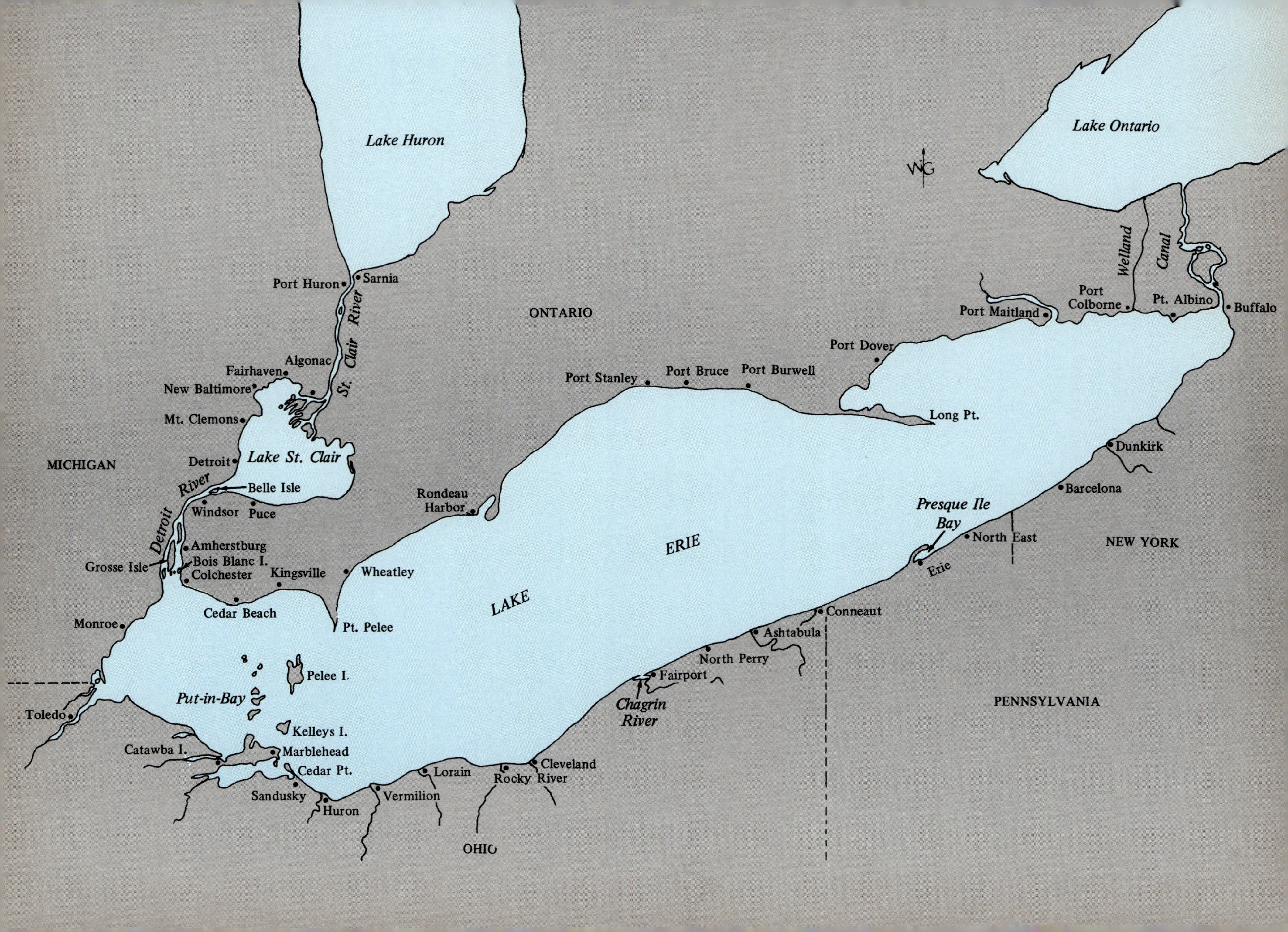
Lake Huron
Lake Ontario
WG
Port Huron
Sarnia
St. Clair River
ONTARIO
Welland
Canal
Port Colborne
Pt. Albino
Buffalo
Port Maitland
Port Dover
Port Stanley
Port Bruce
Port Burwell
Long Pt.
Algonac
Fairhaven
New Baltimore
Mt. Clemons
Lake St. Clair
Detroit
MICHIGAN
Detroit River
Belle Isle
Windsor
Puce
Amherstburg
Grosse Isle
Bois Blanc I.
Colchester
Kingsville
Wheatley
Rondeau Harbor
Dunkirk
Barcelona
Presque Ile Bay
North East
NEW YORK
ERIE
LAKE
Erie
Monroe
Cedar Beach
Pt. Pelee
Conneaut
Ashtabula
North Perry
Pelee I.
Fairport
Chagrin River
Put-in-Bay
PENNSYLVANIA
Toledo
Kelleys I.
Catawba I.
Marblehead
Cedar Pt.
Cleveland
Lorain
Rocky River
Sandusky
Vermilion
Huron
OHIO

are running less than three feet. Fortunately, Lake Erie is quick to calm down; it can go from a three-foot chop to dead calm in a matter of hours.

Seiches. The lake lies along the path of the prevailing westerly winds. This accident of geography exposes its full length to these winds and gives rise to a phenomenon called a **seiche** (pronounced *sayshh*). Strong westerly winds can pile the water up at the Buffalo end of the lake while water levels at the western end around the islands can drop a foot or more. A decrease in wind speed, or a shift in direction, may allow the water to slosh back; sometimes this causes unusually high water levels for a short period of time in the island area. Smaller seiches occur in the shallow western end of the lake with northerly or southerly winds. Deep-draft sailboats may find themselves temporarily aground in some harbors due to seiche action. Unlike tides, seiches cannot be predicted; they occur completely at the whim of weather conditions.

Weather. The cruising season on Lake Erie runs from May to October, with mid-summer temperatures ranging from daytime 80s down to the 60s at night. By late June, the water has warmed sufficiently for comfortable swimming, rising to an average of 73 degrees by mid-August. Because of the lake's position and orientation, it is subject to sudden and sometimes violent afternoon squalls and thunderstorms. It is important to keep track of weather forecasts at all times during the day.

Zebra Mussels. In recent years Lake Erie has seen a growing infestation of tiny zebra mussels, a small bivalve about the size of a fingernail. Some portions of the lake bottom in the island area are almost completely covered by these rapidly-reproducing animals. Expect to find them growing on any hard surface left under water for any length of time. Zebra mussels pose no problem to boats passing through the lake. However, if you plan to spend several weeks cruising Erie, beware of engine overheating caused by zebra mussels clogging cooling water intakes, especially those of I/O outdrives. Regular anti-fouling paint is sufficient to keep these mussels off boat bottoms.

Harbors. When cruising Erie, be prepared to spend most nights tied up at a dock. Most of the harbors are man-made, enclosed by breakwaters thrusting into the lake. These breakwaters usually have lighted aids on them. Anchorages are somewhat limited, and most of the safe places to spend the night have been turned into public marinas or private yacht clubs. The good anchorages are noted in the text. Most of the lake has a mud, clay, or sand bottom that provides good holding for patent anchors. Some rocky areas around the islands cannot be relied upon for overnight anchorage. Check the chart before dropping the hook in the island area, because electric and telephone cables often cross otherwise good anchorages. Hooking one of the cables can cause problems for unwary skippers.

The following pages will take you on a port-to-port cruise along the southern shore, entering the lake from the Welland Canal. From there it will go from Buffalo to the Detroit Light along the southern, American shore. The most popular spots around the lake can become extremely crowded during the peak summer vacation months of July and August. Overcrowding is also normal on the three summer holidays: Memorial Day, Fourth of July, and Labor Day. If you cruise during the busy summer months, call ahead on VHF radio to see if your destination marina has room. Rafting is customary (and often required) where possible in crowded harbors.

Eastern End

The Canadian coast of Lake Erie is almost entirely rural, with commercial fishing ports spaced at intervals, but very few pleasure boat facilities. The extensive commercial fishing on this side of the lake requires that you be on the lookout for fish nets that can pose quite a hazard. They are usually marked by flagged buoys at either end, but sometimes even these are hard to see. Canadian waters also contain underwater gas wells which are marked on the chart. Canadian law prohibits portable toilets on boats; only permanent holding tanks with deck pump-out fittings are permitted. "Y" valves must be disconnected. In recent years these rules have been strictly enforced, particularly at ports in the eastern end of Lake Erie.

Port Colborne. A constant stream of big ship traffic goes through Port Colborne, the Lake Erie entrance to the Welland Canal. Two large grain elevators built on wharves in the harbor make good landmarks. From the lake, enter through the main ship channel after making sure it is clear of commercial shipping. Don't go around the west end of the breakwater that runs parallel to shore; the water in that end of the harbor is skinny at best. To find the full-service marina, continue up the main channel until you reach the grain elevator wharves, turn left, and run close to the end of the wharves. Turn right and run between the westerly wharf and the small separate breakwater to the yacht harbor, the only marina in the area with water deep enough to take sailboats and large power boats.

Note: The main harbor is buoyed as if coming from the sea through the Welland Canal with reds on the port side as you enter from Lake Erie. The channel leading to the marina is buoyed in the conventional way, however.

The marina is about half a mile from downtown shopping and restaurants. There is an attractive historic complex to visit in Port Colborne.

Niagara River. From Port Colborne to the head of the Niagara River some 15 miles east, the coast is rugged with one significant promontory. Point Abino lies about seven miles west-southwest of Port Colborne. The 20-

LAKE ERIE

Point to Point Courses / Distances

Some suggested compass courses and distances for cross-lake passage; all courses given are True and all mileages are in approximate statute miles.
Note that this table should be used only as a guide, not as instruction. Varying conditions of equipment, weather, and wind will, naturally, affect your passage.

From	To	Course	Distance
Buffalo	Dunkirk	224	32
(North Ent.	Erie Harbor Light	231	75
Harbor Buoy	Presque Isle Light	236	77
2 miles, 207)	(5 miles, 140)		
	Long Point	248	60
	(3 miles, 332)		
Dunkirk	Buffalo	044	32
(1 mile harbor	Port Colborne	012	22
mouth, 325)	Erie Harbor Light	237	43
	Presque Isle Light	241	46
	(5 miles, 140)		
	Port Dover	292	46
	Long Point	272	34
	(3 miles, 332)	253	167
Erie	Buffalo	051	74
(harbor ent.	Port Colborne	041	60
bell buoy B1)	Presque Isle Light	291	4
Presque Isle	Conneaut	240	26
	Long Point	012	23
	Port Stanley	300	65
	Southeast Shoal Lt.	258	124
Conneaut	Presque Isle	060	26
(1.5 miles, 347)	Port Stanley	323	55
	Southeast Shoal Lt.	262	99
	Ashtabula	249	13
	Long Point	038	45
Ashtabula	Buffalo	057	114
(1 mile, 343)	Port Colborne	052	99
	Conneaut	069	13
	Port Stanley	336	53
	Southeast Shoal Lt.	264	86
	Fairport Harbor	248	27
	Long Point	045	56
Fairport Harbor	Ashtabula	068	27
(1.5 miles, 357)	Buffalo	059	141
	Port Colborne	055	125
	Port Stanley	003	59
	Southeast Shoal Lt.	271	61
	Sandusky	255	75
	Cleveland	234	30

From	To	Course	Distance
Fairport Harbor	Long Point	052	82
Cleveland Harbor	Fairport Harbor	054	30
(.5 mile, 290)	Port Stanley	020	81
	Rondeau Harbor	170	49
	Southeast Shoal Lt.	297	42
	Marblehead Lt.	272	50
	(South Passage)		
	Kelley's Is. Shoal (B1)	279	46
Lorain	Long Point Lt.	064	133
(.5 mile, 290)	Rondeau Harbor	016	54
	Southeast Shoal Lt.	330	26
	Marblehead Lt.	281	27
	(South Passage)		
	Sandusky	274	24
	Huron	255	18
	Vermilion	248	11
	Kelley's Is. Shoal (B1)	297	25
	Port Stanley	032	94
Vermilion	Huron	260	11
(1 mile, 037)	Southeast Shoal Lt.	350	27
	Rondeau Harbor	023	62
	Port Stanley	036	102
	Kelley's Is. Shoal (B1)	318	20
	Sandusky Harbor Lt.	288	20
	Scott Point Shoal (B1)	297	25
Huron	Vermilion	080	11
(.5 mile, 000)	Lorain	075	18
	Southeast Shoal Lt.	007	27
	Sandusky Harbor Lt.	308	9
	Rondeau Harbor	030	66
	Port Stanley	041	110
Sandusky	Huron	132	9
(channel ent.	Lorain	094	24
buoy B1)	Southeast Shoal Lt.	206	24
	Rondeau Harbor	037	64
	Port Stanley	044	109
	Kelley's Is. Shoal (B1)	012	10
	Kelley's Is. W. Buoy	327	8
Toledo	Put-in-Bay	105	17
(Harbor Lt.)			

Coastline Distances

Approximate Statute Miles

Location	Between Points	Cumulative
South Shore / Detroit River		
Buffalo	0	0
Dunkirk	37	37
Erie, PA	45	82
Conneaut, OH	33	115
Ashtabula	15	130
Fairport	30	160
Cleveland (main entrance)	33	193
Lorain	28	221
Vermilion	11	232
Huron	11	243
Sandusky	14	257
Put-in-Bay	21	278
Port Clinton	12	290
Toledo	40	330
Monroe, MI	21	351

Location	Between Points	Cumulative
Detroit River Light	14	365
Amherstburg	7	372
Trenton	13	385
Wyandotte	5	390
Detroit (Woodward Avenue)	11	401
North Shore		
Buffalo	0	0
Port Colborne	22	22
Port Maitland	18	40
Port Dover	37	77
Port Burwell	62	139
Port Stanley	23	162
Rondeau Bay	49	211
Kingsville	63	274
Amherstburg	31	305

foot limestone cliff supports a light on a white square tower. An earth-mound breakwater on the western side of the point in Abino Bay serves the Buffalo Yacht Club. A second breakwater protects the Buffalo Canoe Club. Limited repairs are available.

The coast from Point Abino to the Niagara River is a series of shallow bays and points of land. A rock awash is located about a mile east of Windmill Point, and a shallow rocky spit extends about a half mile off the east entrance point of Bertie Bay.

The entrance to the Niagara River is almost a mile wide where it joins Erie. Navigation of this river is not recommended without local knowledge of this shallow, rocky river with its tricky currents. At the Peace Bridge the current has been measured at seven knots.

Waverly Shoal, least depth ten feet, is marked by a buoy. It lies in the lake on approaches to Buffalo from Canadian ports. Middle Reefs lie just inside the Niagara River and are marked by buoys and an abandoned lighthouse. The Buffalo water intake crib is located in 14 feet of water. This circular structure carries a lighted aid.

Buffalo Harbor. A three-mile-long breakwater protects Buffalo Harbor from lake waves. It can be entered either at the northern end near the head of the Niagara River or at the southern end between the breakwater and Stoney Point. The south entrance leads to commercial facilities and is used mostly by ships. The north entrance is used by pleasure boats for access to the Black Rock Canal that bypasses the fierce currents in the Niagara River. Just before the entrance to the canal is a fine marina close to the heart of downtown, a good base from which to explore the city. Just inside the canal is a yacht club.

Black Rock Canal. The Black Rock Canal is operated by the Corps of Engineers. The speed limit is six miles per hour. Two bridges (closed clearance 17 feet) respond to one long and one short blast. Do not approach too closely until they are open, because of the current in the canal. At the north end, the Federal Lock will lower your boat about five feet to the level of the Niagara River. Downbound pleasure boats are locked through on the hour; upbound on the half hour. Commercial traffic takes precedence, so it's wise to call ahead to the lockmaster on Channel 12. Boats anticipating transit of the New York Canal system should use the Black Rock Canal to Tonawanda on the Niagara River.

Facilities and attractions. Along the Niagara River and below the Federal Lock are numerous marinas and yacht clubs on both the mainland and Grand Island. Not all of them accept transient boats. Most are not convenient to shopping, but several have restaurants on the premises. On the southwest side of **Grand Island**, facing the Canadian shore, **Beaver Island State Park** has a fine marina, and the park itself has playgrounds, picnic areas, a beach, and a golf course. About a mile beyond the northern end of Grand Island, the river gathers momentum for its plunge over **Niagara Falls**. Grand Island is the effective head of navigation.

Sights to see in Buffalo include the Allentown Historic District of handsome 19th-century mansions, one of which is the Theodore Roosevelt National Historic Site. Other attractions include the excellent art and historical museums and a naval museum that features several World War II naval vessels. Be sure to try the buffalo wings in area restaurants. These spicy chicken wings originated here in Buffalo.

Cattaraugus Creek. Leaving the southern entrance to Buffalo Harbor for the open waters of Lake Erie, you run 23 miles to **Cattaraugus Creek**. The shoreline is rather steep, and deep water is close to shore, but be wary of shoal spots in the vicinity of Sturgeon Point. Cattaraugus Creek is an important local harbor, mostly for smaller boats. Problems with shoaling at the entrance have been reported. A marina located on the west bank of the river offers services and a launching ramp. Two other marinas located upriver are accessible by outboard or shoal-draft vessels.

Dunkirk. Eleven miles west of Cattaraugus Creek lies the port of **Dunkirk**. Look for the stacks of a power plant (lighted at night) just west of the harbor entrance. The channel lies between the power plant and the outer stone breakwater, which is marked by lighted aids. Dockage is available both at the friendly Dunkirk Yacht Club and at the municipal pier. A recently enlarged full-service marina is located at the western end of the harbor. Dunkirk is a very shallow harbor, but DYC members say that they regularly accommodate boats with drafts to six feet. The east side of the city dock is used by a small local fishing fleet. Several restaurants, new hotels, and limited shopping are located within walking distance of the yacht club (be sure to get a gate key before leaving club property).

Barcelona. Leaving Dunkirk you round **Point Gratiot** with its picturesque lighthouse. A rocky bank with less than 20 feet of water extends about a mile from shore between Gratiot Point and Van Buren Point.

The small port of **Barcelona**, 15 miles west of Dunkirk, is not well protected from the northeast and east. A marina in the southwest corner of the harbor offers gasoline. It welcomes transient boats that don't draw more than six feet.

Erie/Presque Isle Bay. Twenty-seven miles west of Barcelona is the city of **Erie**, Pennsylvania, and beautiful **Presque Isle Bay**. The entrance of this important port for cruising boats is on the east end of the Presque Isle peninsula. This long, arching peninsula connects to the mainland at its western end, creating a large protected harbor, Presque Isle Bay. The bay is about four and a half miles long and a mile and a half wide. The city of Erie lies along the southern shore and all of the northern shore is part of Presque Isle State Park.

The park offers a well-protected marina located about a mile and a half west of the harbor entrance in a

LAKE ERIE

dredged basin. No docks are set aside specifically for transients, but the dockmaster can usually find you a berth left open by one of the resident boats. For boat-weary travelers, the park has shoreside diversions: a playground, beaches, hiking trails, and an ecological reservation. But the state park and marina are a long way from the attractions of the city, and no public transportation is available.

Anchorages include the bay north of the state park marina and Misery Bay. However, these sheltered locations are quite shallow and not suitable for large or deep-draft boats. Furthermore, on the park side of the bay a rule states that you may not sleep on your boat within 500 feet of shore, unless you're docked at the marina.

A monument to Commodore Oliver H. Perry is located on the point of land delineating the western side of Misery Bay. Most of Perry's fleet was built in Erie, which is home to Perry's newly-restored flagship, **Niagara**. Erie is in the process of expanding and redeveloping its marinas along most of the shoreline bordering the city. Pleasure boat amenities are concentrated around the old public dock downtown. From here, several restaurants and many of Erie's interesting sights are within walking distance, although shopping is not so handy.

Conneaut. Just about 25 miles west of Erie, you enter Ohio waters and approach the industrial port of **Conneaut**. Two breakwaters extend into the lake, forming a triangle that makes this an easy harbor to enter. Unfortunately, most of the services here are for commercial shipping or small boats. Conneaut is an excellent port of refuge, but offers little else for transient mariners.

Ashtabula. Fifteen miles west of Conneaut lies **Ashtabula**. A commercial port, it nonetheless offers facilities for pleasure boats. Enter between the two breakwaters that form an arrowhead into the lake. Inside, the entrance to the Astabula River lies to the west of the commercial docks. First-time visitors have been known to mistakenly go up the ConRail slip. The river entrance is marked by a flashing red light. Just upstream from the mouth you pass under an overhead conveyor with 100-foot clearance. The Fifth Street Highway Bridge opens on the hour and half hour. Two commercial marinas and a yacht club are located just upstream from the Fifth Street Bridge. These marinas are at the edge of a heavy industrial district, but the old commercial neighborhood nearby has been restored. It is now occupied by shops and restaurants. Downtown Ashtabula is two miles up the river near the highway.

Fairport Harbor (Grand River). Thirty miles west of Ashtabula at the mouth of the Grand River, **Fairport Harbor** is both a deepwater commercial port and a yacht harbor. Pleasure boats must travel about a mile upstream to reach their docks because heavy commercial activity dominates the river mouth.

Newcomers should always enter this port through the main shipping channel, especially in foul weather or darkness. This entrance is well-marked with lighted aids. Entering the open eastern end of the breakwater is possible, but be wary of the easterly breakwater which is in disrepair and is often submerged during stormy weather. In settled weather, you can anchor in the outer harbor behind the east breakwater.

Friendly yacht clubs and marinas make Fairport a good stopover. Shopping, a Laundromat, and restaurants are all nearby. A short cab ride takes you to the movies and stores at the Market Mall and to the Fairport Marine Museum, located in an old lighthouse on the east side of the mouth of the river. Sailors will enjoy a visit to the sales and administrative offices of Tartan Yachts at Grand River. Shallow-draft boats can explore upriver, past the railroad bridge.

Just west of Fairport Harbor you pass **Headlands Beach State Park**, reportedly one of the finest beaches on Lake Erie. It is local practice to anchor out for a swim. Stay outside the buoyed swimming areas and keep a weather eye out—you're in unprotected waters.

Mentor. Four miles west is **Mentor Harbor**, privately owned by the Mentor Harbor Yacht Club, which extends privileges to members of reciprocating clubs. The club is reported to be among the most charming in the country. A marina, open to transient mariners, is located on the eastern lagoon and marked by buoys. The entrance channel to Mentor Harbor has a silting problem and churns up in heavy northwest-to-northeast winds.

Chagrin River. The **Chagrin River** presents a pleasantly rural, tree-lined shoreline virtually in the backyard of Cleveland's busy metropolitan area. Yachts wishing to avoid spending a night in the big city may find this a good stopping-off point. But the harbor entrance can be difficult in strong northerly winds, when a vicious chop and breaking seas can develop off the river mouth. The entrance also tends to silt up. Nevertheless, the Chagrin River is popular, especially for power boats; depths are insufficient for sailboats beyond the yacht club at the river mouth.

A good landmark for finding the Chagrin River en-

SUTHERLAND MARINE

Sutherland Marine
First on the River
Since 1956

Ashtabulas Oldest Full Service Marina

Dead South — Thru Main Opening - ¼ Mile.

970 Bridge St. Ashtabula, Ohio 44004
(216) 964-3434   VHF Ch 16

trance is the battery of smokestacks rising from the electric plant just west of the river. Don't mistake the plant's water intake canal for the river entrance. Every year several boats make this dangerous mistake. Upstream on the Chagrin, beyond the yacht club, are several marinas and yacht clubs for boats with shallow draft.

Cleveland

An industrial metropolis that has seen hard times, **Cleveland** is now making a strong comeback. The waterfront is a major focus of the city's revival, resulting in constant changes and construction. Although not a traditional cruising destination, the city nevertheless has many cultural amenities and waterfront attractions that make it worth visiting.

Cleveland Harbor. Cleveland's waterfront is protected by a five-mile-long breakwater that creates the harbor. You may take one of three entrances: at the far northeast end, through the main entrance opposite the mouth of the **Cuyahoga River,** or through the Edgewater entrance at the far southwest end. Approaching from either end you'll see Cleveland's landmark symbol, the Terminal Tower. At night the top half of this gray stone building is illuminated with floodlights. Just to the east of it is an equally impressive red stone tower, the Sohio office complex. Both buildings can be seen from a considerable distance offshore.

Cruising boats approaching from the east normally enter the east entrance which is marked by a flashing white light in a white tower on steel skeleton legs. The main entrance is used by commercial shipping, but is handy when approaching the city from the north or west. It is well-marked with lighted aids, the most conspicuous of which is a lighthouse structure (formerly occupied) on the west pierhead. Both the east entrance and the main entrance can be used in all weather. The Edgewater entrance should be used only in calm conditions.

Entering from the east, the city's East 55th Street Marina offers protected dockage. No berths are set aside for transients, but the harbormaster can often find overnight space. Although the facilities are excellent, there is no shopping or entertainment within walking distance. Several yacht clubs that offer transient accommodations to members of reciprocating clubs are located just west of the Cleveland Municipal Light Plant. They are entered through a channel between the Burke Lakefront Airport and the mainland.

The East Basin between the airport and the mouth of the Cuyahoga River is home to a variety of commercial docks, the U.S. Coast Guard, the Corps of Engineers, and the Naval Reserve. The most conspicuous landmark is Municipal Stadium, home of the Cleveland Indians and Cleveland Browns. The area between the stadium and East Ninth Street Pier is currently being redeveloped into a waterfront complex that will include a marine musuem and small boat harbor.

The Edgewater Basin is connected to the main harbor by a semi-protected passage, partially open to allow access to the lake, and thus not fully protected from lake storms. Inside this basin you will find a state park marina and a yacht club offering transient dockage to members of reciprocating clubs.

The public land on Cleveland's waterfront has been turned over to the state of Ohio to be developed as an urban park. All of the public marinas are run by the Ohio Division of Natural Resources. Charted anchorages in Cleveland Harbor are used by commercial shipping. Due to heavy boat traffic, overnight anchorage anywhere in the harbor is not advised.

Cuyahoga River. Navigable for five miles upstream, the Cuyahoga River flows through the heart of Cleveland's industrial district. This alone would make an interesting side trip, but the river is also fast becoming the focus of the city's night life. Entrance to the river is directly opposite the main harbor entrance, marked by a white art deco tower at the abandoned Coast Guard station on the west bank.

Immediately inside the river is a railroad lift bridge that restricts all but the smallest vessels. It opens for pleasure craft on the hour and half hour when such openings do not interfere with railroad traffic. Immediately upstream on the east bank are a variety of restaurants and night clubs, the bulk of which offer free dockage to patrons. Overnight dockage is not available.

A variety of railroad and highway bridges cross the Cuyahoga River. All but the smallest boats will have to signal for the draws to be raised. Because of the closeness of the bridges, each has a different whistle signal. Signs are posted on each bridge explaining the appropriate signal.

Just upstream of the first railroad bridge on the west side is the entrance to the **Old River**. Years ago, the Old River was the main channel of the Cuyahoga, but a new entrance was cut, and the old channel is now a dead end. A short distance up the Old River is a full-service marina.

Cleveland ashore. Although the waterfront marinas are separated from the heart of downtown Cleveland by expressways, railroads, and industrial and commercial installations, a taxi ride to any of Cleveland's attractions is well worthwhile. You can take a tour by carriage or on foot. The view from the top of the Terminal Tower is spectacular on a clear day. The former train station in the base of the Terminal Tower is currently being renovated into a galleria of shops and restaurants. Nearby are two major department stores and specialty shops.

A short distance up Euclid Avenue is the Old Arcade, a 19th-century enclosed mall of structural iron and glass, where elegant shops surround a central atrium on five balcony levels. A little farther along Euclid is Cleveland's restored theater district, known as Playhouse Square. The theaters here give performances year round. Four miles away at (Case-Western Reserve) University Circle are six outstanding museums, including Cleveland's world-famous art museum. Severence Hall, home of the reknowned Cleveland Orchestra, is also located here.

Cleveland to Port Clinton

Except for a few industrial enclaves, the Ohio shore west of Cleveland becomes increasingly residential and recreational. **Rocky River**, six miles west of Cleveland's main harbor, is the suburban location of a yacht club which occupies an island in the river. Transient dockage is available to members of reciprocating clubs. The river entrance is marked by a high bluff on the western side and a low breakwater on the east that may not be seen until you are quite close. Waves reflecting off of the bluff may cause breaking seas in the entrance. Check the river current before attempting to dock. It can run upstream or downstream depending on seiche action. A small anchorage is immediately inside the entrance, but it can be uncomfortable under some conditions. Upstream from the yacht club, beyond the 49-foot highway bridge, are several more marinas.

Lorain. Twenty miles west of Rocky River, **Lorain** is an industrial city with growing recreational amenities. This harbor was once a major shipbuilding port, but now serves pleasure craft almost exclusively. The entrance is between arrowhead breakwaters protected by a disconnected section of breakwater. The main lighthouse structure has been restored by volunteers and is now being used as a symbol of the city's rebirth.

A relatively new municipal marina is located just east of the mouth of the Black River. Limited transient dockage can be found here, but transient buoys are provided in the anchorage for a small fee. Additional transient dockage can be found just inside the mouth of the Black River at the Lorain Yacht Basin.

Much redevelopment is occuring in Lorain. The former dry docks of the American Shipbuilding Company are now a full-service marina. Another full-service yard is located three miles upriver from the pierhead.

Beaver Creek. Five miles west of Lorain at the mouth of **Beaver Creek** are several marinas. Only the first one can accommodate sailboats and larger power boats. Two marinas for power boats under 25 feet are beyond the low, fixed highway bridge less than a quarter mile upstream. A privately maintained set of range lights helps locate the entrance, but don't try this harbor in rough weather unless you're familiar with the channel.

Vermilion. Ten miles west of Lorain, **Vermilion** marks the beginning of the Lake Erie Islands area. This quaint old town with its residential lagoons is a favorite of cruising mariners. The river entrance is protected by a detached breakwater that runs parallel to shore across the mouth. The approach can be confusing to the uninitiated at night, although the detached wall is well marked with lighted aids. The large ball-shaped water tower, painted silver and carrying the symbol of the town's high school, is a well-known landmark.

In front of the city waterworks, you'll see a small amount of public dockage on the right bank. Neither water nor electrical hookups are available, although you can refill your water tanks or pump out your holding tank here. Fender well to protect yourself against wakes from the constant parade of passing boats. Dockage is limited to 24 hours. Two yacht clubs here offer transient accommodations to members of reciprocating clubs. If you cannot find dockage at the waterworks, continue upstream to the area just below the highway bridge, where you'll find all sorts of commercial dockage. All marinas catering to sailboats are located below the fixed highway bridge. Power boats with a clearance of less than 12 feet can continue under the bridge to find several more full-service marinas.

The town of Vermilion is noted for its collection of shops and boutiques—everything from Swiss music boxes to macrobiotic food is available. The shops are within walking distance of all public dockage. The city is also the home of the **Great Lakes Historical Society** and its fine museum of Great Lakes history. The museum store is an authorized NOAA chart dealer.

Several good restaurants are in town. The excellent Hungarian restaurant turns out goulash and paprikas worth standing in line for. After dinner, stroll around the corner for a homemade ice-cream cone.

When you leave Vermilion, keep a watchful eye out for the two buoys marking the water intake cribs just west of the entrance. A scant three feet of water is available over the crib closest to shore.

Huron. Ten miles west of Vermilion, **Huron** is the southernmost port on the Great Lakes. Like so many harbor towns around Lake Erie, Huron combines commercial and recreational boating. The industrial side of the Huron River is on the east, and the town with its marinas and other attractions lies on the west bank.

The approach. A good landmark is the cement plant on the east side of the entrance. On most days, it puts out a plume of pure white steam that can be seen for 20 miles or more. A long breakwater extends offshore along the west side of the entrance channel; behind it is a large, semicircular spoil area. The east wall is much shorter, and both breakwaters contain lighted aids to navigation.

About a half mile upstream on the west side of the river is one of the finest transient marinas on Lake Erie, the Huron Small Boat Mooring Basin, with full services for your boat. Nearby are all sorts of shoreside amenities for the crew, including gift shops, restaurants, bike rentals, and an Irish pub. The floating docks which formerly kept visitors awake with the squeaking of hinges have been replaced with much quieter equipment.

The city's yacht club accepts transients with I-LYA

affiliation. Nearby are a boatyard and a marine store specializing in sailboat needs. Power boats can continue upriver beyond the highway and railroad bridges to several more full-service marinas. If you are cautious, the Huron River is navigable for several miles upstream from the bridges, a pleasant trip through rolling farm country.

A few miles west of the Huron entrance is a marina associated with a resort that also offers golf, tennis, a beach, restaurants, and evening entertainment. The creek is difficult to enter in rough seas and has a controlling depth of five feet.

Sandusky/Sandusky Bay. Sandusky Bay, 15 miles long by five miles wide, is one of Lake Erie's few natural harbors. The entrance, at the west end of the bay, is identifiable from a distance by the 333-foot space needle ride at Sandusky's outstanding Cedar Point Amusement Park. Closer in, the big hill of the world's tallest roller coaster can also be seen, especially at night with its strings of lights. Cedar Point forms the southern protecting arm of the bay, and a breakwater extends northeast from that point about a mile into Lake Erie. This low-lying wall is easy to overlook in rough weather. Keep a sharp lookout for the box-like tower on stilts at the end; it carries the Sandusky pierhead light and a foghorn. Waves reflected off this breakwater can cause rough going in the entrance. Give the stone rip-rap a wide berth when you enter Sandusky Bay.

Keep a lookout for commercial shipping in the entrance channel. Large lake freighters make regular visits to the Lower Lake Coal Dock located at the western side of downtown Sandusky. Ships entering or departing the harbor announce their intentions in security calls on VHF Channel 16.

Anyone unfamiliar with this entrance is advised to stay within the marked channel. A moving sandbar extends well off Bay Point on the northwest side of the entrance. Because this bar moves with wave action, it is not marked. The entrance to Sandusky Bay is well marked by the Mosley Channel range lights. Carry the first range as you enter along the breakwater and turn to port when the second range lines up off your starboard quarter. This back range can be carried all the way to the commercial docks in downtown Sandusky.

Shortly after making the turn to port in the Moseley Channel you can leave it and run parallel to Cedar Point to reach the excellent marina at the Cedar Point Amusement Park complex. The marina is entered from the southeast on a northwest heading through the marked breakwaters. Report to the gas dock area to receive a transient dockage assignment. All regular docks have water and electricity. The amusement park gate is within walking distance of the marina, which also offers an excellent restaurant. Since this is a popular place during vacation season, arrive early in the day to assure dock space.

Sandusky. The city lies on the southern shoreline of the bay just inside Cedar Point. The city's municipal marina at Battery Park lies just east of the Lower Straight Channel. Marina reconstruction has moved the entrance of this harbor to the northeast wall facing Cedar Point. Continue straight inside the marina to the gas dock for a transient dockage assignment. Just outside the marina is Battery Park with picnic space.

Immediately adjacent to Battery Park Marina are two yacht clubs. To the southeast is the Sadler Sailing Basin, home of the Sandusky Sailing Club. Just west is the brand new marina of the Sandusky Yacht Club.

Several full-service marinas are located well to the east southeast of Battery Park. Although the chart shows shoal water, large boats can reach these marinas

---

battery park marina

701 E. WATER STREET   SANDUSKY, OHIO 44870
419 625-6142

• seasonal & transient dockage • gas, diesel & pumpout • restaurant, lounge & outdoor cafe • restrooms, showers & laundry • ships store, marine supplies & groceries • park, picnic area & shelter house • electricity, water & dock carts • tennis courts & wave action pool • easy access & 24 hour security • highest standards for cleanliness • 270° view of Sandusky Bay • accommodations for rendezvous • located in downtown Sandusky •

CEDAR POINT MARINA

SANDUSKY, OHIO   (419) 627-2334

DOCK AT AMERICA'S ROLLER COAST®!

This summer, chart your course to the Cedar Point Marina and treat your crew to 364 acres of fun at Cedar Point. New for 1990: Blast off into outer space adventure on Disaster Transport, a scream in space!

- Year-round marina
- Two waterfront restaurants
- More than 700 slips
- Marina Store
- Fuel docks
- Complete repair shop
- Close to Cedar Point and Lake Erie Islands

LAKE ERIE

with local knowledge. Private buoys mark the preferred channel. Power boats with less than 21-foot clearance can go under the Cedar Point causeway bridge to several boat-in restaurants and a hotel.

The downtown Sandusky waterfront is undergoing rapid reconstruction. At least one major new marina is well underway and other boating amenities are planned. An excellent public launching ramp is located at the western edge of downtown near the coal docks. Several ferries operate from the city dock. One goes to Cedar Point if you are unable to find dockage there and still want to visit the amusement park. Others go to the Erie Islands and to Canada.

Sandusky Bay. This large bay can be thought of as a large shallow lake connected at one end to Lake Erie. Weather conditions affect it completely differently from the way they affect the big lake. Winds that rile the lake may hardly ripple the bay, while at other times the bay can be extremely choppy when Lake Erie is quite calm. The water is thin even in the deepest parts of Sandusky Bay. Gunkhole cruising should be restricted to shoal-draft craft such as outboards and outdrive power boats. Wind-driven seiches, described earlier in this chapter, can cause major changes in water level.

Powerboat skippers can cruise through the railroad bridge and under the two highway bridges to the upper stretches of the bay. From there, shoal-draft boats can continue up the **Sandusky River** as far as **Freemont**. The trip takes most of a day but provides plenty of scenic river cruising. Note that while NOAA charts still show three bridges across Sandusky Bay, there are now only two. The middle lift bridge was removed during the winter of 1989-90.

A major new state launching ramp is located on the northern side of the bay behind Johnsons Island. This island served as a prisoner-of-war camp for Southern officers during the Civil War. Only the camp's graveyard remains, along with a statue of a Confederate soldier gazing forever southward. Look for it at the southeast tip of the island.

With care, the enterprising mariner can find a variety of potential overnight anchorages in Sandusky Bay. Much of the bottom is mud or sand with good holding qualities. In choosing an anchorage, check the weather and be sure of your depth. Keep in mind that this bay has considerable small boat traffic. Anchoring overnight is not advisable anywhere in the vicinity of Cedar Point or the city of Sandusky.

The Island Area

From Marblehead to Port Clinton. The **Marblehead** Peninsula forms the north shore of Sandusky Bay, separating it from Lake Erie. Running roughly due east and west, the peninsula is formed of limestone, and much of the interior has been quarried over the past 150 years. A number of marinas suited only for small fishing craft are sprinkled along the Marblehead shoreline.

Just north of Bay Point on the lake side of the peninsula is a locally famous fish restaurant (charted) with its own docks. Water alongside is reported to be more than eight feet deep. As you approach, watch for a shoal spot about 300 feet directly off the entrance.

Beyond the restaurant, on the northeast tip of the peninsula, Marblehead Lighthouse can be seen from a long distance. Built in 1821, this is the oldest working lighthouse on the Great Lakes. Tours are scheduled for the last Saturday of the month, June through August, in 1990. Visitors will be allowed to climb the tower, but you'll have to come by car as off-lying rocks make landing from the water unsafe even in a small boat.

Watch for big ships. As you cruise along the north side of the Marblehead peninsula, be especially watchful for ships. Lake freighters steam directly up to a stone loading dock to load stone from the quarry. Just west of the stone dock is the landing for ferries serving Kelleys Island. They operate on a half-hour schedule all summer.

Continuing west from the ferry dock you come to **Lakeside**, Ohio, a Chatauqua-type resort operated by the Methodist church. On summer evenings, a carillon plays hymns, making a delightful counterpoint to an evening's sail. The Lakeside dock is rough and not suitable for pleasure craft.

West of Lakeside is another full-service marina with limited transient berths. You'll recognize this facility by the sunken ship used as a breakwater and a cluster of yellow buildings, one with a rounded top.

East Harbor. Several small marinas are found along the Marblehead shoreline west of Lakeside. Few offer transient accommodations. The entrance to East Harbor is located where the land begins to bend northward to form the **Catawba Island** peninsula. It is protected by stone walls marked with lighted aids to navigation. The north shore of East Harbor is a state park and the harbor itself is a public fishing and game refuge. Depths in East Harbor are limited; skippers of deep-draft vessels should exercise caution entering here. You can anchor overnight near the state park, although you must be aware that the muck on the bottom doesn't always make good holding ground. Be sure to rig an anchor light as this harbor is used almost 24 hours a day by fishermen during the summer.

Dockage. With the exception of one marina located immediately to your left after you enter East Harbor, most of the commercial marinas are located on the southern shoreline. Follow the buoyed channel to stay in relatively deep water. Boats in the channel are restricted to a no-wake speed, but those operating outside the channel can travel faster. Most of the docks in East Harbor are privately owned and belong to cottagers. The easiest way to spot a commercial marina is to look for a fuel dock carrying an oil company sign. The state park offers no dockage in East Harbor, and the launching ramp is restricted to those using the campground.

West Harbor. The shoreline between East and West harbors is actually a low-lying barrier island made of lake sand. The entire stretch is an excellent beach with an off-lying sandy bottom that gives good holding to patent anchors. This is an excellent place to anchor for a swim, but it is too unprotected for overnight anchorage. Avoid the buoyed areas marking the state park swimming beach.

Most of the dockage available in this area is located in **West Harbor**. The main entrance is between the stone rip-rap piers of an arrowhead breakwater. Lighted aids mark the entrance and lighted buoys guide you up the channel. Do not stray from the marked channel, because depths go from eight feet to virtually zero. The buoyed channel leads from the entrance through the center of West Harbor, which is virtually a landlocked lake.

West Harbor is home to more than 5,000 boats, and is ringed with full-service marinas; although sailboat services are scanty, since the majority of the boats are power. Most marinas offer limited transient accommodations. An excellent public launching ramp (which you can use for a fee) is also located here. Anchoring is not recommended in West Harbor due to the high volume of boat traffic and poor holding in the soft ooze.

The old entrance to West Harbor was through the Gem Beach Channel, to the west of the new entrance. This channel remains in service, but can be used only by low clearance power boats because of the 20-foot Harbor Island bridge.

Catawba Island. More than 150 years ago when the first European settlers arrived, **Catawba Island** was in fact an island. Since then, the land has been filled in, turning it into a peninsula.

Cruising westward, be sure to go outside **Mouse Island** when you go around the tip of Catawba—there are rocks and sandbars between the tiny island and the mainland. Also, keep a lookout for the Put-in-Bay ferry, which docks just behind the west side of Mouse Island.

You'll find three major marinas on the west side of Catawba Peninsula, as well as private harbors that are not open to transient boats. The Catawba Island Club restricts overnight dockage to its own members, but the other two marinas welcome transients. Their entrances are guarded by sunken breakwaters marked by private buoys. Local knowledge is beneficial. At night, or if you draw more than four feet, go to Port Clinton for dockage. The Catawba Island State Park offers an excellent public launching ramp.

Cruising yachts should stay well offshore when going from Catawba Island toward Port Clinton. As the chart shows, this is a shoal area despite its appearance of open lake. Marinas along this stretch of the Catawba Peninsula are geared for small fishing boats.

Port Clinton. Located at the mouth of the **Portage River, Port Clinton** is the commercial center for the peninsulas and islands. The entrance lies between two stone breakwaters that extend for several hundred feet into the lake; both walls have lighted aids. Local skippers use the stack of the waterworks and a radio relay tower behind it as a range to guide them into the entrance. Be careful, though: While this range does provide a rough approximation of the center of the channel at the entrance, following it blindly could put you aground on the west side of the channel farther inside.

This port is home to the world's largest jet catamaran ferry, capable of exceeding 35 miles per hour. It docks just upstream of the entrance on the west side of the river. When operating at high speeds, this ferry normally displays a flashing yellow strobe light between its hulls in addition to the normal running lights. Mariners should be aware that this vessel is moving across the lake much faster than it appears to be. A second, coventional ferry also operates from the same dock.

Mariners with I-LYA affiliation will get a warm welcome at the Port Clinton Yacht Club. A small city dock is opposite the yacht club, but is only capable of handling two boats at most (one space is almost always filled by the city's police boat). You must go through the highway bascule bridge for transient dockage, repairs, and other marine services available here. The bridge opens for pleasure boats on the hour and half hour; the signal is one long and one short blast. Don't be in too much of a hurry to sound your horn. The bridge tenders keep a good lookout and usually open without any prodding.

Three major marinas are located on the north side of the bridge. All manner of marine supplies and repairs are also available. Deep-draft boats should not go upstream beyond the railroad bridge and should stay in the marked channel at all times. Low-rise power boats can gunkhole the Portage River almost to the town of **Oak Harbor**, if they proceed with care. Clearance under the railroad bridge is 13 feet in the open position.

The Portage River is broad and slow-moving above Port Clinton. At the city, it narrows into a restricted channel for about a mile before reaching the lake. The result of this constriction can be currents of unexpected strength. Usually, the current moves downriver, but when the lake level is rising rapidly because of the seiche action, the current can be reversed, causing turbulent conditions in the channel. Be especially cautious just upstream from the highway bridge.

The Islands.

Like stepping stones between the United States and Canada, the Erie Islands comprise a popular cruising and fishing ground. Most of the islands are privately owned, so mariners should take care not to trespass. But four of them welcome visitors and provide amenities for cruising boats. These spots are apt to be crowded, however, especially on summer weekends, so it's best to arrive early in the day. Despite the density of boats, the islands still convey a soothing rural ambience.

LAKE ERIE

Put-In-Bay (South Bass Island). This island is about three miles north of the Catawba Peninsula. Most people refer to it as **Put-In-Bay**, although this name is technically incorrect. Put-In-Bay is the harbor on the north side of the island and the name of the island's only town. However, years of misuse have blurred the distinction, and now island, town, and harbor are all commonly called by the same name.

During the War of 1812 Commodore Perry anchored his fleet here just before the Battle of Lake Erie. Today, the battle fleet has been replaced by a pleasure fleet that numbers in the hundreds. The 352-foot tall monument to Perry's victory is visible for 25 miles and is the dominant landmark in the area.

Always enter Put-In-Bay by rounding the eastern end of **Gibraltar Island**. Never go between the west side of Gibraltar and **South Bass Island**; a line of rocks just below the surface connects the two. Owned by Ohio State University and used as a research station for studies of Lake Erie, Gibraltar Island is not open to the public.

Most cruising boats head for the public marina near the center of town. The docks are maintained by the town of Put-In-Bay. Fees are collected for both hourly and overnight dockage. Rafting is required, but limited to three boats deep. Never tie up to the outside walls of this basin. Waves in the bay and the wakes of passing boats can lift a moored craft onto the pier, causing major damage. Always go inside the basin. Electricity and water are available dockside, but the number of boats using this harbor usually is greater than the number of outlets available. Smaller, shallow-draft boats can use the small piers close to shore. Larger boats should stay on the outer piers.

Free dockage is available at the state park docks at the far western end of the bay. These are in shallow water and close together, so are limited to boats under 25 feet and with shoal drafts. Stay in the buoyed channel along shore to avoid the shallows between Gilbraltar and South Bass. No electricity or water is available at dockside here, but there are restrooms with flush toilets. The state docks are more than a quarter mile from the bright lights of downtown Put-In-Bay. The long walk to town discourages many people from using them, so you can often find space here when the marina downtown is full.

The Crew's Nest is a private club that offers daily memberships on weekdays only. The daily membership allows use of a club dock and limited use of club facilities such as the restaurant. Three Crew's Nest dock complexes are scattered around the harbor. Check with the dockmaster at the office for a space assignment. Transient dockage can also be obtained at The Boardwalk just west of the city marina.

You can spend the night on the hook in Put-In-Bay just the way Commodore Perry did. Many people prefer this solution to the noise and crowded conditions of the marinas. You can pick up a private mooring if the owner is away, or use your own ground tackle in the designated anchorage area behind Gibraltar Island. A free dinghy landing is located downtown between the city marina and The Boardwalk pier. Use caution in your dinghy, however, because the ferry to Middle Bass Island also uses this slip, as do boats approaching The Boardwalk fuel docks. The dinghy landing is a rocky beach that usually requires at least one member of the crew to get his feet wet.

South Bass Island. The island is almost entirely recreational. In addition to the mariners who swarm there on summer weekends, cottage inhabitants also swell the small year-round population, as do day-trippers who come from the mainland by ferry. A rental bicycle, moped or golf cart are nice ways to tour the island—beyond the bustling village, it's a peaceful place—or you can take the narrated train tour. Almost everyone heads for the Perry Monument, where park rangers tell the story of his famous victory in the 1813 Battle of Lake Erie. The view from the top of the monument is magnificent on a clear day. Sometimes you can see the tall buildings of Cleveland and Detroit. Downtown, you'll find a wide variety of boutiques, taverns, and restaurants with live entertainment. Heineman's Winery makes a variety of wines and juices from grapes grown on South Bass. Tours of the winery and Crystal Cave (the world's largest geode) are available.

Middle Bass Island. There is only one transient harbor on **Middle Bass Island**, the Lonz Winery marina. Don't confuse the marina with the small boat basin on the south side of the island near the winery building. This small basin is not suitable for even temporary dockage because of surge, and it is roped off. Go around the east side of the island to find the marina. The entrance is pointed directly at **Ballast Island** and is plainly marked on the chart. It is guarded by two rusting steel walls on which privately maintained flashing harbor lights are usually mounted. Larger boats should wait until the channel is completely clear of other traffic before entering. Observe the No Docking signs. They mark the locations of underwater obstructions. The marina provides no services and collects day or overnight fees. The winery offers tours and tastings in its Gothic cellar, and there are pleasant country lanes to walk on the island. Ice and limited grocery items can be obtained at the ferry dock.

Kelleys Island. In approaching this island, four miles from Marblehead, stay a half mile offshore. Several shoal areas are located along the eastern side of Kelleys Island. The boats you observe closer in are usually fishing. On the north side of the island, Kelleys Island Shoal and Gull Shoal are charted and well marked with buoys.

The great attraction of Kelleys, the largest American island in Lake Erie, is a large cove on the north side which shelters one of the best beaches on this part of the lake. On weekends, hundreds of boats anchor here for picnics, swimming, or water-skiing. Unfortunately, the bottom is now thin sand over rock and offers poor holding for an overnight stay, except in the calmest of weather. The best place to anchor is in the western end of the bay near the state park swimming beach. (The swimming area is buoyed off, and boats are not permitted to enter.)

Two marinas are located on the southern side of the island facing Marblehead. Immediately downtown is the Kellys Island Public Marina, a collection of formerly-private docks. Look for the barn-shaped building of Popeye's for a landmark. The marina office is located at the head of the stairs next to the stone house just west of Popeye's. This marina offers limited services, but has the advantage of being close to downtown shops and restaurants.

The other marina is tucked into the southeast tip of the island. The entrance runs almost due east and west; it is protected by two stone walls marked with lighted aids. Report to the gas dock just past the cannon on your left for a dock assignment. All transient docks are on the walls of the basin and rafting is required. Electricity and water are available, as well as restrooms, showers, and pump-out.

Kelleys is an excellent island for exploring by bicycle or golf cart, both of which are available for rent at several locations. The most famous natural features are the Glacial Grooves in the state park on the north shore. These grooves dramatically show the power of Ice Age glaciers that were once a mile thick here. Other attractions include the ruins of an old winery, as well as a fine new winery offering tastings in a garden setting.

Pelee Island. The largest island in Lake Erie and the southernmost spot in Canada, **Pelee** is primarily an agricultural community surrounded by water. At first glance, little would seem to attract cruising boats. Yet thousands of American yachts clear through Customs here each year. Some come to buy Canadian beer and spirits at lower prices; others are looking for a bargain in English china or fine woolens. But the majority come looking for the quiet, slow pace of life that characterizes this island.

The easiest Customs office to visit is at West Dock on the west side of the island. This is a commercial wharf made of concrete and steel, and a more efficient destroyer of gel coats has yet to be invented. Even good fenders are not always enough because the pier extends straight into the lake with no protection. In rough weather, avoid West Dock; go straight to the yacht harbor and report to Customs by telephone.

Another place to report to Customs is Dick's Marina, tucked into the southeast corner of the island. This marina is suitable for small boats only and cannot accommodate boats larger than 25 feet.

The yacht harbor at Scudder on the north side of the island is tucked behind the picturesque wooden granary on the government wharf. There are only 18 slips available to transients here and they are often occupied. Additional dockage can be had along the granary wharf outside of the area used by the ferry to the mainland. Overnight anchorage can also be attempted in fair weather.

Pelee Island is located in one of the most active commercial fishing areas in Lake Erie. Literally thousands of feet of fishing nets are strung out in the Canadian waters around this island. Usually they are far enough below the surface to cause no problems, but not always. Most nets are strung in a straight line with poles marking each end. These poles are supposed to have flags, but often the cloth has weathered away. Small black floats between the poles support the net, which hangs on tarred rope underneath.

Fish weirs and pound nets are located in several spots along the west shore of Pelee north of West Dock. Made of wooden pilings driven into the lake bottom with netting between, they are not lighted or marked in any way. Stay at least 2,000 feet offshore to avoid these structures.

Western Lake Erie

Lake Erie is most shallow at its western end. The low, marshy land is cut by numerous small creeks. It is a fine environment for wildlife—much of the land is protected in refuges—but it's not so good for cruising mariners. Keep well offshore until heading directly for your destination.

Danger Zone. Just west of Port Clinton, an artillery firing range danger zone lies off the Ohio National Guard's **Camp Perry**. Restricted Area I is close to shore and is used every day from April 1 to November 30, between 8:00 a.m. and 5:00 p.m. Restricted Area II is used only sporadically. The latest information on these zones is published in the *Local Notices to Mariners* by the Ninth District Coast Guard. Notices of firing in both ranges are also posted at local marinas, printed in local newspapers, and broadcast over NOAA Weather Radio. The range safety officer can be reached on VHF channel 16. A flashing white strobe light on the range control tower signals firing in either impact zone. This light is bright enough to be seen for at least six miles in daylight.

Heading westward from Port Clinton, the shoreline is dominated by the 500-foot-tall cooling tower of a nuclear power plant on **Locust Point**. Lake depths are shallow close to Locust Point, so it's best to stay several miles offshore. None of the small streams or marinas in this area is suitable for large boats.

West Sister Island lies nine miles north-northwest of the cooling tower. This island is a federal wildlife sanctuary—do not go ashore. Game wardens monitor activity on the island and will arrest anyone caught onshore without permission.

Cooley Canal (Anchor Pointe). Eight miles southwest from West Sister Island is a large, round structure housing a water intake for the city of Toledo. In 18 feet of water about two miles offshore, this water intake crib makes a good reference point for finding the entrance to the **Cooley Canal**, which can be difficult to locate. The entrance lies southwest of the intake structure on a

LAKE ERIE

course of approximately 218 degrees True. A series of private lights on the breakwaters mark the entrance. Most of the harbor is taken up by a condominium-style marina where skippers own their docks. Transient mariners are welcome for short stays. A restaurant and a full-service marina overlook the lake. Other marinas and the launching ramp located farther inland are suitable only for small, shoal-draft boats.

Toledo. The Maumee River, the largest flowing into the Great Lakes, enters Lake Erie through broad, shallow, Maumee Bay. On the river banks at its mouth, the city of **Toledo** is an important industrial port. But there are also attractions for the cruising mariner here.

The Toledo Channel actually begins eighteen miles out in the bay, but pleasure boats coming from the east can enter it nine miles from port at the Toledo Harbor Light. This is a large square building with a round lighthouse attached. Follow the channel buoys carefully, because there are unmarked spoil areas on either side. Within four miles of the harbor, a lighted range comes into view.

At the river's mouth, commercial docks are located on the south side. Opposite on the north bank, a basin you can enter between the Coast Guard Depot and the Naval Reserve Station has two yacht clubs. A little farther upstream on the same side is a full-service marina. The river banks become industrial once again as you pass through four opening bridges to reach downtown. The two railroad bridges open on demand. The Craig Memorial Bridge, which carries I-280, opens from three minutes before to three minutes after the hour and half hour, except at 7:30 a.m. and 4:30 p.m., when it remains closed. One mile beyond, the Cherry Street Bridge opens 15 minutes later.

Just past the Cherry Street Bridge on the north bank, Toledo's handsome new SeaGate development graces the foreshore, backed up by some impressive new skyscrapers. The development includes Promenade Park, a hotel, and Portside Festival Marketplace. During the winter of 1989, Portside went into receivership, and many of the shops have closed temporarily until the economic problems are solved. Nevertheless, Portside is still an excellent destination, with several fine restaurants nearby. A large number of floating docks welcome visiting yachtsmen, although the supply is never adequate on weekends. Water and electricity are available. A commercial marina is located on the east bank almost directly across the river.

From Portside, downtown Toledo is within walking distance. The city's first-rate art museum is a cab ride beyond downtown. It includes not only famous paintings, but an outstanding collection of artistic glasswork. Across the river from Portside is a straight-deck Great Lakes freighter, now open as a museum.

The Maumee River is navigable for several miles upstream, where industrial gives way to residential and another yacht club. After two opening bridges and one high level span, 45-foot and 37-foot fixed bridges will deter sailboats with taller masts.

Toledo Beach. Immediately northwest of the mouth of the Maumee River is shallow North Maumee Bay and the Ottawa River. A variety of small-boat amenities are located here, but local knowledge is necessary. Tiny Turtle Island with its abandoned lighthouse is half in Ohio and half in Michigan.

About six miles northwest of Toledo Harbor Light is a large, full-service marina and a yacht club in the dredged-out mouth of **Sulphur Creek**. They are just over the state line into Michigan. The harbor entrance range is hard to pick up from offshore, but the power plant stacks two and a half miles to the south give you a clue as to its location. When you get close enough, the marina buildings are conspicuous. Members of I-LYA are welcome at the yacht club. The full-service marina can arrange limited transient dockage.

Bolles Harbor (La Plaisance Creek). Three miles north of Toledo Beach, **Bolles Harbor** is a Michigan small-craft harbor of refuge. A dredged, buoyed channel and lighted aids lead through the shallows of La Plaisance Bay into **La Plaisance Creek**. Near the entrance is a Michigan Waterways Commission launching ramp, and upstream are two commercial marinas and a yacht club. There are a couple of convenience stores within walking distance, but the city of Monroe is about three miles away.

Monroe (River Raisin). This harbor has a fine, deepwater entrance, but little else to recommend it. Commercial ships deliver coal to the power plant at the mouth of the river and there are few services for transient boats. The turning basin above the power plant is a potential harbor of refuge and could be used as an anchorage with caution. Only low-rise boats can proceed upstream beyond the I-75 highway bridge.

This northwest corner of Lake Erie is quite marshy, with a number of creeks that flow into the lake. A couple of them have small yacht clubs or marinas, but for the most part this area is difficult to navigate without local knowledge. From Bolles Harbor, it is preferable to keep to the open lake until you reach the Detroit River Channel, covered in the next chapter. Now the narrative returns to the east end of Lake Erie to describe the Canadian coast.

Ontario Shore

In contrast to the United States side, the Canadian coast of Lake Erie is almost entirely rural, with artificial commercial fishing ports spaced at intervals, but very few pleasure boat facilities. The extensive commercial fishing on this side of the lake requires that you be on the lookout for fish nets that can pose quite a hazard. They are usually marked by flagged buoys at either end, but sometimes even these are hard to see. There are also underwater gas wells, only some of which are marked by buoys. They are concentrated at the two ends of the lake, as shown on the chart. The shipping lanes run closer to the Canadian shore between the Welland Canal and Pelee Passage, separating Pelee Island and the Ontario mainland, the only deep-draft route through the Erie Islands at the shallow west end.

Port Colborne. Port Colborne, the Lake Erie entrance to the Welland Canal, sees a constant stream of big-ship traffic in and out of the harbor. Two large grain elevators built on wharves in the harbor make good landmarks. Enter through the main ship channel after making sure it is clear of commercial shipping. Don't go around the west end of the breakwater that runs parallel to shore; the water in that end of the harbor is skinny at best. To find the full-service marina, continue up the main channel until you reach the grain elevator wharves, turn left and run close to the end of the wharves. Turn right and run between the westerly wharf and the small separate breakwater to the yacht harbor, the only marina in the area with water deep enough to take sailboats and large power boats.

Note: The main harbor is buoyed as if you were coming from the sea through the Welland Canal, with reds on the port side as you enter from Lake Erie. The channel leading to the marina is buoyed in the conventional way, however.

The marina is about half a mile from downtown shopping and restaurants, and Port Colborne offers an attractive historic complex for you to visit.

Port Maitland. From Port Colborne to **Port Maitland**, 15 miles west, the coast is broken by points and shallow bays. Visible from the lake is Sugar Loaf Point with its tree-covered knoll, about a mile west of Port Colborne. Anchorage in Moulton Bay is good, but the bay is protected from westerly winds only. Don't stop here under other conditions.

Port Maitland was the entrance to the first Welland Canal, and remains of the old canal can still be found a short distance up the **Grand River**. More recently, it was the home of a fishing fleet, but almost all the commercial traffic is gone now, leaving the harbor with the appearance of a ghost town.

During storms from the south or southwest, lake water surges up the Grand River. When the wind shifts or drops, the water rushes back out, causing strong currents in the harbor entrance. Maitland Harbor is subject to silting and the actual depths may be less than those shown on the charts.

The Dunnville Boat Club is up the Grand River, with a controlling depth of six feet. This small club, on your right as you approach the town, has a small cupola showing a blue light as a beacon to welcome cruising boats. Mariners are welcome to use the club's kitchen and restrooms. A grocery store and other shops are within walking distance.

Long Point Bay. This area is a fisherman's and naturalist's delight. It's enclosed by 18-mile **Long Point**, a sand spit built by wind and wave action over the centuries. On the lake side, Long Point has a continuous sand and gravel beach backed by dunes and forest. The bay side is less well defined and tends to marsh and wetland. It's a haven for migrating and nesting birds, and in season, turtles come ashore to lay their eggs. A small portion of the peninsula is part of an Ontario provincial park.

The best anchorage is behind Bluff Bar, about seven and one half miles west of Long Point Light. A flashing green light buoy near the tip of the bar helps to identify it in this otherwise featureless area. The anchorage shoals off quickly, so don't go too far in. Set your anchor in 12 to 15 feet. In a north or northwest wind, the anchorage is untenable.

Long Point Bay supports both sport fishing and commercial fishing. Many of the marinas in the villages on the mainland side are best suited to small boats, but there are a few places for cruising mariners.

Port Dover. Commercial fishing, yachting, and a resort community come together in Port Dover. Claiming to be the world's largest freshwater fishing port, this small town has a fleet of tugs to prove it. Several marinas and a yacht club are located up the Lynn River beyond the commercial fishing wharves at the mouth. A large beach to the west of the harbor entrance has been attracting vacationers for generations.

All of the yacht facilities are above the highway bridge (24-foot clearance closed), which opens on the hour and half hour. A 8,000-volt power line crosses the

---

WATERWAY GUIDE
ACTUAL NASA LANDSAT SATELLITE PHOTOS

Our exceptional lithographic prints are reproductions from actual NASA Landsat Satellite photos. Taken from 570 miles in space, these high quality infrared photos are perfect for framing or as an accurate record of a memorable voyage.

Send payment with order to:

WATERWAY GUIDE
BOOK DEPARTMENT
6255 Barfield Road
Atlanta, GA 30328

____ Cape Cod Area ($9.45)
____ Chesapeake Bay Area ($9.45)
____ Long Island Area ($9.45)

Order Now. Quantities Limited.

NAME _____
ADDRESS _____
CITY _____ STATE ____ ZIP ____
PHONE (___)

LAKE ERIE

river just above the yacht club. Vertical clearance is reported at 69 feet.

Turkey Point. About ten miles west of Port Dover there is a marina that accommodates cruising boats at Turkey Point. Just beyond the point, the channel begins from the main part of Long Point Bay into Inner Bay. Inner Bay is shallow and best suited to power boats with little draft.

Port Rowan. This is the village center for Inner Bay.

Several marinas are scattered in and around the area. Most of them have buoyed channels leading to their docks that range from five to eight feet deep.

Port Burwell. It's a long haul from the shelter of Long Point Bay around the shoals off Long Point to the next harbor west, Port Burwell. The distance from Port Dover is 62 miles. Although tugs work out of Port Burwell, the harbor at the mouth of **Big Otter Creek** silts badly and probably shouldn't be attempted by boats with more than a three-foot draft. There is no marina

Lake Erie		SEASONAL / YEAR-ROUND	SAIL / POWER / BOTH▲	LARGEST VESSEL ACCOMMODATED	NO. OF TRANSIENT BERTHS	MARKED ENTRY CHANNEL	APPROACH DEPTH (Reported)	DOCKSIDE DEPTH (Reported)	GAS★ / DIESEL● / BOTH▲ FUEL BRAND	RAILWAY / LIFT CAPACITY (in tons)	ENGINE REPAIRS: Gas★ / Diesel● / Both▲	PROPELLER / HULL REPAIRS	LAUNCHING RAMP	MARINE SUPPLIES / GROCERIES / ICE	LPG★ / CNG● / BOTH▲	110V★ / 220V● / BOTH▲ MAX AMPS	SHOWERS / LAUNDROMAT	PUMP-OUT STATION	RESTAURANT / SNACK BAR	RADIO WATCH—VHF (CB)
BUFFALO																				
1. Anchor Marine	(716) 773-7063	Y	▲	40			12	7	MOB	★	L		★	PH		MI	★30	S		S	
2. Beaver Island State Park	773-3271	S	▲	40	80		6	6									★20	S	●	RS	
3. Harbor Place Marina	876-5944	Y	▲	100	10	●	18	12		▲	50	R	▲	PH		MGI	★50	S		RS	16
4. Pier Aus-Tel and Rich Marine	873-4060	Y	▲	100				10	MOB	▲	L	R	▲	PH		MI	▲30	S			
5. Erie Basin Marina*	842-4141	S	▲	100	22	●	29	23	NOC			R	▲	P		MGI	▲100	S	●	S	
6. RCR Yachts	856-6314		S	45	2	●	18	12			20		▲	P		MI	★20	S		R	
DUNKIRK																					
7. Stefan's Rec., Inc.	366-3388	Y	▲	30	4	●	5	5		★	2	R	★	P		MI	★			R	
8. Dunkirk Yacht Club	366-9789	S	▲	50	6	●	8	7	YACHT CLUB							GI	★15	S	●	RS	
9. Bart's Cove*	366-8243	S	▲	40	2	●	10	7	PEN	★	7	R	★	PH		MGI	▲30			RS	16
ERIE																					
10. R.D. McAllister & Son	(814) 452-3201	Y	▲	100	6	●	7	7	MAR	▲	50		▲	P		MI	▲50	SL		RS	16
11. Gem City Marina	459-8184	S	▲	60	3	●	8	8			25										
12. Community Boating Center	(216) 998-6272	S	▲	40	5	●	10	5			12	R	★	H		MGI	★30	SL		R	16
13. Commodore Perry Yacht Club	(814) 454-9106	S	▲	42	6	●	10	8			10					I	★110	SL	●		
14. Presque Isle State Park	838-1417	Y	▲				10	8		★		R								S	
15. Perry's Landing Marina	455-1313	S	▲	100	6	●	16	12	IND	▲	35		▲	P	●	MI	▲50	SL	●	RS	
ASHTABULA																					
16. Sutherland Marine (p. 144)	(216) 964-3434	Y	▲	100	6	●	15	11	SOH	▲	15		▲	P		MI	▲50	S		RS	16
17. Jack's Marine, Inc.	997-5060	Y	▲	210	8		8	8	76	▲	30	R	▲	P		MGI	▲50	SL	●	RS	16/9
FAIRPORT TO CHAGRIN RIVER																					
18. Rutherford's Landing	352-8122	S	P	50	1	●	6	4	MOB	▲	L	R	▲	PH		MGI	▲			S	
19. Bolton's Marine Sales, Inc.	942-7426	Y	P	43	6	●	10	6		★	30		★	P		MI	★30	S	●	RS	
CLEVELAND																					
20. East 55th Street Marina*	361-1157		▲	40	4	●	35	8	PEN	▲						MGI	▲50	S	●	S	16
21. Sailing, Inc.	361-7245	Y	▲				14	10			L		▲	PH		M	★20				
22. D'Poo's on the River	579-0828	Y	▲	35	4	●	14	10	RESTAURANT DOCK											R	
23. Jim's Steak House	241-6343	Y	▲	100	12		24	24	RESTAURANT DOCK							I	▲30			R	
24. Channel Park Marina	631-5000	Y	▲	40			18	10	MAR	★	20	R				I	▲	S	●	S	
25. Edgewater Marina	961-1111	Y	▲	45	8	●	18	7	SOH	▲	L	R		H		I	★30	S			
26. Edgewater Yacht Club	281-6470	Y	▲	50	8	●	10	10	SOH	▲	L					I	★30	S		RS	16
LORAIN																					
27. Beaver Park Marina	282-6308	S	▲	40	8		6	6	MAR	▲	30	R	★	P		MGI	▲	S		RS	
28. Copper Kettle Marina	282-6301	Y	P	32	10	●	8	6	SHE	★	6		★	P		MI	★30	S		RS	19
VERMILION																					
29. Valley Harbor Marina	967-5225	S	P	40	4		8	6	SHE	★	20	R	★	P		MGI	★30	SL	●	S	
30. Romp's Water Port	967-4342	S	P	34	10		10	7	MAR	★	9		★			MGI	★15	SL	●	R	
31. McGarvey's Riverview Restaurant*	967-8000	Y	▲	100	10		12	8	RESTAURANT DOCK											R	
32. Vermilion Power Boats, Inc.	967-4100	Y	▲	44		●	6	5	MOB	▲	30		▲	P		MI	★30	S	●	RS	9
33. Vermilion Boat Club	967-6634	S				●			YACHT CLUB												
34. Municipal Water Works	967-4114	S							24-HOUR DOCKAGE												
35. Vermilion Yacht Club*	967-3255	S	▲	68	2	●			CIT	▲				YACHT CLUB		I	★50	S			

To provide the most complete and accurate information, **all facilities have been contacted within the past year.** If an asterisk (*) appears, it indicates a facility which did not respond to our requests for information (these listings may not reflect current conditions). Although facility operators supplied this data, we cannot guarantee accuracy or assume responsibility for errors. Entrance and dockside soundings tend to fluctuate. Always approach marinas carefully. Reference numbers on spotting charts indicate marina locations. ✓ Member American Boat Builders & Repairers Association.

LAKE ERIE

here. Tie-up is available among the tugs on the inner sides of the breakwaters. The surge is bad in strong south and southeasterly breezes.

Port Bruce. Located on **Catfish Creek** ten miles from Port Burwell, this harbor is identified by a break in the sand bluffs visible from offshore. Port Bruce is a cottage resort without a real village. You can tie up along the west wall beyond the inner end of the breakwater; or you can try the small-boat marina just before the highway bridge. Watch here, too, for surge in southerly winds. The harbor can be difficult to enter in heavy seas.

Port Stanley. The large harbor at Port Stanley serves both fishing and pleasure boats. It is identified from offshore by oil tanks and grain silos. Proceed through the buoyed channel past the commercial wharves and follow **Kettle Creek** to the highway bridge that opens on the hour and half hour. Beyond it is a marina and a small, friendly yacht club. They are both within convenient walking distance of the village shops.

Lake Erie	Phone	Seasonal / Year-Round	Sail / Power / Both	Largest Vessel Accommodated	No. of Transient Berths	Marked Entry Channel	Approach Depth	Dockside Depth	Railway / Lift Capacity	Gas / Diesel / Both — Fuel Brand	Engine Repairs	Launching Ramp	Propeller / Hull Repairs	Marine Supplies / Groceries / Ice	LPG / CNG / Both	110V / 220V / Both — Max Amps	Showers / Laundromat	Restaurant / Snack Bar	Pump-Out Station	Radio Watch VHF (CB)
HURON																				
36. American Boat Medics	(419) 433-3911	Y	P	29	3		18	18	SHE	★		★		MI	★			RS		16
37. Harbor North Marina	433-6010	Y	▲	40		●	20	15	SHE	▲	10		▲	PH		MGI	★15	SL	R	10
38. Holiday Harbor Marina	433-2140	Y	P	45	10		6	6	SHE	★	20	R	★	P		MI	★30	S	●	RS	16/68
39. Huron Municipal Boat Basin*	433-3858	S	▲	70	100	●	12	8								I	★30	SL	●	RS
40. Banner Yachts*	No Listing	S	▲	100	50		8	8		▲	35		▲	PH	●	MGI	★50	SL	●	RS	16
41. Huron Lagoons Marina	433-3200	Y	P	53	10	●	18	8	GUL	★	20	R	★	PH		MI	★30	S	●	R
SANDUSKY TO PELEE ISLAND																					
42. Cedar Point Marina (p. 147)	627-2334	Y	▲	125	175	●	10	8	SOH	▲	50	R	▲	P		MGI	▲50	SL	●	R	16
43. The Harbour Marina	626-3611	S	P	65	25	●	7	7	SHE	★						MGI	★50	SL	●	RS	16
44. Venetian Marina	625-2515	Y	▲	43		●	7	6	76	★	25		▲	P		MI	★30	SL	●	RS
45. Battery Park Marina (p. 147)	625-6142	Y	▲	70	100	●	6	5	SOH	▲						MGI	▲50	SL	●	RS	16
46. Clemons Boats	684-5365	S	P	35			4	4	CIT	★	L		★	PH		M	★30			
47. Lakeside Marine, Inc.	798-4406	Y	▲	70	30		8	5	SOH	★	50		▲	PH		MGI	▲50		●	
48. Gem Beach Marina	797-4451	S	P	42	10		5	5	MAR	▲	35		▲	P		MGI	★30	S		S
49. Foxhaven Marina	797-4654	S	P	43	20		7	7	MAR	▲	20		▲	P		MI	★30			R
50. Chafee's Marina	797-4521	S	▲	40			7	6	PENZ	★										
51. Winke's Boat Storage	797-4618	S	P	40	15		11	8	SHE	★	20		★	P		MGI	★30	S		RS
52. Dick's Marina*	(519) 724-2024	S	▲	50	20		8	6	ESS	★						I	★30			S
53. Pelee Island Yacht Club	724-2195	Y	▲	150	50		25	25		▲		R	▲					SL	●	R
PORT CLINTON																					
54. Brands' Marina	(419) 734-4212	Y	▲	75		●	8	8	MAR	▲	150		▲	P	●	MI	★50	S	●	RS	16
55. Clinton Reef Marina	734-3107	Y	▲	80	50		15	9	SOH	★	35	R	★	PH	●	MGI	★50	S	●	RS	68
TOLEDO TO TOLEDO BEACH																					
56. Anchor Pointe Boat-O-minium	(519) 836-2455	S	▲	60	30	●	9	7	SUN	▲	50		▲	PH		MGI	▲50	SL	●	RS	16
57. Harrison Marina	(419) 729-1676	S	▲	50	10	●	34	14	SHE	▲	26		▲	PH		MGI	▲60		●	S
58. Brenner Marine	691-4663	Y	▲	46	5	●	7	6	AMO	★	L	R	▲	PH		M	★30			
59. Harbor Marine	(313) 241-2833	Y	▲	45	2	●	8	6	STA	▲	24		▲	PH		MGI	★30		●	RS
60. Monroe Marina	243-4483	S	▲	34	44	●	9	6									▲30			R
61. Toledo Beach Marina	243-3800	Y	▲	75	10	●	25	14	76	▲	50		▲	H		MGI	▲60	S	●	RS	16
ONTARIO SHORE																					
62. Casper's Landing	(519) 322-2288	S	P	40	100	●	5	5	TEC			R				MGI	★30	S	●	RS	68
63. Leamington Municipal Marina	326-0834	S	▲	60	150	●	25	15		▲		R	▲	P		MI	★30	SL	●	RS	68
64. Marlon Marina, Inc.	(416) 834-6331	Y	▲	40	10	●	5	5	IND	★	20	R	▲	PH		MGI	★30	SL	●	R	68
65. Port Colborne Marine	835-1774	Y							MARINE SUPPLIES											
66. Hoover's Marina*	(519) 587-2776	S	▲	45	6		6	6	ESS	★		R				I	★20			RS
67. Bridge Marine Services	583-1611	S	P	40	5		10	10	PC	★	25	R	▲	PH		MI	★30	L	●		68
68. Turkey Point Marine Basin	426-6795	S	▲	45	20	●	6	6	SUN	▲		R	▲			MGI	★30	SL	●	RS	68
69. Big Bass Canada Marina	586-7411								PC									L		
70. Port Stanley Marina, Ltd.	782-3481	S	P	36	20		6	9	ESS	★	R	▲	PH	★	MGI	★15	SL	●	S
71. Rondeau Bay Marina, Ltd.*	674-5931	S	▲	45	5		11	6	BP	★		R				GI	★20			RS
72. Erieau Marina, Ltd.	676-4471	Y	▲	100	70	●	12	16	PC	▲	L	R	▲	PH		MGI	★30	RS	●	R	68

To provide the most complete and accurate information, **all facilities have been contacted within the past year.** If an asterisk (*) appears, it indicates a facility which did not respond to our requests for information (these listings may not reflect current conditions). Although facility operators supplied this data, we cannot guarantee accuracy or assume responsibility for errors. Entrance and dockside soundings tend to fluctuate. Always approach marinas carefully. Reference numbers on spotting charts indicate marina locations. ✒ Member American Boat Builders & Repairers Association.

Lake Erie

Rondeau Bay (Erieau). One of the best harbors on the north side of Lake Erie is Rondeau Bay at **Erieau**, a long 45 miles from Port Stanley. This bay resembles a small lake cut off from Lake Erie by a broad peninsula. The outside of the peninsula extends nearly five miles into the big lake in the form of a broad point. The entrance to the bay is on the southwest side of the point in between two steel-sheeted piers. South winds can cause the water level in the bay to rise considerably and when the wind shifts, the water in the bay flows outward, setting up currents in the channel that are tricky for small boats.

Immediately to your left after you enter the harbor, in the first slip running west off the entrance channel, you'll spot a marina. A short walk from here is the town of Erieau, where you'll find a grocery and restaurant. Beyond the marina is an enclosed basin with dockage for the fishing fleet that operates from here.

Rondeau Bay has beaches, Rondeau Provincial Park, and reportedly excellent fishing, but no chart or soundings. It's unwise to take a cruising boat into the bay, but you can enjoy it by dinghy.

Wheatley. Thirty miles from Rondeau Bay, Wheatley is a substantial commercial fishing harbor, without services for pleasure boats. It does provide refuge in deteriorating weather, however. A large fish-packing plant is a conspicuous landmark.

Point Pelee. From Wheatley, the shoreline dips southward for nearly nine miles to form Point Pelee, a narrow finger of land extending into the lake. A sand spit extends for about a half mile off the point, and the water continues shallow for another five miles to **Southeast Shoal**. Yachts can cross the shoal water by staying well off the point, but such a crossing should be undertaken only in daylight when the lake is calm. Stay at least two miles offshore. Navigating in the shallow water off Point Pelee may be preferable to entering the main shipping channel at Southeast Shoal, where you'll encounter freighters.

Leamington. On the western side of Point Pelee is Leamington, largest town on the Canadian shore of Lake Erie. A new marina is east of the government dock inside the breakwater.

Kingsville/Cedar Creek. The harbor at **Kingsville** is entirely commercial, with only a rare space at the far inside end for a pleasure boat. The recreational harbor for Kingsville is at **Cedar Creek**, two miles west. Sandbars building up at the entrance limit draft to five feet, although there is more depth in the channel and in the harbor itself. An overhead power cable close to the entrance has a vertical clearance of 48 feet. You'll find a public dock, a yacht club, and a marina here. The park on the outer side of the creek has a sandy beach. Downtown Kingsville is three miles from this harbor.

From Cedar Creek, it's twenty miles to the Detroit River Light, where the next chapter begins.

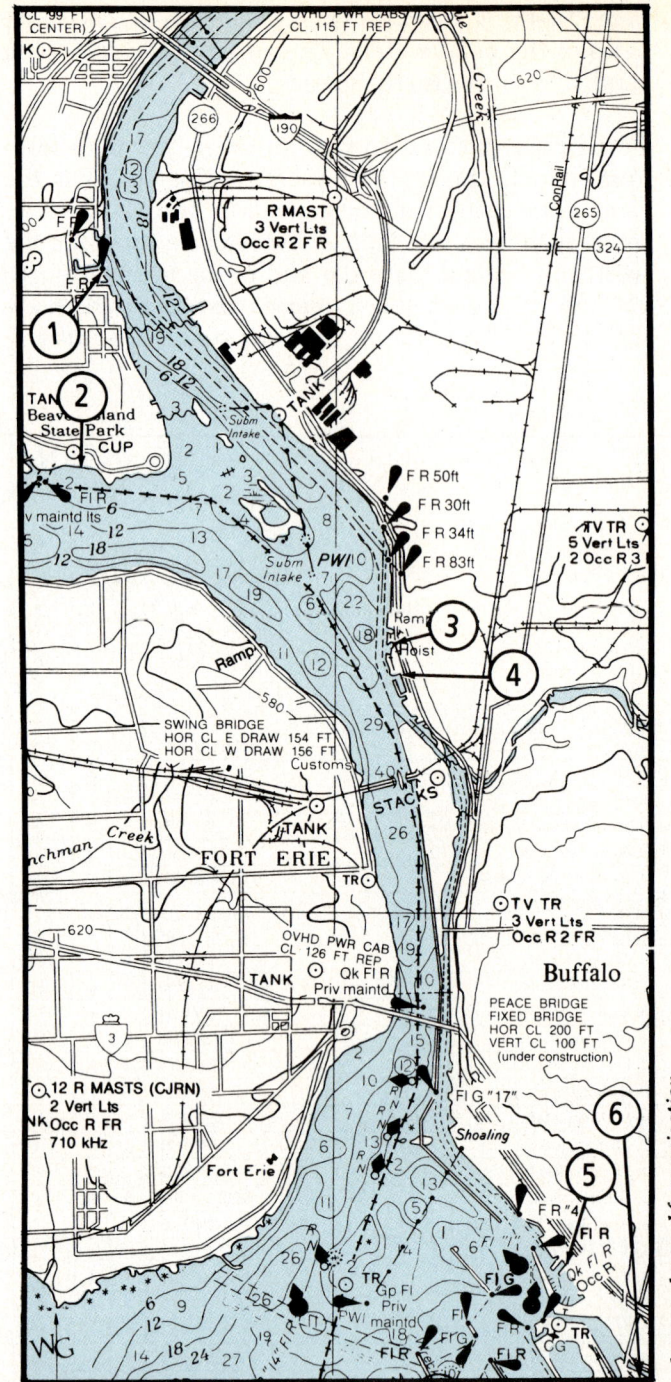

Chart 14822, edition 25

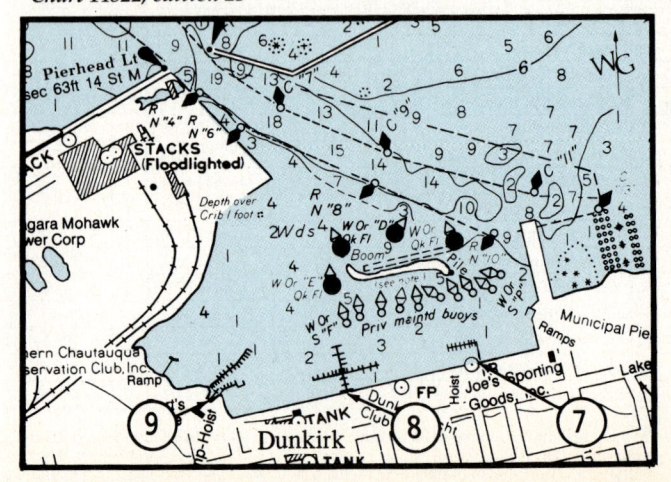

Chart 14823, edition 23

LAKE ERIE

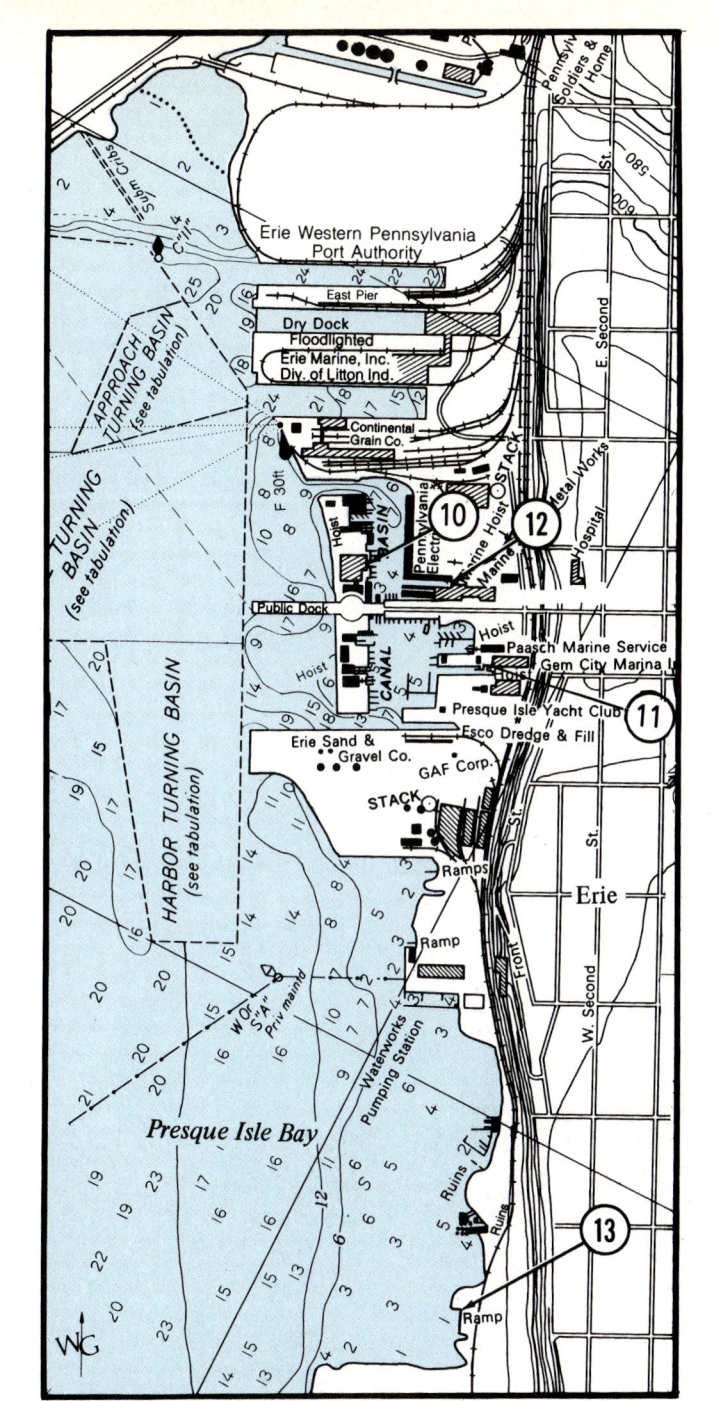

Chart 14835, edition 27

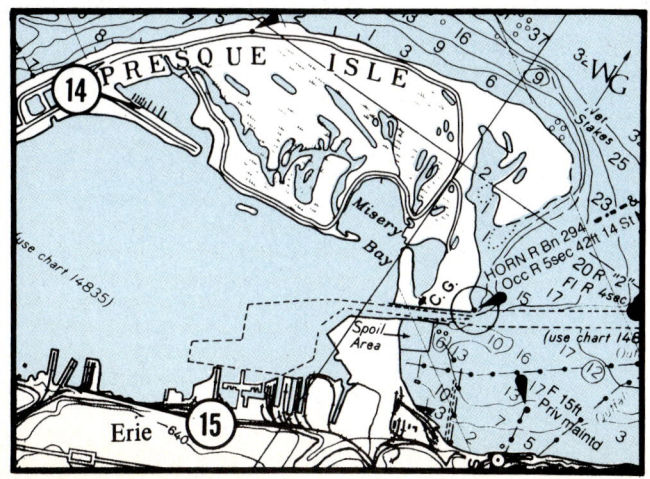

Chart 14824, edition 21

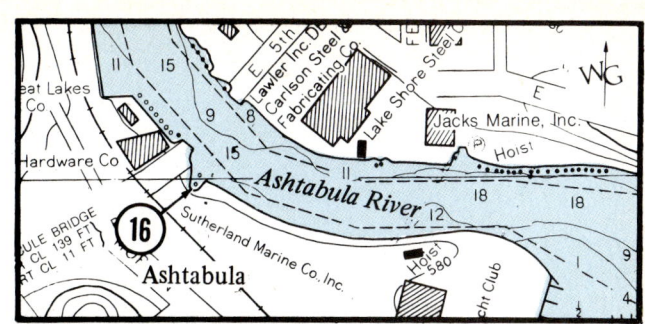

Chart 14836, edition 23

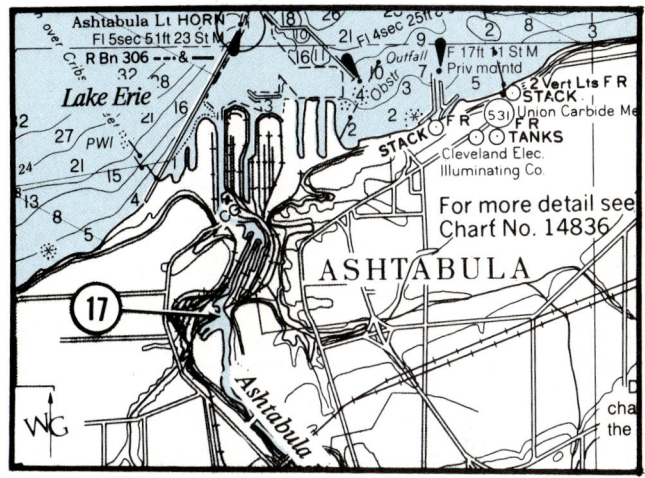

Chart 14825, edition 20

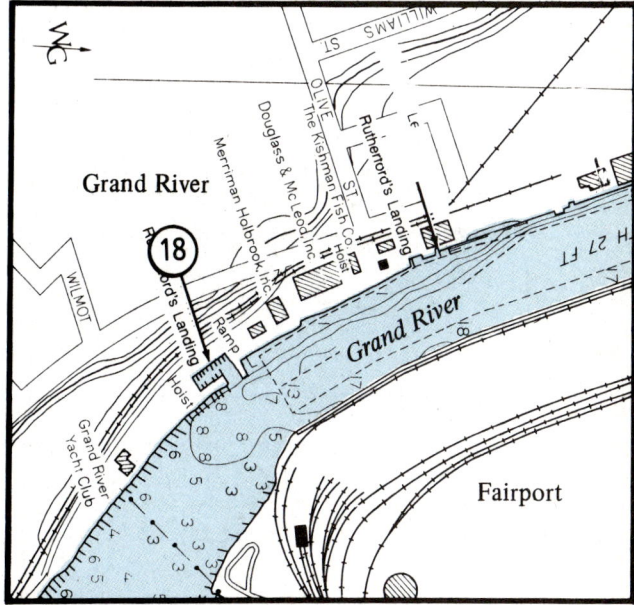

Chart 14837, edition 22

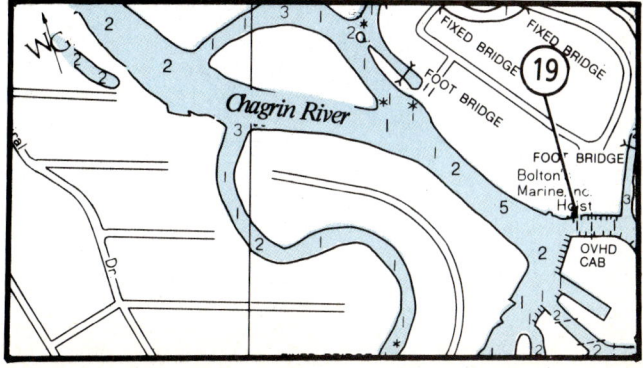

Chart 14825, edition 20

GREAT LAKES EDITION — Under no circumstances are these charts to be used for navigation. — 157

LAKE ERIE

Chart 14839, edition 30

Chart 14839, edition 30

Chart 14839, edition 30

Chart 14839, edition 30

Chart 14826, edition 22

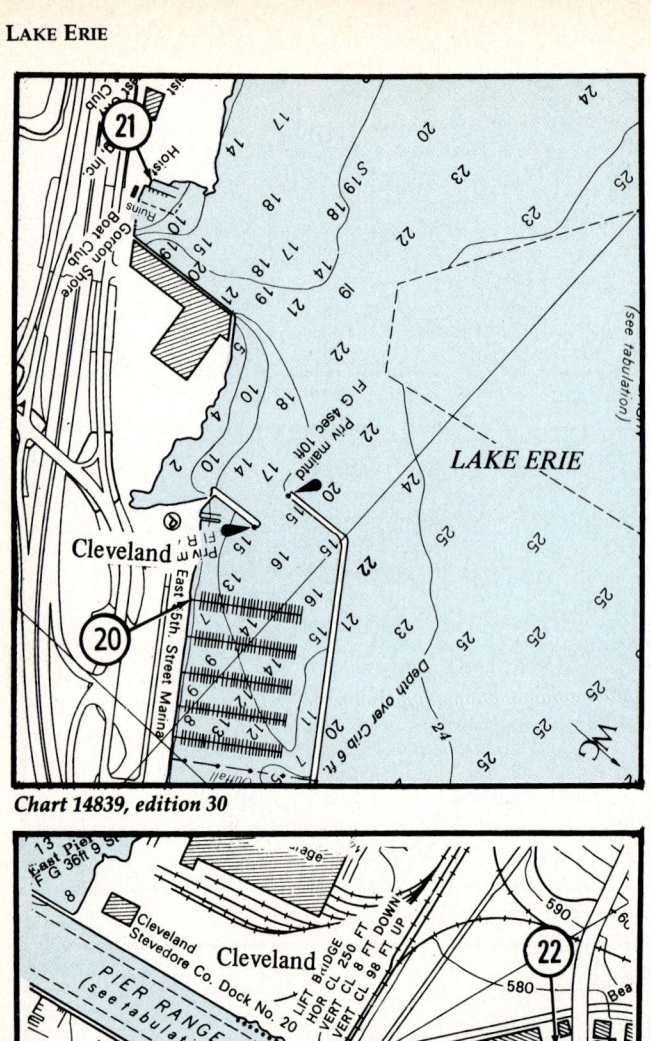

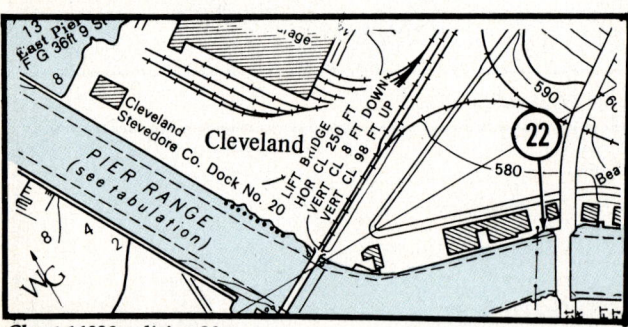

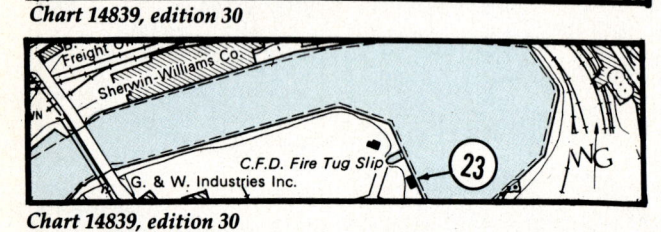

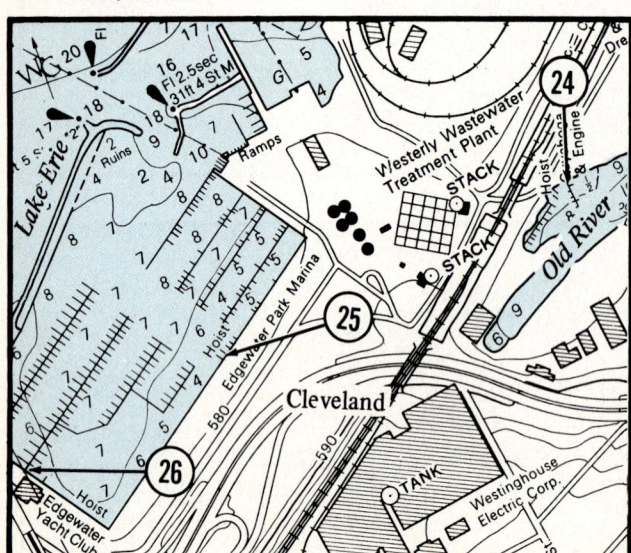

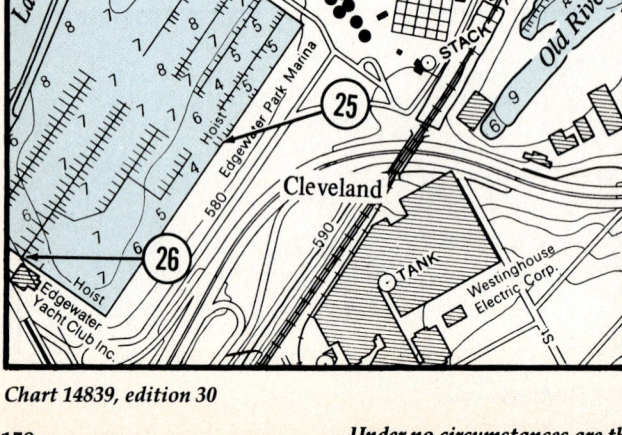

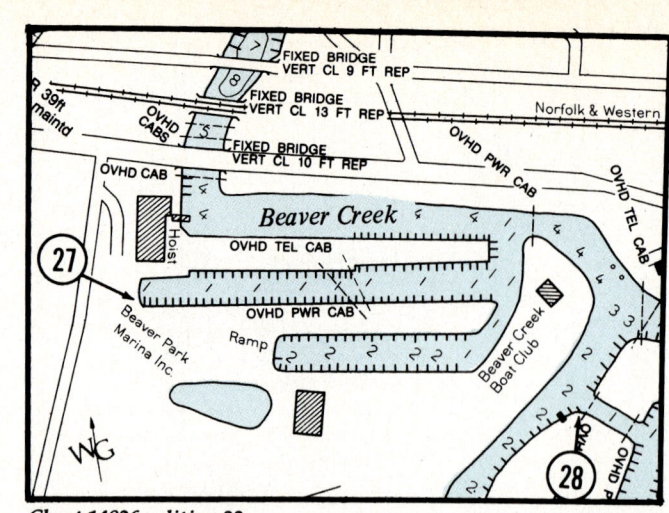

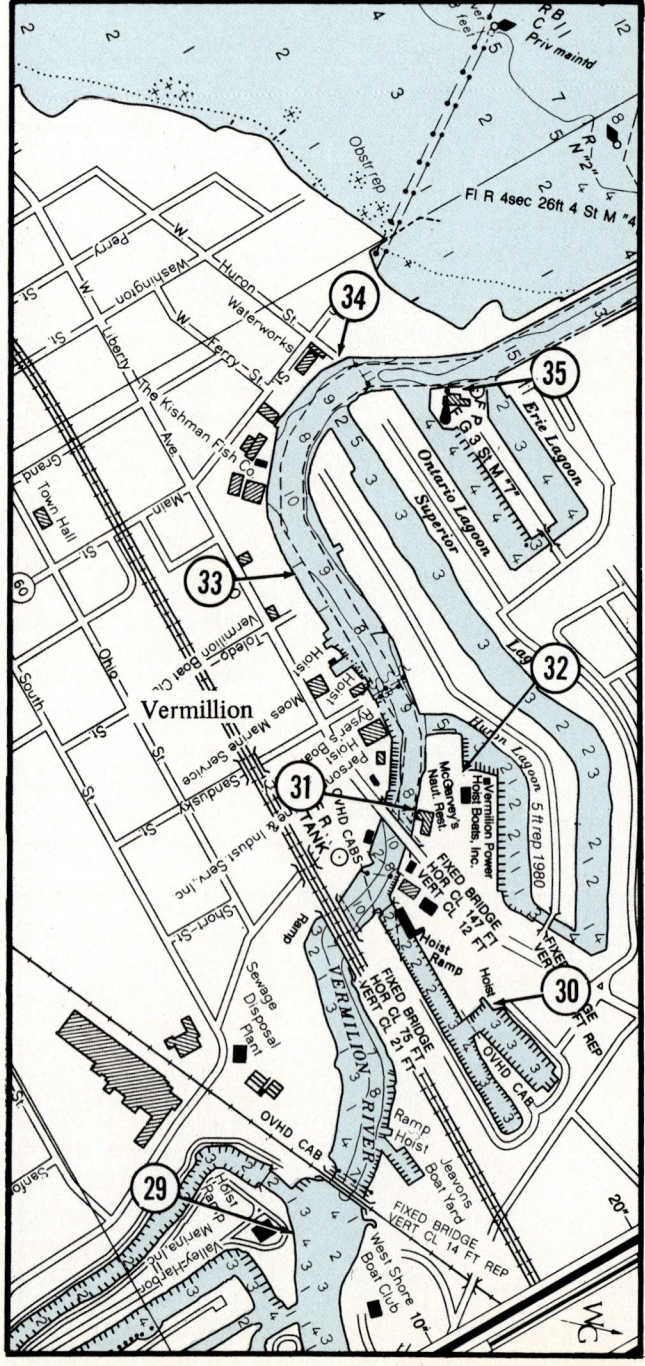

Chart 14826, edition 22

158   Under no circumstances are these charts to be used for navigation.   WATERWAY GUIDE / 1991

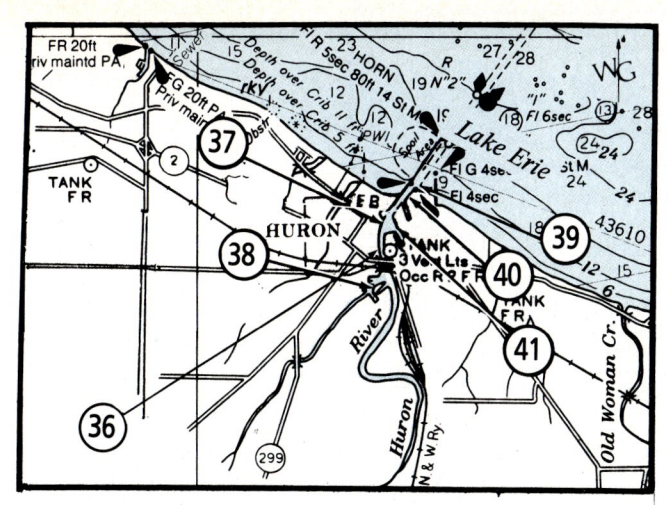

LAKE ERIE

Chart 14830, edition 18

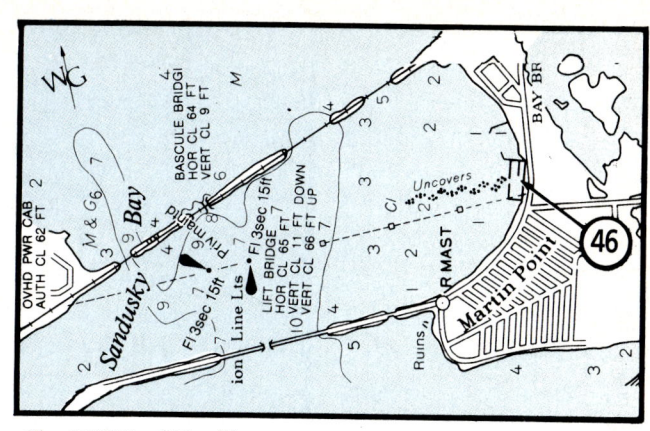

Chart 14844, edition 25

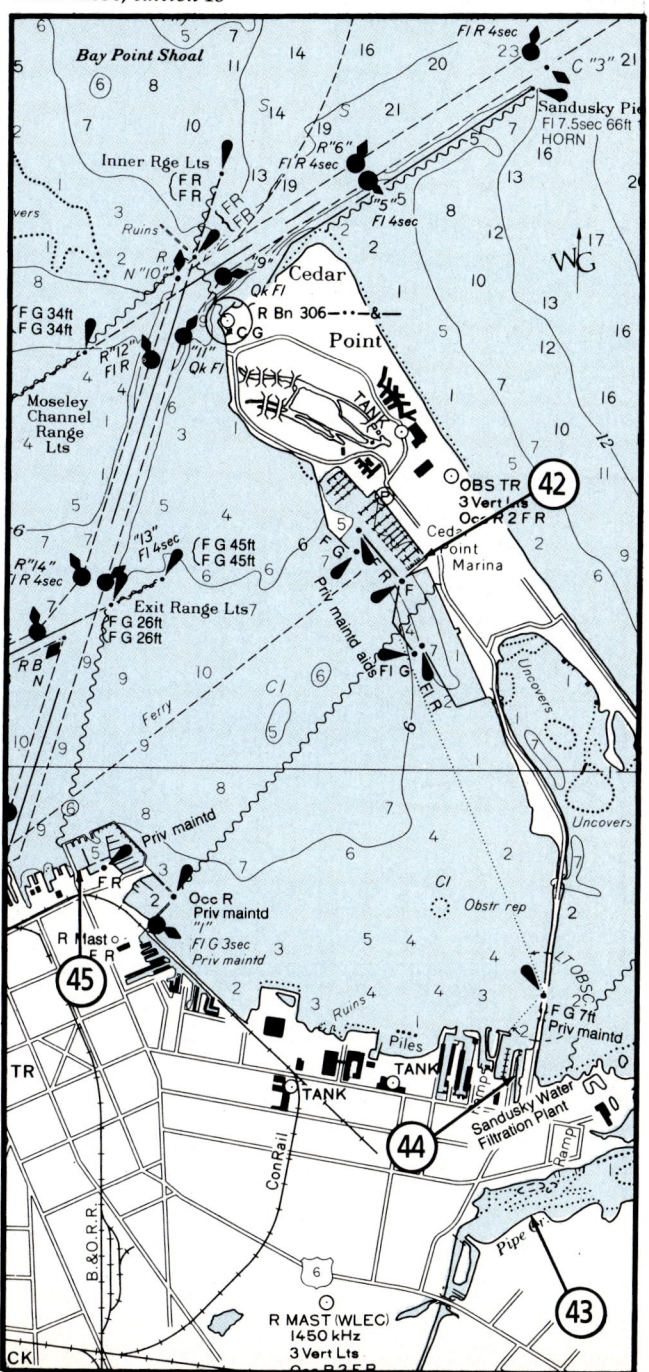

Chart 14842-SC, edition 7

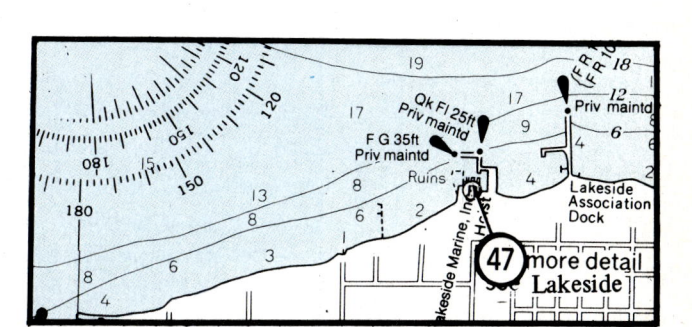

Chart 14842-SC, edition 7

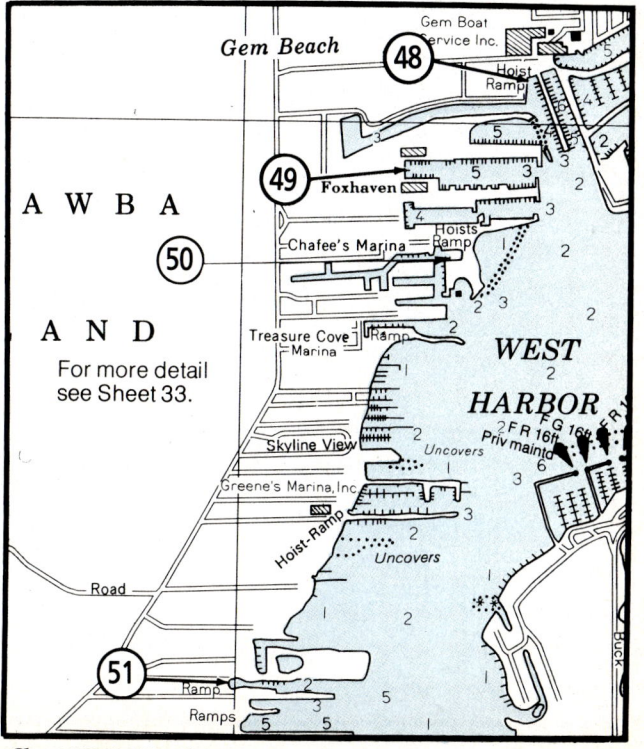

Chart 14842-SC, edition 7

GREAT LAKES EDITION *Under no circumstances are these charts to be used for navigation.* 159

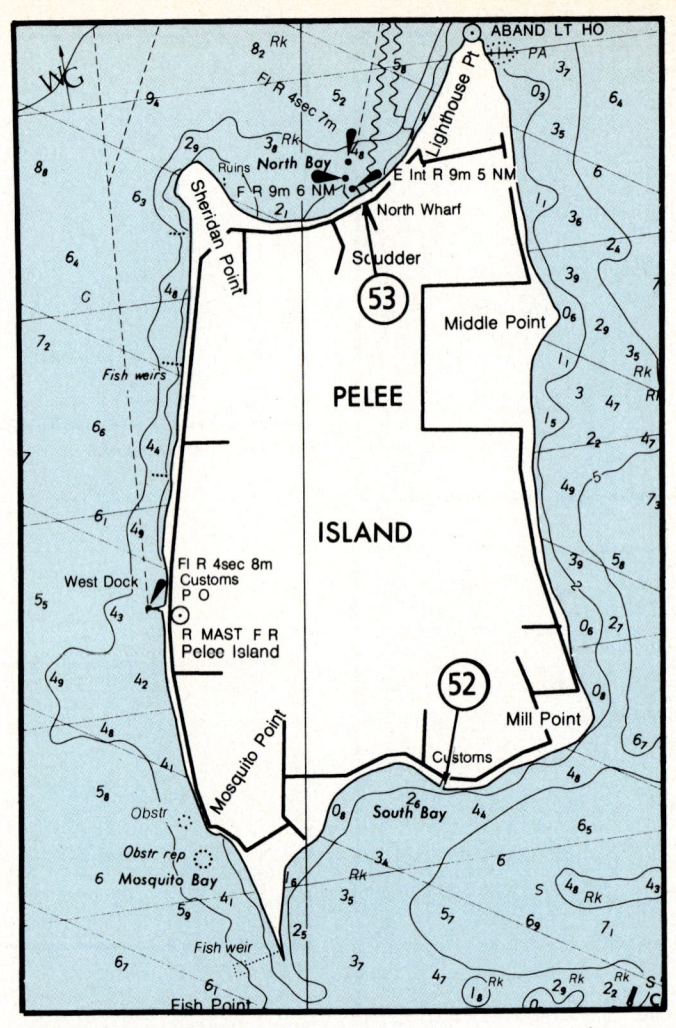

LAKE ERIE

Chart 14830, edition 18

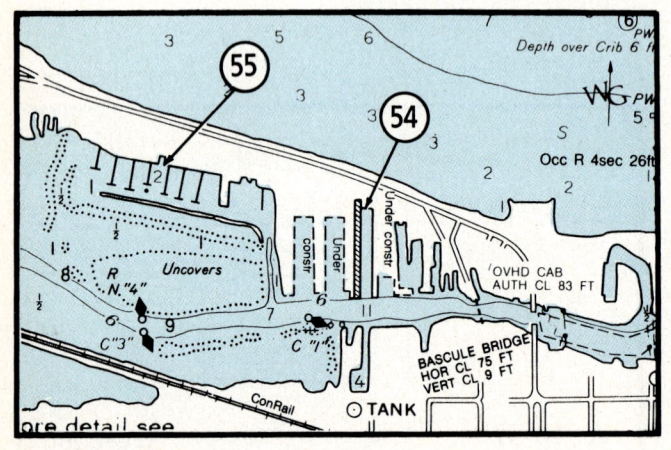

Chart 14846, edition 7

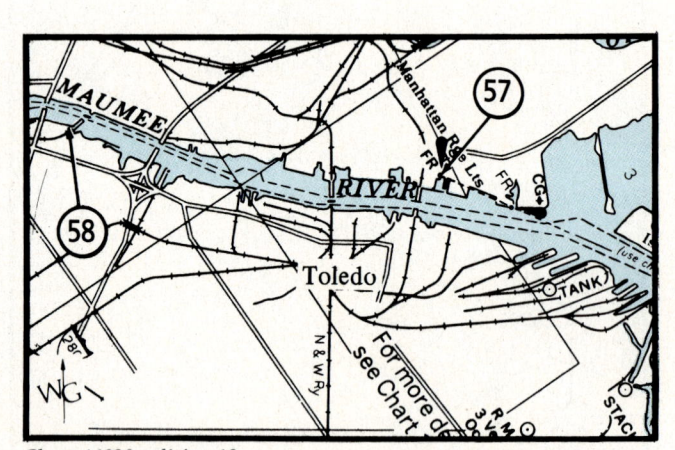

Chart 14830, edition 18

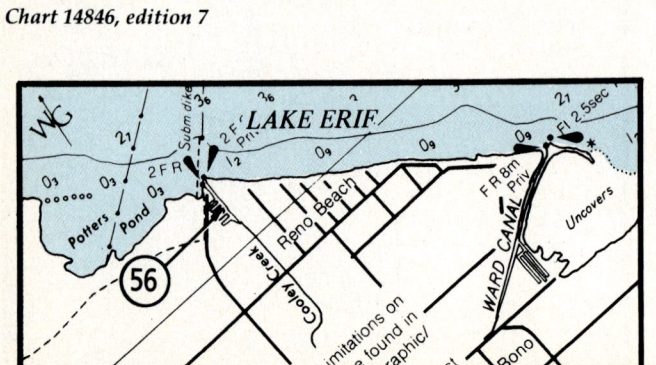

Chart 14830, edition 18

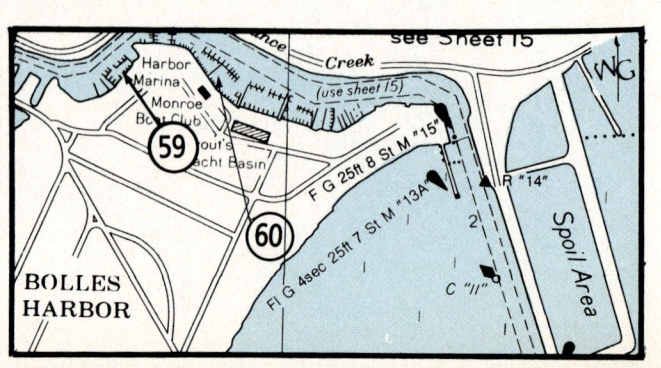

Chart 14846-SC, edition 7

Under no circumstances are these charts to be used for navigation.

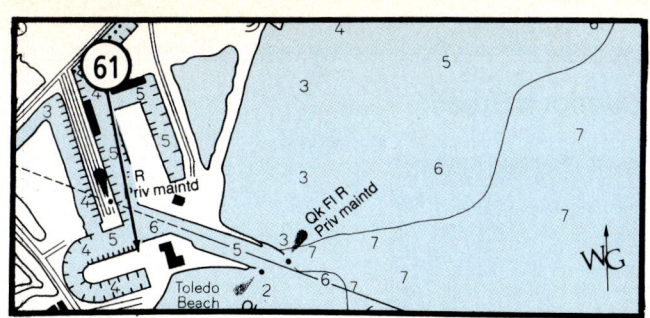

LAKE ERIE

Chart 14846-SC, edition 7

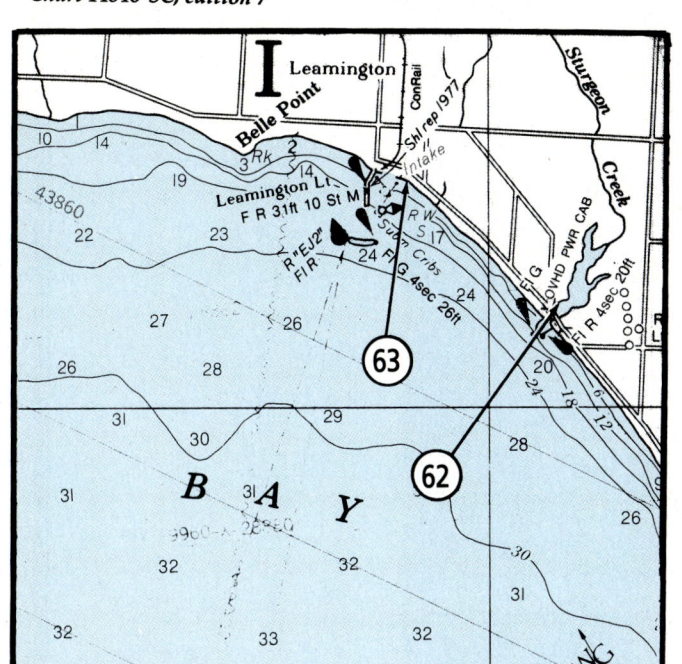

Chart 14830, edition 18

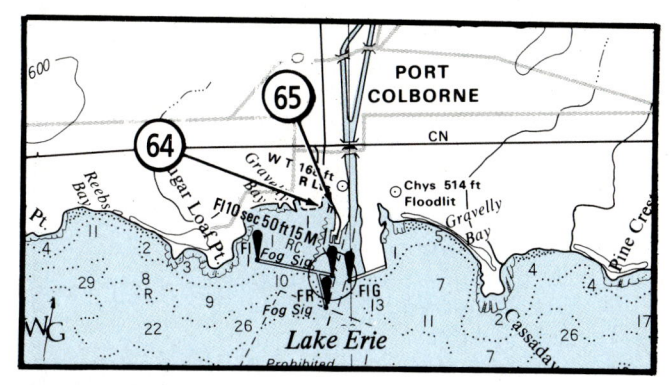

Canadian chart 2101

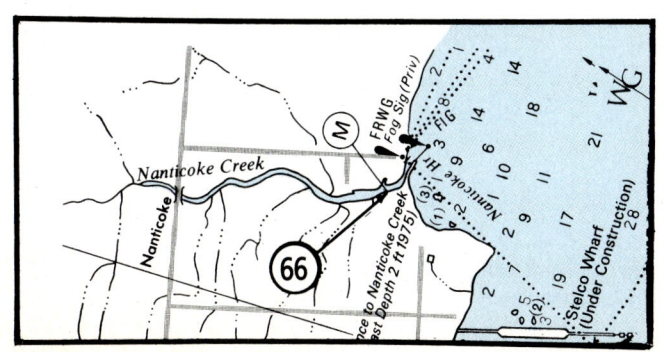

Canadian chart 2110

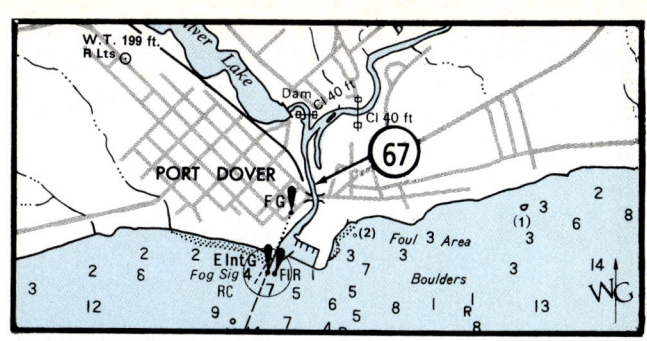

Canadian chart 2110

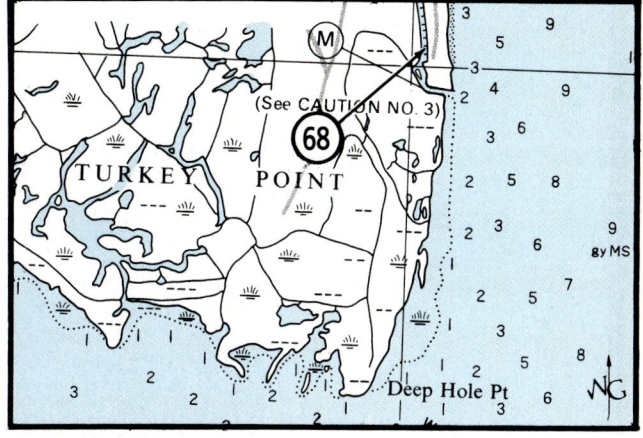

Canadian chart 2110

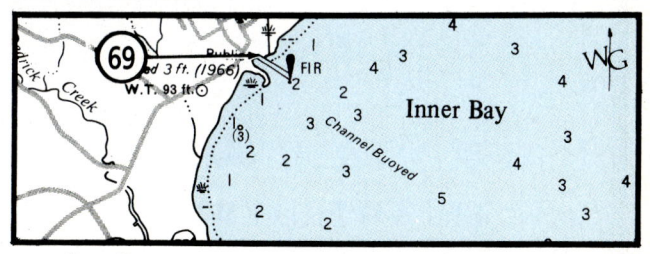

Canadian chart 2110

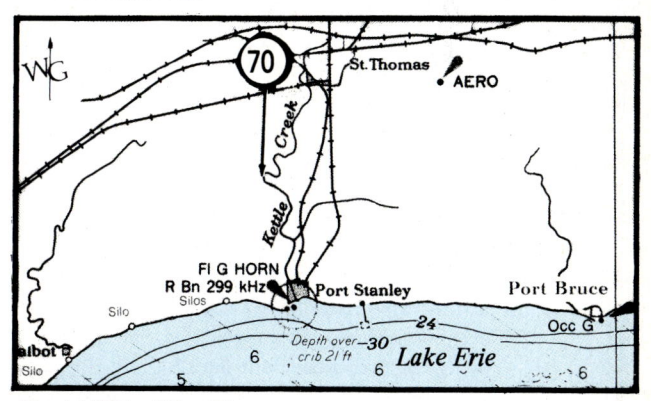

Chart 14820, edition 38

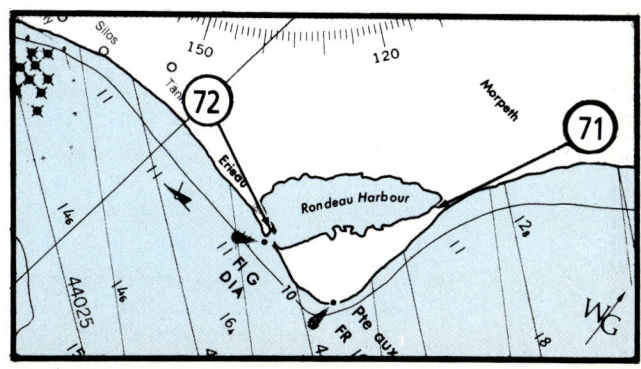

Chart 14820, edition 38

GREAT LAKES EDITION *Under no circumstances are these charts to be used for navigation.*

Available from The Overlook Press:

THE OVERLOOK ILLUSTRATED DICTIONARY OF NAUTICAL TERMS
GRAHAM BLACKBURN

With all the beauty and consistency of Blackburn's earlier works, and in his inimitable style, this dictionary is a useful well-illustrated reference with more than 2500 entries.

From Able Seaman to Z Twist, this comprehensive and practical source book of nautical subjects is a handy guide for all lovers of ships, boats, and the sea. Clearly written entries, cross-referenced, explain the parts and equipment of vessels old and new, places aboard ship, orders, directives, and maneuvers involved in sailing all kinds of boats, and other lore and language relating to the sea and the vessels that sail it. "A straightforward, concise dictionary which concentrates on sailing terms new and old. The definitions are clear and precise, and the illustrations add substantially to understanding the terms." (*Library Journal*)

GRAHAM BLACKBURN is an expert sailor and has written nine books, including *The Illustrated Encyclopedia of Ships, Boats, and Vessels*, published by The Overlook Press.

Reference/Recreation
368 pages; 6 x 9
615 line drawings

SBN: 124-9   *Cloth* $27.95
SBN: 950-9   *Paper* $9.95

To order, send check or money order to: The Overlook Press, RR1 Box 496, Woodstock, New York 12498. Add $2.65 postage and handling for first book, $.90 for each additional book.

Detroit River/ Lake St. Clair/St. Clair River

CHARTS: 14848, 14849-SC, 14850, 14851-SC, 14852, 14853, 14854, 14865.

The connection between Lake Erie and Lake Huron runs through two rivers with a "little great lake" in between. With a total drop in water level between Huron and Erie of nine feet, there is considerable current in both rivers, but the lake is placid when the wind doesn't whip up. All three waterways see heavy traffic in both freighters and pleasure boats, but each has distinctive characteristics.

Detroit River Cruising Conditions

Current in the Detroit River averages about a knot, but is stronger in constricted areas or as the result of unusual weather conditions. The river seems to "steer" local winds so they follow the channel; sailboats often find the wind right on the nose despite the twists and turns of the channel. If the wind is with the current, the river remains calm. However, if wind and current are opposed, a harsh chop and sizeable waves can develop.

Slower pleasure craft will be overtaken by large freighters. Always keep a sharp lookout astern, because big ships are almost silent when approaching bow-on. When being overtaken, get as far to the starboard side of the channel as possible. There is usually more than enough water for everyone. Sometimes you can slip outside the buoyed channel to avoid a freighter, but do this only as a last resort, unless you have local knowledge. Do not cross close behind a moving freighter; the wash from large ships can upset cruising boats.

To ease traffic congestion in the lower reaches of the river, shipping is divided into upbound and downbound channels. Upbound, it follows the Amherstburg Channel along the Canadian shore. The Livingston Channel, which runs between scrubby islands and spoil banks, is for downbound traffic. Pleasure boats are not bound to follow the big ship rules, although most do.

Upbound Passage/Lake Erie To Detroit

Most cruising boats follow the main ship channels when transiting the Detroit River. The following pages will detail this main route. Later pages focus on the attractions and marinas on the U.S. and Canadian shores.

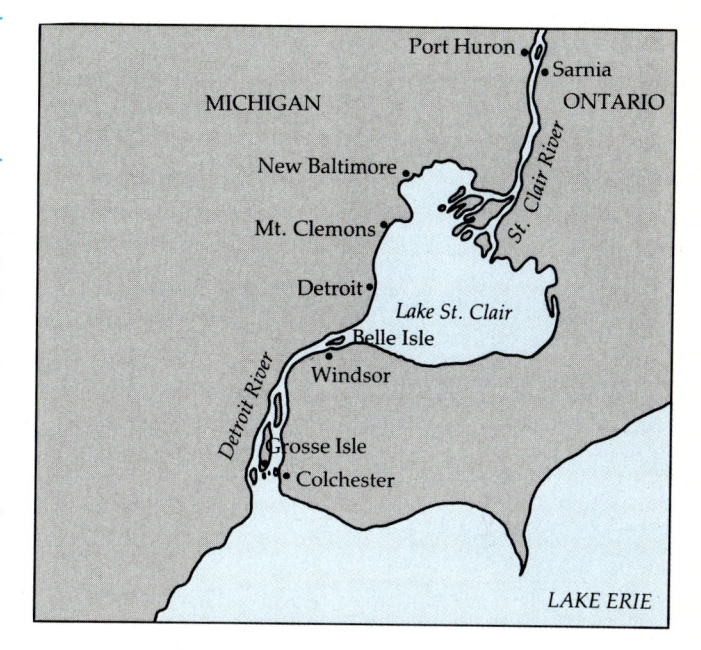

Detroit River Approach. Most cruising boats head for the big white tower of the Detroit River Light when approaching the river from Lake Erie ports. The light and its radio beacon are located about three miles offshore and are visible for about 22 statute miles. From well offshore, the twin cooling towers of a nuclear power plant provide the first landmark. The entrance channel is well-marked with lighted buoys. Following the channel here is pretty much a matter of ticking off the numbered aids as you pass.

Amherstburg Channel. A little less than two miles north of the Detroit River Light is the Detroit River Pier Light marking the beginning of the Amherstburg Channel. A lighted range on the Canadian mainland guides you up the center of the Amherstburg Channel to the southern end of Bois Blanc Island. From there, the Limestone Reach Channel turns slightly left with another set of lighted ranges and lighted buoys to guide you.

Ballards Reef Channel. North of Crystal Bay, the main ship channel crosses Ballard Reef. Two-way commercial traffic will be encountered starting in the Ballards Reef Channel. It pays to keep a close watch on the buoys here; check each one as you go along and use the lighted range on Grosse Ile shore to guide you. There

GREAT LAKES EDITION   163

HEARST MARINE SAILS AHEAD OF THE FLEET

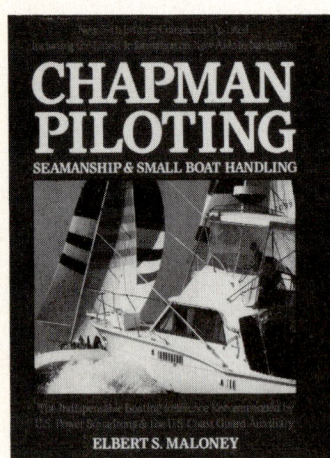

"The Bible of Boating"
Elbert S. Maloney
With the 59th edition, CHAPMAN'S continues its tradition as the most up-to-date, comprehensive, and authoritative book available for recreational boaters. This new edition contains the latest word on the new system of navigational aids and developments in the fast-changing fields of marine electronics, radar, and communications.
Deluxe Edition
$50.00/0-688-09252-7
Standard Edition
$29.95/0-688-09127-X
Over 1500 photos and illustrations
18-page index   Appendixes
Glossary   678 pages

Bernard Gladstone and
Tom Bottomley
BOATKEEPER and MORE BOATKEEPER are confirmed leaders in the fields of marine maintenance, improving performance, and saving time in repairs and upkeep.
$17.95/0-688-03565-5   Illustrations
288 pages [BOATKEEPER]
$18.95/0-688-07645-9   Illustrations
203 pages [MORE BOATKEEPER]

Sid Stapleton
STAPLETON'S POWERBOAT BIBLE is a distillation of the best advice on how to put together a boat tailor-made to any boat owner's cruising needs and then how to plan for the perfect cruise.
$22.95/0-688-08448-6   Photos
Illustrations   448 pages

Joanne A. Fishman
The definitive guide to buying, maintaining, and achieving peak performance in the high-speed powerboats that are the fastest growing segment of the powerboat market today.
$25.00/0-688-08209-2   Photos
Illustrations   224 pages

Hearst Marine and the USPS have teamed up to produce the perfect reference for the seventy-two million people who participate in recreational boating throughout the United States. From the basics of docking to the complexities of plotting a course, navigating, and anchoring, this lively video, produced by an Emmy Award-winning crew, covers everything contained in the six-week USPS basic boating course. Whether you're a beginner learning the fundamentals of boating or an expert brushing up on a particular area, the UNITED STATES POWER SQUADRONS' BOATING COURSE FOR POWER AND SAIL is the perfect reference.
$39.95/0-688-09126-1 80-minute video/
240-page book

Revised Edition
Conrad Miller and Elbert S. Maloney
Considered the leading guide to everything electrical on board, this revised edition incorporates all of the new developments and equipment in this fast-changing field.
$18.95/0-688-08132-0   Illustrations
560 pages

Hearst Marine Books

are shallows extending up to the edge of the dredged route and you can go aground without ever realizing you have left the channel.

Fighting Island Channel. This wide channel runs almost due north from the northern tip of Grosse Ile starting at the Fighting Island Light. This is a wide, quiet stretch of river that requires only keeping track of the passage of buoys. A shoal area extends west and north from Mamajuda Light. The channel passes between Grassy and Fighting islands to reveal a water intake crib on the east side of the channel that, from a distance, looks like a ship.

Main River to Detroit. Above Fighting Island, the river slowly sweeps eastward until the Canadian shoreline eventually lies surprisingly to your south. Both banks are lined with heavy industry and steel mills served by a variety of large lake freighters. Be particularly wary of commercial traffic entering the river from the Rouge River. Anchorages marked on the chart in this part of the river are intended for large freighters and are not recommended for pleasure craft. Just south of the Ambassador Bridge you may discover the *J.W. Wescott*, the nation's only floating post office. It delivers mail and supplies on the move to the big ships. The Ambassador Bridge is the longest international suspension bridge in the world; clearance is 100 feet at the center.

Ontario Shore

Amherstburg. Amherstburg is an historic Canadian town. It was the British naval base for the fleet that Commodore Perry defeated in the Battle of Lake Erie. Not only can you tour the Fort Malden National Historic Site, but you can also see the North American Black Historical Museum, which commemorates the settlement of refugee slaves in the area. Also located here are several restaurants, gift shops, art galleries, and two marinas.

Bois Blanc Island. Across the channel from Amherstberg, Bois Blanc Island is home of the popular Boblo (an Americanized corruption of Bois Blanc) Amusement Park, which dates from 1898. It was recently modernized and now has 75 rides, shows, and attractions. A large marina on the west side of the island offers transient accommodations. The best way to reach this marina is to go around the north end of Bois Blanc.

Crystal Bay. Just above Bois Blanc Island is **Crystal Bay**, a large cove in the shape of an arrowhead pointing upstream. Although the water is shallow, this is one of the few protected anchorages on the lower stretches of the Detroit River. Plow-style anchors are preferable in the weedy bottom, but others work with coaxing. Overnight anchorage is best as deep in the bay as your draft

---

Galley Stoves

Galley stoves should never be taken lightly. Something you're going to be using every day deserves some thought.

Many stoves have a number of good qualities, depending on factors such as the space available, your own temperament, and your budget for stoves. However, the more burners, the better. Some cooks can make do with one burner, but they are few. And of those few, all could do an even better job with more burners.

Some may point out that when camping, one fire can be made to make do. But a camp fire is many fires and properly made, can serve many purposes. With one burner, you have one source, one heat—and that's all.

Sometimes you have little choice because of space, but most of the time, you can rearrange things to accommodate two burners rather than one. If by doing so you could get the kind of galley stove to suit you, it would be worth the effort.

William Morrow & Co., Inc. Reprinted by permission.

---

will allow. Always set an anchor light, because there is boat traffic all night. Children will enjoy exploring by dinghy the channels hidden in the west wall. Often, a floating hamburger stand can be found here. Unfortunately, during the day Crystal Bay is a favorite haunt of water skiers and speed boats. All this activity can make the bay unattractive for a lunchtime stop, especially on weekends.

Ballards Reef to Windsor. Instead of following the main channel, you may want to explore the charted channel running east of Fighting Island. Plenty of deep water exists on the east side of Fighting Island, but the channel is mostly unmarked, and it's easy to find yourself aground in the marshes around Turkey and Grass islands. A variety of marinas and small boat harbors can be found along the Canadian shoreline inside Fighting Island.

LaSalle. In and around the quiet village of LaSalle, a number of marinas are set on a series of long, narrow inlets leading from the lake. Many of them offer dockage with electricity and not much more. But there are some full-service facilities as well, and one is associated with a large restaurant.

Windsor. Thanks to a bend in the river, the city of Windsor is actually south of Detroit, making it the only Canadian city south of the United States boundary. Like Detroit, Windsor is an auto town, as well as the site of a major distillery. A park development is located along the downtown waterfront, offering a superb view of the Detroit skyline across the river. Windsor's large municipal marina and a yacht club are located at the east end

KEAN'S YACHT MARINA

SHIP'S STORE, WITH GROCERIES, LIQUOR & MORE
RESTROOMS, SHOWERS, AND LAUNDRY
SUMMER AND WINTER STORAGE AVAILABLE
8 GAS DOCKS, AND PUMP OUT SERVICE
MASTER CARD, VISA, AND AMOCO ACCEPTED
CALL (313) 822-4500
TRY OUR DELI!!

of the city. Bus or taxi will take you to downtown Windsor's shops, restaurants, night clubs, art gallery, and the Hiram Walker Historical Museum.

Michigan Shore.

The Michigan shore of the Detroit River is much more urbanized and industrial than the Ontario side. Nevertheless, you'll find numerous marinas here, since Michigan boasts the largest number of boat registrations in the nation. The lower reaches of the river are filled with islands and channels perfect for gunkhole cruising.

Metro Park South (Maple Beach). A well-marked channel leads to this public dock, which offers only limited space. Although there is a gas pump for park vehicles, a court order prevents the park from selling fuel. No other amenities or stores are within walking distance.

Gibraltar. Gibraltar is primarily a residential suburb on the mainland opposite Grosse Ile. Two full-service marinas cater mostly to power boats. To reach them, continue upriver past west of low-lying Celeron Island and east of Horse Island. Stay offshore until sighting the lighted aids which mark the channel into the marinas. Avoid Brownstone Creek without local knowledge.

Grosse Ile. The largest island in the Detroit River, Grosse Ile is mostly residential, with the exception of the Municipal Airport, located on a former Naval Air Station. Three yacht clubs are on the island and offer transient accommodations to members of reciprocating clubs.

Trenton Channel to Detroit. A couple of miles beyond Gibraltar, you enter deepwater Trenton Channel between the mainland and Gross Ile. Two bridges connecting Grosse Ile with the mainland open on request with one long and one short blast. The river becomes increasingly industrial and commercial as you move upstream to Detroit. You'll pass several marinas and yacht clubs tucked in among the commercial facilities. Most offer limited transient accommodations.

Detroit. Detroit's downtown waterfront combines park and promenade with some monumental buildings. It is anchored at the west end by Cobo Hall, a massive exhibition center, and on the east by the gleaming towers of the Renaissance Center, with an impressive skyline to back it up. Two marinas here offer great views, but little protection.

All the rest of Detroit's marinas are beyond the 32-foot fixed bridge leading to Belle Isle. Sailboats and large power boats should go around the north end of Belle Isle and not attempt to pass beneath this bridge. Mariners who pass under the bridge must be alert for the buoys marking Scott Middle Ground. On the mainland inside the island are several full-service marinas, a pub-

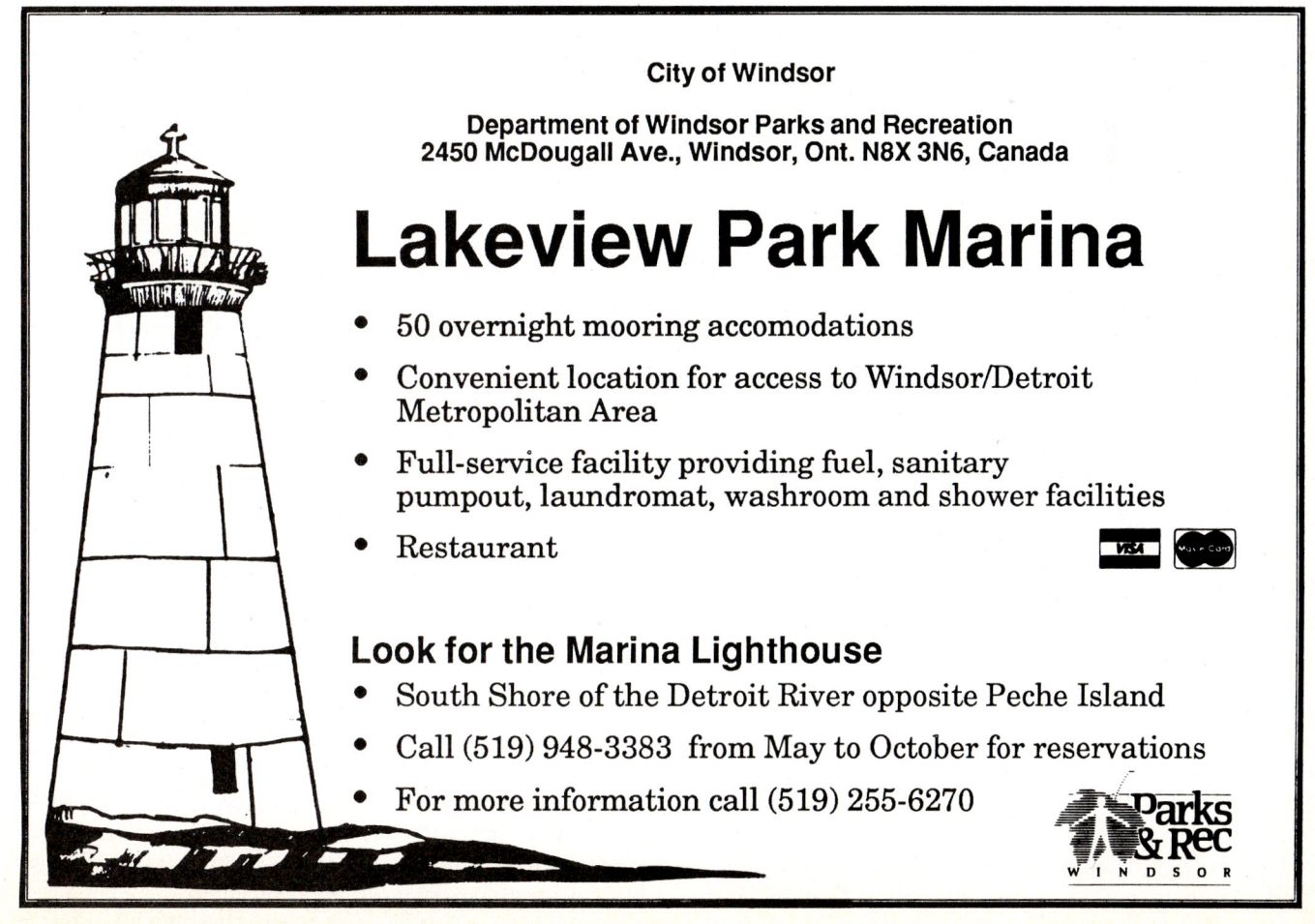

City of Windsor

Department of Windsor Parks and Recreation
2450 McDougall Ave., Windsor, Ont. N8X 3N6, Canada

Lakeview Park Marina

- 50 overnight mooring accomodations
- Convenient location for access to Windsor/Detroit Metropolitan Area
- Full-service facility providing fuel, sanitary pumpout, laundromat, washroom and shower facilities
- Restaurant

Look for the Marina Lighthouse

- South Shore of the Detroit River opposite Peche Island
- Call (519) 948-3383 from May to October for reservations
- For more information call (519) 255-6270

Parks & Rec WINDSOR

DETROIT R./LAKE ST. CLAIR/ST. CLAIR R.

lic launching ramp, and yacht clubs. Two more yacht clubs are located on the Detroit side of Belle Isle. There is little shopping near these facilities, and their neighborhood surroundings are somewhat run down. For travel to the city's attractions, it's best to take a taxi.

Belle Isle is an exquisite park, designed by Fredrick Law Olmstead. It features sports facilities, beaches, walking trails, a zoo, and a Great Lakes marine museum. Downtown, the city's waterfront park, Hart Plaza, is home to ethnic festivals every summer weekend, in addition to events at Cobo Hall, Joe Louis Arena, and Ford Auditorium. A couple of miles north, along Woodward Avenue, is the Cultural Center with the Detroit Institute of Arts and several museums. Detroit also has a variety of fine restaurants, shops, and night clubs, especially in the Greektown district.

Lake St. Clair.

Almost round, at 24 miles by 26 miles, Lake St. Clair is also very shallow, with a maximum depth of 21 feet. Most places have less than that. It is possible to be out of sight of land with less than fifteen feet of water under the keel. The shallow nature of the lake dictates a steep chop in high winds. St. Clair is also subject to seiches, when strong winds cause the water to pile up on the downward side of the lake at the same time the depth on the upwind side decreases. Shifts of two to four feet can occur in this way. Seiches are most common in Anchor Bay at the north end of the lake. Another problem that can occur on Lake St. Clair is poor visibility, due to the combination of a low, featureless shoreline, summer haze, and air pollution.

Most of the time, however, the lake is pleasant. On any summer weekend, especially on the Michigan side of the lake, the water will be covered with craft of all kinds, from tiny, open fishermen's runabouts (fishing is a major sport on the lake) to big sailing schooners. Traffic can be a hazard.

The ship traffic across the lake is predictable, however. Freighters must keep guardedly to the dredged channel that crosses on the diagonal for sixteen miles from the Detroit River to the marshy delta of the St. Clair River, known as the St. Clair Flats. The dredged, buoyed St. Clair Cutoff Channel leads for another six miles through this maze to the natural South Channel of the river and on upstream. Cruising mariners who don't plan a stop on Lake St. Clair can also follow this route.

The Michigan Shore.

The Michigan side of the lake is suburban as far as the Clinton River. Beyond, the population thins out to small villages.

Grosse Pointe. North of Windmill Point at the Detroit River entrance there are five communities with the name or prefix Grosse Pointe. Most of them are well-to-do, and some impressive mansions and estates line the lakeshore. The marinas you see belong to each of the respective communities and are open only to their residents. But there are two yacht clubs that accept members of reciprocating clubs.

St. Clair Shores calls itself the "Boating Capital of Michigan." A string of marinas, large and small, and numerous ancillary services line the waterfront. Approaching from the south, give Gaukler Point a berth of about a mile and a half; the outer end of the rock ledge off the point is marked by a lighted buoy. Note the "No Wake" speed limit extending 1,300 feet off the waterfront of St. Clair Shores. Although restaurants are handy to the marinas, food shopping is not close by.

Huron-Clinton Metropolitan Beach Park interrupts the line of suburbs at Point Huron. Black Creek, flowing into the lake just north of the point, is the site of the park's excellent marina. The approach channel has a controlling depth of five feet, and should be entered from the buoy about two miles offshore. There is also a range to guide you in. Dockage is limited to 48 hours on a first-come, first-served basis. The park includes a golf course, roller skating, and an extensive beach, none of which is very close to the marina, however.

Clinton River. Two miles beyond Point Huron, the Clinton River leads to the city of Mount Clemens. This river, too, has a controlling depth of five feet, and the buoyed channel should be entered from deep water out in the lake. Both sides of the river are lined with marinas and services, but most of them do not accept transients for overnight dockage. The city is seven miles upstream from the mouth of the river. The passage is limited by three-foot depths and 21-foot overhead clearance. Just north of the Clinton River entrance is a large full-service marina directly on the lake.

Anchor Bay/Fair Haven. Beyond the Clinton River you are well into Anchor Bay, jammed with local boats. It seems that Detroit residents have discovered this attractive, protected cruising area. The western shore of Anchor Bay is lined with trees and cottages; its northern side is thick with marshes and low islands. Part of the bay is a wildlife refuge. The marshes still support a wide variety of shore birds despite constant encroachment by developers.

The bay has a maximum depth of about 11 feet, but is much shallower in places. Anchor Bay is separated from the main lake by a bank with a minimum depth of eight or nine feet.

The northern side of Anchor Bay is packed with marinas and other small-craft amenities. At the mouth of the **Salt River**, at **New Baltimore**, and at **Fair Haven**. But only the latter, in the northeast corner, offers transient accommodations. The village is eleven miles from the outer channel buoy off Point Huron, and some unmarked spots have only three feet at chart datum. If draft permits, there are several marinas along a pleasant country channel west of Swan Creek. Fair Haven is only four or five miles from the north channel of the St. Clair River Delta.

The Ontario Shore

In contrast to the Michigan side, the Ontario shore of Lake St. Clair, beyond the pull of Windsor, is quite rural and becomes more so as you move east and then north to the St. Clair River. The sand bottom on the south and east sides of the lake comes very close to the surface, so that approach channels to the harbors begin a mile or more from shore. Few of them carry more than five feet.

Pike Creek enters the lake about four miles from the Detroit River entrance; two marinas and a sailing club—dockage is available if you draw less than five feet—are located a short distance upstream. The water tank at the Hiram Walker distillery, illuminated at night, makes a good landmark for Pike Creek.

The **Puce River** enters the lake four miles farther along the shoreline. The entrance is difficult to find, but some markers are privately maintained by the local marina. The entrance can be located by watching for the new watertower, painted blue, and the bright orange building on the shore. At night, a bright light marks the entrance to the river. Upstream lies the marina and the community of Puce.

Distances
Approximate Statute Miles

Location	Between Points	Cumulative
Detroit River Light	0	0
Amherstburg	7	7
Trenton, MI	13	20
Wyandotte	5	25
Detroit (Woodward Ave.)	11	36
Mount Clemens	35	71
St. Clair Flats	15	86
Algonac	14	100
Marine City	7	107
St. Clair	7	114
Port Huron / Sarnia	12	126

Continuing eastward along the shore, you come to the town of **Belle River**. A new marina operated by the town has been constructed here. Easily visible during the day, it is marked by a bright light at night.

The **Thames River** empties into the southeast corner of Lake St. Clair, through a buoyed channel that begins one and a half miles out in the lake. Once inside the river, depths go to six feet. There are two marinas and a yacht club off side channels of the river. This lovely river is navigable 20 miles to **Chatham**; where new

JEFFERSON BEACH
MARINE STORE

COMPLETE SELECTION OF SAILBOAT AND POWERBOAT HARDWARE
DECKSHOES • CLOTHING
U.S. AND CANADIAN CHARTS
SWAGING AND RIGGING
NAUTICAL BOUTIQUE
INTERLUX PAINTS
ELECTRONICS

24400 JEFFERSON, ST. CLAIR SHORES — NEXT TO BROWNIES

OPEN 362 DAYS A YEAR
778-8180

MICHAEL SHERIGAN, PROPRIETOR

Pleasure boats must share the St. Clair River with large freighters. Use caution.

amenities, including shopping, parks, and docks, are being developed. Two bridges open during daylight for boats proceeding to Chatham.

Mitchell Bay. The northeast corner of Lake St. Clair is flat and marshy, with rich aquatic and bird life. A rather complicated channel for smaller, shallow-draft craft leads to an attractive public marina at the settlement of Mitchell Bay.

Another buoyed channel leads through shallow water to the mouth of **Chenal Ecarte**, part of the St. Clair River delta system. You can poke along it to reach the St. Clair and, by way of **Sydenham River**, cruise to the city of **Wallaceburg** about ten miles upstream. Mariners are well received here with dockage for 100 boats, with easy access to shopping, restaurants, a museum, and a pool.

Note that this passage to the Sydenham River is limited by a 20-foot overhead power line. Cable ferries also run on either side of the Sydenham, which pose a hazard when the ferries are in motion and the cables come to the surface.

St. Clair River

The St. Clair River flows for 39 miles between Lake Huron and Lake St. Clair, descending six feet in the process. The four-mile current at the upper end diminishes at the broad delta to about one and a half miles per hour. Freighter traffic can be heavy in the river, but there is plenty of room and depth to keep out of their way along the sides of the channels. The scenery is mostly rural and dotted with summer cottages in the lower stretches. Some big industry appears as you near the cities of Port Huron and Sarnia.

The Delta Channels. As discussed earlier, if you're coming directly from the Detroit River or the southern part of Lake St. Clair, you'll take the six-mile St. Clair

---

SET YOUR COURSE FOR Wallaceburg

On Sydenham River - Lake St. Clair
Public Docking with full facilities
Museum - Glass Outlet - Parks
Accommodations - Shops - Restaurants

For further information and reservations

Contact: **Wallaceburg Tourist Bureau,**
786 Dufferin Ave.,
Wallaceburg, Ontario. N8A 2V3
(519) 627-1603 & (519) 627-8000

DETROIT R./LAKE ST. CLAIR/ST. CLAIR R.

Flats Cutoff Channel to South Channel. Note that the tall, white towers lining the way are located 190 feet outside the channel in shallow water. Unlit buoys mark the channel's actual boundary. Just beyond the junction with South Channel is a marina on Harsens Island.

North Channel comes in from Anchor Bay and runs between marshland and summer cottages for ten miles to its junction with the main stem of the river at the resort village of **Algonac** on the north side of North Channel. Two ferries cross North Channel from Algonac, one to Harsens Island and the other to Russell Island.

After these channels all join beyond Algonac, the river runs straight, wide, and deep for 28 miles to Lake Huron and forms the border between the United States and Canada. A couple of miles past the junction, Chenal Ecarte leads off on the Canadian side. After eight miles it meets the Sydenham River and after eight more, Mitchell Bay in Lake St. Clair, as described earlier. At the junction of the St. Clair River are two marinas, the only ones on the Canadian side of the river until Sarnia.

Marine City. On the banks of Belle River, flowing into the St. Clair on the Michigan side, are several small marinas suitable for an overnight stop. Depths run to five feet.

St. Clair. Eight miles farther on, the salt mining town of St. Clair has become something of a resort. Pine River, which flows into the St. Clair south of the main part of town, is identified by the salt company at its mouth. Immediately inside the river, the highway bridge opens on the hour and half hour. Beyond it is a Michigan Waterways Commission marina in the heart of town. Another mile and a half upstream is a marina in a country setting. There are fine shops and restaurants in St. Clair. The well-known St. Clair Inn has dockage right on the river, but it is quite untenable because of the wakes from passing ships.

Port Huron offers to cruising mariners a yacht club, private marinas, and several well-equipped municipal docking areas. All the facilities are located on the **Black River**, which is identified by a large gravel pile on the south bank. The railway bridges across Black River generally stand open, and the highway bridges open on the half hour between 9:00 a.m. and 5:30 p.m. Most of the accommodations are located close to downtown, shopping, and restaurants. Port Huron features an interesting Museum of Arts and History, and their annual Blue Water Festival is a gala event.

Sarnia. Across the river from Port Huron, Sarnia, Ontario, is a major industrial city, whose oil refining and petrochemical plants you will have passed on your way upstream. One of Sarnia's large marinas is located in Sarnia Bay, the other in a protected basin a little farther on. Both are well equipped and just a short walk to shops, restaurants, a motel, and bus service. Downtown Sarnia is only a 15-minute walk away. In a sheltered basin directly off Lake Huron is a yacht club and another marina in a suburban location.

At this northern end of the St. Clair River, the current runs swiftly, especially around the base of the high level Blue Water Bridge. It can exceed four or five miles an hour and is worst in the middle of the river or on the American side. Low-powered vessels should navigate closer to the Canadian east shore when passing under the bridge. Shortly beyond it you are in Lake Huron, covered in the next chapter.

Transient Boaters Prefer

SARNIA BAY MARINA

- 24 hour security
- 190 transient slips
- walk to restaurants and floral gardens
- groups welcome
- city bus at door

Reservations accepted:
SARNIA BAY MARINA
P.O. BOX 700 CORUNNA,
ONTARIO, CANADA N0N1G0
May to Oct. 1-519-332-0533
Nov. to Apr. 1-519-862-2291

PORT HURON MARINAS

On the Black River

Harbormaster
100 McMorran Blvd.
Telephone: (313) 982-0200 year round
or (313) 985-5676 & (313) 984-4075
May 1 — November 1

SERVING THE BOATER

dock attendants · cart shuttle service
ice · charts · showers · restrooms
transient accommodations
gasoline & diesel fuel
holding tank pump - out
marine channels 9-16-68
water · electricity · CATV
boat service center

GREAT LAKES EDITION

Detroit R./Lake St. Clair/St. Clair R.

Detroit River / Lake St. Clair / St. Clair River

		SEASONAL / YEAR-ROUND	SAIL / POWER / BOTH▲	LARGEST VESSEL ACCOMMODATED	NO. OF TRANSIENT BERTHS	MARKED ENTRY CHANNEL	APPROACH DEPTH (Reported)	DOCKSIDE DEPTH (Reported)	GAS★ / DIESEL● / BOTH▲ FUEL BRAND	RAILWAY / LIFT CAPACITY (in tons)	ENGINE REPAIRS: Gas★ / Diesel● / Both▲ LAUNCHING RAMP	PROPELLER / HULL REPAIRS	MARINE SUPPLIES / LPG★ / CNG● / BOTH▲ GROCERIES / ICE	110V★ / 220V● / BOTH▲ SHOWERS / MAX AMPS	RESTAURANT / LAUNDROMAT PUMP-OUT STATION / SNACK BAR	RADIO WATCH—VHF (CB)
DETROIT RIVER																
1. Ford Yacht Club*	(313) 676-8422	S	▲	50			5	5			PRIVATE YACHT CLUB					
2. Humbug Marina	676-6633	Y	▲	55	20	●	5	7	STA	▲	L	▲	PH	MGI	★30	SL	●	S	16
3. Damark Marine	676-2880	Y	▲			●		10			20	▲			★		R	16
4. Mike's Marine Supply	675-5150	Y	▲				5	5		MARINE SUPPLIES						
5. Mill Cove Marina, Ontario	(519) 252-7289	S	▲	30	10	●	10	10	ESS	▲	3	★	PH	MGI	★15	SL	●	RS
6. Anderson Harbor Lite Tavern, Ontario	736-5555	Y	▲	50			6	6		RESTAURANT DOCK				R
7. Duffy's Tavern & Motor Inn, Ontario	736-4301	S	▲	80	18	●	14	7	SHE	★		R	★	P	MGI	▲	L	●	RS
8. Port O'Call Marina*	No Listing	S	▲	65	100									I	★15		RS
9. Wyandotte Harbor of Refuge*	No Listing									MUNICIPAL DOCK—FISHING PIER					
10. Island View Marina, Ontario	(519) 734-7058	S	▲	50	6	●	10	5		★	10	R	★		MI	★30	S	●	RS
11. LaSalle Marina	734-1345	Y	▲	55		●	22	10	SHE	★	40	R	▲	PH	MGI	▲20	SL	●	RS
12. River's Edge Marina	(313) 386-3353	S	▲	45	6	●	18	10		★	14	R	▲	PH	●	MGI	★30	S	●	S
13. Memorial Park Marine*	267-7143	S	▲	57		●								I	★30	SL	●
14. Kean's Detroit Yacht Harbor ✓ (p. 166)	822-4500	Y	▲	50	10	●	8	7	AMO	★	15		▲		MGI	▲30	SL	●	RS	16
15. Riverside Marina, Ontario*	(519)	S	▲	40	5	●	10	4	ESS	▲		R	▲	PH	MGI	★15		
16. Lakeview Park Marina, Ontario (p. 167)	948-3383	S	▲	85	30	●	20	10	TEX	▲		R			I	★30	SL	●	R	68
17. Rendezvous Tavern*	735-6021	S	▲			●	20	12		RESTAURANT DOCK					
LAKE ST. CLAIR / MICHIGAN SHORE																
18. Jefferson Beach Marine Store (p. 169)	(313) 778-8180	S	▲	200	300	●	20	20						M			
19. Mike's Marine Supply	778-3200	Y	▲				5	4		MARINE SUPPLIES					
20. Michigan Harbor, Inc.	775-0852	S	▲	60	30	●	9	7	AMO	▲	25	R	▲	PH	MGI	★30	S	●	S
21. Metro Beach Metropark	463-4581	S	▲	100	170	●	8	6			R			I	★30	S	●	S	16
22. Boca Grande Marina, Inc.	463-BOCA	Y	▲	70		●	7	7	MAR	▲	15		▲	P	MGI	★30		●	R	16
23. Excel Marina	463-6126	Y	▲	55		●	11	8	76	▲	L	R	▲	PH	MI	★30		●
24. Belle Maer Harbor	465-4534	S	▲	83	10	●	7	7	76	★	40		▲	P	GI	▲100	SL	●	RS
25. Captain's Cove Marina	949-6660	S	P	35			10	10	76	★	L	R	▲	P	MGI	●30		●
26. Fair Haven Marina, Inc.	725-8396	S	▲	48	10	●	5	5			25		▲	PH		▲30			16
27. Kip's Cove*	725-6718	S	▲	50		●	5	5	MOB	★	L		▲	PH	MGI	▲30	SL	●	R
28. Bay Shore Boat Club	725-0043		▲	45	10		12	8	STA	★	L	R	▲	PH	MGI	★30	SL	●	S	16
29. Harmony Marina Motel	725-1331	Y	▲	35	3	●	10	6				★		MGI	★20	SL	●	R
LAKE ST. CLAIR / ONTARIO SHORE																
30. St. Clair Parkway Marina	(519) 354-8423	S	▲	50	10	●	6	4	TEX	★		R			I	★	S	●	R
31. Deerbrook Marine, Ltd.	728-1123	S	P	30	10	●	12	6			10	R	★	P	★	MGI	★20		●	S	68
32. Belle River Marina*	728-2245	S	▲	35	27	●	12	12		★					MGI	★30	S	●	RS	9
33. Bell's Puce Marina, Inc.	735-0404	S	▲	60	20	●	5	5	TEX	★	30	R	▲	PH	MGI	▲30		●	R	68
34. Ted Dudley's Marina	735-3786	Y	▲	30	2	●	4	4			10	R	▲	PH	MGI	★20		●	R
35. Pud's Place	735-9561	S	▲	40	3	●	5	7	SHE	▲	L		★		MGI	★30		●	S
ST. CLAIR RIVER																
36. Al D'Eath Marina, Inc.*	(313) 748-9943	S	▲	50	8		5	5	MOB	▲	L		★	PH	I	★30		●
37. Sassy Marina	794-9333	Y	▲	120		●	13	13	AMO	▲	100		▲	P	I	▲50	SL	●
38. Lyle's Marina	794-4460	S	P	38		●	5	5	MOB	★		R	★	PH	MI	★		●
39. Algonac Harbour Club	794-4448	S	▲	60	30	●	8	8	SUN	▲			★	P	MGI	▲50	SL	●	RS	16/17
40. St. Clair Boating	(519) 677-5625	Y	▲	40	100	●	10	10	SHE	▲	L	R	★	PH	I	★50		●	S
41. St. Clair Municipal Marina*	329-4125		▲							▲						●
42. St. Clair Marina	(313) 329-9407	Y	▲	70		●	8	8	SHE	▲	40	R	▲	P		▲30	S	●	R
PORT HURON / SARNIA																
43. Mike's Marine Supply*	987-1420	Y	▲	55			8	8		MARINE SUPPLIES					
44. City of Port Huron Marina (p. 171)	982-0200	Y	▲	130	85	●	28	15	MOB	▲		R			I	▲60	SL	●	RS	16/9
45. Sarnia Bay Marina (p. 171)	(519) 332-0533	S	▲	80	190	●	27	8	ESS	▲		R			I	★30	SL	●	R	68
46. Bridgeview Marina*	337-3888	Y	▲	85	30	●	30	10	PC	▲	25	R	▲	PH	MI	▲20	S	●	R
47. Sarnia Yacht Club	337-7175	S	▲	45		●	6	6	ESS	▲					MGI	★30	S	●	R
48. Lake Huron Yachts, Ltd.*	344-0572	S	S	60	10	●	10	10	ESS	▲	L		▲	PH	▲	MGI	★30		●	S	16

To provide the most complete and accurate information, **all facilities have been contacted within the past year.** If an asterisk (*) appears, it indicates a facility which did not respond to our requests for information (these listings may not reflect current conditions). Although facility operators supplied this data, we cannot guarantee accuracy or assume responsibility for errors. Entrance and dockside soundings tend to fluctuate. Always approach marinas carefully. Reference numbers on spotting charts indicate marina locations. ✓ Member American Boat Builders & Repairers Association.

172 WATERWAY GUIDE / 1991

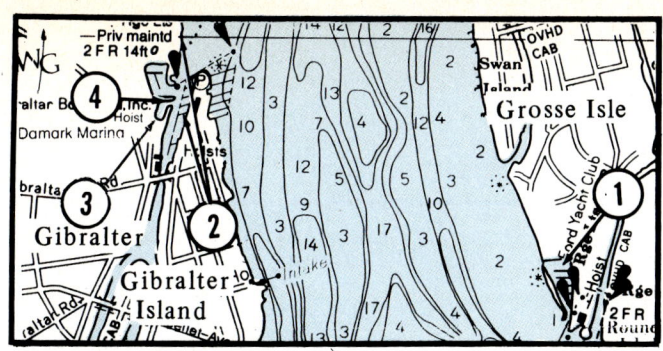

Detroit R. / Lake St. Clair / St. Clair R.

Chart 14848, edition 46

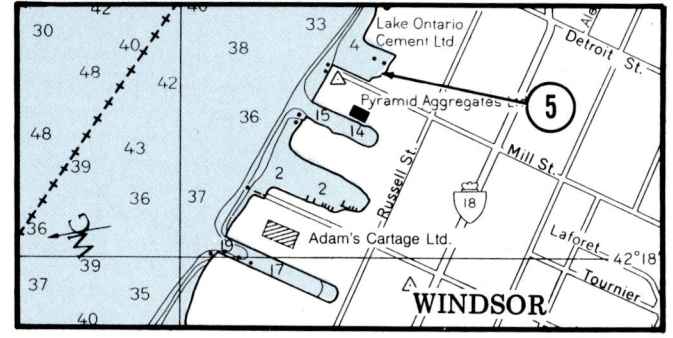

Chart 14853, edition 8

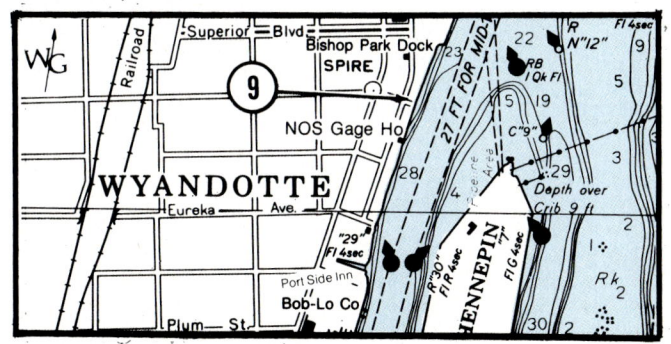

Chart 14848, edition 46

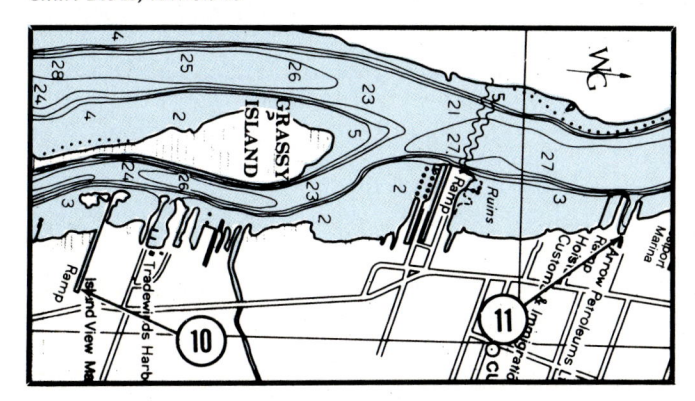

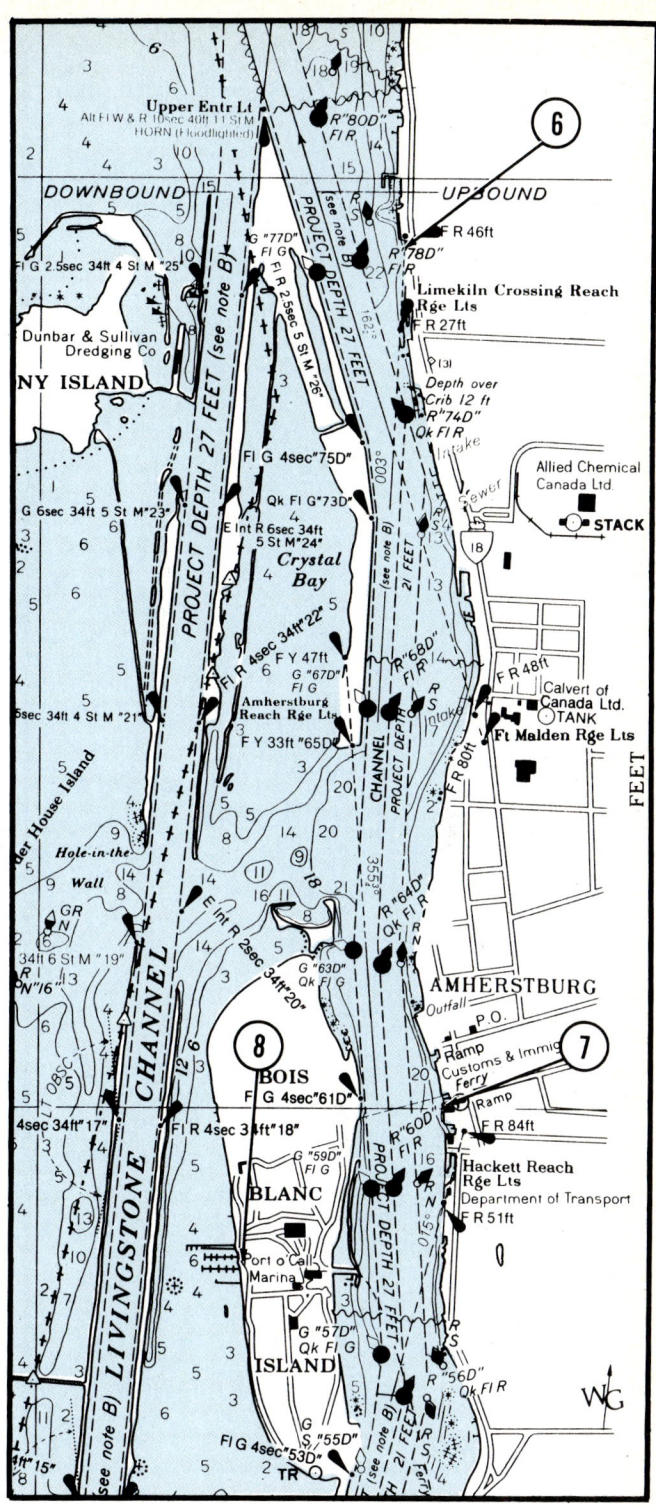

Chart 14848, edition 46

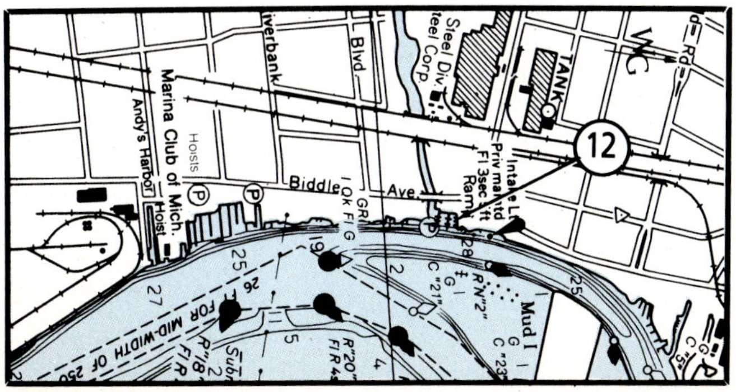

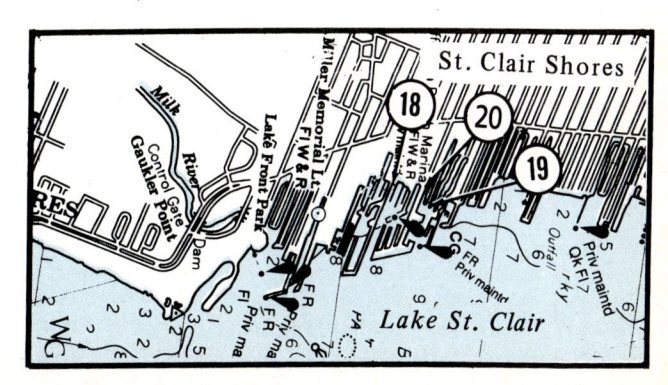

Chart 14850, edition 41

GREAT LAKES EDITION — *Under no circumstances are these charts to be used for navigation.*

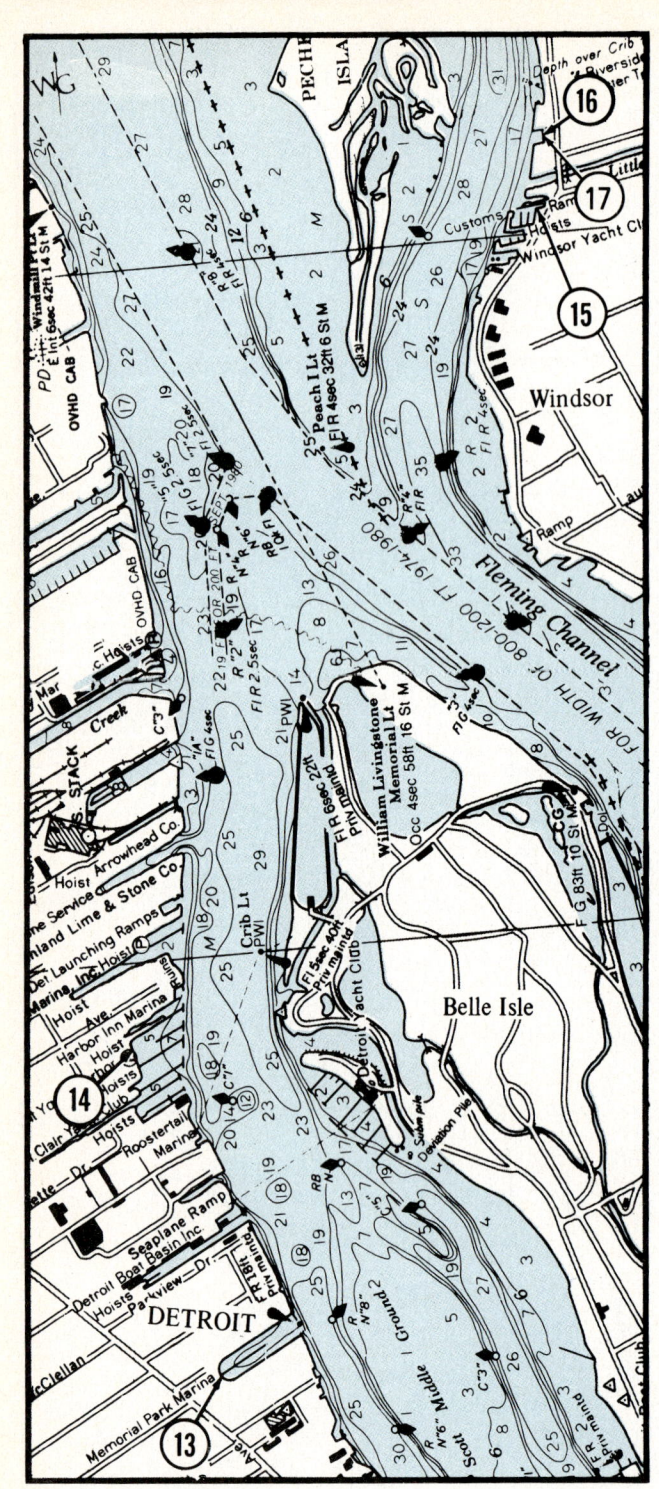

Detroit R./Lake St. Clair/St. Clair R.

Chart 14848, edition 46

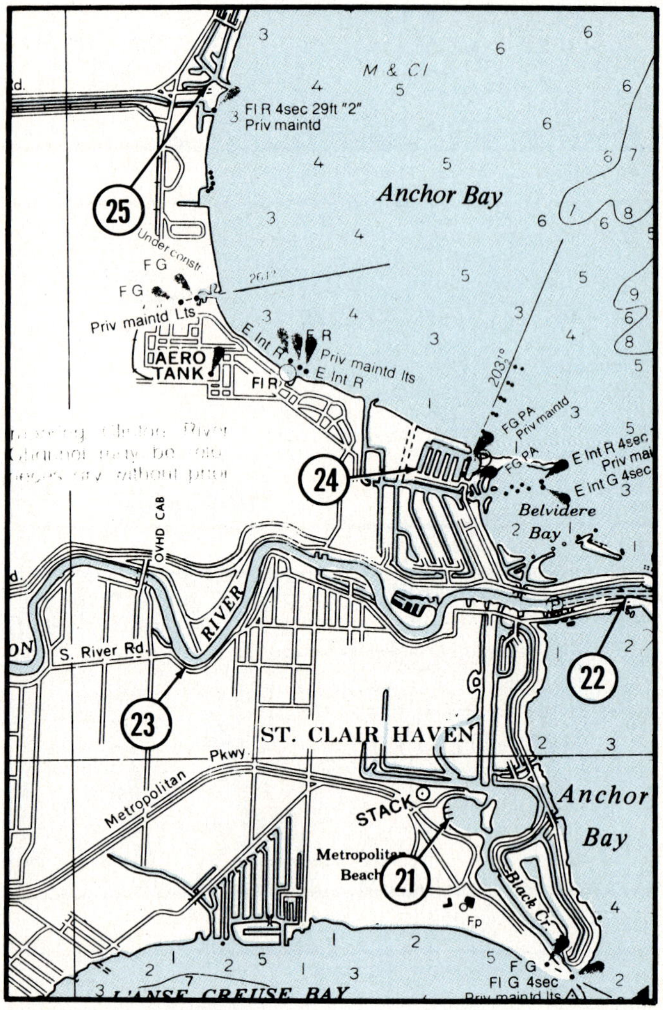

Chart 14850, edition 41

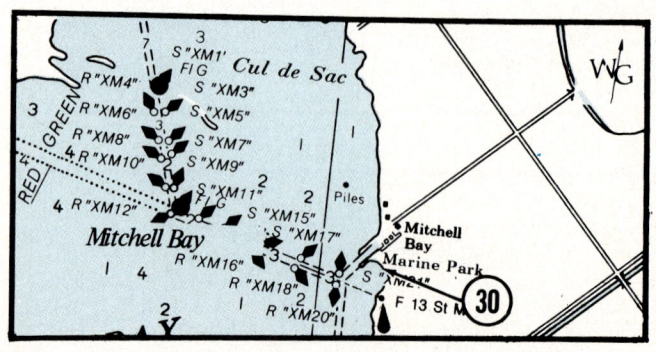

Chart 14850, edition 41

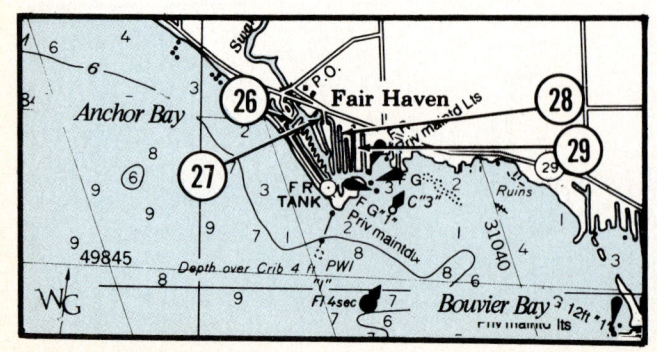

Chart 14850, edition 41

174   Under no circumstances are these charts to be used for navigation.

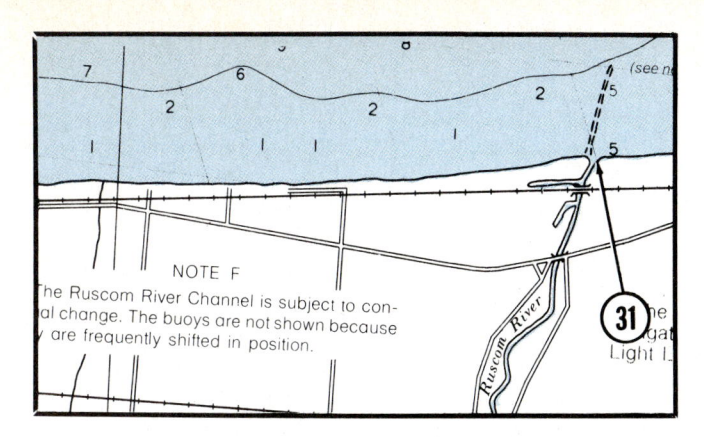

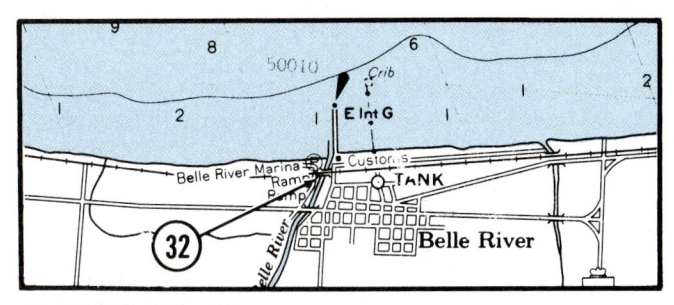

Detroit R./Lake St. Clair/St. Clair R.

Chart 14852, edition 34

Chart 14850, edition 41

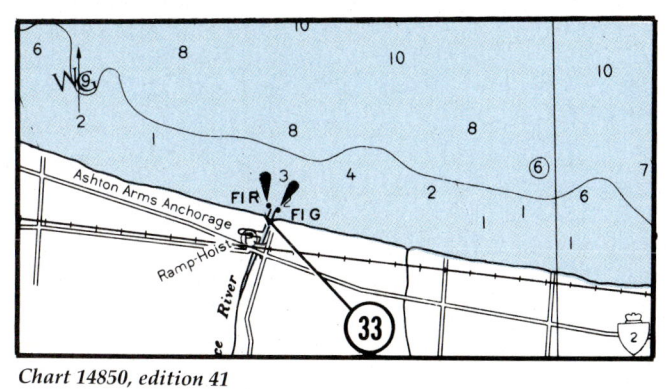

Chart 14850, edition 41

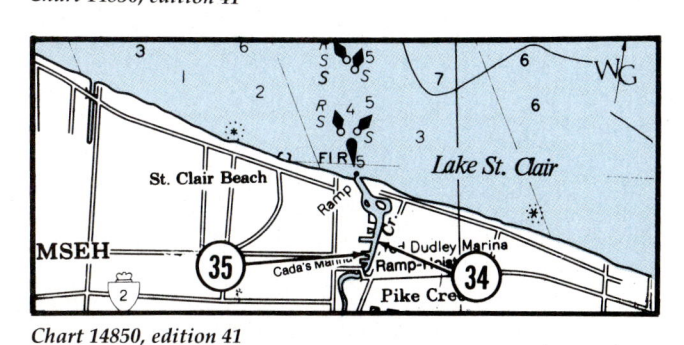

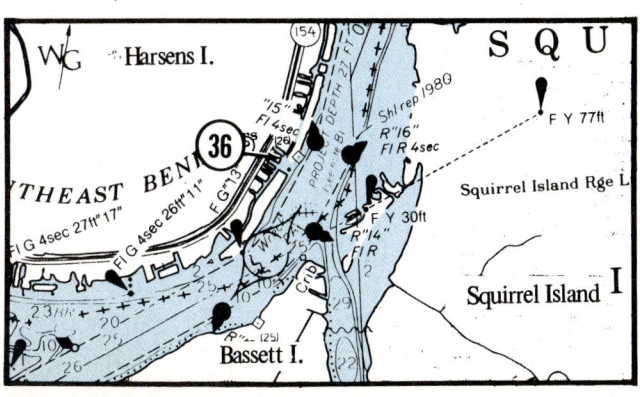

Chart 14852, edition 34

Chart 14850, edition 41

Chart 14852, edition 34

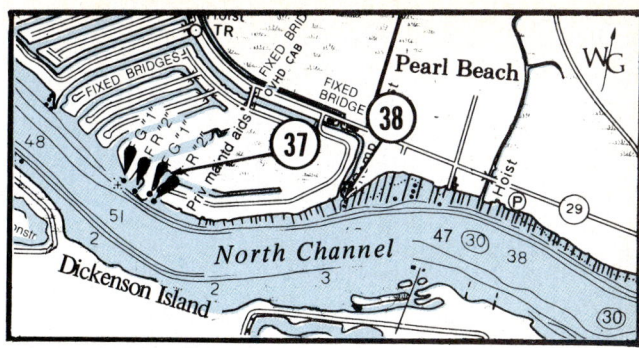

Chart 14852, edition 34

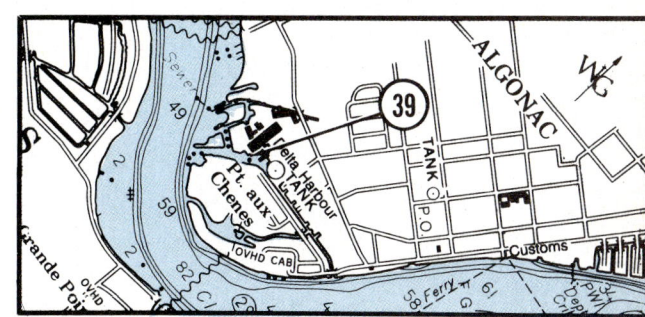

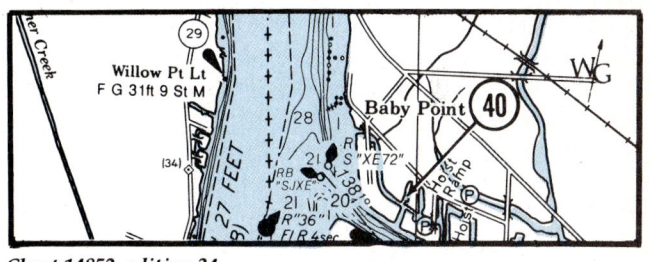

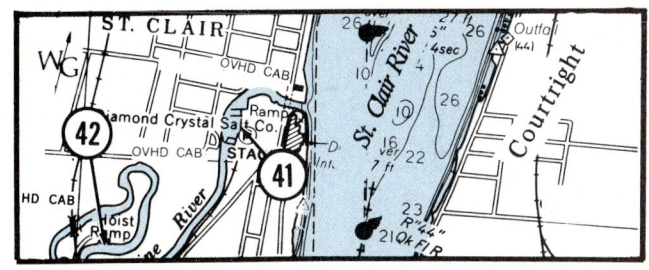

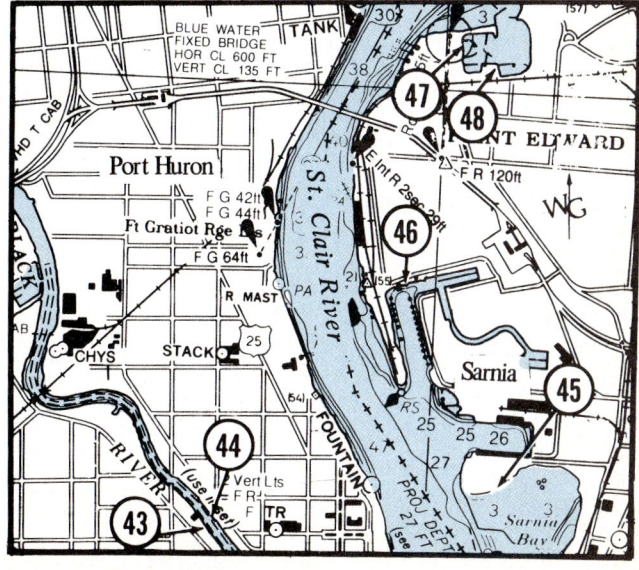

Chart 14852, edition 34

GREAT LAKES EDITION *Under no circumstances are these charts to be used for navigation.* 175

MICHIGAN
St. Mary's River
North Channel
Hessel
St. Ignace
Les Chenaux Is.
Drummond I.
Straits of Mackinac
Mackinac I.
DeTour Pass
Cockburn I.
Manitoulin Island
Bois Blanc I.
Mackinac City
Cheboygan
Little Traverse Bay
Burt Lake
Mullett Lake
Huron Beach
Rogers City
Petoskey
Providence Bay
South Baymouth
Georgian Bay
Presque Isle
Tobermory
Alpena
Thunder Bay
LAKE HURON
Harrisville
MICHIGAN
South Hampton
Oscoda
Port Elg
E. Tawas
Kincardine
Au Gres
Standish
Port Austin
Caseville
Saginaw Bay
WG
Harbor Beach
Bayport
Goderich
Sebewaing
Bay Park
Bay City
Bayfield
Saginaw
Port Sanilac
Grand Bend
Lakeport
Lexington
Port Huron
Sarnia
St. Clair River
ONTARIO

Lake Huron

CHARTS: 14860, 14862, 14863, 14864, 14865, 14867, 14869, 14880, 14881, 14882, 14885, 14886-SC; Canadian: 2235, 2273, 2274, 2290, 2291, 2292, 2297, 2298.

Lake Huron, second largest of the Great Lakes, divides into three major segments, each with a different character. The main body of the lake, roughly 100 miles wide by 160 miles long, lies in a north-south orientation. The shores taper almost to a point at the St. Clair River and are smooth with few natural harbors. The international boundary bisects the lake, but the small towns on each side have much in common: their origins; their current mixture of traditional occupations such as farming, manufacturing, and fishing; their artificial harbors; tourism; and the stretches of beachfront resort property that lie between them.

Recreational boating is big on this part of the lake. Local sailboats, racing from clubs on Michigan's Saginaw, Tawas, and Thunder bays, and from Ontario's harbors of Kincardine, Bayfield, and Grand Bend, fill a busy summer calendar. The mid-season extravaganza is the Port Huron-to-Mackinac race in July. Fishermen set out by the fleet in boats of all sizes, especially in the more sheltered waters of Michigan's Saginaw Bay and the Fishing Islands of Ontario. For the cruising sailor, the orientation of the lake affords favorable winds—predominantly southwest to northwest—no matter which way you point. At the **Straits of Mackinac**, the lake turns west and the shorelines as well as freighters and pleasure boats converge, for the passage into Lake Michigan.

Georgian Bay, entirely in Canada, has been called the sixth Great Lake, and it does present in small version all the variety of Lake Huron. One of the world's great cruising grounds, it is both a destination for mariners from distant ports and a residence—at its southern end—for a growing fleet of its own.

In the all Canadian North Channel, the scenery explodes with a powerful impact. A panorama of islands, carved from granite and adorned by northern forests, is backed on either shore by mountains or bluffs. Sheltered from the fetch of Lake Huron proper, the seas are kind to both sailboats and power boats.

Cruising Conditions

Lake Huron's great appeal for the cruising mariner is the variety of its natural features and the absence of large cities and congested urban areas. But this variety also brings some special cruising conditions. Lake Huron conforms to the general Great Lakes weather pattern—summertime high-pressure systems of fairly long duration, punctuated by lows coming through from the southwest. Daytime temperatures can reach the high 80s and 90s but, except for unusual heat waves, onshore breezes bring night temperatures down, especially on the northern and eastern shores. The northern reaches of the lake are perceptibly cooler than the southern, but it is possible to have chilly days and downright cold nights anywhere on the lake. Water temperature rises over the course of the summer, from south to north, reaching its highest temperature in September. By early July swimming in the northernmost shallows is comfortable at 68 degrees.

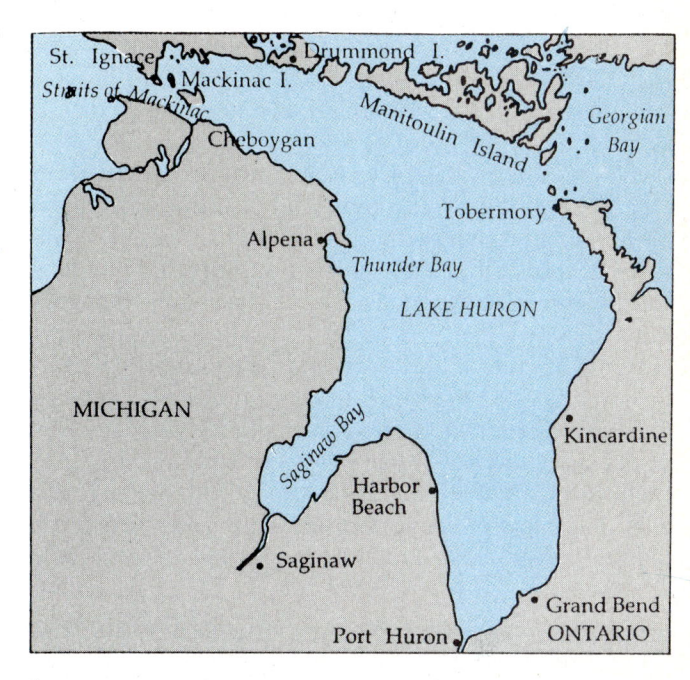

Prevailing westerly winds make Lake Huron and Georgian Bay (with their north-south orientation) superb sailing waters. But their great fetch along the main axis can raise perilous seas when a gale comes up, especially at the two extremities and on the leeward shores. A layer of shipwrecks on the lake's floor testifies to the power of this inland sea. While summer winds are mostly benign, skippers should keep a constant weather watch.

Late afternoon thunderstorms are likely to arise from the southwest or northwest. The changing cloud formations usually signal what is to come, but these storms can be violent on all parts of the lake. Occasionally stormy weather will come from the northeast, especially in the Georgian Bay-North Channel area.

On all the Great Lakes, fog is most common in late June and early July, when warmer air currents move across the water's cool surface. On Lake Huron, fog oc-

LAKE HURON

curs most often at the northern end. The Straits of Mackinac are especially vulnerable because of the complex juncture of land formations and currents, and similar conditions prevail in the passage off the Bruce Peninsula between Lake Huron proper and Georgian Bay. Although most likely to roll in late at night or in the early morning and burn off by midday, fog can occur at any time and any place. On Lake Huron proper, however, it's rare for fog to last as long as a full day in summer.

Navigation on Lake Huron can run the gamut from long-distance dead reckoning and celestial sighting to gunkholing and rangefinding with trees. Special conditions are described in each section. On the lake as a whole, annual fluctuations in water level must be taken into account when you're closing with shorelines and entering harbors. Chart soundings are accurate and sufficiently detailed in most cases, but in Canadian waters some old-fashioned charts—dating from very old surveys using outdated water-levels—are still in use.

In the more remote areas there are few navigational aids, but boats cruising northern Lake Huron reap the benefit of very long hours of daylight. Darkness falls about 10:00 p.m. in mid-summer. In the main body of the lake, the coastlines are almost devoid of natural landmarks, so you must often rely on the stacks and tanks shown on the chart, in addition to dead reckoning, to spot a harbor mouth. The breakwaters at all the artificial harbors on the Michigan side are marked by entrance lights, and the docks are lighted. On the Canadian side you'll find ranges in addition to lighted aids at each artificial harbor, but the ranges are not always on the breakwaters.

The boating season on Lake Huron depends on the hardiness of the sailor. For some it is year-round. However, early June to early October are the customary limits to extended cruising. In more remote locations, marinas may not be open before June and after September, although the public docks on both sides of the border ensure at least a place to tie up. For early and late season cruising, a cabin heater, in addition to warm clothing, is a must, and it can be a comforting accessory even in summer. Although the days are shorter at the two ends of the season, the air is often clear and bright, and the harbors uncrowded.

You can plan a Lake Huron cruise in many ways.

Distances
Statute miles (approximate)

From	To	Miles	From	To	Miles
Port Huron/Sarnia	Harbor Beach	60	Rogers City	Meldrum Bay	60
	Goderich	65	Meldrum Bay	Little Current	60
	Tobermory	165		Thessalon	35
Harbor Beach	Alpena	95	Tobermory	Little Current	65
	Rogers City	140		Killarney	50
	Tobermory	110		Byng Inlet	60
Goderich	Harrisville	100		Parry Sound	80
	Tobermory	110		Midland	100
Bay City	Goderich	135		Owen Sound	80
	Tobermory	160	Owen Sound	Killarney	105
	Rogers City	160		Byng Inlet	90
Harrisville	Tobermory	95		Parry Sound	75
	Rogers City	80		Midland	70
Alpena	Mackinac Island	120	Midland	Killarney	120
	Meldrum	90		Byng Inlet	80
	Tobermory	90		Parry Sound	60
Rogers City	Mackinac Island	55	Parry Sound	Killarney	90
	Hessel	50			

Parry Sound distance refer to the city itself.

Location	Between Points	Cumulative	Location	Between Points	Cumulative
Michigan Shore			Mackinac Island	17	412
Port Huron/Sarnia	0	0	St. Ignace	6	418
Port Sanilac	33	33			
Harbor Beach	32	65	**Ontario Shore**		
Bay City	102	167	Port Huron/Sarnia	0	0
Saginaw (off channel)	13		Goderich	65	65
Au Gres	30	197	Kincardine	36	101
East Tawas	24	221	Southampton	30	131
Au Sable	21	242	Tobermory	63	194
Alpena	49	291	Great Duck Island Can	69	263
Presque Isle Harbor	47	338	De Tour	50	313
Rogers City	17	355	Port Dolomite	23	336
Cheboygan	40	395	St. Ignace	28	364

You can plan a Lake Huron cruise in many ways. You can follow all the coasts and their indentations, cross from end to end, or combine open-water cruising with coasting. Many people, on limited vacations, take the length or breadth of the lake in one long passage, in order to spend more time anchoring among the islands of Georgian Bay and the North Channel. Others prefer dockside amenities and linger in the towns and villages.

While each port town is covered in our pages, it is impossible to describe all the anchorages. From the Fishing Islands of Lake Huron to the Thirty Thousand Islands of Georgian Bay, to the Bay of Islands in the North Channel, thousands of possibilities exist for gunkholing and anchoring.

Michigan Shore

Lake Huron didn't always have its present shape. Before the last Ice Age it was much larger and covered what became the thumb of Michigan's mitten. The old lake bottom left rich soil for the farms which developed in the mid-19th century after the lumber barons removed the thick forests. Then, after the hot, dry summer of 1871, several small fires merged into a huge conflagration that raged for two long days across the thumb, destroying villages, farms, and immense stands of uncut timber. Miraculously, few lives were lost and the settlers rebuilt. A decade later the tragedy repeated itself, with the mass of fallen timber from the previous fire providing seasoned tinder for the new blaze. This time the fire claimed several hundred lives and millions of dollars worth of property across the entire peninsula. The American Red Cross had been organized just three weeks earlier; this fire was its first relief project.

The local people still talk about these events, perhaps because life here has been so quietly prosperous ever since. The coastal villages present a serene face to summertime visitors.

Lexington. Settled in the 1830s, **Lexington** was the first village along this shore. However, the town's artificial harbor is the newest on the Michigan side of the lake. It is a convenient 20-mile run from the St. Clair River.

Port Sanilac. This harbor is about a dozen miles north of Lexington. There is some dispute about the origin of its name; some say Sanilac was a Wyandot chief, others say that he was a 17th-century French-Canadian trapper. The town was called Bark Shanty for its first 17 years, because the earliest arrivals, in 1840, were men from Detroit who tanned bark on the beach. As the town grew, its citizens petitioned the Post Office for a more dignified name.

In 1951 Port Sanilac was the first harbor of refuge built under the sponsorship of the Michigan Waterways Commission. You can anchor in the protection of the breakwater, opposite the state dock. The commercial marina offers a marine store, repairs, and a launch ramp, and the village has a full complement of shops. The local historical museum is housed in an 1872 mansion donated to the county by sea captain Stanley Harrison, grandson of the builder. Port Sanilac honors Independence Day in style, and on the last weekend in July the annual summer festival mounts a full program of events, displays, contests, and food.

Harbor Beach to Port Austin. Thirty miles beyond Port Sanilac, **Harbor Beach** also underwent a name change from Sand Bay about 20 years after the harbor was built in 1877. The largest man-made harbor in the world, it was intended as a refuge for shallow-draft lake freighters and to serve the large Hercules Power Company plant. There is a Michigan Waterways Commission marina at the north end of the harbor, about a mile from downtown shopping.

It's about 30 miles to the next port of call, and north of Harbor Beach the rock-strewn coastline shoals out much farther. You should keep about three miles offshore as you round the top of the thumb.

If your boat has very shallow draft, however, and can hug the coast past **Pte. Aux Barques Light**, you might find your way into the unmarked small boat harbor at **Grindstone City**. Tie-up is available along the jetty or at one of the two small boat marinas. Between 1880 and 1930, grinding stones ranging from three pounds to six tons were quarried and shaped here to supply industrial firms around the world. The natural stone of this unique geological formation couldn't compete with later development of carborundum and emery, so the once-thriving city became first a ghost town, and then a summer place. Many grindstones still lie along the shore for the curious beachcomber.

Port Austin. At Port Austin is a summer resort at the mouth of shallow Bird Creek. There is a Michigan Waterways Commission marina in the outside artificial harbor. Despite breakwaters, there can be considerable surge in high northeast winds. On the approach to Port Austin, give Port Austin Reef a wide berth. At Port Austin you have reached the southeastern entrance to **Saginaw Bay**. This approximately 25-by-50-mile indentation of Lake Huron is relatively shallow, which can make for anxious piloting, especially when strong winds parallel the northeast-southwest axis of the bay and raise or lower the water levels by as much as four feet near the southern end. The fishing is superb, however. Legend has it that sturgeon were once so plentiful, especially in spring when they went up the tributaries to spawn, that the local folk caught them with spears, pitchforks, and clubs. Commercial fishermen might net eighty, 150-pounders in one cast. The sturgeon are gone, but enough bass and perch are left to crowd the reef contours with sportfishermen on summer weekends.

Caseville. A longtime resort town, **Caseville** still jumps with activities for all ages, including a fun slide, two miniature golf courses, a roller rink, numerous restaurants, and shops of all kinds. Most of the dockage here is seasonal, but transients are accommodated at the Waterways Commission dock, the newest in town. All of this lies at the mouth of the **Pigeon River**, protected by a breakwater, with a channel dredged to six feet.

Bay City. The ship channel leading to the Saginaw River is easy to spot by the stacks and derricks of Lake Huron's only large industrial complex, **Bay City/Saginaw**. A short distance inside the entrance you'll find yacht clubs on both shores and a large marina just upstream. About six miles and as many bridges upriver (vertical clearance ranging from seven to 30 feet) are two marinas in **Bay City**.

The trip up the river can be fascinating; you'll pass industrial installations of all kinds. Of special interest to mariners is the Gougeon Brothers plant. The Gougeons are best known for their pioneering work in epoxy and wood building material. Unfortunately, most of the marinas are far from shopping, restaurants, and other services in this city of 50,000, but cabs are available.

Between 1850 and 1890 an estimated 31 billion feet of lumber was cut from the extraordinarily rich forests of the Saginaw Valley. **Saginaw** ultimately had 74 sawmills with sawdust piles up to 40 feet deep. **Bay City**, despite its 36 sawmills, was where the lumber barons built their palaces. Some say the town spawned 98 millionaires. You can still walk along the street where they lived, admire the lavish architecture, and learn more of their story at the Historical Museum of Bay County, 1700 Center Avenue. Center Avenue ranks among the most splendid boulevards of Victorian mansions in the United States.

Saginaw River. It's about 22 miles from the mouth of the river to the junction of the **Tittabawassee** and the **Shiawassee** rivers in the city of Saginaw. In the open places between the industrial centers of the two cities, the low flatland is devoid of the forest that once shut out the sky. The scene is bucolic, with stretches of parkland on the port side and only a few houses scattered among the woods and fields. The river is deep and channeled for big ships. There are 11 more bridges after Bay City, with 14-foot clearance at the lowest of the fixed spans near the end of the run. There are no marinas in Saginaw.

Bay City/Au Gres. The west side of Saginaw Bay is low, shallow, and marshy, with bars extending out from shore and little to attract the mariner other than a marina at Linwood. Near the top of the bay, about 25 miles from the Saginaw River, **Point Au Gres** thrusts out toward deeper water, and just northwest of it a buoyed channel leads through four-foot depths to a marina for small boats. The entrance to the **Au Gres River**, about two and a half miles north of the point, is protected by a breakwater, with a dredged, buoyed channel leading to the river mouth. Some two miles upstream, a Waterways Commission marina is located just below the highway bridge, and is handy to shops, a Laundromat, and restaurants in the village of **Au Gres**. There is also a county historical museum here, located in an 1897 two-room schoolhouse.

East Tawas, at the southern end of Tawas Bay, has a Waterways Commission marina connected to an elaborate breakwater. The breakwater is a favorite perch for fishermen in great numbers. At the head of the dock, a city campground is squeezed in between Highway 23 and the waterfront. Consequently, shoreside and dockside jump with activity most of the summer, and the sand beach next door swarms with families. The dock is convenient to downtown shopping and restaurants. East Tawas has a historical museum, as do many of these lakeside towns.

The bay is not suitable for anchorage, but there is a marina on the far point in a quieter location for boats of shallow draft.

If you like to hike or bike, the Michigan Shore-to-Shore Trail begins here and winds for 125 miles to Lake Michigan. Trout and salmon are the prize catches in Tawas Bay during spring and fall, with perch abundant all summer.

Oscoda/Au Sable. From Tawas Point northward the strand is almost continuous. Several generations of cottagers and resort visitors have enjoyed the soft, white, powdery sand of this beach. At Au Sable Point, just eight miles from Tawas Point, you are officially out of Saginaw Bay. Thirteen miles beyond is the lighted entrance to the **Au Sable River**. Sometimes the current flows very swiftly at the river mouth, depending on control of the dam upstream.

The villages of **Oscoda** and **Au Sable** flank the river a short distance from the entrance. A water tank at each helps identify the river entrance from offshore. Several marinas and a yacht club provide a network of services. All but one marina is beyond the highway bridge (fixed at 23 feet), where the channel's controlling depth is three feet. Village shopping is not within easy walking distance from the marinas, but a restaurant and a miniature golf course are located on the south side just beyond the bridge.

The Au Sable River was a major thoroughfare for logs in the lumbering years, but as reforestation (begun in 1909) has restored its banks, it has become one of Michigan's favorite canoeing rivers. Despite the dams, which require short portages, most of the riverside is wild and beautiful. Canoe rentals are available in the village of Oscoda.

Harrisville. About 18 unobstructed miles north of Au Sable is the peaceful village of **Harrisville**, with a Waterways Commission marina. The harbor is entered between breakwaters from the north side. Within the harbor are both a beach and a playground. But if you are among those who like to walk for miles on clean, open sand, keep heading south from the dock until you get tired.

Harrisville shopping, including a bakery, is just a few blocks from the harbor. On Saturday afternoons, free band concerts are given on the courthouse lawn.

Alpena. It's 30 miles from rustic Harrisville to the relatively citified atmosphere of Alpena. Rocky shoals reach out as much as two miles from shore along this stretch, so don't hover too close, especially as you enter **Thunder Bay**. Unfortunately, there is no protected anchorage in this pretty indentation of the coast, but a marina is under Partridge Point on the west side of the bay.

The lighted and buoyed channels in Alpena Harbor lead to the commercial piers in the Thunder Bay River and to the Huron Portland Cement docks beyond. The pleasure boat harbor lies just to the south of the river entrance, behind a breakwater marked by a light. It is entered from the southwest, with a sharp turn to port just inside the breakwater. The city-owned, Waterways Commission-built dock is operated under lease by a private firm. You'll find a well-stocked marine store and complete boatyard services. The hospitable yacht club is next door.

Alpena, one of the most attractive stops on the main part of Lake Huron, is an excellent port for restocking the boat, for general shopping, for medical care if needed, and for entertainment. A downtown mall is located next to the docks, and additional city shops are just a few blocks away. Restaurants, movies, a roller rink, and tennis courts are all within easy walking distance, as is the Thunder Bay Theatre, a resident professional company. For scuba divers, the Thunder Bay Bottomland and Preserve includes several shipwrecks to explore. An excellent museum is a cab ride away.

Alpena to Presque Isle. At one time this area was covered with warm salty seas. Billions of tiny organisms lived in these waters, and when they died, their skeletal remains sank to the bottom. Today those skeletons are being raised again in the form of limestone, mined from beds hundreds of feet thick, to feed the steel mills of the lower lakes. The limestone deposits along the shores of upper Lake Huron begin at Alpena. The cement loading piers here are fairly conventional, but farther up you will see huge conveyor belts and elaborate overarching apparatus that bring raw limestone directly from vast quarries to waiting ships. The very names of the harbors convey their purpose: Rockport (no longer used), Stoneport, Calcite Harbor, and Port Dolomite.

From Alpena it is about 55 cruising miles to the next harbor with dockage, but there are a number of places to anchor in between. Some shelter can be found between **Thunder Bay Island** and **Sugar Island** at the north end of Thunder Bay, but if much sea is running, the roll is likely to be uncomfortable. A better spot can be found about 17 miles on, under **False Presque Isle**. This spot is open to the southeast, but fully protected from the more commonly prevailing southwest to northeast winds. Unless you're using the anchorage, it's best to round Thunder Bay Island on the outside, then gradually work your way toward shore, coasting at least a mile off by the time you reach **South Nine Mile Point**. That way you will avoid the long bank of nasty shoals lying north of Thunder Bay.

Presque Isle Harbor. The best anchorage in this part of Lake Huron is at **Presque Isle Harbor**, or in **North Bay** on the other side of the near-island. In both cases, best protection is in the southern part of the anchorage.

The entrance to Presque Isle Harbor is guided by a lighted range on a course of 274 degrees True. The marina on the north side has been closed for years and the docks have fallen into disrepair. The property is owned by the Michigan Department of Natural Resources, and there have been plans to rebuild a marina. But meanwhile, a restaurant is on site, and you can tie up the dinghy at the old docks and walk down the road towards the end of the peninsula. Branching off to the right, a beautiful forested track will lead you to the old **Presque Isle Lighthouse**. Built in 1840, it was used only 30 years before being decommissioned. It is open to visitors.

Rogers City. Eighteen miles beyond Presque Isle, **Rogers City** is easily identified from the water by immense piles of limestone a mile and a half to the south. The Waterways Commission docks are in a city park with a beach, playground, tennis courts, and a band shell where you can enjoy a free concert on Saturday afternoons. On Independence Day, the park hosts a gala celebration, topped off by fireworks, of course. As you leave the park to head downtown, a quarter mile away, the side of a big shed is covered with notices of commercial services available. In addition to the usual shops, including a bakery, there are several restaurants and a movie theatre in town. The Laundromat is not within convenient walking distance, but the historical museum is close by.

Hammond Bay. Beyond Rogers City, the coastline follows the northwest curve that began back at Presque Isle and sweeps gracefully around **Hammond Bay**. Just beyond this indentation, 20 miles in a straight line from Rogers City, the Waterways Commission has placed a small-boat harbor of refuge, known as Hammond Bay. There is no town or commercial activity here. The area is undeveloped, but the important dockside services are there, as well as a nice beach.

Straits of Mackinac

The Great Lakes system is a series of steps from Lake Superior, 602 feet above sea level, through successively lower lakes and the St. Lawrence River to the sea. Lakes Huron and Michigan share the same water level. Only the bed of an ancient river, widened over the centuries by the persistence of water and the scouring of ice, has kept the passage open, and today a strait four miles wide separates the two peninsulas of Michigan. This strait carries a name venerated in Indian lore, Mackinac (pronounced Mack-in-aw), "the Turtle," whose back supports the world, according to one tradition. The Straits of Mackinac, like all narrow passes, have long been considered an area of strategic importance.

Lake Huron

Cheboygan. This harbor is the southern gateway to the Straits. Cheboygan was an especially important lumber town in the mid-to-late 19th century and its convenient river-mouth harbor is still a commercial asset. Today the town is also a tourist center.

The first thing you are likely to see as you enter the harbor through the dredged channel on a lighted range of 212 degrees True, is the Coast Guard Cutter *Mackinaw*, docked at her berth. The 290-foot vessel is equipped with six 2,000 horsepower engines used to break up ice floes that impede ship passage in late fall and early spring. A new marina is across the harbor.

The drawbridge has a vertical clearance of nine feet, but opens for six minutes either side of the quarter and three-quarter hour during the day in summer, and at other times on demand with one long and one short blast.

You'll find both commercial marinas and a Waterways Commission dock along the river in Cheboygan. A convenient walkway leads from the Commission dock to the downtown shopping area, which includes restaurants and a movie theater. Just a few blocks away is the Cheboygan County Historical Museum, housed in the town's former jail. The Cheboygan Opera House was recently restored and offers a variety of theatrical presentations.

Bois Blanc Island. Five miles across South Channel from Cheboygan is the Straits' largest island, **Bois Blanc**—long ago corrupted to "Bob-lo." Most of the island is owned by the State of Michigan, but a settlement of devoted summer residents lies along the south shore, served by a daily mail boat from Cheboygan. Behind the breakwater the Waterways Commission maintains a long wooden dock for pleasure boats. There aren't any services here, but they do offer a country store, a friendly bar, and pleasant walking among the rich woods of the island.

The Inland Waterway. From the port of Cheboygan it is possible to cruise for 36 miles through a series of inland rivers and lakes almost to Lake Michigan. The pretty passage is limited to boats with three-foot draft and sixteen-foot height.

The passage begins at the Cheboygan River Lock with a lift of thirteen feet. One long and two short blasts signal the lockmaster. The Cheboygan River leads to Mullett Lake. About half way along is a marina, and a popular restaurant in an old inn. Several coves are suitable for anchorage in the ten-by-three-mile lake.

From Mullett Lake, the twisting channel of Indian River leads to Burt Lake. The town of Indian River has several marinas and some good restaurants. The course across large Burt Lake leads to the twisting Crooked River, which in turn connects to Crooked Lake. A small lock is at the junction. Crooked Lake is small, but can kick up a nasty chop in high winds. From there a narrow channel leads into Pickerel Lake, but there is no outlet here for Lake Michigan, only two miles away. A marina on Crooked Lake will transport boats overland to Lake Michigan if they are under 25 feet and weigh less than 5,000 pounds.

Mackinaw City. It was here in 1715 that the soldiers and traders of New France established the fortified village which grew to be the most important military outpost in the west and the great emporium of the fur trade. When the British moved the fort to Mackinac Island in 1781, the village and fur trade went with it. Mackinaw City's revival came in the next century with the railroad ferry terminus, placed here where the Straits barred direct conection with Michigan's upper Peninsula. Then in 1957, the engineering feat previously deemed impossible was accomplished. "Mighty Mac," once the world's longest suspension bridge, was completed, linking Michigan's long-separated peninsulas. Since then, railroad car ferry traffic has declined, and the ferrying of motor vehicles has disappeared. But tourist passenger ferry traffic to the island is brisker than ever—Mackinaw City is a full-scale tourist town.

The great bridge is a beacon for 20 miles in either direction, and just east of it, **Mackinaw City** features a large marina. Enter from the north between two lights, and turn abruptly to starboard once you're inside the breakwater. A new vessel has taken up permanent residence in one of the slips. The precise reconstruction of the sloop *Welcome*, first launched for the fur trade in 1775, is open to visitors. A few blocks away, painstaking archaeological research, begun in 1959, continues on the site of the original Fort Michilimackinac. When you pass through the stockade gate you'll find yourself in the old French village, risen again on the stone foundations that lay buried for so long. As you wander among the fur traders' houses, the church, the commandant's house, and the other buildings, you will learn of the stirring events that took place on these premises.

In addition to history, Mackinaw City offers a soft sand beach with a beautiful view of the Straits and the bridge, a miniature golf course, shops of all kinds, and several restaurants close to the marina. The town is one of the few places on the American shores of Lake Huron from which fishing tugs still put out, and the prize they bring back can be purchased fresh or smoked. Haulout and repairs are available at a marine service located near the ferry docks.

St. Ignace. Directly across the Straits, at the other end of the bridge, is the village of St. Ignace. Father Jacques Marquette established a mission here in 1671. A tombstone marks his grave overlooking the water; the surrounding park commemorates the works of the mission. The Michigan Waterways Commission harbor at St. Ignace is a smaller version of the one across the Straits. It gets less traffic, perhaps because it is not very convenient to shopping, although a sprawling business district is a few blocks away. A number of tourist ferries run from St. Ignace.

Mackinac Island. Despite the scenic attractions of the mainland ports, The Island is indisputably the area's big draw. Although only three miles by two, its brooding height dominates the Straits. Approaching from any direction, you can understand why the Indians held Mackinac Island sacred.

Ferries and giant lake freighters churn up the water where the passage narrows. The most constricted place is at Round Island Passage Light, precisely where you enter the harbor. Somehow the architects of this Waterways Commission harbor have never quite figured out how to protect the docks at Mackinac Island from the considerable disturbance. It can be an uncomfortable place to lie if the wind and sea are coming from the east. Yet the drawing power of the island is such that pleasure craft will race each other for a slip, which is assigned by loudspeaker to each boat as it approaches the dock. Then they'll bounce all day in the wash from the ferries, and pay premium dockage fees for the privilege. (When those pleasure boats are joined by racers from Port Huron or Chicago during the last two weekends in July, dock space is virtually impossible to come by; the island belongs to the fleet.)

You'll find much to do ashore on Mackinac Island. Wandering and soaking up the atmosphere of the well-preserved 19th-century village is a favorite pastime. Motor vehicles are prohibited, and the thoroughfares are given over entirely to the placid pace of pedestrians, carriages, and bicycles. During the day the village streets—all two of them—teem with "fudgies". These are the tourists who come over for the day and carry home boxes of fudge from the numerous candy shops.

You can walk backward in time inside the historic buildings of John Jacob Astor's American Fur Company and the home of Robert Stuart, his agent. These are not reconstructions, but the original structures preserved and maintained. Each has a fascinating, often surprising story to tell, as does the William Beaumont Memorial. Dominating the village from the bluff above is **Fort Mackinac**, much of it just as His Majesty's soldiers left it. Farther east along the shore you'll find the Indian Dormitory and Ste. Anne's Church. The park across from the dock boasts lilacs planted by the French traders.

In addition to its historic sites, the island has beautiful hiking and horseback riding trails in its interior. A bike ride around the eight-mile shore road is a must. Several fine old hotels are located on this resort island. The most famous is the Grand Hotel, which opened in 1887 and has the longest piazza in the world. All of the hotel dining rooms are open to the public, and additional restaurants and many gift shops are in town.

A final note: Stop at Mackinac Island for its ambience, not for service. Gas is available only at the high, rough former coal dock during limited hours, and the marina does not have showers.

Les Chenaux. West of the bridge, the Straits of Mackinac gradually broaden into Lake Michigan, but no adequate shelter is available on this side. Eastward from Mackinac Island, a lovely archipelago lies off the north shore of the Straits. Les Chenaux translates as The Channels, but misunderstanding of the French has rendered it The Snows. True, much snow falls on the islands in winter, but it is the maze of channels among them that is their distinguishing characteristic. There are three entrances to Les Chenaux: West, Middle, and East.

The first entrance lies a dozen miles from Mackinac Island. You'll wind along the main buoyed channel among low, wooded islands and inlets to emerge 18 miles later at the East Entrance.

You can also meander among the side channels, marked by private buoys maintained by the Les Chenaux Islands Association. Controlling draft on the main channel is seven feet, but poking into some of the side channels will give you a clearer view of the double life of the islands. Gracious summer cottages with charming, old-fashioned boat houses on the western reaches, and newer, more modest cottage developments toward the east, are interspersed with uninhabited coves and islands rich with bird life.

You can choose from a number of anchorages, depending upon the draft of your boat. **Marquette Bay** on the west end and **Government Bay** near the east are two favorites. All are easy to enter, requiring only that you watch your depthsounder in conjunction with the chart.

Two towns on the mainland serve Les Chenaux. **Hessel**, at the head of West Entrance, has a Waterways Commission dock and commercial facilities offering repairs and marine supplies. Hessel is a quiet little village, with a good grocery store and a homey restaurant. **Cedarville**, a few miles to the east, offers more shops and Les Chenaux Historical Museum. But the village's only dock is for small boats and expressly prohibits overnight mooring. Caution: The main channels leading to Hessel and Cedarville West and East entrances respectively, are buoyed as if returning from sea to town. Thus, in the middle stretch between them the buoyage may be reversed, depending on the direction of your course. Watch carefully.

After you depart the East Entrance to Les Chenaux there are no protected harbors along the north shore of Lake Huron for another 20 miles or more. By then you are in **St. Marys River**, the link between Lake Huron and Lake Superior.

The Ontario Shore

The Canadian side of Lake Huron is the shore of spectacular sunsets viewed from broad sand beaches. First settled in the 1830s, the rich agricultural land (known then as the Huron Tract) was cleared of its virgin forest. The mouths of the rivers flowing down to the lake became ports, first for shipping the timber, and then for transporting the crops of the farmers and the catch of the fishermen. As elsewhere on the lakes, when the railroads extended westward to the shoreside villages, the commercial importance of these harbors declined. Fishing tugs were usually the only boats to be seen. Their catches, too, were shipped by rail, and later by

LAKE HURON

truck. By the latter part of the 19th century the shores of the Huron Tract were discovered by another group, residents of the growing mid-Ontario cities seeking relief from summer heat who possessed the wealth to build second homes on the shore. Summer colonies sprouted and continue their growth to this day.

Cruising up the Canadian shore of Lake Huron, you can alternate stops between lively summer resorts and quaint working towns for the first 125 miles. Then, beyond **Chantry Island**, the shoreline is transformed, and so are the settlements. Here the even sand bluffs and beaches of the southern two-thirds give way to the irregular, island-studded coast of the **Bruce Peninsula**, the 55-mile long promontory creating Georgian Bay. The rugged, coniferous north country begins, agriculture is left behind, and settlements are smaller and more modest than those farther south. The **Fishing Islands** still yield the livelihood they have for 150 years, though the catch is now greatly reduced. Not for many years has Main Station Island hosted a forest of masts or even a bevy of steam tugs. To cruise up this coast of Lake Huron is like cruising backward in time.

Caution: Charts 2290, 2291 and 2292 are based on surveys dating from the turn of the century and show depths in fathoms. Furthermore, those depths and the heights shown relate to a water level chart datum no longer in use. Subtract one half or one and a half feet from the charted soundings to conform to current usage. Consult the notes on each chart for specific instructions.

When navigating this part of the lake, keep in mind that you are on a lee shore, and watch the weather. Although each harbor has an entrance range, they are small and not readily visible more than five miles offshore. It's best to enter in the afternoon with the sun behind you, or at least somewhat below its zenith. In heavy weather the only harbor on this lee shore that should be attempted by a stranger is **Goderich**. The most conspicuous hazard is **Kettle Point** and its reef, extending some two miles. It is an easy point to guide you, however, as the St. Clair River drops astern and the graceful arch of the Blue Water Bridge hangs on the horizon for many miles.

Port Franks. The first harbor north of Sarnia, Port Franks is suitable only for very shallow-draft boats. The harbor has no breakwater and can shoal to three feet. A sandbank close to the channel entrance shoals to as little as one foot. If you can get inside, you'll find dockage, a quiet village to explore, and the **Au Sable River**, which is navigable by dinghy for several miles.

Grand Bend is a pleasant 20 miles from the Blue Water Bridge, where the coast bends sharply northward. Vivid orange paint on the ends of the piers protecting the dredged river channel augments range in bringing you in. Fuel, ice, and pump-out are available on the pier. But for overnight dockage, proceed about a half mile upriver to the long town dock on the north side (the yacht club is opposite on the southern bank). Depths of six feet are available alongside, with dockside electricity, and heads and showers just beyond the top of the stairs leading up the bluff from the dock. The river carries nine feet to the highway bridge, and if you can get under its 20-foot clearance, a full-service marina lies just beyond.

Grand Bend may drowse in winter with a population of 780, but in summer it comes alive as ten times that number are attracted to its broad, soft beach. The town is then transformed into a lively entertainment center with a roller rink, miniature golf course, children's rides, tennis, as well as shops, restaurants, and evening entertainment, all very near the dock. Yet the steep river bluff, on which the main street is perched, shields the dock from traffic and helps maintain the quiet of the setting. Grand Bend also offers one of the infrequent opportunities on Lake Huron to attend summer theater. True to the spirit of summer stock, the Huron County Playhouse, where a professional group performs nightly, is in a converted barn two miles from the village.

Bayfield, the second oldest settlement on the lakeshore, discovered in 1830, was popularized by prosperous summer cottagers early in this century. Within the past few years it has been discovered by the wandering tourists who crowd its historic inns and good restaurants, gift and antique shops. Most recently Bayfield has become one of the best-equipped yacht harbors on the lake. The marina on the river features a restaurant and other resort amenities. Although all the dockage is new and well built, the finger piers are very short, so you'll have to back in or get on and off from the bow.

The town of Bayfield was built on the bluff, rather than on the river that bears its name. It is a pleasant walk of about one mile up the hill and over the highway bridge, through charming residential streets to the shopping area. If you're out for an evening stroll, go across the bridge and follow the road to your right all the way to the lakefront park and its spectacular view of the setting sun.

Goderich. Twelve miles beyond Bayfield, Goderich is the largest town on Huron's Canadian coast. It is also the oldest, founded in 1827 by one of Ontario's most colorful characters, Dr. William "Tiger" Dunlop, known for his escapades as a British Army surgeon in India.

Goderich never became the major port its founder envisioned, but the discovery of rich salt deposits in 1866 gave the town an important industry that flourishes to this day. In fact, the Sifto Salt Mine is the first thing you see upon entering the harbor. The mine penetrates 1,760 feet underground and far beneath Lake Huron, producing 50 percent of all the rock salt mined in Canada. What is most clearly visible from offshore, however, is the big grain elevator that stands at the head of the harbor.

Inside the northern breakwater, snuggled under the mine buildings, is the municipal marina, known appropriately as Snug Harbor. The mine's salt (which inevitably sifts onto nearby boats), the grain elevator, and the retired lake freighters placed there for grain storage may make Goderich sound like an unappealing industrial harbor. But the lovely municipal beach, just on the other side of the southern breakwater and crowded with riotous children, dispels that impression.

Despite the breakwaters, a strong west wind creates a surge in the harbor. A buoyed channel, leading off to port from the main channel just before the salt mine, carries eight feet as it follows the outside of a long spit of land up the **Maitland River** for about a mile to a marina where hardly a ripple from the big lake is felt at the dock. Goderich is the last port on this side of Lake Huron where big-boat haulout and major repairs are available. It's 174 miles up and around the Bruce Peninsula to the next such repair yard, at Wiarton, Ontario, in Georgian Bay.

Neither marina is very close to downtown Goderich, but taxis are available. The unusual town square was the architectural creation of Tiger Dunlop and his literary friend and associate John Galt. The town "square" is actually an octagon centered by the county courthouse amid spacious lawns and venerable trees. Eight streets radiate to form the downtown shopping and restaurant district. Goderich's sights include the enormous collection of the Huron County Pioneer Museum and the Huron Historic Jail.

Kincardine. Once a furniture town, Kincardine is today more closely associated with the Bruce Nuclear Power Development—one of the world's largest—a few miles north of town. The quiet old-fashioned ambience of the town remains, however, and the small harbor is one of the most picturesque on this coast. In the lighthouse on the side of the **Penetaugore River** bluff at the inner end of the harbor is a marine museum operated by the Kincardine Yacht Club, which also operates the marina.

The main street of town, with a choice of restaurants and a Laundromat, is only a couple of short blocks from the waterfront. For recreation, Kincardine offers tennis courts, a bowling alley, a movie theatre, and a lovely beach. On Saturday evenings, Kincardine's Scottish Pipe Band parades down Main Street to perform in the Victoria Park Bandshell right behind the marina.

Port Elgin, twenty-two miles north of Kincardine, is a different sort of place. It is definitely a resort town, for both cottage and hotel visitors. The business district sits a considerable distance back from the harbor, so it's not handy for shopping, but the waterfront offers a number of attractions. Clustered around the municipal marina and the large beach are snack bars, restaurants, a cocktail lounge, tennis courts, a playground, a miniature golf course, and amusement park rides. Port Elgin is not very scenic; but it's a good stop for active recreation, and the dockage is good.

Only five miles farther north, **Southampton** marks the outlet of the **Saugeen River**. Southampton was originally a fishing town, then a lumbering and furniture manufacturing center. Today it is a nice blend of market center and resort. Its special attraction is the well-executed **Bruce County Historical Museum**, featuring an 1851 log house and an 1873 log school.

Unfortunately, Southampton's yachting amenities don't match the harbors farther south. They consist mainly of concrete government wharves along the river bank, with nine-foot depths alongside and washrooms in the little park adjacent. For boats that can get under the 29-foot fixed bridge, a marina just beyond offers the usual services.

On the approach to Southampton you pass **Chantry Island**, a federal bird sanctuary. It is fringed with boulders, however, and can be closely approached only by shallow-draft boats. You must round it and leave it to starboard when approaching Chantry Island from the south or west, as the passage between the island and the mainland is foul.

Bruce Peninsula

Southampton, on a straight line with Owen Sound 25 miles to the east, anchors the base of the **Bruce Peninsula**. This remarkable triangle of land, which narrows to six miles across at its tip 60 miles north of Southampton, presents two completely different faces to the boats cruising its shores. On the Lake Huron side, the land slopes gradually from its limestone spine, meandering seaward in a maze of islands and small peninsulas as if uncertain where land ends and water begins. **Sauble Beach**, 12 miles beyond Southampton, is the last out-

---

Town of Port Elgin
on Lake Huron

100 berths on wall & floating docks
• electrical outlets, fresh water •
washrooms & showers • pump-out
• gas and diesel fuel • airfield •
beach attractions • shopping center • taxis
• welcome to home fleet activities

TOWN OF PORT ELGIN
P.O. Box 550 Port Elgin, Ontario N0H 2C0
Tel: (519) 832-2008
Chamber of Commerce (519) 832-9101

Lake Huron

post of the luxurious Lake Huron strand. It has no harbor, although a treacherously shifting channel into the Sauble River does lead to a couple of small-boat marinas. You could launch a very shallow-draft boat here for an excursion on a very good day.

The Fishing Islands. The islands' incredible bounty was first revealed in 1831 to Alexander McGregor of Goderich, who was astonished to see the herring and whitefish schools so thick that their bodies were lifted out of the water. He quickly established his fishing enterprise here to supply the growing city of Detroit and erected the first building on the Bruce Peninsula on Main Station Island.

Fishing tugs still cast their nets in the intricate network of channels, coves, and reefs among the islands, but these days sportfishermen are more numerous, putting out their small boats from resorts on the mainland. One or two of these harbors are approachable by visiting boats on a calm day with the sun high overhead or declining in the west. Others require local knowledge to thread the reefs. You will find no soft sand here, and a grounded keel hits solid rock.

The offshore run. The direct offshore run north up the coast from Port Elgin or Southampton to Cape Hurd is a clear passage of 55 miles. Once at the cape, cruising skippers have a choice of channels into Georgian Bay. Use modern Chart 2274, with soundings in feet, for navigation. If visibility is good and seas calm, **Cape Hurd Channel** is the most direct route and is adequately buoyed. In rough weather **Devil Island Channel**, although a greater distance to travel, offers a range to guide you. The next two channels north, **McGregor** and **North Channel**, are not buoyed. The main ship channel lies considerably farther out of the way, passing around the north end of **Cove Island**, the largest in the passage, where the major lighthouse stands.

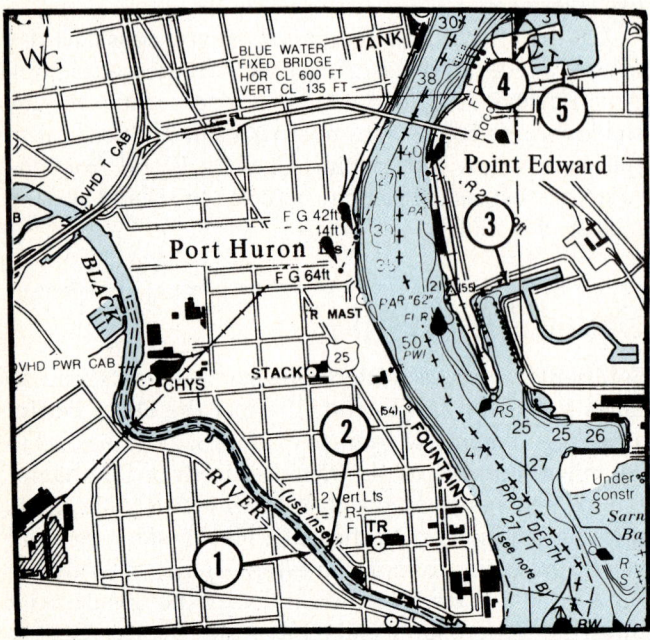

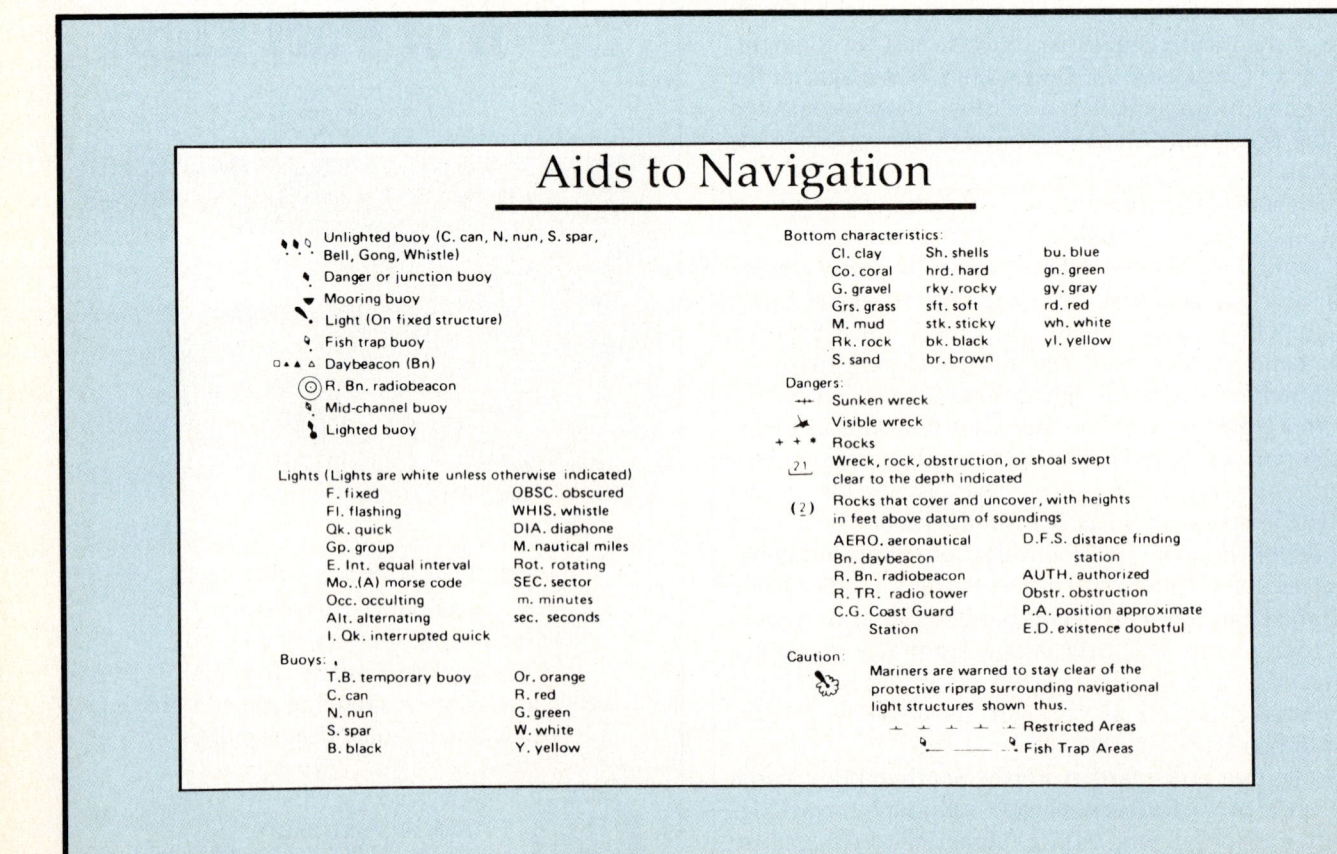

Chart 14852, edition 34

Aids to Navigation

Unlighted buoy (C. can, N. nun, S. spar, Bell, Gong, Whistle)
Danger or junction buoy
Mooring buoy
Light (On fixed structure)
Fish trap buoy
Daybeacon (Bn)
R. Bn. radiobeacon
Mid-channel buoy
Lighted buoy

Lights (Lights are white unless otherwise indicated)
- F. fixed
- Fl. flashing
- Qk. quick
- Gp. group
- E. Int. equal interval
- Mo. (A) morse code
- Occ. occulting
- Alt. alternating
- I. Qk. interrupted quick
- OBSC. obscured
- WHIS. whistle
- DIA. diaphone
- M. nautical miles
- Rot. rotating
- SEC. sector
- m. minutes
- sec. seconds

Buoys:
- T.B. temporary buoy
- C. can
- N. nun
- S. spar
- B. black
- Or. orange
- R. red
- G. green
- W. white
- Y. yellow

Bottom characteristics:
- Cl. clay
- Co. coral
- G. gravel
- Grs. grass
- M. mud
- Rk. rock
- S. sand
- Sh. shells
- hrd. hard
- rky. rocky
- sft. soft
- stk. sticky
- bk. black
- br. brown
- bu. blue
- gn. green
- gy. gray
- rd. red
- wh. white
- yl. yellow

Dangers:
- Sunken wreck
- Visible wreck
- Rocks
- Wreck, rock, obstruction, or shoal swept clear to the depth indicated
- Rocks that cover and uncover, with heights in feet above datum of soundings

- AERO. aeronautical
- Bn. daybeacon
- R. Bn. radiobeacon
- R. TR. radio tower
- C.G. Coast Guard Station
- D.F.S. distance finding station
- AUTH. authorized
- Obstr. obstruction
- P.A. position approximate
- E.D. existence doubtful

Caution: Mariners are warned to stay clear of the protective riprap surrounding navigational light structures shown thus.

Restricted Areas
Fish Trap Areas

LAKE HURON

All the channels around Cape Hurd are separated by treacherous unmarked reefs, and you should not try to cross from one channel to another. Furthermore, currents up to five or six knots can run through all these channels, especially after a strong wind shift.

But this description may sound more intimidating than it should. Entrance into Georgian Bay is not difficult, and the high, wooded islands that guard the tip of the Bruce Peninsula foretell the splendor that lies beyond.

Lake Huron

		SEASONAL / YEAR-ROUND	SAIL / POWER / BOTH▲	LARGEST VESSEL ACCOMMODATED	NO. OF TRANSIENT BERTHS	MARKED ENTRY CHANNEL	APPROACH DEPTH (Reported)	DOCKSIDE DEPTH (Reported)	RAILWAY / LIFT CAPACITY (in tons)	GAS★ DIESEL● BOTH▲ FUEL BRAND	ENGINE REPAIRS: Gas ★ Diesel ● Both ▲	PROPELLER / HULL REPAIRS	LAUNCHING RAMP	MARINE SUPPLIES / GROCERIES / ICE	LPG ★ CNG● BOTH▲	110V ★ 220V ● BOTH ▲ MAX AMPS	SHOWERS / LAUNDROMAT	PUMP-OUT STATION	RESTAURANT / SNACK BAR	RADIO WATCH—VHF (CB)
PORT HURON / SARNIA																				
1. Mike's Marine Supply*	(313) 987-1420	Y	▲	55			8	8				MARINE SUPPLIES				★30				
2. Port Huron River Street Marina	982-0200	S	▲	65	70	●	10	7		MOB	▲			GI		★30	S	●		16
3. Bridgeview Marina*	(519) 337-3888	Y	▲	60	100	●	15	10		SHE	▲	L	R	▲	PH	MGI	▲50	SL	●	R
4. Sarnia Yacht Club	337-7175	S	▲	45		●	6	6		ESS				MGI		★30	SL	●	R	
5. Lake Huron Yachts, Ltd*	344-0772	S	S	60	10	●	10	10		ESS		L		▲	PH	▲	MGI	★30	S	●	S	16
MICHIGAN SHORE																				
6. Lexington Harbor	(313) 359-5600	S	▲	60	30					STA	▲	HARBOR OF REFUGE		★30		●	R	16
7. Port Sanilac Marina	622-9651	Y	▲	40		●	11	5		AMO	★		▲	P		MGI	●	S		RS	16/68
8. Port Sanilac Harbor	622-8818	S	▲	100	38	●	12	6		SHE	▲	HARBOR OF REFUGE	G	★30	SL		RS	16
9. Port Austin Harbor*	(517) 738-8712	S	▲	45	36	●	7	7		BOR	★	HARBOR OF REFUGE	★		S		RS	16
10. Hoy's Saginaw Bay Marina	856-4475	Y	▲	34	10	●	8	6		MOB	★	40	R	★	P	▲	MGI		S		RS	16
11. Caseville State Dock	856-4590	S	▲								★	HARBOR OF REFUGE	★		S	●		16
12. Sunset Shores Yacht Club	686-2900	S	▲	50	10	●	8	9				R				I	★30	SL	●		16
13. Brennan Marine	894-4181	S	▲	65	20	●	15	10		MAR	▲	50		▲	P	●	MI	★30	S	●	R	16
14. Hoyles Marina	697-4415	Y	▲	48	10	●	5	8			▲	15	R	▲	P		MGI	★30	S	●	R	
15. Au Gres Yacht Club	876-8155	S	▲	50	25	●	6	6		76	▲		R	▲	P		MI	★30	S	●		16
16. Au Gres Harbor	876-8729	S	▲	75	28	●	5	6		STA	★	HARBOR OF REFUGE	★		S		RS	16
17. Inland Marine	876-7185	Y	P	36								R	★			M			RS	
18. Northport Marina	876-8929	S	▲	36		●	4	5		76	★		R				MI	★30		●		(11)
19. East Tawas Harbor*	362-2731		▲	45	68		15	15		MOB	▲	HARBOR OF REFUGE	★		S	●		16
20. Jerry's Marina, Inc.	362-3939	S	▲	40	8	●	4	5		MOB	▲		R	★			MGI	★30	S			
21. North East Michigan Marine	739-4411	S	P	45	5	●	5	5		SUN	▲	18		▲	P		MI	▲	S		RS	16
22. Fellow's Marine	739-2525	S	P	60	20	●	6	6		AMO	▲			★	P		MI	●	S		RS	16
23. Harrisville City Dock*	724-5242	S	▲	50	65	●	12	5		MAR	▲		R	▲			GI	★30	S	●	RS	16
24. Partridge Point Marina	354-3535	S	▲	60	20	●	8	12		MAR	▲	50	R	▲	PH		I	★50		●	RS	16
25. Arnold's Marina*	No Listing	S	▲	70	25	●	9	9		AMO	▲	L	R	▲	PH	▲	MGI	▲	SL	●	RS	16
26. Rogers City Small Boat Harbor	734-3808	S	▲	60	50	●	9	8		AMO	▲		R				GI	★30	S	●		16
27. Hammond Bay Harbor*	938-9291		▲	60	12		9	5			★	HARBOR OF REFUGE	★		S	●		16
CHEBOYGAN																				
28. Bridge Marina	(616) 627-7878	S	▲	60	12	●	12	12			▲				P		MGI	★60	S	●	RS	16
29. Walstrom Marine	627-7105	Y	▲	80	12	●	25	15				70		▲	P		M	▲50	S	●	RS	16/9
30. Rivertown Marina and City Dock	627-6831	S	▲	100	40	●	10	8			L						G	★30	S	●	RS	16
INLAND WATERWAY																				
31. Anchor In Marina	627-4620	Y	▲	50	12		12	12		AMO	★	30		★	P		M	★30	SL	●	S	16
32. Indian River Marina	238-9373	Y	▲	42	20		5	5		AMO	▲	20	R	★	P		MI	★		S	●	R	
33. Windjammer	347-3918	S	P	33		●	3	3		STA	★		L	R	★	H		MI	★	S		(19)
STRAITS OF MACKINAC																				
34. Shepler's Marine Service	436-5025	Y	▲	120	25	●	12	10			▲	15	R	▲	P		M			●	RS	
35. Mackinaw City Harbor*	436-5269	S	▲	92	78	●	14	14		AMO	▲	L	▲	PH	★	MGI	▲30	SL	●	R	16
36. St. Ignace State Dock*	(906) 643-8131	S	▲	60	14			8		STA	★		HARBOR OF REFUGE	★		S			16
37. Mackinac State Dock*	847-3561	S	▲	60				8			★		HARBOR OF REFUGE	★30		S	●		16
38. Hessel Marina	484-2672	S	▲	70			14	12		AMO	★	L	▲	PH	★	MGI	★		S	●	R	16
39. E.J. Mertaugh Boat Works	484-2434	Y	▲	42	4	●	12	9		AMO	★	L	▲	PH		MGI	★30			R	
ONTARIO SHORE																				
40. Grand Bend Government Wharf	No Listing	S	▲	70	300	●	10	6									★30	S		RS	
41. Harbor Lights Marina	(519) 565-2149	S	▲	60	90	●	12	8		ESS	▲	L	R	▲	PH	★	MGI	★30	SL	●	RS	16
42. Maitland Valley Marina*	524-4409	S	▲	80	70	●	10	12		ESS	▲	L	R	▲	PH		I	★30	S	●	S	68
43. Snug Harbor Municipal Marina	524-6878	S	▲	100	20	●	28	24		ESS	▲		R	▲	H		MGI	▲	S	●	S	(9)
44. Kincardine Government Dock*	396-4336		▲					8			★						MGI	★			RS	
45. Port Elgin Marina (p. 185)	832-2008	S	▲	100	100	●	12	15		ESS	▲		R	▲	PH	★	MGI	★15	SL	●	RS	68

To provide the most complete and accurate information, **all facilities have been contacted within the past year.** If an asterisk (*) appears, it indicates a facility which did not respond to our requests for information (these listings may not reflect current conditions). Although facility operators supplied this data, we cannot guarantee accuracy and assume responsibility for errors. Entrance and dockside soundings tend to fluctuate. Always approach marinas carefully. Reference numbers on spotting charts indicate marina locations. ⌁ Member American Boat Builders & Repairers Association.

GREAT LAKES EDITION

LAKE HURON

Chart 14862, edition 24

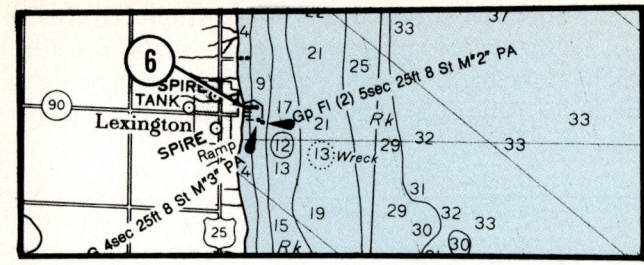

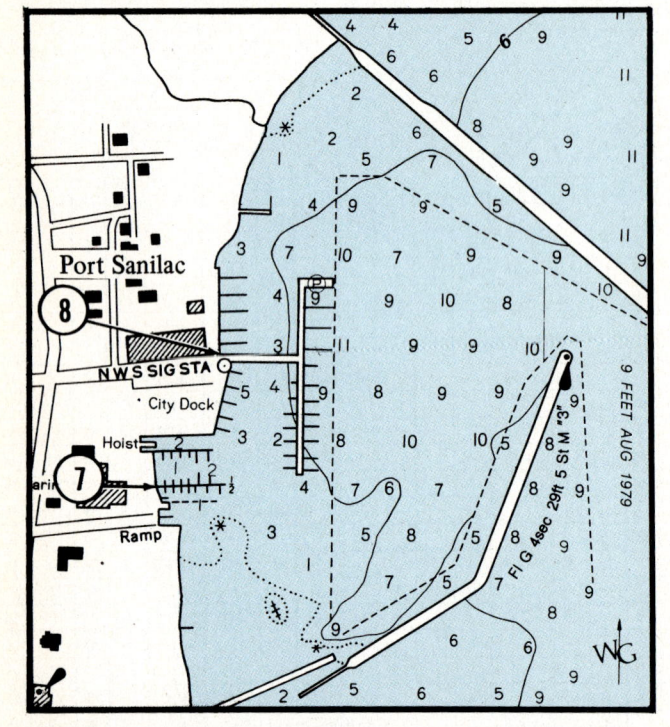

Chart 14862, edition 24

Chart 14863, edition 24

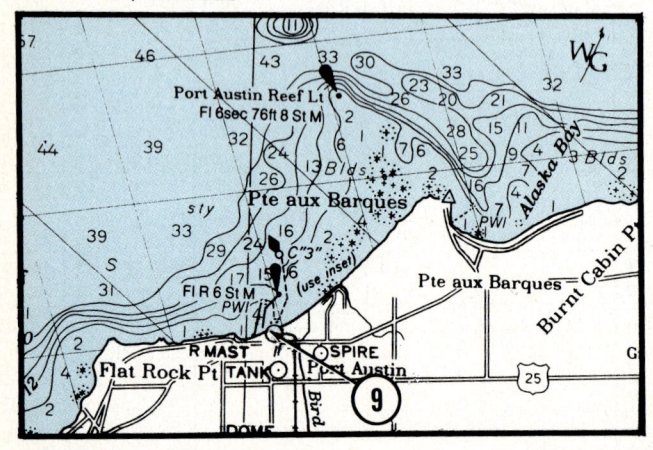

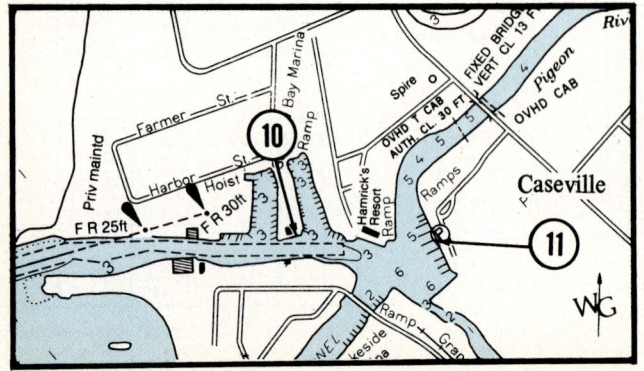

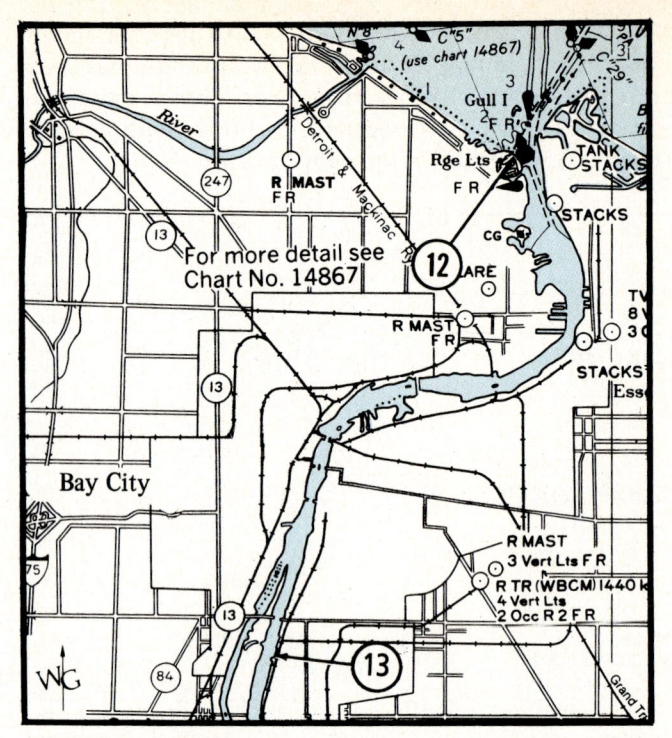

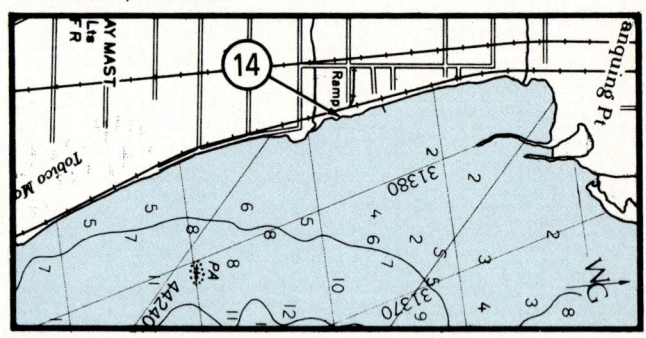

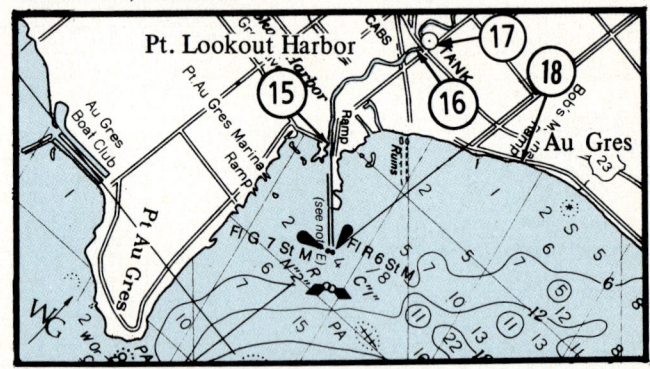

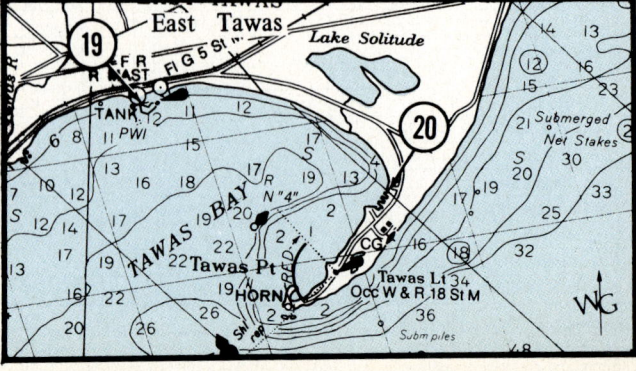

Chart 14863, edition 24

Chart 14863, edition 24

Chart 14863, edition 24

Chart 14863, edition 24

Chart 14863, edition 24

188   *Under no circumstances are these charts to be used for navigation.*   WATERWAY GUIDE / 1991

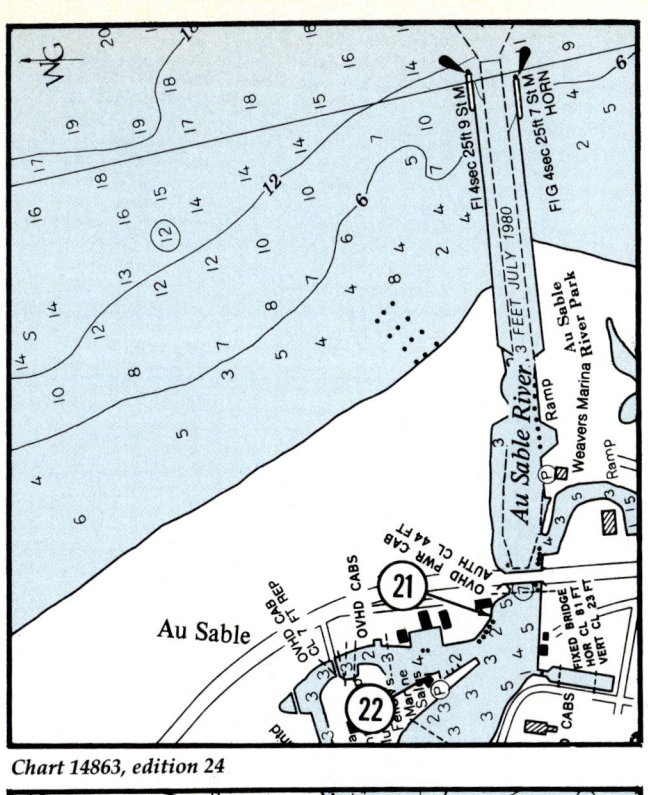

LAKE HURON

Chart 14863, edition 24

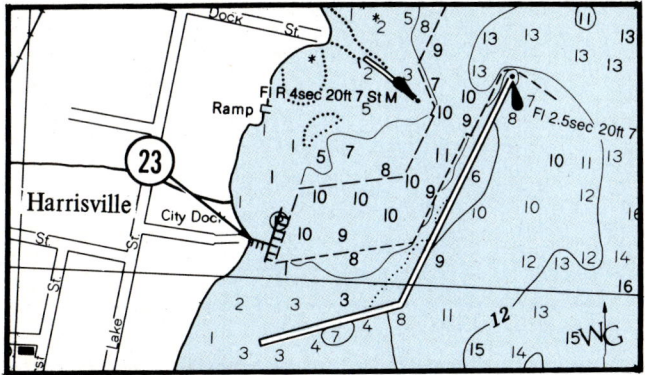

Chart 14864, edition 22

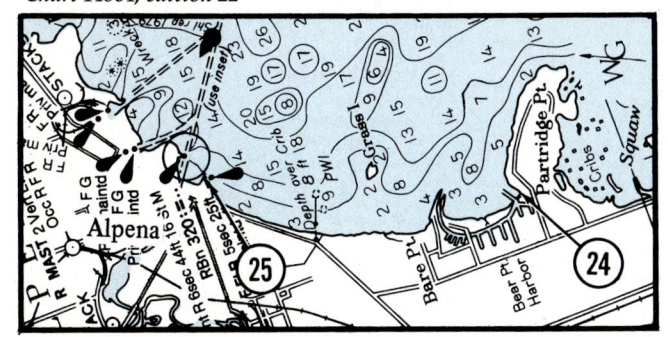

Chart 14864, edition 22

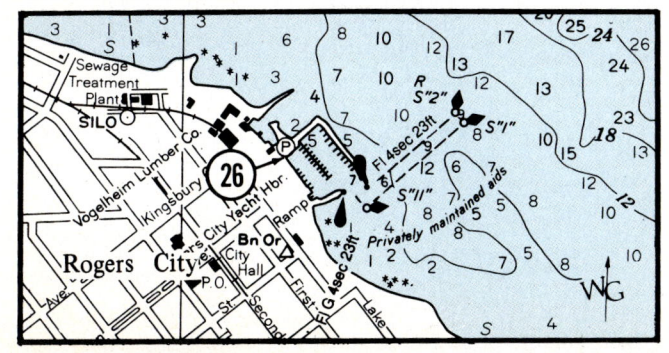

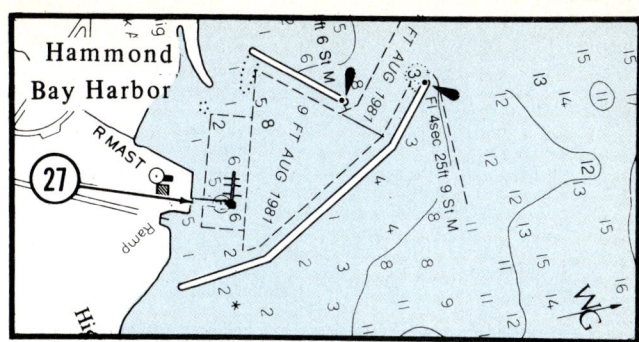

Chart 14864, edition 22

Chart 14881, edition 24

Chart 14886-SC, edition 7

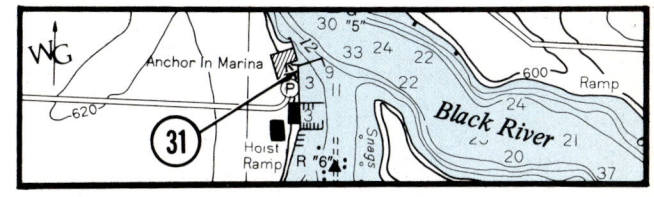

Chart 14886-SC, edition 7

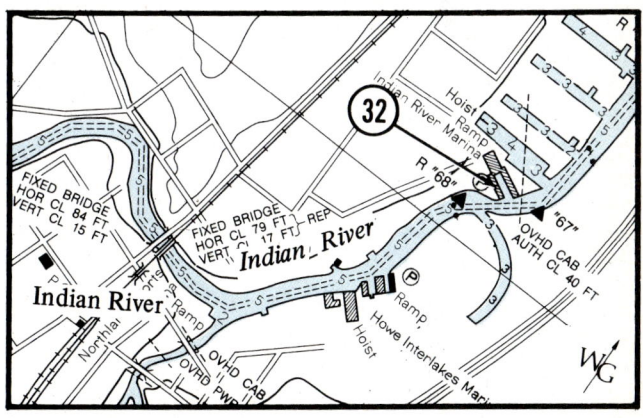

Chart 14886-SC, edition 7

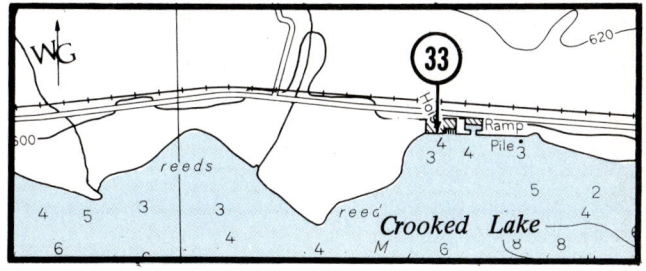

Chart 14886-SC, edition 7

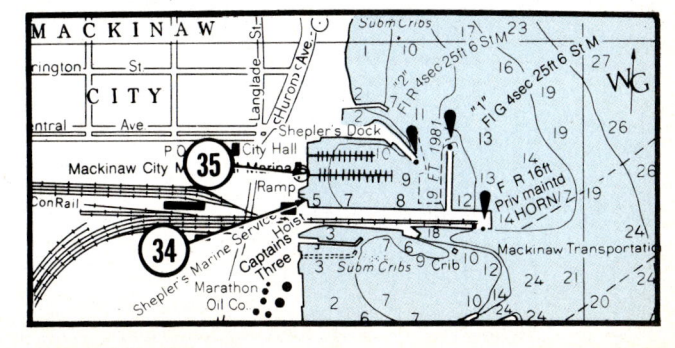

Chart 14881, edition 24

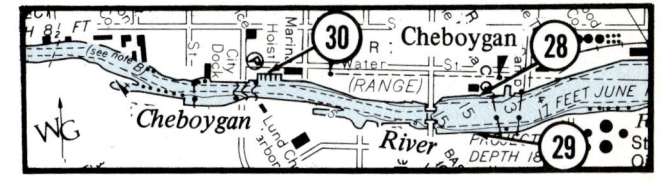

GREAT LAKES EDITION *Under no circumstances are these charts to be used for navigation.* 189

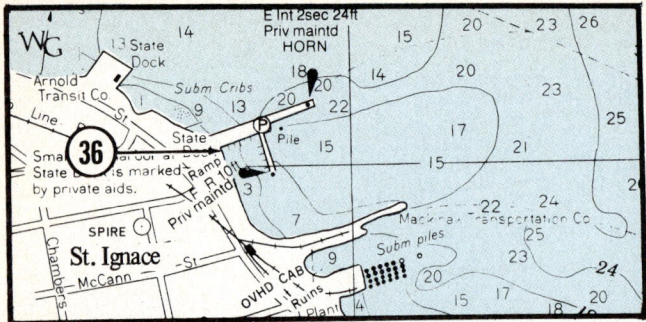

LAKE HURON

Chart 14881, edition 24

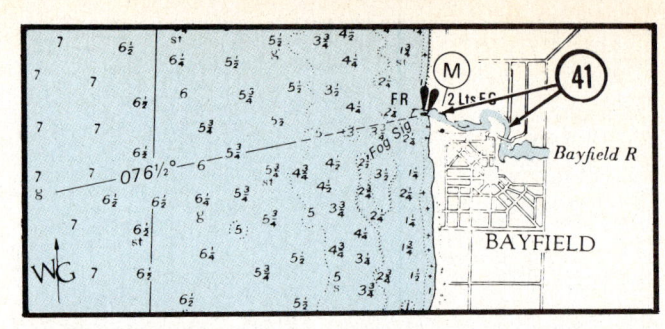

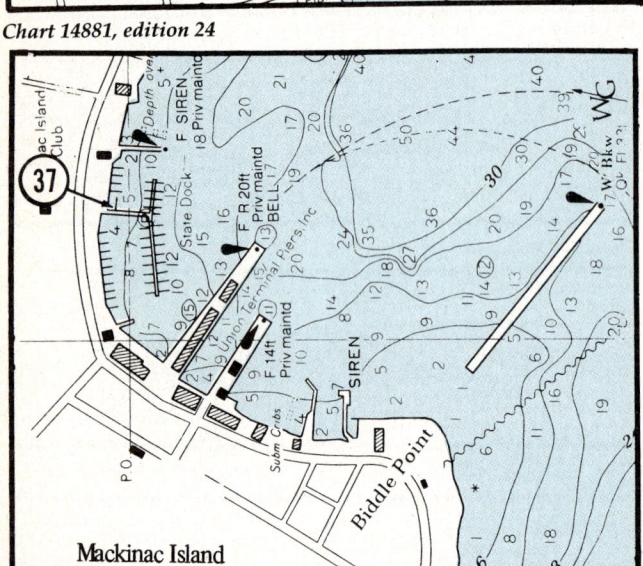

Chart 14881, edition 24

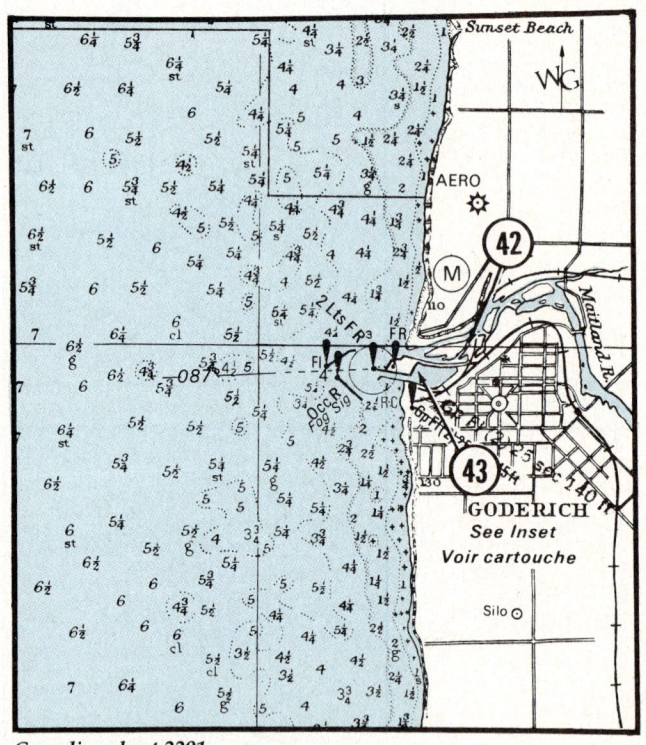

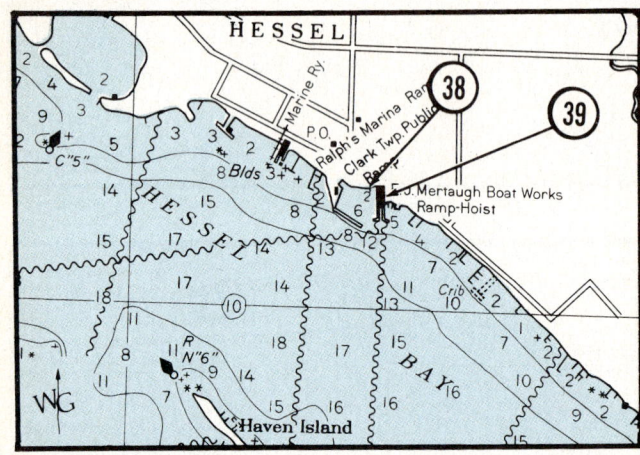

Chart 14885, edition 16

Canadian chart 2290

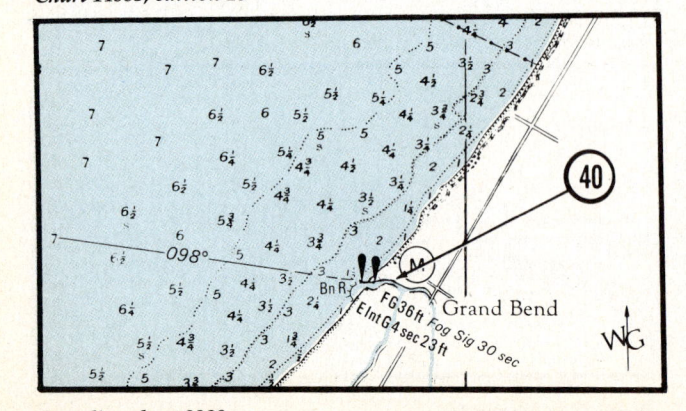

Canadian chart 2290

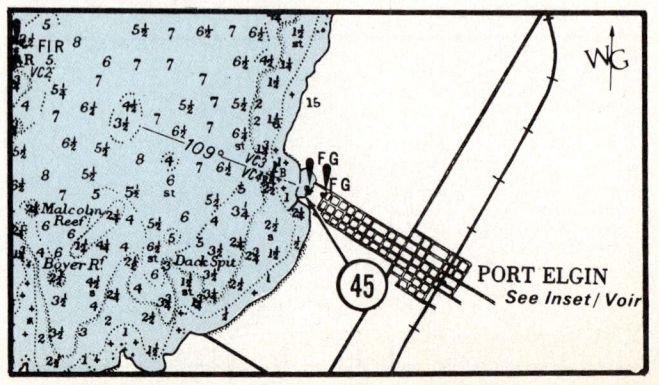

Canadian chart 2291

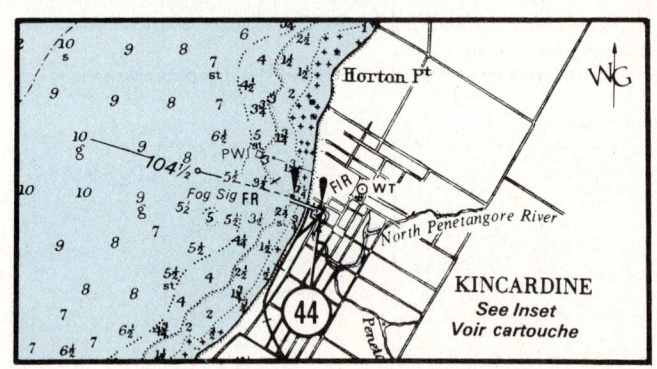

Canadian chart 2291

Canadian chart 2291

190 Under no circumstances are these charts to be used for navigation. WATERWAY GUIDE / 1991

Lake Michigan/Eastern Shore

CHARTS: 14880, 14881, 14900, 14901, 14902, 14905, 14906, 14907, 14911, 14912, 14913, 14926-SC, 14930, 14932, 14934, 14933, 14935, 14937, 14938, 14939, 14942.

Lake Michigan, 320 miles long by 50 to 80 miles wide, offers an unusually broad range of possibilities to the cruising mariner. You can make cross-lake, open-water passages which will test all of your navigational skills, or if you want relatively calm, relaxed cruising, you can harbor-hop your way to various ports along the shore. If you want the classic cruising adventure of discovering remote anchorages in isolated harbors, cruise the far north shore of the lake (the southern shore of Michigan's Upper Peninsula). If you want the company of fellow mariners, discover the popular harbors on the eastern shore.

You can take an urban cruise; the southern end of the lake gives you an impressive glimpse of what was once known as the "heartland of industrial America;" Chicago and Milwaukee offer all the attractions of sophisticated cities.

If you're a fisherman, you'll find the deep lake teeming with potential catch. Thousands of mariners trailer their craft to a handy ramp, spend the day zipping from one hot spot to another while enjoying the sun and air, and return with a fine catch.

Cruising Conditions

In summer, prevailing winds are westerlies, and thunderstorms leap up quickly, so keep a careful weather watch. The lake can build up a steep, uncomfortable chop in what seems like no time.

The **eastern shore** of Lake Michigan (entirely in Michigan except for one corner in Indiana) is lined with sandy beaches studded with high dunes. Many lakes behind the dunes have had outlets dredged though to Lake Michigan, creating fine, safe harbors. Entering during a westerly requires careful boat handling, since waves can break across the entrance channel.

The westerly winds have given a different cast to the **western shore** of the lake, bordered by Illinois and Wisconsin. Here the sand has been removed, leaving a rocky shoreline with few harbors, many of which are artificial. If the wind blows from the northeast-southeast quadrant, these harbors are subject to surge, as waves swarm up through the entrance channels.

Lake Michigan, like the other Great Lakes, is full of commercial traffic. You must keep a lookout for these floating monsters whenever you're near the shipping lanes. Post a radar reflector so that a big ship's radar might pick up your comparatively tiny craft.

Beaver Island to Frankfort. By common understanding, Lake Michigan begins at the Mackinac Bridge. There is no harbor in the Straits of Mackinac west of the bridge, however. Beaver Island, forty miles from the bridge, is the closest destination.

Beaver Island. The largest island in Lake Michigan, this summer resort is known as "America's Emerald Isle." It welcomes daily ferry boats loaded with tourists who come to hike the trails or rent bikes to see the island. The countryside is wooded, grassy, and dotted with farms and abandoned buildings. Newer homes line some shore areas.

The center of the town of St. James is a dusty road lined with flat-topped storefronts dating from the 1800s. Nearby, a well-operated, town-owned marina has good docks which are well-protected but open to strong southeasterly winds. Anchoring in the northern end of the harbor, however, provides excellent protection from all directions.

The island's unusual history is revealed in the museum next door to the old Mormon jail. In the mid-1800s James Strang founded a Mormon settlement here and crowned himself king. His reign was short-lived, however. He was assassinated by his followers, and Beaver Island was left to the Irish who settled and remained. Visitors will also find a toy museum and a marine museum across the street.

Fishing is good here. The whitefish are plentiful in the waters off the island's sandy shores. You can even

Distances
Statute miles (approximate)

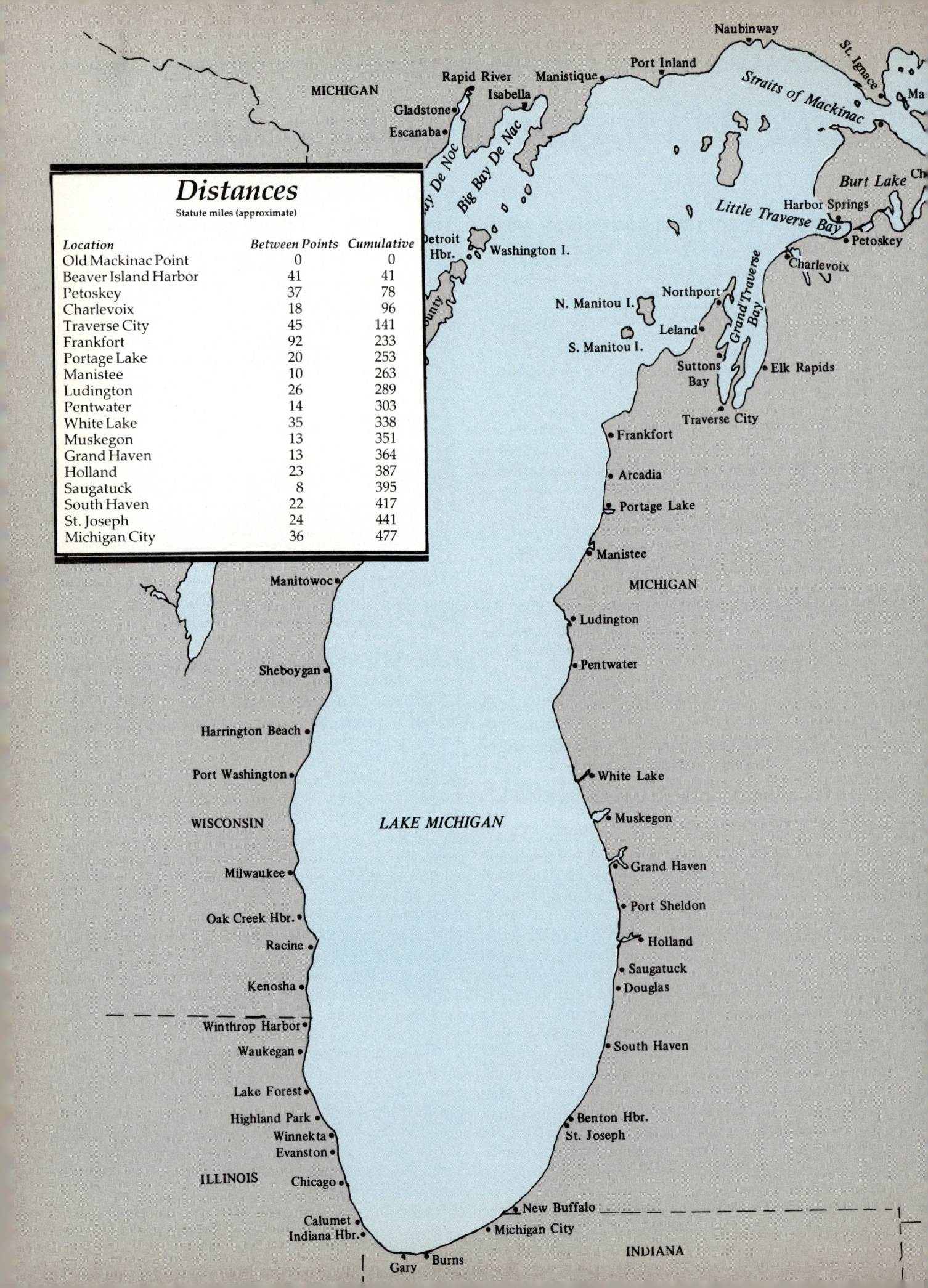

Location	Between Points	Cumulative
Old Mackinac Point	0	0
Beaver Island Harbor	41	41
Petoskey	37	78
Charlevoix	18	96
Traverse City	45	141
Frankfort	92	233
Portage Lake	20	253
Manistee	10	263
Ludington	26	289
Pentwater	14	303
White Lake	35	338
Muskegon	13	351
Grand Haven	13	364
Holland	23	387
Saugatuck	8	395
South Haven	22	417
St. Joseph	24	441
Michigan City	36	477

go to one of the Indian fishermen's net sheds on the beach to buy fresh fish. These Indians have tribal rights and the exclusive franchise to commercial fishing in these waters. Fresh produce from local farmers is also available, as are homemade baked goods and jellies.

Several campgrounds, motels, and restaurants are located on the island. The lodge specializes in freshly caught whitefish and homemade cheesecake. A local pub has been the gathering place for sailors and powerboaters alike for more than 25 years.

Harbor Springs. Southeast of Beaver Island is Little Traverse Bay, with the towns of **Harbor Springs**, on the north shore, and **Petoskey**, on the south. These charming harbor towns welcome visitors with excellent accommodations, shopping, dining, and sandy swimming beaches.

Harbor Springs is 38 miles from Beaver Island. The direct course takes you across shipping lanes leading to Grays Reef Light. Steer a course south of the Dahlia Shoal green can. As you near the town you'll see a line of impressive homes along the peninsula that creates the large, deep, natural harbor. Then, as you round the point, the picture-postcard town climbs up the bluff, fronted by a harbor filled with moored boats.

At the waterfront there's a municipal marina flanked by two commercial marinas. This is a popular cruising destination, making transient space scarce. The commercial marinas take reservations, but the city dock doesn't, so it's wise to arrive early. Anchorage is available in the harbor, but the water is deep and the shallower spots are taken up by moorings.

Petoskey. Just four miles south across the bay from Harbor Springs, Petoskey has a municipal dock about a half mile from town. A privately maintained buoy marks the shallow waters, but you can be assured of a 12-foot approach. Fuel is available along with showers, pump-out, electricity and propane next door.

An historical museum and a park with a playground are next to the marina, but the heart of town is an uphill walk away. The historic Gaslight District, famous for its art galleries, and specialty shops make the town a pleasant stopover. There are several good restaurants and a movie theater.

Charlevoix/Lake Charlevoix. Cruising southwest from Little Traverse Bay for 20 some miles brings you to Charlevoix. A good landmark is the Medusa Portland Cement plant, west of the harbor entrance.

Entrance is between breakwaters into the **Pine River** which leads into **Round Lake**. The U.S. Highway 31 bridge spans the river; it opens 24 hours a day to one long and one short blast, but from 6:00 a.m. to 6:00 p.m. the bridge will only open on the hour and half hour. In an emergency, blow five blasts. This river can have a considerable current, depending on the wind direction.

Charlevoix is a picturesque harbor town. Boathouses, private docks, and massive old summer homes line the shores of Round Lake. Passing beneath the opened bridge you'll see an excursion boat on the left that cruises on Lake Charlevoix, and to your right you'll see the ferry to Beaver Island. Just beyond is the municipal marina, always busy and usually filled to capacity. Its location is ideal: right in town, with groceries, laundry, and restaurants a short walk up the hill. Fuel is available next door and specialized marine services are around the harbor.

Because docking space is always at a premium in town, many mariners elect to anchor just off the dock, where the depth is considerable and sufficient scope can be a problem. The designated anchorage for the area is on Round Lake's north shore just below the lumber company.

Round Lake channels into Lake Charlevoix, which is 14 miles long with two arms: the northern one is headed by **Boyne City**, 13 miles up; the southern arm reaches 13 miles to **East Jordan**. These are the places to go if the hustle and bustle of Charlevoix are not to your liking. Lake Charlevoix is a fine cruising ground in its own right, with deep water and much less sea than the big lake. Its shoreline is hilly and pastoral.

Entering Lake Charlevoix you'll see a large, full-service marina on the west shore; approach the fuel docks to see if they have room for transients. Getting a slip is more likely if you arrive early in the day.

Oyster Bay, across from the marina and Two Mile Point, is a good anchorage. You'll find good holding in 12-foot depths.

The narrower, southern arm of the lake begins at **Ironton**, where you'll see a cable ferry crossing. Pass over the cable with special care and caution, and don't attempt to pass at all when the ferry is in motion and the cable is close to or above the surface. In East Jordan there are public docks with shops and nearby restaurants.

Boyne City, at the foot of the northern arm of Lake Charlevoix, has municipal docks in a park on the north side and a marina associated with a condominium development on the south. Both are convenient to Boyne City's shops and restaurants. Horton Bay is a popular anchorage not far from Boyne City.

Grand Traverse Bay. Lake Michigan's Grand Trav-

---

bellinger marine service

Sales • Service • Parts • Accessories

Johnson Motors • OMC Stern Drive
20 Ton Algonac Haul Out
Hull and Mechanical repair
AMOCO Gas & Diesel Fuel

In the Harbor
Charlevoix, Michigan 49720
Phone (616) 547-2851

Lake Michigan/Eastern Shore

erse Bay is ten miles wide by 32 miles long, and is divided by a narrow peninsula creating an east and west arm. The scenery varies from rocky, wooded areas to pastoral farmlands and orchards. This is cherry country, and in spring, the display of bloom on the hillsides is spectacular.

Elk Rapids. About two thirds of the way down the East Arm, the village of Elk Rapids at the mouth of Elk River has a Waterways Commission marina close to shops, restaurants, and a movie theater. At the foot of the East Arm you'll find a marina with a beach and restaurant.

Traverse City. At the foot of the West Arm, **Traverse City** is the largest city in the northern Lower Peninsula of Michigan. The public marina is in a waterfront park, complete with a natural history museum, a small zoo, and a beach. Besides being a diversified business center, Traverse City is a rapidly growing resort with all the overnight accommodations, restaurants, and theater that goes with it.

A couple of miles out of town, on the west side of West Arm, lies a commercial marina in an artificial basin shared with a municipal dock for seasonal use only.

Marion Island, about seven miles north of Traverse City off Mission Peninsula, provides a fine anchorage

Cross-Lake Distances and Courses

The table below is a selection of major cruising stops in Lake Michigan and the distances between them. It is not a complete list of ports and is intended solely as a guide to cruise planning. All distances have been figured along the most direct course consistent with safe, normal navigation. *All figures are approximate statute miles.* Actual mileage traveled will depend on variations of course, speed, boat, weather, currents, and other cruising conditions. Courses are given in True degrees.

From	To	Course	Distance	From	To	Course	Distance
Frankfort	Manistee	190	26	White Lake	Milwaukee	252	75
	Big Sable Point	200	40		Racine	237	78
	Sturgeon Bay Canal	281	50		Kenosha	233	86
	Kewaunee	258	63		Waukegan	225	98
	Manitowoc	241	75		Chicago	210	120
	Sheboygan	230	95	Muskegon	Little Sable Light	341	34
	Port Washington	223	116		White Lake	337	12
	Milwaukee	216	130		Grand Haven	158	15
Manistee	Frankfort	010	26		Holland	168	32
	Big Sable Point	216	15		Saugatuck	170	40
	Sturgeon Bay Canal	308	60		South Haven	177	58
	Kewaunee	284	55		Benton Harbor	185	78
	Manitowoc	260	65		Michigan City	195	106
	Sheboygan	242	72		Sturgeon Bay Canal	337	118
	Port Washington	231	94		Kewaunee	327	100
Ludington	Big Sable Light	335	8		Manitowoc	313	90
	Little Sable Light	192	20		Sheboygan	302	76
	Sturgeon Bay Canal	324	70		Port Washington	282	75
	Kewaunee	304	60		Milwaukee	260	75
	Manitowoc	289	58		Kenosha	240	85
	Sheboygan	257	60		Waukegan	231	95
	Port Washington	241	80		Chicago	214	110
	Milwuakee	228	100	Grand Haven	Little Sable Light	338	45
	Racine	218	106		Muskegon	338	15
	Kenosha	216	116		Holland	176	20
	Waukegan	212	128		Saugatuck	176	30
	Chicago	202	150		South Haven	186	46
White Lake	Little Sable Point	340	20		Benton Harbor	190	66
	Muskegon	157	12		Michigan City	200	98
	Grand Haven	157	25		Sturgeon Bay Canal	336	130
	Holland	165	44		Kewaunee	328	115
	Saugatuck	168	50		Manitowoc	316	100
	South Haven	174	68		Sheboygan	304	86
	St. Joseph	182	88		Milwaukee	269	80
	Sturgeon Bay Canal	337	108		Racine	254	76
	Kewaunee	325	90		Kenosha	248	84
	Manitowoc	310	78		Chicago	220	104
	Sheboygan	292	68	Holland	Little Sable Light	344	63

LAKE MICHIGAN/EASTERN SHORE

that is especially popular on weekends. Two buoys, a can off **Tucker Point** and a nun off the north end of Marion Island, mark shoaling to less than two feet. A can marks a shoal off the southwest end of the island; anchorage is best off the eastern shore in **Bowers Harbor**.

Suttons Bay is an indentation of the shoreline about half way up the West Arm. The resort village at the foot of the bay has a public marina in rather shoal water. The marina is in a park with a beach and a playground. Village shops, restaurants, and a movie theater are only a few blocks away. Anchorage is possible just south of the marina.

Northport, fifteen miles farther north, is a more sophisticated resort village with gift, antique, and art shops as well as grocery stores, restaurants, and cocktail lounges. The Waterways Commission marina is set in a park a couple of blocks away from these attractions. When entering the harbor, leave the red nuns and flashing red bell of Northport Point close to starboard to avoid the unmarked shoals north of Bellow Island.

Leland. From Northport it's a 25-mile run around the top of the Leelenew Peninsula to Leland. Approach Leland Township Harbor from the south; a marked breakwater protects the entrance. Once inside there is a spacious marina. Small boats can also anchor in the northwest corner of the harbor.

From	To	Course	Distance	From	To	Course	Distance
Holland	Muskegon	348	32		Port Washington	311	105
	Saugatuck	180	8	South Haven	Milwaukee	298	90
	South Haven	188	26		Racine	278	84
	Benton Harbor	197	50		Kenosha	280	76
	Michigan City	206	80		Waukegan	268	76
	Sturgeon Bay Canal	334	146		Chicago	242	72
	Kewaunee	331	130	Benton Harbor	Little Sable Light	358	106
	Manitowoc	324	114		Muskegon	005	76
	Sheboygan	312	98		South Haven	028	22
	Port Washington	297	92		Holland	017	48
	Milwaukee	282	84		Michigan City	219	34
	Racine	268	76		Sturgeon Bay Canal	348	190
	Kenosha	261	80		Kewaunee	343	170
	Waukegan	251	82		Manitowoc	338	150
	Chicago	228	90		Sheboygan	331	128
Saugatuck	Little Sable Light	345	72		Port Washington	321	112
	Muskegon	350	40		Milwaukee	312	90
	Holland	000	8		Racine	304	74
	South Haven	190	20		Kenosha	296	70
	Benton Harbor	200	80		Waukegan	284	66
	Michigan City	209	75		Chicago	254	56
	Kewaunee	332	140	Michigan City	Little Sable Light	008	136
	Manitowoc	323	120		White Lake	012	116
	Sheboygan	315	106		Muskegon	015	108
	Port Washington	300	96		Grand Haven	020	96
	Milwaukee	286	86		Holland	026	80
	Racine	272	78		Saugatuck	028	75
	Kenosha	266	80		South Haven	034	56
	Waukegan	255	80		Sturgeon Bay Canal	355	210
	Chicago	232	86		Kewaunee	351	188
South Haven	Little Sable Light	350	88		Manitowoc	347	170
	Muskegon	357	56		Sheboygan	344	144
	Holland	009	26		Port Washington	337	122
	Benton Harbor	208	22		Milwaukee	331	98
	Sturgeon Bay Canal	343	172		Racine	328	80
	Kewaunee	337	152		Kenosha	322	72
	Manitowoc	329	136		Waukegan	313	60
	Sheboygan	323	116		Chicago	287	30

LAKE MICHIGAN/EASTERN SHORE

> ## Nautical Terms
>
> **Ekeing.** The shipwright's term for an extra piece of wood joined on to a baulk or beam to lengthen it. The word comes from the same distant root as does "augment," meaning "to enlarge," and gives us the expression "to eke out," meaning "to make something last by stretching it."
>
> From *The Overlook Illustrated Dictionary of Nautical Terms*. Copyright © Graham Blackburn 1981. Reproduced by permission of the Overlook Press, Lewis Hollow Road, Woodstock, NY 12498.

"Fish Town," a national landmark district, is Leland's main attraction. Ancient ice and fish shanties now house an operating fish house and a leather goods store, as well as fudge and specialty shops. Lining the dammed Leland River you'll find fine dining spots and, in town just a block away, a grocery store, a bookstore, and other shops to provide all the supplies you need. The ferry to South Manitou Island leaves from here.

North Manitou Island was once owned by private interests but is now part of the Sleeping Bear National Lakeshore. The island is expected to have public park areas and dockage, or at least a designated anchorage in the near future.

South Manitou Island. The crescent-shaped bay on the east side of this island, 16 miles west of Leland, was for many years a favorite of the lumber schooners seeking shelter along the main track up and down Lake Michigan. Now it's an anchorage for pleasure boats, as long as the wind doesn't blow from northeast through southeast. Then it becomes an uncomfortable lee shore. As you approach, be careful of **Pyramid Point Shoal**; pass north of its green can.

South Manitou Island is part of Sleeping Bear National Lakeshore Park, though some of the island is still privately owned. The water is deep very close in, so you can drop the hook in 30 feet of water and nearly touch the sandy, wooded beach. You won't find docking, fuel, or pump-out facilities here; however, the park service does have a substantial dock where you are permitted to tie up for 15 minutes to pick up or drop off passengers. Go to the island fully equipped; only limited camping supplies are available here. Plan to return with your garbage; Park Service regulations require visitors to take their trash back to the mainland.

You can take a motor tour of the 5,000-acre island or hike it yourself. Points of interest include an 1871 abandoned lighthouse which has been restored and is open to the public for tours and lectures at posted hours, and the wreck of the *Francisco Morazon*, a Liberian freighter which ran aground in 1960. The massive cedar forests here are alone well worth a trip ashore.

Frankfort to Muskegon. The 480-foot high Sleeping Bear Dunes between Leland and Frankfort are a magnificent sight. They dramatically announce the beginning of a long coastline bordered by dunes and soft, sand beaches all the way to Indiana at the foot of Lake Michigan.

Many harbors on this coast are actually lakes which have been opened to Lake Michigan by dredging channels through sandbars. Breakwaters are fixed to keep the channel open and protected. The channels often have two- or three- mile-per-hour currents that can flow in either direction, so care is needed when entering.

Frankfort is the first of these typical harbors. Lake Betsie is one and a half miles long by a half mile wide. On the north Frankfort shore is both a commercial and a municipal marina with shopping close by. Across the lake, in Elberta is another marina and a condominium complex with an occasional slip for transients. The combination of high dunes and soaring winds make Frankfort a national center for hang gliding.

Arcadia, a sleepy little town ten miles south of Frankfort, is a pleasant layover. Approaching from the north you'll see "High Hill," a ridge of sand dunes; approaching from the south you'll spot another high dune and see that the entrance is relatively flat by comparison. Once inside the harbor, turn north into the arm of the **Arcadia River**. Stay in the center of the channel; a bar has built up somewhat on the south side. The Waterways Commission Marina is on your starboard hand and beyond it, at the head of the harbor, is a limited-service marina and a campground. You can anchor across from the city dock in 14 feet. The little village five blocks away has several shops and a diner. Wildflowers line the streets of clapboard houses, and a park with tennis courts is nearby.

Portage Lake. Cruising south along the lake you'll see heavily wooded terrain interspersed with white sandy beaches. Portage Lake, lined with summer cottages and boathouses, measures about three and a half miles long by a mile wide, with depths ranging from 15 to 60 feet. You'll find it ideal for anchoring out, but the area is also popular with waterskiers and fishermen, so choose a spot with them in mind. Watch out for the shoal extending southward from North Point.

Note that as you approach the marina on the south shore, at least 12- to 15-foot depths are available, but your depthsounder may indicate otherwise—depending on the density of the seaweed cover. A courtesy car is sometimes available at the marina to take you to the village of Onekama, where you'll find a swimming beach, a park, tennis courts, and several stores.

Manistee. The harbor channel here is actually the last mile and a half of the Manistee River. It leads past homes and small marinas catering to fishermen in Manistee Lake. The town is on the south bank and has a Waterways Commission Marina convenient to downtown. Two highway bridges with 23-foot clearance and a railway bridge that usually stands open must be cleared for entrance into the lake. The bridge tenders respond to one long and one short blast. At the north end of the lake is a full-service marina. The lake is deep, except in the river delta in the northeast corner, but anchoring is ill-advised, because the bottom is foul.

Manistee is an exceptionally well-preserved town. A portion of the downtown shopping area is on the National Register of Historic Places. You can visit the county historical museum, and an old opera house here is still used as a theater. It's just 60 miles across the lake from the Sturgeon Bay Ship Canal, if you're planning to go over to the Wisconsin side, and Manistee is served by airlines and bus lines, if you need to change crews.

Ludington. Big Sable Light is 17 miles south of Manistee. It sits on a spit of sandy shoreline that juts out into the lake. The 106-foot light is an important aid to navigation. Its light can be seen 19 miles away.

The town of **Ludington**, with an excellent municipal marina, is about seven miles south of the light on the north shore of **Pere Marquette Lake**. The harbor is only about 55 miles across the lake from Manitowoc and Two Rivers, making it a popular destination for cruisers criss-crossing the lake. The marina is close to downtown shops and restaurants.

A trip aboard the tugboat *Annie*, moored nearby, makes an interesting day excursion. You might be able to board *Annie* to cross the lake and catch a bus to travel to **White Pine Village**, a historic settlement with buildings dating back to the 1840s. The village blacksmith shop, fire barn, and trapper's cabin are some of what you'll see on the Heritage Tour.

Anchorage can be found near the small yacht club, by the moorings across from it, or in the southwest corner of the lake—all in 15 feet of water.

Pentwater. Fourteen miles from Ludington, Pentwater is a charming lakeshore town on the fringes of the dunes. On the north shore of Pentwater Lake, the village has a yacht club, a Waterways Commission marina, and a couple of commercial marinas. The lake is deep and unobstructed, with the most sheltered anchorage in one of the bays on the south side.

Ashore you'll find all the accoutrements of a lakeside summer resort. Art galleries, macrame shops, and jewelry stores are interspersed with a bakery, meat market, and grocer. There's even a caterer on Hancock Street who specializes in box lunches. If you need to re-provision fruits and vegetables, remember you're in the heart of some of Michigan's finest orchards and farmlands.

Traveling south from Pentwater you'll pass two shipwrecks. The *Anna C. Minch* lies buried about two miles from the south pierhead with 18 feet of water over her. In 1940 a November storm brought her down. Just south of **Little Sable Light**, ten miles from Pentwater, the wreck of *Novadoc* lies in about 20 feet of water marked by a green can buoy.

White Lake. Another pleasant stop, 20 miles south of Little Sable, is **White Lake,** with its twin cities of **Montague** and **Whitehall.** The lake is about two miles across at its widest point and is six miles long.

The White Lake Yacht Club, in the southwestern corner of the lake, is a favorite with many Lake Michigan mariners because of its friendly people and charming old clubhouse. The club has the oldest operating sailing school in the country.

A marina is on the port side in Montague as you move up the lake to the twin towns. Several additional marinas are on the Whitehall side, including a Waterways Commission dock. These are close to shopping, restaurants, and the Howmet Theater.

Muskegon to Michigan City.

Although the natural features of the lakeshore change little from Muskegon to the south, the towns grow bigger and busier and the harbors are more crowded with resident boats. **Muskegon** is a substantial city on the south shore of Muskegon Lake, four miles long, by two miles wide. Just past the channel from Lake Michigan, the south shore suburban village of Lakeside has a yacht club and a couple of marinas. Across the lake, in North Muskegon, is another large marina.

Proceeding toward downtown Muskegon, you'll pass commercial facilities that surround the municipal marina. Spotting this marina may be difficult because the entrance is narrow and at an angle obstructed by a breakwater. Keep a watch out for Hartshorn Light, a red flashing light just south of the marina entrance. You can tour several historic buildings or the first-rate art museum in Muskegon.

Grand Haven/Spring Lake. Grand Haven is just 13 miles south of Muskegon. Here you'll see wide stretches of sandy marshlands, then towering trees lining the shore. The channel into the Grand River is deep and wide, but can be very rough in bad northerly weather. A marina is just inside the harbor entrance on the north side. Farther on, the city marina is located in the heart of downtown Grand Haven. Not only are shops and restaurants handy, but a Harbor Trolley is convenient for a city tour or a ride out to the beach. The historical museum is next door to the marina. From your slip at

---

BARRETT BOAT WORKS INC.
(616) 842-1202

OPEN 7 DAYS
TRANSIENT DOCKAGE $20 PER NIGHT
GAS DOCK * PUMP OUT * POOL * BATH HOUSE
CONVIENCE STORE * COMPLETE MARINE STORE
SERVICING MERCRUISER, OMC,
YAMAHA & VOLVO ENGINES
VISA * MASTERCARD * AMERICAN EXPRESS * MOBIL

Dealers for:
Johnson * Tollycraft Yachts * Zodiac * Regal Boats

821 W. SAVIDGE STREET
"Just through the Spring Lake Bridge"

LAKE MICHIGAN/EASTERN SHORE

the marina or from the nearby grandstand, you can observe Grand Haven's major attraction: A colored water musical fountain and light show that entertains visitors nightly during the summer months.

From Grand Haven you can follow the buoyed river upstream to Spring Lake. The railroad bridge is usually open, and the 25-foot highway bridge opens for three minutes before and after the hour and half hour. To starboard is an elaborate marina with resortlike amenities. If you follow the channel to port, you will find a couple of additional facilities, but a 34-foot fixed bridge prohibits tall-masted boats from entering Spring Lake. This is a suburban, residential area, and there are some nice coves for anchoring in the lake.

Holland/Lake Macatawa. Twenty miles south of Grand Haven is one of the most popular cruising areas in Michigan. **Lake Macatawa** is conveniently located 90 miles from Chicago, and many Windy City mariners cruise over for the weekend to enjoy this lake-within-a-lake.

Two resort towns flank the entrance from Lake Michigan. On the south shore is a full service marina and yacht club. Although no shopping is nearby, restaurants are available. In the village of Ottawa Beach on the north side of Lake Macatawa, you'll find a marina near the state park and beach. Farther up the lake on the north side, Big Bay opens up with two large resort marinas.

At the far end of the five-mile lake, the city of **Holland** has a marina on the south shore and a number of tourist attractions. Holland was settled by the Dutch in the 1840s, and its annual Tulip Festival in May attracts thousands of visitors from around the nation. Windmill Island is a beautiful downtown park that includes an authentic working Dutch windmill, a miniature Dutch village, a carousel, and wooden-shoe dancing performances. Toward the outskirts of town are two wooden-shoe factories and a tulip farm you can visit.

Saugatuck/Douglas. On Kalamazoo Lake and the Kalamazoo River that connects it to Lake Michigan, you'll find one of the most popular boating communities on the lake. Ninety miles across from Chicago and Milwaukee, this is a convenient destination for mariners from those areas. The breakwatered entrance to the river is actually about a mile north of its natural outlet. If you're coming from the south, watch out for old pilings (marked by a buoy) at that outlet.

A hand-cranked chainlink ferry crosses the river from downtown Saugatuck. It's a convenient way to get to the beach from town. Mariners should be sure to wait if the ferry is in motion before continuing up or downstream.

Saugatuck, on the port shore as you move upstream and into the lake, is the larger and busier of the twin villages. It has several marinas and a yacht club. All are convenient to the gift, art, and antique shops, restau-

---

All Seasons Marine, Inc.

IN-OUT RACK SERVICE
SALES, SERVICE, AND STORAGE
MAINTENANCE OF ALL KINDS, DOCKAGE
COMPLETE SHIP'S STORE

- Full Service Marina
- Marathon Premium Gas & Diesel
- Certified Mechanics On Duty
- Rack Storage
- AWL-GRIP Coatings
- Rigging
- Sails & Sail Repair
- Emergency Repairs
- Storage & Dockage
- Complete Ship's Store
- OPEN 7 days a week
- CNG
- Car Rental
- Transient Slips

powered by merCruiser — best selling stern drive in the world
LUND
MERCURY OUTBOARDS
AVON inflatable boats

234 BLACK RIVER ST. • P.O. BOX 431 • SOUTH HAVEN, MI 49090
TELEPHONE (616) 637-3655
FAX: (616) 637-3938

LAKE MICHIGAN/EASTERN SHORE

rants, and night spots. You may also enjoy the historical museum and summer theater.

Douglas, across the lake, is quieter. It also has a couple of marinas, several restaurants, and the museum ship *Keewatin*, a former luxury passenger vessel.

South Haven. Twenty miles from Saugatuck, the village of **South Haven** is on the Black River. On the north bank you'll find a Waterways Commission marina and a commercial establishment. Across the river and closer to downtown is the yacht club. The marine museum is at the bridge (which opens on the hour and half hour). Beyond it is yet another marina.

For a day off the boat, take the sightseeing tour of southwestern Michigan sponsored by the South Haven Chamber of Commerce. The bus tour includes a visit to the Maritime Museum, a local vineyard, Cook Nuclear Center, and Deer Forest.

St. Joseph/Benton Harbor. More industry is visible along the shore as you approach the mouth of the St. Joseph River, 22 miles from South Haven. About half a mile from the entrance is a Waterways Commission marina on the port side. It's convenient to the beach, but not to shopping. The railroad bridge beyond it usually stays open, and the highway bridge opens for three

Lake Michigan / Eastern Shore	Phone	Seasonal/Year-Round	Sail/Power/Both	Largest Vessel Accommodated	No. of Transient Berths	Marked Entry Channel	Approach Depth	Dockside Depth	Railway/Lift Capacity	Gas/Diesel/Both Fuel Brand	Engine Repairs	Propeller/Hull Repairs	Marine Supplies	LPG/CNG/Both	110V/220V/Both Max Amps	Showers/Laundromat/Ice	Restaurant/Snack Bar	Pump-Out Station	Radio Watch VHF (CB)
BEAVER ISLAND TO TRAVERSE CITY																			
1. Beaver Island Marina*	(616) 448-2252	S	▲	35			12	6		★		HARBOR OF REFUGE			★30	S	●		16
2. Walstrom Marine	526-2141	Y	▲	120	20		15	15	PHL	▲	30		▲	P	MI	▲50	S	●	RS	16
3. Harbor Springs Marina	526-5355	S	▲	200	38	●	30	9				R			I	▲50	S	●	RS	16
4. Irish Boat Shop ✓	526-6225	Y	▲	50	24	●	12	10	PHL	▲	25	R	▲	P	●	MI	★30	S	●	RS	16
5. Petoskey Municipal Marina	347-6691	S	▲	60	20	●	10	9	MOB	★		R			GI	★30	S	●	RS	16
6. Charlevoix Marina	547-3272	S	▲	110	39	●	20	12		▲	L	HARBOR OF REFUGE			▲30	S	●		16
7. **Bellinger Marine (p. 193)**	**547-2851**	**Y**	**▲**	**80**	**3**		**20**	**12**	**AMO**	**▲**	**20**		**▲**	**P**	**MI**	**▲50**			**RS**	
8. Fairport Marine Electronics	547-6553	Y	▲	85	4		20	8				MARINE ELECTRONICS			▲50	S	●	RS	16
9. Irish Boat Shop ✓	547-9967	Y	▲	67	15	●	20	10	TOT	▲	35	R	▲		●	MI	★30	S		R	16/71
10. Boyne City Municipal Marine	582-6611	S	▲	60	16	●	6	8				R				★30	S	●	RS	16/9
11. East Jordan Marina	536-2166	S	▲	30	8		20	10								★30	S	●		
12. Elk Rapids Harbor*	264-9920		▲							★		R	HARBOR OF REFUGE			★30	S	●		16
TRAVERSE CITY																			
13. Duncan L. Clinch Marina*	922-4903	S	▲	100	35	●	15	20	76	▲		R			I	▲30	S	●		16
14. East Bay Marina	938-2131	S	▲	35			12	6	SHE	▲						★30		●	R	
15. Grelickville Marina	946-5463	S	▲				7	5		★						★30		●		
16. Sail North, Inc.	922-3000	S	▲	36	2		6	6				▲	PH		MGI	★30	S			16
SUTTONS BAY TO LELAND																			
17. Suttons Bay Marina*	271-6703	S	▲	40	6	●	25	10	TEX	★		R			GI	★20	SL	●	RS	68
18. Northport Municipal Marina*	386-5411	S	▲	60	45	●	12	10	AMO	▲						★30	S	●		16
19. Northport Bay Boat Yard	386-5151	Y	▲	50			40	8			25	R	▲	P		M			●	RS	16
20. Leland Marina	256-9132	S	▲	35			7	5		▲						★30		●		16
FRANKFORT TO PENTWATER																			
21. Jacobson Marina	352-9151	S	▲	150	30	●	18	12	PHL	▲			▲	P	MI	▲50	SL	●	RS	16
22. Frankfort Municipal Marina*	352-9051	S	▲	95	40	●	35	10	STA	▲		R			GI	▲30	S	●	RS	16
23. Betsie Bay Marina, Inc.	352-7200	Y	▲	75	16		10	8	TOT	▲	30		▲	PH	MI	★50	SL	●	R	16
24. Elberta Municipal Marina*	352-9504	S	▲	35	10	●	20	10				R				L	●	R	
25. Veteran Municipal Marina*	No Listing		▲	40			5	5	TEX	▲					I	★30	S	●		
26. Onekama Marine ✓	889-4218	Y	▲	45	10		14	10	MAR	▲	RL		▲	PH	MGI	★30	S	●	R	16
27. Manistee Municipal Marina*	723-6491			40			14	9		★					MGI	★30	S	●		
28. Moonlite Motel & Marina	723-3587	S	P	40		●	22	15	76	★			★		I		S	●	RS	
29. Fisherman's Center	723-7718	S	P	36	6		10	7		▲		R	★	P	MI	★			R	16/9
30. Ludington Municipal Marina*	843-9611	S	▲	98	40		12	11		▲					GI	▲50	S	●		16
31. Thompson Marina, Inc.*	843-9888	S	▲	60	10	●	25	4	ZEP	★		★		PH	MGI	★120		S		16
32. Ludington Yacht Club*	843-9904	S	▲	40			5	7		▲						★30	S			
33. Star Port Marina	845-7692	S	P	40		●	35	5	MAR	★		R	★	P	MI	★20	S	●		16
34. Pentwater Yacht Club*	869-8921	S	▲	60	4		14	14							MGI	★20	L		R	
35. Pentwater Marina	869-8301	S	▲	45	20		20	6							MGI	★30	SL	●	RS	
36. Snug Harbor Marina	869-7001	Y	▲	100	40	●	30	15	STA	▲	15		▲	PH	★	MGI	▲50	SL	●	RS	16

To provide the most complete and accurate information, **all facilities have been contacted within the past year.** If an asterisk (*) appears, it indicates a facility which did not respond to our requests for information (these listings may not reflect current conditions). Although facility operators supplied this data, we cannot guarantee accuracy or assume responsibility for errors. Entrance and dockside soundings tend to fluctuate. Always approach marinas carefully. Reference numbers on spotting charts indicate marina locations. ✓ Member American Boat Builders & Repairers Association.

GREAT LAKES EDITION

LAKE MICHIGAN/WESTERN SHORE

minutes before and after each hour and half hour.

Beyond these bridges is a full service marina. Then, past the next highway bridge (opens for three minutes before and after the quarter and three-quarter hour) are two more marinas. None of these marinas is within walking distance of St. Joseph's downtown. Benton Harbor is largely industrial.

New Buffalo. Twenty-five miles south of St. Joseph, this is the last port of call in the state of Michigan. If yours is a deep-draft boat, pay particular attention when entering this harbor. The channel is prone to shoaling, and a mud flat extends northward into the main channel just before the full-service marina's entrance channel. The village is about a half mile away.

Michigan City. About five miles south of New Buffalo, you enter Indiana waters, and about five miles farther is Michigan City at the south end of Lake Michigan. One of the largest marinas on the lake is situated in the city park which also houses a zoo, tennis courts, and a band shelter. Reservations aren't accepted; slips are available on a first-come, first-served basis. The **Old Lighthouse Museum** and swimming beaches are close by. This harbor is home to the Tri-State sailboat races and the In-the-Water Boat Show.

Lake Michigan / Eastern Shore

37. Sail Point Marina	869-7551	S	▲	50	12	●	18	4			▲	H	MI	★30	SL		R	16
WHITE LAKE																		
38. Wesley Marine Services	(616) 894-6909	S	▲	50			15	6		30	▲	PH	MI	★30	S	●		16
39. Skipper's Landing, Inc.	893-4525	Y	▲	50	10	●	11	11	STA	▲	L	▲	PH	MGI	▲30	SL	●	RS	16
40. Crosswinds Marina & Restaurant	894-4549	Y	▲	85	5	●	13	8	AMO	▲	50	▲	P	MI	▲50	S	●	RS	16
41. South Shore Marina	893-3935	S	▲	20	5				SUN	★	L	★	H	MI	★50	S	●	S	
MUSKEGON TO GRAND HAVEN																		
42. Torresen Marine, Inc.	759-8596	Y	▲	65	2	●	12	12	STA	▲	60	R	▲	P	▲	MGI	★30	S	●	RS	16
43. Pointe Marine Association	744-3236	Y	▲	44	5	●	7	6	SUN	★	15		▲	P		MI		S	●	R	16
44. Hartshorn Marina	724-6785	S	▲	45	36	●	15	11				R				MI	●	S	●	R	16/9
45. North Shore Marina	842-1488	Y	▲	80	15	●	8	10	MOB	▲	30		▲	P		MI	★30	S	●		16/9
46. Grand Haven Municipal Marina	847-3478	S	▲	60	70	●	20	10		★		R				I	★50		●	RS	16
47. The Wharf Marina	842-5370	Y	▲	45	2	●	5	5	SHE	★	15		▲	P		MI	★20	SL	●	RS	16
48. Grand Isle Marina	842-9330	S	▲	100	15	●	20	8	AMO	▲	70	R	▲	P	▲	MGI	▲50	S	●	RS	16/9
49. Holiday Inn	846-1000	S	▲	60			9	18	MOB	▲						I	★30	S		R	
50. Riverbend Marina	842-8600	Y	▲				8	6		★	L		▲	H		GI	★30				
51. **Barrett Boat Works** (p. 197)	842-1202	Y	P	60	10		15	12	MOB	★	39		★	PH		MGI	★30	SL	●		16
52. Grand Valley Marina	837-6389	S	P	36			10	10		★		R				GI	★30	S			
HOLLAND / SAUGATUCK																		
53. Parkside Marina	399-2020	S	▲			●	17	5	MOB	▲	L					GI	★30	S			16
54. Eldean Shipyard	335-5843	Y	▲	100	30	●	20	17	AMO	▲	75		▲			MI	▲50	SL	●	RS	
55. Easter Marine Svc.*	335-5520	Y		34		●	22	20	SUN	●	L	R	▲	PH		M					
56. Bayshore Marina, Inc.	786-9300	Y	▲	70	20		18	6	MOB	▲	20		▲	P		MI	▲50	SL	●	RS	16
57. Anchorage Marina	399-1800	Y	▲	60	20	●	9	6	MAR	▲	80		▲	PH		MGI	▲50	SL	●	RS	16
58. Casa Loma	857-8701	Y	▲	60		●	12	6									▲50	S			
59. Saugatuck Yacht Service	857-2151	S	▲	60	10		12	12	SHE	▲	30		▲	P		MI	▲30	SL	●	R	
60. Singapore Yacht Club	857-2442	S	▲	60	8	●	15	10								GI	★30	SL	●	R	
61. Tower Marine	857-2151	Y	▲	80	20		10	10	SHE	▲	60		▲	P		MI		S	●	RS	
62. West Shore Marina	857-2181	Y	▲	35				13			L						★30				
SOUTH HAVEN TO MICHIGAN CITY																		
63. Municipal Marina*	637-3171	S	▲	60	30	●	22	10	MAR	▲	L	R	▲	PH	★	MGI	▲30	S	●	R	16
64. **All Seasons Marine, Inc.** (p. 198)	637-3655	S	▲	80	6		20	20	MAR	▲	35		▲	P	●	MGI	▲50	SL	●	RS	16
65. West Basin Marine*	983-5432	S	▲	50	5	●	24	19	CIT	▲	L		▲	PH		MI	★30		●		
66. Harbor Isle Marina	982-0812	Y	▲	65	10		10	10	MOB	▲	65		▲	PH		MGI	★30	SL	●		
67. Brian's Marine Svc.	983-0760	S	▲	36	5		20	10	MOB	★	50	R	★	P		MGI	★	S	●	S	
68. Pier 1000 Ltd. Marina	927-4471	Y	▲	55	10	●		6		▲	60		▲	P	▲	MI	▲50	SL	●	RS	
69. Oselka's Marina	469-2600	Y	▲	56	10		8	10	AMO	★	35		▲	P		MGI	▲30	SL	●	RS	16/77
70. Washington Park Marina	(219) 872-1712	S	▲	150	15	●	10	10	66	▲		R				I	▲50	SL	●	RS	16

To provide the most complete and accurate information, **all facilities have been contacted within the past year.** If an asterisk (*) appears, it indicates a facility which did not respond to our requests for information (these listings may not reflect current conditions). Although facility operators supplied this data, we cannot guarantee accuracy or assume responsibility for errors. Entrance and dockside soundings tend to fluctuate. Always approach marinas carefully. Reference numbers on spotting charts indicate marina locations. ✓ Member American Boat Builders & Repairers Association.

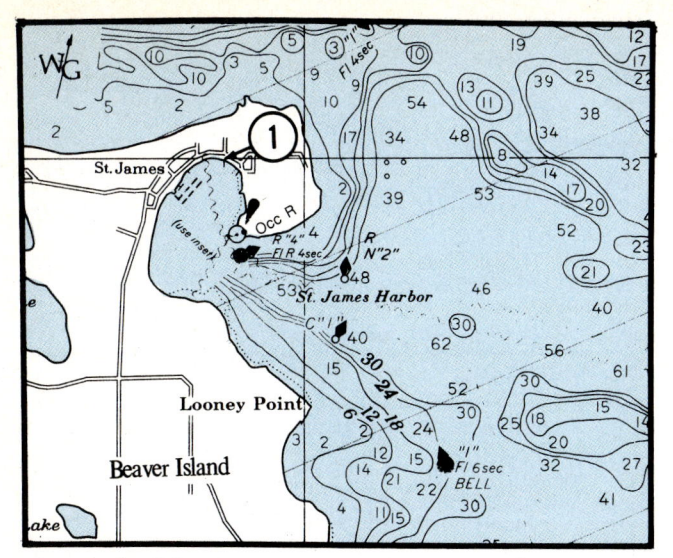

Lake Michigan/Eastern Shore

Chart 14911, edition 15

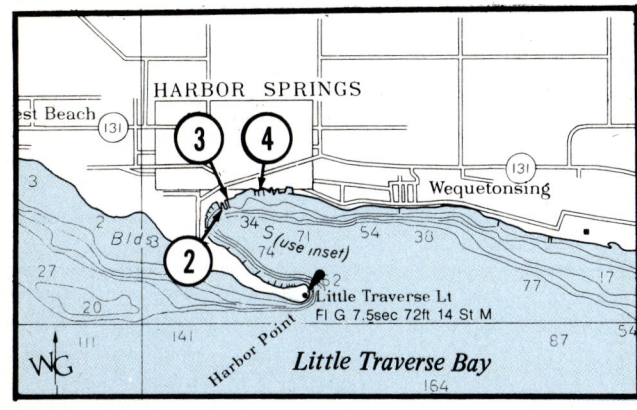

Chart 14913, edition 14

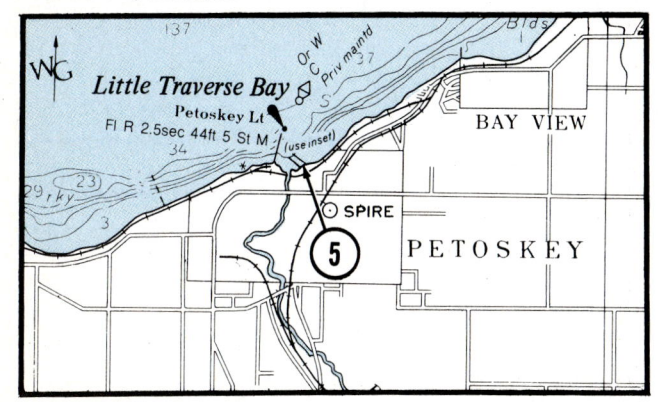

Chart 14913, edition 14

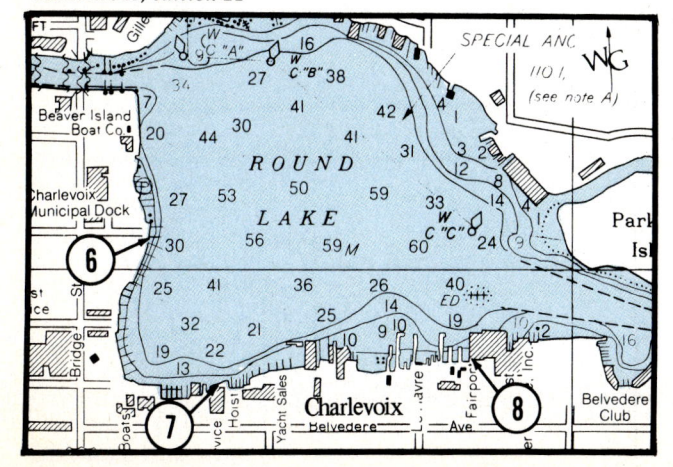

Chart 14942, edition 22

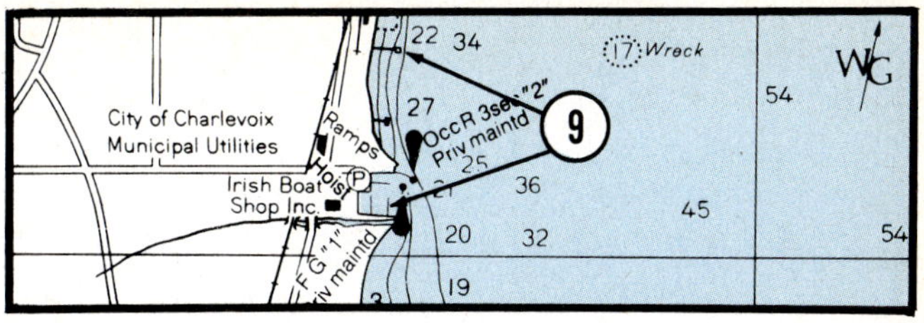

Chart 14942, edition 22

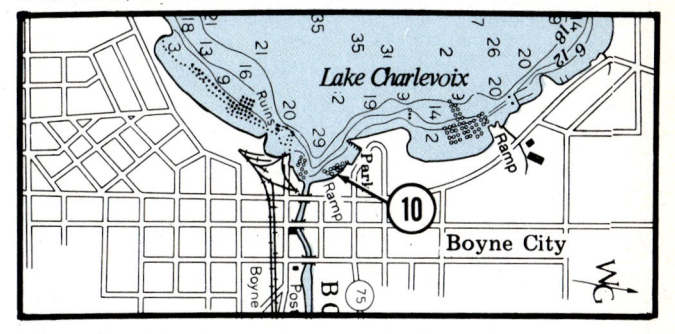

Chart 14942, edition 22

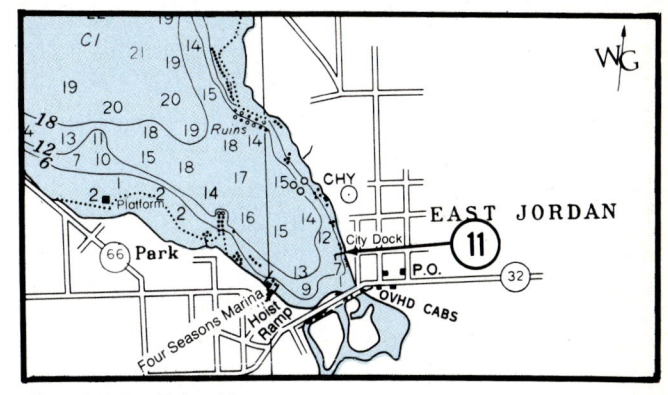

Chart 14942, edition 22

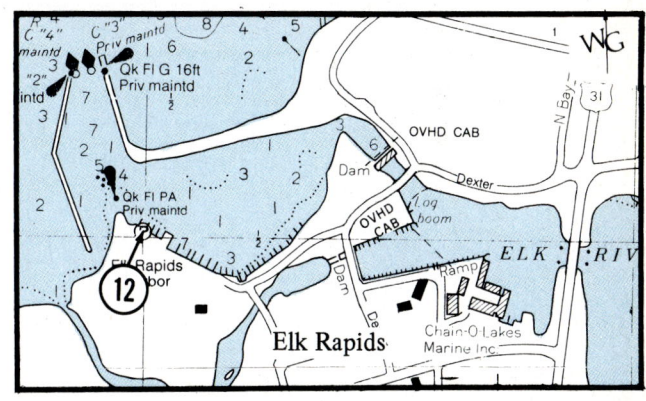

Chart 14913, edition 14

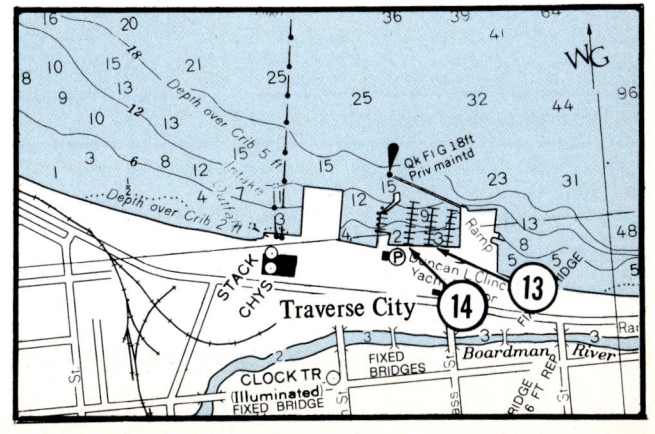

Chart 14913, edition 14

GREAT LAKES EDITION   *Under no circumstances are these charts to be used for navigation.*

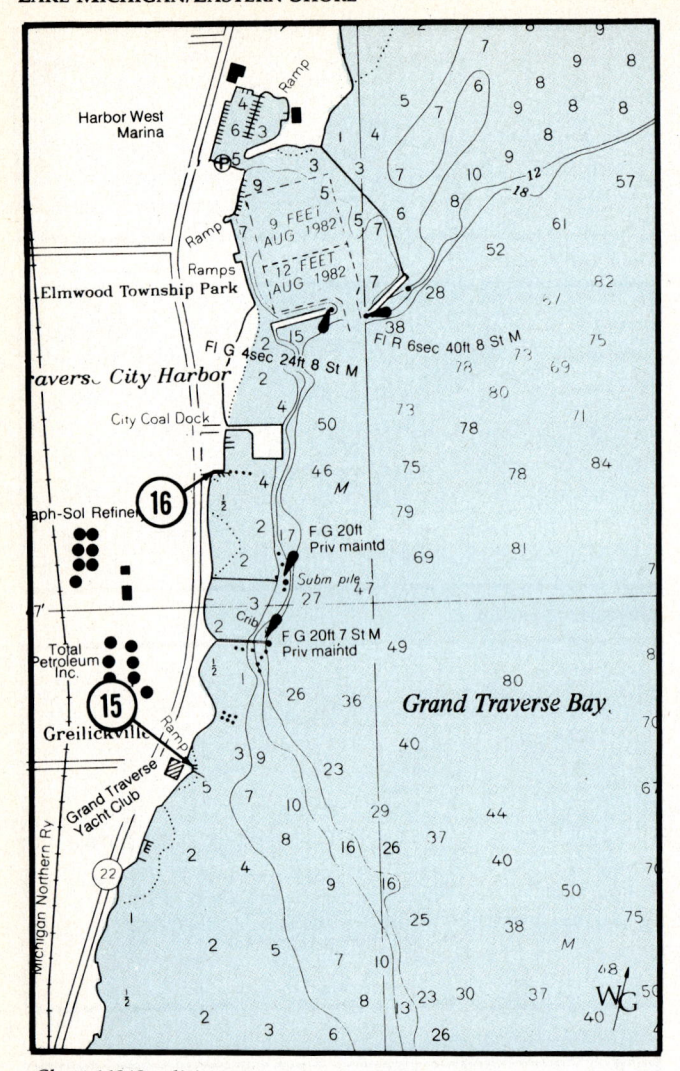

Lake Michigan/Eastern Shore

Chart 14913, edition 14

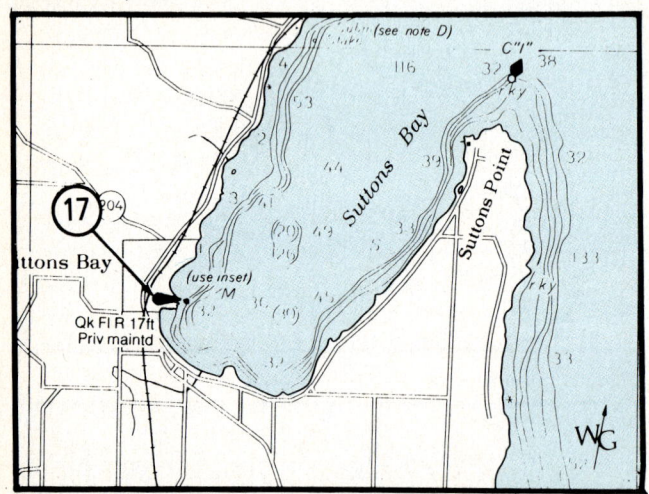

Chart 14913, edition 14

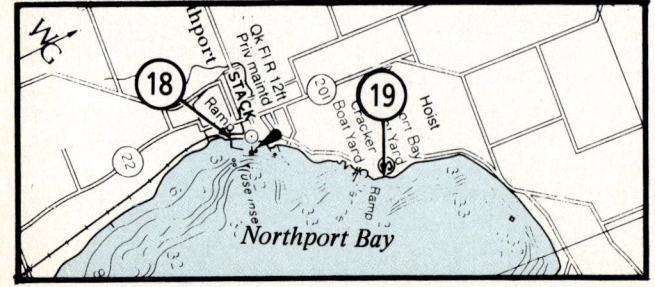

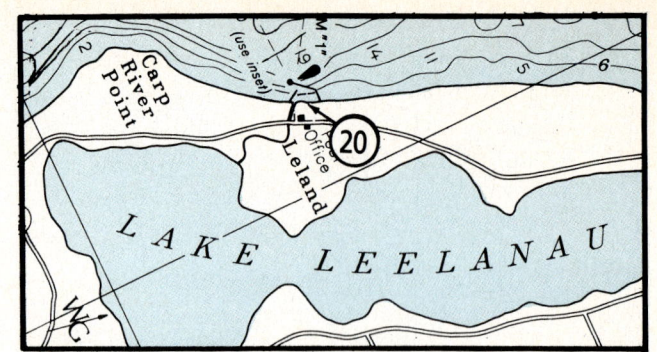

Chart 14913, edition 14

Chart 14912, edition 14

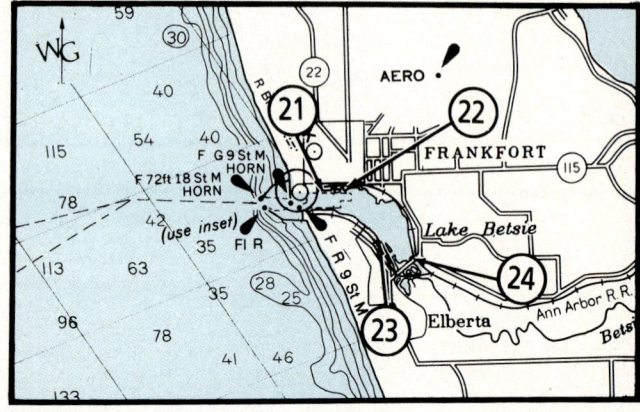

Chart 14907, edition 20

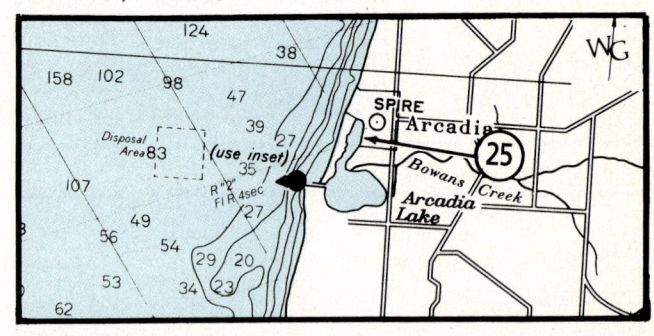

Chart 14907, edition 20

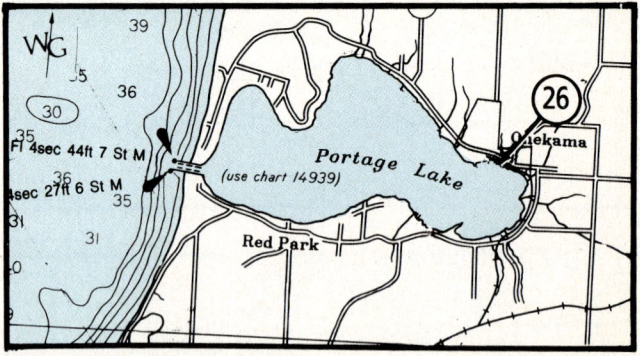

Chart 14907, edition 20

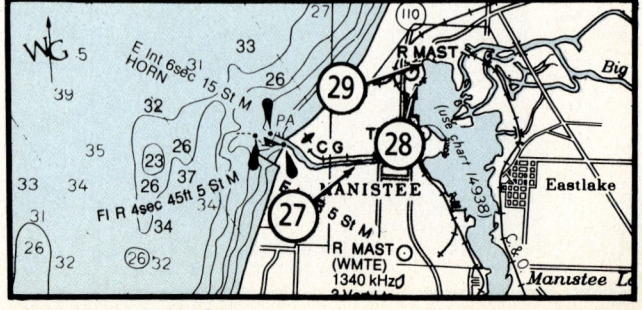

Chart 14907, edition 20

202   Under no circumstances are these charts to be used for navigation.   WATERWAY GUIDE / 1991

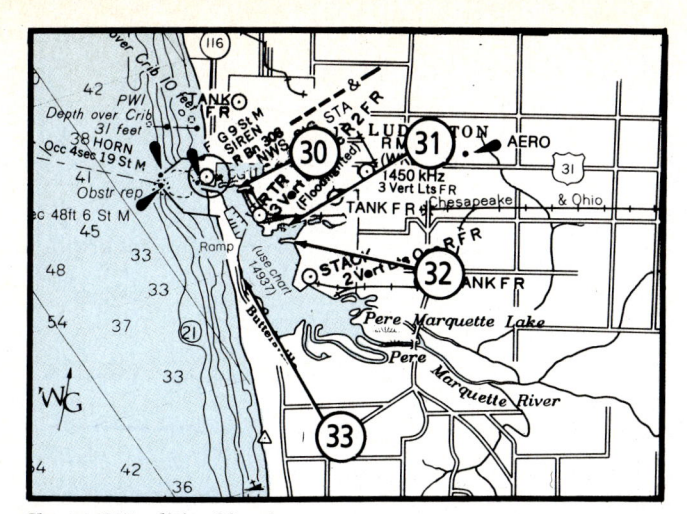

LAKE MICHIGAN/EASTERN SHORE

Chart 14907, edition 20

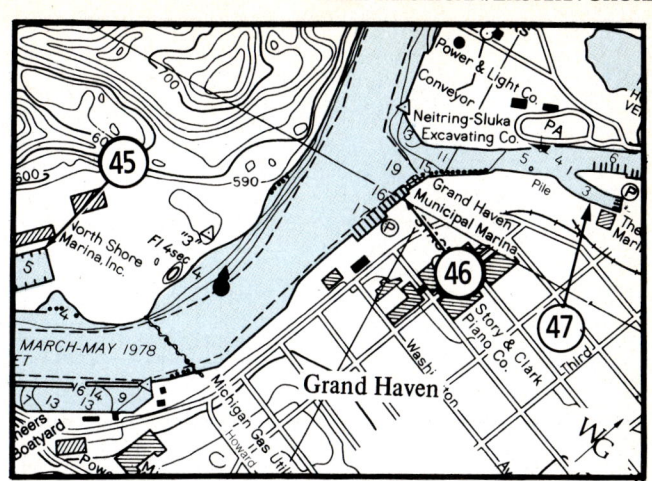

Chart 14933, edition 20

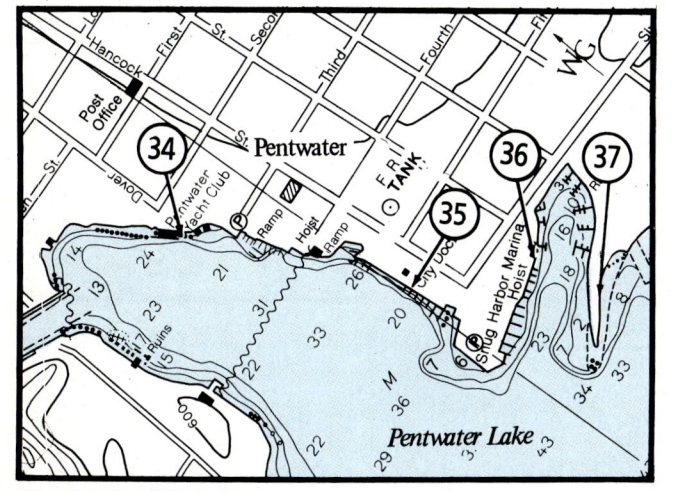

Chart 14907, edition 20

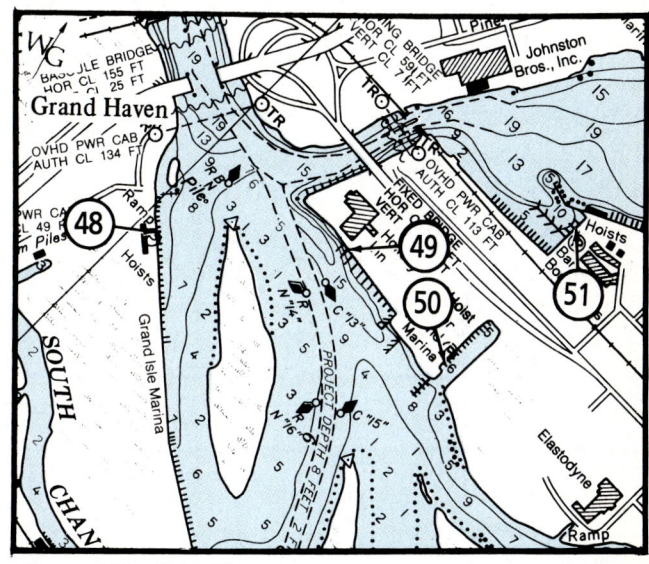

Chart 14933, edition 20

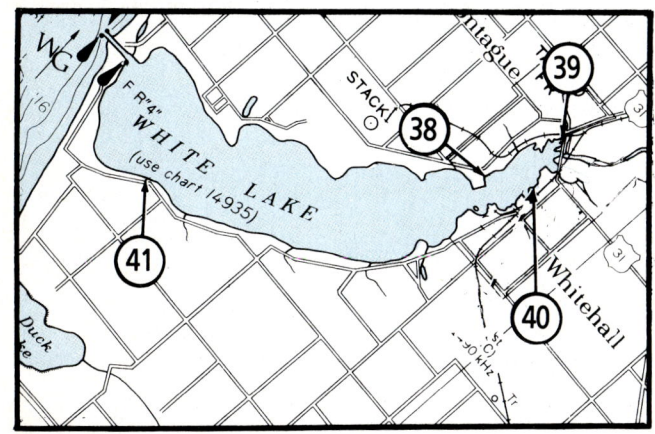

Chart 14906, edition 20

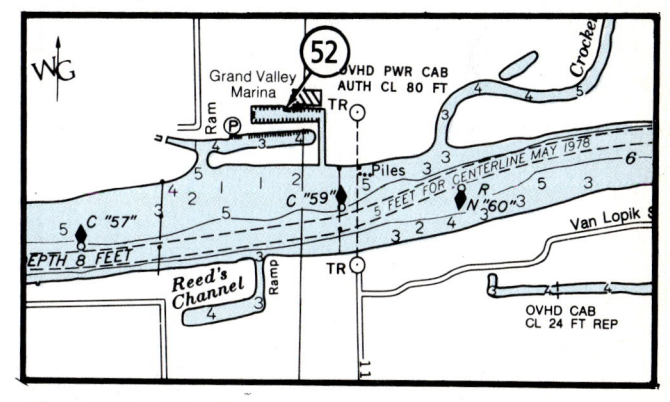

Chart 14933, edition 20

Chart 14906, edition 20

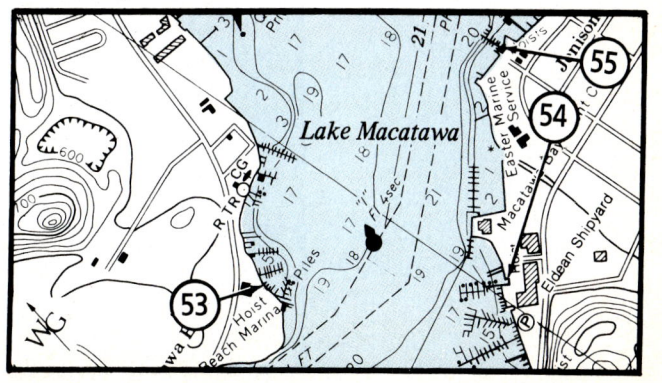

Chart 14932, edition 19

GREAT LAKES EDITION *Under no circumstances are these charts to be used for navigation.*

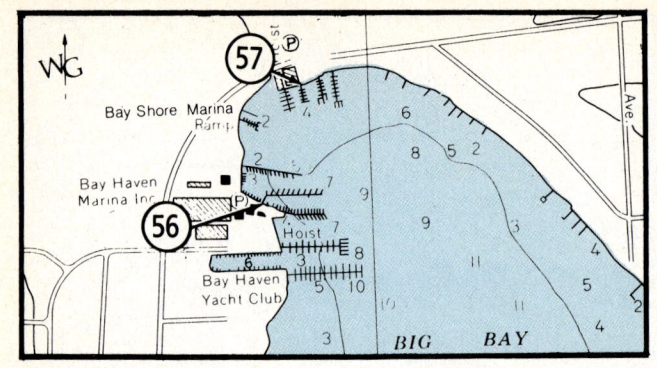

Lake Michigan/Eastern Shore

Chart 14932, edition 19

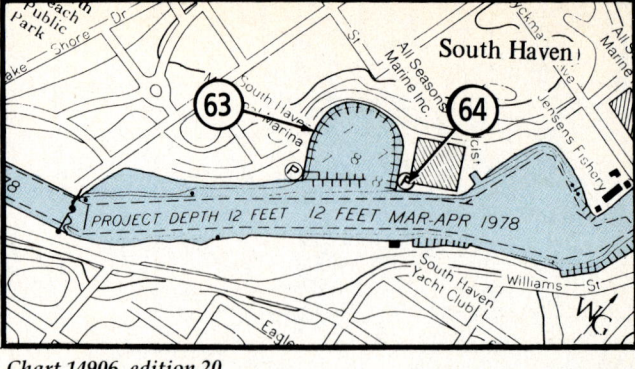

Chart 14906, edition 20

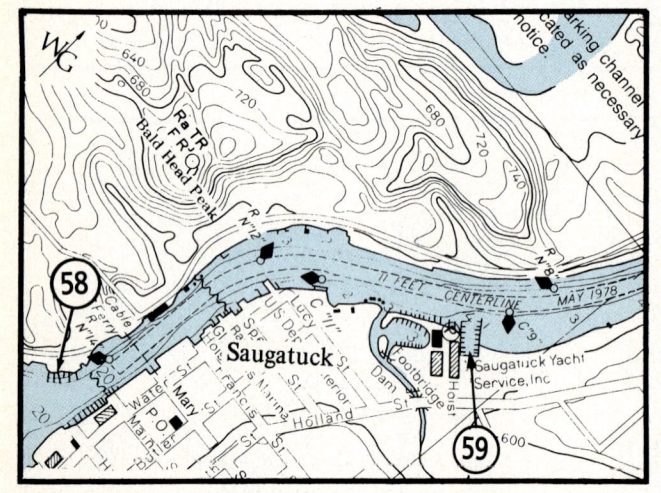

Chart 14906, edition 20

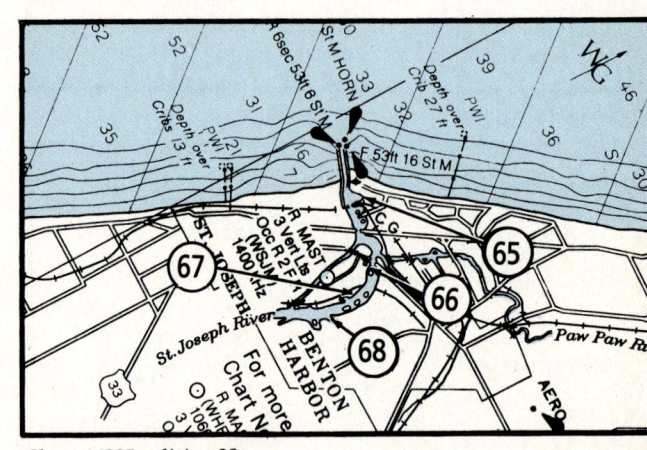

Chart 14905, edition 23

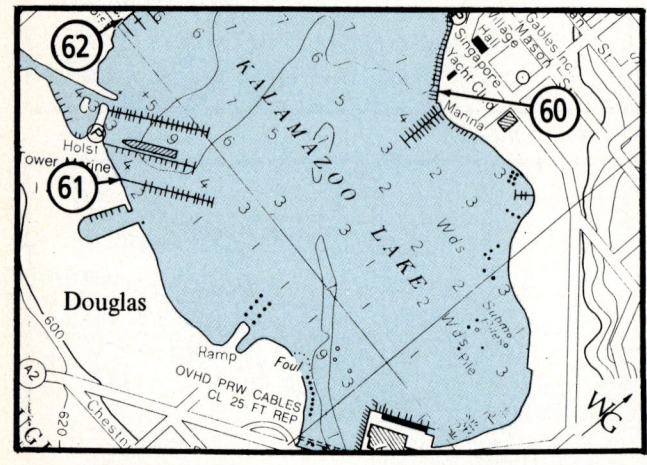

Chart 14906, edition 20

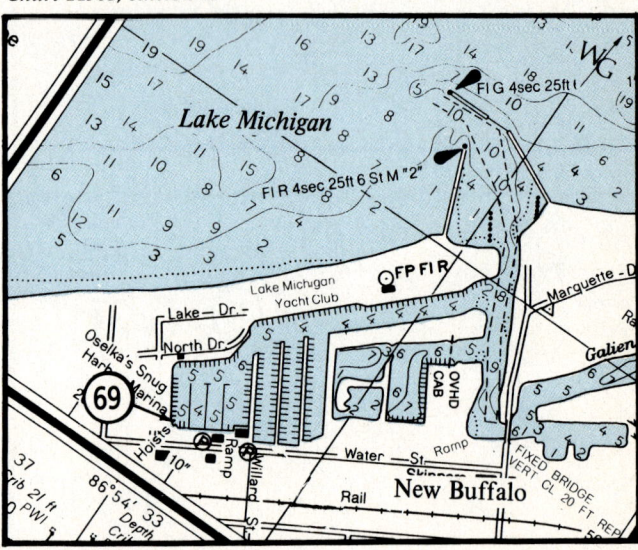

Chart 14905, edition 23

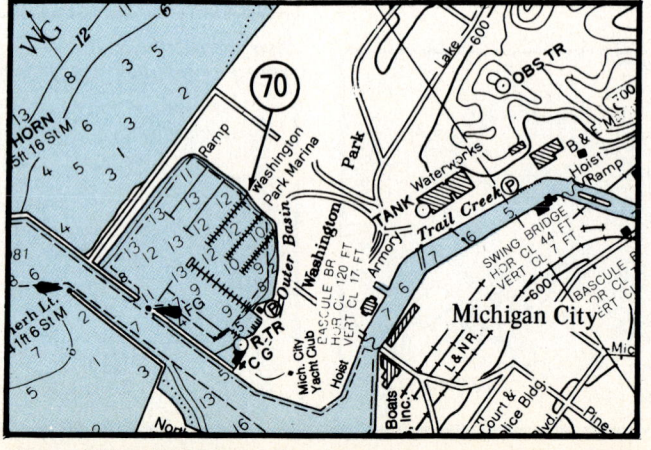

Chart 14905, edition 23

204   *Under no circumstances are these charts to be used for navigation.*   WATERWAY GUIDE / 1991

Lake Michigan/Western Shore

CHARTS: 14880, 14881, 14900, 14903, 14904, 14908, 14909, 14910, 14915, 14916-SC, 14917, 14918, 14919, 14922, 14924, 14925, 14928, 14929, 14930.

Where dune country ends west of Michigan City, Indiana, the march of industry begins. With only a few interruptions, it continues up the west shore of the lake for the next 125 miles. Then smaller cities and towns give way to Wisconsin's rural countryside and the resort areas of the Door Peninsula and Green Bay. There are few natural harbors on this west coast of the lake. Most of the ports are artificial basins, some in dredged river mouths, sheltered by lighted waterways.

Chicago

Third largest city in the nation, Chicago is exciting architecturally, culturally, and recreationally. Its magnificent waterfront is almost entirely parkland, backed up by the soaring skyscrapers that have made Chicago a world leader in urban architecture. Eight harbors in four parks moor thousands of boats. Virtually no space is set aside for transients, but you can call the dockmaster ahead of time at the harbor of your choice to arrange use of an absent seasonal boat's slip or mooring. The yacht clubs are open only to members of reciprocating clubs. Most of the marinas are not within walking distance of city attractions, and for some, it's even a long walk to the bus line. Taxis are always available.

From south to north, the first park is Jackson, which has two harbors. Jackson Park Harbor has moorings and Star docks and a yacht club in the Outer Lagoon. Inner Lagoon, with depths of four feet beyond a fixed 14-foot bridge, has a similar set of amenities. Fifty-ninth Street Harbor is limited to small power boats by its four-foot depth and fixed ten-foot bridge.

Burnham Park Harbor is identified by massive McCormick Place, Chicago's exhibition center. In a peculiar arrangement, the harbor, surrounded by a land fill, is on the landward side of Meigs Airfield. Planes are not permitted to operate here between 10:00 p.m. and 6:00 a.m., however, so your sleep will not be disturbed by aircraft. On entering the harbor during the day, stay close to the west wall of the channel to clear the flight of planes landing and taking off. A yacht club is located in this harbor, as well as public docks and moorings. The big adventure of Burnham Park Harbor is its proximity to the Adler Planetarium, the Shedd Aquarium, and the Field Museum of Natural History, three of Chicago's most popular attractions. The harbor is also convenient to public transportation.

Grant Park is just north of Burnham Park. The vast Monroe Street Harbor in the southwest corner of Chicago's main harbor consists almost entirely of moorings. Two yacht clubs are also located here. In this harbor, you are closest to the Art Institute and the new maritime museum at Navy Pier. At the bandshell in the park, there are frequent free concerts. This harbor is also the most convenient to all the other amenities of downtown Chicago.

From the main Chicago Harbor itself, a lock and canal leads into the Chicago River, then to the Sanitary and Ship Canal, the Illinois Waterway, and eventually the Mississippi River. Though this waterway isn't covered here, Chicago's marine repair yards are located on the river past the lock.

Lincoln Park, in a residential district about three miles north of the Chicago River, has three harbors. Close to the Lincoln Park Zoo, Diversey Harbor is limited to boats that can clear a 14-foot fixed bridge and has a yacht club as well as public docks. Belmont Harbor, accessible to sail and power boats, has both docks, moorings, and a yacht club, with a public beach nearby.

Wherever you moor in Chicago, you'll find plenty of activities day and night only a bus or taxi ride away. In addition to the museums mentioned, the Art Institute and Museum of Science and Industry are justly world famous. Walking the Magnificent Mile of North Michigan Avenue is a shopper's dream, and Chicago boasts a rich array of outstanding restaurants, theater, concerts, and night clubs.

GREAT LAKES EDITION

Distances
Statute miles (approximate)

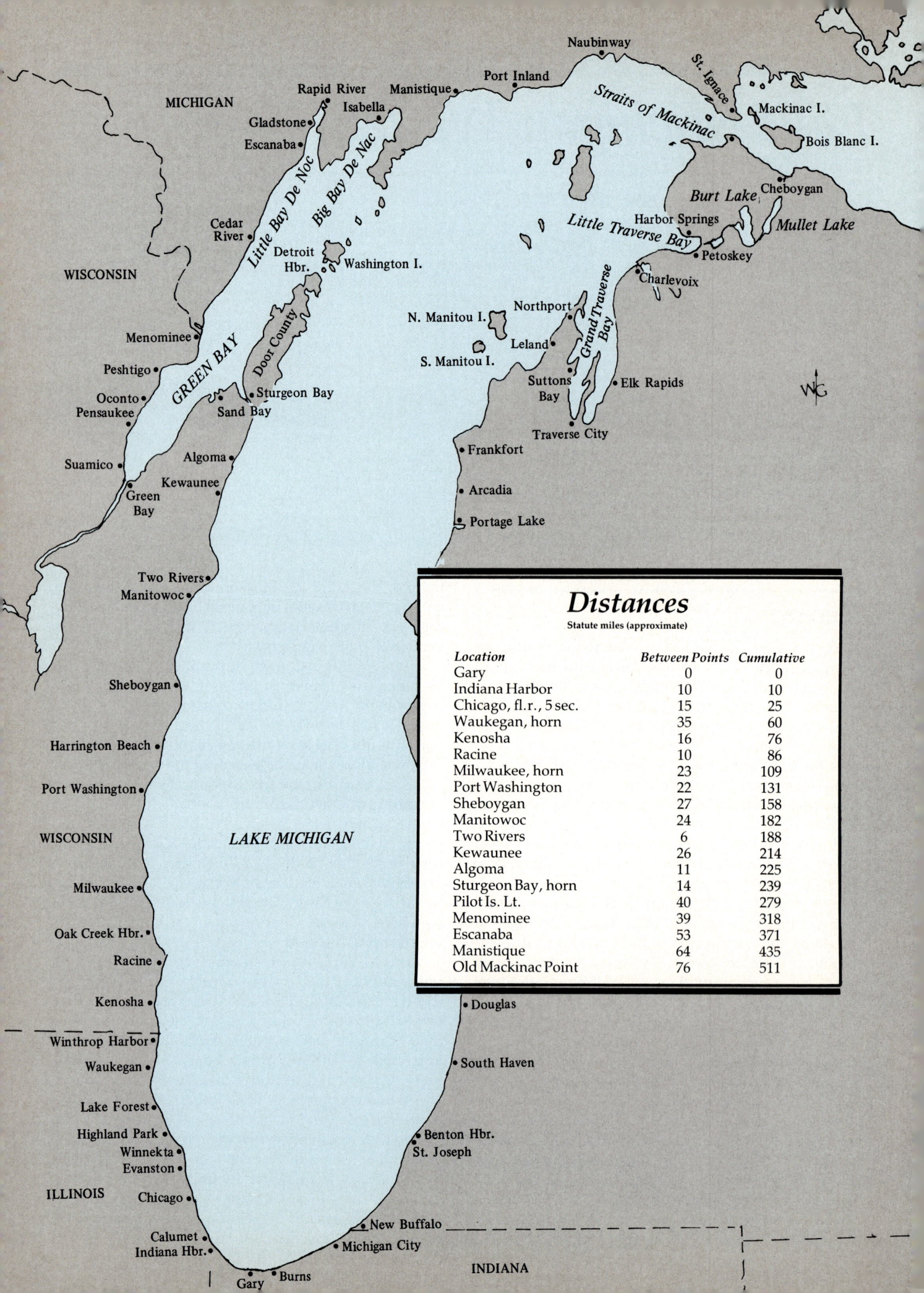

Location	Between Points	Cumulative
Gary	0	0
Indiana Harbor	10	10
Chicago, fl.r., 5 sec.	15	25
Waukegan, horn	35	60
Kenosha	16	76
Racine	10	86
Milwaukee, horn	23	109
Port Washington	22	131
Sheboygan	27	158
Manitowoc	24	182
Two Rivers	6	188
Kewaunee	26	214
Algoma	11	225
Sturgeon Bay, horn	14	239
Pilot Is. Lt.	40	279
Menominee	39	318
Escanaba	53	371
Manistique	64	435
Old Mackinac Point	76	511

Chicago to Milwaukee

The northern suburbs of Chicago do not offer any services to visiting mariners.

Waukegan. Thirty-five miles north of Chicago, **Waukegan** has greatly improved its harbor in recent years. The new breakwaters are well marked. Directly opposite the entrance channel is a yacht club, and at the north end of the harbor is a full-service marina. At the park district fuel dock in the main harbor, you can get directions to a mooring. Enter the city's large new marina at the south end of the breakwater, followed by a turn to port. Ashore are museums to visit and an historic district with interesting art and antique shops.

Runaway Bay. Astride the Illinois-Wisconsin border about nine miles from Waukegan, the full-service marina in a private harbor has shoaled to one foot.

Kenosha. Fifteen miles north of Waukegan, **Kenosha**, Wisconsin, is an industrial town with some commercial traffic in its harbor. To starboard beyond the entrance is the yacht club, and the Holiday Inn across the harbor offers dockage. Where the harbor narrows at its northern end is a marina near the fixed bridge with sixteen feet of clearance. Beyond the bridge is another private marina and the city marina. These marinas are close to a park with a nice beach. A new marina offers 150 slips. Downtown shopping and restaurants are about half a mile away. You can also visit a couple of museums from here as well.

Racine. An industrial skyline rims the shore between Kenosha and **Racine**, ten miles north. About a mile offshore from the harbor entrance, Racine Reef is a set of shoals marked by a light and buoy. If approaching from the north, there are also shoals extending off Wind Point. Racine's harbor has undergone major reconstruction recently. Proceed through the large turning basin; to the south are boats on moorings, and to the northwest you'll see the Racine Yacht Club, which welcomes visiting mariners, except in foul weather. Their docks are relatively untenable for larger craft, and they discourage docking. Moorings are available on the north side of the harbor.

Proceeding up the Root River, you come to another facility before two drawbridges. Dockage is along a bulkhead, which is subject to surge in foul weather. Standoff or breast anchors are recommended. The Main Street Bridge opens on demand every 20 minutes from 6:00 a.m. to 9:00 p.m. (its signal is one long and one short blast). Between the Main Street Bridge and the State Street Bridge is a newly completed marina with limited transient dockage. Beyond the State Street Bridge is one of Lake Michigan's most noted boatyards, Palmer-Johnson.

The amenities on the river are the closest to downtown Racine. The city's popular attractions include the Johnson Wax Building, designed by Frank Lloyd Wright; the building's associated theater, designed by Wright's students; and museums of art and history.

Milwaukee. Wisconsin's largest city is an important seaway port. The 42-story First Wisconsin Center building is a landmark visible from a great distance, and the expansive arch of the Harbor Freeway comes into view as you approach the harbor. The long harbor is enclosed by breakwaters with several entrances.

South Shore Park Harbor can be entered from a southern gap in the breakwater, or you can come from the north through the main harbor to the mooring area and yacht club. Another yacht club offers a restaurant, and a beach is nearby. Transient slips are limited, however.

From the marina, an easy walk through a lakeshore park filled with roller skaters and soccer players takes you to the War Memorial and Art Museum. From the War Memorial you can catch a bus downtown.

Milwaukee is a city with a great many sights to see, including several opulent historic buildings and mansions, art museums, the outstanding Milwaukee Public Museum with life-size dioramas and walk-through exhibits, brewery tours in the town that beer made famous, music, theater, dance, and an array of ethnic restaurants. All summer, festivals are held on the Summerfest grounds at the waterfront.

Milwaukee to Sturgeon Bay

As you move up the coast, the large industrial cities give way to smaller towns and rural Wisconsin.

Port Washington. New and expanded marinas have in recent years made this attractive town, 25 miles from Milwaukee, a popular cruising destination. A public marina and a private marina are located in the two basins that form the harbor. Both are convenient to downtown, with its well-known seafood restaurant and maritime museum. Stone Croft, a European shopping village with a restaurant, is a cab ride away.

Sheboygan. An industrial city, with not much to offer tourists, **Sheboygan** is located 26 miles north of Port

---

Nautical Terms

Ghoster. A very lightweight sail—which might well be blown away in stronger winds—used in very light airs. If a regular sail were used in light wind conditions, the wind might not be able to lift the sail, much less drive it.

© The Overlook Press. Reprinted by permission.

Cross-Lake Distances and Courses

The table below is a selection of major cruising stops in Lake Michigan and the distances between them. It is not a complete list of ports and is intended solely as a guide to cruise planning. All distances have been figured along the most direct course consistent with safe, normal navigation. *All figures are approximate statute miles.* Actual mileage traveled will depend on variations of course, speed, boat, weather, currents, and other cruising conditions. Courses are given in True degrees.

From	To	Course	Distance	From	To	Course	Distance
Chicago	Big Sable Light	020	160		Michigan City	148	84
	Ludington	022	156		Chicago	173	64
	Little Sable Light	023	144	Milwaukee	Frankfort	036	140
	White Lake	030	120		Ludington	048	97
	Muskegon	034	114		Manistee	042	117
	Grand Haven	040	108		White Lake	072	78
	Holland	048	95		Muskegon	080	80
	Saugatuck	052	90		Grand Haven	089	83
	South Haven	062	77		Holland	102	88
	Benton Harbor	074	60		Saugatuck	106	89
	Michigan City	107	38		South Haven	118	93
	Sturgeon Bay Canal	004	208		Benton Harbor	132	96
	Kewaunee	002	181		Michigan City	151	104
	Two Rivers	000	158		Port Washington	357	29
	Manitowoc	359	156		Sheboygan	009	55
	Sheboygan	358	132	Port Washington	Frankfort	043	119
	Port Washington	353	107		Manistee	051	98
	Racine	353	64		Ludington	061	80
	Kenosha	347	54		Muskegon	098	77
	Waukegan	340	38		Grand Haven	106	84
Waukegan	Big Sable Light	031	136		Holland	117	94
	Ludington	032	130		Saugatuck	120	97
	Pentwater	035	122		South Haven	137	105
	Little Sable Light	035	112		Benton Harbor	141	112
	White Lake	045	100		Michigan City	337	124
	Muskegon	051	96	Sheboygan	Frankfort	050	95
	Grand Haven	059	93		Ludington	077	60
	Holland	071	86		White Lake	112	68
	Saugatuck	075	84		Muskegon	118	78
	South Haven	088	78		Grand Haven	124	87
	Benton Harbor	104	70		Holland	132	102
	Michigan City	133	64		Saugatuck	135	106
	Chicago	107	38		South Haven	143	118
Kenosha	Big Sable Light	032	120		Benton Harbor	151	130
	Ludington	036	117		Michigan City	164	146
	Pentwater	040	108		Chicago	178	132
	White Lake	053	86		Manitowoc	006	26
	Muskegon	064	87		Two Rivers	013	29
	Grand Haven	068	86	Manitowoc	Manitou Passage	052	96
	Holland	081	82		Frankfort	061	79
	Saugatuck	086	82		Manistee	080	66
	South Haven	100	79		Ludington	099	60
	Benton Harbor	116	75		Pentwater	110	64
	Michigan City	142	76		White Lake	130	79
	Chicago	167	54		Muskegon	133	90
Racine	Big Sable Light	033	112		Grand Haven	136	102
	Ludington	038	108		Holland	141	118
	Little Sable Light	042	88		Saugatuck	143	123
	White Lake	057	81		South Haven	149	137
	Muskegon	064	80		Benton Harbor	158	150
	Grand Haven	074	80		Michigan City	167	169
	Holland	088	79		Chicago	179	156
	Saugatuck	092	80		Sheboygan	186	26
	South Haven	107	80		Two Rivers	051	6
	Benton Harbor	124	78				

LAKE MICHIGAN/WESTERN SHORE

Washington. North of the Sheboygan River entrance in the artificial harbor, is a yacht club that welcomes visitors. Some marine services are provided up the river. A ten-foot fixed bridge here opens on the quarter hour, but on the half-hour during rush hours.

Manitowac. Twenty-four miles north of Sheboygan, **Manitowac** has an excellent expanding municipal marina. The city has a long shipbuilding tradition, including the production of luxury Burger yachts. The maritime museum reflects this tradition in its quality exhibits. The submarine on display was one of the many built here during the second World War.

Two Rivers. A few miles beyond Manitowac, Two Rivers is a fishing town, with a museum devoted to that enterprise. The confluence of the Twin Rivers forms the harbors, but the marinas facilities are in the West Twin River, below and above the bascule bridge. Tennis courts, a beach, and downtown shopping are convenient to the marinas.

Kewaunee. About 25 miles from Two Rivers, **Kewaunee** has city dockage below and above the highway bridge, which opens on one long and one short blast. Both marinas are close to downtown, where sights include the County Historical Museum and Old Jail and the world's largest grandfather clock.

Algoma. This is one of the few towns along this shore of the lake with an operating fishing fleet, and the narrow river is lined with various fishing tugs and charter boats. The bright red light on the pierhead is a popular subject with amateur photographers. The town is on the shores of the Ahnapee River and the approach is straightforward. Just inside, the marina is within walking distance of stores and supplies.

Ashore you'll find the "Living Lakes Exposition," and Mrs. Gray's Doll Museum attached. Also, you can tour the Von Stiehl Winery, famous for its fruit wines native to this region.

Sturgeon Bay Canal. Carved out of the spindly Door County Peninsula, this canal was built to allow freighters access to Green Bay without having to navigate the shoal-ridden **Ports Des Morts Passage** at the northern tip of the peninsula. For the fleet of cruising boats on Lake Michigan, it offers easy and safe entry into Green Bay's protected waters. The eight and one-half mile channel is well-marked and lighted, buoyed from Lake Michigan with reds on the starboard hand. The speed limit in the canal is five miles per hour, but currents can run faster than that in either direction.

About three tree-lined miles from the canal entrance is a resort with dockage on the north shore. Beyond it,

From	To	Course	Distance
Two Rivers	Manitou Passage	052	88
	Frankfort	062	75
	Manistee	083	62
	Ludington	104	57
	Pentwater	114	61
	White Lake	133	78
	Muskegon	137	89
	Grand Haven	140	101
	Saugatuck	145	123
	South Haven	152	137
	Benton Harbor	159	151
	Michigan City	169	170
	Chicago	180	158
	Sheboygan	193	29
	Manitowoc	231	6
Kewaunee	Manitou Passage	064	72
	Frankfort	078	62
	Manistee	104	58
	Ludington	124	61
	Pentwater	132	70
	White Lake	145	93
	Muskegon	147	104
	Grand Haven	148	116
	Saugatuck	152	141
	South Haven	157	156
	Benton Harbor	163	171
	Michigan City	171	192
	Chicago	002	181
	Sturgeon Bay Canal	021	30
Sturgeon Bay Canal	Manitou Passage	080	56
	Frankfort	102	58
	Manistee	128	65
	Ludington	144	76
	Pentwater	148	87
	White Lake	157	113
	Muskegon	157	124
	Grand Haven	156	137
	Holland	158	155
	Saugatuck	160	162
	South Haven	164	178
	Benton Harbor	168	195
	Michigan City	175	217
	Chicago	185	208
	Waukegan	189	176
	Racine	189	150
	Milwaukee	192	133

a 42-foot bridge opens on the hour and half hour. Past the town, the canal widens as it opens into the reaches of Sturgeon Bay and then Green Bay. On the port side is Potawatomi State Park and just before you reach Green Bay itself, Sawyer Harbor, also to port, offers sheltered anchorage to shoal draft boats.

Sturgeon Bay. The town of Sturgeon Bay is an interesting combination of resort and industry, in the form of massive shipbuilding. Eastward of the 14-foot Michigan Street Bridge, which opens on the hour and half hour, is a full-service marina with tennis courts and a picnic area on the south shore. On the north side, the famous Palmer-Johnson custom boat-building yard offers transient accommodations. Both of these facilities are convenient to downtown shopping, restaurants, and the historical and art museums. The marine museum is on the outskirts of town near one of the city's two huge shipbuilders.

Door Peninsula/Green Bay

A different kind of cruising awaits you along the shores of the Door Peninsula than is found along the Lake Michigan coast below. The Door is geographically part of the Niagara Escarpment. It encloses **Green Bay** with steep limestone bluffs on the west side, while its eastern shore slopes gradually into Lake Michigan, with off-lying shoals. The coastal villages of this beautiful finger of land are mostly summer resorts, although a fair amount of commercial fishing remains. The interior is still largely farm and orchard.

Bailey's Harbor. Watch out for fish net stakes as you move northward 20 miles from the Sturgeon Bay Ship Canal to Bailey's Harbor. Come into the harbor carefully on the range lights and channel markers. When you're fairly well inside, a turn to starboard leads you to the Bailey's Harbor Yacht Club, which is a fine resort.

Baileys Harbor Yacht Club & Resort
BAILEYS HARBOR, WISCONSIN 54202
PHONE 414-839-2336

OPEN TO THE PUBLIC

Our modern marina welcomes both transient and seasonal craft. We have 24' - 40' floating piers and also can accommodate larger boats.

Full Service Hook-up • Water • Gas & Diesel Fuel
Pump Out • Showers & Dressing Rooms • Laundry
Ice • Bike & Car Rental • Dining • Lounge • Pool
Tennis • Waterview Hotel • Villas

GATEWAY TO THE FAMOUS DOOR COUNTY CRUISING AREA

Established 1944

- Located in the city between the bridges
- 17 acres with 120,000 sq. ft. under roof
- 3 travelifts and 3 lift wells to 50 ton capacity
- Large ship's store including nautical furnishings
- 275 slips in Sturgeon Bay and Fish Creek
- Service and repair of all types
- Picnic park area

- Yacht club located on premises
- 50 people to serve you
- 6,000 sq. ft. parts department
- Indoor and outdoor storage
- Large selection of boats on hand at all times
- Tennis courts

Southwest Side of Canal
We monitor Channels 16 and 9

OCEAN ALEXANDER • FORMULA • BOSTON WHALER • SILVERTON
KONG & HALVORSEN ISLAND GYPSY • MAKO • JOHNSON O/B • INFLATABLES

STURGEON BAY YACHT HARBOR

NAUTICAL DRIVE • STURGEON BAY, WISCONSIN 54235 • PHONE 414-743-3311
OPEN 7 DAYS A WEEK

The harbor tends to silt up, however, so deep-draft vessels should inquire about depths. All the amenities of the hotel are available to transient mariners, including tennis, swimming, and rental bikes to tour the quaint village or a nearby nature preserve.

Rowley Bay. Another attractive resort with marine services, as well as a long list of shore activities, Rowley Bay lies about 15 miles from the sea buoy off Bailey's Harbor. Here, too, hazardous shoals require careful attention to navigation and buoyage.

The Door Peninsula ends at a jagged peak of land separated from Plum Island by the infamous **Ports Des Morts Passage**, Death's Door. Its killing combination of winds, shoals, rocky shoreline, and cross-currents shouldn't be challenged. Pay close attention to navigational aids and be on the lookout for fishing net markers. Large freighters plow the passage into Green Bay and a stream of car ferries leave from Gill's Rock to Washington Island.

Washington Island. Washington Island is the largest of the chain trailing off the tip of the Door Peninsula. Once farmed, it is now mainly a summer resort, with three harbors available to mariners. In the southeast corner, is a private harbor with transient accommodations available. Although depths are good, the entrance is narrow.

Enter Detroit Harbor, the main harbor for Washington Island, from the west or southwest past Detroit Island. Keep to the marked channel until you are opposite the ferry dock. Marinas are on either side of the ferry dock, where you can rent mopeds or take a ride on the Cherry Train. The village is two miles inland. Another marina lies across the harbor on the east side, and Peterson Bay at the north end of Detroit Island provides a good anchorage.

The north side of Washington Island, **Jackson Harbor**, is small and shallow, but does have a small marina. It must be approached from the west. One of the main attractions of this area is the ferry to Rock Island State Park, a beautiful wilderness park with hiking trails and the ruins of a Chicago millionaire's estate.

potatoes, and sometimes onions, depending on the persuasion of the chef. The dish is prepared in a spectacular way and served with cole slaw and fruit pie for desert. Be sure to indulge.

Ellison Bay. Cruising south on the Green Bay side of the peninsula, the northernmost harbor is **Hedgehog** at Gill's Rock. Homeport to the commercial and charter fishing fleets, it provides no services for transients.

Just six miles south is picturesque Ellison Bay; you'll see docks for visiting mariners just as you enter the tree-lined harbor. The quiet little town is within easy walking distance from the harbor; rows of summer cottages line the shore.

Sister Bay, six miles south of Ellison Bay, is the next little village, but this one explodes in summer with shoppers at its trendy boutiques, gift shops, antique shops and a number of restaurants (watch for goats grazing on the thatched roof of one of them). A beach and tennis courts provide recreation.

The water is deep close to shore, but beware of the rocks surrounding the Sister Islands. The marina on the north side of Sister Bay is the only full-service yard on the peninsula. The village has dockage for transients in a park setting convenient to town.

Ephraim. Cruising south from Sister Bay keep to the east of the Sister Shoals by following the shoreline. **Ephraim**, just five miles away, has several docks available for visiting mariners, all located on the eastern shore of **Eagle Harbor**. The sunset view from this horseshoe-shaped bay is magnificent; looking inland you'll see spindly white church spires and steeples rising high from stands of birch and sumac.

Anderson's Dock, an historic site, is the municipal marina, and next door is the yacht club. A little beyond is another marina. All are close to village shopping, art galleries, and restaurants. You can also visit two historic buildings in town.

Peninsula State Park. Between Ephraim and Fish Creek, the shoreline juts out as Peninsula State Park, with hiking trails and a golf course. Shanty Bay on the

Door Peninsula/ West Side

The wooded, limestone bluffs, a few islands, and a close succession of picturesque villages make this part of Green Bay a favorite cruising ground. Most of the harbors, however, are not completely protected on the west and northwest, and are subject to considerable surge in high winds. Nevertheless, these harbors get very crowded in summer, and advance reservations are advised.

The Wisconsin Fish Boil is a unique local gastronomic delight presented by at least one restaurant in almost all of these harbors. It's a set dinner of whitefish,

CAL MARINE INC.
DOOR COUNTY

1024 Bay Shore Drive Sister Bay, WI. 54234
(414) 854-4521

ONE BLOCK NORTH OF MUNICIPAL DOCK
SALES • STORAGE • SERVICE

LAKE MICHIGAN/WESTERN SHORE

north side is exposed to north and northeast winds, but is a pretty anchorage in settled weather. Across the bay, **Horseshoe Island** is a small clump of trees huddled around one of the snuggest harbors in all of Green Bay. The sandy shore is snarled with trees and provides the perfect backdrop for anchoring. A small-boat dock is provided for visitors, but not for overnight use. Ashore you can follow a hiking trail around the island.

Chambers Island. Sitting just about in the center of Green Bay, Chambers Island has a large harbor ideal for anchoring in anything but northerly winds. When

Avoiding Lyme Disease

Walking in woods and brush with bare legs invites ticks to seek an acceptable host. They wait at low levels on leafy brush until attracted by the heat and gasses emitted by passing animals or people. Ticks are eyeless and cannot distinguish color or selected hosts. You and your pets are vulnerable to Lyme Disease carried by deer ticks and transmitted by their bites.

Lyme Disease is named for the community in Connecticut where it was first identified by the Yale School of Medicine. Another prominent center of the disease is Cape Cod and the islands of Massachusetts. About 92 percent of all cases of Lyme Disease are concentrated in just eight states: New York, New Jersey, Pennsylvania, Connecticut, Massachusetts, Rhode Island, Wisconsin, and Minnesota.

Protect yourself by following these sensible precautions:

★ Wear light-colored clothing, against which ticks can easily be seen.

★ Always wear trousers when walking in tall grass or brush. Tuck cuffs into socks.

★ Avoid walking through any trackless patch of brush or on a deer trail. Walk in the center of any road or path in brushy areas. Avoid brushing against low foliage.

★ Inspect for ticks frequently while walking. They move quite rapidly.

★ Check your pets for ticks. Your pet can carry and drop them. Use tick repellent for your animals.

★ Use high-strength DEET repellent on clothing, not on skin.

★ Be alert to ticks year-round, although they are most prevalent during the months from April through October.

★ Learn to recognize the tick species and their juvenile forms.

★ Keep abreast of new knowledge about the disease.

If bitten—don't panic.

Only a small percentage of ticks carry disease. Prompt removal is advisable, but ticks often stay on your skin for as long as 24 hours before biting, and infection will not occur for several hours. Remove the

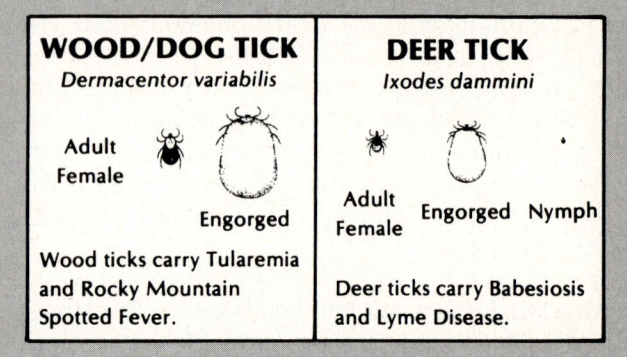

WOOD/DOG TICK
Dermacentor variabilis
Adult Female
Engorged
Wood ticks carry Tularemia and Rocky Mountain Spotted Fever.

DEER TICK
Ixodes dammini
Adult Female
Engorged
Nymph
Deer ticks carry Babesiosis and Lyme Disease.

attached tick by a direct upward pull, grasping the head, but not squeezing the body. If squeezed, the body fluids and bacteria will be released and spread. Wash your hands and disinfect the bite with alcohol. Save the tick in a closed jar.

See your doctor if an expanding or unusual red or red-rimmed rash develops or you suffer flu-like symptoms that persist in the form of a general malaise, fatigue, fever, and possible joint or facial pains. Remember to report the tick bite.

Bear in mind that you may be bitten without knowing it. If you are suffering from any of the above symptoms which do not go away, you may be infected. Pregnant women should be particularly alert to these symptoms. If in doubt, a blood or urine test is recommended. State and research labs provide the most reliable tests. Insist upon these tests.

Early detection and treatment with antibiotics is usually effective in treating Lyme Disease. Do not delay treatment if you have symptoms or have a real reason to believe that you have contracted the disease. Untreated disease leads to very serious late symptoms, which are difficult to treat. They include cardiac, neurological, arthritic, paralytic, or mental symptoms.

The disease is too new to know the full range of its effects. Ongoing research will produce new information for a number of years. Keep abreast of the latest information.

For more information about ticks, call the extension specialist at the Dukes County Cooperative Extension at (508) 693-0694.

For more information about Lyme Disease, call either the Massachusetts Department of Public Health at (617) 727-0049; or the Lyme Borreliosis Foundation in Tolland, Connecticut 06084, at (203) 871-2900.

From a brochure prepared by The Martha's Vineyard Lyme Disease Action Committee, Box 1696, Oak Bluffs, MA 02557.

✳ WATERWAY GUIDE NEEDS YOU!

To report hazards, misrepresentations of services, compliments, and comments on what you've observed in your travels on the water.

Marina or anchorage_____
On the (body of water)_____
Nearest big town_____State_____
When visited_____ Appearing on WATERWAY GUIDE page number____
Name of your boat_____Type of boat_____Homeport_____
Comments/Suggestions_____
_____
_____
_____

Name_____
Address_____
City_____State_____Zip_____

- -

✳ WATERWAY GUIDE NEEDS YOU!

To recommend **restaurants** *to other mariners traveling on the ICW.*

Name of restaurant_____
Address_____
City_____State_____Phone_____
Nearest marina or anchorage_____On the (body of water)_____
Walking distance from marina: No_____Yes_____If yes, how far?_____
Type of food (continental, French, seafood, sandwiches, etc.):_____

	$	$$	$$$	$$$$
Approximate price per meal	$1-7	$8-12	$13-20	$21-

Credit cards_____Reservations_____Dress_____
Name_____
Address_____
City_____State_____Zip_____

- -

WATERWAY GUIDE *and* CHARTBOOKS *are available from your marine dealer or directly from* WATERWAY GUIDE, *Inc. Indicate items you want and then send in this card with check, or call 800-233-3359 to order. Dealers send for special rates.*

GUIDEBOOKS
- ☐ SOUTHERN 1991 FLORIDA AND GULF COAST — $27.95
- ☐ MID-ATLANTIC 1990 CHESAPEAKE BAY AND ICW — $25.95
- ☐ NORTHERN 1990 NEW YORK TO MAINE — $25.95
- ☐ GREAT LAKES 1991 — $27.95

CHARTBOOKS
- ☐ NEWPORT TO CANADA — $49.50
- ☐ NEW YORK WATERS — $49.50
- ☐ CHESAPEAKE & DELAWARE BAYS — $79.95
- ☐ NORFOLK TO JACKSONVILLE — $54.95
- ☐ JACKSONVILLE TO MIAMI — $45.50
- ☐ LOWER FLORIDA AND THE KEYS — $49.50
- ☐ FLORIDA'S WEST COAST — $49.50
- ☐ MARINE BUYERS' GUIDE (30th Edition) — $34.95

Check enclosed _____add $3.00 postage for each item. Total _____

BUSINESS REPLY MAIL
FIRST CLASS   PERMIT 11077   ATLANTA, GA

POSTAGE WILL BE PAID FOR BY ADDRESSEE:

Communication Channels, Inc.
WATERWAY GUIDE, EDITOR
6255 Barfield Road
Atlanta, GA 30328-9988

NO POSTAGE NECESSARY IF MAILED IN THE UNITED STATES

BUSINESS REPLY MAIL
FIRST CLASS   PERMIT 11077   ATLANTA, GA

POSTAGE WILL BE PAID FOR BY ADDRESSEE:

Communication Channels, Inc.
WATERWAY GUIDE, EDITOR
6255 Barfield Road
Atlanta, GA 30328-9988

NO POSTAGE NECESSARY IF MAILED IN THE UNITED STATES

Send all orders to:

WATERWAY GUIDE
Book Department 79
6255 Barfield Road
Atlanta, GA 30328

PRE-PAYMENT REQUIRED

NAME_____

ADDRESS_____

CITY_____ STATE_____ ZIP_____

PHONE ( )_____

Georgia Residents: Add 5% Sales Tax.

winds are from the north, anchor in the lee of the island, where you'll find some good beachcombing. It's 11 miles to either Ephraim or Fish Creek from Chambers, making it a popular spot to drop the hook for lunch. A lighted bell buoy marks a shoal that runs north of the island; also watch for fishing markers.

If you're approaching from the north you'll see the **Strawberry Islands** on your port side. If you are coming from the south, follow the markers through **Strawberry Channel**.

Fish Creek, locally pronounced "crick," is the busiest and most commercial of the Door's tourist towns. But its gift shops, boutiques, craft shops, artists' studios, and restaurants have a charm of their own. The Peninsula Players is the oldest stock company in the nation, but you'll have to take a three-mile taxi ride to catch a performance.

In approaching the harbor, pay close attention to the shoals surrounding the Strawberry Islands. Pass to the east and keep at least a half mile offshore. On entering you will see many boats on moorings; these are all private. A marina lies immediately to starboard inside the harbor, and the City Dock is farther into the bay. Both are convenient to village attractions.

Egg Harbor. Egg Harbor is six miles south of Fish Creek and 13 miles north of the entrance to the Sturgeon Bay Ship Canal. Its broad bay has a panoramic view framed by forests of oak, maple, birch, and sumac. The village dock is at the foot of town, and some space for transients is available at the local resort. (Call regarding water depths before approaching.) Egg Harbor doesn't have much to offer, except a hardware store, a bakery, and some small eateries. You can anchor in plenty of water anywhere in the bay but be wary, because it's wide open to the north.

Green Bay. The city at the foot of the bay with the same name is a busy seaway port, with a diversified industrial base. Its harbor is the mouth of the Fox River. The bay shoals in its lower reaches, and the well-buoyed ship channel begins ten miles from the harbor. Just before the high fixed bridge crossing the harbor, a turn to port leads to a friendly yacht club. This is a long taxi ride from downtown Green Bay, but a nice beach is a reasonable walk away.

The numerous bridges crossing the Fox River operate on a complicated schedule; it's best to consult the *Coast Pilot*. About a mile upstream from the entrance, the Holiday Inn offers dockage and hotel privileges. This is the closest facility to downtown shops and restaurants. A mile and a half farther on is a full-service marina in a residential location. You can visit several museums in Green Bay, in addition to the usual commercial amenities of a substantial city.

Oconto. The western shore of Green Bay is low and marshy, with shoals reaching far out into the bay. It's best to follow the ship channel as far as you can toward Oconto, about 30 miles from Green Bay. The combination yacht club and municipal marina up the river provides minimal services. It's about a mile from town, but features some historic buildings and a museum.

Marinette/Menominee. The twin industrial cities are on either side of the Menominee River, which forms the Wisconsin-Michigan border, about 20 miles north of Oconto. Keep well offshore until you enter the channel.

A deeply dredged channel leads up the river for a couple of miles to a full-service marina on the Marinette side. Downtown shops and restaurants are close by, as is a park with a logging museum. Across the river in Menominee is the Mystery Ship Seaport Museum, devoted to the resurrected *Alvin Clark*, the oldest merchant vessel afloat. But the Michigan Waterways Commission marina in Menominee is on the bay front, about a mile northeast of the river entrance.

Lake Michigan North Shore

The north coast of Lake Michigan is entirely in Michigan waters. It extends from Little Bay de Noc, the northern extension of Green Bay, to the Mackinac Bridge. The harbors here are fewer in number and more widely separated than elsewhere on the lake. Beyond Big Bay de Noc, you're on a lee shore in southerly winds blowing up the long sweep of Lake Michigan, so pick your weather carefully when crossing.

Escanaba. Fifty miles north of the Menominee River, Green Bay narrows into Little Bay de Noc. The city of Escanaba on the west shore is an iron loading port. The commercial harbor is on the north side of conspicuous Sand Point, while a well-sheltered basin on the south side encloses the Waterways Commission marina and the yacht club. Pay close attention to the navigational aids on your approach to the harbor, because of numerous unmarked shoals. Furthermore, iron in the region causes magnetic disturbances and compass deviations.

The marina is located in a park with a beach, tennis courts, and the historical museum. Downtown shopping and restaurants are about a mile away.

Gladstone. Seven miles farther into the bay, the friendly little city of Gladstone also has a Waterways Commission marina in a sheltered basin about a mile southwest of Sanders Point. The entrance is narrow, but depths range to seven feet. This marina is in a park with playground, beach, and tennis courts. Downtown shops and restaurants are a few blocks away.

Fayette. Big Bay de Noc continues the limestone bluffs of the Door Peninsula on its eastern shore, but the west side is foul with rocks and shoals. Follow the buoyage carefully when passing around Peninsula Point between Little and Big Bay de Noc. Almost in the north-

LAKE MICHIGAN/WESTERN SHORE

east corner of the bay, Fayette State Park preserves the former ghost town of **Fayette**.

Built in 1867 for iron smelting, Fayette thrived for some 25 years until the local hardwood petered out. The site was abandoned, but the stone work of the furnaces survived, and many of the town's other buildings have been restored to comprise a fascinating historic park. Fayette is a popular cruising destination for Michigan and Wisconsin mariners. Snail Shell Harbor is well protected by its surrounding limestone bluffs. A kind of dockage is arranged around the old pilings of the iron days, but most boats anchor in the bay.

Manistique. Since Manistique is a 50-mile run from Fayette across the open lake, watch the weather forecast before setting out. The harbor is at the mouth of the Manistique River, with a Waterways Commission marina a short distance upstream. The village is nearby.

Naubinway. Another village harbor, Naubinway, is 45 miles northeast of Manistique. To get there, pass through the large shoal area of northern Lake Michigan, marked by buoyage and several big lighthouses to guide the freighters through. A small Waterways Commission marina is located at Naubinway, as are a general store and a restaurant.

From here, it's about fifty miles to the Mackinac Bridge, with no shelter on the way. **Beaver Island**, where the previous chapter began, provides the closest harbor, 25 miles away.

Lake Michigan Western Shore

		Seasonal/Year-Round	Sail/Power/Both	Largest Vessel Accommodated	No. of Transient Berths	Marked Entry Channel	Approach Depth	Dockside Depth	Fuel Brand Gas/Diesel/Both	Railway/Lift Capacity	Engine Repairs: Gas/Diesel/Both	Launching Ramp	Propeller/Hull Repairs	Marine Supplies/LPG/CNG/Groceries/Both	110V/220V/Both	Showers/Laundromat	Max Amps	Pump-Out Station	Restaurant/Snack Bar	Radio Watch–VHF (CB)
CHICAGO																				
1.	59th Street Municipal Harbor	No Listing	S	▲					★							I				
2.	Burnham Park Municipal Harbor*	(312)294-4614	S	▲					★	L						I			●	
3.	Marina City Marina	467-1855	Y	P	60	4		20	6	66	▲	L		★	PH	MGI	▲50	L	●	RS
4.	AAA Boatyard*	276-0330	Y	▲	100	15		21	14		18			▲	PH	▲	MG	★60		●	R
5.	Diversey Municipal Harbor*	327-4430	S	P							★					I			●	
6.	Belmont Harbor	281-8587	S	▲							★					I	★		●	
WAUKEGAN TO RACINE																				
7.	Waukegan Yacht Club*	623-4188	Y	▲	60			15	12					YACHT CLUB						
8.	Larsen Marine	336-5456	Y	▲	60	5		15	10	MOB	▲	30		▲	P	●	MI	★30	S	●	R	16
9.	Trident Marina*	(414)694-1200	Y	▲	70	15	●	6	10	SHE	▲	L		▲	PH	MI	▲30	SL	●	S	
10.	Holiday Inn*	658-3281	S	▲	45			7	5					HOTEL DOCK		GI	★30			R	
11.	Kenosha Yacht Harbor	656-8066	S	▲	44	3	●	25	9			R					★		●	R	
12.	Great Lakes Yacht Sales, Inc.	654-0207	Y	▲	50	2		23	13		★	25		▲	PH	MG	▲30	S		RS	16
13.	Villa Marina*	652-9400	S	P	40	2		12	15	66	★			▲		MI	▲50	S		RS	16
14.	Racine Yacht Club	634-8585	S	▲	45			10	10					YACHT CLUB			★30	S			16
15.	Pugh Marina	632-8515	Y	▲	50	5	●	9	6		▲			R	▲	H			S	●	
16.	Belle Harbor Marina	633-8777	Y	▲	65	4	●	11	7			L		▲	PH	MI	★30	S	●		16
17.	Palmer Johnson Marina	632-2724	Y	▲	65	10	●	12	10		▲	30		▲	H	MI	▲30	S	●	S	16
MILWAUKEE TO PORT WASHINGTON																				
18.	Harbor Marine	273-7020		▲	65	12	●	30	18		▲	L		▲	PH	MI	★30		●		16
19.	Admiral's Wharf, Inc.	276-0793	S	▲	60	10	●	20	10	COD	★	L		★	PH	GI	★20		●		9
20.	McKinley Park Marina	273-5224	S	▲	60			15	10		▲		R			MI	★30	S	●	RS	16
21.	Port Washington Marina	284-6606	S	▲	50	27	●	10	10	STA	▲		R	▲	P	GI	★30	SL	●		16
22.	Port Marine*	284-3574	S	▲	50			16	15			R		▲	PH	MGI	▲30	L	●	R	16
SHEBOYGAN TO ROWLEY'S BAY																				
23.	Sheboygan Yacht Club / Delano Ramps	458-6601	Y	▲	65	10	●	12	12	MOB	▲	L					★10	S		R	16
24.	The Wharf Sheboygan Inc.	458-0051	Y	▲	30	2	●	13	11	MOB	★					GI	▲20		●	S	
25.	Manitowac Marina	682-5117	S	▲	100	40	●	25	10	CIT	▲	35	R	▲	P	●	MGI	▲50	SL	●	RS	16
26.	Seagull Marina & Campgrounds	794-7533	S	▲	50	20		14	14	76	▲		R	▲	PH	MGI	★30		●	R	16
27.	Twin Cities Marine	793-2715	Y	P	25	10			12	MOB	★		R	★		MI	★30	S	●	RS	16
28.	Kewaunee Landing Marine	388-5100	S	▲	40	18		9	8	SHE	▲		R	▲		★	MGI	★30	S	●		16
29.	Fisherman's Point Marina	388-5100	S	▲	50	50	●	9	9	SHE	▲	35	R	▲	PH	MGI	▲50	SL	●	RS	16
30.	Algoma Marine	487-3443		▲	35	10		9	6		▲	L	R	★	H		MI	★30	S	●		16
31.	Sturgeon Bay Yacht Harbor (p. 210)	743-3311	Y	▲	100	35	●	22	9	MOB	▲	50	R	▲	P	★	MI	▲50	S	●	R	16

To provide the most complete and accurate information, **all facilities have been contacted within the past year.** If an asterisk (*) appears, it indicates a facility which did not respond to our requests for information (these listings may not reflect current conditions). Although facility operators supplied this data, we cannot guarantee accuracy or assume responsibility for errors. Entrance and dockside soundings tend to fluctuate. Always approach marinas carefully. Reference numbers on spotting charts indicate marina locations. ✒ Member American Boat Builders & Repairers Association.

# LAKE MICHIGAN/WESTERN SHORE

Aids to Navigation

- Unlighted buoy (C. can, N. nun, S. spar, Bell, Gong, Whistle)
- Danger or junction buoy
- Mooring buoy
- Light (On fixed structure)
- Fish trap buoy
- Daybeacon (Bn)
- R. Bn. radiobeacon
- Mid-channel buoy
- Lighted buoy

Lights (Lights are white unless otherwise indicated)
- F. fixed
- Fl. flashing
- Qk. quick
- Gp. group
- E. Int. equal interval
- Mo..(A) morse code
- Occ. occulting
- Alt. alternating
- I. Qk. interrupted quick
- OBSC. obscured
- WHIS. whistle
- DIA. diaphone
- M. nautical miles
- Rot. rotating
- SEC. sector
- m. minutes
- sec. seconds

Buoys:
- T.B. temporary buoy
- C. can
- N. nun
- S. spar
- B. black
- Or. orange
- R. red
- G. green
- W. white
- Y. yellow

Bottom characteristics:
- Cl. clay
- Co. coral
- G. gravel
- Grs. grass
- M. mud
- Rk. rock
- S. sand
- Sh. shells
- hrd. hard
- rky. rocky
- sft. soft
- stk. sticky
- bk. black
- br. brown
- bu. blue
- gn. green
- gy. gray
- rd. red
- wh. white
- yl. yellow

Dangers:
- Sunken wreck
- Visible wreck
- Rocks
- Wreck, rock, obstruction, or shoal swept clear to the depth indicated
- Rocks that cover and uncover, with heights in feet above datum of soundings
- AERO. aeronautical
- Bn. daybeacon
- R. Bn. radiobeacon
- R. TR. radio tower
- C.G. Coast Guard Station
- D.F.S. distance finding station
- AUTH. authorized
- Obstr. obstruction
- P.A. position approximate
- E.D. existence doubtful

Caution: Mariners are warned to stay clear of the protective riprap surrounding navigational light structures shown thus.

- Restricted Areas
- Fish Trap Areas

Lake Michigan Western Shore

		SEASONAL/YEAR-ROUND	SAIL/POWER/BOTH	LARGEST VESSEL ACCOMMODATED	NO. OF TRANSIENT BERTHS	MARKED ENTRY CHANNEL	APPROACH DEPTH (Reported)	DOCKSIDE DEPTH (Reported)	RAILWAY/LIFT CAPACITY (in tons)	GAS★DIESEL●BOTH▲ FUEL BRAND	ENGINE REPAIRS: Gas★Diesel●Both▲	LAUNCHING RAMP	PROPELLER/HULL REPAIRS	MARINE SUPPLIES	LPG★CNG●BOTH▲	110V★220V●BOTH▲ GROCERIES/ICE	SHOWERS★MAX AMPS	RESTAURANT/SNACK BAR	PUMP-OUT STATION	RADIO WATCH—VHF(CB)
32. Palmer Johnson Inc.	(414) 743-4412	Y	▲	50	12	●	12	10		▲	30		▲	P	●	MI	★30	S	●	RS	16
33. Nelson Shopping Center	839-2326	Y	▲				7	6	CIT				R		★	MGI	★	L		R	
34. Bailey's Harbor Yacht Club (p. 210)	839-2336	S	▲	65	30	●			UNI	▲			R			I	▲30	SL	●	R	9
35. Wagon Trail Marina and Resort	854-2385	S	▲	35	20	●	12	6		★			R			I	★30	SL	●	R	16
WASHINGTON ISLAND																					
36. Kap's Marina	847-2640	S	▲	46	30	●	7	7	AMO	★	30	R	▲	PH	●	MI	★40	S	●	R	9
37. Island Outpost	847-2395	S	▲	90	12		7	7								M	★20			RS	16/68
38. Shipyard Island Marina	847-2533	Y	▲	65	15	●	7	7	AMO	▲	35	R	▲	P		MI	★50	S	●	R	16
39. Moorings of Njord Heim	847-2459	S	▲	60	30	●	7	8		▲				▲	P	MGI	▲50	SL	●	RS	16/68
40. Jackson Harbor	847-2511	S	▲	60	26	●	13	6	STD	▲			R	▲		MGI	▲30	S	●	R	
GREEN BAY / EASTERN SHORE																					
41. Weborg' Wharf	854-2428	S	▲	35	12		7	5	CIT	★			R			I	★30				
42. Liberty Grove / Ellison Bay Town Dock*	854-4603	S	▲	35	10	●	7	5					R				★20				
43. Anchor Marine, Inc.	854-2124	Y	▲	37	5		8	6	UNI	▲	12		▲	P	★	MI	★15	S	●	RS	16
44. Cal Marine (p. 211)	854-4521	Y	P						AMO	★			★	PH		M				R	
45. Sister Bay Dock*	854-4457	S	▲	55	15		30	8					R			GI	★30			RS	16
46. Ephraim Yacht Harbor	(414) 854-4014	S	▲	65	10		8	8		▲						I	▲30				16
47. Alibi Dock	868-3789	S	▲	90	40		20	12	MOB	▲				▲		MI	▲50		●	RS	
48. Fish Creek Municipal*	868-3909	S	▲	46			15	10	TEX	★			R			GI			●		
49. Egg Harbor Municipal Dock*	No Listing		▲	40			20	5		★			R			G	★20		●		
GREEN BAY / WESTERN SHORE																					
50. Holiday Inn City Centre Marina	437-5900	S	▲	50	10	●	28	12								GI	★30	SL	●	R	16
51. Green Bay Yacht Club	432-0168	Y	▲	48	3	●	8	5		★	25	R				I	★30	S	●	RS	16/9
52. Great Lakes Marine Center	494-3303	Y	▲	40	5		7	5		★							★30		●		
53. Skinner's	(715) 732-4466	Y	▲		2				TEX	▲	L	R	▲			G	★30		●		
54. Menominee Memorial Marina	(906) 863-8498	S	▲	60	20	●	16	9		▲			R		●	MI	★30	SL	●	RS	16
NORTHERN SHORE																					
55. Escanaba Marina	786-9614	S	▲	40		●	15	8	MOB	▲			R			I	★30	S	●		16
56. Gladstone Yacht Harbor	428-4915	S	▲	50	5	●	8	8	MAR	★			R		★	MGI	▲30	S	●	RS	16
57. Fayette State Park	644-2603	S	▲	100		●	10	13					R			GI					
58. Manistique Marina*	341-6841	S	▲	30	5	●	8	5		★							★30		●		16

To provide the most complete and accurate information, **all facilities have been contacted within the past year.** If an asterisk (*) appears, it indicates a facility which did not respond to our requests for information (these listings may not reflect current conditions). Although facility operators supplied this data, we cannot guarantee accuracy or assume responsibility for errors. Entrance and dockside soundings tend to fluctuate. Always approach marinas carefully. Reference numbers on spotting charts indicate marina locations. ⌐ Member American Boat Builders & Repairers Association.

GREAT LAKES EDITION 215

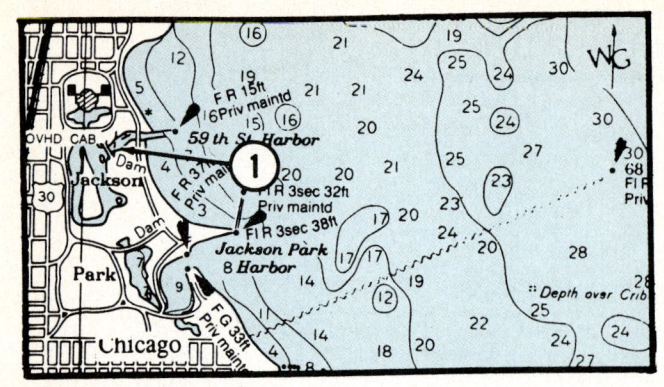

Lake Michigan/Western Shore

Chart 14927, edition 18

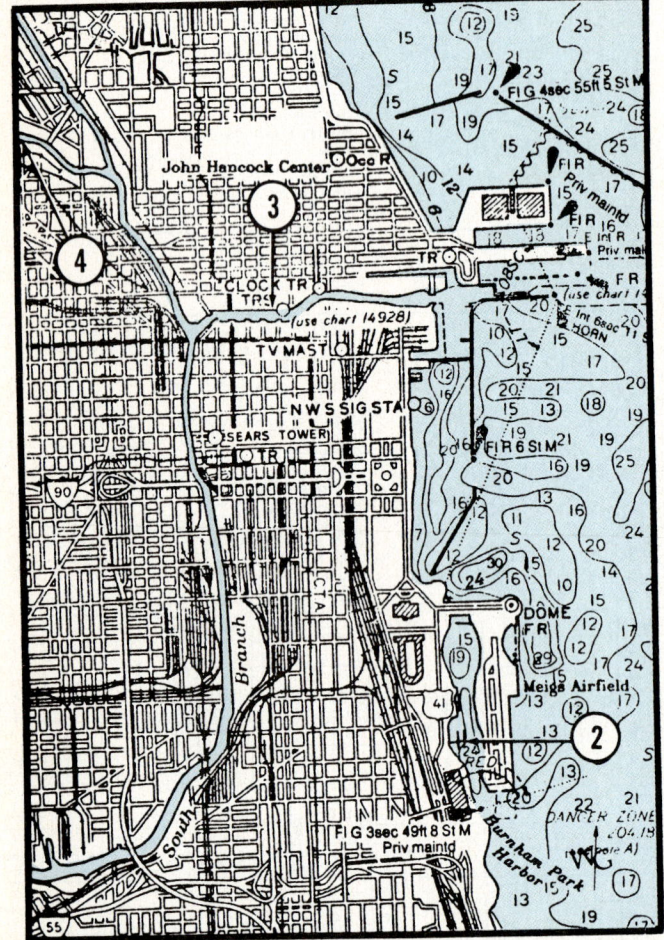

Chart 14927, edition 18

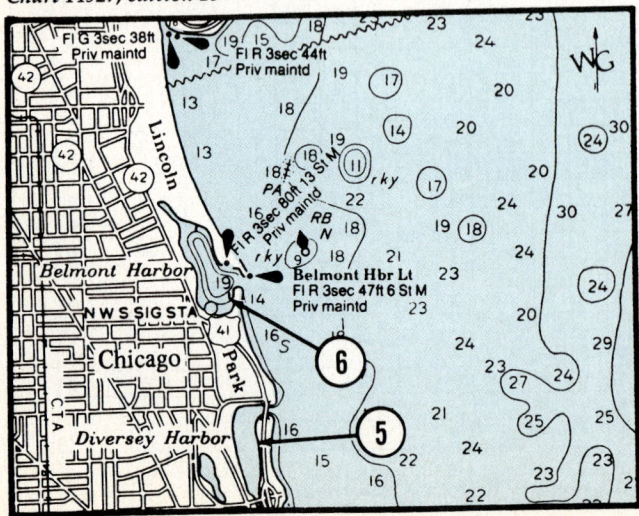

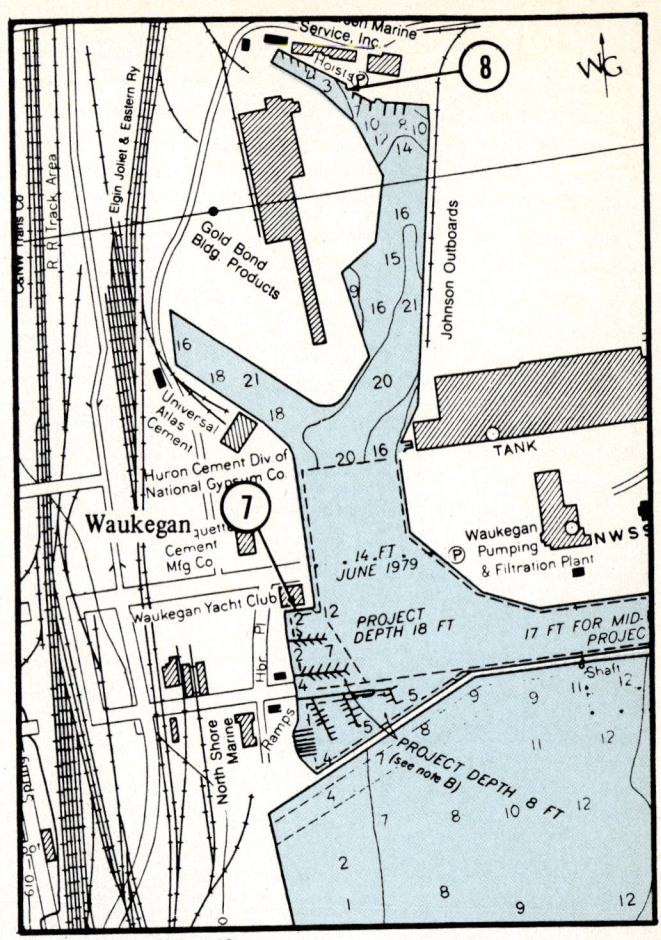

Chart 14927, edition 18

Chart 14904, edition 19

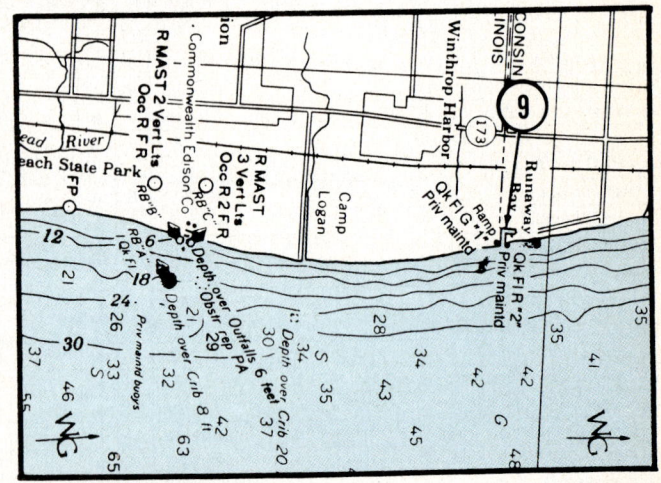

Chart 14904, edition 19

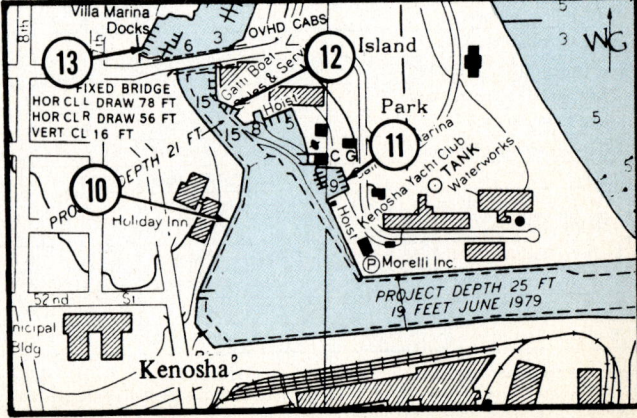

Chart 14904, edition 19

216   *Under no circumstances are these charts to be used for navigation.*   Waterway Guide / 1991

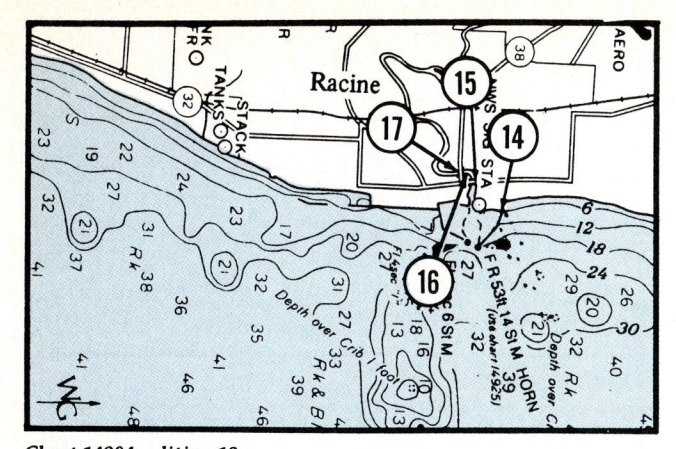

Lake Michigan/Western Shore

Chart 14904, edition 19

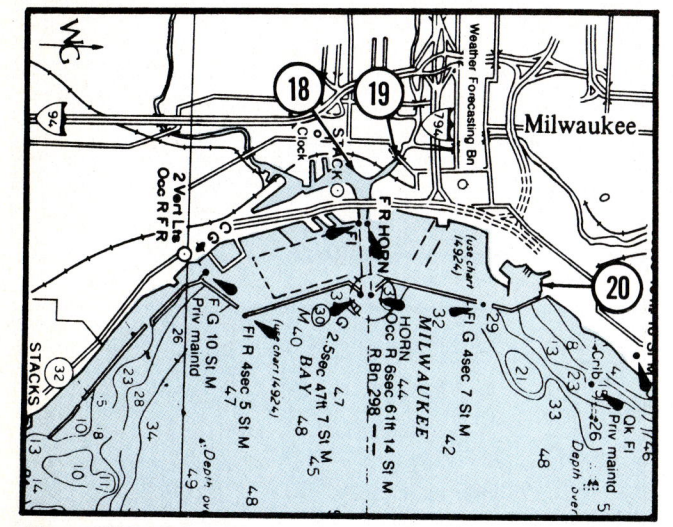

Chart 14904, edition 19

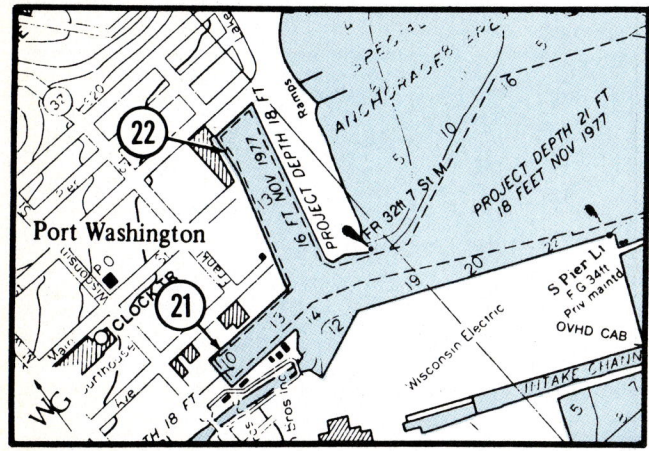

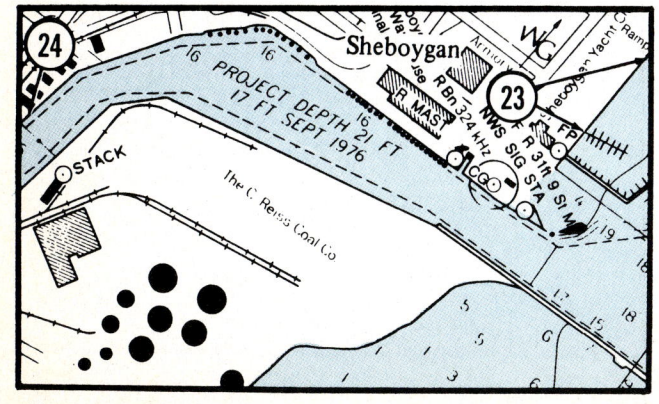

Chart 14904, edition 19

Chart 14922, edition 15

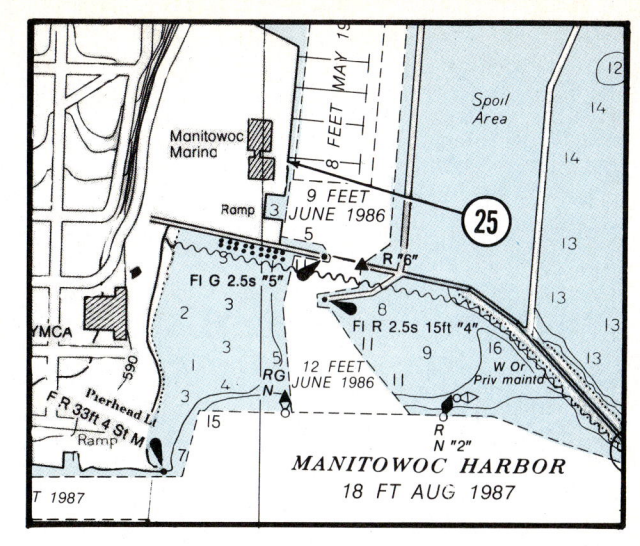

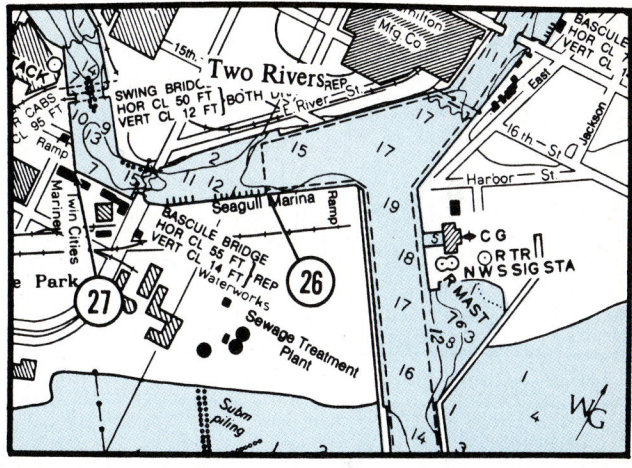

Chart 14903, edition 19

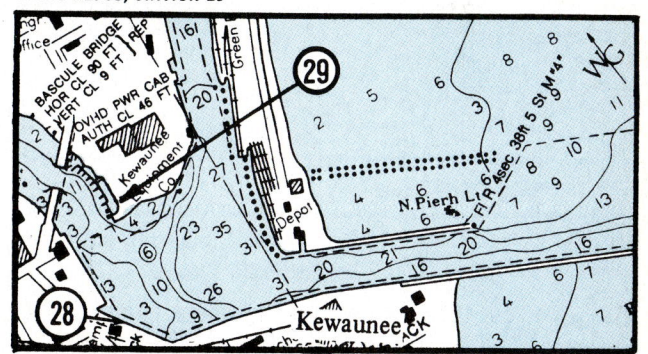

Chart 14903, edition 19

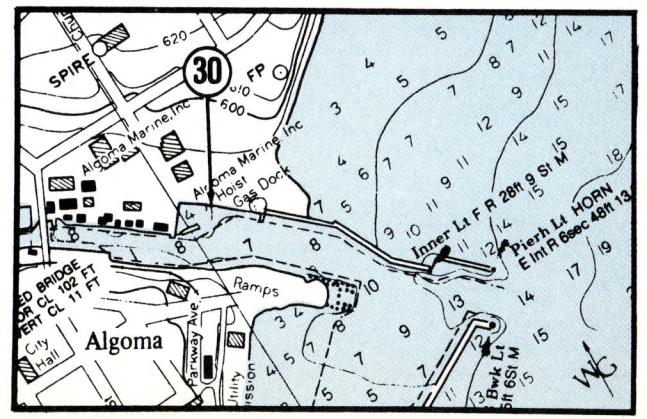

Chart 14910, edition 17

GREAT LAKES EDITION — *Under no circumstances are these charts to be used for navigation.*

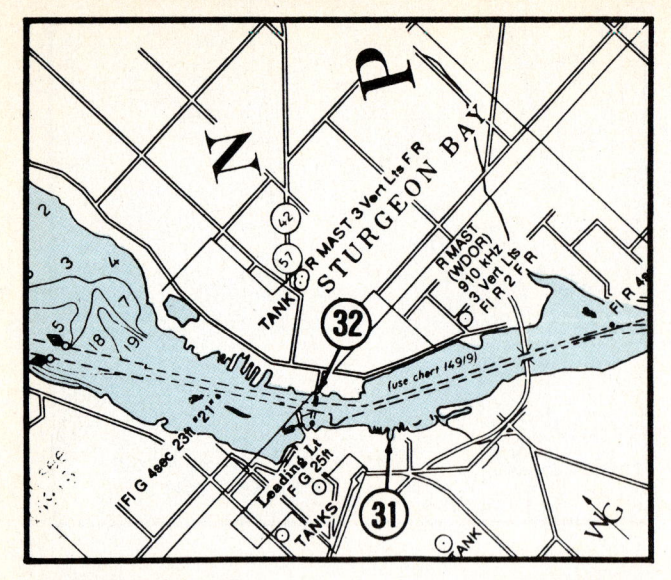

LAKE MICHIGAN/WESTERN SHORE

Chart 14910, edition 17

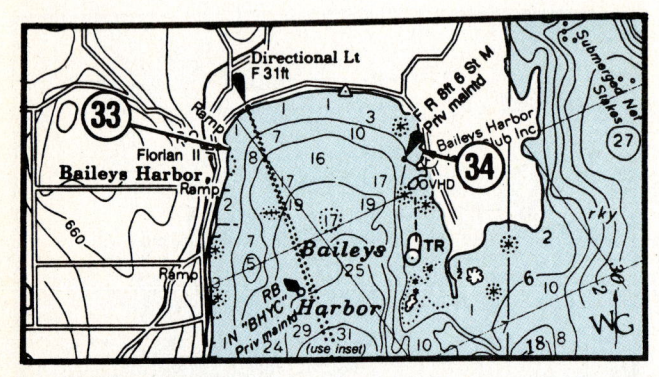

Chart 14909, edition 15

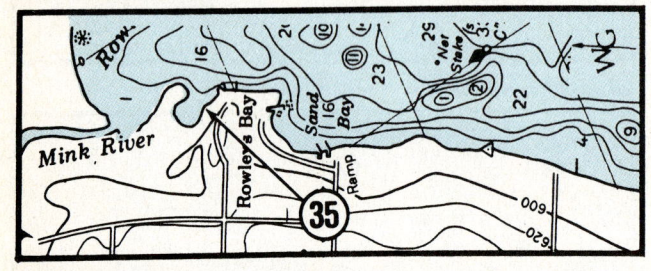

Chart 14909, edition 15

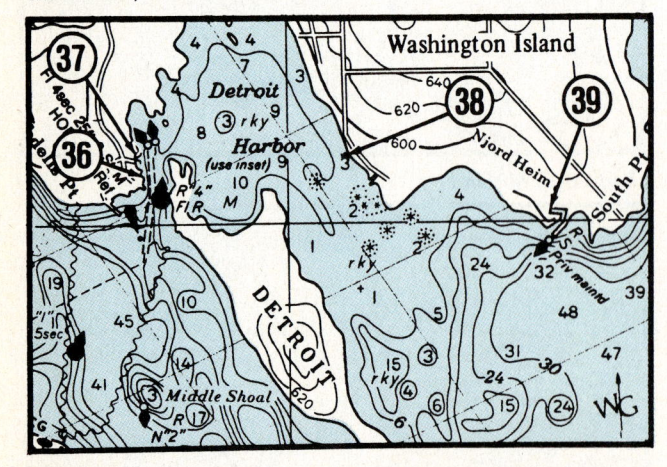

Chart 14909, edition 15

Chart 14909, edition 15

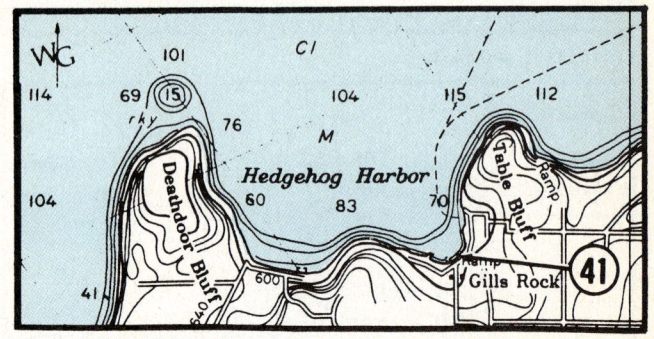

Chart 14909, edition 15

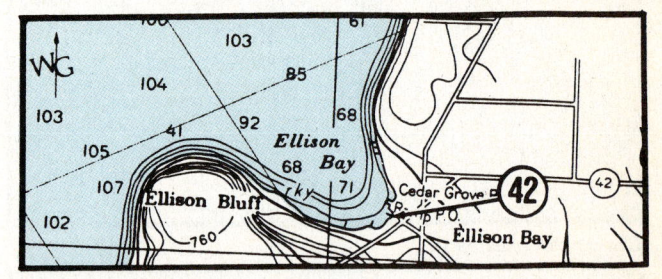

Chart 14909, edition 15

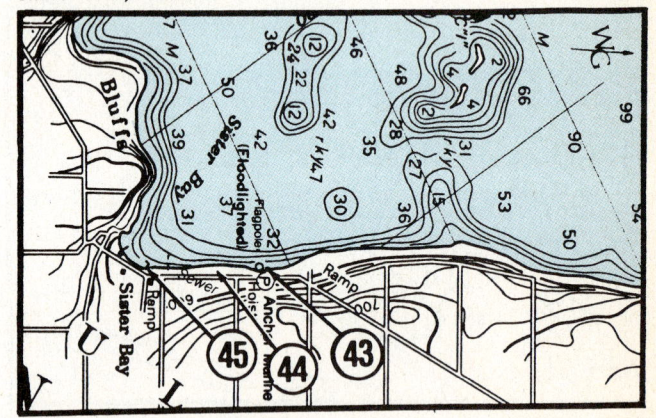

Chart 14909, edition 15

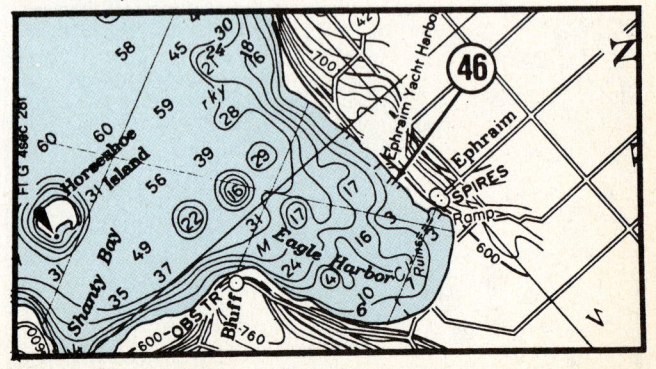

Chart 14909, edition 15

Lake Michigan/Western Shore

Chart 14909, edition 15

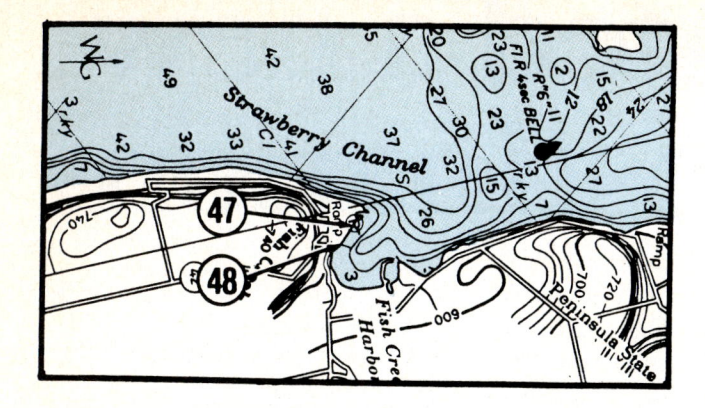

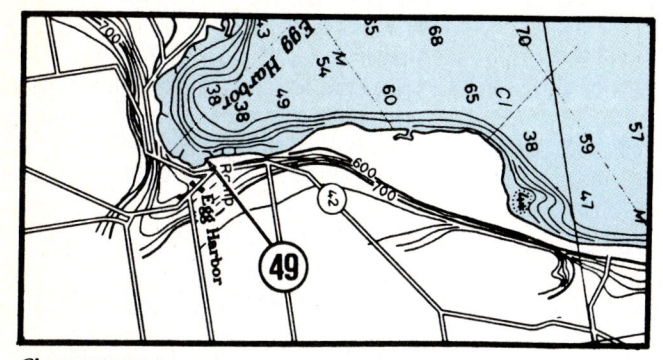

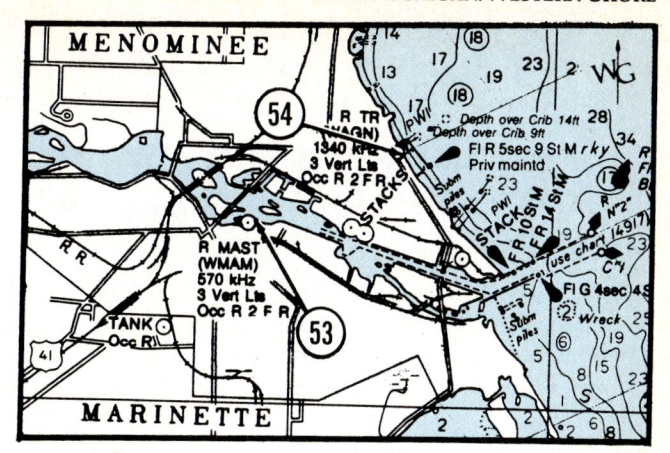

Chart 14909, edition 15

Chart 14908, edition 15

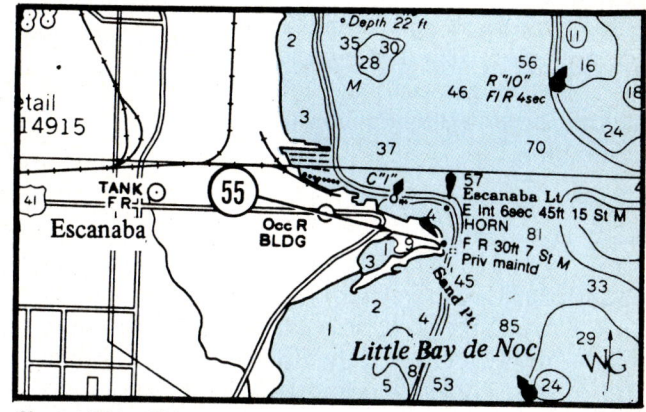

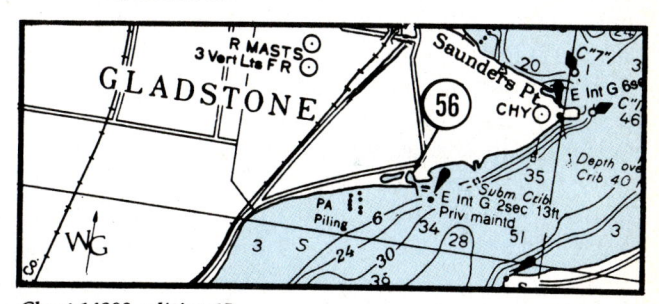

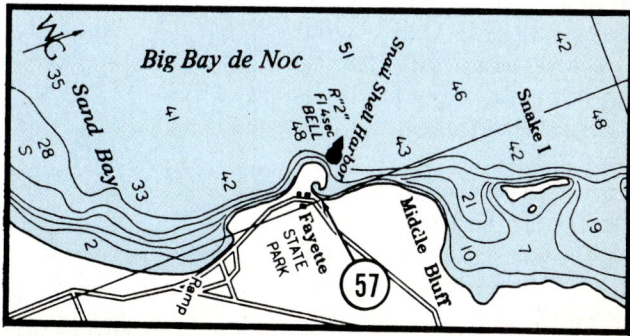

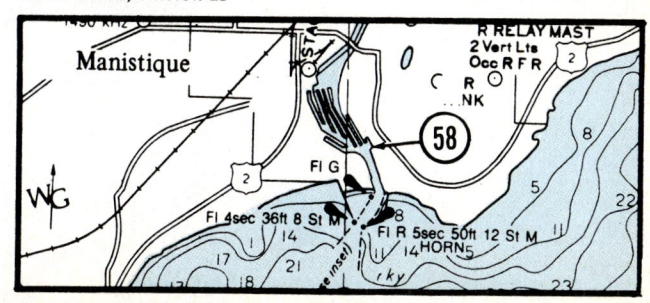

Chart 14908, edition 15

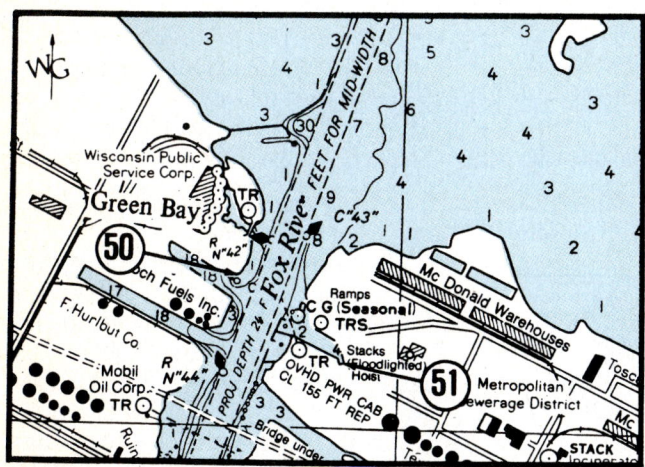

Chart 14918, edition 21

Chart 14908, edition 15

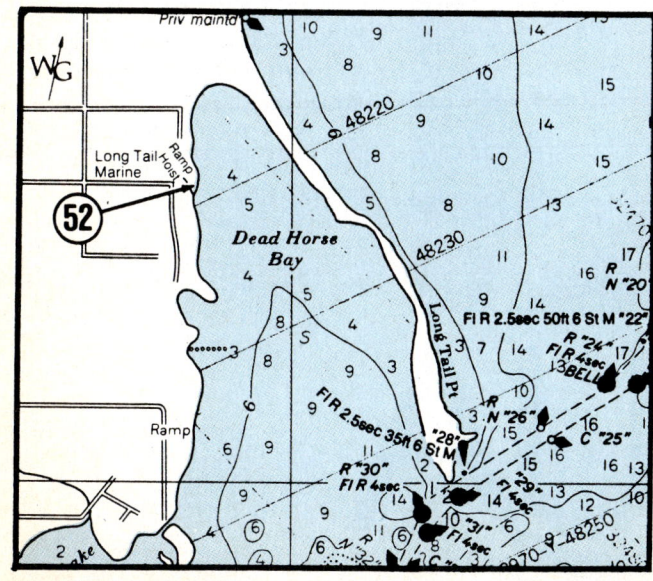

Chart 14910, edition 17

Chart 14908, edition 15

GREAT LAKES EDITION — *Under no circumstances are these charts to be used for navigation.*

We've created a new boating destination

It's called Aqua Yacht Harbor. Have you ever cruised the beautiful Tennessee River? Come explore the clean waters, the quiet coves, the scenic hills, the historic cities and enjoy the friendly people for the best boating you'll ever know. The skiing, swimming and fishing don't get any better than in the tranquility of the Tennessee. You'll enjoy making Aqua Yacht Harbor your destination.

Over the seasons or overnight, yours to enjoy.
Aqua Yacht Harbor is one of the finest inland waterway marinas in the U.S.A. Its large protected harbor is strategically located at the north end of the Tennessee Tombigbee Waterway. Northern boaters find it to be the perfect location for in-water winter dockage.

If you want to fly into the area, Savannah, Tennessee's airport is only minutes away, with a 5,000 foot runway, and our courtesy vehicles are only a phone call away.

Hospitality fits any size.
Facilities, services and hospitality. If that's what you're looking for, look no further. Aqua Yacht Harbor is the perfect location for year-round boating. As the area's largest full service marina, we cater to cruising yachtsmen as well as weekend boaters. Aqua Yacht Harbor is the ideal stopping point for north- and south- bound cruising yachts. Its management are professional yachtsmen who see to it that your boat is serviced by courteous, experienced and knowledgeable personnel, using quality products as if your boat were their boat.

Aqua Yacht Harbor has it all.
Full service marina facilities at Aqua Yacht Harbor include:
- Approach depth 25'...12' dockside at normal pool
- 600 covered and open slips accommodating vessels up to 120', plus 25 transient slips
- Gas, diesel, lubricants, pumpout. Fuel capacity 36,000 gallons with six gasoline pumps, four diesel high speed delivery pumps, all with in-line filtration
- Major credit cards honored
- 50 amps 220V and 30 amps 125V service
- Showers, restrooms, laundry, ice
- Cable TV & phone hookups
- Ship's stores, groceries, snacks, marine supplies
- Harbor view restaurant
- Courtesy cars
- Boat washing service
- Divers available
- Two travel lifts up to 70 tons
- Experienced mechanics for both gasoline and diesel engines
- Complete full service yard with over 11,000 parts for both sail and power, including state-of-the art sandblasting and painting facilites
- Dry storage up to 30'
- Fully equipped service van for quick response and dependable maintenance when underway
- Parts department with extensive inventory
- Home of Pickwick Yacht Club
- 18 hole Winfield Dunn golf course just 6 minutes away
- Monitors VHF Ch. 16, open year round

Transients are always welcome.
More than 1,000 feet of transient slips provide enough room for cruising clubs, groups or boatercades.

Our rates are 50 cents per foot per night, plus tax. This includes electricity and water (new hubble 50 amp and 30 amp service).

For reservations or information contact:
Aqua Yacht Harbor, Route 4, Box 530, Iuka, MS 38852 or call (601) 423-2222 or after hours (601) 423-2605.

Formerly Greenwater Marina on Pickwick Lake in Yellow Creek. Just 2200 yards (1.25 miles) west of Tennessee Tombigbee Waterway Island Upper Daymark 448.7

AQUA
YACHT HARBOR

Advertisers' Index

A
Albany Yacht Club, 29
All Seasons Marine, Inc., 198
Allstate Insurance, 6, 7
American Boat Builders, 228
Aqua Yacht Harbor, 220

B
Baileys Harbor Yacht Club, 210
Barrett's Boat Works, 197
Battery Park Marina, 147
Bellinger Marine Service, 193
Blain's Bay Marina, 56
Brewerton Boat Yard, 58

C
Cal Marine, Inc., 211
Catskill Marina, 28
Cavallario's Steak House, 89
Cedar Point Marina, 147
Collins Bay Marina, 71

D
Dawson's Marina Ltd., 104
Delegal Creek Marina, 9
Denison Marine, 10
Digitial Marine, 1

E
East Shore Marina, 73
Ess-Kay Yards, Inc., 59

G
Grand Banks Yachts, Ltd., 17
Gulf Plating, Inc., 14

H
Hansen Insurance, CV4
Harbourfront Marine, 74
Hibiscus Harbor, 61
Hubbell Incorporated, CV2
Hutchinsons Boat Works, 88

J
Jefferson Beach Marina, 169
The Jockey Club, 16
John Ray and Sons, 28
Johnson Boat Yard, 62

K
Kean's Yacht Harbor, 166

L
Lake Ontario Marina, 71
Lakeview Park Marina, 167
Lock 12 Marina, 45

M
Marinco, Inc., 4

O
Ontario Marine Operators, 76
Oswego Marina, 60

P
Plattsburgh Harbor Marina, 48
Point Bay Marina, 47
The Poplars Inn, 57
Port Huron River Marina, 171

R
Raritan Engineering Co., 14
Riveredge Resort, 89
Riverview Marine, 27
Rondout Yacht Basin, 26

S
Safe Captains USA, 9
Sarnia Bay Marina, 171
Schuyler Yacht Basin, 45
Shady Harbor Marina, 28
Skinner's Harbour, 58
Smith Boys, Inc., 62
The Store, 75
Sturgeon Bay Yacht Harbor, 210
Sutherland Marine, 144
Switlik Parachute Co., 2

T
Tarrytown Marina, 24
Town of Port Elgin, 185

W
Wallaceburg Tourist, 170
Watermakers, Inc., 15
West Shore Marina, 25
Westport Marina, 47

GREAT LAKES EDITION

Tossing this trash overboard could leave death in your wake.

Throwing a few plastic items off a boat may seem harmless enough. What's one more six-pack ring, plastic bag, or tangled fishing line?

Actually, it's one more way a fish, bird, seal, or other animal could die.

Fish, birds, and seals are known to strangle in carelessly discarded six-pack rings. Sea turtles eat plastic bags—which they mistake for jellyfish—and suffer internal injury, intestinal blockage, or death by starvation.

Other plastic trash can be dangerous, too. Birds are known to ingest everything from small plastic pieces to plastic cigarette lighters and bottle caps.

Birds, seals, sea turtles, and whales die when they become trapped in old fishing line, rope, and nets.

Plastic debris also can foul boat propellers and block cooling intakes, causing annoying—sometimes dangerous—delays and causing costly repairs.

So please, save your trash for proper disposal on land.

That's not all you'll be saving.

To learn more about how you can help, write: Center for Environmental Education, 1725 DeSales Street, N.W., Suite 500, Washington, D.C. 20036.

A public service message from:
The Center for Environmental Education
The National Oceanic and Atmospheric Administration
The Society of the Plastics Industry

Index

A

Abeel Island, NY, 57
Admiralty Island, Ont., 87
Ahnapee River, WI, 209
Albany, NY, 29
Albion, NY, 63
Aldolphus Reach, Ont., 72
Alexandria Bay, NY, 40, 89
Algoma, WI, 209
Algonac, MI, 171
Allen Point, VT, 48
Alonquin Island, Ont., 73
Alpena, MI, 181
Amherstburg, Ont., 165
Amherstburg Channel, Ont., 163
Amherst Island, Ont., 72
Amsterdam, NY, 56
Anchor Bay, MI, 168
Anchor Pointe, OH, 151
Arcadia, MI, 196
Arcadia River, MI, 196
Ashbridges Bay, Ont., 73
Ashtabula, OH, 144
Ashtabula River, OH, 144
Au Gres, MI, 180
Au Gres River, MI, 180
Au Sable, MI, 180
Au Sable River, MI, 180, 184
Aubrey Island, Ont., 87

B

Baie Comeau, Que., 93
Baie Eternite, Que., 93
Bailey's Harbor, WI, 210
Baker Island, Ont., 72
Baldwinsville, NY, 60
Ballards Reef Channel, MI, 163
Ballast Island, OH, 150
Balsam Lake, Ont., 103
Bannerman's Island, NY, 25
Barcelona, NY, 143
Barnhart Island, NY, 91
Barrie, Ont., 104
Bassin Louise, Que., 92
Bateau Channel, 87
Battery, NY, 24
Battlefield, NY, 71
Bay City, MI, 180
Bay of Quinte, Ont., 69, 71
Bay Point, OH, 147
Bayfield, Ont. (Lake Huron), 184
Bayfield Bay, NY, 87
Bayfield Island, NY, 87
Beaches, The, Ont., 73
Beacon, NY, 26
Bear Mountain, NY, 25
Beauharnois Canal, Que., 91
Beaurivage, Ont., 86
Beaver Creek, OH, 146
Beaver Island, MI (Lake Michigan), 191, 214
Beaver Island State Park, NY, 143
Belle Isle, MI, 167
Belle River, Ont., 169
Belleville, Ont., 72
Belmont Harbor, IL, 205
Beloeil, Que., 50
Bensford Bridge, Ont., 101
Benson Landing, NY, 46
Benton Harbor, MI, 199
Bertie Bay, Ont., 143
Big Bay, MI, 198

Big Bay, Ont., 72
Big Chute, Ont., 105
Big Island, Ont., 72
Big Otter Creek, Ont., 154
Bird Creek, MI, 179
Black River, MI, 171, 199
Black River Bay, NY, 71
Black Rock Canal, NY, 143
Black Rock Lock, NY, 64
Blainsville, Que., 91
Bluffers Bay, 73
Bobcaygeon, Ont., 102
Bois Blanc Island, MI (Detroit River), 163, 165
Bois Blanc Island, MI (Lake Huron), 182
Bolles Harbor, MI, 152
Bolsover, Ont., 103
Boucherville, Que., 92
Bowers Harbor, MI, 195
Bowmanville, Ont., 72
Boyne City, MI, 193
Braddock Bay, NY, 79
Breakneck Point, NY, 26
Brewerton, NY, 58
Bridge and Lock Manners, 115
Brighton, Ont., 72
Brockport, NY, 63, 79
Brockville, Ont., 90
Bronte Harbour, Ont., 75
Bronte Creek, Ont., 75
Brother Islands, Ont., 72
Brownstone Creek, MI, 167
Bruce Peninsula, Ont., 178, 184, 185
Buckhorn, Ont., 102
Buffalo, NY, 64, 143
Burleigh Falls, Ont., 102
Burlington, VT, 48
Burlington Bay, Ont., 75
Burlington Bay, VT, 41, 48
Burnham Park Harbor, IL, 205
Burt Lake, MI, 182
Button Bay, VT, 47

C

Camelot Island, Ont., 87
Cameron Lake, Ont., 103
Camp Perry, OH, 151
Canal Lake, Ont., 103
Canoga, NY, 61
Cap a l'Aigle, Que., 93
Cape Gaspè, Que., 94
Cape Hurd, Ont., 187
Cape Hurd Channel, 186
Cape Vincent, NY, 40, 87
Cardinal, Ont., 90
Carleton Island, NY, 87
Caseville, MI, 179
Castleton-on-Hudson, NY, 28, 42
Catawba Island, OH, 148, 149
Catfish Creek, Ont., 155
Catskill, NY, 27
Catskill Creek, NY, 27
Cattaraugus Creek, NY, 143
Cayuga Lake, NY, 60, 61
Cayuga-Seneca Canal, NY, 54, 60
Cedar Creek, Ont., 156
Cedar Island, Ont., 87
Cedar Island, VT, 48
Cedar Point, OH, 147
Cedarville, MI, 183
Celeron, Island, MI, 167
Centre Island, Ont., 73
Chagrin River, OH, 144
Chambers Island, WI, 212

Chambly Canal, Que., 41, 49, 92
Champlain Canal, 42, 43
Champlain Waterways, 43
Chantry Island, Ont. 184
Charlevoix, MI, 193
Charlotte, VT, 47
Chatham, Ont., 169
Chaumont, NY, 40, 71
Chaumont Bay, NY, 71
Cheboygan, MI, 182
Cheboygan River, MI, 182
Chemung Lake, 103
Chenal Ecarte, , Ont., 170
Chequaga Falls, 62
Chic-Choc Mountains, Que., 94
Chicago, IL, 205
Chicago River, IL, 205
Chicoutimi, Que., 93
Chimney Point, VT, 46
Chipman Point, VT, 43, 46
Chippewa Bay, Ont., 90
Clayton, NY, 40, 89
Clear Lake, Ont., 102
Cleveland, NY, 58
Cleveland, OH, 145
Cleveland Harbor, OH, 145
Clinton River, MI, 168
Clyde River, NY, 54
Coast Guard, 116
Coboconk, Ont., 103
Cobourg, Ont., 72
Coeymans, NY, 28
Cohoes, NY, 55
Cold Spring, NY, 25
Confederation Basin, Ont., 71
Conneaut, OH, 144
Constantia, NY, 58
Converse Bay, 41, 48
Cook Bay, Ont., 104
Cooley Canal, OH, 151
Cornwall, Ont., 40, 91
Corps of Engineers, 132
Cote St. Catherine, Que., 91
Cove Island, Ont., 186
Coxasackie Island, NY, 28
Cow Island, Ont., 101
Crescent, NY, 55
Croil Island, NY, 91
Crooked Lake, MI, 182
Crooked River, MI, 182
Cross Lake, NY, 60
Croton Point, NY, 24
Crowe Bay, Ont., 100
Crowe River, Ont., 100
Crowes Landing, Ont., 102
Crown Point, NY, 43, 47
Crystal Bay, MI, 163
Customs, 130
Cuyahoga River, OH, 145

D

Daley Island, NY, 56
Deep Bay, VT, 41
Deer Bay, Ont., 102
Deer Island, Ont., 90
Deschaillons, Que., 92
Deseronto, Ont., 72
Detroit, MI, 167
Detroit Harbor, WI, 211
Detroit Island, WI, 211
Detroit River, MI, 163
Devil Island Channel, 186
Distance Tables:
   Chambly Canal, 46
   Champlain Canal, 46
   Detroit River, 169
   Erie Canal, 55

   Great Lakes, 123
   Lake Champlain, 46
   Lake Erie, 142
   Lake Huron, 178
   Lake Michigan, 192, 194 206, 208
   Lake Ontario, 78
   Lake St. Clair, 169
   St. Lawrence Seaway, 92
   Trent-Severn Waterway, 102
Door Peninsula, WI, 209, 210
Douglas, MI, 198, 199
Dunderberg Mountain, NY, 25
Dunkirk, NY, 143

E

Eagle Harbor, WI, 211
East Harbor, OH, 148
East Jordan, MI, 193
East Tawas, MI, 180
Eastern Gap, Ont., 73
Egg Harbor, WI, 213
Eighteen-mile Creek, Ont., 78
Elberta, MI, 196
Elk Rapids, MI, 194
Elk River, MI, 194
Ellison Bay, WI, 211
Endymion Island, Ont., 87
Ephraim, WI, 211
Erie, PA, 143
Erie Basin, 64
Erie Canal, 40, 43, 54
Erie Islands, 149
Erieau, Ont., 156
Escanaba, MI, 213
Esopus Creek, NY, 27
Esopus Island, NY, 27
Esopus Meadows, NY, 27
Essex, NY, 41

F

Fair Haven, MI, 168
Fairport, NY, 63
Fairport Harbor, OH, 144
Fairyland Island, Ont., 90
False Presque Isle, MI, 181
Fayette, MI, 213
Fenelon Falls, Ont., 103
Fighting Island, Ont., 165
Finger Lakes, NY, 60
Fish Creek, WI, 213
Fishing Islands, Ont., 184,186
Fonda Terminal, NY, 56
Forestry Islands, Ont., 73
Fort Edward, NY, 45
Fort Frontenac, Ont., 71
Fort Mackinac, MI, 182
Fort Malden, Ont., 165
Fort Michilimackinac, MI, 182
Fort Ontario, NY, 69
Fort Plain, NY, 57
Fort Ticonderoga, NY, 42, 46
Foundry Cove, NY, 25
Fox River, WI, 213
Frankford, Ont., 99
Frankfort, MI, 196
Frankfort, NY, 54, 57
Freemont, OH, 148
Frenchman Bay, Ont., 73
Fulton, NY, 59
Fultonville, NY, 56

G

Galop Canal, Ont., 90
Gananoque, Ont., 87

GREAT LAKES EDITION   223

Gannon Narrows, Ont., 103
Garden Island, VT, 48
Gasport, NY, 64
Gem Beach Channel, OH, 149
Genesee River, NY, 63, 79
Geneva, NY, 62
George Washington Bridge, 24
Gibralter, MI, 167
Gibralter Island, OH, 150
Gladstone, MI, 213
Glen Ross, Ont., 99
Glens Falls, 45
Glen Water, Que., 91
Glenora, Ont., 72
Gloucester Pool, Ont., 106
Goderich, Ont., 184
Goose Bay, NY, 90
Government Bay, MI, 183
Grand Bend, MI, 184
Grand Haven, MI, 197
Grand Island, NY, 143
Grand River, MI, 197
Grand River, OH, 144
Grand River, Ont., 153
Grand Traverse Bay, MI, 193
Grass Island, Ont., 165
Great Lakes Historical Society, 146
Green Bay, WI, 210, 213
Grenadier Island, Ont., 71, 87
Grimsby, Ont., 76
Grindstone City, MI, 179
Grindstone Island, NY, 87
Gros Cacouna, Que., 94
Grosse Isle, MI, 163, 167
Grosse Pointe, MI, 168
Gulf of St. Lawrence, Que., 93
Gull Island, NY, 75
Gull Shoal, OH, 150

H

Hamilton Harbor, Ont., 75
Hamilton, Ont., 75
Hammond Bay, MI, 181
Hanlan Point, Ont., 73
Harbor Beach, MI, 179
Harbor Springs, MI, 193
Harbourfront, Ont., 75
Harlem River, NY, 24
Harrisville, MI, 180
Harsens Island, MI, 171
Harwood, Ont., 101
Hastings, Ont., 100
Hastings-on-Hudson, NY, 24
Hay Bay, Ont., 72
Headlands Beach State Park, OH, 144
Healy Falls, Ont., 100

Heart Island, NY, 89
Hedgehog Harbor, WI, 211
Henderson Bay, NY, 40, 71
Herkimer, NY, 57
Hessel, MI, 183
Himmansville, NY, 59
Holland, MI, 198
Holley, NY, 63
Horse Island, MI, 167
Horseshoe Island, WI, 212
Horton Bay, MI, 193
Hospital Creek, VT, 47
Houghtaling Island, NY, 28
Howe Island, 87
Hudson Falls, 45
Hudson River, NY, 43
Humber River, Ont., 75
Huron, OH, 146
Huron-Clinton Metropolitan Park, MI, 168
Hyde Park NY, 27

I

Iberville, Que., 48
Ile-aux-Noix, Que., 48
Ile aux Coudres, Que., 93
Ile d'Orleans, Que., 93
Ile Perrot, Que., 91
Ile St. Quentin, Que., 92
Ilion, NY, 57
Illinois Waterway, IL, 205
Indian River, MI, 182
Indian River, Ont., 101
Inner Bay, Ont., 154
Iona Island, NY, 25
Ironton, MI, 193
Iroquois Lock, NY, 40, 90
Irondoquoit Bay, NY, 79
Ithaca, NY, 60, 62
Ivy Lea, Ont., 87

J

Jackson Park Harbor IL, 205
Jackson Harbor, WI, 211
Johnsons Island, OH, 148
Juniper Island, Ont., 102

K

Kalamazoo Lake, WI, 198
Kalamazoo River, MI, 198
Kawartha Lakes, Ont., 102
Kawartha Park, Ont., 102
Kelleys Island, OH, 148, 150
Kempfelt Bay, Ont., 103

Kenosha, WI, 207
Kettle Creek, Ont., 155
Kewaunee, WI, 209
Kincardine, Ont., 185
Kingsland Bay, VT, 41, 47
Kingston, NY, 27
Kingston, Ont., 71
Kingsville, Ont., 156
Kirkfield, Ont., 103
Klein Island, NY, 60

L

La Plaisance Creek, MI, 152
La Salle, Ont., 165
Lac St. Louis, Que., 91
Lac St. Pierre, Que., 92
Lagoons The, Ont., 73
Lake Champlain, 43, 45, 97
Lake Charlevoix, MI, 193
Lake Couchiching, 104
Lake Erie, 64, 139
Lake Fleet Island, Ont., 87
Lake Huron, 177
Lake Katchewanooka, Ont., 102
Lake Macatawa, MI, 198
Lake Michigan, 191, 205
Lake Ontario, 40, 69
Lake St. Clair, 163, 168
Lake St. Francis, Que., 91
Lake Scugog, Ont., 103
Lake Simcoe, Ont., 103
Lakefield, Ont., 102
Lakeside, MI, 197
Lakeside, OH, 148
Lancaster, Que., 91
L'Anse a Valleau, Que., 94
Leak Island, Ont., 87
Leamington, Ont., 156
Leland, MI, 195
Leland River, MI, 196
Les Chenaux Islands, MI, 187
Lexington, MI, 179
Lighthouse Pond, Ont., 73
Lincoln Park, IL, 205
Lindsay, Ont., 103
Little Bay de Noc, MI, 213
Little Chute, Ont., 106
Little Falls, NY, 57
Little Lake, Ont., 102
Little Sodus Bay, NY, 80
Little Traverse Bay, MI, 193
Liverpool, NY, 60
Lockport, NY, 64
Locust Point, OH, 151
Long Island, Ont., 101
Lonqueuil, Que., 91
Long Point Bay, Ont., 153
Long Sault, Ont., 91

Lorain, OH, 146
Lovesick Lake, Ont., 102
Lower Buckhorn Lake, Ont., 102
Lower Straight Channel, OH, 147
Ludington, MI, 197
Lynn River, Ont., 153
Lyons, NY, 54, 63

M

Mackinac Island, MI, 182
Mackinaw City, MI, 182
Mail Drops, 128
Maitland River, Ont., 185
Malletts Bay, VT, 41, 47, 48
Mallorytown Landing, Ont., 87
Manhattan, NY, 24
Manistee, MI, 196
Manistee Lake, MI, 196
Manistee River, MI, 196
Manistique, MI, 214
Manitowoc, WI, 209
Maple Beach, MI, 167
Marblehead, OH, 148
Margaret Island, Ont., 100
Marine City, MI, 171
Mariner's Handbook, 113
Marinette, WI, 213
Marion Island, MI, 194
Marlboro, NY, 26
Marquette Bay, MI, 18
Marsoui, Que., 94
Mary Island, Ont., 90
Matane, Que., 94
Maurice River, Que., 92
Maumee Bay, OH, 152
Maumee River, OH, 152
McCrackens Landing, Ont., 102
McDonald Island, Ont., 87
McGregor Channel, Ont., 186
McMasterville, Que., 50
McPhee Bay, Ont., 104
Mechanicville, NY, 42, 45
Medina, NY, 64
Menominee, MI, 213
Mentor, OH, 144
Mermaid Island, Ont., 87
Metrics, 131
Metro Park South, MI, 167
Metropolitan Beach, MI, 168
Mexico Bay, Ont., 69
Meyersburg, Ont., 99
Michigan City, IN, 200
Middle Bass Island, OH, 150
Middle Ground Flats, NY, 28
Middleport, NY, 64
Milwaukee, WI, 207
Minetto, NY, 59
Misery Bay, NY, 143
Mitchell Bay, Ont., 170

Mitchell Lake, Ont., 103
Mohawk River, NY, 40, 55
Monroe, MI, 152
Montague, MI, 197
Mont Louis, Que., 94
Montezuma, NY, 60, 62
Montezuma Marsh, NY, 60, 63
Montour Falls, NY, 61, 62
Montreal, Que., 40, 91
Montreal Island, Que., 92
Morristown, NY, 90
Moseley Channel, OH, 147
Moulton Bay, Ont., 153
Mount Julian, Ont., 102
Mouse Island, OH, 149
Mullett Lake, MI, 182
Murray Canal, Ont., 72
Muskegon, MI, 197
Muskegon Lake, MI, 197

N

Narrows, The, Ont., 104
Naubinway, MI, 214
Navy Islands, Ont., 87
Neuville, Que., 92
New Baltimore, MI, 168
New Baltimore, NY, 28
New Buffalo, MI, 200
New Hamburg, NY, 26
New London, NY, 58
Newark, NY, 63
Newburgh, NY, 26
Newcastle, Ont., 72
Niagara Falls, 143
Niagara-on-the-Lake, Ont., 77
Niagara River, 60, 64, 77, 141
North Bay, MI, 181
North Channel, Ont., 186
North Germantown Reach, NY, 27
North Manitou Island, MI, 196
North Maumee Bay, OH, 152
North Muskegon, MI, 197
North Pond, NY, 40, 69
North Tonawanda, NY, 64
Northport, MI, 195
Nyack, NY, 24

O

Oakville, Ont., 75
Oakville Creek, Ont., 75
Oak Harbor, OH, 149
Oak Orchard Creek, NY, 78
Oconto, WI, 213
Ogden Island, Ont., 90
Ogdensburg, NY, 40, 90
Olcott, NY, 78
Old River, OH 145
Oneida Lake, NY, 40, 58
Oneida River, NY, 54, 58
Onekama, MI, 196
Onondaga Lake, NY, 54, 59, 60
Orillia, Ont., 104
Oriskany Battlefield, NY, 58
Oscoda, MI, 180
Oshawa, Ont., 72
Ossining, NY, 24
Oswego, NY, 40, 59, 69
Oswego Canal, NY, 40, 54, 59
Oswego River, NY, 40, 59
Otonabee River, Ont., 101
Ottawa Beach, MI, 198
Ottawa River, OH, 152
Ottawa River, Ont., 91
Oyster Bay, MI, 193

P

Palisades, The, NY, 24
Palmyra, NY, 63
Partridge Harbor, NY, 41
Peekskill, NY, 25
Pelee Island, Ont., 151
Penetaugore River, Ont., 185
Peninsula State Park, WI, 211
Pentwater, MI, 197
Pentwater Lake, MI, 197
Peray Reach, Ont., 99
Pere Marquette Lake, MI, 197
Peterborough, Ont., 101
Peterson Bay, WI, 211
Petoskey, MI, 193
Phoenix, NY, 59
Pickerel Lake, MI, 182
Picton, Ont., 72
Piermont, NY, 24
Pigeon Lake, Ont., 103
Pigeon River, MI, 180
Pike Creek, Ont., 169
Pine River, MI, 193
Pittsford, NY, 63
Plattsburgh, NY, 41
Point Abino, Ont., 143
Point Breeze, NY, 78
Point Gratiot, NY, 143
Point Pelee, Ont., 156
Pointe Anicet, Que., 91
Pointe au Cedre, Que., 91
Pointe-aux-Trembles, Que., 92
Pollepel Island, NY, 25
Port Austin, MI, 179
Port Bruce, Ont., 155
Port Burwell, Ont., 154
Port Clinton, OH, 149
Port Colborne, Ont., 141, 153
Port Credit, Ont., 75
Port Dalhousie, Ont., 76
Port Darlington, Ont., 72
Port Des Morts Passage, WI, 209
Port Dover, Ont., 153
Port Elgin, Ont., 185
Port Ewen, NY, 27
Port Franks, Ont., 184
Port Henry, NY, 41, 43, 47
Port Hope, Ont., 72
Port Huron, MI, 171
Port Kent, NY, 47
Port Maitland, Ont., 153
Port Ontario, NY, 69
Port Rowan, Ont., 154
Port Sanilac, MI, 179
Port Severn, Ont., 106
Port Stanley, Ont., 155
Port Washington, WI, 207
Port Weller, NY, 77
Port Whitby, Ont., 73
Portage Lake, MI, 196
Portage River, OH, 149
Port des Mortes Passage, 211
Porte de Valleyfield, Que., 91
Porter Bay, VT, 47
Potawatomi State Park, WI, 210
Poughkeepsie, NY, 26
Prescott, Ont., 90
Presque Isle Bay, PA, 143
Presque Isle Harbor, MI (Lake Huron), 181
Presqu'ile Bay, Ont., 72
Prinyers Cove, Ont., 72
Public Coast Marine Operators, 122
Puce, Ont., 169
Puce River, Ont., 169
Pultneyville, NY, 80
Put-In-Bay, OH, 150

Q-R

Quebec City, Que., 92
Quinte's Isle, Ont., 72
Race, The, NY, 25
Racine, WI, 207
Rack Island, Ont., 100
Radiobeacons, 121
Red Mills, Ont., 90
Repentigny, Que., 92
Restaurants, 134
Rice Lake, Ont., 100
Richelieu River, Que., 40, 43, 48, 92
Richelieu-Chambly Canal, 43
Rideau Canal, Ont., 91
Rideau Waterway, 60
Rimouski, Que., 94
Rip Van Winkle Bridge, NY, 28
Riviere au Renard, Que., 94
Riviere du Loup, Que., 94
Roach Point, Ont., 100
Rochester, NY, 68, 79
Rock Island State Park, WI, 211
Rockport, Ont., 87
Rocky River, OH, 146
Rogers City, MI, 181
Rome, NY, 40, 58
Rondeau Bay, Ont., 156
Rondout Creek, NY, 27
Root River, WI, 207
Rosedale, Ont., 103
Rouge River, MI, 165
Round Islands, 89
Round Lake, MI, 193
Rouses Point, NY, 41
Rowley Bay, WI, 211
Rules of the Road, 114
Runaway Bay, WI, 207
Russell Island, MI, 171

S

Sackets Harbor, NY, 40, 71
Saginaw, MI, 180
Saginaw Bay, MI, 179
Saginaw River, MI, 180
Saguenay, Que., 93
St. Clair, MI, 171
St. Clair River, MI, 163, 170
St. Clair Shores, MI, 168
St. Ignace, MI, 182
St. James, MI, 191
St. Jean, Que., 41, 48
St. Johnsville, NY, 57
St. Joseph, MI, 199
St. Joseph River, MI, 199
St. Lambert, Que., 91
St. Lawrence River, 40, 43
St. Lawrence Seaway, 41, 60, 86
St. Marys River, 183
St. Ours, Que., 50
St. Regis Islands, Que., 40
Ste. Anne des Monts, Que. 94
Salaberry-de-Valleyfield, Que., 92
Salt River, MI, 168
Sandusky, OH, 147
Sandusky Bay, OH, 148
Sandusky River, OH, 148
Sarnia, Ont., 171
Sauble Beach, Ont., 185
Saugatuck, MI, 198
Saugeen River, Ont., 185

Saugerties, NY, 27
Sawmill Bay, NY, 71
Sawyer Harbor, WI, 210
Schenectady, NY, 55
Sciota, NY, 56
Scudder, Ont., 151
Seiches, (Lake Erie) 141
Seneca Canal, NY, 62
Seneca Falls, NY, 62
Seneca Lake, NY, 62
Seneca River, NY, 54, 60
Sept Isles, Que., 93
Severn Falls, Ont., 105
Severn River, Ont., 104
Sheboygan River, WI, 209
Sheboygan, WI, 207
Shelburne, VT, 41, 48
Shelburne Bay, VT, 41, 48
Sillery, Que., 92
Sister Bay, WI, 211
Sister Islands, WI, 211
Sleeping Bear Dunes, MI, 196
Snug Harbor, Ont., 184
Snake Island, Ont., 73
Sodus Bay, NY, 80
Sorel, Que., 41, 43, 50, 92
Soolange Rapids, Que., 91
South Bass Island, OH, 150
South Haven, MI, 199
South Manitou Island, MI, 196
South Shore Canal, Que., 91
South Shore Park Harbor, WI, 207
Southampton, Ont., 185
Southeast Shoal, Ont., 156
Sparrow Lake, Ont., 105
Spectacles, The, Ont., 87
Spencerport, NY, 63
Spring Lake, MI, 197, 198
Spuyten Duyvil Creek, NY, 24
Squaw Island, NY, 64
Stave Island, VT, 48
Stockport Middle Ground, NY, 28

Stone Croft, WI, 207
Stony Lake, Ont., 102
Stony Point, NY, 23, 25, 46
Storm King Mountain, NY, 25
Straits of Mackinac, MI, 177, 181
Strawberry Island, WI, 213
Sturgeon Bay, WI, 210
Sturgeon Bay Canal, WI, 209
Sturgeon Lake, Ont., 102
Sturgeon Point, NY, 143
Sugar Island, MI, 181
Sulphur Creek, MI, 152
Summerland Island, Ont., 90
Summerstown, Que., 91
Suttons Bay, MI, 195
Swan Creek, MI, 168
Swift Rapids, Ont., 105
Sydenham River, Ont.,
  (Lake St. Clair) 170
Sylvan Beach, NY, 54
Syracuse, NY, 59, 60

T

Tadoussac, Que., 93
Talbot, Ont., 103
Talbot River, Ont., 103
Tappan Zee, NY, 24
Tar Island, Ont., 87
Tarrytown, NY, 24
Tawas Bay, MI, 180
Thames River, Ont., 169
Thompson's Point, VT, 47
Tittabawassee River, MI, 180
Thousand Islands, 86
Three Rivers Point, NY, 59
Thunder Bay, MI 181
Thunder Bay Island, 181
Toledo, OH, 152
Toledo Beach, OH, 152

Tonawanda Creek, NY, 64
Toronto, Ont., 73
Toronto Islands, Ont., 73
Traverse City, MI, 194
Treadwell Bay, VT, 41
Trent River, Ont., 72, 99
Trent-Severn Waterway, Ont.,
  60, 72, 99, 108, 199
Trenton, Ont., 72, 99
Trenton Channel, MI, 167
Trois Rivieres, Que., 92
Troy, NY, 29, 40
Troy Lock, NY, 29
Tucker Point, MI, 195
Turkey Island, Ont., 165
Turkey Point, Ont., 154
Turtle Island, MI, OH, 152
Tuscarora Bay, Ont., 78
Two Rivers, WI, 209

U

Union Springs, NY, 61
Upper Nyack, NY, 24
Useful Publications, 129
Utica, NY, 56, 58

V

Van Buren Point, NY, 143
Van Shaick Island, NY, 29
Vermilion, OH, 146
Vischer Ferry, NY, 55

W

Waddington, NY, 90
Wallace Point, Ont., 101
Wallaceburg, Ont., 170

Walter Island, NY, 59
Wards Island, Ont., 73
Washago, Ont., 104
Washington Island, WI, 211
Waterford, NY, 43, 54
Waterford Flight, NY, 55
Waterloo, NY, 62
Watkins Glen, NY, 62
Waukegan, IL, 207
Waverly Shoal, Ont. 143
Wayneport, NY, 63
Weather Information, 118
Welland Canal, 60, 76, 153
Wellesley Island, NY, 40, 89
West Harbor, OH, 149
West Point, NY, 25
West Sister Island, OH, 151
Western Gap, Ont., 73
Westport, NY, 41, 47
Wheatley, Ont., 156
White Lake, MI, 197
White Pine Village, MI, 197
Whitehall, MI, 197
Whitehall, NY, 42, 43, 45
Whites Bay, NY, 71
Wide Waters, The, NY, 63
Wiley-Dondero Canal, 91
Willsboro Bay, NY, 47
Wilson, NY, 78
Windmill Point, Ont., 143
Windsor, Ont., 165
Wolfe Island, Ont., 87
Woodbine Park, Ont., 73
World's End, NY, 25

X-Y-Z

Yonkers, NY, 24
Youngs Point, Ont., 102
Youngstown, Ont., 78
Zebra Mussels, 141

Features

Avoiding Lyme Disease, 212
Galley Stoves, 165
Locking Procedures, 30
Navigating Below Sorel, 93
Pets On Board, 91

Vital Statistics:
  Erie Canal, 58
  St. Lawrence Seaway, 41
  Trent-Severn Waterway, 103
Welland Canal, The, 76

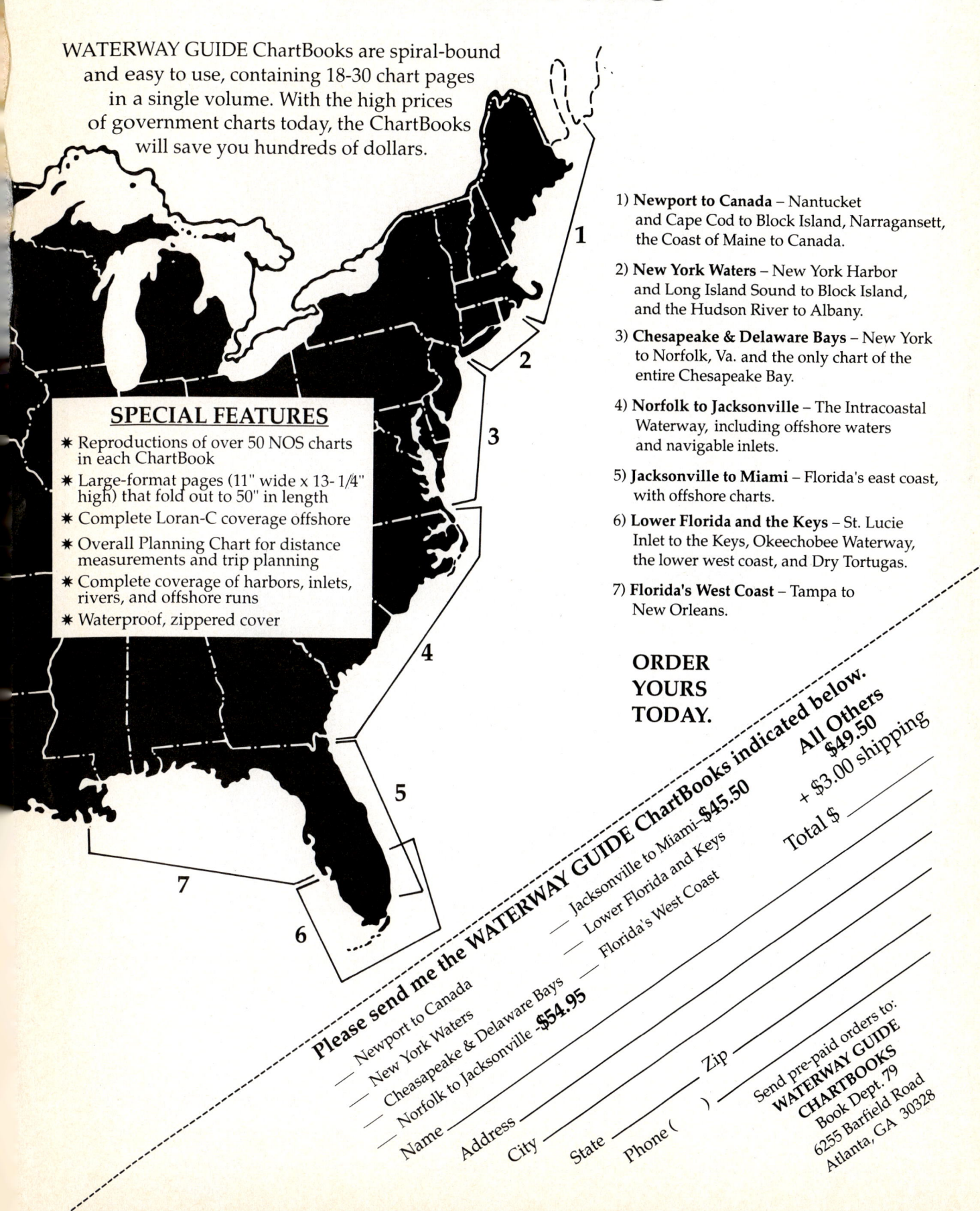

WATERWAY GUIDE ChartBooks

WATERWAY GUIDE ChartBooks are spiral-bound and easy to use, containing 18-30 chart pages in a single volume. With the high prices of government charts today, the ChartBooks will save you hundreds of dollars.

SPECIAL FEATURES

* Reproductions of over 50 NOS charts in each ChartBook
* Large-format pages (11" wide x 13-1/4" high) that fold out to 50" in length
* Complete Loran-C coverage offshore
* Overall Planning Chart for distance measurements and trip planning
* Complete coverage of harbors, inlets, rivers, and offshore runs
* Waterproof, zippered cover

1) **Newport to Canada** – Nantucket and Cape Cod to Block Island, Narragansett, the Coast of Maine to Canada.

2) **New York Waters** – New York Harbor and Long Island Sound to Block Island, and the Hudson River to Albany.

3) **Chesapeake & Delaware Bays** – New York to Norfolk, Va. and the only chart of the entire Chesapeake Bay.

4) **Norfolk to Jacksonville** – The Intracoastal Waterway, including offshore waters and navigable inlets.

5) **Jacksonville to Miami** – Florida's east coast, with offshore charts.

6) **Lower Florida and the Keys** – St. Lucie Inlet to the Keys, Okeechobee Waterway, the lower west coast, and Dry Tortugas.

7) **Florida's West Coast** – Tampa to New Orleans.

ORDER YOURS TODAY.

Please send me the WATERWAY GUIDE ChartBooks indicated below.

___ Newport to Canada
___ New York Waters
___ Cheasapeake & Delaware Bays
___ Norfolk to Jacksonville –$54.95
___ Jacksonville to Miami–$45.50
___ Lower Florida and Keys
___ Florida's West Coast

All Others $49.50
+ $3.00 shipping

Total $ _____

Name _____ Address _____ City _____ State _____ Phone ( ) _____ Zip _____

Send pre-paid orders to:
WATERWAY GUIDE CHARTBOOKS
Book Dept. 79
6255 Barfield Road
Atlanta, GA 30328

What qualities do you look for in a boatyard when your boat needs service?

Very likely, an ABBRA member has these qualifications.*

AMERICAN BOATBUILDERS & REPAIRERS ASSOCIATION, INC.
Serving The Marine Industry Since 1940

715 Boylston Street • Boston, MA • 02116 • 617-266-6800

*American Boatbuilders & Repairers Association, Inc. members are denoted by a (✓) check in the facilities listings of this publication.